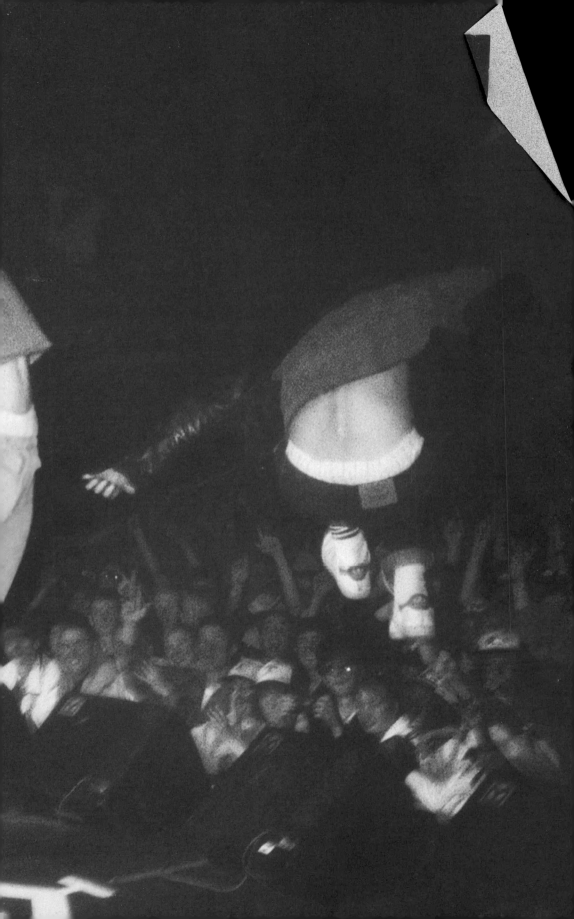

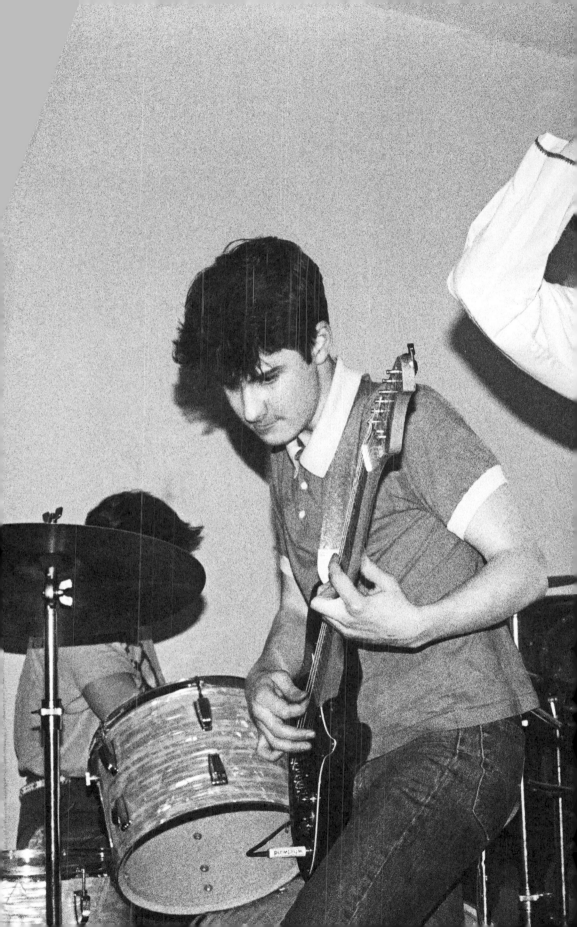

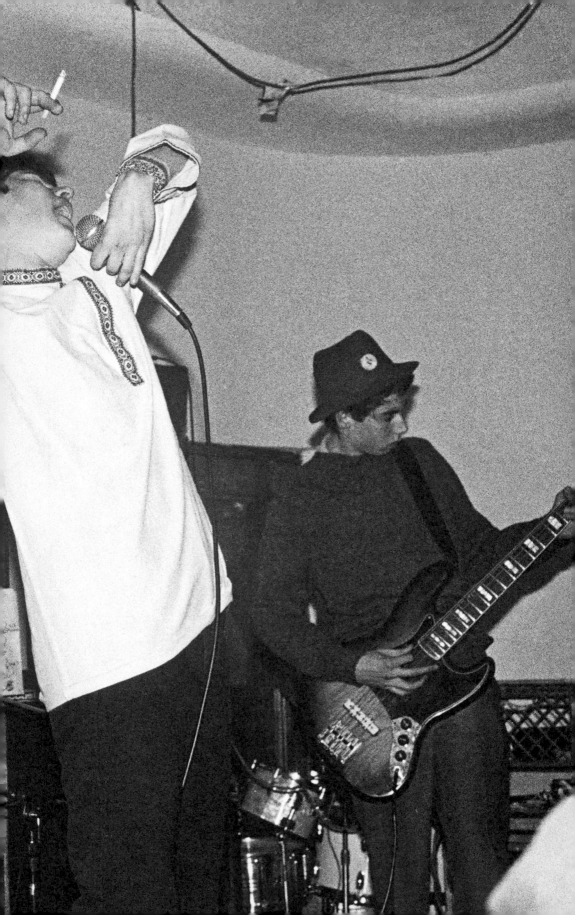

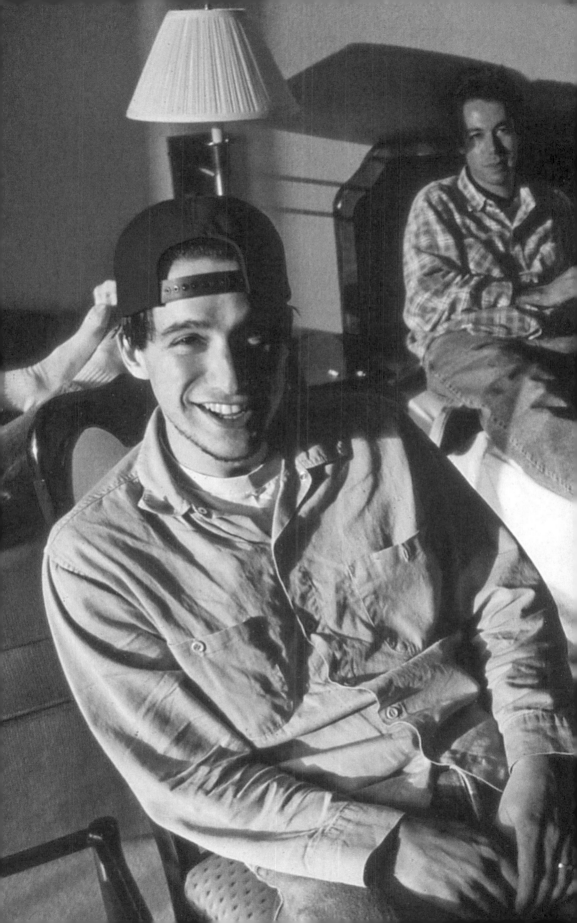

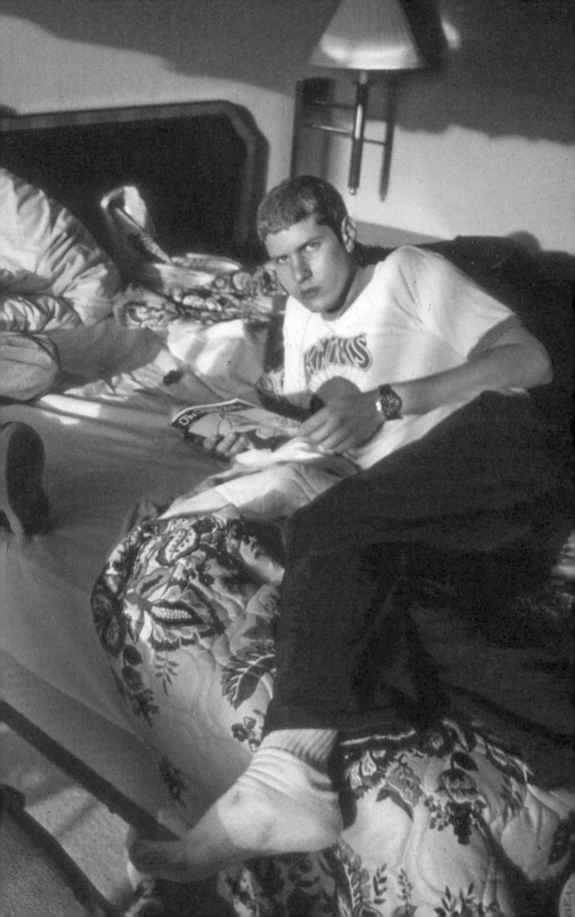

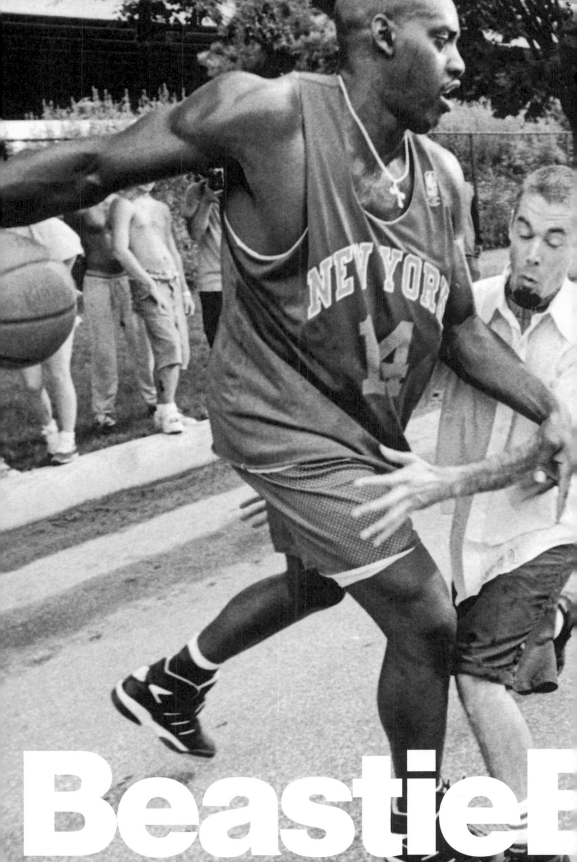

Michael Diamond / Adam Horovitz

oysBook

Spiegel & Grau | New York

Contents

Contents (cont'd)

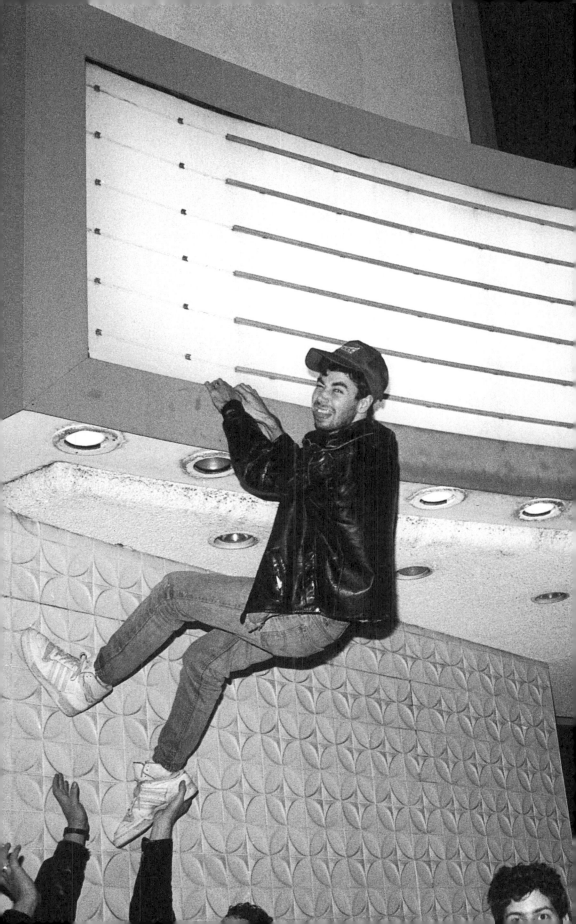

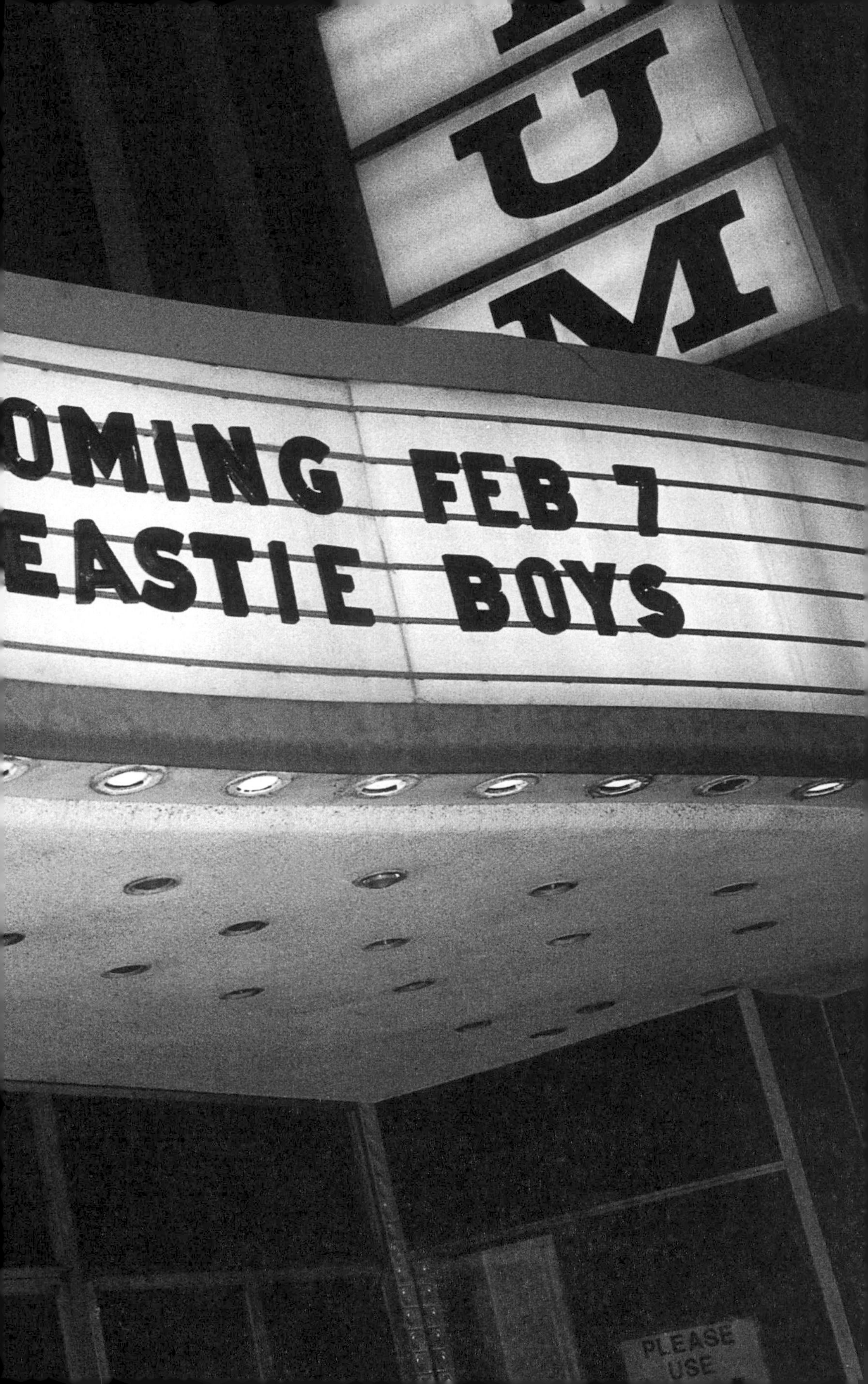
U
M
OMING FEB 7
EASTIE BOYS
PLEASE
USE

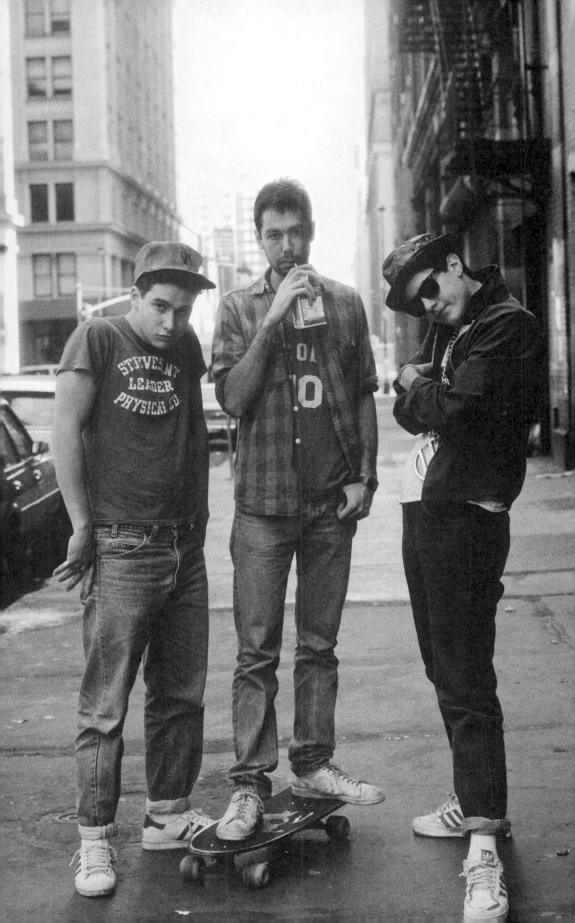

Wild Card (An Introduction)

Adam Horovitz

We all have different types of friends, right? There's the one that's kind of an asshole but fun to be around once in a while. Fun to get drunk and talk shit with, but you'd never actually call on them for physical or emotional help 'cause they're just unreliable. (And kind of an asshole.) Or there's the friend you see once in a while and it's a nice hangout and you're always like, "I should spend more time with that person," but for some reason . . . you don't. Then there's that true friend, the one you'd be on the phone with forever. The one that helps you move, or meets you at the hospital, or has a permanent spot on their couch for you just in case you ever need it. Those type of friends are rare, we all know. BUT . . . there's an even rarer friend: the one that gets you motivated. The one that not only gets themselves going and doing great things but says: we should *all* get together and do *this*. And then does it. Adam Yauch was that type of friend. A once-in-a-lifetime type of friend. The friend that makes it happen. The friend that inspires you to go big.

We all see things differently. We each experience an event in our own way. This book is how Michael "Sweet Lou" Diamond and I remember what happened to us. Yauch had talked about wanting to document our band, but, sadly, without him here, me+Mike are gonna have to do it alone. I say "sadly," well . . . because of the obvious. Adam passed away in 2012. But it's additionally sad because, if any of the three of us saw things with a unique perspective, it was Yauch. He was truly a wild card. Someone who, in my mind, was like . . . "Shit . . . I'm gonna walk to the top of the Empire State Building with cameras taped to my shoes . . . I'll carry you up there piggyback-style . . . It'll be funny . . . let's go." He was the rare person who actually does all the crazy things they say they're gonna do. And does them even crazier than you'd imagine. For instance . . .

Yauch got into snowboarding in the late '80s. He met some other people that were into it and would go snowboarding with them. But not like how a regular person would do it. He met someone who knew someone in Alaska, and this person in Alaska would fly them to the top of an un-snowboarded-on mountain in a helicopter . . . they'd jump out of the helicopter, with their snowboards attached, and head down the mountain. That's a crazy thing to even dare yourself to think of, let alone say you're gonna do. Or do. Or have done.

The first time we went to Australia was in 1992. To me, Australia was a foreign land. Not only had I never been there, I don't think I had ever met anyone who was Australian. What happens there? I had no idea. The flight took, like, sixteen hours. And when we arrived, we went through customs and all that stuff, got outside, exhausted from the flight, and a little nervous about

being in a new place so far away from home. I just wanted to get to either a bed or a cup of coffee. As we left baggage claim and headed out to find a taxi, Yauch tells us that he met someone on the flight, and that they had some friends who were all meeting up to go snowboarding somewhere hours and hours (of more traveling) away. And since our first show wasn't for a couple days, he was gonna cut out and hang out with these people for a bit, and see us all at sound check before the show. Wait . . . WHAT!?! At that point in my life I liked to think of myself as a spontaneous kind of person, but this was a little too next-level. I just did not understand this behavior.

Yauch wanted to see the world. So he did. He went to India and looked around. Saw things, met people. While on one of his trips there, he got in touch with the plight of the people of Tibet. He was so moved by their culture and what they had endured, and continue to endure, he came back home and wanted—*needed*—to let people who didn't know know. So he put together a big concert. Not just a show, but a fucking massive benefit concert in Golden Gate Park in San Francisco. And that was just the start. He ended up having a bunch of these shows all over the world. Huge concerts in baseball stadiums. With huge bands like U2. Yeah, he could get in the door (and on the snowboard helicopter in Alaska) because he was famous, but not many people can rally so many others to work for free. Especially for some "weirdo" cause like nonviolence. Passion and compassion. Yauch had 'em.

Yauch, Mike, and I have spent more time with each other than with our own families. REALLY. When we were kids, all we'd do is hang out with each other and do stuff. Dumb kid stuff. Like doing nothing all day. And

when we got serious about being a band, and writing and recording music, we'd meet basically every day, five days a week, to work. And on weekends we'd just hang out together anyways 'cause, you know, you gotta eat, right? So add those days up for thirty-five years and that's a lot of getting to know someone. So like . . . when it comes to my friend the rapper Mike D, I *know* him. Like, basically everything. I know what sounds he makes when he eats (he mumbles to himself and hits the spoon against his teeth). I know the exact and precise time to say something fart-related that will make him spit up his food or drink. Every time. I kind of always know what he's gonna say next. And he knows me just the same. He knows I'm always running late. He knows I have terrible B.O. because I haven't bathed in a while. He knows I've got some long-winded cockamamie story about something stupid and stressed-out, like my dog shitted twelve times in the living room and I had to take her to the vet and whatever. *Every*-thing. But Adam Yauch . . . ? A puzzle. A conundrum. A labyrinth of ideas and emotions. An enigma . . . A *wild card*.

After thirty years of friendship, I never knew what he was gonna do or say next. He was a living contradiction of people's idea of how, or what, you're supposed to be or do. He's the Buddhist guy who's telling me how last night he was at this after-after-party for some fashion show. And he's the "Fight for Your Right to Party" guy who went trekking through Nepal on a discovery quest. He once told me that the main draw to him about the Dalai Lama was that he was a funny dude. Obviously there were other reasons he was drawn to spirituality, faith, and Buddhism, but the funny-dude part made perfect sense to me, coming from Yauch. Funny is very important.

When you're a "celebrity" people see you as a certain thing. Or rather, in a certain way. But certain personal traits aren't on display. Things you might not know about that person. Like . . . Yauch was an information tornado. Winding through the world, drawing in as much as he could and as fast as possible. For example . . . when we were kids, it wasn't enough to just play the guitar. He needed to know how it worked. What makes an electric guitar make sound through that amplifier? Something about the metal-threaded coils attached to the guitar, and when the metal strings vibrate against them and when the cord from the guitar is plugged into an electrical source . . . Oh my God . . . he's explained it to me maybe seven different times, and I will *never* understand. Rick Rubin gave him the name Techno Wiz because he understood things technologically.

But again . . . wild card. Russell Simmons also used to say that Yauch was the James Dean of our band because he was smooth with the ladies (in the '80s). Remember, this was before the Internet and Internet billionaires, so someone who was into technology *and* smooth with the ladies did not really exist yet.

Me+Mike were always slightly different from Yauch. Maybe it's because we're both the youngest of three-kid households. When you have older brothers or sisters you don't develop as much time or space for a fully formed thought process. It's way more physical than reflective. It's more about fighting to get

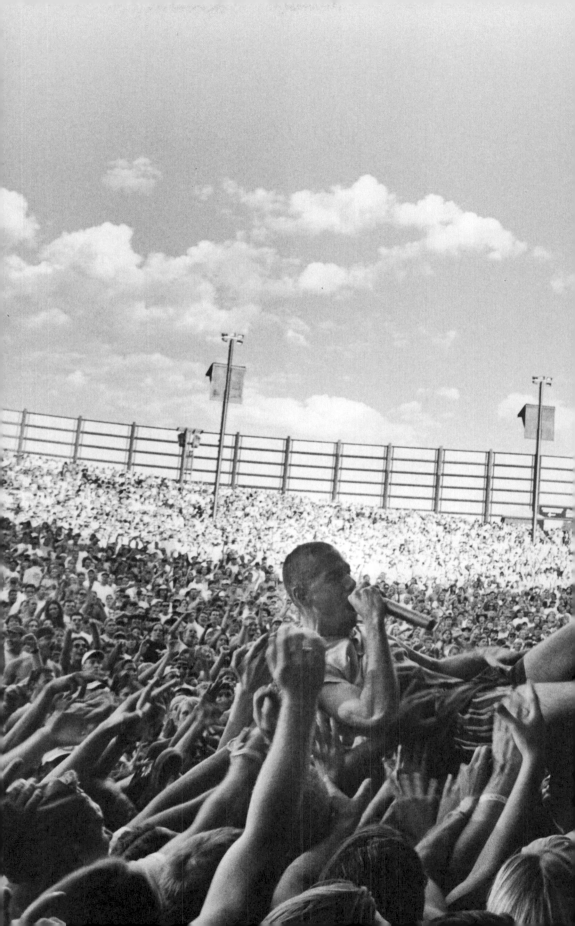

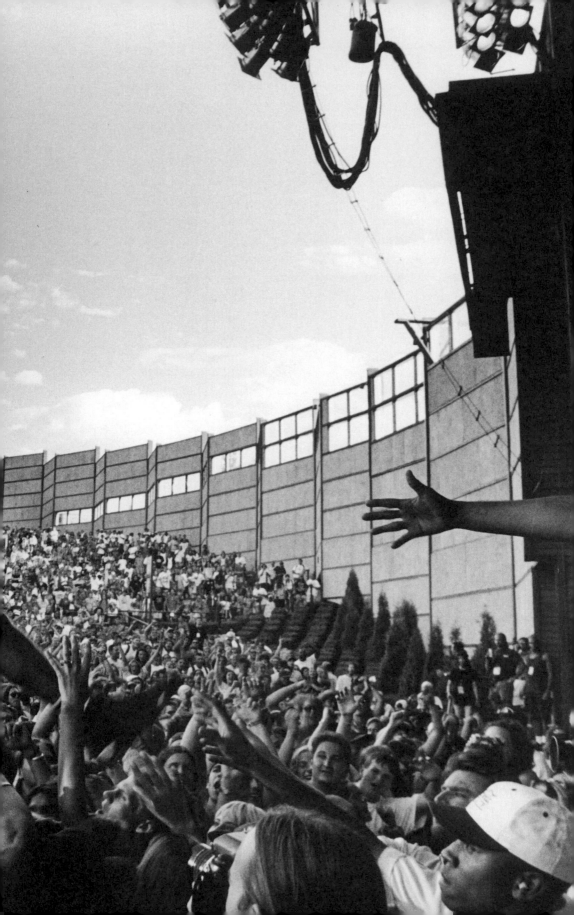

space in the car, or figuring out how to not get tormented, or following your older siblings around trying to just keep up. Yauch was an only child, with really smart, funny, and encouraging parents. He had the space to think and understand. For so many reasons, we were lucky to have this band. But one of the reasons me+ Mike were lucky is that we didn't have to figure out a lot of shit because Yauch already knew it.

Once a week, for thirty years, Yauch would say something like, "Oh yeah, I heard about this camera that takes a 360-degree picture. We should stand on a corner and take one of those. It'd look so cool to see NYC like that." *Where* did he hear about that camera? Where did he "hear" about so many things, so often? I want to reiterate this pre-Internet thing. Besides what your teachers are talking about in school, if you didn't have a #ComputerSmartPhoneTablet with a #UnlimitedDataPlan . . . how the fuck would you know anything about what you *really* wanna know? But Yauch had knowledge of things that I didn't even know I should *want* to know about. Maybe it's because I'm just not a good payer of attention, but Yauch, since the day I met him, had knowledge, had insight into so much outside our teenage world. He could pull out little gems of information just as casually as you'd pull a cough drop out of your coat pocket. He had an understanding of things like history and science, and nature, and food, and music, and even just . . . life, like how to navigate living in a big, sketchy city. He was a lot older than just the one and a half years that separated us.

All groups of friends have stories they've told each other. We've all seen some crazy-ass shit. Been in really weird situations. Gone places. Done stuff. Took breaks. Went away. Came back. Told each other what happened while we were there. But one little detail of a Yauch vacation has always stuck with me. He was in India. He was sitting in a park, and a monkey came along and stole his shoe. The monkey climbed up a tree, wouldn't give it back, and taunted Yauch with his own shoe for, like, half an hour. Then finally threw it at him and ran off. Who does that happen to? A monkey stole your shoe!?! Not a bar fight/ motorcycle crash/blew something up/smashed a gun with a sledgehammer/ jumped out of a helicopter (all of which also happened to Adam) but . . . India/ monkey/shoe taunting?

For me, the reason why Beastie Boys stayed together for so long and had so much fun being a band is because Yauch+Mike are the family members I *wanna* see. They're my two other brothers I love, and can depend on. And, yes, they're also my jerk friends that make shit jokes. They're my friends that I'm with all day but then call later that night and stay on the phone for an hour and laugh with. And all three of us in the end were the friends that inspired one another to go big. So yeah, it sucks that this book about us and our band isn't coming from all three of our perspectives, but me+Mike will do our best to let you know what happened.

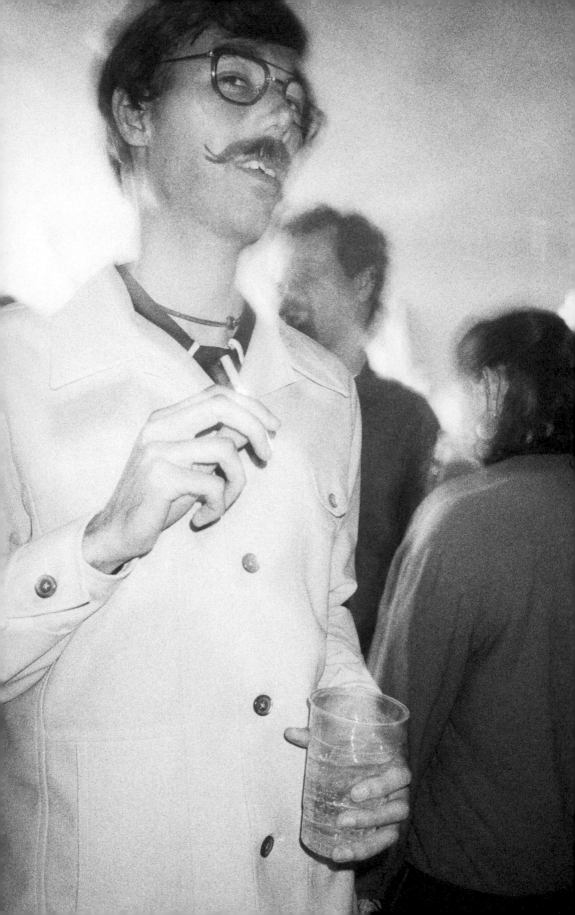

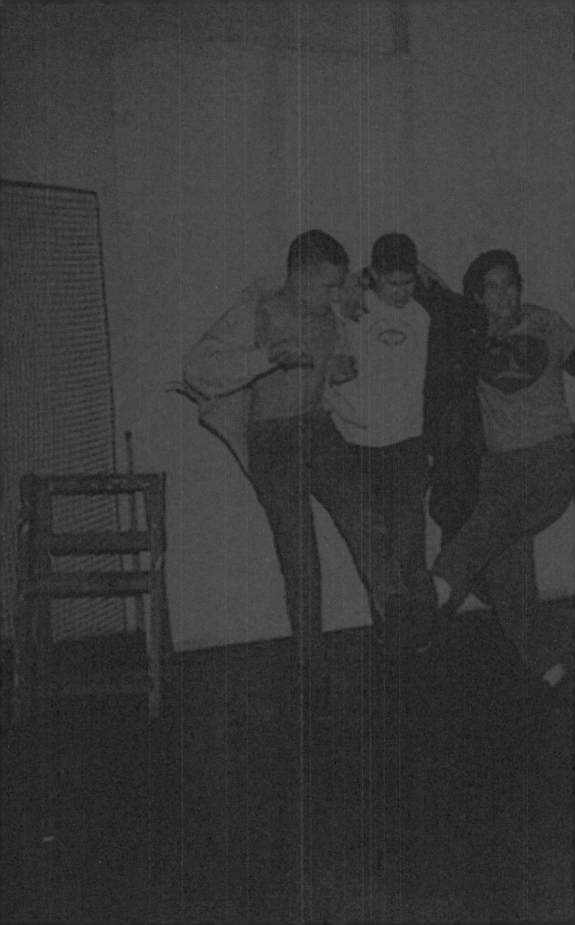

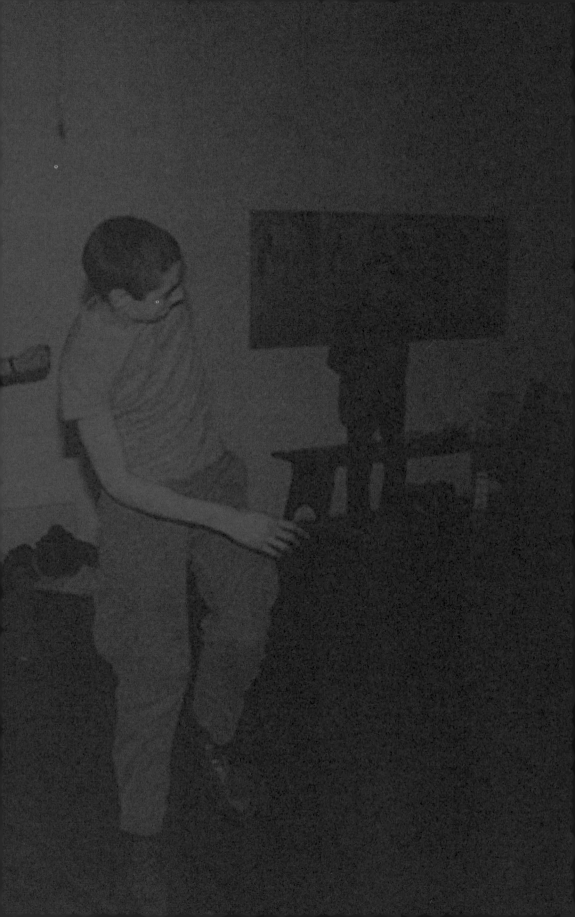

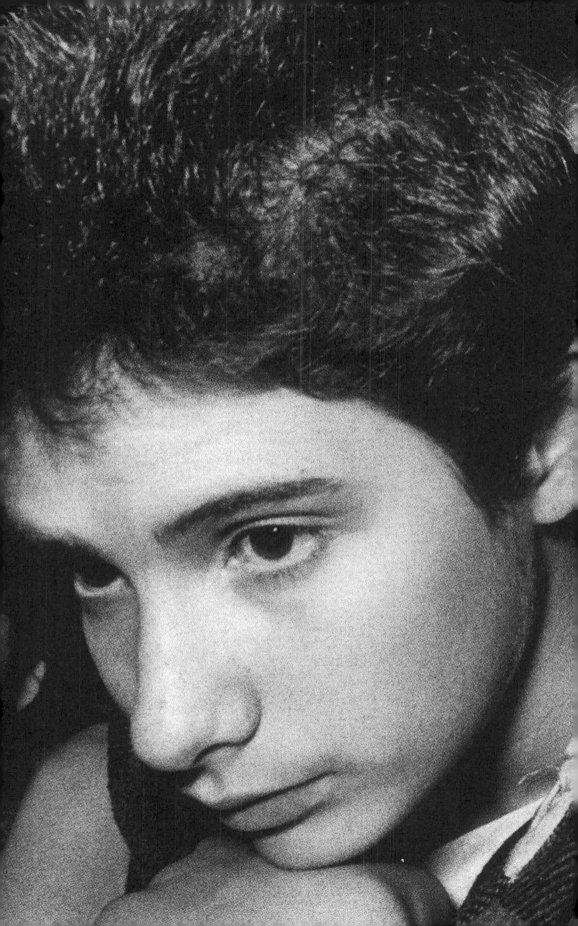

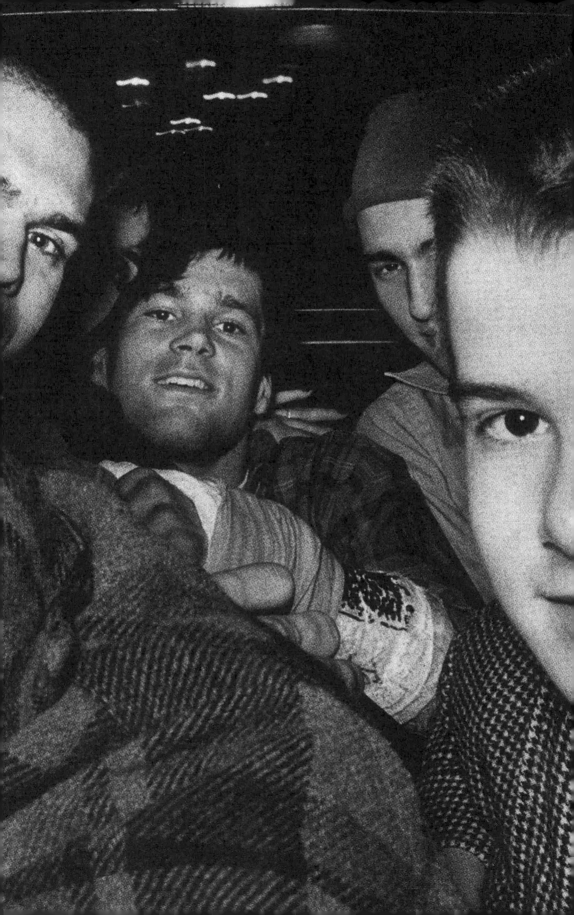

BEASTIE REVOLUTION

LUC SANTE

It is 1981 in New York City: a distant planet, hard to see now. **Beastie Boys** is just being embryonically formed in a rehearsal space somewhere. Elsewhere, **Butthole Surfers**, **Cro-Mags**, **Mötley Crüe**, **Napalm Death**, **Run-DMC**, **Sonic Youth**, and **Wham!** are likewise coagulating. In hospitals in other American cities, **Beyoncé Knowles**, **Alicia Keys**, **Britney Spears**, and **Justin Timberlake** are being born. **Ronald Reagan** has, since January 20, been the fortieth president of the nation. The personal-listening cassette device known as the Walkman has been available in the United States since the previous summer, but it isn't cheap and not many people have one. Instead, music is ambient throughout the city. It is everywhere, whether you like it or not. A song will come on WBLS as you're climbing the stairs from the subway station and you'll catch it on a radio playing in a passing car, picked up by the outdoor speakers at a bodega, continued by a boombox hefted on the shoulder of somebody going the other way, resumed by another boombox in the basket of a bicycle weaving in and out of traffic, concluding in the pizza parlor you've just entered for a slice.

Maybe the song is "The Adventures of Grandmaster Flash on the Wheels of Steel," and it's brand-new, first time you've heard it, so when you hear it in bits and pieces mixed with car horns and sirens you don't realize at first it's all the same number—it sounds like an extended mix of "Good Times" by **Chic** with assorted other radio stations cutting across it, playing **Blondie**, **Queen**, **Spoonie Gee**. That seems entirely plausible because it's the sort of thing that happens all the time in New York City. Just as you can walk down one street and hear a single station emanating from every

12

broadcast device, you can walk down the next block and hear charanga over here and Philly soul over there and skank down this way and doo-wop down that. The street itself can function as a mixing deck. If there's a really strong cut in the wind that week, it will serve as a moving backdrop, apparently always somewhere on the airwaves, while other sounds happen across it like billboards in a car window, or quotes dropped in by a DJ. And "Good Times" has been audible somewhere seemingly every minute for the past two years.

It's a world that runs on radio. In the city, radio is a constituent element of the public landscape, as much as the buildings and the trucks and the signs and the people on the street. You hear the frantic Teletype jingle of WINS—"Give us twenty-two minutes and we'll give you the world"—traffic reports and weather and murder and war all delivered in the same flat, dry announcer voice. You hear "Spanish" radio (the word "Hispanic" isn't much used yet), and if you're a *blanco* you might not know if what you're hearing is Rican or Dominican, salsa or bachata or merengue or guaracha. What you hear most of all is WBLS or WKTU or, as of halfway through 1981, WRKS: KISS FM. Those stations constitute what is not quite yet referred to as "urban contemporary," and it's still mostly disco, which accounts for, among other things, the omnipresence of "Good Times." What they don't play is rap, which continues to be despised by the eminences of African American radio, such as BLS's **Frankie "Hollywood" Crocker**, formerly renowned for his golden ear. So you probably wouldn't be hearing "The Adventures of Grandmaster Flash" on the radio unless whoever owned the radio was hip enough to tune in to **Mr. Magic (John Rivas)**, who has been hosting his *Rap Attack* on WHBI, which has been devoted to "leased-access ethnic programming" only for about a year.

Hip hop—then known as "rap"; "hip hop" became an umbrella term that covers rapping, DJing, graffiti, and break dancing—isn't the first successful urban sound to be scorned by the media. It happened to street-corner vocal harmonizing in the mid-1950s, until it was finally exhumed five years later and marketed as "doo-wop." More recently it happened to punk, a phenomenon you could have entirely missed, for years, if you hadn't visited a certain handful of bars and record stores. But hip hop is all over the streets anyway. Those boomboxes aren't just radios. Mixtapes rule. Which is why you can take in brand-new 12-inch releases on the fly before you're necessarily even aware of what you're hearing. Mixtapes also account for, say, the middle-aged Ukrainian guy walking down St. Mark's Place blasting **Merle Haggard**. Try finding **Merle** on the radio anywhere in New York City.

If you're some punk-ass white kid in Youthville—which this year is bounded by Third Avenue, Fourteenth Street, Avenue B, and Delancey Street—you may not know anybody in the Bronx, so when you hear one of those brand-new 12-inch rap releases flying out of somebody's boombox on the street and it cuts you to your marrow, how

do you find out what it is? Well, you can go to Disc-O-Rama on the east side of Union Square, a branch of a chain that moves records in and out as comprehensively and impersonally as bread and milk, and you might get lucky—but you might just end up buying something else on the strength of its name or its label. Or, if you are inclined to travel, you will sooner or later make your way up to Downstairs Records, in Midtown, which, at least at first—it moves a few times—is actually located in a subway arcade. The store isn't that big, but they seem to stock everything, and they always know what you're talking about. Just repeat the one rhyme you're sure you caught off that last thing you heard, and without hesitation the guy behind the counter will retrieve it from a case, like magic. And sometimes, especially if you're buying dance beats, the record has little or no information on the label. Is it a bootleg, a promo, a test pressing? You may never know. The most brilliant mix you ever heard only seems to exist on one sliver of vinyl. For all you know, only six copies were ever pressed. And then your apartment is burglarized and the record disappears, forever.

A lot of hip hop is basically rumor at this point. There are of course the hits, underground and otherwise, as there have been since **Spoonie Gee** and **Kurtis Blow** and the **Sugarhill Gang** manifested themselves two or three years ago. But you know the real action is happening in the Bronx and Harlem, in parks and community youth clubs and common rooms in the projects and sometimes in cocktail lounges. Things go down that go unrecorded, as MCs and DJs try to top one another: unrehearsed epiphanies simply occur. Maybe you were lucky enough to catch the **Cold Crush Brothers** versus the **Fantastic Five** at Harlem World, or **Flash** versus **Crash** at the Audubon Ballroom, but

maybe you weren't. And if you know about all this but aren't there, the records can sometimes sound like just a captured sliver of something huge, although that's been the case forever with recordings of music with a large improvisational component—the same was true of **Charley Patton** and **Charlie Parker**. There are many fantastic records out there, but what's so striking about hip hop right now is its gigantic untapped potential. Most of the rap you hear involves people talking over grooves, mostly at a walking tempo, mostly fronting. There's not really a lot of non-fronting lyrical content going on—the only "conscious" record anybody can think of is still last year's "How We Gonna Make the Black Nation Rise?" by **Brother D and Collective Effort**. The standard of production still very much follows the early Jamaican template: hit tune minus vocals plus talkover. This year the MCs are all over **Taana Gardner**'s "Heartbeat" and **Tom Tom Club**'s "Genius of Love," and you can see why, because those are both grooves that can last all day long.

"Heartbeat" has a full stop right in the middle of the bass line—three steps leading up to it and three steps away again, making it like a slow-grind minuet. **Taana** is calling out to the world from the crag her passion has abandoned her on, until every once in a while a tinkly synthesizer sprinkles glitter and she's surrounded by a party. And "Genius of Love" is the same kind of stagger-step, just a touch faster. It has an indefatigably bright synth hook—with a stop in the middle—and a bottom like a brick shithouse. You can run all kinds of additional sound material through that setup without causing any real damage. **Tom Tom Club**'s best idea, though, is the tender chapel-girl harmonies. In addition to being a solid jam, "Genius" is also a happy pill, very good for the street. Notice also where those two jams originated. "Heartbeat" is a product of disco standard-bearers West End Records, and it was given its definitive club mix by **Larry Levan** at the Paradise Garage—the pope and Vatican of gay dance culture. "Genius," by contrast, is the work of **Tina Weymouth** and **Chris Frantz**, late of **Talking Heads**, who emerged from CBGB, the punk manger over on the desolate Bowery. Cultural fences seem to be breaking down all over, and influences are running in every possible direction. It seems as if every strain of urban music is folding into a cult of the groove, what **Linton Kwesi Johnson** calls "bass culture."

Not everybody's gotten the news quite yet, though. Remember "Disco sucks"? Outside lower Manhattan, people who maybe in a few short years will be blasting **Run-DMC** are still fiercely and monomaniacally devoted to the old definition of rock 'n' roll. On May 28 a herd of them boo **Grandmaster Flash and the Furious Five** off the stage as they are attempting to open for **The Clash** at Bonds International Casino on Times Square. This comes as a shock to everybody downtown, although more than anything it reflects the usual white folks' denial when it comes to inbred racism; black people aren't especially surprised. The fact is that the pan-racial, omnisexual groove religion is pretty new even downtown. It wasn't until 1978 or so that it even occurred to the regulars at CBGB that almost everybody who played there was white. And it's only

now that the **Funky Four Plus One More** are playing the Mudd Club (not to mention *Saturday Night Live*). Even so, there's no question that many musicians and music lovers have been listening broadly all over town. Some onetime CBGB regulars make their way to the reggae dance clubs downtown, Isaiah's and then Negril, or to take in salsa at the Roseland or Corso Ballrooms, or to the astonishing series of gay dance clubs—the Paradise Garage, the Loft, the Gallery—that boast unsurpassable mixes, sound systems, dancers, and enthusiasm.

The salsa rooms are daunting: you are never dressed right, and sometimes you're not even allowed in because you're wearing sneakers, and once you're there your honky feet cannot follow the steps. But soon enough **Ray Barretto** and **Tito Puente** also come to the Mudd Club, where it's all right for hipsters to make all sorts of flailing attempts at dancing. It's bracing to see those bands there: **Barretto**'s jackhammer piano louder than any other instrument; **Puente**'s lead singer, a bull of a guy whose collar and cuffs pop out from his suit coat as he punches the air and addresses incantations to someone invisible over his head. The gay discos can be daunting too, because of how easy it is to be utterly outclassed by the skill level of the other dancers—the extreme is the Nickel Bar, a pickup joint on Seventy-Second Street where **Robert Mapplethorpe** is known to go look for models, in which no one who is not a teenage athlete would even think of getting on the floor. But after a certain time spent in discos the mood of sheer abandon overtakes self-consciousness. The physical presence of the music is so much deeper—the bass more enveloping, the flow more liquid, the breaks more apocalyptic—than you are used to hearing anywhere else. You fall into it as if it were water on a hot day. At the

Loft there is no liquor, just fruit juice, cheeba, and the occasional psychedelic punch. There is even effective ventilation, and a lightness of atmosphere that goes with it. You might float home the next morning in broad daylight.

You're most likely to see more of your post-punk friends at the reggae clubs, because Jamaican music has been a constant presence in all your lives since the **Wailers** broke stateside in '73, and major artists come through New York City regularly. In fact you just saw **Lee Perry** and **Culture** at Irving Plaza, **Perry**, spliff in hand, crowing and raving and citing scripture in front of a wall of skank as dense as anything **Phil Spector** ever built. But the dance clubs aren't especially meant for your kind—they are the first signs of a Jamaican diaspora that will only keep increasing as people flee the unrelenting sectarian violence on the island. White kids go to the clubs expecting Rastafarian hippie-radical vibes and instead get served slackness, which not only is rude and sometimes obscene but rides on purposefully shallow, singsong, insanely repetitive hooks that crawl under your skin almost against your will, **Yellowman** and **General Echo** and **Papa Michigan** and **General Smiley** leering their way through repurposed nursery rhymes the meanings of which elude you for the longest time—although once you've figured out that the word they're saying is "punanny," it doesn't take you a year to work out what it signifies.

You also sometimes go dancing at the Squat Theatre on Twenty-Third Street, which is run by an extended family of Hungarian expats. When they are not putting on plays, they provide a home for what gets called punk jazz. The genre consists of R&B-based dance music, played tight with sharp edges and unlimited skronk by avant-garde jazz veterans. The "punk" thing is presumably in reference to the **Lounge Lizards**, who actually got labeled "fake jazz" because they are twenty-five-year-old white amateurs, although they acquit themselves pretty well. All these bands—**Joe Bowie**'s **Defunkt**, **Oliver Lake**'s **Jump Up**, **Luther Thomas**'s **Dazz**—take their cue from the **Lizards** in terms of material and basic approach. It is unusually populist territory for a crowd of guys who all have artistic and even familial links with the **Art Ensemble of Chicago** and **Ornette Coleman**'s constellation and jazz cred as long as your arm. The stuff they play is crazy danceable, always on full alert, and with more bristles than a brush. It's like **James Brown**'s band backing up **Albert Ayler**. You're pretty sure it'll be the next big thing. How could it miss?

And there are a million other clubs where a couple of years ago there were, like, three. The Mudd Club is the center of the known universe. It's changed a lot since it opened on Halloween 1978 and remained a pretty intimate bar-disco for at least a year. It wasn't crowded but it was very, very loud. People had *X*s in place of eyes. Watches stopped working just inside the door. Saturday night could stretch into Wednesday. Drink tickets were legal tender, and dollars were good mainly for rolling into cylinders. Friendships were forged that might last for hours, possibly days. Your coat, tossed in a

corner, was as good as gone. And then the place hyperinflated on celebrities and drink-ticket speculation. But amazingly it didn't crash, instead reinventing itself as a concert location, nicely scaled and with an excellent sound system. One afternoon you go there looking for a friend who's supposed to be rehearsing for that night's event, but when you open the door it's just you and **Nico**, on the stage with her harmonium, the rest of the room pitch-dark. You listen transfixed as she plays her entire show.

Normally, the Mudd Club is like Grand Central Station. If you're looking for anyone—they're not answering their phone and are absent from their usual haunts—you'll eventually see them come through. You see **Jean-Michel Basquiat** and **Anya Phillips** and **Lydia Lunch** and **John Sex** and **Lisa Rosen** and **Fab 5 Freddy** and **John Lurie** and **Andy Warhol** and **Sophie Vieille** and **Klaus Nomi** and **Futura 2000** and **Felice Rosser** and **Boris Policeband** and **Mary Lemley** and **Lee Quinones** and **Patti Astor** and **Kristian Hoffman** and **Adele Bertei** and **Lady Pink** and **Ronnie Cutrone** and **Rammellzee** and **Debbie Harry** and **Rene Ricard**, and **Anita Sarko** on the decks and **Haoui Montaug** at the velvet rope, the wisest and most poetic doorman ever. Later you will have breakfast with all of them at Dave's Corner at Canal and Broadway, where **Betty**, who has been working there for maybe forty years, sports a blond bouffant helmet, edged with a flip, over a face you seem to remember from a **Dorothea Lange** photograph.

A couple of blocks farther, just around the corner on West Broadway, is Tier 3, which has a broad clientele overlap with the Mudd Club but couldn't be more different. It was a bar and grill once, and bands play in what was the dining room—there is

no stage, and the audience begins about a foot from the mic stands. There is a room upstairs the same size where people just drink and talk, and another on the third floor where they show movies, usually by customers. The ambience of the club is as chill as if it were happening in your own living room. It's so low-key and unpretentious—and there is never a velvet rope—that it feels like a secret, even though a great many visiting acts from the UK (**The Raincoats**, the **Slits**, **Young Marble Giants**, **A Certain Ratio**) play there before appearing on larger stages uptown, this in addition to the hometown scene: **Bush Tetras**, **8 Eyed Spy**, the **Futants**, the great **DNA**, who appear to be reinventing pop music from scratch in some Lascaux cavern of their imaginations.

It's certainly a far cry from the aggression that marks so many other places, the frenzied door scenes and dance-floor territoriality you can find at the Peppermint Lounge or Danceteria or Bonds—all of them ambitious omniclubs with multiple levels and multiple bars and plenty of video monitors and VIP lounges that perhaps contain even more exclusive VVIP accommodations within. You visit those places, with their high prices and incessant status competitions, and think you've maybe been given a glimpse of the future—but you push the thought out of your mind. Just a few years ago, there was a clean division between downtown nightlife and uptown nightlife, with Studio 54 heading the latter, and the two sides did not mix. The downtown people drank beer and wore sneakers and listened to rock 'n' roll, while uptown they wore designer outfits and ran through several months' rent worth of cocaine in the course of a night and did some version of the hustle to disco numbers sugared with synthesized string sections. Now it's all one, thanks in part to the cult of the groove having swept the island of Manhattan.

CBGB, which might have been founded by the Visigoths in the third century, has outlived all the competition and by this time seems as if it will last forever. Visiting firemen of all statures still play there, some of them arena acts that play unannounced sets just for the glory and the cred. Even so, most nights there nowadays feature stacks of bands, seven or eight of them end to end maybe sharing a drum kit. You may go there now only to see your friends play—it's a rite of passage; all new bands are seemingly required to play CB's once—but you are guaranteed to go at least a couple of times a year. Its opposite number, Max's, site long ago of the **Velvet Underground**'s last stand and more recently a representation of punk so institutionalized it featured drinks named after popular stars of the day—champagne and stout was called a **Patti Smith**—comes undone this year. The fledgling **Beastie Boys** plays there on its last night, opening for **Bad Brains**.

But sometimes you think that punk itself may be hovering on the edge of extinction. That's certainly what **John Lydon**, formerly Rotten, would like to see happen, and this year he does his level best to push it over. His band **Public Image Ltd**, which played a couple of galvanizing shows last year, at the Palladium and, incongruously, at the Bowery

19

metal club Great Gildersleeves, is this year booked at the last minute for a set at the Ritz, a turn-of-the-last-century dance palace once called Webster Hall that has recently opened with a view to booking touring acts just below the arena level. The line outside starts to form at noon, and you can walk by and feast your eyes on the current look of suburban adolescence, all Perfecto jackets and stiff hair and dog collars and safety pins through the cheek. Eventually the doors open and everyone files in and waits. And waits some more. And waits some more after that. Three hours later a semblance of a show begins. The stage is almost completely covered by a giant video screen, behind which lurk the three members of the band and a few walk-ons. Aimless prerecorded videos are shown, along with murky live footage from behind the screen; the band tosses off rudimentary versions of a few numbers from its latest release, *Flowers of Romance;* at one point somebody puts the record itself on the turntable for a while. Occasionally it seems as though the throat-clearing has ceased and a recognizable performance is about to begin, but whenever that happens everything stops dead, to be followed by shambolic video effects and semi-musical doodling. As the audience becomes restive, the band begins to taunt it, with increasing intensity, daring it to start a riot. And the band gets its wish. Bottles and then chairs are thrown, the video screen is yanked off its mount, the equipment slides off the stage, the band members barely escape with their lives. It is by merest chance that the injuries are relatively minor and that no one is killed.

But just look at what else has been coming out this year from formerly rock-identified precincts: **Blondie**'s "Rapture," **Kraftwerk**'s *Computer World,* **Soft Cell**'s cover of "Tainted Love," **Brian Eno** and **David Byrne**'s *My Life in the Bush of Ghosts,* the **Human**

League's "Don't You Want Me," the first singles by **ESG** and **Liquid Liquid**, **A Certain Ratio**'s "Do the Du (Casse)," not to mention the **B-52s**' misunderstood *Mesopotamia*, the release of which will be delayed for a year. Any of these can slide into a rotation that also includes **Grace Jones**'s "Nightclubbing," **Prince**'s "Controversy," **Teena Marie**'s "Square Biz," and **Rick James**'s "Super Freak," not to mention assorted items by **Afrika Bambaataa**, **Grandmaster Flash**, and the **Treacherous Three**.

And it isn't just music that appears to be on the cusp of a transformation. The city is poised on much the same kind of brink. For years, almost since the end of the war, it has been increasingly given over to the poor, while anybody who can scrape together a down payment has headed off to the suburbs. Whole neighborhoods have been virtually abandoned, entire clusters of blocks set on fire, sometimes on multiple occasions. The blocks east of Avenue B look like the aftermath of war—it's probably around now that a bar called Downtown Beirut opens on First Avenue. Social services barely function; the streets are filthy and heaped with trash; there are so few cars parked on the Lower East Side that stolen whips get dumped there and torched. Many taxi drivers will not take you east of First anywhere below Fourteenth Street. Chances are that you've endured at least part of the winter with no heat. And drugs are rampant, probably at an all-time peak. Heroin and cocaine are ridiculously cheap and available, and all kinds of people who should know better are getting themselves strung out, some of them fatally. Friends are stealing from friends; bands dissolve when members start hocking equipment—there are many more stories circulating about that sort of crime than about people getting mugged. And this is also the year that an unknown cancer begins to be spotted among gay men, just a few dozen at first.

At any rate, the city has up to now been the ideal place for artists and musicians, for young people trying to figure out life and getting there by pushing at any and all boundaries of custom and habit and even good sense. You can live for very cheap; rent an apartment of more than one room for less than $200 a month; buy furniture and clothes secondhand; get a job, in a record store or a bookshop, that pays the bills and allows for a social life and occasions for shoplifting. You and your friends can take a share in a rehearsal space for almost nothing, as long as you are willing to freeze in the winter and broil in the summer. You can get some gigs going in any of the myriad clubs—there's one for every fractional taste—and if nobody will give you a record contract you can cut and press and distribute a single yourselves without falling into penury. You can advertise your gigs with photocopied fliers wheatpasted on walls and the plywood coverings of shuttered shops and atop paid advertisements on the sides of bodegas. Maybe if yours are clever enough you can attract some people other than just your friends. Even as you hope you might win some sort of pop-music jackpot, you know you'll probably never make any money, even if you get a record contract and go on to tour college towns and the Scandinavian countries. Hundreds of the bands

that appear on bills at downtown clubs will do so only once before they break up over money disputes or matters of dogma. Or change their lineup because of personality problems. Drummers are scarce, and worth their weight in 40s of Olde English.

But none of that is a tragedy, because you can afford to fail. You can change your style and your name over and over again. You can branch out into painting or Super 8 movies and see whether any of it clicks, and if it doesn't you can try something else. You can maintain a reasonably decent life at the bottom, secure in the knowledge that if you jump out the window down there you won't get hurt. There may be people around who are actually planning a career, but if so they're keeping mum about it. Anybody who would really prefer to live in a more secure environment or continues to dream of plush settings probably pulled up stakes and moved west years ago. But you're starting to notice a tinge of hysteria in the air. People can be heard fronting about how bold it is of them to be living on the edge. You never used to hear that sort of talk—used to be that youths from elsewhere who moved downtown realized pretty soon that they had entered a neighborhood of families and old people, Dominicans and Ukrainians and Chinese, who really didn't care about their artistic ambitions or romantic lowlife fantasies, and that they owed their neighbors a good deal of discretion and respect. Now you've got people making up brand names for their assumed neighborhoods—Alphabet City, for example, as if they were already packaging the eventual action-adventure based on their early years of struggle.

Nobody is conscious of it yet, but major change lies just around the corner. Very soon—next year, maybe—the building you live in will be bought by a speculator who will flip it, probably to someone else who will flip it again, and so on down the line until its sale price is ten or twenty times more than the initial speculator purchase. And at some point a buyer, having invested so much and knowing that the combined rents of the building will not allow him to recoup in this lifetime, will start making efforts to get you out, by fair means or foul. And when he does so he will put in new drywall and reconfigure the layout so that he can insert a bathroom and get the tub out of the kitchen. And then he can rent the place out for three or four or five times what you had been paying. And so your club will become a bank, your rehearsal space a parking garage, your greasy spoon an eyeglass boutique, your dive a sports bar. Even if you manage to stay, you will feel like a ghost.

But all that lies in the future—some of it in the near future. In the meantime youths continue to start bands, to fuck up, to change names, to change appearances, to change styles. Enormous numbers of them continue to be obsessed with music. Even if music isn't your gift or your strong suit you are obsessed with music, and even if you are completely incapable of making any music yourself, you want to live inside it. It's the primary language of your time, the major medium of exchange, the principal commodity. It's the public face of sex, the legal drug, the emotional prosthetic. It rules

and shapes every waking moment of your life. Music is ambient everywhere outside, and it is ambient at all times inside your head. And all the music around you is in the process of becoming one music, a great river of groove, embellished variously, identified by matters of instrumentation or echo or use of electronics or details of vocal styling. As surely as a certain kind of thin, dry guitar and a certain nasal delivery mark a thing as British, and as surely as a staccato vocal attack and a capital use of cheap electronics mark something else out as Jamaican, so the sound that this year immediately registers as New York all over the globe is principally composed of the scratching and mixing and jumping and fading and rhyming of hip hop.

There are little pockets of that sound starting to happen in other cities across the country, but they're embryonic as yet. Rap right now is a direct, mimetic product of the streets of New York City, embodying the city's verbal agility and aggression, its constantly fractured barrage of traveling sounds, its abrasive textures and juxtaposed incongruities, its densely layered strata of information. And it's only just becoming apparent how much more can be done with the fundaments of the style: how much stripping down, speeding up, pulling in of other sounds musical and otherwise, and how much textual complexity and nuanced attitudinizing and justified protest and seductive strategizing and flat-out indictment can be brought to the talkover. It is occurring to people all over the city that rap is a sound that can be *carved*. And so it is occurring to three young city kids, lately in the punk-rock business, that they can use it to make anthems and stage sketch comedy and arrange pinpoint-precise repartee that wears a stupid hat to conceal its sophistication—and that's just the beginning.

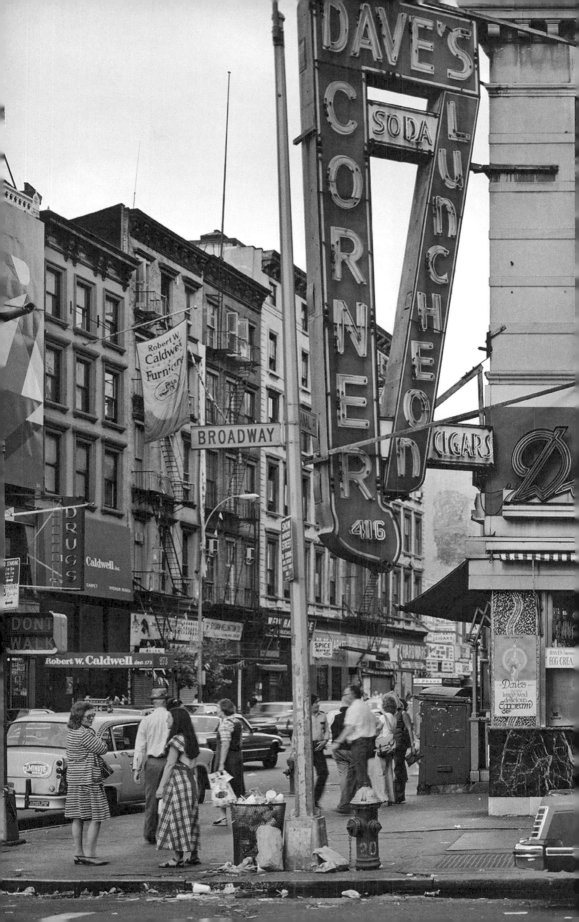

ENTRANCE
AROUND CORNER

JOBBERS ISAAR SCHRADER EXPORTER
LACES EMBROIDERIES TEXTILES

e's Restauran

Dave's
IMPROVED
EGG CREAM

ALL BEEF
FRANKFURTERS

| 35 | Coke 35 | Chola LIME RICKEY 45 | Calcina HOT KNISHES 65 | ALL BEEF FRANKS 65 |

DAVE'S
CORNER

$1.99
LUNCHEON SPECIAL
CUP OF SOUP
PLATTER OF THE DAY
with coffee
MONDAY to FRIDAY

MONDAY to FRIDAY 6 A.M. to 11 P.M.
2 EGGS SCRAMBLED or FRIED ONLY 70¢
TOAST & COFFEE
75 120 1

PIX
PIX
PIX

(AH)

Since electricity . . . happened . . . every generation of kids has had this, like, magical electronic moment in time. For our generation it was the dawn of video games. Pong was a huge fuckin' deal. *Major*. Space Invaders, Asteroids, Robotron, and so on. *But* . . . for us here in New York, the

real suspended-in-time magical electronic-game moment happened right after school on Channel 11 (WPIX): the live-on-air video game known to us as . . . **PIX**. Every New York City fifth grader in 1978 was abuzz about that shit.

All day at school, we felt like chain smokers on a seventeen-hour flight. When school let out at three you would bust your ass to get home to tune in. Then you'd frantically call the station's phone number to try to get on the show. But it would never happen for you. The number was always busy. You'd keep calling back until that day's game started but some lucky kid who called just before you got to play. The TV screen would turn into what now would look like the most basic and primitive video

game, but back then it was *so* futuristic. There'd be a sort of cannon at the bottom of the screen, and all of a sudden, a spaceship would pass quickly across the top of the screen, and that lucky mthrfkr would have to shout "PIX!" at the perfect time to make the cannon shoot at the spaceship. No one ever timed it right. No one ever hit that spaceship. It was wildly weird. And it was the best.

In our little ten-year-old minds, we imagined the backstories of all these other kids that got lucky enough to play PIX, but were so shitty at it. Some kids seemed like they were drunk or high and would just mumble "PIX" like, rrree-aall slow and kind of lispy too. Way after the spaceship had already passed. "Pikths." You also had the kid who had

way too many friends that wouldn't shut up in the room, so their screaming in the background would drown out the actual rallying cry of PIX. But my favorite kid did what I for sure would've done as soon as that shit commenced . . . just start rapid-fire screaming:

PIXPIXPIXPIXPIXPIXPIXPIXPIXPIX!!!!

You'd *have* to hit that spaceship, right? But *no one ever did.* Was it rigged? Would WPIX really do that to us kids? I mean, they didn't *need* to have this game. It was just in between whatever cartoons they were showing. We would have watched *Hong Kong Phooey* at 3:15 anyways. So why not let us win once in a while?

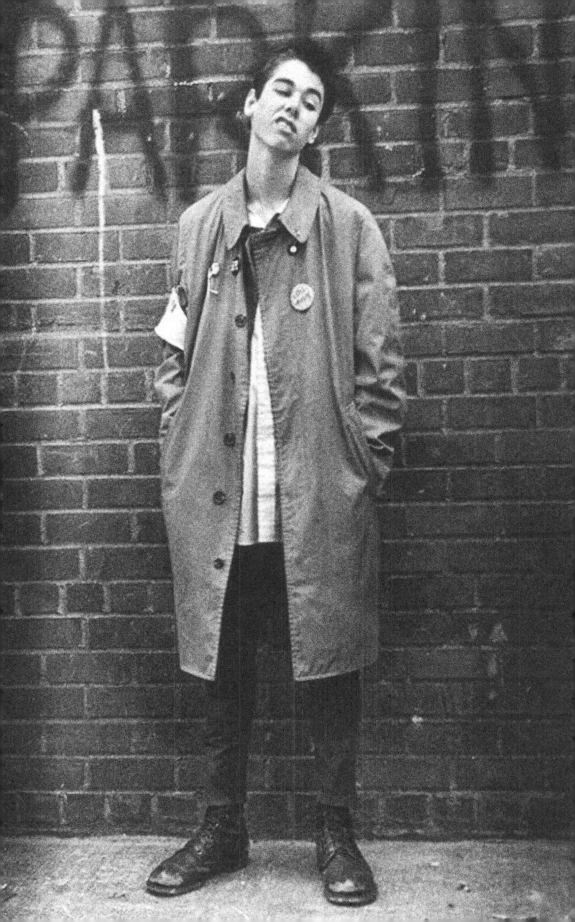

The Other Kid at the BAD BRAINS Show

Michael Diamond

The thing about being the punk-rock kid at school was that you'd have no friends. You looked like a weirdo with ill-fitting, torn-up, and stenciled button-down shirts from the Goodwill store and a safety pin as an earring, and you would get laughed at. I lived near the Hayden Planetarium, on Central Park West, and I'd have to walk by it to get to the Eighty-First Street subway. On Friday nights, the planetarium hosted Laser Rock shows, where they played Pink Floyd's *Dark Side of the Moon* in its entirety, accompanied by lasers. (P.S., they still do this.) So when I wanted to take the subway to a show on Friday, I'd have to walk past the planetarium, where large groups of dudes stood around smoking pot in denim jackets with the sleeves cut off and Floyd art on the back. I'd be greeted immediately with "Hey, faggot!" and other catcalls; in a few instances, an actual chase was involved. It felt like everyone else was into Pink Floyd, Zeppelin, or the Who. But when you first discover punk, it's sort of your *job* to hate classic rock. So there was no common ground. Which, in retrospect, is a little surprising; it's not like I went to a big public high school in Middle America. I went to a "progressive school" in New York City; all three of us did. Mine was a small, hippie-liberal school called Walden. It was really hard to get into trouble there. If I didn't do my homework, I was confronted with: "Interesting choice, Michael . . . why did you choose not to do the assignment?" Yauch went to a place in Tribeca named Elizabeth Seeger (named for Pete Seeger's aunt, which tells you a lot). Seeger was so progressive it made Walden look like West Point. I think smoking pot at lunch might have been a sanctioned option? And Horovitz went to CAS, or City as School. This was barely school at all. He got credit for doing stuff like

running errands for a recording studio, being a prep cook, and interning for an artist.

Of course, none of us knew each other yet. But despite all that educational open-mindedness, there were so few punk kids that even in the vastness of NYC we were almost destined to eventually meet. But that was later. . . .

My first punk-rock friends were two other kids at my high school. One had spiky hair, acne, and a pale Irish complexion—the most classically British-punk-looking New Yorker I'd ever met. His name was John Berry. The other kid was the exact opposite: a heavyset, nerdy Jewish kid with glasses, named Jeremy

Shatan. He was less immersed in the fashion and lifestyle than John and I were; he just loved the music.

By the time I befriended these guys, I'd already been a serious record nerd for as long as I could remember. I came from a decidedly nonmusical household. Visual art was always around; my dad was an art dealer, and my parents would constantly have artists over for very spirited discussions about painting and art history. Music was just not part of the conversation; it was not something that was on my parents' radar at all. But I had two older brothers, and my musical initiation came through them.

My brother David had a stack of Motown 7-inches, so from a very early age I got super into the Jackson 5. Through my brothers I also got into the Beatles and Neil Young's

Here's a perfect illustration of the kind of parents we had, and the kind of freedom they gave us: When our friend Tania Aebi (one of the Bag Ladies) turned eighteen, she wasn't sure what she wanted to do. So her dad—a Swiss-German eccentric who lived in SoHo—made an offer: he'd either pay for her college education or he'd get her a sailboat. But if she took the sailboat, she had to sail around the world.

By herself.

And she had no sailing and navigation experience.

And he wasn't going to flat-out buy the boat for her either—he'd just give her a loan so she could do all of this, even though she'd expressed zero interest in sailing, like ever. So what did she do?

She fucking sailed around the world by herself even though she had no idea how to sail or navigate.

First American woman and the youngest person up to that point ever to do it. Took her two years.

So maybe there *was* a method to our parents' madness?

(NB: I was always a little scared of her dad, though, tbh.) (MD)

Everybody Knows This Is Nowhere and Stevie Wonder's *Songs in the Key of Life*. I look back on it now, those are all really good records—great records actually, pillars of pop music. But identity-wise, none of it was *mine*.

Kiss was the first band I embraced as my own. (Possibly because my brothers were a little too old for them. And maybe a little too smart.) I found Kiss exciting for the same reasons that millions of other American preteen boys did—great riffs, comic-book imagery, and a shitload of fire-breathing. (Also: blood.) I remember staying up to watch *Kiss Meets the Phantom of the Park*, a ninety-minute TV movie that involved an evil amusement-park owner, a Kiss concert, and cyborgs.

Wikipedia: "For years after its airing no one who worked for the group was permitted to mention the film in their presence." (MD)

The next pivotal band for me—and again I have my brothers to thank—was The Clash. They spoke to me in so many new ways. The music was raw and intoxicating. I don't think at that age I could necessarily understand or relate to the band's politics per se, but there was something vital and real about them. I went to see them play on the *London Calling* tour in 1980, and they were incredible. But watching them play I never felt like that could be me. They were too cool, too unattainable, too culturally different. They were British, with a whole different set of political and social realities. Which didn't mean I couldn't go and dance and have fun and be in awe at their show, but they remained on a pedestal.

Hardcore was different.

For me, the watershed band was Bad Brains. I remember hearing the "Pay to Cum" 7-inch and being totally blown away by it. It was faster than anything I'd ever heard, by a wide margin, but it was still a real song, still had enough pop melody that I loved it.

Pre-cellphone/smartphone, kids actually had to call each other's houses. This was as embarrassing as you'd imagine. When you were a fourteen-year-old kid calling up a friend's house, you had to make small talk with whatever parent or sibling picked up before actually talking to your friend. The most embarrassing would be when my mom picked up a phone from another spot in the house and would just start dialing before she realized I was already on the phone. (Kids: landlines back then'd be like if you shared the same cellphone number with your parents, and they could listen in or interrupt anytime you were on a call, and their calls rang on your phone. Srsly y'all would have died. At my house, there was a phone in the hallway outside my room with a super-long cord. I would pull the cord all the way into my room and close the door so I could keep my punk-rock life secret.) (MD)

Once John Berry and Jeremy Shatan and I found each other, the three of us would talk about music every day and get together whenever we could to listen to new 7-inches or cassettes. John Berry and I were both determined to figure out how to dress like Joe Strummer and Mick Jones on the cover of the first Clash album, with their homemade clothes that had slogans spray-painted on them. We tried to change our look. We'd go together to the Salvation Army on Ninety-Sixth between Broadway and West End, trying to make our own bondage pants. We made a horrible job of it. We bought button-down permanent-press shirts for 89 cents and tried to cut them up and spray-paint them and made bad stencils.

We also read everything we could find about punk and hardcore, which wasn't much: *The Face* magazine and the NYC free weeklies *SoHo Weekly News* and the *Village Voice*. The last two were particularly useful because in addition to articles, they contained concert calendars, and in the back pages were ads for all the upcoming shows. It was in one or both of those weekly papers that, sometime in late 1980, we found an ad announcing a Bad Brains show at Botany Talk House, a tiny dive bar in Chelsea. By this time, I'd already spent countless afternoons alone in my bedroom dancing like an idiot to "Pay to Cum." We were in.

If I remember correctly, John and I ended up going, but not Jeremy. So the two of us walk into the Botany Talk House. Though in our minds Bad Brains was a huge deal, that night there were all of maybe twelve people there, and only two of them seemed our age. One was easily the coolest person I'd ever seen, kind of like *intimidatingly* cool. Homemade bondage pants. Homemade leather jacket with **LOUD FAST RULES** and various band names painted on the back. Heavy black eyeliner around his

"Loud Fast Rules!" was the great first single by NYC hardcore pioneers the Stimulators. (MD)

eyes. This would turn out to be Nick Marden, bassist in the NYC hardcore band Even Worse, later of the Stimulators. Nick was maybe three years older than us, but that was enough to make him seem like he was from a different generation. Especially with those clothes; it would have been one thing if he just bought that shit at Trash and Vaudeville on St. Mark's Place, but he *made* it. He was invested like that. I was a young teenager *trying* to be punk-rock; here was a guy who actually *was*.

The only other kid our age was wearing a black trench coat, a couple of small homemade band buttons, and black combat boots. At that stage of my life, I was super shy. I mean, I wouldn't start a conversation with *anyone*, never

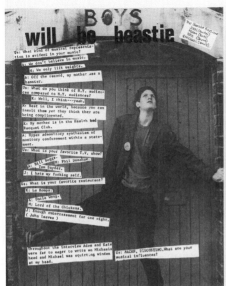

mind a stranger. But John was much more comfortable socially than I was, so he just goes over and starts talking to the kid. He was our age, it turned out, and his name was Adam Yauch.

We didn't have long to talk before Bad Brains started playing. It was the rowdiest, fastest, most ear-shattering show I had ever seen, and I loved it. We all did. Afterward, John and I wrote down our phone numbers for Yauch.

We all started talking on the phone frequently, saw each other at shows, and, along the way, found other punk kids that became our friends; soon we evolved into a bigger clique of like-minded outcasts.

The principals were me, Berry, Shatan, Yauch, and a group of girls we called the "Bag Ladies" because they only bought clothes at thrift stores, seemed determined to layer these clothes in ever-more-unlikely ways (think: a skirt over a pair of jeans), and would cruise around with all manner of stuff in bags on the go: Jill Cunniff, Gabby Glaser, Kate Schellenbach, Tania Aebi, Arabella Field, Rhana Harris, Kate Stearn, Sarah Cox. Tania and Jill also had their own zine, *Decline of Art*. I remember them teaching us how to fake hand-stamps so you could sneak into shows.

Yauch and I would sit around and listen to records endlessly and laugh about shit. He was quiet, but with an unflappable intensity and focused enthusiasm—whether for a record or an activity, he'd keep pushing you to listen, keep going until shit was accomplished. He just had a greater degree of determination and decisiveness than the rest of us. He was also funny; it'll probably make no sense to you, but my favorite mannerism of his was this thing he and his friend David Wade would do. Back then, after somebody did something ridiculous or was the subject of a stinging insult, most kids would say "*burn!*"

(It was like the 1980s version of "owned" or "rekt.") But Yauch and Wade had their own version of this, where they'd do this weird hand motion and say "*boof!*" It was nonsensical and totally hilarious.

You'd make the "OK" hand sign, put the circle (that your pointer finger and thumb would make) next to your eye, then bring that circle right down to the person who had fallen down, dropped their food, or got snapped on. Then say "boof" in a weird low tone. (AH)

If we had grown up almost anywhere else in the world, our crew wouldn't have had such a steady flow of amazing events that we could all go to, unaccompanied by parents. First of all, in other cities you'd have to drive to shows, which automatically meant a parent. And second, because all of our parents were artists or intellectuals, they gave us an unusual amount of freedom. It was still kinda the '70s, in terms of parenting. My mom had certain time structures, like, you know, I couldn't be out late on a weeknight. And I had to be clear about where I was and where I was going. But her basic attitude was, *If your*

One time I stayed out all night without calling my mom, and she (understandably) lost her mind when I got home. Just got super fucking pissed and grounded me.* So I learned the hard way: there *were* limits. (MD)
*Yes, even Mike D gets grounded. *Boof.* (AH)

schoolwork doesn't suffer, you can do whatever you want. If it does, we have a problem.

Everybody in our crew had parents that were, in one way or the other, similarly lenient.

So even though we were barely just teenagers, we got this powerful shared experience of going to punk shows, running around deserted downtown Manhattan, and becoming close friends in the process. It sounds corny, but it was magical. And after a while, something began to dawn on us as our lives became increasingly organized around bands and shows.

We should try doing this ourselves.

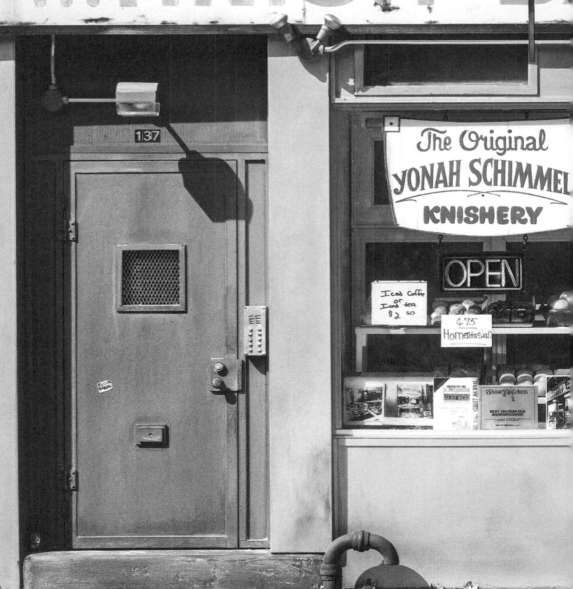

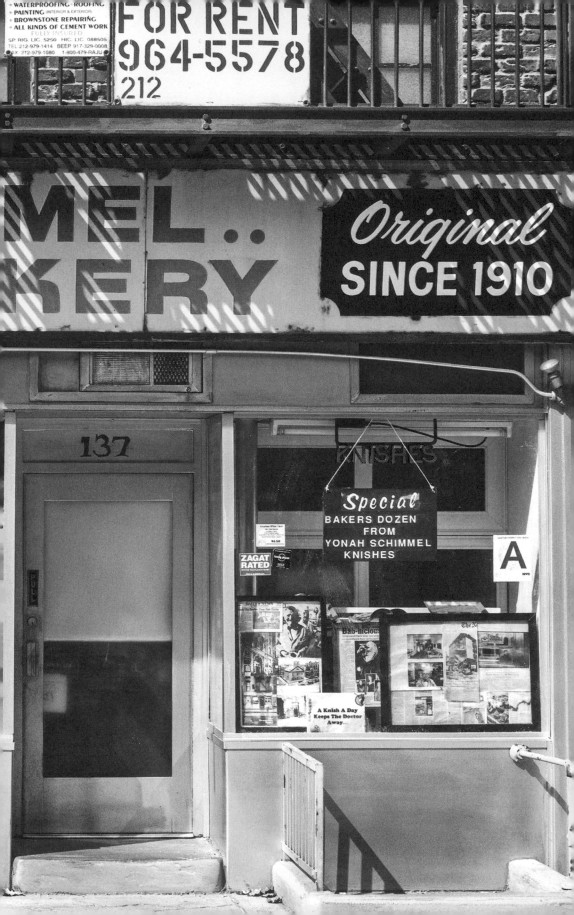

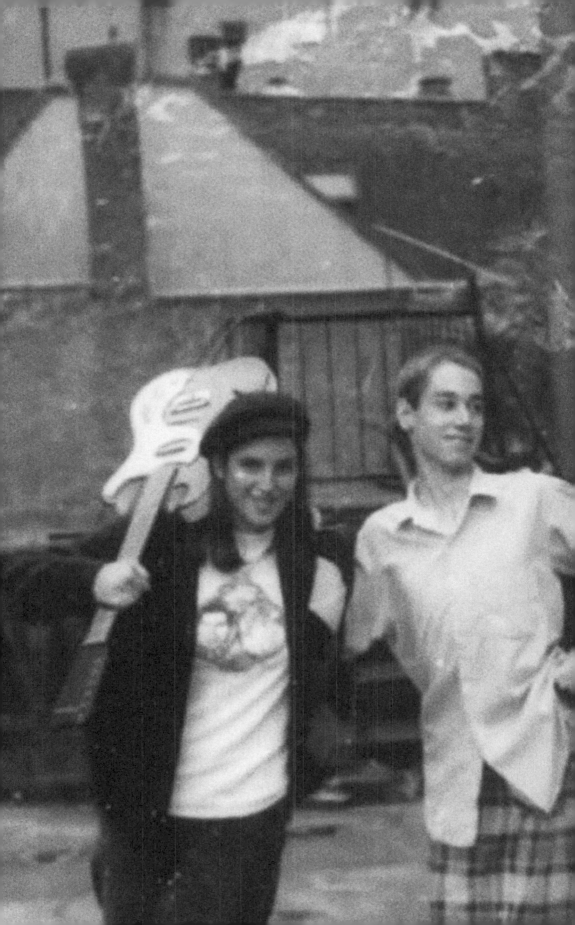

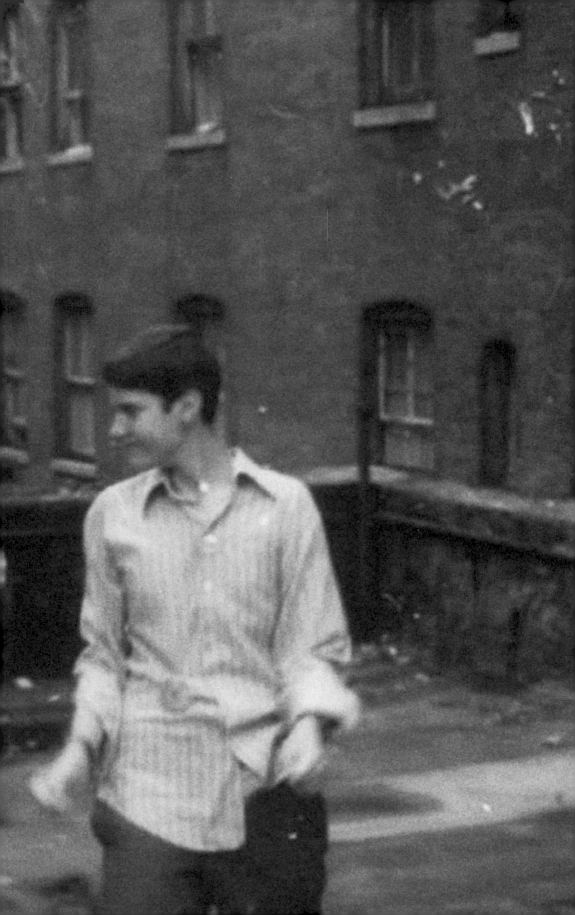

Well, Back in My Day...
(AH)

Wearing a backpack was *not* cool. I mean, unless there's textbooks in there and you're actually going to, or coming from, school. Otherwise, DO NOT WEAR ONE. And on your way to and from school: having on both backpack straps was square. It could only hang from one strap, on one shoulder, and you had to have buttons on your backpack. Band buttons. Not too many, just a few. Five was the limit for sure. You couldn't appear as though you were trying too hard. The minutiae of dumb details in a fifteen-year-old's mind are fantastic. So . . . being that I often cut school, I had to just carry a bunch of shit around in my pockets. You know, with the no-backpack rule and everything. And by "shit," I mean my tapes and my Walkman. There was a different connection to your music back then. The cassette-tape era. You had to plan your day around your cassettes. How many could you fit in your pockets? (Obviously, winter was an easier time 'cause you had way more storage options . . . jackets, coats, down vests, etc. More pockets.) You had to think this shit through. What did you wanna listen to that day? Who were you gonna run into, because you did not wanna get busted with only the Psychedelic Furs' *Talk Talk Talk* tape on you. Even though you loved that shit. You had to have the cool shit on you, just in case. You might end up at someone's apartment and wanna put some music on. You had to have variety. Oh, and also . . . remember, this is the '80s so there's no baggy anything. It's just tight pants with bulging rectangular pockets. *No, that's not a knot of cash in my pocket*, it's the Minor Threat (A side) / Black Flag (B side) tape, and the Slits (A side) / Marvin Gaye's greatest hits (B side), and so on. Having eight cassette tapes shoved into your front and back pants pockets, walking around all day, is a schleppy look. I WOULD HAVE FUCKING LOVED THE SHIT OUT OF HAVING AN IPHONE. For real. Anyone who's trying to convince you that tapes are cool, and that iPhones are corny, is dead wrong. I can tell you from experience, *and* with a professional's opinion: the cassette vs. vinyl vs. CD vs. mp3 argument is boring. If I made you a mixtape and you've just heard the J.B.'s song "Pass the Peas" for the first time . . . the song would be just as fucking awesome if I emailed you an mp3 instead. I promise. Being able to scroll and click to get to the next song is a wonderful new feature. "Yeah, but . . . mp3s sound terrible." Who cares?! Try Scotch-taping a broken cassette tape four or five times in different places on the tape, and then listen back to that after it's been in various linty pockets for a year and a half. To me, the only thing that's really missing with the iPhone is that physical relationship to your music.

If I added it up, I feel like I've wasted 261 solid hours of my life just watching cassette tapes rewinding and fast-forwarding. There was no drag and

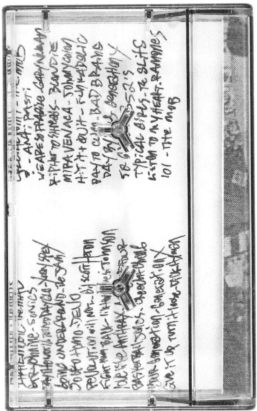

drop onto a playlist to make a mixtape. To record X-Ray Spex's song "Identity" onto a tape, you had to listen to the whole song as you recorded it. So a whole album took a while. Jimmy Spicer's song "Adventures of Super Rhyme" is, like, fifteen minutes long. Just that one song. Maybe *that's* why my attention was so limited when it came to doing homework. If I had fuckin' iTunes I would've had time to *read* the book for school instead of glancing at the Cliffs Notes. Or asking my best friend, Arthur Africano, to describe what happened in that book, because he would actually read the books for homework. You couldn't just Google search for a podcast to listen to. No Spotifying anything. You had to wait until the radio show you wanted to tape came on (Tim Sommer's *Noise the Show*, the Red Alert show, the Mr. Magic show, the Gil & Pat Bailey show, etc.) and then actually sit there for the whole hour that it took to tape it. Live streaming meant just that. If your stereo couldn't record what the radio was playing, you'd have to put a tape recorder right up next to the speakers so you could tape that radio show you wanted.

The physical thing of taking the record out, cueing up the song you wanna record on the turntable, letting it play, pushing the Play+Record buttons on the cassette recorder at the perfect time (you don't want a lot of dead airspace on your tape), then repeating that for 45, 60, or 90 minutes was an all-day/all-night event. It might've been the most physical labor I've ever done in my

life. And if the tape you were making was meant to be a gift for someone, it took serious focus. It was rarely just about sharing songs via a cassette. It's way bigger than that. Artistic decisions, emotional decisions, and, depending on who you're making it for, strategic decisions went into its making. For certain people, you gotta remind them that you have a way better record collection than they do. And this tape I'm giving you now will show and prove it. (Not that it's a competition . . . but it always is.) You could keep it brief with a 30-minute tape. But maybe that's too brief. The 90-minute tape is a bit much. It can get tiresome, unless that tape was meant for background music. The 120-minute tape is for obsessive-compulsives with too much time on their hands. In my opinion, the 60-minute tape is the best of the cassette-tape lengths. You're putting work in but not going overboard. (If you have romantic intentions, don't get creepy. For sure go with the 60.)

Cey Adams: If you happen to be reading this, it's my belief that you still owe me a 60-minute tape from 1984. I came home one day and you left me a dollar and a note that said, "I took a blank cassette, here's the $." I appreciate that you didn't just take the tape knowing that I probably would never notice. And that you left the dollar, but remember . . . my room was on the fifth floor and so I had to go down four flights and walk over to Hudson Street to get a new blank tape. A dollar is not the same thing as a cassette tape, no matter if a cassette tape cost a dollar. To put it in terms that you could better comprehend: imagine if you came home and opened the fridge, and instead of that banana pudding that was in there waiting for you, you'd find a note I'd left and $2.50 in its place. Not the same thing, right? (AH)

After you finished making your tape, you'd have to make a cover for it. You couldn't just have the white TDK sleeve with song titles. You'd want your tapes to have cool covers like your LPs, flyers, and fanzines. The outside cover would be some kind of picture you'd cut out of a magazine, or your science book, or whatever. You'd Scotch-tape it to the blank cover that came with the cassette so that you could write down the songs on the tape on the back. And then you'd doctor up the actual tape itself. You'd draw a few different colors for outlines around the band's name, or the title you'd given the mixtape. (Paint pens were a game changer when they came out.) It was a process. But you know, you can fit more tapes in your pockets without the cases, so the tapes themselves gotta look fresh. Oh, also . . . very important . . . *the tabs*. Every blank cassette tape has these two little rectangular plastic tabs on top. You can record on a tape only if the tabs are still there. If the tabs have been taken off, like every store-bought album on cassette, you'd have to put Scotch tape, or a sticker, over where the tab was. The top left corner, that's the Record tab on the side of the tape you're recording. So . . . when you're done, don't forget to pop the tabs, or peel the tape off the popped tabs, or else you're gonna record over what's on the tape on accident. Like how I have a tape of The Jam's *Sound Affects* that I recorded me+Yauch having a super boring conversation over. Funny now, but aggravating then. If you were reading this when you were in high school in 1981 you would really thank me for saving you the time of figuring all this out for yourself. Not only was it not cool to wear a backpack, it was really uncool to be like, *Hey . . . um . . . can you show me how to do this thing that I don't know how to do?* Also . . . who would you ask? An older kid? No way. Pre-YouTube you were on your own.

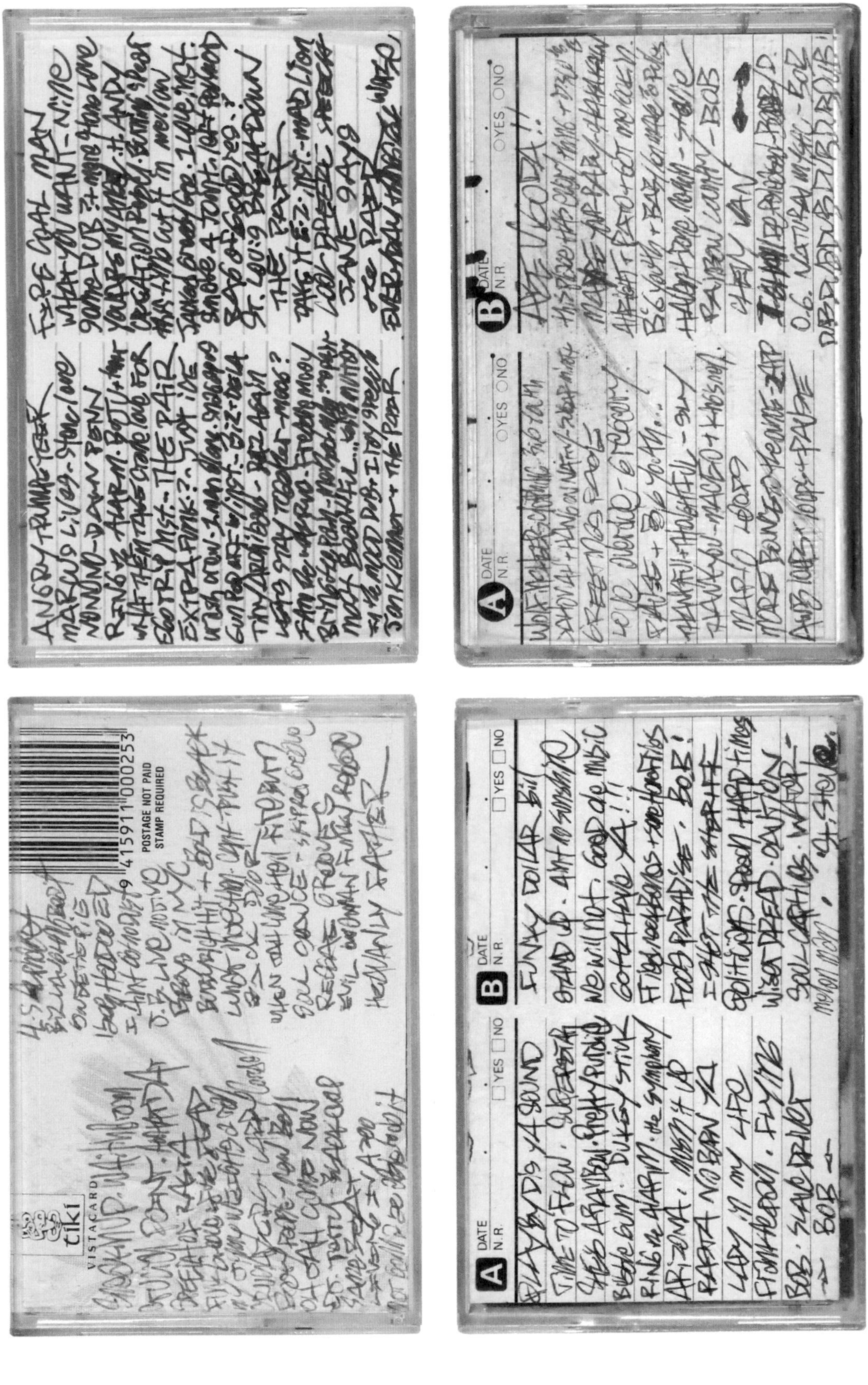
tiki
VISTACARD
POSTAGE NOT PAID
STAMP REQUIRED

Cassette-tape upkeep is fucking delicate. After carrying the same tapes in your tight, linty pockets for months, and playing them a thousand and one times . . . the tape would inevitably get wound up and stuck in the tape heads. Everything would stop. Through the little window on the cassette, you could see the gears of the tape moving around like a dryer at the laundromat. Suddenly, you would see the tape you'd spent hours making all bunched up. That moment felt like when a computer freezes and a sad-face image shows up on the screen. You'd have to stop whatever you were doing and deal with this dire situation immediately. The tape would be all squished up into the machine. Mangled. Taking it out was like pulling 60 minutes of wet fettuccine out of a dog's mouth. It was as though the tape and tape deck were mad at you for being a careless and impatient teenager. "Damn kids! Always rewinding and fast-forwarding. Just let the songs play all the way through or it's gonna break." To fix that tape, you'd have to gently and painstakingly pull the tape out of the deck. Knowing when to force it and when to go real slow. And finally, when you'd get all the tape out . . . you'd get a tiny Phillips-head screwdriver and unscrew the screws holding the tape's housing together. You'd open it up, cut the tape at its most damaged point, unravel the tape, put a tiny piece of Scotch tape on a table, match up both ends of broken tape, join the two cut ends with that tiny piece of Scotch tape, screw the housing back together, and then . . . *the pencil.* You'd have to wind the cassette tape back into its housing so it'd be ready to play again. The pencil was the perfect tool to fit inside the cassette's little plastic gears. So you'd sit there and wind, and wind, and wind, and wind, and wind.

On tour I always used to bring Scotch tape, a pencil, and a big Swiss Army knife (that my sister gave me in the early '80s) with me, in case a tape broke. The Swiss Army knife had a pair of scissors and the perfect tiny little Phillips-head screwdriver. And also, you know, most hotels would screw their windows shut so you couldn't throw shit out or do whatever they didn't want you to do out their windows. Like smoke pot and throw fireworks. Or teakettles, Scotch eggs, furniture, etc. The Swiss Army is ready for action. (AH)

It seems like it's just so easy to know things now. To know about movies, or art, or music, or food preparation, or the 1950s roller-derby circuit. But in 1978, junior high school . . . besides what was on the seven available TV channels, or WPLJ radio, we didn't know anything. Important. About life. Like sex. And what you're supposed to do and how to have it. Or anything else, really, that we actually wanted to know. The library on Tenth Street didn't have what I was looking for at age fifteen. In 2000-whatever, if you want to learn how to play a song on the guitar, someone's on YouTube waiting to teach you how to play that exact song. Or build that record shelf, or how to have sex and what it looks like. Does all the accessible information give you confidence as a junior high schooler, or is it too overwhelming? Like . . . *you're supposed to know how to do this already, dumbass.* Your "record" collection is supposed to be all-encompassing of your fifteen-year-old world. You don't have to figure out where did this come from, or how do you do this? Google will tell you that (insert whatever current band that a current fifteen-year-old would listen to here) was totally inspired by The Strokes, who were inspired by Television, who were inspired by . . . and so on. So, you can have Brenda Lee on your iPhone

because in a random search, the band that you love was inspired by so+so, and they did this+that, and that someone loved Brenda Lee. Within minutes, you would have all of that backstoried information. And within minutes you're now listening to Brenda Lee's voice for the first time and you're like, OH SHIT! With the iPhone you no longer have to worry that some square would think *you* were a square for carrying around that Psychedelic Furs *Talk Talk Talk* tape in your pocket because it'd be buried deep amongst 12 billion mp3s.

I'm not trying to be all . . . Well, back in my day we had to carry blocks of ice up a mountain made of shards of broken glass just to get to drink a *Hatful of Rain*. But it's true that the physical relationship to music was different. There was more touching, holding, caressing, and finessing. Making, listening to, and caring for cassettes is *the most* hands-on and personal music listening experience. For sure. You don't just listen; you're very involved. I do miss that, but I don't miss schlepping all those fucking tapes around in my tight, bulky pockets like a scrub. And like so many really close friendships . . . sadly, me+my tapes have drifted apart. All that said, the experience of a fifteen-year-old kid obsessing over music is basically the same as it's been since the fuckin' gramophone or player piano. Endless hours sitting in bedrooms, or on stoops (or whatever the suburban equivalent is to a stoop), waiting for a friend to show up. Waiting for something to happen. Waiting to have sex. Waiting to understand your weird parents. Waiting to understand anything in the world. Waiting to go somewhere else. It all needs a soundtrack. Your soundtrack. Since forever in time, we've all had our . . . "I just got dumped," "I'm gonna break up with you," "I'll love you forever," "No one gets it," and "Entrance to the party" songs. It's just easier to physically carry them with you now.

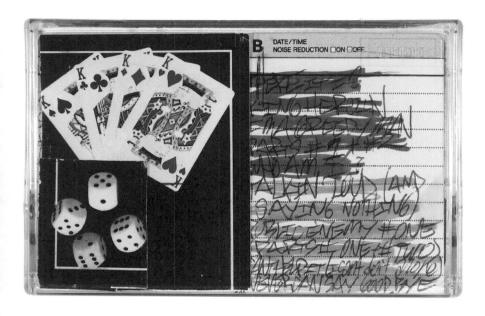

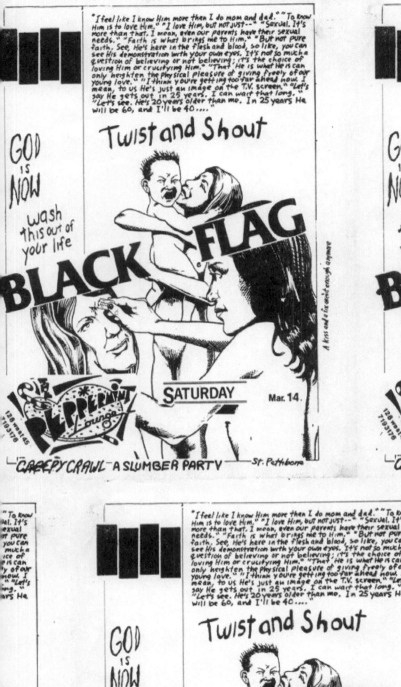
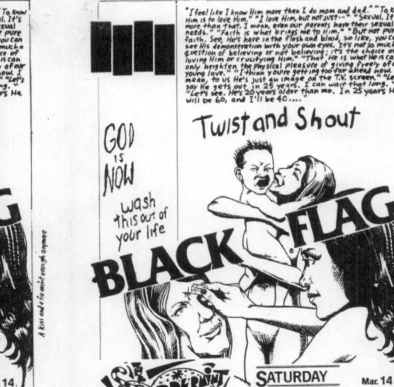

Black Flag at the Peppermint Lounge
(MD)

Back in '81, the area near Times Square was straight-up suspect. The Lower East Side, where we often hung out, may have been more dangerous, but Times Square was somehow scarier; on the LES, the drug dealers were busy with a steady stream of dedicated customers. They were not hustling us, whereas in Times Square, it was always on full display—a carnival of live sex shows, porn theaters, and third-run kung-fu movies attended by feral masturbators. Not a hood that we would visit for pretty much any reason. Until sometime in January or February 1981, when it was announced that the Peppermint Lounge, a club on West Forty-Fifth Street that was renowned for being an incubator for the dance craze "The Twist" in the early 1960s, would be hosting the first-ever East Coast performance by Black Flag.

I fucking loved Black Flag. Before I got their first EP, *Nervous Breakdown*, I had listened to many hours of punk rock, but this was something radically different: noisier, super-aggressive, and dissonant, with lyrics filled with paranoia and anger. Some of the ingredients had existed before—in bands like the Stooges, the Ramones, Black Sabbath, and the Dead Boys—but no one had put it together into anything like *this*. I mean, at the time, I had absolutely no frame of reference for Greg Ginn's incredible guitar playing. It was like some terrifying alien assault of squeal. When I listen now, it has more in common with the free jazz of Archie Shepp to me than the crunch of the Sex Pistols' Steve Jones; as a thirteen-year-old, I couldn't really compute, but I fucking loved it. *Nervous Breakdown* was a birdcall to so many of us who were too young for the first wave of punk and craved an outburst of pure noise that we could call our own.

So as soon as the announcement went out, life became *Black Flag is coming, Black Flag is coming*. Our crew was completely amped. We got our HC uniforms on—our boots and our cuffed-up jeans, our white T-shirts—and headed to the club, ready for . . . well, I guess we had no idea what we were ready for. I guess that's the point. But whatever we were expecting, it was nothing like what we found.

First of all, the Peppermint Lounge was not small; the stage alone was bigger than most of the clubs we went to. This was not home court, like walking into CBGB or A7. The punk scene we were part of was essentially a small handful of art kids, and there were a few of them at the Black Flag show—including, I'd find out later, Adam Horovitz, whom we hadn't yet met. Mostly, though, the Peppermint Lounge was filled with gladiators we'd never seen before—tons of suburban kids (mostly dudes) from Long Island and New Jersey and Queens, attracted not only by the music but by its rage. With two

hundred(ish) angry youths in the room, some maybe fucked up and ready to go off, the show was like a powder keg waiting for a match—a gathering of outcasts who'd been waiting their whole lives for this moment.

When the band eventually took the stage, the match was lit: it was as loud, abrasive, and straight-up exciting as a show could be. Shit was jumping off. I remember Greg Ginn's clear Lucite guitar, with the band's "four bars" logo painted on it. I remember how Robo's cymbals were flat and not tilted. I remember how bass player Chuck Dukowski was missing a tuning peg, so he used pliers to put his bass in tune.

Mostly I remember that it was the first time I'd seen kids really slam-dancing/moshing. It was amazing and it was terrifying. It turned out the dudes who actually really *knew* how to mosh that night were a dedicated hardcore crew from Washington, DC, who drove up in two vans to see the show—even though Black Flag was playing DC three nights later. Among them were Minor Threat singer Ian MacKaye; his younger brother and member of the Faith, Alec MacKaye; Henry Garfield, singer in State of Alert; and a bunch of other DC/Dischord Records associates. I'd later become friends with most of them, but their attitude that night was, *Fuck New York and everyone in it. We hate you.* They were really intimidating, they knew it, and all of that came out in the first hardcore pit I'd ever witnessed. Our crew was literally pushed against the back wall like scared kids at a high school prom by the chaos and energy of the music and the pit in a way we had never seen before. By the end of the show, both the band and its audience were soaked through with sweat. Shirts dripping, gasping for air, wondering what the fuck just happened. It was perfect.

I guess every generation of music fans in every city has a moment that, in hindsight, stops time and focuses the energy of everyone in attendance. For us, it was Black Flag at the Peppermint Lounge. In retrospect, maybe the most impressive thing about the show is how many bands formed at that moment and in the aftermath. It inspired Yauch and John and me to form Beastie Boys a few months later. It inspired Adam Horovitz to form the Young and the Useless. Thurston Moore was there; he was already playing around with Kim, but they didn't debut as Sonic Youth until later that

I was there with Nick Cooper. The place was super-duper packed. It felt very football team/dude-ish. And I 100% remember seeing all you guys in the back of the place doing silly dances, making fun of people, and cracking up. You looked like the fun kids to hang out with. I remember 'cause I saw Jill and Kate, whom I recognized from around my neighborhood. It might quite possibly be the night that Michael Louis Diamond, Adam Nathanial Yauch, and I were first introduced. (AH)

Black Flag weren't dressed like punks. That was cool to me. I couldn't afford Doc Martens and a whole punk kit. So my beat-up sneakers and lame button-down shirt were fine. They kind of looked like the weird kids who hung out in that weird room in my high school. The one with that weird thing called a computer. It was as if those kids from the computer room were playing Ramones songs, really fast and really loud. (AH)

From a 1981 review that was printed in a zine called *Critical List*: "DC people were the rowdiest dancers, occasionally clambering on a stage over 5 ft. high & falling back into the crowd. Dez thanked DC punks for coming to the show. Most of the New York crowd, minus a select few, were pretty lame. By the end of the show everyone there knew people were up there from DC and most felt intimidated. The show was probably one of the greatest we've ever seen, and it will be a long time before we forget it." (MD)

Not that I ever went to a high school prom. (Or maybe this show *was* my prom?) (MD)

year. And that summer, DC punk and mosher Henry Garfield, who was seeing Black Flag for the first time that night, would join the group as its singer under the name Henry Rollins. To him and all of us in the audience, that night in March changed what we thought was possible.

Boys (and a Girl) Entering Anarchistic States Toward Inner Excellence

(MD)

My first band was actually called Young Aborigines. It had formed before the Black Flag show, as early as 1979 or 1980. Lineup: me on drums, John Berry on guitar, Jeremy Shatan on bass, and Kate Schellenbach on percussion. We met Kate at some point in the context of going to shows—Stimulators, Irving Plaza, Tier 3. She was easily the smartest member of the Young Aborigines. She went to Stuyvesant High School, a big, competitive magnet school for math-and-science nerds. She lived in a loft on West Fourteenth Street, back when lofts were actually raw and cold, and when there was no glamour whatsoever to be found on Fourteenth Street—mostly what you'd find were stores lining up to sell velvet Elvises and other textile-art masterworks.

We never got around to getting a full-time singer. We tried a couple, but nothing ever quite worked, and it was a job that none of us wanted. We just wanted to be in a band and make music. We were not yet completely consumed with hardcore 7-inches and going to hardcore shows. Young Aborigines was inspired by the Slits, the Young Marble Giants, Gang of Four, Public Image Ltd—all this post-punk stuff that we loved. But with no singer and no experience, we couldn't do much except practice, which we did as often as we could for months and months.

Our practice space was the third floor at John Berry's house on the northwest corner of 100th and Broadway. How do I even *begin* to describe this place? Start with the fact that it was an old, squat, three-story wooden structure in the middle of a concrete jungle, like someone had forgotten to tear the place down when they were building the rest of the modern city. Also, for a wood building, it was ancient, literally a hundred years old; it had been a saloon in the late 1800s—*before the streets up here were even fucking paved*—and the place looked and felt like it hadn't been touched since. It was a dilapidated, sagging, slant-roofed structure of rotting wood, parked in a sea of concrete, brick, and steel. At that point, there was a greasy Cuban-Chinese restaurant on the ground floor (that's right, Cuban-Chinese). John and his dad lived above the restaurant.

John's bedroom, where we practiced, was the building's third-floor loft; the second floor was a single open room, but not like a glamorous designer loft. Large windows were set in rotting and splintered wooden frames. Fading and chipped paint covered the clapboard. Every piece of furniture looked like it had been found on the street. There was even a hammock hanging over one of the windows.

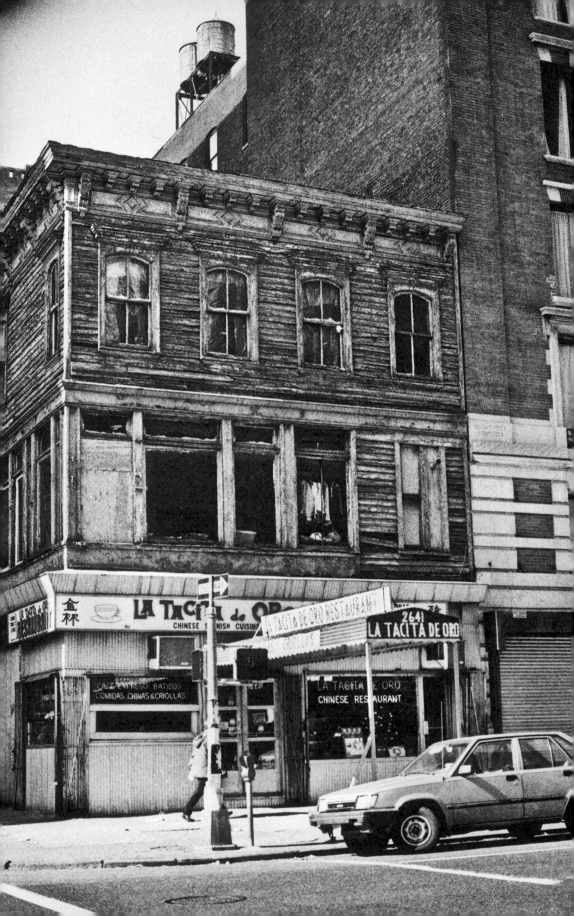

If ever there was a person destined to live in this building, it was John Berry's dad. He was a man from another era. He worked as editor in chief of *Library Journal*, and he was a 1930s-style left-leaning intellectual with a serious work ethic and clothes to match. Worn blue jeans. Button-down oxford shirt and tie. Always a Harris-tweed blazer, complete with elbow patches. Framed pictures of Che Guevara, books on Lenin and Trotsky, and pamphlets about the IRA lay around the house. He was radical without the chic, like something out of a Studs Terkel book, and he was as pragmatic and grouchy as any other hardworking single dad during, say, the Depression might have been. Every night, he would get home from work and want his glass of scotch. He'd often follow it with half of a pin joint. I'm not talking Kush or Indo; this was 100% leafy shake that legit smelled like burning leaves. Then he'd prop his feet up, literally, and start reading, in this big room filled with the books and ephemera of a socialist intellectual librarian. And we knew better than to disturb this important state of unwind; he gave John and all of us a long leash, but when he got home, band practice was over.

Upper Broadway at that time was like a multicultural mixtape. Salsa blaring on one block, a JVC boombox playing rap outside a housing project on the next, sounds of AM broadcasts from Panasonic clock radios coming out of opened windows on the next. Across 100th Street from John's place was this large residential hotel—politely known as an SRO (single-room occupancy) building, and impolitely known as a flophouse. Shit would really go down there.

It seemed like every afternoon or evening, cops would appear for some kind of drug raid or prostitution shakedown or domestic disturbance or who the fuck knew what. One day, John and I sat on his roof and witnessed someone, in the heat of an argument, throw a small sink out of a very high window; we watched as it plummeted and crashed on the 100th Street sidewalk.

The constant hubbub across the street worked out well for us, though, because it allowed us to play music as loud as we wanted. Who was going to make a noise complaint when people across the street were using sinks to play Depth Charge? We were pretty far down the precinct to-do list. So we'd just set up and practice after school on the third floor, where John lived. When we weren't actually practicing, our whole cast of characters just hung out and played music full blast.

Yauch didn't play in Young Aborigines, but he was around so much that he was our unofficial fifth member and one-man tech crew. We called Yauch the techno wiz for a reason: he somehow knew how to do all this handy technical shit, everything from wiring a '70s flashbulb so it could be detonated as an explosive to fixing a microphone cable with a soldering gun. As for instruments and amps, he actually had an understanding of how that stuff worked, how it should be set up and treated. Which the rest of us did not.

At some point after the Black Flag show at the Peppermint Lounge, he started egging us on to form a "side" band, one that dispensed with the arch post-punk artiness and instead played straight hardcore, the new style forged by Bad Brains that we loved so much. We even had a name ready to go: Beastie Boys.

Actually, we were a button before we were a band. All of us were obsessed with the slightly older punk-rocker Nick Marden, the cool kid at the Bad Brains show the night I met Yauch. Nick did a great job of making his own buttons — or, to use the punk-rock term, badges. One afternoon while fooling around on our instruments and talking about a band name, we all came up with Beastie Boys. BEASTIE was an acronym for Boys Entering Anarchistic States Toward Internal Excellence. (Don't ask; no idea.) While the acronym alone made no sense, it made even less sense when combined with "Boys," since the acronym already contained that word; now the name was ridiculous *and* redundant. (And also incorrect, since we had a girl drummer.)

Anyway, it stuck. The next time I saw Yauch, he'd already made our first-ever badge, before we'd even practiced a single time.

Meanwhile, the Young Aborigines, like any typical high school band, had an epic months-long run of practices, played two shows in one night, then promptly broke up. The two shows were on Friday, June 19, 1981. One was at 171A, a punk-rock recording studio. The other was at a club downtown somewhere, opening for an L.A. punk band called UXA. There were, at most,

The bass player in UXA was a guy from Brooklyn named David Danford, aka Bosco. He's best known to the general public as the bassist in the Darby Crash Band to whom Darby (the infamous singer of the Germs) addressed his suicide note: "My life, my leather, my love go to Bosco." I later became friends with Bosco (RIP) and played with him in the bands Big Fat Love and Flophouse Society Orchestra. (MD)

53

five people at each show, including Yauch, our one-man road crew. I can't remember exactly why we broke up after those shows, and it may not have been as well articulated as all that. We all wanted to be in a band, yet none of us in Young Aborigines were driven enough to take it anywhere. But Adam Yauch was. The simplest way to put it is that Beastie Boys took over and Young Aborigines faded away. Beastie Boys had actually started to practice once in a while, and the pace increased after the Aborigines split up. I'd been nominated singer—since this was hardcore, actual singing ability wasn't so important; Kate switched from percussion to drums; John still played guitar; Jeremy wasn't as psyched on hardcore as I think we were, so Yauch called it, kinda like shotgun: "Bass." Even though Yauch was a year older than us, he was still like a puppy, with hands and feet that were way oversized for his body. He also had the look down: rolled-up, straight-legged blue jeans. Green army jacket. Oxblood Doc Martens. Hair cut short.

Years later, I still vividly remember bassist Darryl Jenifer from Bad Brains grabbing Yauch's hands and going, "These are bass player's hands! Look at these long fingers!" (MD)

Writing hardcore songs is not that complicated, right? *Do this part eight times, do that part four times, repeat it once, the end.* Pretty quickly, we had about twenty minutes of original music. Most of our practices were at the 100th Street shanty; sometimes we'd have them in Yauch's bedroom at his parents' home in Brooklyn Heights. Unlike Berry's place, Yauch's was clean and well designed. His father, Noel, was an architect and an amazing cook, so I'd always happily stay for dinner after messing around with music. Looking back, I still can't believe that Noel and his wife, Frances, were tolerant enough to let us make the racket we did up in that bedroom. God bless them.

In 1987, after *Licensed to Ill* became a huge hit, Noel Yauch described those early days to the *L.A. Times*: "The funny thing is, when I was Adam's age, I came to New York to be an abstract painter and my parents . . . thought I was nuts. I look at Adam now and the whole thing seems to be history repeating itself. The words that want to come out of my mouth are the words my father was saying to me . . . and I am trying not to say them." (MD)

We were coming up on Yauch's birthday. August 5, 1981. He was turning seventeen. We still hadn't played a gig as Beastie Boys. One day after practice, he motivated us

My mom, on the other hand, had this to say in the article: "I was at this party the other night, and this man went on and on about how the Beatles had ruined Western civilization for the last twenty years. I listened for a while and finally said, 'If you had problems with them, you ought to hear my *son's* band!'" (MD)

all by saying, "Hey, let's have my birthday party at John's loft and play at it." Seemed like a good enough idea at the time; our equipment was already there, for starters.

So the word went out. *Yauch's birthday party, 100th Street loft.* Maybe two dozen people showed up. Us, the Bag Ladies, a few of Yauch's oldest friends, and Dave Parsons and his girlfriend, Cathy, from a newly opened and really cool downtown record store called Rat Cage. We sat around listening to records, just hanging out, talking, drinking beer, smoking cigarettes. Eventually we moved John's bed against the wall so that we had a dance floor of sorts, and got up the courage to put on our instruments and play.

And yeah: it did take courage, especially being a singer for the first time. It was embarrassing to put yourself out there, being an awkward teenager with-

out any real experience, performing a few feet away from the friends you see on the regular and whose taste you respect and trust. I was usually pretty shy and quiet, so to be yelling lyrics into a mic felt deeply foreign. I remember looking down at the floor a bunch because I wanted to make as little eye contact as possible.

But what I quickly discovered about singing was this: it's a different part of you. It's not like me having an actual conversation with you, or me being in a taco restaurant nervously trying to say hi. You're in a totally different context, and it's a band, you know—so it's kind of like a gang. You don't want to be afraid, and pretty soon, you're not.

We made it through some or maybe all of the songs we'd written, probably starting and stopping each one a few times because we would mess up or forget a part. Eventually, we made it through our set. Phew. What a fucking relief. I don't think we knew what to feel after. Then Dave from Rat Cage came up to us and said he had an idea: *Why don't you guys make a record and I'll release it?*

This seemed crazy and unfathomable. Us, make a record? That you could buy in a store? We had just played our first show in front of other people as Beastie Boys. And now this guy from a great record store wants us to make an actual record? For him?

What?

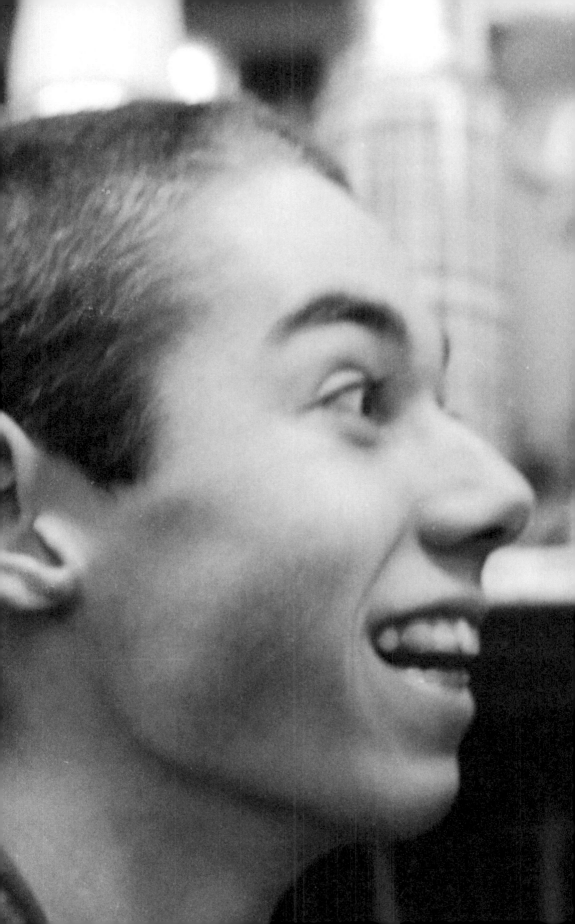

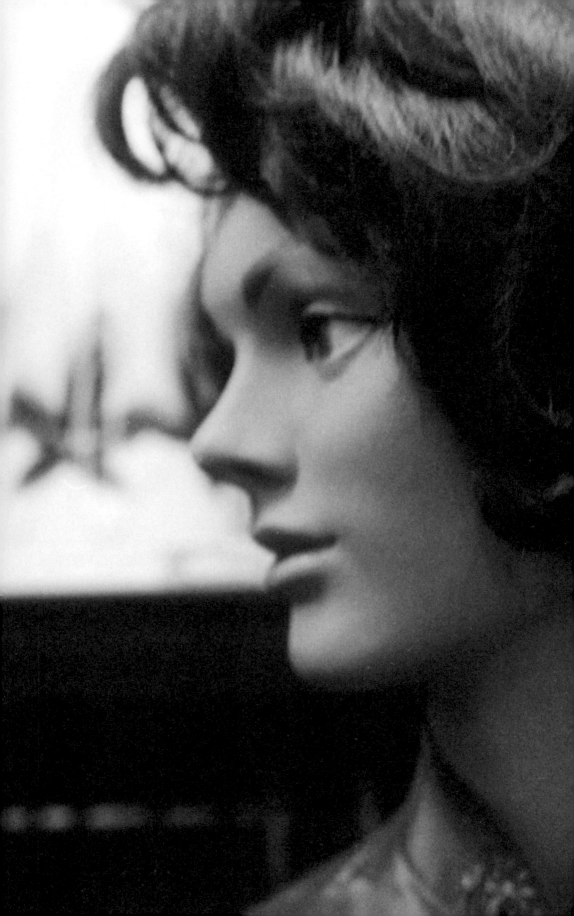

A Rubber Band Was Involved
(MD)

Did I mention we made a demo sometime before our first show? We made a demo sometime before our first show. Yauch's determination single-handedly made it happen. The idea was that a cassette of songs—combined with a photo and maybe a fake flyer for a nonexistent show—would get us gigs. Somehow, Yauch convinced Gregory Crewdson and Eric Hoffert from the Speedies to bring their TASCAM Portastudio 4-track to the 100th Street loft. This was 1981, and the Portastudio—which had only been out a couple of years—was a revolutionary piece of gear. Before that, if you wanted to record anything with four tracks, you'd need a reel-to-reel recorder, which also required a separate mixing desk and a reel of tape from, like, a pro audio store. In other words, you actually needed to know a thing or two. But the Portastudio would fit in a back-pack and recorded onto a cassette, which you could get at any corner bodega. It was basically idiot-proof. That shit democratized the recording process in a way that's hard to overstate.

They brought over their 4-track, plus a few mics, and we recorded. Two of the demos got played on *Noise the Show*, a half-hour weekly NYU-radio hardcore show hosted by Tim Sommer. Getting on the radio seemed kind of inconceivable to us, and then it actually fucking *happened*. WNYU miraculously reached my family's apartment on the Upper Upper West Side; one day I tuned in and heard Tim Sommer screaming about our song "Egg Raid on Mojo." Then the song itself came on, and I was so excited that I started solo moshing in my own bedroom, stage-diving off my bed. After the song ended, I ran into the hallway where the phone was, dialed Yauch's number, took the phone (with its twenty-foot-long cord) into my room, and, catching my breath, tried to explain to Yauch what I had just heard.

Sommer would later go on to become an A&R man at Atlantic Records and sign Hootie & the Blowfish. You can hear his voice sampled on "Heart Attack Man" from *III Communication*. (MD)

Such (extremely limited) exposure aside, the demo was—in the words of the wise Biz Markie—"just a demo." It wasn't great, but it got the job done. It was the first time we'd heard each instrument and the vocals isolated. I remember being freaked out by just how unforgiving it was. When we played live, the volume, crappy club monitors, adrenalized moshing, and general chaos covered everyone's flaws. Recording did the opposite—exaggerated them, shone a light on them. Nowhere to hide.

Dave's offer to record us took a while to actually happen. It's not like Walter Yetnikoff from CBS Records was signing us, you know what I mean? It was Dave's first record too. He had to figure shit out.

The Rat Cage store was in the basement of 171 Avenue A. On the first floor was a long, narrow former storefront that had been taken over by these two Southern guys, Jerry Williams and Scott Jarvis. They'd relocated their punk band, Th' Cigaretz, from North Carolina to NYC, at which point the group promptly broke up. So Jerry and Scott turned their apartment into a multi-use musicians' space: there was a stage at one end, a sound booth with recording equipment up in a loft at the other, and a bunch of dirty, ripped-up couches in between. After that, it became a combo practice space, makeshift recording studio, and—after Jerry hooked up with them to produce their fucking incredible self-titled first album—unofficial HQ of Bad Brains. To us, the fact that Bad Brains had recorded there made the space almost sacred.

Jerry had this great Southern drawl, but he'd also apparently been picking up some of the Rastafarian patois that Bad Brains would use, so he spoke in some weirdly accented hybrid language of uncertain origin. He had long gray hair, even though he was probably in his mid-thirties. Long beard, with a rubber band involved. Super tall and wiry. Just generally fit right in among the other downtown eccentrics. Scott was super nice and a little more conventional than Jerry. Faded blue jeans, Converse All-Stars, a haircut that was definitely his own handiwork, and a bit of a Southern twang as well. I always attributed his humility and friendliness to being Southern. Certainly it wasn't the result of living in the East Village.

At some point in the fall of 1981, Bad Brains was heading out on tour and Jerry was going with them, so Dave Parsons arranged for us to use the

studio to record our EP. Scott had stuck around and would be the engineer and de facto producer. (Read: designated adult.) When we finally showed up to record, the process was so new that *literally everything* was fun. *Oh, we need to pound the motherfucking kick-drum for thirty minutes straight to make sure it sounds good? Awesome!*

Bad Brains had taken a bunch of equipment with them on tour, so 171A was about as bare-bones as a studio could be. Basically just a 4-track reel-to-reel recorder and a mixing desk to operate it. That said, you'd need experience to understand how to route the mixer onto the different tracks, and there were five or six mics that needed to be sub-mixed onto one track. It wasn't until pretty well into recording that it became clear that Scott hadn't done this very often. To his credit, he was honest about it; he basically said, *This is not my studio, I'm just a drummer who kind of knows how everything works, we'll figure this out.* And he did; I don't remember him fucking anything up.

It took us a day or two to record everything. We set up on the stage at the far end of the room, as though we were playing a show. I was out front with a mic. Kate was behind me on the drums. Yauch was playing his first Fender Jazz bass, but—in order to record things with separation (in case we wanted to change or fix anything)—it was plugged into a direct input so there was no amplified signal that would bleed into the drums or vocal mics. John Berry was on his Cherrywood Gibson SG, also through a DI. If I remember correctly, we finished all the basic tracks in a day, and most of the overdubs and vocals. The remaining work may have been finished the next day, or the next weekend, or whatever, but it was fast. Compared to the amount of time we would spend recording albums in the future, it was a fucking nanosecond.

I don't remember having any sort of specific ambition with the record. It's not like we were thinking, *Oh, it should sound like this.* Again, we weren't too serious about the "hardcore aesthetic"; we loved the music and the energy, but our idea was to fuck with all the dogmatic shit that accompanied it. The lyrics I wrote were the most ludicrous and silly things I could come up with—whatever seemed funny to us at that time. We had no serious agenda, in contrast to almost every other hardcore band. Which was sort of the idea. To take our small step toward breaking down a predictable formula. The fact that *Polly Wog Stew* captured what we were doing and it sounded way more professional than we could have imagined—that was good enough for us.

Example: "Holy this, holy that / Holy funky big fat rat / Holy piss, holy crappers / Jill Cunniff, holy snappers." (MD)

Once we finished recording, the plan was to mix everything at 171A sometime over the following few weeks. But in the time between recording and mixing, whoever had the lease on 171A—whether it was Jerry Williams or Scott or Bad Brains or all three—lost it. I don't know if they couldn't pay the rent, or didn't want to, or whatever. In any case, we got a call from Dave telling us that the studio was out of business. We were like, *Holy shit, what happens to the stuff we recorded? Like, how does that work?* We were worried that Scott had left the

A. BEASTIE BOYS
   TRANSIT COP
   JIMI
   HOLY SNAPPERS

B. RIOT FIGHT
   ODE TO...
   MICHELLE'S FARM
   EGG RAID ON MOJO'

KATE -- DRUMS, Backing Vocals, Washboard
ADAM -- BASS, Backing Vocals, Acoustic Guitar
JOHN -- GUITAR
MICHAEL -- LEAD VOCALS, Cow Bell
BACKING VOCALS -- Dave, Id, Dave P., Nick

RECORDED AT 171A STUDIO
ENGINEERED BY SCOTT JARVIS
PRODUCED BY BEASTIE BOYS AND SCOTT JARVIS
FRONT PHOTO BY ROBIN MOORE
BACK PHOTO BY ARABELLA FIELD
AND SPECIAL THANKS TO TOM, ANDRES, DAVE AND CATHY

© and ® of The Beastie Boys,1982

tape behind or a landlord repossessed it or something. Once we realized that *Yes, he has the tape but we'll have to mix it at his apartment now,* we calmed down a bit.

At least until we saw his apartment.

New York is (obviously) known for its small apartments, but even by New York standards, Scott's was tiny. It was one of those East Village specials: a single room of maybe 350 square feet, and to fit anything besides a bed in there, you have to build a loft where you can put your mattress, and usually there's some fucked-up feature in the overall design, like the bathtub's in the kitchen or the toilet's in the shower. If you didn't live in New York and see that shit all the time, you'd think it was some cartoon exaggeration of a tiny apartment. But it wasn't; we all crammed into this awkward loft-bed zone and mixed *Polly Wog Stew* there—the 4-track tape machine set up on a small dresser, speakers to the left and right, sending signal out through the same small mixing board we used to record. The only effect I remember having was an old Roland Space Echo, which you can hear deployed on the song "Jimi."

Making the artwork—in those days, you had to do it with an X-Acto knife and ruler—and printing it took some time. The record was pressed in England. By the time we finally got everything back and released it, it was the summer of 1982. It felt really good to hold a fucking thing you'd made in your hands. I remember taking a few copies to school. Not to show to anybody or anything like that—just to have, like, this secret source of confidence and pride in my backpack.

The fact that it took almost a year to get done would have seemed like a long time, except we were in school and leading fifteen-year-old lives. And we'd also occupied ourselves with a new challenge in the meantime: playing live shows somewhere besides John Berry's loft.

Transit Cop—Inspired by real-life events. Yauch and I were riding the 4 or 5 train from Borough Hall into the city one night to go see a show. The train was empty, so Yauch was hanging and swinging from the bars. We were talking and laughing. We stopped at a station, and two transit policemen walked into our train car and right up to us and started yelling at Yauch: "Hey, what do you think you are doing? Swinging around like a fucking monkey? If we catch you doing it again, we're giving you a ticket." We were bothering no one; the train was empty. Damaging nothing. This was just two dickheads fucking with us because we were punk-rock kids with boots and spiked hair.

Riot Fight—This and "Ode To" were probably our most fake political-type songs. I mean, we liked Discharge and Crass, but we had no political agenda ourselves, so "Riot Fight" was really just a tribute song, I guess, and also us kinda laughing at that stuff at the same time—part tribute, part satire.

Michelle's Farm—The Michelle in the title refers to our friend Michelle Ford, who was part of our crew of show-going, stamp-faking teenagers, also one of the Bag Ladies. She lived in Brooklyn and had no farm.

Egg Raid on Mojo—The closest this EP comes to a pop single, or maybe even just a song. Also based on a true story. Mojo was a large dude who used to go to a lot of the same shows as us. He was also one of the only black kids we'd see at them. At 6'4", wearing bondage pants and a leather jacket and a beret, he stuck out pretty easily. He was nice enough, but it freaked us out a bit that he would totally switch up his look depending on the type of show he was seeing, from punk to hardcore to ska to full-on Blitz Boy. Mojo was an alternative fashion chameleon.

After we'd seen him around a bunch, he got a job working the door at an after-hours club called Berlin, which shared its loft space with another club called Reggae Lounge. The place was kind of awesome: loud dub and reggae through a legit sound system on one side, new wave on the other. Since we knew Mojo from around, once he started working there we figured, *Cool, he'll definitely hook us up and let us in for free.*

NOPE. We go there one night and he's out front wearing a flowing white pirate's blouse, like fucking Adam Ant or some shit, and he completely pretends not to even know us. No parting of the velvet rope, no "What's up guys, come in." We were like, *What the fuck?* Anyway, justice served: at some point—we ambushed Mojo outside where he was working the door, pelted him with eggs, and then ran.

We never egg raided him, no matter what anyone says. That never happened. (Kate Schellenbach)

1 - BEASTIE GO!

2 - E.G.G RAID ON MOJO

3 - HOLY SNAPPERS!

4 - BEASTIE REVOLUTIO...

5 - OED TO POLY WOG S...

6 - FINE QUALITY!

7 - PURPLE HAZE!

8 - MICH' FARM!

9. TRANSIT COP!

10 RIOT FIGHT

! = END THE SONG!

BEASTIE BOYS

5 RING CIRCUS

FEATURING

REAGAN YOUTH • THE BLESSED
ARTLESS • YOU SUCK

GREAT GILDERSLEEVES 331 BOWERY

SUNDAY • APRIL 24 Eight PM

THE YOUNG & THE USELESS

STIMULATORS

P.S.I. FORCE

AGNOSTIC FRONT

FRIDAY SEPT. 3

OPEN TEN PM
UNTIL......

ARMAGEDDON
113 Jane St.   924-7030

RAT CAGE RECORDS PRESENTS

ALL ☆ AGES!

NECROS

BEASTIE BOYS

REAGAN YOUTH

DAY AY 6th

PLUS
DJ MUSIC
REFRESHMENTS
H.C. ARTSHOW
RAT CAGE
(FUN & GAMES)

DOORS OPEN
8 PM
$5.00

TALLER LATINO AMERICANO LOFT
9 WEST 21st ST.

PLEASE, NO VIOLENCE!! AND REMEMBER, IT'S JUST GOOD CLEAN FUN!

RAT CAGE RECORDS PRESENTS

• SAT. NOV 20
MATINEE STARTS AT 3:30

BEASTIE BOYS
REAGAN YOUTH
THE YOUNG AND THE USELESS

• SUN NOV 21 •
MATINEE STARTS AT 3:30 PM
FROM PHOENIX ARIZONA

MEAT PUPPET
BLOODCLOT!
FRONTLINE
CBGB

BOWERY AT BLEECKER

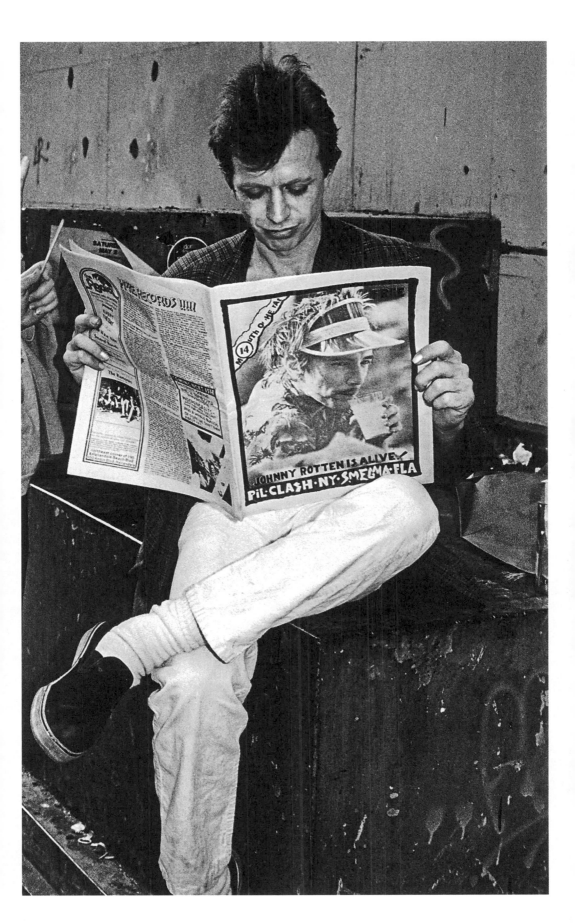

Mouth of the Rat

(AH)

Dave Parsons owned and ran the Rat Cage along with his girlfriend, Cathy. Dave was older than all of us kids who hung out at the store. He was a grown-up. He'd lived other lives before any of us met him. He was from Florida. He'd wanted to be a dancer. He once showed me a picture of himself wearing a ballet costume, in full ballet pose. Maybe he was in midair, even. It was pretty beautiful. And I remember he kind of tucked the little picture away after he showed it to me like you do when you know that particular dream will never come true. He was a little older now and living in New York in a new and different life.

Dave Parsons was not the typical grown-up who treated you like a kid. He wanted to share ideas, and life, with us. He seemed to love both the mundane boredom and the frenetic excitement of our teenage lives. He was just as excited as we were when the new Minor Threat record came out. How cool is that for a grown-up? He'd let us put up our flyers for our band's upcoming shows, sell our homemade fanzines and buttons, and basically let us use his place of business as a teen scene. It was like the New York City punk version of a 1950s movie malt shop.

Safe to assume that if you were there on a Tuesday at one P.M., you were cutting school. But Dave didn't seem to care. Some of us were getting our education at the Rat Cage. Important life lessons like financial studies: How are we gonna get enough money to get French fries and gravy from the 2nd Avenue Deli? Technological research consisted of playing video games at Fun n' Burger down the street. We really did hang out at the Rat Cage *all* the time. I'd like to say that the bulk of our time there was spent in a creative young folks' issues-based think tank, but more factually, our days at the Rat Cage, and in the East Village, were spent trying to come up with something interesting and dumb to do. You know, like breathe in and out really fast and have someone push on your chest to see if you'd pass out.

Anyway, Dave was a dancer, a punk-rock record store owner, and also an artist. He drew the lightning-bolt illustration for Bad Brains' first record cover. (It's been used on a million T-shirts and stickers since then, but I'm pretty sure neither Dave nor Bad Brains ever got any money from any of that.) Dave also had a fanzine when he lived in Florida, called *Mouth of the Rat*. So I guess add writer to the list. (Dave's use of the word "rat" comes from growing up in Boca Raton. I guess people there call it the Rat. I only learned this a year ago on the Google machine.)

When I think of Dave Parsons, my favorite image is him riding around the East Village on his skateboard. He'd ride to the post office up on Fourth

Avenue+Eleventh Street to get a shipment of new records for his store. In the early '80s you didn't see that many punk rockers, or skaters for that matter, and it made young punk-rock me so proud that I knew that funny-looking grown-up punk on the skateboard carrying those heavy boxes. There must've been an easier, more efficient means of product transportation, it's just . . . he wanted to ride his skateboard.

Dave had a connection with a guy in London named John Loder, who had something to do with printing and pressing Crass's records. Crass was a British band, and record label, that was the fuckin' zenith of punk. Their music and record covers were political, smart, and weird. To be down with Crass meant you were punk for real. So, Dave sent the tapes that were recorded at 171A and Scott Jarvis's apartment to England, and the next thing you know . . . a real record: *Polly Wog Stew*. I wasn't in Beastie Boys yet; I had a band called the Young and the Useless. My band loved *Polly Wog Stew* so much that we begged and pleaded with Dave to put out a record for us too. And after ten thousand C'MONs and PLEASEs . . . he did. John Loder also had that record pressed, and I've been lying to people ever since, saying that Crass had a big part of putting our records out. I mean . . . sort of . . . right?

Dave+Cathy actually lived with me and my mom for a little bit. We had an extra room in our apartment, and my mom would rent it out to bring in some $. We had all kinds of people coming through our place. So many that late one night, while Dave+Cathy were staying there, my mom went into the kitchen to get some water, and some guy was kind of standing there in the living-room area. My mom said to him, "Oh, you must be one of Adam's friends." She got the guy a blanket, a Coke, and a slice of pound cake, and told him he could crash on the couch, and said good night. The next morning, the Coke and cake were gone, as well as Dave's Walkman and forty bucks.

Dave+Cathy didn't last long at our place. Things were changing by then. They were breaking up. The Rat Cage was soon closing. And us kids were kind of, sort of, growing up. We were a little older. The malt shop wasn't our scene anymore. We wanted to go out to clubs and get involved with grown-up stuff. And so we lost touch with Dave+Cathy.

By 1984, our new post-teen/pre-grown-up scene was a club called Danceteria. I hadn't seen or talked to Dave Parsons in a year or so. I arrived at Danceteria one night, and was

GRAND OPENING the RAT cage

UNDER

DISCOUNT IMPORT RECORDS·NEW AND USED/BOUGHT, SOLD &TRADED CLOTHES·T-SHIRTS·BADGES·LOCAL SHIT·FANZINES·BOOKS·ETC· 12NOON/1AM 7 DAYS

171 AVENUE A BETWEEN 10TH & 11TH ST. 533-4606

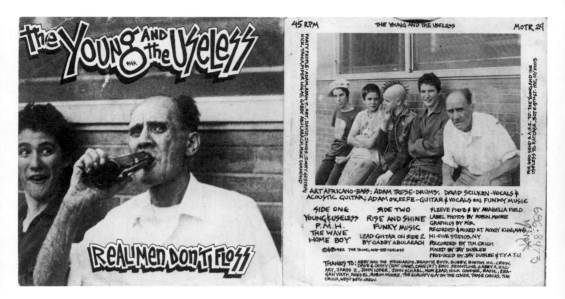

ART AFRICANO-BASS; ADAM TRESE-DRUMS; DAVID SCILKEN-VOCALS &
ACOUSTIC GUITAR; ADAM O'KEEFE-GUITAR & VOCALS ON FUNKY MUSIC

SIDE ONE	SIDE TWO	SLEEVE PHOTOS BY ARABELLA FIELD
YOUNG & USELESS	RISE AND SHINE	LABEL PHOTOS BY ROBIN MOORE
P.M.H.	FUNKY MUSIC	GRAPHICS BY MIR
THE WAVE	LEAD GUITAR ON SIDE 2	RECORDED & MIXED AT MOODY KLING MANG
HOME BOY	BY GABBY ABULARACH	HI-FIVE STUDIOS, NY
		RECORDED BY TIM CRICH
©1982 THE YOUNG AND THE USELESS		MIXED BY JAY DUBLEE
		PRODUCED BY JAY DUBLEE & T.Y.A.T.U.

THANKS TO: ABBY AND THE STODDARDS, BEASTIE BOYS, BUBBY, BOSTON H.C. CREW, DAVE & CATHY (RAT CAGE), DAVE (AT) ERIC, FRONTLINE, GABBY A, HILLARY, JAMES Z., JOHN LODER, JOHN SCHABL, MOM & DAD, NICK COOPER, RAOUL, REAGAN YOUTH, RUSS EL, ROBIN MOORE, THE SCRUFFY GUY ON THE COVER, THOSE CHICKS, TIM CRICH, WEST BETH CREW.

walking around looking for some friends, when I hear a familiar voice call my name. I turn around to see a few women posted by the wall. One of the women kind of pops out, and it's Dave. In full drag. Weird dress, bad makeup, pearls. This was a detail I did not know about him. He introduced me to his date (a woman) and we talked for a moment and then said our goodbyes. It was one of those melancholy moments when you see, like, an uncle, or grown-up that you love and look up to, but you know that you're not gonna see them for a while. Maybe never again. And because you're young, you don't know how to tell someone how meaningful they are to you. And then there was also the whole *Whoa, Dave's cross-dressing now?* thing that sort of threw me off in the moment.

One day, not long after that, Yauch was walking past the Rat Cage and saw the new-wave guy that used to work at the deli on the corner selling all of Dave's stuff. Records, buttons, fanzines . . . everything. Yauch asked him what was up, and he said that Dave had split town. He wouldn't offer up any more information, but it seemed pretty sketchy.

CUT TO: 1987. Life has changed . . . a lot. We're on the *Licensed to Ill* tour. Down in New Orleans. We're at the gig during the day, for sound check, and our friend Dave Scilken rushes in. Wild, with a crazy story to tell us. He was walking around the French Quarter doing tourist stuff. Beignets, chicory coffee, some kind of fruit+alcohol drinks . . . it's a sunny summer day and there's a bunch of different street performers out with little circles of people gathered around each of them. Out of the corner of his eye, Scilken thinks he sees Dave Parsons. There's a small crowd around him and Dave is dressed as Charlie Chaplin. Scilken kind of ducks around a corner and then peeks out to see if it's really him. As he's looking, Scilken realizes that there's a small crowd of people looking at *him* because a mime had snuck up behind him and was mimicking all his shady private-eye movements. When Scilken tells him to go away, the mime

would mime . . . *go away*. He wouldn't stop, so eventually Scilken ran away. But someone went back to find Dave and invited him to our show. He ended up coming as Dave Parsons, not Charlie Chaplin, and we talked for a little bit but didn't really catch up. Some things weren't discussed: why he left NYC/why New Orleans/Charlie Chaplin!?! We all really loved Dave and hoped he was doing okay. We were also total drunk fuck-ups in 1987 and didn't really know how to communicate things like feelings and phone numbers.

It wasn't till the late 1990s when Yauch somehow reconnected with Dave. It turned out the whole Charlie Chaplin/New Orleans thing was fucking crazy. Back at the tail end of the Rat Cage days, after he split up with Cathy, Dave was broke and needed to break out of New York. He had a friend in New Orleans and was like: Fuck it. So he's down there, but he's still broke. His friend had the idea that Dave should go out and do a

Charlie Chaplin routine on the street to hustle some money. Dave was like, "What do I know from Charlie Chaplin?" His friend said, "What's the big deal? You get a funny hat, a cane, and a fake mustache, and you're done. You already look and act like fuckin' Charlie Chaplin . . . it'll be easy." So he put a makeshift Charlie Chaplin outfit together, hit the streets, and Dave Scilken just happened to be strolling around the French Quarter of New Orleans and saw Dave Parsons *on his very first day* as Chaplin. What's even crazier is . . . that same day, someone from Italy (I think) sees him with the funny mustache and hat, twirling a cane, and says that they're having some big Charlie Chaplin festival and that he's a great Chaplin impressionist and asks if he'd like to go to Europe, all expenses paid, to perform? So of course he did. While at the festival, someone from Charlie Chaplin's estate was so impressed with Dave Parsons's performance and likeness to Charlie Chaplin that they asked him if he'd like to move to Switzerland and live in Charlie Chaplin's family estate and be the world's go-to Charlie Chaplin impersonator. Now . . . I could have some of the facts a little off here but . . . I'm telling you . . . that's what Dave Parsons told us. There was a picture of him in fuckin' *People* magazine. Someone showed it to me. For real. It was like a full-page article on a Charlie Chaplin convention. And there was Dave, right in the middle of the page.

By the time Yauch had reconnected with him, Dave Parsons had left his Chaplin days behind. He was no longer at the Chaplin estate, but was living

somewhere else in Switzerland, playing music and now going by the name Daisy. (Or Day-Z, or Donna Lee—I believe the name changed a couple times.) He was transitioning from male to female. I'm not sure how it all worked, specifically, but . . . he really wanted to have gender-reassignment surgery. It turns out that being a Charlie Chaplin impersonator doesn't bring in the kind of surplus of cash it takes to pay for such an operation. He needed some money. He also had cancer. Pretty bad. My understanding of Dave's situation was that he was pretty much dying, and that he wanted to live out the rest of the little time he had left in the body of his choosing. (I'm using the words "he" and "his" because I only knew Dave when he was still going by "he.") So Yauch took care of it. He organized it so that we gave him the money for the operation, but it was under the guise of reimbursement and unpaid back royalties for the *Polly Wog Stew* record from 1982. Dave/Daisy got the operation, and then within a year passed away.

Without Dave Parsons, Beastie Boys probably would've been a punk band for a couple years, and that's it. We never would've taken it seriously. We never would have thought we could do this for a living unless we had made those first couple records for Rat Cage. Dave gave all of us kids somewhere to be. A hangout. A meeting place for music. But most important, he gave us the notion that being a grown-up didn't mean you'd have to give up. You can live many different lives in your one life as You.

A quistionaire interview with the Beastie Boys

MY FAVORITE; by ADAM

Music-None

Movie-Beastie movie

Book-Aeschelus2,Thrasher

Sport-Tenis

Hobby-Building models

Place to be alone-The Woods

Place to visit-Rat Cage

Food-Pigs feet

Entertainment-Hectic low rotation skating

Animal-Sampson

Color-Ulra marine blue

Song-Popcorn by Hot Butter

Sports figure-Lee Majors

Female hero-Michael Diamond

Male hero-His mother

T.V.show-Uncle Wong's

T.V.star-Leon Redbone

Porno movie-The Farmer's Daghters

Band-Steely Dan

Political figure-Dave Insurgent

Person I know-Jack Rabid

Sex symbolpistol- Sid vicious

My Favorite: by Michael

Music-Gregorian chants

Movie-Fast Times at Ridgemont High

Book-Auto bography of Gertrude stein by Alice
                                                   Period
Sport-Low rotation football,jugling,fencing

Hobby-Spitting

Place to be alone- My Hootie

Place to visit-Adam's house

Food-Zucchini casserole w/ carrot sause

Entertainment- M.T.V.

Animal-Sampson

Color-Hawiian print, Paisly

Song-They owe us a living-Crass,Shaft-Issac
                                            Hayes
Sports figure-Russel, Adam Yauch

Female Hero-Debbie Does Dallas

Male Hero-Jas Rah "Hard" Alvin

T.V.Show-Good morning America

T,V.Star-Magilla Gorilla

Porno movie-Sex Mash w/ Deago,The Hard Way

Band-Reagan Youth,Minor Threat,CURTIS MAYFIELD
                                            Crass
Political Figure-John Watson

Person I know-Haile Selassiie I

Sex symbol-Kate schellenbach

BEASTIE BOYS INTERVIEW Cont.

My Favorite: by Kate	My Favorite: by John
Music-Music with soul(not soul)	Music-Ukrainian
Movie-Road Warior	Movie-A night at the Opera
Book-Beowulf	Book-Tropic of Cancer
Sport-Answering the Phone	Sport-LaCross
Hobby-Playing	Hobby-Paint by number sets
Place to be alone-Danceteria	Place to be alone-the Bathroom
Place to visit-Orient(Long Islan)	Place to Visit-the Park
Food-B.B.Q.RIbs	Food-Hot Dogs and Beans
Entertainment-Watching People	Entertainment-Broadway Shows
Animal-Capiraba	Animal-Dog
Color-Grey+the Like	Color-Yellow
Song-B.I.N.G.O.	Song-Brother can ya' spare a dime
Sports figure-Budgie	Sports figure-Reggie
Female Hero-Anabella	Female Hero-Brook Sheilds
Male Hero-MOJO	Male Hero-Scott Baio
T.V.Show-Facts of Life,Live at 5	T.V.Show-People's Court
T.V.Star-Jessica Savage	T.V.Star-Mork from Ork
Porno movie-Salo(140 days of Sodom)	Porno Movie-Chinease Baby-sitters
Band-Banshees,U.K.Dekay,3 Way Studpile	Band-Meat Men
Political figure-Tip O'neal	Political Figure-Ted Kennedy
Person I know-You	Person I know-Arabella
Sex Symbol-John Berry,of course	Sex Symbol-Nina

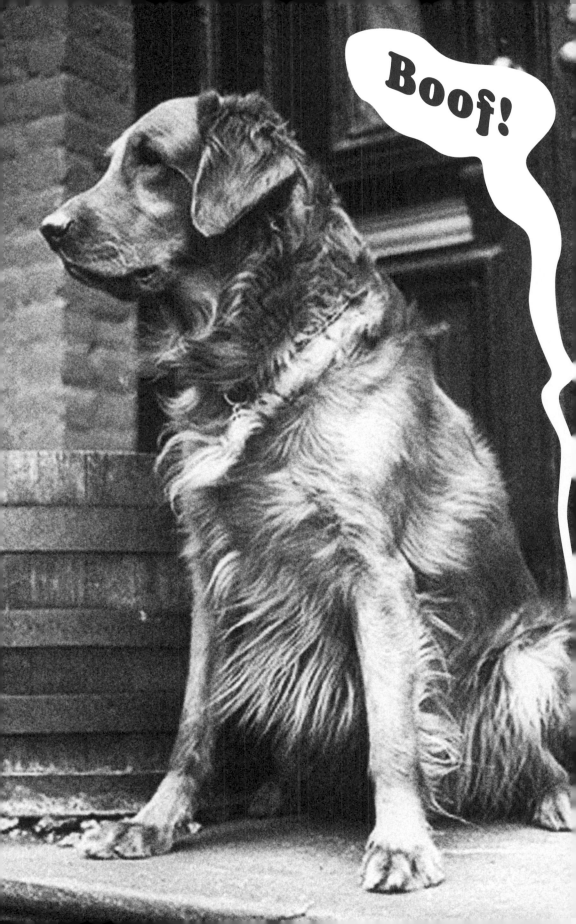

Samson's Pizza

(AH)

I joined Beastie Boys in 1983. John Berry wasn't into it anymore, so he quit.

To me he always felt a little cooler and more mature than us. He had friends with names like Danny Vegas, hung out at different places with different people, and you could tell that the hardcore scene was not his . . . how you say . . . milieu. And so he moved on. At this point I was hanging out with Mike and Adam and Kate all the time, and so I guess since I was standing there . . . I was the new guitar player. *My* band, the Young and the Useless, had run its course, and the joke at the time was that I was being called up to the big league from the minors.

For John Berry, it was kind of like the joke was over and he wasn't laughing anymore, like when you fall asleep to an episode of *Three's Company* and wake up, like, why was I ever watching this? Hardcore seemed kind of serious and limiting to John. He was branching out, going from listening to punk and post-punk to folk and American roots and blues music, and the whole hardcore formula and attitude, I think, seemed kind of childish to John. He wanted to go to Polish bars and listen to Ramblin' Jack Elliot while we were at a CB's hardcore matinee being all straight-edge. (MD)

When I joined, we would have band practice at Yauch's house. It was a beautiful old brownstone on a nice, quiet street in Brooklyn Heights. We kept all of our equipment up in Adam's room on the top floor. Like I said, the house was beautiful, but old. As in, really creaky wood floors and stairs from the 1800s. After every show we played, we'd have to get everything back to Brooklyn and lug it all up to Adam's room and do it without making a sound because his parents were asleep in their bedroom, which was right below his. Really . . . there's no way to be silent and carry guitars, and amps, and drums, and cymbals up flights of creaky stairs. Especially when being carried by a bunch of dumb, loud teenagers who think they're doing a great job of being quiet and really truly believe that Yauch's parents are asleep. But . . . we never heard a "Shut the fuck up!" from the second floor. Maybe Noel and Frances Yauch are just the heaviest sleepers of all sleepers ever. More probably, they're just wonderful parents.

You know those people who tell you that they did all kinds of elaborate and crazy shit? The more details they give you the more you know they're just making it up as they're telling you? Yauch was not one of those people. One of the first times I went over to his house, we were up in his room, and he told me this story of how, when he was a kid, he and his friend Brian blew up the backyard. The story involved a ton of firecrackers that had been used to make a sort of bomb to blow up the wooden fence that separated the Yauchs' yard from the neighbor's. Because, you know, kids often wonder . . . can I blow that up? He said that when he was maybe twelve, he had one of those Wile E. Coyote TNT-detonator/push-a-bar-into-a-box explosion things. Adam's parents can testify to the actual realness of this. It is a fact. He had one. (Where and how does a twelve-year-old get a detonator?)

So Adam+Brian attached some kind of wires to the twelve-year-old's makeshift bomb and put it on the fence. They had the wires go through the yard, up the back of the house, into the window of Adam's bedroom, and connected it to the Wile E. Coyote detonator box. Deep breath. They pushed the push bar down and . . .

FUCKIN' BOOM! They did it. It actually worked. They blew up the fence.

> The explosion was on the ground in the yard. Not the fence. Loud noise but no destruction. Adam found the detonator on the street. It was wood, painted red, and looked like a stage prop. Noel and I never knew it was something that actually worked until the big bang. (Frances Yauch)

The thing that's awesome about being a kid is that there's never a bigger picture. There's so many "Can I's," like *Can I blow up this fence?* but rarely a "What happens after?": *What would happen if I actually did blow up this fence?* Ramifications aren't really part of a twelve-year-old's lexicon. Even Adam Yauch, who always seemed to be three steps ahead, didn't think of the important peripherals to this detonation. I mean . . . his parents were home. They would hear an explosion in their backyard, so naturally they'd run out there to see what the hell had just happened. They'd see the wires that led from the blown-up fence, went through the yard and up the side of the house and directly into their son's bedroom. Now, that is some dumb shit.

There'd always be some tasty leftovers in Yauch's fridge, and so sometimes after band practice in Adam's room, we'd sit around the dining-room table downstairs and eat. Samson the dog would be down there, below the table, waiting for fallen scraps and snacks. My main memory of Samson is the pizza incident. I wasn't there when it happened, but after Yauch told me the story, every time I saw that dog, I pictured it. And even now . . . I see random golden retrievers on the street and think of the Samson pizza incident. One night, when no one was looking, Samson stole a whole pizza off the table. Right out of the box. Adam and his parents chased the poor dog around the kitchen and dining-room area trying to get the pizza from him. But Samson was like, *Fuck it. This shit is mine.* He knew that if he stopped running or put the pizza down, it'd be over. So he just ran around dragging a whole pizza from his mouth, trying to eat it all as fast as he could while in motion. Now, in case you've forgotten . . . dogs don't have hands. They're not like marathon runners who can get handed cups of water while they continue on their way. Dogs can't do that. Put yourself in poor Samson's place and imagine Adam Yauch and his mom and dad chasing you around the room trying to get an entire pizza out of your mouth while you're trying to eat it without using your hands. After a minute the pizza fell apart and landed on the floor, but Samson managed to hold on to one last slice. He kept running while he chewed. Head up, nose held toward the sky, proud and ashamed, but determined. The visual: imagine how you'd look if you tried to chew water. Yauch said that in that moment Samson reverted back to a wolf. He stopped running and dropped the slice of pizza on the floor. He stood hovering over it and let out a protective growl. The Yauch family backed off and let Samson get his slice.

FUN FACT
Yauch said that when Samson would climb up the front stoop of the house, he'd cut a fart with each step he took.
    Pause on that for a moment.

I mean, c'mon . . . family is family, right?

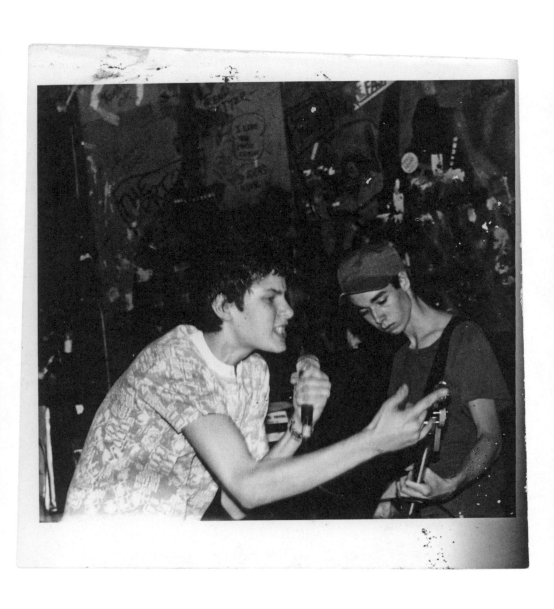

HARLEY+ERIC CASSANOVA WITH SOME
SHIT WRITTEN ON THEIR FOREHEADS

GARY/DR. KNOW

I KNOW IT'S NOT MARK RONSON
BUT IT'S FUNNY TO SAY IT IS

JIMMY GE

BERRY
?

JOHN WATSON

ALVIN SPALVIN
?

NOT SURE IF THIS IS
ACTUALLY YAUCH

HR
?

DAVID WADE
?

NO WAY THAT'S
SARAH COX, RIGHT?

A7

(MD)

We needed gigs. So Yauch and I got a little package together with the demo we had made on 100th Street, some stickers, and a photo. We kinda played it off like *Yeah, we play shows, look at this one we got coming up.* You could say we made up for whatever we lacked in skill and experience with hustle and ambition—the ethos of hardcore in a nutshell. And our little act of false bravado worked: we landed a weekend slot at New York City's only real hardcore room, A7.

A7 was on the ground floor of a tenement building at the corner of Avenue A and Seventh Street, across the street from Tompkins Square Park. I have no idea what the folks who lived upstairs could have thought, but I guess that's just how shit was on the Lower East Side then, before "noise complaints" or "quality of life" offenses.

Pretty much every NY hardcore band got its start at A7. Reagan Youth had played their first show there. Kraut, Adrenaline OD, Agnostic Front, the MOB, Even Worse, and a hundred other bands of disaffected teenagers all played their first shows in this dingy ground-floor space.

Playing A7 was like setting up in your friend's living room. Your friend's *small* living room—the club was actually smaller than John Berry's loft. Couches lined the walls, and a low, small stage sat in one corner. The audience wasn't really separate from the performers; we were all part of this house party. So we got there,

The then vs. now is difficult to put into perspective. We were *literally* kids. On our own. There was all kinds of booze and drugs going in and out of those places, and no proud parents mouthing the words to the songs from the back of the room. No minivan drop-off "see you laters." Who was the adult that told the fourteen-year-old kid . . . "Okay, we got six other bands playing tonight, you guys gotta be onstage at midnight"? Where were our guardians? There was never a conversation between any of us kids and our parents, where our parents were like . . . "Oh, you have a gig tonight? On a Tuesday? That's cool. Oh, wait, don't you have school tomorrow?" (AH)

set up, and just started playing. When things got going, the crowd of twelve or so people would use the couches to launch off of, sort of stage-diving into the room, like many a suburban youth would later do in their garage. Our performance was neither triumph nor disaster. We made it through. Mission accomplished, and another late-night train or cab ride home. We had played a "real" show.

Our next show was opening for Reagan Youth at Trude Heller's in November 1981.

The Young and the Useless had our first official gig at A7 too. We got "onstage," got ready to play our few songs to the very few people/friends that were there. Maybe ten people. Maybe. My friend Dave Scilken, the singer, was really nervous. We counted the song off . . . 1, 2, 3, 4 . . . and as we're about to play our very first song at our very first "professional" gig, two of our friends jumped up onstage and tackled little Dave Scilken. Right before he's about to start singing. It was actually the greatest way to be initiated into the world of performance. With your friends on top of you. (AH)

There were a few dozen people in the audience, not just our small group of friends, and that made me feel way less embarrassed and self-conscious. I looked

out once we started playing, and people were into it, starting to mosh, jump around, and crash into each other. This was pretty exciting when you didn't know what you were doing, and it was all kind of a goof anyway. John had been kinda skeptical about the whole thing, but there was a moment when Yauch and he looked at each other and probably thought, *Holy shit, people seem to be into this.* To top it all off, toward the end of our show, all of a sudden I see fucking Bad Brains singer HR join the crowd, moshing around. *Into it!* That was crazy. I mean, we loved and revered Bad Brains so much, and here was HR actually into *us*.

Even crazier: backstage afterward, HR comes in and says hi, then very quietly and humbly asks if we would like to open a show for them the next month at Max's Kansas City—the final show at the club, which was closing the next day. *What?!* A legendary band shutting down a legendary venue and we get to play too? *Three months after our first fucking show?* We went from goofing around, throwing some hardcore songs together up at 100th Street, to playing these shows with people that we totally looked up to and respected. Insane.

Playing Max's Kansas City was intimidating, for a couple of reasons. One, because of how we perceived it historically, with the punk history and lineage from the Velvet Underground to the Ramones to Devo to now. And two, the guys who worked there were these big biker-looking guys, and we were little skinny kids and the overall vibe was of a harder, older crowd of drugs and booze. We were actually very innocent for it all—it felt scary and menacing, but I don't think we really processed why.

We came on first, only played three songs, and our performance sucked. At the Trude Heller's show, the audience's energy had been contagious, and we fed off that; at Max's, the audience never seemed to lock in or care, and we responded in kind. To cap things off, we were so young and inexperienced (read: dumb) that we left our equipment there overnight so we could pick it up the next day—only to discover when we returned that most of it had been stolen. So, yeah, that sucked too.

But the momentum of those two shows mattered. Over the next year, we played tons of shows with a host of other esteemed colleagues, old and new—Bad Brains, Misfits, Reagan Youth, Swans, Sonic Youth, Necros, the Stimulators, Live Skull. After a while, there's only so much of a rush you can get from, say, playing a hardcore matinee at a bar that smells like stale beer, urine, and cigarettes, but it felt like we were a real band playing real shows, with a real hardcore 7-inch and maybe even a few fans.

Then something happened that made us throw away everything we'd already built.

Hip hop came downtown.

Hip Hop Goes Downtown
(MD)

Our parents lived all over the city, but we were downtown kids. Record-store-shopping, club-hanging, show-going, hand-stamp-forging downtown kids. A big pack of teenagers, girls and boys, going out to clubs practically every night. The drinking age in New York was eighteen and never enforced. You could be thirteen and get into a club no problem. If you were tall enough to see over the bar, you could get a drink.

Originally, we'd go to clubs to see shows by bands we loved; at some point, we started going more just to dance, and to hear the new music that DJs would play. Clubs like Danceteria, Area, or the Mudd Club had DJs who spun every kind of music imaginable. They started playing rap, particularly Grandmaster Flash's "The Adventures of Grandmaster Flash on the Wheels of Steel," Treacherous Three's "Body Rock," the Sugarhill Gang records, Kurtis Blow's "The Breaks," and Jimmy Spicer's "Adventures of Super Rhyme."

Harlem and the Bronx were closer to my parents' apartment than the downtown clubs, but I would've been way too intimidated to go to Harlem World to witness the culture where it began. Instead the culture came to us. Rap groups and DJs from Harlem and the Bronx started to perform downtown. One night at the Rock Lounge, much to our excitement, Funky Four Plus One More performed. Not only had we never seen a rap group in person; I don't remember having seen any on video or TV either. Rap was still underground, with the exception of Blondie's homage "Rapture."

That night at Rock Lounge, we had this real geek anticipation of seeing the show, same as we would for a Clash concert at the Palladium. And Funky Four delivered. Lil' Rodney C and Sha-Rock were both incredible MCs. If you've never heard their single "That's the Joint," you should put this book down right now and listen to that shit because it's incredible. The band's routines, the fast switching between their vocals, and the mix of their voices were so magical. They killed it. We left the club that night feeling high, like we'd seen and heard and danced to something entirely new.

The real turning point for us was when we started going to this club on Second Avenue in the East Village called Negril. Negril was a reggae club but they started having a hip hop night on Thursdays. The first time we went, the DJs were Afrika Bambaataa and Jazzy Jay, with the Rock Steady Crew dancing. Everyone rolled thick with full posse, so you had this crowded little club that was a convergence of cultures—a funny and amazing blend of downtown characters, hip hop pioneers, and curious musicians. I remember seeing Terry Hall from the Specials, the English DJ Don Letts, and Billy Idol in the mix.

We were still just kids and these guys were big stars to us—people we'd only seen on the cover of *The Face* magazine and *NME*. Add in the Rock Steady Crew and everyone that Bambaataa brought from the Bronx, and we were seriously intimidated.

Nothing could have prepared us for Afrika Bambaataa. To us, club DJs were people who played single records and maybe made sure the beats matched between songs so that everybody kept dancing to that disco sound. Bam was doing something entirely different; he was the first guy we'd seen who took small parts of a bunch of different records and mixed them together into an entirely new song—one that he made his own. He was an insane combination of curator, improviser, and musician. A true breakbeat DJ. It's common today, but at the time we'd never seen or heard anything like it.

Even more revolutionary, to us, was the breadth of music he'd play. He might start with a seamless mixing of breakbeat b-boy classics, but then he'd throw in everything from Gary Numan's "Films" to Aerosmith's "Walk This Way" to Toni Basil's "Mickey," from Michael Jackson to Kraftwerk to Yellow Magic Orchestra to Soul Sonic Force. To Bambaataa, it didn't matter what the group looked like or what they were about, just what a record or a groove sounded like and what he could do with it. The breadth of his DJ sets is still unparalleled.

I think our brains short-circuited. It had never occurred to us that so much different music from so many different worlds could all live together, with the sum being (far) greater than the parts. Bam also had DJ Jazzy Jay in tow, and Jay was a next-level vinyl manipulator. Again, we innocent teenagers had never witnessed such finesse: quick vinyl "scratches," superfast cross-fade

moves, beat juggling, beat matching. Taking parts of songs and repeating them, manipulating two copies, going back and forth. Cutting in or mixing a sound, a vocal line, or a horn stab to create something totally new. Bam was like a master orchestra conductor, Jazzy Jay his main musician, and the sounds and beats and words and melodies of crates and crates of records were the notes of their symphony. The shit was crazy, so good, and so well done. Our world was forever changed.

I don't know how any of us got to sleep that night. Maybe we were just wrung out from dancing. We couldn't wait until the next week. Any other club night now seemed a bit less exciting. We'd seen the future and wanted more of it.

The next week we went and it was the same crazy mix of characters, but the club was noticeably more packed. And this time a group performed. The Treacherous Three. If there was one rap group we *loved* at the time, it was the Treacherous Three. We'd studied and tried our best to memorize every single word and every rhyme on the 12-inch records they had out. "Body Rock" was an anthem. We loved that shit so much.

And here they were, onstage, in a tiny club, just a few feet away, performing the songs that we couldn't get enough of. "We got something new, we got something new." They were fucking great. If you've never heard "Body Rock" or "The New Rap Language," you should once again put this book down right now, find them online, and listen to those shits, because they are fucking incredible. We rapped along with every lyric and stood amazed when they went off

into routines and freestyles we'd never heard before. Their voices and styles were varied and still formed one amazing whole. This second week at Rock Lounge was even better than the first. Rap, in all its far-reaching ambition, was now It. Our hardcore punk world simply couldn't compete anymore. How much louder and faster and rulier could bands get? So much of hardcore is about limits— shorter, simpler, more speed, more volume—whereas breakbeats and hip hop are all about the limitless—limitless possibilities, limitless imagination. Punk rock had changed our lives, but hardcore had served its purpose. Now all we wanted was to be our own version of the Treacherous Three.

No turning back.

White-Boy Bouillabaisse
(An Archaeology)

It is a white man's world, they say. No sane white man would dispute it. But it wasn't a white boy's city, not in those days. And, as William Carlos Williams correctly forecast, the pure products of New York City in the 1970s go Crazy Eddie. Which is, actually, a good thing. To "go Crazy Eddie" is to pick up the material of the sidewalks, the vibrant sarcasm and hostility of the street encounter, and to sell it as your own—to make it your preemptive shield for navigating the zone. Crazy Eddie might be the very first white rapper, after all. To invite him aboard is to take on the homeopathic dose of urban madness, the inoculation—you ingest a little eye-dropper of Crazy Eddie, wear punk-nerd apocalypse on your sleeve in order to keep from locking it too hard in your heart. The city is writing the rules, the A train is already in screeching motion, and you? You're just reading the map, or trying to, through the layers of dripping tags and the scratchiti. Try to keep a sense of humor about the situation. When you gaze into this polyglot stew, the polyglot stew gazes into *you*.

Zoom in on three specimens yanked from the mad camouflage of their environs, plopped instead into the petri dish of a Quaker summer camp in the woods of Pennsylvania, just weeks after the July 1977 blackout, Summer of Sam. This is Friends with a capital F, as in "The Religious Society of." You know, the guy on the oatmeal box. Camp Onas, based on the Quaker principle of Simplicity, a largely no-frills outpost, hippie counselors in tie-dye, campers sleeping in double bunks in huge open-sided army surplus tents pitched on rough wooden platforms. The place was commonly mocked as "Camp One-Horse," though there were, in reality, zero horses. Or "Camp Onus, Where the Responsibility for Having Fun Is on You." Few facilities, but for a city kid just getting out of Brooklyn for four weeks of the summer, Camp One-Ass could save your life.

Standard uniform here might be: Lacoste and Keds, worn in homely preppie sincerity—or a black concert tee and ripped jean jacket, if you wanted to suggest you were capable of cutting a class and hanging out in the park. The jean jacket could be painted with a zeppelin if you had the skills. If not, alter your high-top Chuck Taylors by scribbling those pretzeled Led Zep symbols, or the Who's bull's-eye logo, with a blue ballpoint.

Hold up: destroy a perfectly good pair of white high-top Chuck Taylors? Not these three lads. They're Caucasoid as the next man, but these guys come from the tribe that keeps a toothbrush in their back pocket in order to keep their suede Pro-Keds looking fresh.

Who knew when you would get another pair? Some degree of street recognition has come over these three: here, west of the Delaware Water Gap, standing on a dusty baseball diamond in the woods, Brooklyn's in the house. In fact, the three boys had more in common than they knew, Kings County smartasses with Jewish mothers and goyim dads.

Spoiler alert: only one of this troika's a future Beastie Boy.

Let's not trouble yet over which, just hover at a middle distance and catch a hint of what they're saying.

"Yo, yo, you got a tag? Let me see what you write—"

"Where'd you find this kid? Why you hanging out with a dude from the kids' tent? What's your name, kid? I'm calling him Yo-Yo."

"He's cool, man, he's okay."

"I just never heard a white kid say 'yo' before."

"You got a tag? You can write?"

"Sure I got a tag. What d'you listen to?"

"I don't know, the Jackson Five, whatever's on the radio."

"You hearda Ramones—'Beat on the Brat'?"

"Who's a Ramones?"

"Never mind, what's your tag? Show me your tag. Or is that Pilot just for show?"

"Where? You got a black book?"

"What's a black book? Find a wall."

The Camp Onas boys' bathrooms and showers were housed in a concrete and cinder-block structure, the walls of which constituted the only decent substrate for miles around. Being, correspondingly, the only knucklehead for miles around, the kid with the marker ("Yo-Yo") tagged with as much style and flourish as his young hand could muster, the others looking over his shoulder and egging him on.

He'll be trying to no avail to buff his own tag the next morning, smearing it around with a cloth in an ever-widening swirl of ink and turpentine, two fuming counselors over his shoulder. In mercy, let's zoom out. One of these guys, the tall one, writes the tag SAKE, though he's smart enough not to do it here, a Flatbush kid, terrific at basketball, in fact the only white kid to start for the legendary Riverside Church squad. He'd go on to manage 3rd Bass, then later to produce Nas's *Illmatic*.

And "Yo-Yo," he'd be named by none other than *Rolling Stone* magazine as the first white rapper, the earliest reported entry on a timeline culminating, at the time of the article in question, in Eminem.

But it's the third, kid named Yauch, who's a nascent Beastie.

So this was, what, some kind of precognitive summit meeting? Could the birthplace of "White Rap" (for whatever *that* term's worth) be the Pennsylvania woods, a Quaker summer camp? Or are we just looking at three white boys, momentarily to be sprung from this sanctuary, dumped back in Ed Koch's cauldron?

Cut: back to the city. Where, weirdly enough, this remains a *Quaker* story. The Religious Society of Friends has run a private school in Downtown Brooklyn since just after the Civil War: Brooklyn Friends School, K through 12. Though a Quaker institution, BFS doesn't really stress religious training; the student body is diverse, weighted heavily Jewish, like the more expensive and desirable Brooklyn "Episcopal" private school St. Ann's, a few blocks off in Brooklyn Heights.

But what difference a few blocks can make! St. Ann's is situated in the impregnable Heights, on the preferred side of Court Street, a neighborhood tree-shady and placid, adjunct to Manhattan and navigable for white boys of nearly any stripe. Brooklyn Friends, on the other hand, is stranded on cul-de-sac Pearl Street, in the thick of Brooklyn's ancestral downtown. Here's Fulton Street, a ghetto-lively black and Hispanic corridor of wig shops, dress shops, pizza-slice and Jamaican meat-patty joints, its sidewalks an open-air flea market of knockoff and black-market mercantile activity, the possibility of shadiness of a decidedly non-tree variety.

Fulton, just before it meets Flatbush Avenue and Junior's famous cheesecake restaurant, is anchored by the buzzing hive of record stores, sneaker shops, and self-styling sociological potentialities known as the Albee Square Mall ("The truth is brutal/ Your grandma's kugel/Kings County is my stomping ground/The Albee Square Mall/ Brooklyn Downtown"). Downtown Brooklyn's a zone that's for safety's sake non-white-boy-indicated, though its allure can hardly be overlooked. Any white boy in that particular time-space vicinity can attest to individual indices of attraction-fear-coping, to private mental route-schemes mapped to avoid, say, the Hoyt-Schermerhorn subway station, or to skirt the corner of Willoughby and Jay Streets.

All three of our Camp Onas boys are destined to pass through Brooklyn Friends School. The special mix of 1970s granola-Pacifist-philosophy-drenched youngsters sent out to run the Downtown Brooklyn gauntlet, against a backdrop of the vivid, violent, vibrant collapse of NYC's social and material infrastructure, might be a machine for producing white rappers—or, at the very least, let's consent that it is a machine for producing teenage ironists of a deep and uncanny variety.

One of our Camp Onas boys has taken the full course: writing graffiti, fabricating markers out of felt chalkboard erasers, and writing MC rhymes. Taken with a side-order of cheeba and malt liquor, these activities leave school studies a distant contender for last place. Unathletic—white boys being largely unpicked for anybody's team anyway—and certainly not a dancer; the Hustle, the Bus Stop, and the Bump had given way to the Freak, the Patty Duke, and the Rock, all beyond his capacities even to attempt. As for fighting? Well, he'd most definitely proven he could *take* an ass-whipping many times over; giving one back, however, was a skill eluding him. *But . . .* he had the gift of gab. Could spit some fly shit. His slick tongue had been winning snap battles, ranking sessions, and "Yo Mama"

ciphers since third grade. Seated on the stoop with his best friend, Alonzo, he would listen to horrible-sounding bootleg twelfth-generation dub cassettes of live MC battles and Zulu Nation jams from Alonzo's cousin, who lived uptown. The white boy and his black friend memorized and mimicked every routine, the L Brothers and the Furious Five, as well as local MCs with names unrecorded in any ledger.

Soon these two are part of a crew, but in the big yard of IS 293, they're hardly the big dogs. The white boy rhymes on the humble, and chooses to stick and move before the real Hard-Rocks show up. By now Sugarhill has dropped "Rapper's Delight" and the game is changed, overnight every kid is an MC or a DJ, and even those not owning a single record, let alone equipment, begin calling themselves "DJ Master Willy-Will." Just being able to rhyme doesn't guarantee you a pass anymore, everybody rhymes, and winning a battle easily leads to getting jumped and robbed.

Hell, just daring to wear your sneakers with the laces wide and untied gets you confronted.

"Oh, word? What, you think you hard, homeboy?! Yo, you ain't hard . . . you *soft!*"

The white boy in question, formerly known as "Yo-Yo," is garbed in burgundy twill Lee jeans with sharp creases all the way up the legs and a burgundy Le Tigre polo shirt buttoned all the way up. The laces in his Puma Clydes match his shirt and pants. Best not be in the wrong place at the wrong time.

More white boys for you to consider:

This one's flipped as hard in the punk direction as the other's gone b-boy. Arrived at Edward R. Murrow High School, he's taken the first option to acquire the snap-on studded dog-collar necklace, and painted his leather jacket with the words WHITE RIOT—not, actually, a phrase destined to play so well on the sidewalk, and he gets himself quickly stomped for it by a trio of homies. How to explain British punk, anarchy, the working-class solidarity of it all? A misunderstanding. Yet who can command the context of the street? But at night in Manhattan, at CB's or the Mudd Club, or just on a stoop on St. Mark's, the context claims itself, approving glances from kids mobbing around in the same garb and you've found your tribe for a minute, maybe much more than a minute.

Another white boy is first to form a band, or in earshot anyhow he seems the first. His reward, with his bandmates, is to be declared royalty. In those days the fresh and barely competent are gigging within minutes of finding a rehearsal space, opening for punk legends at Max's Kansas City and then allowed to hang in the back room with dregs of the Warhol scene—or maybe not even dregs, the new scene barely laid over the top of the former, and ready to begin taking its photograph immediately. Turning schoolmates into a fan club, the Speedies are so famous they're already a breakfast cereal. . . .

Another band, Upper West Siders, LaGuardia High School of Music & Art boys, a four-piece of three brothers and their friend B. Sloan on his handcrafted electric bass,

devote themselves to funk and soul harmony, develop a little charisma, their stage act worked around the littlest brother, drummer Michael, who sings in a voice-not-yet-changed Michael Jackson sort of way. Miller, Miller, Miller & Sloan, who opened for The Clash at Bonds Casino and were scouted by Rick Rubin in his early canvassing for a white rap band to mold (the brothers told him they were unwilling to jettison their bassist in favor of canned beats). They'd quickly carved out a place as the White Teenage Funk Band Most Likely to Succeed, no small accomplishment at Music & Art, a hotbed of talent convergence from all boroughs: Mackie Jayson was there, a great graffiti writer as well as the drummer who would help create the NYHC sound. The Kangol Crew, which included Slick Rick and Dana Dane, also the Fresh 3 M.C.s. Coming along behind in the M&A freshman class were MC SERCH and David "SHADI" Scilken, later in a certain punk band called, right, the Young and the Useless. . . .

The kid once briefly nicknamed "Yo-Yo" (the unfortunate nickname doesn't actually persist, is instead quickly layered behind dozens of assumed identities, graffiti and rap monikers), after being shifted by a worried parent from public school to Brooklyn Friends, falls in again with the tall one, the basketballer. He manages to convince his friend that disco was not dead, but had morphed into something harder and funkier—Spoonie Gee, the Crash Crew, Kurtis Blow, Super Rhyme, the Treacherous Three were all in heavy rotation.

Though he doesn't play himself, Yo-Yo joins the b-ball squad: Clinton, Kenny, Bernard, and a dude named Kagel. Yo-Yo spits one of his little Grand Master Caz–inspired rhymes for Kagel in the gym locker room, and right there Kagel suggests they link up after and go to his crib, just across Flatbush Extension back behind the Williamsburg Savings Bank. Kagel's a DJ, and the house is a treasure trove of musical wonders, not only turntables, mixer, and a mic, and wild stacks of vinyl, but a piano and gold records on the wall.

"Oh, yeah, my mom's Betty Carter."

Yo-Yo's too abashed to say he doesn't know who that is, but he sure does recognize the name Ray Charles next to hers on the gold plaque. . . .

Here's another white boy who, having flunked out—really, he'd never even attended classes at all, so there was nothing to flunk from—is placed instead in an alternative high school, one based on an internship model, with the insanely appropriate name City-as-School. Hey, the city certainly has been schooling you, so why not get some official credit for it? CAS reveals itself as another nexus for like-minded teenage heretics, a superb breeding ground for punk bands. . . .

Another white boy's more retiring and bookish, the future book writer with the world's largest target painted on his back, such that parents advise their sons not even to walk down the street with him; one cruel dad even nicknames him "Muggable Mike." Yet he'd quietly tabulate his yokings, years later turning them into his signature motif, his

street credential—a version of Crazy Eddie as the long con, taking what the street gives you and wearing it as your perverse badge. . . .

So many others. The Park Slope filmmaker with the novelist dad and the film-critic mom (and here, by the way, is another key to the self-morphings of these white boys: so many with one or both parents the painter, the playwright, the poets and set designers, mostly not famous or even close to "making it," but with the capacity to impart the suggestion, to set an example for making your confusion into culture, making something for show, *putting on a show*—).

The novelist who'd go on to wear his multiplicitous yokings like gold stars, in the same book he'd portray a gathering of white punk boys leaping around a couch in delirious japing wonder at the energy and idiocy coming off a newly acquired 12-inch Sugar Hill label first-pressing of "Rapper's Delight." You recognized the sound, you let it into your body, and you held it at mocking arm's length at the same time: the special cognitive dissonance of the white boy possessed by culture not possessible by him.

When the needle dropped on "Cooky Puss," it was that same moment, distilled to vinyl. Beastie Boys had shouted back at the sound that had invaded their nervous systems. Tom Carvel, the ice-cream merchant turned pitchman, was another Crazy Eddie, his idiotic pitch like some sonic mercantile graffiti thrown up everywhere you went. (A white boy in Clinton Hill was originator of the riddle "How does Tom Carvel take a shit?"—the punch line being not verbal but instead to squat and mime squeezing out a dump in a long soft-serve swirl, as if into a cake-cone toilet. . . .)

Yo-Yo's first time hearing "Cooky Puss" was when it was thrown into a DJ's mix—the *Zulu Beats* show on WHBI, late-night. The track was weird, seemed to be poking fun at hip hop, but Yo-Yo and his crew rocked with it anyway. By this time Mel Brooks and Rodney Dangerfield both had rap records out, and then there was Shawn Brown's "Rappin' Duke," with a black dude doing his best to *sound* white. Hell, as far as the larger universe was concerned, every rap jam that hit the radio was "Flying Purple People Eater" or "The Streak"—a novelty hit. There still weren't that many *actual* hip hop records on wax—if you wanted to rock a mega-mix for hours, everything went in there. Why begrudge some local punks your age their turn at the mic?

Next couple of years, Yo-Yo saw the Beasties at various clubs and parties, or hanging downtown with some of his boys. He heard a few little singles they dropped here and there, but nothing really made noise until early 1986. The Latin Quarter nightclub was crazy, a small venue packed with all the hip hop stars of the day, as well as the most notorious drug dealers and stick-up kids of the five boroughs. There was no VIP section or separate, secured, roped-off areas; everyone was equal. You'd witness robberies, slashings, and even shootouts inside. Crooklyn terrorized the dance floor, snatching gold chains at will. Yo-Yo was cool with the worst offenders from Fort Greene and Lafayette Gardens; he never had any problems there, though he could count the white boys he saw there

on one hand. MC Serch was the only other Caucasoid you could consider a regular. So it stood out, the night a white kid ran in straight up to the DJ booth with a record in his hand. Yo-Yo was talking with Biz Markie and his boy Romeo when DJ Red Alert put the needle on that record: "Hol' it now, Hol' it now, Hol' it now! Hit it! Hit it! Hit it! Hit it. . . . YO LEROY!" and then that beat. The reaction was immediate. The hardest Hard-Rocks were on the floor wilding. Everybody was doing the Wop.

There were always a couple of records that made Brooklyn get real stupid. The first few notes would signal it was time to form like Voltron and go Rambo. Records like Cut Master DC's "Brooklyn's in the House," Stetsasonic's "Go Stetsa pt1," and Audio Two's "Top Billin'." These songs were audio malt liquor; they could make you wanna smack your own mama. The Beasties automatically joined this pantheon of riot-starters. They knew how to incite a crowd. Yo-Yo himself? More graffiti writer than MC in the end, he'd dissolve into legend.

In truth, the Beasties had accidentally made the first gangsta rap album. It's not too wild a claim. If gangsta rap is identifiable by first-person crime narrative, misogyny, drug and alcohol glorification, and over-the-top violence, then they had done it for sure. A few stray singles one could point to first, notably Schoolly D out of Philly, but in New York dudes were not claiming to be criminals on records. Quite the opposite in fact, hip hop was aspirational, MCs wished to be seen as suave and debonair, lovers, not muggers. Ricky D said "Callin' me a thief? Don't even try it," and Doctor Ice of UTFO rhymed "Me? The Doc? A hood? A rock? Runnin' round the street robbin' people on the block? Nah. That's not my style, to crime I'm not related, as far as I'm concerned I'm too sophisticated." The only real crime-rhyme you heard out of New York was in third person, and cautionary, the "Did-Don't-Da-Don't-Di-DON'T DO IT!" type of tale exemplified by Melle Mel and Duke Bootee. The reason wasn't exotic: most cats in NYC actually lived in harsh conditions and hoped to elevate above. Live in the hood, avoid cops and robbers, just get in your front door, and you didn't dream crime, you dreamed limousines and fly parties.

In New York it was understood that the Beasties weren't serious. They weren't shooting piano players any more than the Ramones had actually beat on brats with baseball bats. Outside of New York, it wasn't always so clear if they got the joke, in which kids from the right side of the tracks glorified the fouler aspects of ghetto living. Rick Rubin grasped the trick of shocking suburban parents and getting banned from venues in Middle America, a marketing plan modeled on Alice Cooper and the Sex Pistols more than Afrika Bambaataa or the Cold Crush Brothers.

That was the intention. Gangsta rap was the unintended consequence. Out west, *Licensed to Ill* blasted from every car driving by with the boomin' system. In the invention of L.A. rap, you can hear the influence. Some cats even adapted Mike D's trademark nasal whine. Ice-T admitted that "6 in the Mornin'," originally a B-side, intentionally had a

Beastie Boys–type sound. And the Bay Area? Forget about it—Sir Mix-a-Lot's "Posse on Broadway" is essentially a "Paul Revere" cover.

Back, one last time, to Brooklyn Friends School. Was it just the peculiarity of the locale, the contrast to the code of pacifism taught there, or was there something uncanny in that school's role as player in some of the most unnerving and violent incidents stalking the white-boy mind? Two kids corralled from Fulton Street in what might seem another trite shakedown for pocket money, instead subjected to torture and rape. A parent murdered in her sleep in her renovated brownstone. Other tales might be unknown, private wounds, humiliations tended behind closed doors.

Penny-ante traffickers in nostalgia advertise Bloomberg's gleaming city as fallen from some '90s peak of danger and excitement, but if you knew the '70s, you're unimpressed. The city was already gentrified in the '90s. The '70s were serious; the world we knew was something else, no matter how tired you might be by now of the testimony of aging white boys. For all the gory fun and provocation, all the John Carpenter horror lurking in "sticking up old ladies with the handgun or the sawed-off," in the impostures of the white boy lay a seed of real fear—on this, we must insist. It was the Beastie Boys' special legacy, as theatrical pretenders, juvenile actors playing juvenile delinquents, that freed them to tell of what they knew in the form of giddy cartoons, to indulge in code-switching of the *Mad* magazine variety. That they had an exit option—their whiteness, that is—meant they could dabble, and their dabbling was their genius.

You can read plenty on the relationship between Islam and hip hop, Judaism and hip hop, even Buddhism and hip hop. But did the nonviolent philosophies of the Quaker religion have a part in the creation of some of the most violent music ever recorded?

Hey, Richard Nixon, another Quaker product, was also known to drop some bombs.

R.I.P.

DAVE "SHADI" SCILKEN,

YVES "SEID" BREWER,

ADAM "BARD" YAUCH,

BETTY CARTER,

ELLEN FIELD,

EDWARD R. MURROW,

AND RICHARD "TRICKY DICK" NIXON.

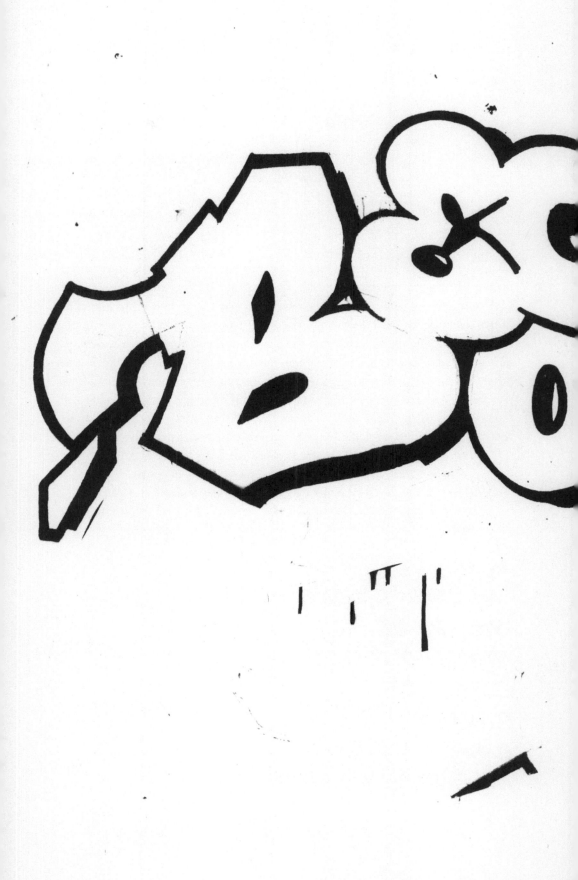

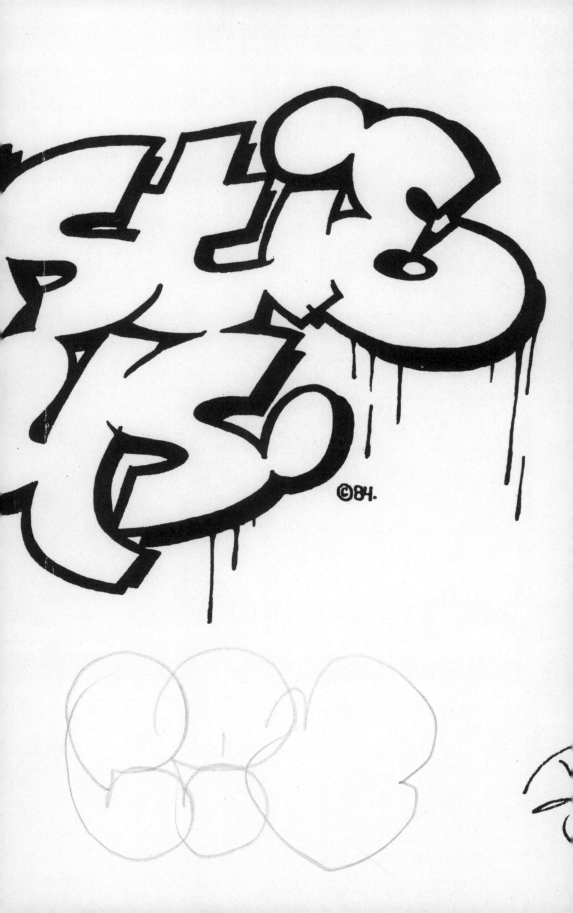

©84.

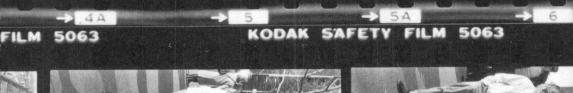

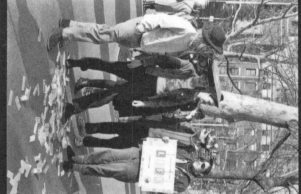
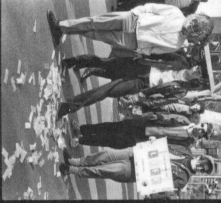

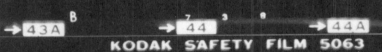
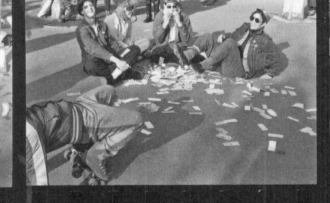
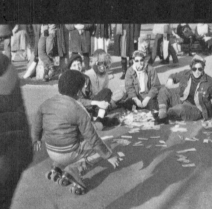

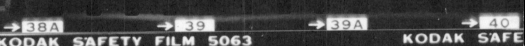

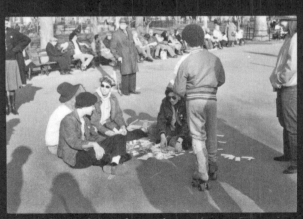
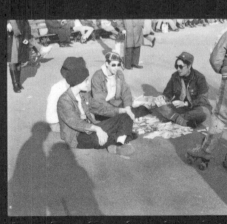

13A →14 →14A →15

KODAK SAFETY FILM 5063   KODAK SAFETY FILM

→18A →19 →19A →20

KODAK SAFETY FILM 5063   KODAK

→23A →24 →24A →25

KODAK SAFETY FILM 5063

The Making of "Cooky Puss"
(AH)

It's tough for NYC kids to like, or love, anything. It's just not cool. Whatever you do, you have to show the outward appearance of . . . *Yeah, pizza's okay. You know, it tastes good but, like, I was eating pizza like since back in the day so . . . whatever.* Admiration is from a kind of distance when you're a teenage child of "artsy-type" divorced parents from Manhattan. The idea behind our song "Cooky Puss" was that we were making fun of Malcolm McLaren's song "Buffalo Gals." That song was massive in our circle and scene. The clubs of NYC, downtown '83. We actually loved that song and listened to it every day and danced to it every night. Why make fun of it? We had to.

Adam Yauch's parents had an old friend, Doug Pomeroy, who ran a recording studio in Manhattan called Celebration. A name I have only grown to appreciate in this very moment I'm writing this. Celebration was a studio for recording jingles for commercials and stuff. A real grown-up place of business. As a favor to his old friends the Yauchs, Doug Pomeroy would let their son's band come in and he'd record us, after hours, for a couple nights. For free. So we recorded all the new songs we had in, like, twenty minutes. But he'd said we could use the studio for two nights so we were gonna make Actually, I had to bring an envelope of cash, like $200, to pay somebody? The night janitor? (MD) the most of it. As we listened to these new songs we had *just* recorded, we realized that they were pretty bad. They weren't hardcore songs, they were oddly Goth-ish and just sort of, well . . . pretty bad. We had a song called "Bucket of Cheese." We did a cover of the Cockney Rejects song "Subculture" because Yauch loved that song. We had a kind of love song/ode to Samson the dog in the style of a song that Mike, Kate, and I loved called "King of Kings" by a band called the Pack. The semi-Goth lane was not our comfort zone, and we kind of knew in the moment that the songs were bad, but since we had more time in the studio, we were gonna make *something*.

In the early '80s there were these TV commercials for an ice-cream place called Carvel. More specifically, for a specialty cake they made called Cookie Puss. The voiceover was this weird high-pitched space alien saying, "Hello, my name is Cookie Puss," followed by a slurring man's raspy voice talking about the merits of the cake and the establishment. Allegedly the voice was that of Mr. Tom Carvel himself. The ads were super cheap and seemed homemade, and we loved them. Kind of obsessed with them, really. Why was Cookie Puss a space alien? For St. Patrick's Day they'd take a Cookie Puss cake, add a little green frosting on top, and have an ad for a different cake named Cookie O'Puss. On Father's Day they'd make Fudgie the Whale. It was a cake decorated to look like a whale, using

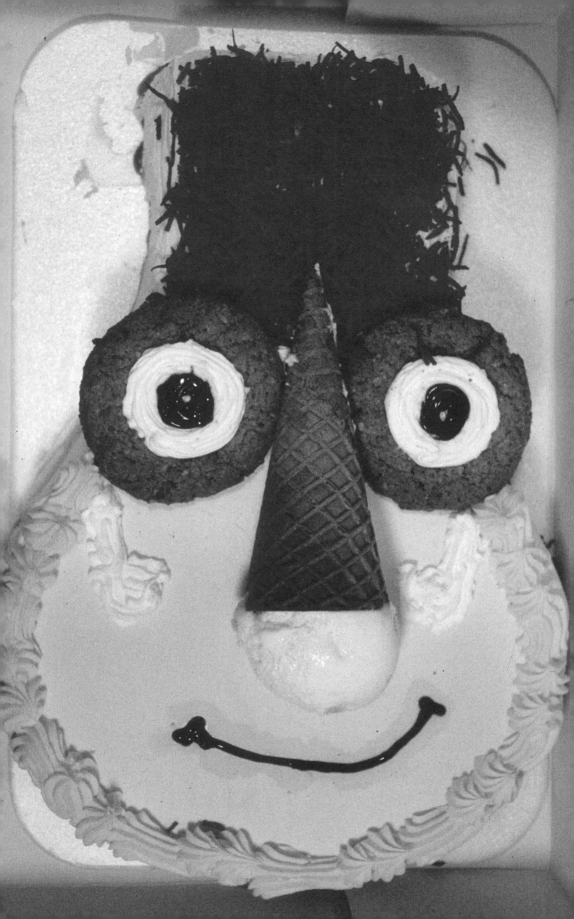

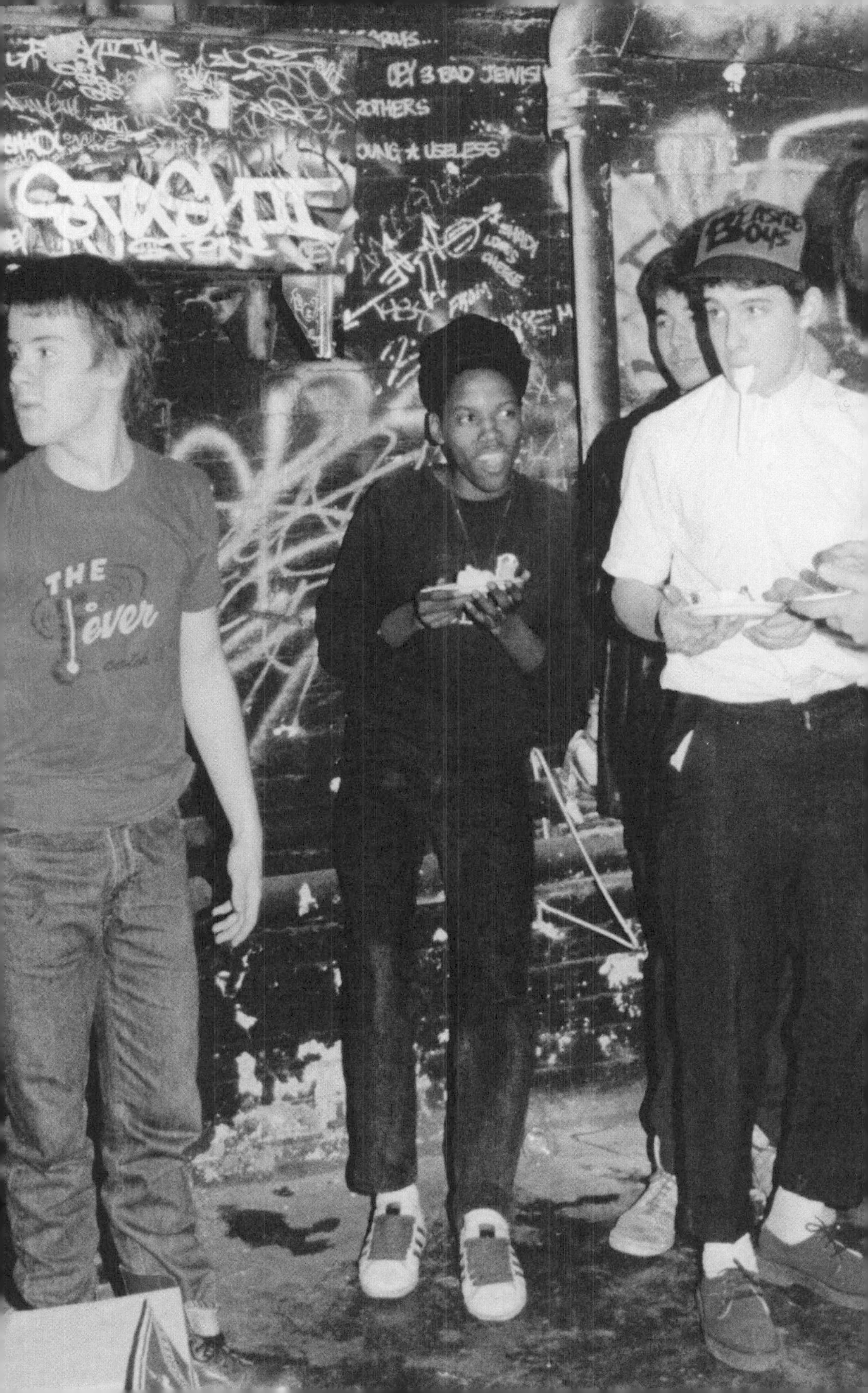

ROTHERS
USELESS
THE

the same Cookie Puss cake mold, and they'd write "To a Whale of a Dad" on it. For Christmas, they'd put a Santa hat on Cookie Puss and have a new ad for that. The cakes and commercials were so cockamamie and grimy and unprofessional that I guess we were drawn to their punkness. So since we had this extra time in the recording studio . . . let's make fun of our current two most favorite things, Cookie Puss and "Buffalo Gals," and write a song about them.

We made a track that was basically just Kate playing a danceable beat, Yauch playing a simple distorted bass line, and we added some shitty attempts at scratching records on top of that. I don't know whose idea it was to call Carvel and curse out the person on the phone, but I was the one to make the call. We recorded it, and that was our song. It's actually pretty fucked-up. Sadly, when you're a teenager, you don't think about those things too much. You know, other people's feelings. Like the telephone operator and the woman working at Carvel that I called and harassed and screamed at. (Can I formally apologize right here and now? I'm sorry.) There's a definite line between funny prank call and being mean. Just randomly calling and cursing a woman out on the phone is not cool. But Adam, Mike, Kate, and I thought it was funny at the time. We were just so psyched to be a band, in a recording studio. We were teenagers with a ton of teenage energy. As you get older, you form a filter for what's a great idea and what's not. And so most of the dumb shit falls by the wayside. Which is probably for the best, but as I said . . . we thought it was funny at the time.

We made another song that night called "Beastie Revolution." Basically it's just us making a goofball reggae song. We loved dub reggae and so we had to make fun of it to not appear infatuated. We scrapped the other songs we'd written and recorded and decided to release a 12-inch single of "Cooky Puss" (with "Beastie Revolution" as the B-side) on Rat Cage Records. And for whatever reason, people liked it. Our friends started to tell us that they heard DJs playing "Cooky Puss" in clubs. Mark Kamins or Anita Sarko was playing it at Danceteria. Johnny Dynell at Area. Allegedly, Afrika Bambaataa was playing "Cooky Puss" at the Roxy. (I meant to say Roxy's. If you're from New York you always leave off the superfluous words and add an apostrophe *s* after the name of a place. Like if you're going to Carnegie Deli, for instance, you'd say that you were going to Carnegie's. Or to Roxy's instead of the Roxy.) Things were changing for us now. We were becoming a hardcore band that wasn't a hardcore band. Now we had an actual 12-inch record like the bands, singers, and rappers that we *loved*. Not like we were huge or anything, but other people besides our fifteen friends had heard this song.

Going out to clubs was suddenly different now. It wasn't just that we were receiving more attention, but we were a little older too. Hanging out had a new and added meaning: meaning . . . sex. Just a year before we were out at clubs and shows to see bands and hang out with other kids. Maybe flirt a little. (Making out was a huge deal.) But now it was on and poppin'. The transformation from kid to little grown-up person. That thing when you break

off from your friends at the end of the night. Now when we said goodbye we weren't going home . . . to bed. . . . Now we were looking for a potentially illicit and grown-up good night. Leaving the group *with someone else.* Man, that was great. Being young and getting it on. But I digress. . . .

One night this kid comes over to me in Danceteria's second-floor stairwell and starts to talk to me about "Cooky Puss." He says that his uncle is Tom Carvel and that we don't need to worry about any legal issues because he'll talk to his uncle about it and tell him that we're cool and that it'd be cool and all that. I was sixteen, and professional legal issues weren't really on my radar yet. (Also . . . it's not illegal to write a song about a cake. Is it?) But as it turned out, the slurry, raspy voice from the TV commercials really was the kid's uncle, and he was cool with our song about his product. How nice is that? There's no real point to me telling you this detail other than it being fantastic that there was an actual, for real, Tom Carvel. And that somewhere in his brain, Beastie Boys exists. Right in there next to Cookie Puss, Cookie O'Puss, and Fudgie the Whale.

P.S. Cookie Puss is fucking delicious.

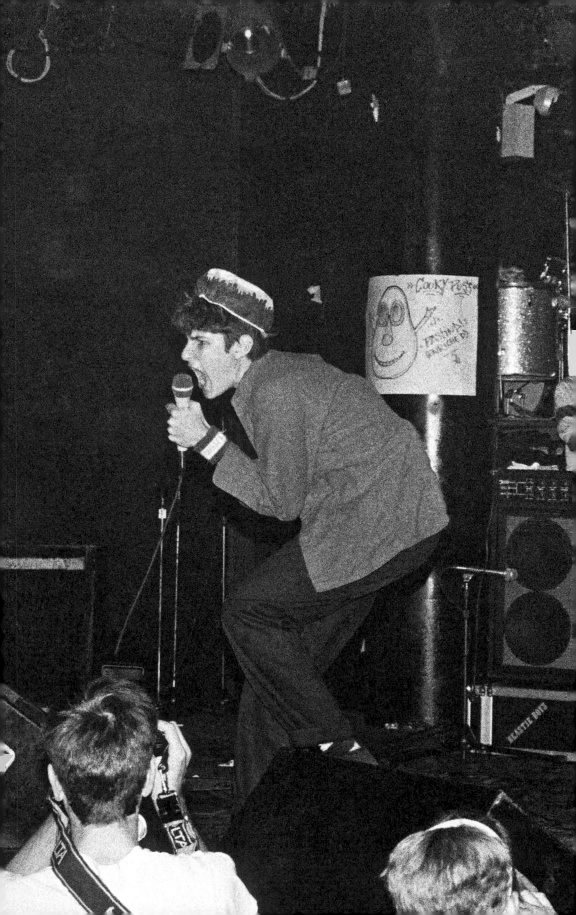

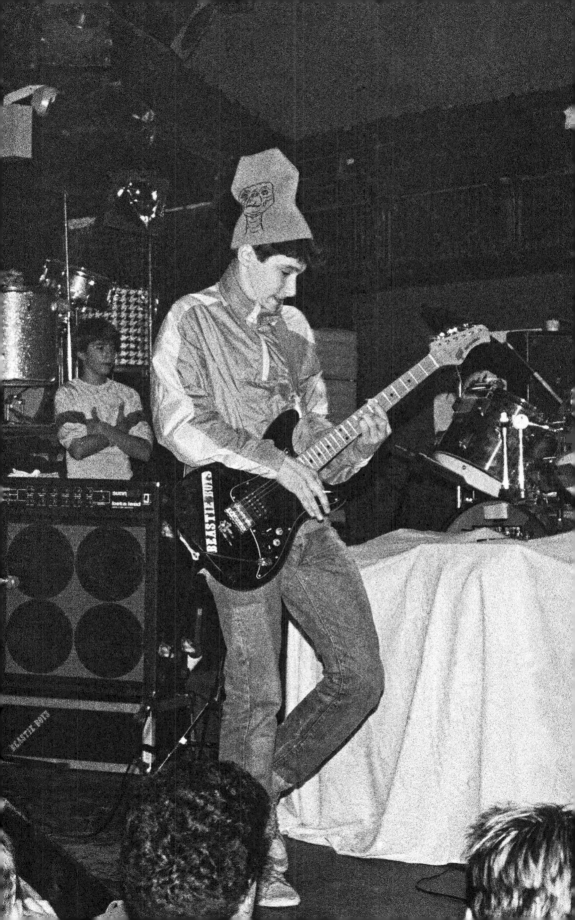

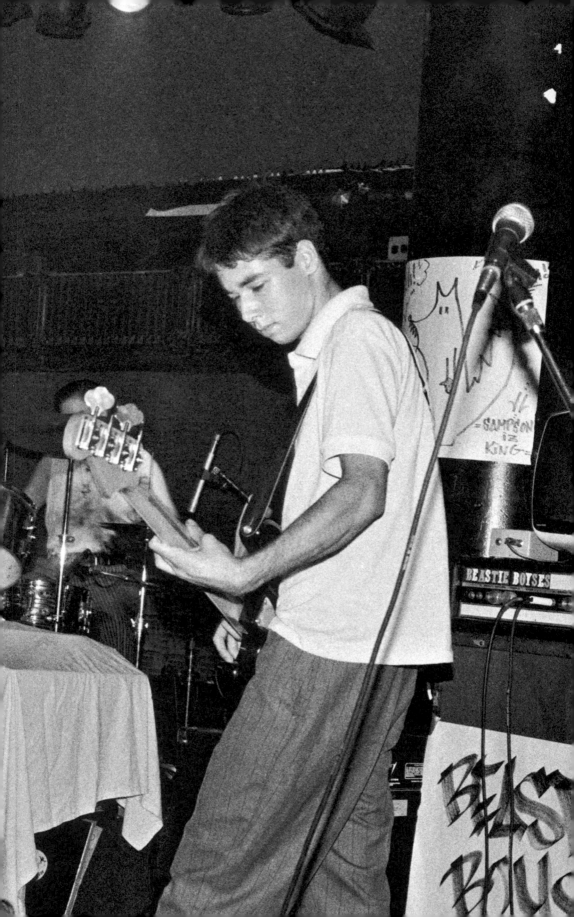

PLEASE EAT ME

AL COMEY. BUSBOY, MUDD CLUB: "Say what you want about Cookie Puss, he was one chill motherfucker."

JANE TRILLING. COAT CHECKER, IRVING PLAZA: "Cookie never talked about his childhood. I know he was from the Midwest, a town called Carvel. A lot of small minds, to hear him talk of it. They used to make fun of him because he was mixed. 'What are you? Are you ice cream, or are you cake?' Stuff like that."

DAISY MEEKS. CASHIER, CANAL JEANS: "Might as well have been from outer space, he was so far out."

GARY DELUXE. PERSONALITY: "New York is always too expensive, and people always keep coming. No matter when you come, you've already missed it. Cookie Puss was one of these seekers."

DEV TREMORS. DRUMMER, SHOOT THE HOSTAGES: "I'm not trying to make a case for New York City from '81 to '85 as some magical wonderland. I mean, it was no Cleveland '77. But let's just say that New York City between '81 and '85 was a great place to be young, and to make music."

ANGIE DUST. DJ, WNYU's NEW AFTERNOON SHOW: "I didn't get Cookie Puss at first. Still don't."

BOB PLOTNIK. OWNER, BLEECKER BOB'S RECORDS: "Sure, he worked here. I let him sleep in the back sometimes, when he was between things. He swept up. Wasn't that good at it. I don't know if it was laziness or what. You'd see him just standing there staring at the LPs on the wall. Staring like an idiot. Last straw was when I caught him holding a copy of *Metallic K.O.* up to his ear. I was like, 'What the hell are you doing?' He just smiled."

CHASE "CHAZ" CHASERTON. PROJECTIONIST, THE PYRAMID CLUB: "He claimed he could listen to vinyl without a turntable. That it was easy once you got the hang of it."

DEV TREMORS: "It got so I'd have to steer him through the East Village, avoiding certain blocks, because he'd have to stop wherever people were selling their shit on the street. LPs, clothes, porno mags. Who'd want to buy someone else's used porno mags? But Cookie, he'd have to stop when he saw some freak selling records. Merengue, polka, funk, he didn't care."

FLORIAN GOODE. COLLEGE ROCK BUYER, TOWER RECORDS: "He was a bit of a hustler."

GREIL MARCUS. CRITIC: "He told me he knew someone who was selling Bob Dylan's jockstrap. You know, from *The Basement Tapes*? Of course I was interested. We met at the Holiday Cocktail Lounge. Anyway, he rooked me."
[OPENS JEWEL-COVERED BOX]
"I mean, does this smell like Bob Dylan's jockstrap to you?"

DEV TREMORS: "He was a mix, a mutt. When you looked at him, you saw what you wanted to see. From one angle, a cake. From another, ice cream. Chocolate. Vanilla, whatever your taste. Black. White. Cookie Puss."

AL COMEY: "Nothing he liked more than watching TV. Watching TV and sniffing glue. *Video Music Box*. Ed Norton, Ted Knight. Mr. Ed. 'You know Ted Knight is up to some kinky shit when he's off the air,' he'd say."

FLORIAN GOODE: "You got all types of people in this city, that's what makes it unique. You got your blacks, your Puerto Ricans. Italians and Jews. Ice-cream cakes. Each one an instrument in the symphony of the city."

MADGE FELLOWS. BARTENDER, PALLADIUM: "He still owes me ten dollars."

GEZA BINS. BASSIST, SHOOT THE HOSTAGES: "At the time, he was dating Lydia Lunch's dermatologist. I don't know how she got tickets, but the Germs were playing on *Saturday Night Live*. Belushi was a fan. Things like that actually happened in this city. Anyway, they tore the place up. His girlfriend was appalled. She was this uptight Scarsdale type, skinny little thing. Cookie loved it. He used to say, 'This is just punk energy waiting to be transformed into something else.'"

GLORIA MEADOW. LYDIA LUNCH'S DERMATOLOGIST: "We came from different worlds. I was this suburban white girl from outside Philly. He was an ice-cream cake. We tried . . . but sometimes love just isn't enough."

DEV TREMORS: "You make a personality out of everything you suck into your orbit—parents, friends, teachers, songs, TV shows, movies, your neighborhood. All that stuff, you mix it together, and it becomes your identity. That's the best music, the stuff that makes the new connections between everything that everyone else is putting out."

GRACE GRACELESS. TCHOTCHKE WRANGLER, LOVE SAVES THE DAY: "We met at a Clash show. Bonds, when Grandmaster Flash opened for them. Stuff like that actually used to happen."

RIFF RANDELL. PUBLICIST, LOLLAPALOOZA, 1993–96: "You didn't want to get Cookie started on The Clash, obviously middle-period Clash, or else you'd be up all night. Rap! Rockabilly! Gospel! Dub! He had this theory that Sandinista! was actually a quadruple album, and that the fourth record was lying in a vault somewhere. That they would release it when the world was ready. They started out as a punk band and then something beautiful happened."

GLORIA MEADOW: "He was a sweet guy. Maybe too sweet."

EVAN PARKER. DENTIST: "I heard he came up with the drumbeat for Strafe's 'Set It Off,' but I'm not sure if that's true."

AL COMEY: "He was running around with Basquiat. Tagging up the city. You'd see his handiwork all over—'CP,' for Cookie Puss. But the thing was, he used chocolate syrup. Squirting. The next time it rained it would just wash away."

FLORIAN GOODE: "He'd start raving whenever 'World Destruction' came on, that Afrika Bambaataa–Johnny Rotten song. 'This is the future of music—big beats and guitars!' Where punk was transformed by rap music, or rap music was transformed by punk energy, or maybe it was not one thing acting on the other but the two things just coming together into something new. He thought all music would be like that one day."

DEV TREMORS: "Needless to say, it didn't happen that way, but the vibes were out there. If you picked up on them."

PAZ TROUT. CIGARETTE GIRL, THE WORLD: "His synthesizer arrangement of 'Baby Let Me Bang Your Box' was a minor club hit in Germany."

<u>**Coco LaCroix. Procurer, Save the Robots:**</u> "At the time, Cookie was working as Ugly George's personal assistant. Ugly George was this guy who'd go around, he had this public access show and he'd ask women to take their clothes off on camera. Go around the city, going up to women. A precursor to the kind of weird Internet celebrities you have nowadays, but back then it was crazy. Cookie thought the whole thing was fabulous, really DIY. 'If it doesn't exist, make it.' Guitars on top of a beatbox—good, go, do it."

<u>**Al Comey:**</u> "One time this guy he grew up with was visiting. Fudgie, I think his name was. Big guy. We were standing outside CB's and he said, 'You know, one day this is just going to be condos for rich people.' We laughed, of course, how could you not, the way the Bowery was in those days. And he was wrong, of course. CB's is a *clothing store* for rich people."

<u>**Coco LaCroix:**</u> "It was November 1984. The night Reagan got reelected. He was going off. 'Fuck the Great American Songbook. Give me the Great American Mixtape.'"

<u>**Jeff Chambers. Accountant, 99 Records:**</u> "Cookie was always going from one job, and then he'd get fired, and then he'd find another gig. Somehow he stumbled into a job working for the vending company that serviced the candy machines in NYU dorms. That's how he met Rick Rubin. Rubin got his hand stuck in one machine trying to steal some Ho Hos, and that's how they met. Cookie brought the jaws of life."

<u>**Evan Parker:**</u> "It was Cookie Puss's idea to put that little white kid into Run-DMC's video for 'Rock Box.' He was like, 'This record is going to take over the country.' They needed 'a Trojan Horse,' is what he called it. Watching MTV, those kids out there in the Midwest, they'll see this little white boy hanging out with these b-boys and it'll just seem natural."

<u>**Dev Tremors:**</u> "He was really into the idea of that little white kid, sure. Wrote a TV pilot for a Saturday-morning cartoon show called *The Amazing Adventures of Run-DMC and Jim-Jim*. Flew out to L.A. and everything. Nothing ever came of it."

<u>**Florian Goode:**</u> "He said, 'The New Style is every style that has come before, recombined.' You know that story about how everyone who saw the Ramones started a band? Well, everyone who sniffed glue with Cookie started on a genre-bending musical odyssey."
<u>**Interviewer:**</u> "Like who?"
<u>**Florian Goode:**</u> "I didn't agree to talk to you so I could be attacked."

<u>**Jeff Chambers:**</u> "What actually happened the night that Cookie Puss met Beastie Boys remains a mystery. Something went down, everyone agrees on that. Now, of course,

everyone says they were there at Downtown Beirut that night. Like Woodstock, or the Sun Ra–Sonic Youth show at SummerStage, or that Shoot the Hostages show where Dev Tremors stapled the Chihuahua to his chest. History."

Coco LaCroix: "Oh, to have been a fly on the wall."

Evan Parker: "It was not recorded, obviously. There were no photographs. But after that night, everything was different."

Riff Randell: "I don't think they ever met again."

Florian Goode: "In a certain sense, he was their Pete Best."
Interviewer: "What sense would that be?"
Florian Goode: "Get out of my house."

Evan Parker: "For a long time after, in certain trendy downtown art circles, 'Speaking to Cookie Puss' was slang for smoking marijuana. You know, cheeba, sinsemilla."

Grace Graceless: "I don't know what happened to him."

Angie Dust: "He started hanging with this rough crowd. The whole downward-spiral thing, hitting the hard stuff—hot fudge, sprinkles."

Al Comey: "I heard he melted."

Dev Tremors: "The last time I saw him was at the Ritz, when it was still the Ritz and not that club or whatever it is now. It was Beastie Boys and Murphy's Law. *Licensed to Ill* had just come out, but it hadn't broken yet. 'Party' was maybe a video already, but it hadn't blown up. It was a great show. Really mixed crowd, the way clubs were in those days. B-boys, what you'd call white hipsters nowadays, teenagers, punks, club heads. All these crazy cats. Mosh pit bringing them all together. Like magic. And there was Cookie Puss, just standing there in the middle of it, smiling his head off. It was a great night. One of those New York nights that stay with you, no matter what happens later."

Riff Randell: "We lost touch after that. You grow up, settle down. Don't stay up all night anymore. Life happens."

Daisy Meeks: "Back to outer space, I'm telling you. His work here was done."

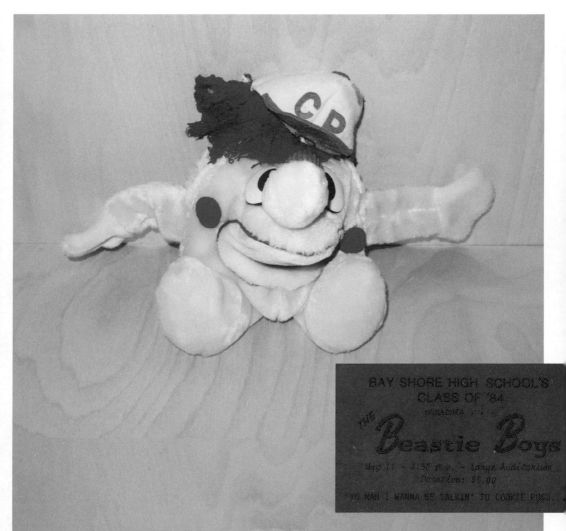

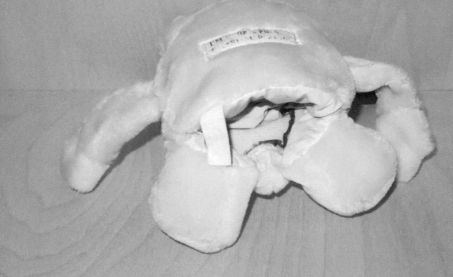

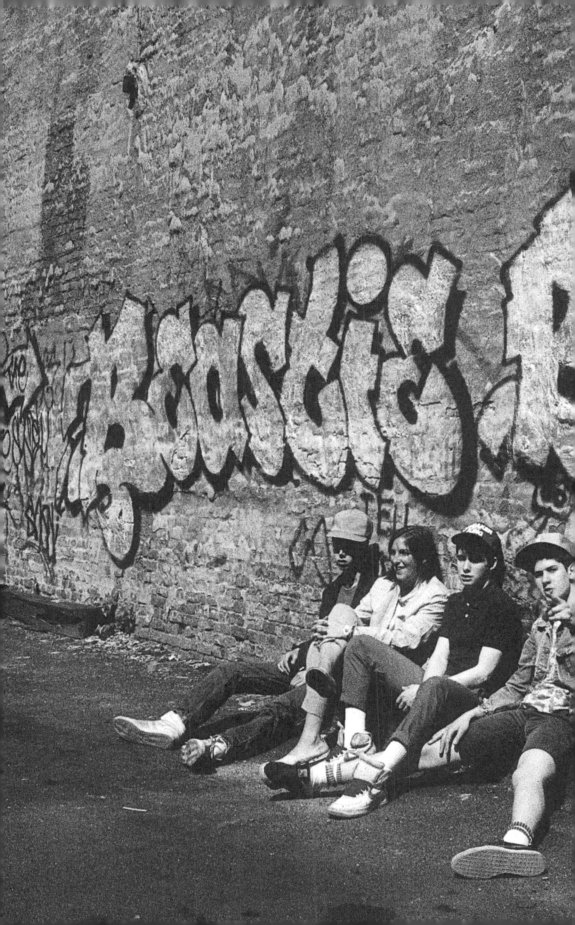

British Airways
(AH)

So one day I'm at my friend Tammy's apartment (Tammy Toye, sister of downtown supermodel Terri Toye). It's 1983. I'm supposed to be in school. But I'm not. I'm at Tammy's apartment. On Eighteenth Street. We're just hanging out. The TV's on, but it's sort of in the background. All of a sudden, I hear our song "Beastie Revolution" (the B-side of the "Cooky Puss" single) playing from that background. *Wait, what? No way.* I rush to the TV, turn it up, and . . . "OH SHIT!!! THAT'S OUR FUCKING SONG!!!" Playing in an ad for British Airways?! I was freaking out. *Did that shit really just happen?* Yes. Our song really did just play on a commercial for an airplane on TV. I have no idea what happened in the ad. It was a total blur. In slow motion, it happened in an instant.

I called Yauch, Kate, and Mike right away. *Yo! How crazy is that . . . Wait up . . . you can't just use someone's music for an ad without getting permission.* I mean . . . we were new to the "industry," but shit . . . British Airways . . . !?! Where's our money!?! Mike's mom had a friend who had a friend who knew someone in a law firm, and they said that there was this young guy that had just started, fresh out of law school, and that he'd be perfect for us to talk to. So we did. He appeared to be basically our age, but seemed like he was trying really hard to look, and act, like a grown-up. He contacted the lawyers for British Airways, and I guess they realized that they fucked up, and were quick to pay us a settlement. Adam, Mike, Kate, and I got ten grand each. Besides random jobs here and there, a few dollars playing gigs, and my job at the ice-cream store (did I mention that I worked at an ice-cream store?), this was the first real money I'd *ever* had. Long dollars. This shit was HUGE for me. I never had a nice guitar, and so fuck it . . . I'm gonna get one. The one I'd wanted forever was a black Rickenbacker. The same one that Paul Weller from The Jam played. I'd been eyeing a used one at Rogue, this music store my mom's friend owned. It cost $250. So when I got my British Airways money, I went up there with exactly two hundred and fifty dollars. I had definitely never had that much cash in my pocket before. When I got there I was all ready to get the cool Paul Weller Rickenbacker but . . . I saw this drum machine they were selling for the same price. By then we were all *really* into rap music, and all the best new rap records were using drum machines. "Rockin' It," "F.R.E.S.H.," and "Sucker MC's" were for sure made with a drum machine, so I wanted one. I had no idea that we would actually ever really make rap music, but for some reason I said fuck it. I mean, I already had the Hondo guitar my mom and her friends gave me for my twelfth birthday, and it worked just fine, so I bought the drum machine instead.

I'm not sure why, but this particular drum machine drew me in. Maybe 'cause it was selling for the exact amount of money that I had in my pocket. Maybe it was the forces of nature, but this shit just looked really cool. No one I knew had a drum machine, and I wanted to have one. This one, the Roland TR-808.

That same 808 later became the house 808 at Chung King studio, where us, Run-DMC, LL Cool J, and a bunch of other rappers recorded. (AH)

I can't believe the randomness of it all. The TV just happened to be on, and it was playing loud enough for me to hear the commercial. Us just fucking around, having fun late one night at Yauch's parents' friend's recording studio, making stupid songs like "Cooky Puss" and "Beastie Revolution," would turn into me having the cash to buy the very drum machine that would later make the beat for songs like "Brass Monkey," Run-DMC's "Peter Piper," and a bunch more songs that you might know and enjoy.

Another wild part of the British Airways thing was that later it turned out the person responsible for selecting our piece of music for that TV ad was this guy from a band called Haysi Fantayzee. And just a couple years before I met Tammy and went to her apartment and heard this TV ad . . . I was a kid at home listening to the Haysi Fantayzee record on my shitty Emerson brand turntable/radio/cassette/entertainment system in my bedroom. I mean . . . how does this type of stuff happen? This shit should be in a book, right?

Cereal
Milk
Ice cream
eggs
Rye bread
Bagels
Olive oil

THE MONEY MAN.

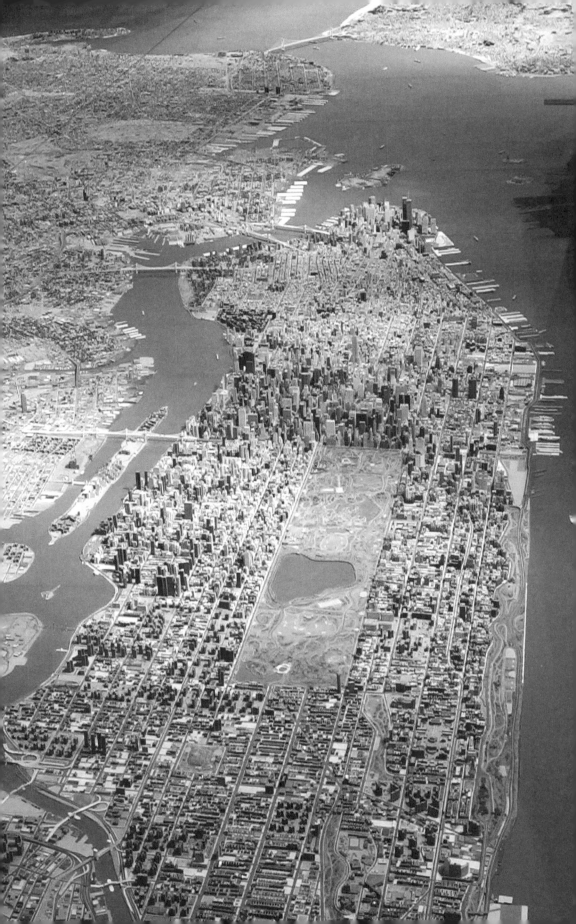

The  (AH)

Yauch was the first to leave the city. He went to Bard College in upstate New York. He didn't really leave, though, 'cause it seemed like he came back home every weekend. I didn't know much about his life up there other than he lived in a dorm, and that there was a kid who had a radio show and Yauch threw a smoke bomb into the studio during his show 'cause he thought it would be funny and that the kid would think so too. But the kid *really* didn't think it was funny, and went on a two-minute, on-air, cursing rampage about Yauch. Which actually made the thing way more funny. (Damn you, podcasts! Why weren't you around then? This parenthesis could be a link!) Yauch set up a show for us at Bard, and so we all went up there a few months into his freshman year. We also just wanted to see what college was like. I remember us being so psyched that there was this mess-hall kind of place where the food was free. *You mean we can just take as many of these mini boxes of Rice Krispies as we want, and we won't get in trouble?* Yauch was basically like . . . "Yeah, no one gives a shit about the cereal. They're pretty content with the tuition money they're getting."

Yauch actually played us a tape of it back then and it was fucking funny as shit. (MD)

Yauch was two years older than me, and so he did a lot of stuff first. Not only leave NYC, but also own a car. Yauch had some money saved and bought a beat-up old black MG sports car from the '60s. It was SO COOL. Well . . . it *looked* really cool. And when you were riding in it, it was awesome. But as far as dependability and safety and stuff like that, it was not so much like . . . you know . . . up-to-date. I remember that Yauch was very particular about starting it up and letting it sit for a long while before he would drive off in it. "I know it's freezing outside and the heat doesn't work in here but . . . just wait."

The first time he drove his new MG down to the city, he went around trying to find people to show it off to but no one was around. He drove to my apartment but I wasn't home. My mom was, though, so Adam drove her around the entire circumference of the island of Manhattan. Just the two of them. Cruising. When I finally got home and my mom told me about it, it made me so happy. My mom never learned how to drive, and I know she loved being in cars. What it must have meant to her to have her little son's friend pick her up and take her out on the town. But that was Yauch. He wasn't doing anyone any favors. He just loved living and sharing experiences. And the same went for my mom.

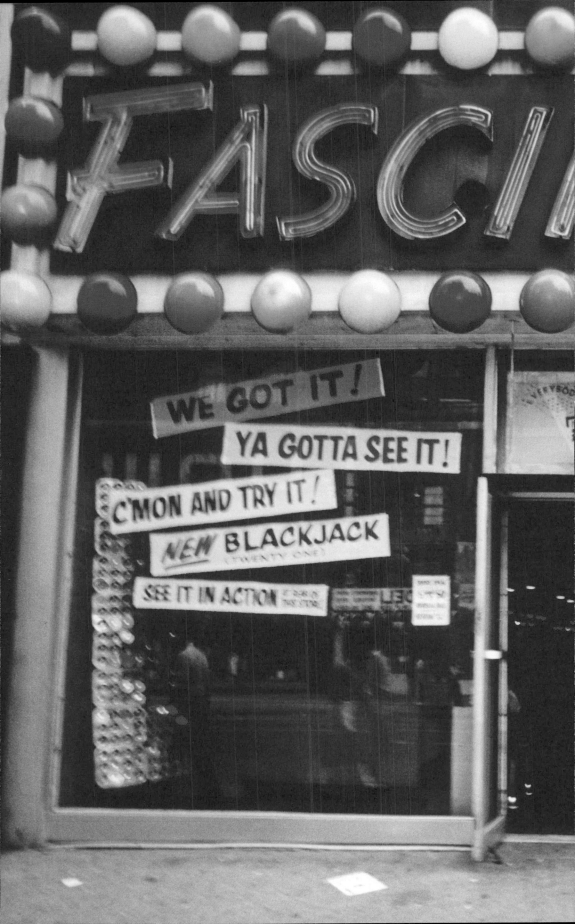

ATION
WE GOT IT!
YA GOTTA SEE IT!
C'MON AND TRY IT!
NEW BLACKJACK
SEE IT IN ACTION
JESUS SAID SEARCH THE SCRIPTURES

DJ Double R and His World-Famous Bubble Machine

(MD)

Summer 1983. "Cooky Puss" was getting played in clubs. This was some exciting shit to us.

We wanted to start performing the song live. Never mind that we were a hardcore band with zero experience at playing anything with a funky beat; what were we gonna do for the vocal part, re-create a prank phone call? No. But like one of those inspirational calendars will tell you: great adversity provides great opportunity.

We decided to start rapping.

The decision probably would have happened one way or another. We were totally burnt on hardcore and obsessed with hip hop. But by the time of "Cooky Puss," we had enough of a hardcore audience and were kind of settled into the bass-drums-guitar-vocals format that it took us a while to fully let go; instead, we started with a half step: at future shows, we'd play a twenty-minute hardcore set, then bring on a DJ and do a hip hop set.

We actually did re-create a prank phone call once, at our ill-fated Studio 54 gig. We did a pretend prank phone call with our friend Kecia Benvenuto backstage on a mic, acting like the Carvel lady. At this same gig Mike almost got us beat up for saying something about the Mafia, and then Julian Schnabel and Rene Ricard saved our lives. (Long story.) (AH)

So we needed to find a DJ.

And to teach ourselves how to MC.

To do the latter, we bought every new rap 12-inch as it came out. There still weren't that many—like, maybe one every two weeks—and we would play them on repeat, memorizing every single word, phrase, cadence, and ad-lib. Actually, "on repeat" wasn't even in our vocabulary back then; we'd have to run over to the turntable at the end of every 12-inch, pick up the needle, and drop it back at the beginning. We did this over and over again, dancing around and rapping the whole time. Inevitably, we would try to scratch using our consumer turntables. This did not end well. You would trash the needle and, if you went too crazy, might fuck up the record or even the turntable motor.

I notice that Mike has mentioned dancing several times. Did you know that he studied at Juilliard and the Joffrey? (AH)

None of this could be done on our parents' nicer living-room stereos. One, they wouldn't have it. *Rap music in the living room? Have you lost your mind?* And two, that shit would have been way too embarrassing. I mean, here we were, teenagers trying to learn how to dance and rap. We're talking *seriously* awkward experimentation. Privacy required. Bedrooms only.

Meanwhile, CUT TO:

INT. A HIGH-END BOHEMIAN LOFT IN SOHO—DAY

Cutting-edge modern art hangs on pristine white walls. A tall punk-rock teen with a limp Mohawk talks on a wall telephone in an open kitchen. This is NICK COOPER, downtown punk-rock private school kid, on the phone with his friend Adam Horovitz, who's recently given himself the name THE KING ADROCK.

COOPER: Dude. *Dude.* I'm *telling* you. He is *the guy.* He can DJ. He has all the equipment. Turntables. PA. Drum machine. He even has a fucking *bubble machine.* Everything.

THE KING ADROCK: (O.S.) (*muffled; from the other end of the phone line*) Hold up. Bubble machine?

CUT TO:

Nick leads Adam, Adam, and me over to NYU's Weinstein dormitory, in the middle of Greenwich Village, just off Washington Square Park. Weinstein is an institutional building from the Robert Moses era of NYC construction: soulless, efficient, generic. Brick on the outside; painted cinder block, linoleum floors, and fluorescent lighting on the inside. We're greeted by the dorm receptionist at the front desk. He's a short, stocky guy with thick beard and thicker New York accent. We'd later find out his name: Ric Menello (remember that). He calls up to the dorm room to announce our arrival and issues us passes. This is already some next-level shit for us. High school kids hanging out in a college dorm. In the general vicinity of college-age girls.

We get to the room and knock. The door is opened by a heavyset dude with sleepy eyes and long hair that kinda hangs in his face. It seems clear that he's just rolled out of bed. He looks like a guitarist in some metal band, except he's wearing these weird leather gloves that zip up, which totally creep us out. *This couldn't possibly be him.*

Yep, it's him: one entire side of his tiny dorm room is filled with a complete PA, Cerwin-Vega speaker cabinets with those huge folded horns. Two Technics 1200 turntables (ones you could actually scratch with), a drum machine, and yeah, boys and girls: a bubble machine.

We hired him on the spot. We didn't even know yet if he could DJ or not. But he had the gear. That was enough for us. And that's how we came to work with DJ Double R, known to his friends as Rick Rubin.

Rick was an interesting cat. He was from an entirely different world from us: Long Island. A true suburban kid. Complete with doting, overly protective parents and an unbridled affection for AC/DC and Zeppelin and metal. Turned out that he'd also been part of

AH: He did *not* have a bubble machine. Nick just told us that he did. (The art crowd *loves* bubbles. As do two-year-old children.) But when we met Rick, he said that he had access to a *smoke* machine.

MD: I definitely remember a bubble machine.

AH: There was no bubble machine.

MD: Well, I happen to have Rick Rubin right here . . .

Rick Rubin: I did, in fact, have access to bubbles. The dorm had a machine for parties, as I recall. Seems strange, but it's true.

the NY hardcore scene; we'd seen many of the same shows (including that storied Black Flag show at the Peppermint Lounge), and he'd been in an arty hardcore-adjacent band called Hose. And like us, Rick had also moved on to hip hop. He'd been put in charge of dorm entertainment at Weinstein, which apparently came with a budget, and he promptly used it to hire DJ Jazzy Jay to spin at parties there. That was a huge deal to us—that he even *knew* a real hip hop DJ. He was also ahead of us on rap 12-inches, because while we were going to Rock & Soul or Vinylmania to buy them, he was a member of a record pool: record pools were a service where (real) DJs would pay a fee and get all the new releases ahead of time.

Rick's dorm room soon became our new HQ, our new Rat Cage. We'd spend hours happily going through the fresh crate of records he'd get every week from the record pool. We listened to everything through his large PA speakers. *Really* loud. This never seemed to bother people, though I have a vague memory that when we started hanging out, Rick had a roommate. Somehow, over the ensuing months, he just kind of vanished. No idea why—who wouldn't want to live with a DJ in leather gloves who always had high school kids over to play hip hop at full blast on a concert PA?

We started to map out what the rap part of our live show might look like. We would go through records, all types of records, picking out breaks that we wanted to rap over. Everything from Trouble Funk to AC/DC to John Cougar Mellencamp. Whatever worked. That will always be one of the things that makes me fucking *love* hip hop. It's equal-opportunity. It will take from any person or any source—black, white, Latin, rock, soul, easy listening, jazz, funk, fucking polka—whatever and whomever. By any means necessary. It is all about finding any record that contained two bars of magic.

We'd spend hours in Rick's dorm room, working on the faintest beginnings of our individual MC styles. (Cue the missing montage from the '80s movie *Fame*.) I'll always remember one of the things that Rick said about my rapping: "Mike D needs to sound like he's working hard when he raps." Meaning: for Yauch (the James Dean of the band), rapping was effortless, and it sounded like it. Yauch was a natural. He could effortlessly spit out a flawless re-creation of Spoonie Gee or Frederick MC Count.

For me, as Kool Moe Dee said, "I go to work like a doctor." Rick picked up on that and

I wanted to sound like Jimmy Spicer when we first started rapping. But after hearing myself frontin' on the mic with a fake deep voice (like Jimmy Spicer or Melle Mel), I had to come up with something different. Something that was more me. I had to admit that I'm not a low-voiced smooth talker. I'm more the whiny, upset, screaming type. So the adjustment was made, and I felt way more comfortable on the mic. (AH)

would push me further toward exposing the sweat and effort. We each had our certain default style, and Rick as a producer recognized that.

Rick would usually man the turntables, though sometimes Adam Horovitz would too. Regardless, all of us would shout out records or breaks that we wanted to hear, bobbing our heads and occasionally engaging the Shure SM58 microphone that was on hand.

The first shows we did with a rap set were more like amateur talent shows. They were proper gigs at proper clubs, but we were really just trying to figure it out, dress rehearsal–style. We'd play hardcore for twenty minutes or so as a "band" with our instruments, including Kate on drums. Then we'd leave the stage, Rick would start to scratch, and then all four of us would come back out as MCs. For those first few gigs, Kate would come out and MC with us. She was definitely way less into rap than the three of us were, but I'm not sure we ever had a real conversation with her about the idea of including her less; instead, we just slowly began leaving her out of stuff—a turn of events sometimes encouraged by Rick—and we did so in the least communicative (read: shittiest) way possible.

Our set would be a combo of our own rhymes and covers. We started dressing the part too, sporting fashions straight outta Delancey Street: pullover windbreakers, shell-toe Adidas with fat laces, jeans tapered in tight at the ankles. For one show, at the Pyramid Club on Avenue A, we brought in Mackie, a graffiti artist friend of ours, to create a mural live behind us as we played. This seemed like a good idea until the paint fumes filled the stage and choked us, making it difficult to see or breathe, let alone rap.

At one of our shows sometime around then, we were introduced to Danny Fields—a New York underground legend who had managed the Stooges and

Ramones. We fucking idolized the Ramones, so I was really psyched to meet this guy. He was an unapologetically little dude that reeked of weed. (I liked him already.) But when he opened his mouth, I was devastated. "Kid, this will never work. You're white kids trying to rap? No one will like you. White people will be scared and black people will never accept you." So as Biggie Smalls said in "Juicy," "This album is dedicated to all the teachers that told me I'd never amount to nothing." Challenge accepted. We're gonna get that bubble machine and we're gonna rock the world.

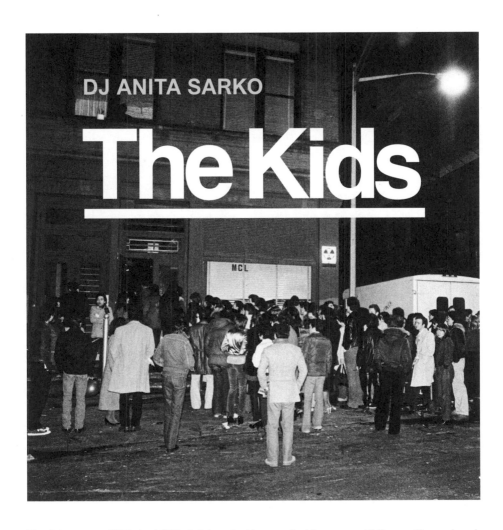

DJ ANITA SARKO

The Kids

Rock Lounge, 1981. An NYC club located in . . . what is now . . . Tribeca. For a visual, check out *Downtown 81*, a film that follows Jean-Michel Basquiat roaming around downtown Manhattan. At one point, he wanders into Rock Lounge. The DJ perched above the dance floor is me. Jean often crashed on my couch during that time, so this was a regular part of his night crawl.

I hated that place. I had only gone there from Mudd Club, where I had been DJing, because Haoui Montaug, who had been the door guy at Hurrah's (the original rock disco), convinced me that we should leave our respective venues to make some real money before we both joined Danceteria co-owner Rudolf Piper at his new venture, Pravda. Only open for one night, Pravda had been immediately shut down by the SoHo Community Board. However, Haoui was convinced it would soon reopen and we would only have to deal with Rock Lounge for a month or two. That seemed like an excellent plan.

Rudolf underestimated the SoHo Community Board: Pravda never reopened. So, here Haoui and I were, stuck at this lame Mudd copycat club, lorded over by the slick-haired, thuggish Howard Stein and Eurotrash poster boy Peppo Vanini, the pair who also co-owned Xenon, a Studio 54 clone. Original ideas were not their forte. *Ha!*

I was miserable. I would end most nights bitterly playing "Sister Europe" by the Psychedelic Furs (listen to the words . . . you'll understand), shedding tears of frustration while Haoui consoled me. Rock Lounge was, for me, rock bottom.

Then, one night, in trooped a swarm of underage teens. There was *something* Haoui loved about them for long enough to forget to ask for IDs. One of the reasons why Haoui was the platinum-standard doorman was his singular taste. Haoui could detect diamonds in the rough (no pun intended?) and knew when to pretend age was not an issue.

"Last Night a DJ Saved My Life"? In this case, it was the other way around. My full-blown existential crisis was happily interrupted as one after another of a seemingly endless train of fresh, adorable, friendly faces appeared at the top of the ladder to my nest, then descended, each greeting me and making requests. I have always hated people in my DJ booths and abhorred requests, but there was just *something* about them that was astonishingly un-annoying.

We made a deal: I would play the punk classics I had played at Mudd if they would agree to remain on the dance floor while I played other sorts of music. I needed the floor filled in case Howard or Peppo walked by. Keeping a floor filled was an issue for me because I didn't play the hits and my methods were disconcerting to many. My style, contrary to other DJs, was to play a vast range of music rather than just one type. Most people thought I didn't know what I was doing and was just slapping on any old record without any thought. Usually, the only people who understood the thread within my segues were musicians. And Larry Levan. Larry told me later that I was the DJ most like him because, even though we played completely different music, "We both like to engage in musical conversations with the dancers and fuck with their minds!"

And so the Kids (as Haoui and I referred to them) became regulars. Every night, they would climb up, one after the other, to say "hello" and then do the same at the end of the night to say "goodbye" and, most important, "thank you." No one had ever thanked me before.

I adored them. Haoui adored them. Howard didn't. "Why do you let in those filthy little children?" Howard would whine to Haoui. Howard, the upwardly mobile son of a mobster whose body had been found in Jamaica Bay minus his head, only approved of uptown preppies and debs, resplendent in their mini-adult garb of suits and ruffles. These people acted entitled and rude and had the lamest musical taste

you could imagine. The antithesis of these young fogies, the Kids wore their regular, extremely casual street clothes to the club, and arrogance was not part of their collective personality. They looked and acted like the well-brought-up teens they were. Howard didn't get it. He was so deeply into appearances that he once eviscerated his wife, Tawn, in front of everyone because she failed to change from uptown clothing to downtown clothing when she went from Xenon to Rock Lounge one night. I think "downtown" meant that she was supposed to wear black and leather . . . or something like that. It didn't matter. Haoui was so contemptuous of Howard's and Peppo's opinions that he just ignored them and kept letting the Kids in.

I would play:

The punk classics: X-Ray Spex, Sex Pistols, the Stranglers, Television, Siouxsie and the Bans

Newer punk (for the Kids to thrash around to): Black Flag, the Cramps. I was happy to obl

Power pop: The Jam, the Go-Go's, Buzzcocks, Jonathan Richman and the Modern Lovers

Post-punk: PiL, Pere Ubu, Killing Joke, Joy Division, New Order, Echo and the Bunnymen, th

New wave: Adam and the Ants, the Brains, the aforementioned Psychedelic Furs, Simple M
the Pretenders, Devo, Elvis Costello, B-52s, Laurie Anderson, Yoko Ono

Anything on ZE Records

Rock: Velvet Underground and solo Lou/solo Cale, Roxy Music and solo Ferry/solo Eno, the N
Bowie, Led Zep, Marianne Faithfull, Hendrix, the Doors, Sly & the Family Stone, John L
Detroiter (I never tired of Detroit rock)

No wave: DNA, Lounge Lizards, Teenage Jesus and the Jerks, James White, Mars

New romantics: Duran Duran, Visage, Spandau Ballet, Blue Rondo à la Turk

Techno-pop roots: Suicide, Wire, Magazine, Kraftwerk, Cabaret Voltaire, Ultravox, Throbbin

African: A lot of Fela, particularly the *Live!* album with Ginger Baker on drums

Jazz: Thelonious Monk, Gil Scott-Heron, Louis Prima and Keely Smith

Funk/R&B: I loved the entire Parliament family, as well as James Brown, Aretha, Otis Redd
Being from Detroit I was *sick* of Motown!

Vintage oddities: Garage rock, the Last Poets, Scott Walker, spoken word—the weirder the t

Early rock 'n' roll/rockabilly: Wanda Jackson, Little Richard, Jerry Lee Lewis, Bo Diddley, B

Reggae: I preferred the more psychedelic types like Dr. Alimantado and dub

Ska: Both the originals and the covers by the acts on 2 Tone Records

And this new music called rap.

ash, the Ramones, the Dead Boys, the Saints, the Damned, Patti Smith, Richard Hell and the Voidoids

they kept their side of the bargain and remained on the floor as I played . . .

kidoo, Teardrop Explodes, Pop Group, Gang of Four, the Fall, Clock DVA

estral Manoeuvres in the Dark, Human League, Bow Wow Wow, Blondie, the Cure, Talking Heads,

s and solo Johnny Thunders/solo David Johansen, the Heartbreakers, Jayne County, the Runaways,

e, the Dictators, Iggy, the Stooges, MC5, Suzi Quatro, Mitch Ryder & the Detroit Wheels—a native

ry Numan

Pickett . . . anything on Atlantic/Stax. Michael Jackson, the Jacksons, Gap Band, Rick James, etc.

ddie Cochran, Chuck Berry, etc.

Rap had entered the consciousness of the Mudd Club due to the efforts of Fred Braithwaite (Fab 5 Freddy) and Glenn O'Brien (then the music editor of *Interview*). Anything on Sugar Hill Records became part of my heavy rotation. As the rap kids from uptown were brought downtown by Fred and Glenn to meet their kindred spirits at Mudd, the uptown and downtown graffiti artists together found a home at Patti Astor and Bill Stalling's Fun Gallery, where they were finally given an inside space to exhibit at, magically transforming themselves from perceived criminals (Defacement! Vandalism!) to *artists*.

Whenever I would play anything besides Stiff Little Fingers and their ilk, the Kids would usually form a raucous conga line. To morons like Howard Stein, seeing a dance floor engaged in this activity was *fabulous*. Uptowners considered the conga line to be a sign that a party was really happening. To downtowners, conga lines were considered so kitsch, they were the height of postmodern mockery.

And so 1981 became 1982. On New Year's Eve in 1981, Rock Lounge booked Killing Joke at the insistence of the staff. We loved Killing Joke. Unfortunately, no one else did. I believe the Ritz had booked the Psychedelic Furs, who had a huge hit that week, so everyone went there. No one showed up at Rock Lounge. Because New Year's Eve is supposed to be such a major moneymaking night, Howard retaliated by firing the entire staff . . . except me . . . the following day. Out of respect, he fired me the day after.

I really didn't care. Unbeknownst to anyone, I was a trust-fund kid (the horror!), so I didn't have to worry about paying the rent. I was finally free of that horrible place! What I did care about was something else: I was told that the Kids, having shown up at Rock Lounge to discover that I was no longer there, allegedly covered the bathroom walls with "This place sucks without DJ Anita." I have no idea if this was true because, obviously, I never went back to check. I believed it at the time, and that cemented the love I had for them tenfold. Nothing speaks louder or truer than loyalty.

I went on to Chase Park, a late-night hangout for the downtown fine-arts crew, and Haoui went to the Peppermint Lounge. The 1982 New Year's Eve act at Chase Park was a disco dolly named Madonna, whom no one had heard of. No one showed up. She was so awful, the staff accused the owner of receiving some backroom favors in order to have booked her. Haoui was doing better at Peppermint Lounge, where, besides doing the door, he created and hosted the "No Entiendes" cabaret. The motto for "No Entiendes" was "If it's good, it's great. If it's bad, it's better."

By 1983, both Haoui and I had landed at the second Danceteria. Happy at last! Haoui decided he needed a co-host for the cabaret. I passed the audition because an owner got me so trashed on Long Island iced teas and coke to calm my nerves, I simulated giving Haoui a blowjob onstage. "No Entiendes" is best known

for being where the newest incarnation of Madonna (now styled and art-directed by Maripol, one of the producers of *Downtown 81* . . . see how this all comes together?) first performed "Everybody," which was produced by Danceteria DJ Mark Kamins. And, to the delight of Haoui, me, and just about everyone else, the Kids . . . under various guises and in various numbers . . . became semi-regular performers at our cabaret. There was Grandmaster Jew, where three of them (the Adams and Mike?)

We were actually called the 3 Bad Jewish Brothers, and it was me, Mike, Josh Cheuse, and our friend Kio Turner. Does it matter? (AH)

dressed in full Hasid drag and performed a rousing take on "My Adidas" called "My Deli." Another time, a much larger group showed up and played children's instruments. I don't recall what the tunes were, but it was brilliant. And then there was the time they concluded their performance by upending the giant round table in front of the stage, drenching all the critics and other journalists who had been sitting there in a mess of cocktails, ice, and cups. These people were not amused. Haoui and I were. And of course "Cooky Puss" was beloved by all.

By 1985, even we referred to the Kids as "the Beasties" (we never used the "Boys" part when speaking of them). I continued to play once a week at Danceteria, but Haoui and I had moved on to Palladium, a massive arts-driven club that was the comeback vehicle for Studio 54's Steve Rubell and Ian Schrager. Haoui was the chief doorperson and I was the DJ for the Michael Todd Room, the VIP room that I co-hosted with Rubell.

The music I was playing between Danceteria and Palladium included:

Industrial: Skinny Puppy, Leather Nun, SPK, the Young Gods, Front Line Assembly, Einstürze

Alternative rock and pop: Swans, Sonic Youth, Big Black, Strawberry Switchblade, the Bang

Go-go: Trouble Funk . . . and I *loved* the Junkyard Band's "Sardines"/"The Word"

Records I picked up from doing international gigs: Brazilian drum schools, Cantonese cove
and "Walk on the Wild Side"

Techno-pop: Soft Cell, Marc and the Mambas, Propaganda, Grace Jones, Pet Shop Boys, Fra

Spoken word: "No Entiendes" regular Karen Finley and others

New wave: (the usual)

House: I was most fond of acid, techno, and gospel house . . . Detroit and Chicago, and the un

And, obviously, **Hip hop** (For both house and hip hop, For the Record and Vinylmania were go

At Danceteria I played:
Hardcore: Black Flag, Bad Brains, Circle Jerks, Suicidal Tendencies, Butthole Surfers, Bad Re

At Palladium, I played:
African: Far more than Fela, though he was still part of it

New Orleans second-line and funk, and soca, and for kitsch value I added the funkier e

Motown (to celebrate mine): Really, I played the disco and Motown as a joke, which was lost o

I have no idea how much of this later music the Beasties paid attention to. By this point, they were already creating their own sound. More important, I believe, was the fact that I controlled the drink tickets. I always kept some aside for the Beasties and their crew.

They no longer made requests or formed conga lines, however. I seem to recall being asked to be in a video by them, but declining because it meant I would have to wake up too early. I had priorities!

I related to these boys and girls. As New York as they were, they still made perfect sense . . . felt comfortable . . . to a former Midwesterner/Southerner. There wasn't a false note . . . no one was "fronting." And that, I believe, was a major key to their universal appeal: they were so damned likable.

At the risk of sounding drearily sentimental: everyone was so proud of them and so happy for their success because, as the Beasties evolved, they (and their gang) went from being precocious, beautifully mannered, high-spirited punks and punkettes (shout-out here to the future Luscious Jackson) to beautifully mannered, startlingly authentic, and supremely creative mensches. So, what was there not to love?

At least, that's how I remember it. . . .

uten, Coil, Test Dept, Foetus, Psychic TV, Chris & Cosey, Die Krupps, Current 93, Nurse with Wound

and the Medics, Dead or Alive, the Style Council, etc.

ɔnna songs, Gerty Molzen—an elderly German woman who covered "Do You Really Want to Hurt Me"

to Hollywood

treasure trove of incredibly filthy records I got from For the Record and Vinylmania

d Kennedys, Flipper, the Misfits, Agnostic Front, etc.

disco (to celebrate Rubell and Schrager's roots)

. This music was all embraced with a fervor that was alarming.

Drink Tickets, Buffalo Gals, and Danceteria

(AH)

1983.

"Buffalo Gals" is the song. Danceteria is the place.

It had everything we were, and everything we wanted to be. Punks, rappers, break-dancers, artists, and weirdos. It was like downtown's version of Studio 54. Grown-ups hung out there doing real grown-up stuff. And us kids were fascinated being so close to it. Danceteria was the closest thing we had in Manhattan to an amusement park. It had so many options of things to get into. You didn't just go there to meet friends. *It* was total excitement, even just walking up to the door. Will you get in? You're only sixteen, but for whatever reason, the doorman, Haoui Montaug, likes you, so you slide in. Once you get inside, you realize that Danceteria isn't just a club. It's an entire building. Like, an eight-to-ten-story ex–factory building. When you're a kid, you remember the details of the places you hang out at all the time, away from home. Out in the suburbs I guess it'd be the woods, or a parking lot, or . . . I don't know . . . the football field bleachers? For us kids in NYC, it was this particular nightclub. And so I, we, remember all these little details. And they're important to us. The layout of Danceteria was like this: The basement was for the semi-devious. Weird stuff would go on down there. Sugar Pie DeSanto's "Down in the Basement"–type stuff but . . . more Goth. The main floor had a bar and was where bands would play; and also where Haoui Montaug and Anita Sarko had their monthly show, "No Entiendes." At Danceteria there was a really cool relationship between us kids and these slightly older grown-ups. And being able to go to this place felt like a privilege. I mean, shit . . . they'd let us in (for free, no less) to see bands like The Raincoats and ESG. Let us be on the dance floor all night. And even get drinks. Really, it was like a super metropolitan teen rec center.

The second floor was the dance floor. Mark Kamins, making it happen. He was the first DJ I'd heard to blend in sound effects with dance music. There was a very specific dance to Danceteria. I could never get it right. My friend Noah Bogen can still do it. He pulls it out once in a while like a drunken card trick. The Danceteria dance is similar to the textbook '80s new-wave dance step, but it has a little more detail. The footwork/floorwork is a little more spread out. A kind of new romantic Safety Dance. Man, I wish I could do that step. Just thinking about it brings me right back to 1983. To the corner of the second floor. Right by the stairwell in the back. Where the action was happening. Little pockets of kids and grown-ups. Having their own scenes. All there, separately together. Me playing the wall. All the cool girls doing that dance step to, like, "Blue Monday" by New Order or slowing the

step down a little for "Genius of Love" by Tom Tom Club. Fuckin' Aqua Net is in the air . . . everywhere. The feeling of that scene, to me, is like an open-face peanut butter and jelly sandwich on a toasted English muffin. Wonderful.

The third floor was a bar (as seen in *Desperately Seeking Susan*), but it also had this kind of lounge area with couches and a bunch of TV sets playing videos. All night. Just random stuff. It seems very '80s now to have a bunch of TVs playing random stuff, but this *was* the '80s. The *early* '80s. And as you know, a decade doesn't really kick in until the beginning of the next one, so this was ahead of its time. And it was also a weirdo place, 'cause the only people in this video lounge area were grown-ups. Like . . . most nights, some grown-up would have nodded off to sleep on one of the couches. (Google: "Spacely NY Punk.") Kids wouldn't hang out in this video lounge, 'cause kids can't sit still. We'd have to sit all day in school, and we'd watch TV at home, so why would we wanna go to a club to sit and watch TV? I wanna be on the second floor, in the corner, hanging out with girls while they did the Danceteria dance.

In the summertime, they'd open up the roof deck and have parties up there. And so, you're sixteen, it's one o'clock in the morning, you're drinking a margarita with your friends and a bunch of grown-ups, and you're looking at the Empire State Building. *It's right there.* All lit up. Just a few blocks away. (In case I haven't made it clear yet, I'd like to spell it out, here and now. I FUCKING LOVE NEW YORK CITY. Love it. Roaches, rats, hot dogs, OTB, the 1 train, weird expensive watch stores, barf on the sidewalk, models with to-go coffees. All of it. Even those shitty street-sweeping Zamboni things. Love. Thank you, Mom+Dad, for having me here.)

There were a few floors between the roof and the third-floor video zone at Danceteria. Those were the secret floors. The no-fly zones. The get-busy spots. The get-high spots. The floors you weren't allowed to go to. I wish I could say that I used to sneak up there and get into all kinds of crazy-ass shit, but I didn't. I was still climbing over the kid side of the fence. But I had seen over to the grown-up side.

You'd think sex would be the child/grown-up divide, but actually . . . it's drink tickets. When someone hands you a drink ticket for the first time . . . shit changes. You're seen differently in the eyes of someone else. The holder of the drink tickets is a person of importance. Of interest. They have been put in the position of power. . . . *Whom shall I grant the right to drink for free?* No way that either Haoui Montaug or Anita Sarko would have given me my first drink ticket. It felt more like Haoui let us hang out at Danceteria 'cause he knew we'd be safer in there than out writing graffiti or something stupid that dumb kids like us would get into.

And so there we were . . . Summertime 1983. On the rooftop of Danceteria, margaritas in hand. Young and ready to live. Looking out over the most glorious city in the world. And our friend Cey gives us a future fabled quote . . . "Wow . . . From up here, I can see the train station. But from down there, I can't see up here."

The Dominatrix Sleeps Tonight—Dominatrix
This one set the standard for the Danceteria dance. When this song came on, all the kids on the second-floor dance floor fell in line. If you don't own this song, go get it, turn the lights down, maybe get a little drunk (just a little), play it, and I'll bet you'll instinctively start doing the Danceteria dance.

Hey DJ—World's Famous Supreme Team
Oddly, this song became a kind of slow-jam romantic cut. This was the song you tried to dance with that special someone to.

Al-Naayfiysh (The Soul)—Hashim
There was a mysterious guy that would shout, "Work that body!" to everyone and no one, when the dance floor got hot. I never got a look at who it was, but this was the song that pushed him over the edge.

Bela Lugosi's Dead—Bauhaus
The basement anthem. For a little while there was a whole separate idea of a club in the basement of Danceteria, called the Bat Cave. It was named and modeled after the Bat Cave Club in London. It was all about this new thing they're calling Goth.

Give Me Tonight—Shannon
This was on the heaviest of rotations on the second-floor dance floor. Kind of more than any other song from that era.

Temptation + Blue Monday—New Order
These songs were what we wanted to be. Modern, electric, and intercontinental.

Shoot You Down—APB
A punk dance-floor crossover. I love it.

White Horse—Laid Back
This song was for grown-ups. It got played every night, but it felt more explicit. It's weird to be sixteen on a dance floor with thirty-year-olds and the song about heroin comes on and you just keep it to yourself that the song frightens you a little.

Din Daa Daa—George Kranz
Oh my God . . . stop playing this song! Every DJ in the world played this song every night. Why? It's awful. For almost half the song, the singer makes these shitty human beat-boxy drum-roll sounds. Mark Kamins (RIP), if you're listening . . . give me some kind of sign as to why you played this record so much.

Jam Hot—Johnny Dynell
Johnny Dynell, one of our own. He was a downtown DJ, and like Anita Sarko and Haoui Montaug, he was one of those cool "grown-ups" that we looked up to. And this 12-inch was gold out there on the second-floor dance floor.

Hip Hop Be Bop—Man Parrish
This was perfect for us kids. The right sound at the right time. Drum machines and synths. Pulsating and blasting.

Moody—ESG
ESG was the coolest band in NYC in '83, no question.

Don't Go—Yaz
Prime-time dance-floor material. If you wanna pack a dance floor, play this song.

Da Da Da—Trio
Damn, this song sounds great booming out of big club speakers.

Lookin' for the Perfect Beat—Soul Sonic Force
Rap wasn't played on the dance floor at Danceteria that much. It was still relatively new, and there were only a few songs that broke through. This one, Soul Sonic Force's "Planet Rock" (of course), "It's Like That" by Run-DMC, "What People Do for Money" by Divine Sounds, and "Request Line" by Rock Master Scott & The Dynamic Three were on a short list of rap records that got spun.

Buffalo Gals—Malcolm McLaren
This song was a real moment. It's what set off hip hop downtown. Of course "The Message" by Grandmaster Flash and the Furious Five was the best, and was what got people hip to rap, but "Buffalo Gals" had the elements that downtown needed. A rap sound, fashion, and a punk white dude to present it. Then Run-DMC could take it from there and make rap music explode.

Hungry, So Angry—Medium Medium +
Change—Killing Joke
These songs were like Snuffleupagus on *Sesame Street*. They only came around once in a while. But when they did we went nuts because these are two great songs.

Money Changes Everything—Cyndi Lauper
They never played this song on the dance floor, but I put this on the list because my best friend, Nadia, had this tape playing on a fucking loop at the ice-cream store we worked at (while we'd be rushing to close up so we could get to Danceteria), so I've heard this song ten thousand times. I love Cyndi Lauper, but I've heard this record too many times.

Genius of Love—Tom Tom Club
Last song of the night. Slow in tempo. Everyone loves this and goes home happy because it is one of the greatest songs ever made.

(AH)

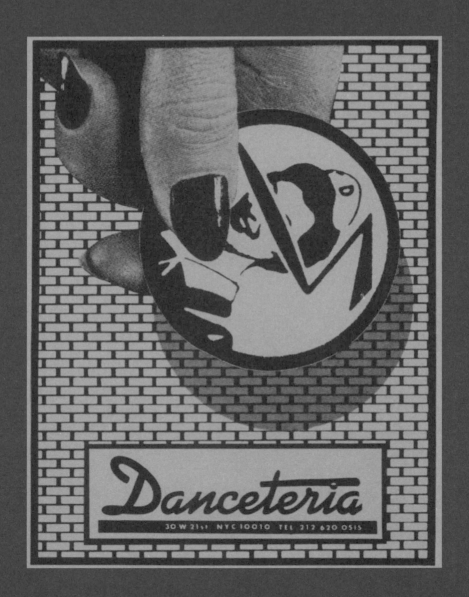

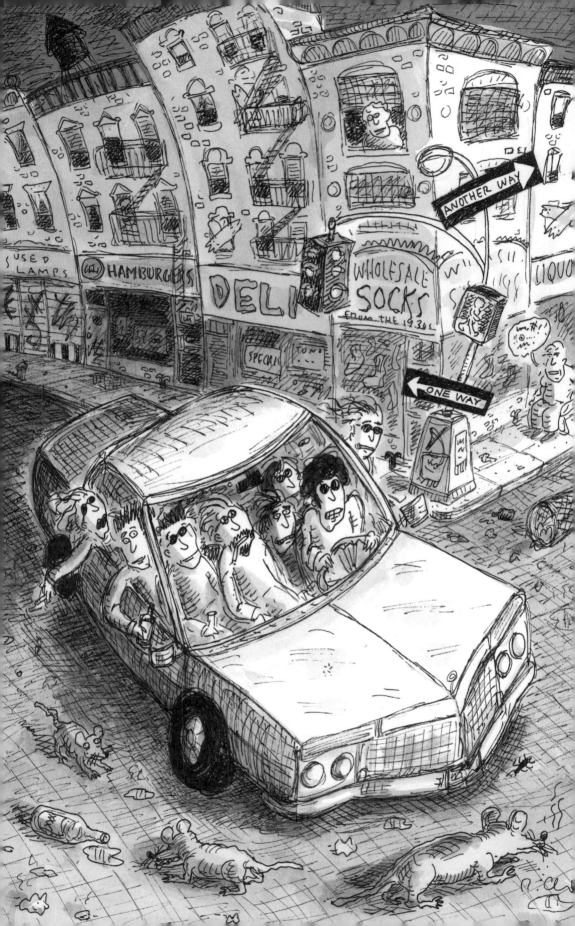

Butthole Surfers Saved My Life
(AH)

Literally.

Well . . . probably.

Potentially.

Me+Rick Rubin went to see them play in NYC at the Ritz, and ended up meeting Gibby Haynes+them hanging out for a minute outside the club. Later that night, Me+Rick were at this after-hours place we used to go to called Save the Robots. (I guess staying out until four A.M. isn't late enough in NYC. These after-hours places would start at four, when the bars closed, and go until tomorrow.) Save the Robots was a grimy place in a deep basement, deep in the East Village. If you saw it in a movie now, you'd swear it was fake. All kinds of drunk freaks, sweating and tweaking, in a stinky graffitied basement blasting nondescript music. In 1984 the deep East Village streets late at night would be empty, except for drug dealers, drug purchasers, and the doorman at *this* place.

So . . . it's 5:32 A.M. Me+Rick are done for the night, and we begin the long walk from the East Side to the West. By now, the sun is starting to come out. The juxtaposition of loud, sweaty, wasted, dark basement party . . . to . . . completely empty cold NYC sidewalks is jarring. It can be pretty unflattering physically and emotionally. So we leave Save the Robots. No one's around. We're walking, and out of my peripheral vision, I notice something. I look back and I see two teenage dudes creeping up on us. One of them is holding a huge knife. Not a switchblade or something, but, like, a big fucking hunting-style knife. I elbow Rick, and he looks back. It's all split-second-type reactions. Neither me nor Rick is known for our hand-to-hand combat prowess. We're more known for, like, making beats and saying weird shit. Neither of those skills is gonna help right now. And these kids are now behind us on the sidewalk, a foul line away. What the fuck do we do!?!

Just as it's all about to go down . . . a *huge* car pulls up to the corner and stops at the red light. In that moment I happen to notice . . . *Oh shit; it's that guy from the Butthole Surfers. Gibby.* So I'm like, "Yo! What's up?! Wanna give us a ride?!" He's driving a two-door, but it's massive. Like a beat-up mid-'70s Buick Riviera. There are a ton of people in there already, but he says something to the effect of . . . "Fuck yeah . . . Hop in!" As we walk toward the car, I look back and see the two knife dudes back away, and walk away.

And so . . . yes . . .

Butthole Surfers saved my life.

(Thank you.)

Rush (Not the Band)
(MD)

The building looked like the place where "Broadway" Danny Rose kept his office. It was on Broadway in the upper Twenties, near Madison Square Park. Today, real-estate developers call the area NoMad; back in the spring of 1984, it was just the cheapest place you could get an office—anybody who could spare a few hundred bucks a month could open up shop. The neighborhood was pure chaos, an open-air market like you might find on the streets of, say, Bangkok: Dudes on every corner selling fake everything. Rolexes, perfume, anything Fila. Whatever was hot. And at night, the area was a derelict ghost town.

The inside was straight out of a noir detective film. All of the offices had old, dark-wood doors with frosted-glass windows that may as well have said "Sidney Falco" on them, and the hallway reeked of Mr. Clean so badly that our noses burned walking in. Back in the day, Mr. Clean was a hallmark of any, umm, lower-tier, aka bummy, NYC building.

This wasn't what we'd been expecting at all.

Yauch and I were there for our first meeting with the biggest hip hop manager on the planet, the owner of Rush Management and the man behind Kurtis Blow and Run-DMC: Russell Simmons. We'd gotten the meeting through Rick Rubin. Russell had been a fan of "It's Yours," a record by T La Rock and Jazzy Jay that Rick had produced and released.

"It's Yours" came out at a pivotal moment in the evolution of hip hop. In 1983, Run-DMC had released their first single, "It's Like That" b/w "Sucker MC's"; before then, records on the dominant rap labels (Sugar Hill, Enjoy) had consisted of MCs rhyming over smooth drums and silky bass lines. (The goal was to make music that would get played on black radio, which was then dominated by R&B.) "Sucker MC's" changed all of that overnight. The song was incredibly basic and stripped down—just a drum machine and rhymes. A real minimal b-boy jam and anthem. Pretty soon, that raw programmed handclap was blasting from every car; the shit took over, and records like "Heartbeat" and "Rapper's Delight" were instantly rendered antique. The future would not be played by musicians; it'd be programmed on TR-808, DMX, and EMU drum machines and Roland synthesizers. And the future had arrived, in the form of songs like "It's Like That," "Sucker MC's," and—more to the point—"It's Yours." Russell couldn't believe that somebody outside his camp had made it, let alone a white college kid from Long Island. It's not like there were a lot of other people making hardcore hip hop records; more exactly, there were no others. No wonder Russell wanted to meet Rick Rubin.

We actually witnessed their introduction sometime in early 1984 at the bar up on the third floor of Danceteria. We were like nervous, spying children. We couldn't hear what was being said; we just watched from afar as Russell consumed multiple screwdrivers and laughed. Russell saw a future in Rick's passion for aggressive and stripped-down rap music. Rick explained us to Russell: *There are these three white rappers, they're still in high school, they come from punk rock but love hip hop even more, all they do is listen to rap.* Russell, in turn, was able to see something beyond what we could see. He saw our potential and, yeah, the color of our skin, and knew that if we were any good, it could give him, as a budding rap mogul, access to all kinds of places that, at the time, effectively excluded underground black music: MTV, pop radio, "rock" music magazines like *Rolling Stone,* and mainstream media in general. An alliance was formed at the bar that night. Def Jam had begun in earnest.

When we went to meet Russell, Rick didn't accompany us to the Rush office for whatever reason. Maybe he was still asleep; he tended to sleep through the afternoon. More mysteriously, Mr. Adam Horovitz wasn't with us either. Maybe he was working at the ice-cream spot or doing

Michael, I refuse to stoop to your petty level of mirth at my expense. I'm sure I was busy that day cataloging my research at the museum. The mysteries of ancient Machu Picchu don't just uncover themselves, you know. It takes long, hard hours. (AH)

something more important, like attempting the high score on Scramble. But Yauch and I were walking on air the whole way over. We worshipped Run-DMC—they were everything we aspired to be as rappers and musicians—and we loved pretty much every other group Russell managed too. He seemed so fucking big-time to us.

The Mr. Clean smell wasn't part of the equation in our fantasy version of Russell's HQ. We'd been imagining a place more like the offices of legendary business-manager-to-the-stars Bert Padell (to whom Russell would in fact soon introduce us).

I remember seeing a big autographed picture of Babe Ruth. Just wanted you to know. (AH)

You can probably imagine Bert's setup: huge, luxurious office on Fifty-Seventh Street, in a neighborhood where wealthy New Yorkers shopped at places like Bergdorf Goodman and FAO Schwarz. Padell had an enormous walnut desk surrounded by gold records on the walls and

extensive memorabilia, all signed by the biggest achievers in their fields. He enjoyed handing guests copies of a vanity-press-published book of poems he'd written called *Bert's Words.*

The reality of Russell Simmons's office at that time was . . . different. We're talking two small rooms. In the front sat longtime Rush staffer Heidi Smith and longtime Rush publicist Bill Adler. Heidi seemed like she'd been around since day one; she was the office grown-up, a straight-laced make-it-happen woman. Bill was a bearded white guy who seemed run down by the thankless task of trying to explain the newest sub-movements in underground hip hop to white journalists. Usually there were a couple of other

assistant/intern-type people around, and maybe a travel agent or tour manager on the phone. (One of the latter was later immortalized by Public Enemy: "At home I got a call from Tony Rome.")

The other room was Russell's office/frequent bedroom/who-knew-what-else. A phone sat on a desk; Russell would sometimes yell into it. There were these two weird and disgustingly soiled futon chairs. I found out later that Russell definitely spent many a night sleeping on these things. His actual apartment was in LeFrak City, a neighborhood in east Queens. (And his room-mate was Andre Harrell, aka rapper Dr. Jeckyll and later the CEO of Motown Records.) After a night downing screwdrivers at Manhattan clubs, why would Russell suffer thirty minutes of potholes on the BQE and LIE and a hefty cab fare when he could just crash a few blocks away at his office?

Here was the domain of the biggest rap music manager on earth—but at that time, being the biggest could only get you a Sam Spade office with hallways smelling like Mr. Clean and a crappy chair/futon thing.

None of this bothered us in the least. First of all, who were we to be snobby about a manager's office? Second, no sooner had we walked into the office than we saw Kurtis Blow. Trying to break-dance. While surrounded by the dudes from Full Force.

Kurtis Blow was *established*. He had gold records for "Christmas Rappin'" and "The Breaks," two early rap records that we'd

memorized beginning to end. The dude seemed *way* older than us. He had Jheri curls on his head and small gold chains around his neck. He was just a big fucking deal, okay—it's worth remembering that DJ Run himself was originally billed (by Russell) as the Son of Kurtis Blow. As for Full Force, if you don't remember them from their days as Lisa Lisa and Cult Jam's backing band and producers, you might remember them as the menacing, muscled-out villains in Kid 'n Play's *House Party* movies. They were an R&B group that spent long hours in the weight room and were no strangers to fringing, beading, and bedazzling the shit out of their wardrobe. They circled around Kurtis Blow as he (somewhat lamely—no offense, Kurtis) tried to emulate real break-dancers. I'm not sure if he was actually spinning on his head or if that's just the version of the story we told everyone, but let's choose to remember it that way. Whatever Kurtis was trying to do, I remember Russell sitting behind his desk, observing the proceedings with clear bemusement.

This was a typical scene at Russell's office: a steady stream of rappers, tour managers, music producers, club promoters, DJs, and miscellaneous small-time hustlers. It was a full-on circus, and Russell was a very-fast-talking P. T. Barnum, selling all the time, alternating between a nonstop barrage of angry phone calls and genuine, supportive, funny conversations with artists. That first visit set the tempo for our interactions with Russell. He charmed us, yelled at some people on the phone, yelled something we couldn't decipher to Heidi in the front room, talked about how Run-DMC would be the first rap group on the cover of *Rolling Stone* and how we would follow behind them and become even bigger. It felt surreal to all of a sudden be part of Russell's nonstop sales pitch. It all seemed so far out of reach, so beyond any of our wildest dreams, so many worlds apart from the downtown culture that we came from. But somehow you walked out of there believing that Russell could pull it off.

RICK RUBIN
RUSSELL SIMMONS

212-420-8666
RUSH 212-620-0577

And he did. Decades later, after our relationship had gone through many ups and downs, we went to meet with Russell for the first time in years. His office was in New York's Garment District, just a few blocks north of that original Rush office. Def Jam and Phat Farm had made him untold millions of dollars. We walked in, and there was Russell, sitting behind that big walnut desk in a proper executive office that might as well have been decorated by Bert Padell, business manager to the stars. I couldn't help but smile. The smell of Mr. Clean had long evaporated from the air.

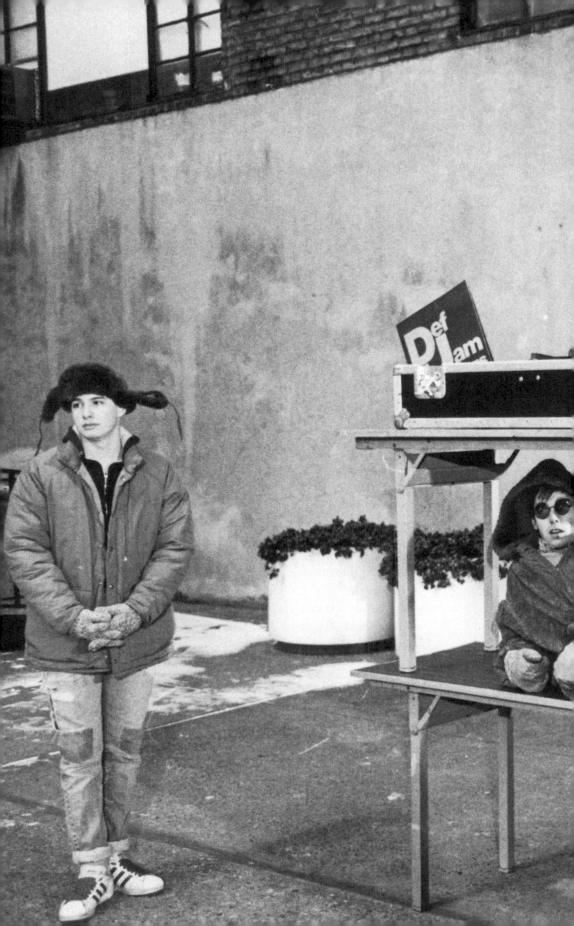

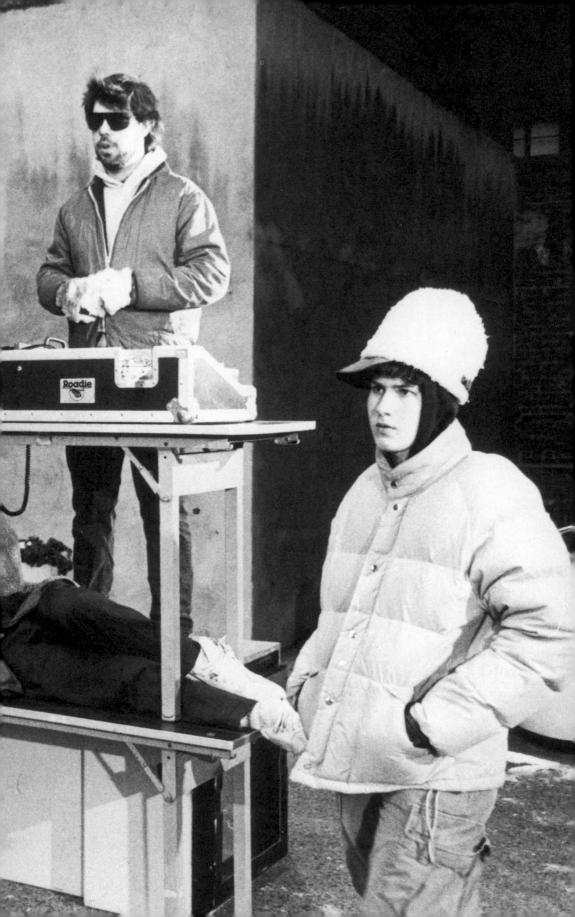

On the Mic at the Fever
(MD)

It started as a night like many others. The five of us—me, Adam, Adam, Rick, and Russell—at Danceteria, bouncing from floor to floor depending on which record was being played where. There was a time, before we met Russell, when he had dabbled in actually producing records; now that we'd started hanging out, it was easy to see why producing hadn't really been for him. Records take patience and focus, the willingness to obsess over small details until they're just-so. Rick had this quality, but Russell was always more interested in big plans and the big picture—already a mogul in the making, completely unable to sit still. On this night, his restlessness—and multiple screwdrivers—led to an idea. *We're going up to Disco Fever. Tonight. Now. And Y'ALL are going to get on the mic.*

Okay. That suggestion probably seems insignificant today, thirty-plus years and countless pop-culture trend cycles later. *So Russell wanted to go to another club, big fucking deal.* But Disco Fever was not just another club. It was the epicenter of hip hop, in the place where hip hop began: the Boogie-Down Bronx. A ton of our heroes made their names and reputations there.

Grandmaster Flash and the Furious Five. Busy Bee. Kurtis Blow. The Treacherous Three. The Sugarhill Gang. And *everybody* would hang out there: musicians, drug dealers, drug users, b-boys, hip hop fans. Things didn't get rolling there until three or four A.M. If your record didn't make it there, you weren't legit. (The owner also had a label called The Fever that released 12-inches by Lovebug Starski and others.) Performing at Disco Fever was a trial by fire. It was OG before OG was an expression. So for Russell to suggest that we, three upstart white teenagers who were just figuring out how to rap, go there and get onstage was akin to making your high school's junior varsity basketball team and then having your coach say that you had to play the 1987–88 Los Angeles Lakers. And win.

That's the great thing about being a teenager, though. You think you're bulletproof. Stupidity and arrogance trump realism and

fear. We loved to rap and were quite honestly feeling ourselves as super-minor-league celebrities within the small world of downtown clubs. But this would be different. *This was fucking Disco fucking Fever.*

We piled into a car and off we went.

We had this idea in our heads that there would be hundreds of people

outside, all behind velvet ropes, desperate to get in. Nope. When we walked up, there was nobody outside at all. Inside, it was basically empty. More like a dressed-up corner bar than Studio 54. I mean, there were seriously maybe a dozen dudes up in that place. And the club reeked of something strange. We were only kids, but we knew what the smell was: menthol cigarettes laced with cocaine. Coco puffs.

I would eventually "inherit" Russell's jacket—meaning that he let me borrow it and I "forgot" to give it back. (MD)

So we got inside and of course Russell knew everybody. He had it wired. He introduced us to Sal Abbatiello, the owner. Sal was also wearing something that the three of us already coveted: a yellow satin Disco Fever jacket. Russell would often show up at Danceteria wearing one, and we thought it was pretty much the coolest hip hop status symbol you could have. Sal and Russell seemed like they had some top-secret funny business going on that we were definitely *not* privy to. It was a "Fellas, please give us a minute" discussion, and they soon disappeared into a back office.

Next thing we knew, we were handed microphones and found ourselves standing in front of the DJ booth, getting ready to MC. Now, you have to understand, it's not like we were standing on a stage. We were sandwiched between the DJ booth and the bar. People were shuffling around, getting drinks, talking, smoking coco puffs, bumping into us. Not necessarily expecting anyone to perform, let alone three Joeys from downtown that nobody knew.

The DJ cued up a record, some kind of instrumental, and we did a kind of freestyle using some rhymes that we'd already been working on. Remember, we didn't have anything out on Def Jam yet; at that point, it was challenging for us to rap in *any* setting, much less this one.

The whole thing lasted maybe three minutes. Three minutes that felt like thirty. Very sweaty palms for all of us. People hardly noticed, and they cared even less. I don't remember anyone cheering or yelling "ho" or dancing or acknowledging our performance in any way. In short, it was nothing like the kind of proto–*8 Mile* experience we'd showed up expecting—or fearing. A couple of years later, in the illustrious major motion picture *Krush Groove*, we performed the song "She's On It" in a fictionalized Disco Fever, in front of a large fictionalized audience; that was more like our imagined version of how this night was supposed to go. In reality, the closest it came was after we left: driving back to Manhattan, we just all kind of looked at each other.

Oh shit. We got on the mic at the Fever.

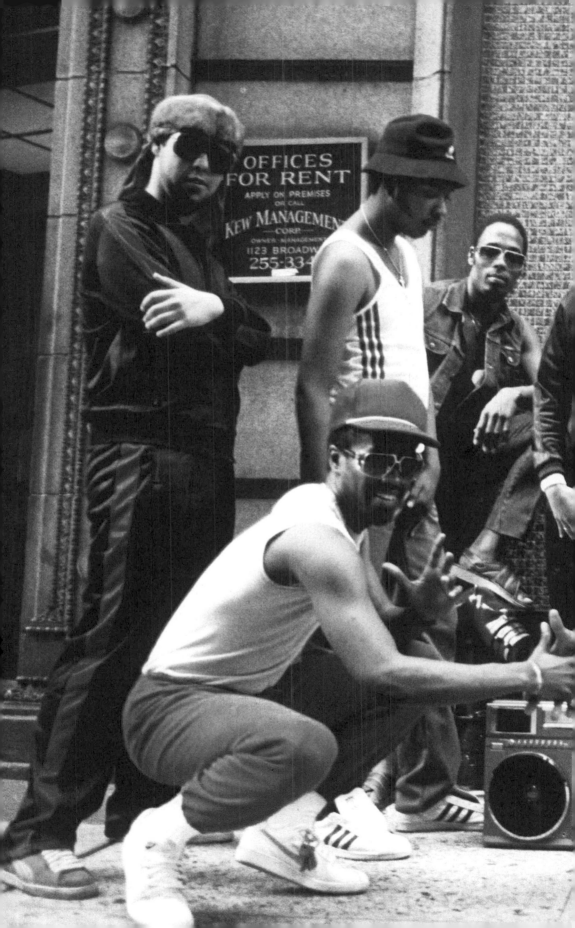

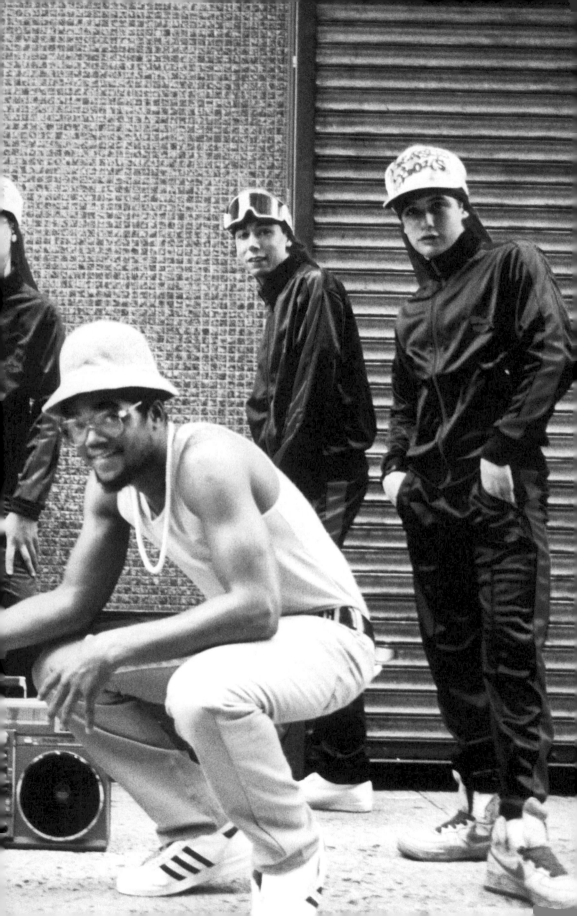

Run and Them

(MD)

Rick, Yauch, Horovitz, and I started running around together a lot. We had a routine: meet up at Rick's dorm; listen to some records; go to Danceteria; hang, dance, scam drink tickets, talk to girls. It was as if going to the club was our job. And we worked.

One night, instead of meeting us at Rick's dorm, Russell invited Rick and us down to Greene Street Recording to visit Run-DMC in the studio. (For those unaware: not only did Russell manage Run-DMC, but his brother is DJ Run—known to his mother as Joseph Simmons.) This was real. This was serious. This was big-time. We idolized Run-DMC more than any other band. When we walked into that studio, we were nervous, intimidated, and giddy with excitement—we weren't just meeting our idols for the first time; we were entering their inner circle and watching them record.

In the control room, we found Russell asleep on a three-seater black leather couch (aka "the leather bad boy"). This was a common place to find Russell at the time. The man was a screwdriver-fueled mogul on the hustle, bouncing from studios to a circuit of clubs to who-knows-what after those clubs to having to wake up in the A.M. to go to meetings at record labels, which at the time were *very* straight and corporate. He had to catch a nap when he could.

Now-iconic producer Larry Smith sat at the board, wide-eyed and freaking out with excitement over the record they were making: *King of Rock*. Like any artist who hears something in his or her own head that no one else is privy to, Larry could be reserved and introverted at times. But there was another side too, where he would seriously flip the fuck out, jumping up and yelling and smiling and saying things to no one at all. *"See, I told you!!!"* And we happened to walk in on one of those moments.

Run and DMC were in the live room, recording backup vocals. We just sat there, watching, listening, and learning. The vocals they were recording were delayed accent words to their own lead tracks. (That thing where one guy raps most of the verse except one or two words, which all the MCs say in unison. You know, "White Castle **FRIES** only come in one **SIZE**.") This accented backup-vocal thing was usually done by using an effect called digital delay on the lead vocal, which makes the one voice sound like several. It can also seem mechanized and a little too perfect when you do it digitally, though, and it had never occurred to us that you could create the effect live. But here were Run and DMC doing exactly that, and it made the song *bigger*—more raw, more powerful, and just sort of more fucking *human*. In short, it sounded incredible; we stole this trick and used it on every one of our own records. One of a thousand things we owe to them.

148

In between vocal takes, they talked to us. You'd be hard-pressed to find three guys more different from each other, personality-wise, than Run and them (as their friends referred to the group). DJ Run—Joe—was totally frenetic, both his energy and his manner of speaking. It makes sense that he ended up becoming a minister, because he had this very charismatic hyper energy going all the time; it sort of needed to get bottled a little bit and pointed at an audience, right? Meanwhile, Daryl (aka DMC) was the complete opposite—he was quiet and seemed to live in his head, like the kid in school who would draw comics in his notebook and walk around in his own reality. In between those two extremes was Jam Master Jay (RIP): a steady, methodical guy and, unsurprisingly, the backbone of the band, the architect of both the sound and aesthetic vision of the group.

It was a huge privilege for us to actually hang out with them, that night and over the next few years. A lot of times, meeting your idols can be disappointing or awkward. With Run-DMC, it was the opposite. They were always super nice and generous, both personally and professionally. It might have helped that we weren't mining the same ground artistically: attitude-wise, we were still punk-rock kids; we were always looking to fuck with people on some level. And Run-DMC wasn't. They were more interested in being the most distilled and absolutely best version of themselves: *We're gonna dress like we do in Hollis, Queens, and make this really stripped-down, raw music and be louder than any other hip hop group you've heard before.* It would take us a while to be completely ourselves in that same way; again, back then, we were just punks. But they were—and will always be—rock stars.

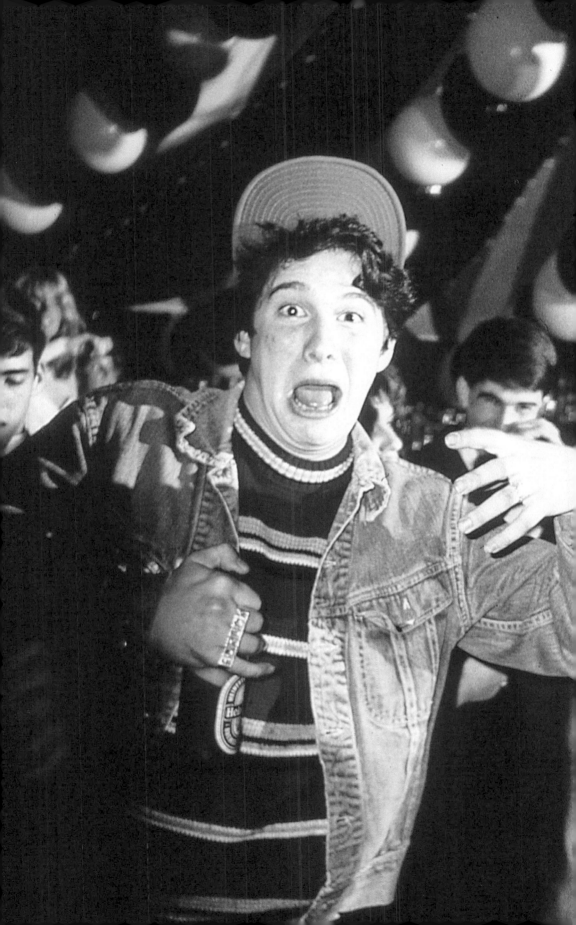

Become What You Hate
(AH)

Imagine if you love ballet and had just given your first-ever ballet recital. Think of just how bad and embarrassing that would be. But . . . you did it! Technically, you are now a dancer. And thus, a peer to Baryshnikov. (Sort of, right?) We had just recorded "Rock Hard," our first rap song, and obviously we didn't think we were on par with the Treacherous Three, the Funky Four Plus One More, or the Furious Five, but we had just made a real rap song with Jay Burnett: the same engineer who recorded Soul Sonic Force's "Planet Rock." And that is legitimately legit. We weren't recording in someone's apartment's loft bed. We weren't sneaking into a parent's friend's studio to record. This was the real deal. We were in a real recording studio with producers and engineers and editors and extra people around to run errands and a fridge with free sodas and black leather couches (leather bad boys) and everything. "Rock Hard" is a terrible song, but you gotta understand, we loved rap music

Leather bad-boy couches are ubiquitous in "fancy" recording studios. It's like some kind of professional dude code. (AH)

and wanted to be rappers so bad. We wanted to be Run-DMC so bad. We really liked it at the time, but listening to it now it sounds like child actors trying desperately to make the words we were saying sound believable.

"First white b-boys we don't regret/There's nothing wrong with your TV set." Russell Simmons wrote that line and kept telling us that we had to say it 'cause it was great, and how b-boy it was, and punk, and all this other stuff. He also really wanted us to say, "I can play the drums, I can play guitar/Not just b-boys, We're real rock stars." And we went along with it. *Okay, man, you're a legit dude in rap. You got fuckin' Kurtis Blow poppin' and lockin' in your office and shit, so if you think saying that is gonna be fresh, fly, wild, and bold . . . okay . . . turn me up in the headphones.* I'd love to blame Rick Rubin and Russell for the quality of this song, but it's us on the mic. We wrote, and said, the rest of the lyrics. We were the rap version of an '80s metal band with big hair and silk shirts, and there should be a link to this song in the dictionary under the word "frontin'."

Perhaps I'm being a little too harsh on this song. It's not that big of a deal. It's just a 12-inch record that sits in a crate of a hundred or so other 12-inches. But it's this song that marks the time when things went haywire for us. This record is the seed that bore *Licensed to Ill*, and is an example to look to for my "become what you hate" theory.

Let's start a band was what we all were saying in 1981. It gave us all something to do. Our circle of friends were girls and boys and no hassles. We loved and respected each other, and the hate we had was for the stereotypical behavior of sell-out rock stars and frat-house types. We thought it was so ridiculous,

we made fun of it. Sloppy drunk dudes trying to creep on young women was repugnant to punks in '81. Unfortunately, when you're a straight guy in your late teens/early twenties, you can easily fall into the stereotype's own trappings. And we fell in. Like, from the high diving board. We got so caught up with making fun of that rock-star persona that we became that persona. Became what we hated. It got so bad that we kicked Kate out of the band because she didn't fit into our new tough-rapper-guy identity. How fucked-up is that!?! When Beastie Boys began, the majority of our group of friends were girls. Like, *the coolest* girls. It's really embarrassing to think that we let them down. Maybe Kate would've eventually just quit the band because we were starting to act like a bunch of fuckin' creeps, but it was just shitty the way it happened. And I am so sorry about it. Friends don't do shit like that.

It took a long time to shake the tough-guy party-bro identity we'd adopted, but looking back on it now, it was really exciting recording this song. We'd committed to the notion that we were now rappers. Rick made the track for "Rock Hard." It was a loop of the intro of AC/DC's song "Back in Black." It was a hard sell because punk rockers hate all that is metalish and burnout. We weren't allowed to like this. But it was like that thing when a little kid won't eat something delicious because they've never tried it before. *Come on, just try a bite of mac+cheese. I know you're gonna like it.* And so we tried it and we liked it. And understood why Rick wanted to sample hard rock/metal. It was like a weight had been lifted off us, and now we could openly enjoy those Led Zeppelin and Black Sabbath records we secretly loved. "Rock Hard" may be a crummy song, but it was a good moment in the trajectory of rap. DJs and producers had started using funk and soul breaks, and even hard rock bands' beats too. Billy Squier's "The Big Beat" is the go-to example. But no one was trying to rap over actual heavy-metal guitar riffs, and Rick Rubin should for sure get the credit for that. Adding yet another layer to the awesomeness that is rap music. Different genres of music combining and creating a new and interesting sound. Shaq and Kobe *can* do great things together. Unfortunately, "Rock Hard" couldn't compete.

Years later, Mike talked to Malcolm Young from AC/DC on the phone to ask if we could clear the sample for a compilation record of ours, and Mr. Young said to Mike, "Look, mate . . . we've been in the game a long time and so have you. 'Back in Black' is one of our top three songs; we can't let you have it." *But* . . . they were extremely generous, and did not retroactively sue us for using their song on a rap record from the '80s that we should've been sued for by the listening audience as some sort of garbage-to-the-ears class-action lawsuit.

Here's the lyrics to "Rock Hard" . . . zoom in:

First white b-boys, we don't regret
There's nothing wrong with your TV set
We're getting loose, we couldn't be harder
Our beats are bigger and better and louder
Got real rock shit, you must admit
Not fake, not false, not counterfeit
I can play the drums, I can play guitar
Not just b-boys, we're real rock stars

When we board your ship, you better hit the deck
You'll walk the plank if you disrespect
If you front on the Rock, best run and hide
If you got static, we'll take it outside
And you start to get dulled by the Beastie Boys
Use real rock beats, show up fake toys
Like claps of thunder from the cumulus clouds
Double R pump the beat and make it real loud

Then scratch it

Heavy-metal tension running through your blood
Too much rock step off the pud
Too much treble mid-range and bass
The beat's so hard it'll hit your face
You'll get crushed hard rock hard beats
Hardcore rhythms for fanatic freaks
Some people say this has been done
We're here, we're now, and the battle's won

Fists of fury in an MC bout
Rock so hard, it'll knock you out
The very first blow is the kick and the snare
The beat's so def that you better beware
When guitar and bass are in your face
The walls crumble down, destroying the place
The finishing touch is the vocals that slam
The final blow in the five-finger jam

Sometimes I write rhythms, rather write rhymes
He writes his and I write mines
Rock 'n' roll rhythms are raunchy and raucous
We're from Manhattan, you're from Secaucus
Mike D, ADROCK, and MCA
Not before long, I can hear you say
In a way these boys got juice
They're goin' off, you know, they love to get loose

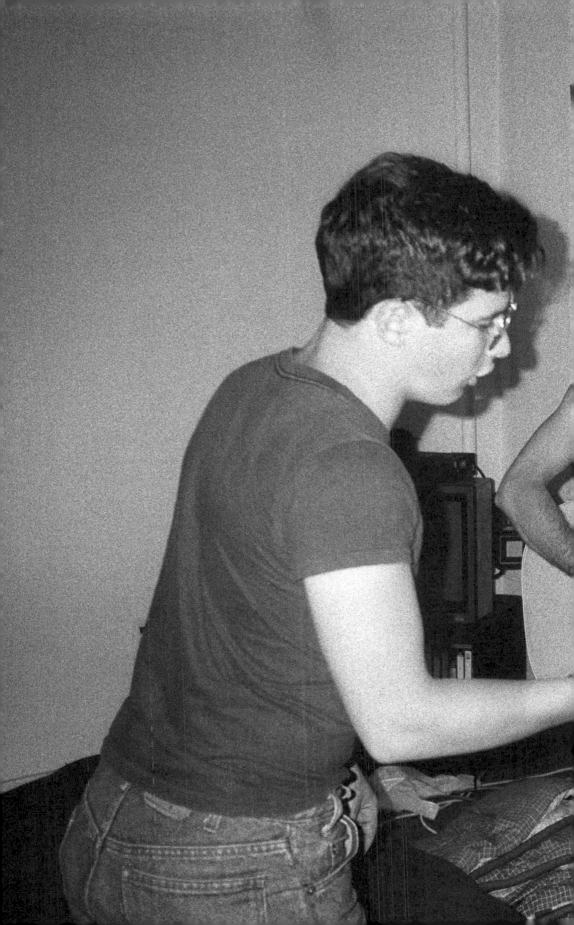

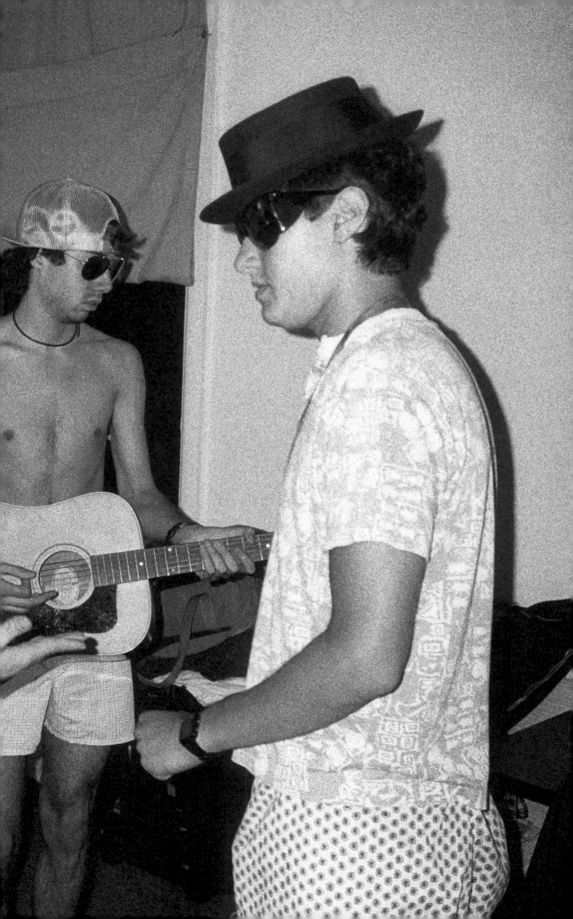

Puppet Show and Beastie Boys
(MD)

This Is Spinal Tap is one of the funniest movies of all time, and it's even funnier if you've been in a band. No matter what situation you find yourself in, at least one of the movie's details—the lying promo dude, the undersized Stonehenge, the cursed drummers, the never-ending backstage-corridor labyrinth—will be directly applicable to a real band's experience. Case in point: our early-1985(ish) show in Philadelphia, presented and sponsored by the pioneering hip hop radio DJ Lady B.

To set the stage: we'd just released our first 12-inch on Def Jam with the b-boy burgundy label, "Rock Hard" b/w "Beastie Groove." In hindsight, yeah—ouch. We hadn't really figured out how to make a good record yet. Our voices were all high in pitch because we were so young, but also because we were forcing our vocals. We weren't remotely relaxed or masterful at our craft yet. (Though I don't know that those things *ever* happened?) But at the time, it seemed pretty cool. We had a real rap 12-inch on a real rap label and the record was going to record pools and DJs and mix shows, and being promoted.

All of which was great, except the record kinda tanked. It didn't seem to be getting played on the radio, and didn't even get played at the same downtown clubs that had played "Cooky Puss" two years earlier. So when Russell called us one day and told us that not only was Lady B playing our record but she wanted us to come down to play a show in Philly she was promoting, we were stoked. And not only because nobody else was paying attention. Lady B was a truly pioneering and powerful woman. At that time, she was one of the only DJs with enough clout and listeners to "break" a rap record—turn it into a hit. If Lady B asked, we were there. The trip seemed like a big deal. Philly was an important hip hop town—I'm thinking like right behind NYC at the time. With its large black population and proximity to NYC, Philly was where rap records first spread to. The support of an influential radio DJ/programmer in Philly could mean a lot to us.

Then Rick—by now not only our DJ but also the co-founder of our label—said that he couldn't make the show. (This became, as you'll see, a recurring theme for the remainder of his time in the band.) But whatever disappointment we felt was immediately gone when he told us who'd agreed to replace him: DJ Jazzy Jay. We were like, *What? You can't do it but* Jazzy Jay *can?* The DJ/record handler/scratch master of choice for Afrika Bambaataa? A member of the Universal Zulu Nation? Jay would be the most veteran, accomplished, and talented DJ we'd ever performed with, by a mile. Rick was a fine DJ, but at the end of the day, he was just a very talented hip hop fan with the right equipment.

Jay was a lifer. We couldn't have asked for a better accomplice to help us win over Lady B's crowd. We headed to Philly.

The first sign of trouble was that the address wasn't even in Philly. It was across the river, in Jersey—Camden or Cherry Hill or someplace like that. We get there only to find that the gig was at a hotel, and not like some grand historic hotel—just a generic chain off the turnpike. The gig itself was in the ballroom. Again, we're not talking the Waldorf-Astoria here, but the kind of small-town hotel ballroom that usually hosts local beauty pageants and puppet shows. No ornate details, just stained carpets and cottage-cheese ceilings and the correct amount of legally required bright-red fire extinguishers and exit signs. From our makeshift green room, we couldn't hear even a small rumbling of people in the ballroom. Still, we were hoping that things might jump off. Lady B showed up; she was very nice and professional, went out to introduce us, and we went onstage.

Staring back at us as we launched into our first song: somewhere between five and eight people. And those people had clearly won free tickets from the radio station, or otherwise been coerced into coming. They didn't care who we were, and they didn't seem interested in our music. What was particularly ironic about the low turnout: anybody who was there witnessed a DJ master class from Jazzy Jay. He was incredible. We'd practiced with him a couple of times, and it was kind of unsettling how easy and effortless it all was for him. Same went for the show; he executed flawlessly. A consummate professional. Which somehow made the whole thing weirder and more embarrassing—we show up with this veteran, iconic DJ, and there's five people there. I've always wondered

This was Jay's only show with us. During this time we had a *Spinal Tap*-ish run of DJs: Rick, Scott Jarvis, Rodger Clayton, Jazzy Jay, "Uncle Jam," DJ Thiggs, Sam Sever, Dr. Dre, Hurricane, and finally Mixmaster Mike. (AH)

if any of the audience members appreciated seeing him in action, or if they paid enough attention to us that they had a good story to tell friends a year or so later, after *Licensed to Ill* became a big deal. But for the three of us, at least, the whole fiasco was worth it just to perform with Jay—even if everything else about the show turned it into one of our many *Spinal Tap* moments. It felt like a super-awkward dress rehearsal that might never end.

That's the other thing we had in common with the Tap: things like disastrous shows—or our first Def Jam record doing less well than a prank phone call set to music we'd recorded two years earlier—didn't faze us in the least. Thinking back on it, I don't remember any of it making us freak out or doubt ourselves, which is weird. You'd think it would have, just in terms of basic common sense.

But I guess we didn't have much of that yet either.

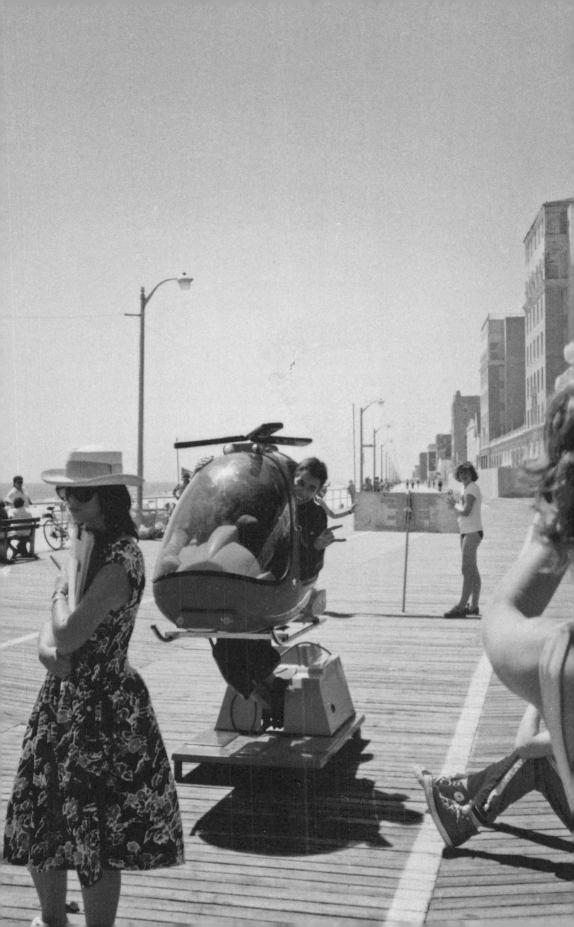

Soundtrack to the Short Film *She's On It*
(MD)

We made another record after "Rock Hard." Our second record for Def Jam: "She's On It." A guitar riff that Rick Rubin played, over a stripped-down beat with us MCing. Before it came out, Rick and Russell made a distribution and marketing deal with Columbia Records. That was a huge fucking deal to us. I mean, *Columbia Records*. Home to Bob Dylan, Bruce Springsteen, Miles Davis, Men Without Hats. Big-time shit.

At the time, Columbia was based in this huge skyscraper in Midtown called Black Rock. We were used to labels that operated out of basement record stores or college dorm rooms. We were also used to making Xerox flyers and putting those up all over downtown NYC ourselves. Now our records were being distributed by a major label with product managers and A&R staff and promotion departments and assistants and Xerox machines and offices whose occupants left expensive cameras lying around that the King ADROCK may or may not have been once accused of steal-

Goddammit, Mike. Let's just not do this again, okay? (AH)

ing, which he vehemently denies. And when "She's On It" got released as our first 12-inch under the new deal, not only were we getting major-label distribution—we got to make a video.

At the time, MTV was a big deal to any teen with cable, but they would only play, like, eight videos, all on microwave rotation. That was it. Huey Lewis and the News, Duran Duran, Night Ranger, Cyndi Lauper. The only two black artists played were Michael Jackson and Prince. Oh, and Lionel Richie. Oh, and Tina Turner. We couldn't imagine ever getting played on MTV, but it didn't matter—we were so out-of-our-minds psyched to be making a video at all. But we also had absolutely no idea what was involved in making a video.

Rick Rubin was into film, and on many nights he'd stay up all night talking cinema with the guy downstairs at the front desk of his dorm, Ric Menello, aka Mr. Ric. (I guess we nicknamed Ric Menello "Mr. Ric" to avoid confusion with Rick Rubin.) Mr. Ric was a short, stocky, bearded New Yorker with a thick Brooklyn accent and a profound film obsession. Actually, forget obsession—he was a savant. Dude knew everything there was to know about all manner of obscure film genres—noir, gore, silent, Jodorowsky. Never shy with an opinion. His attitude about film was the same as our attitude about finding music to sample. We were always looking for two great bars; he would be into something just because of a great scene or a few great lines. It didn't matter what it came from: an art film, a TV series, a studio epic, a forgotten relic of exploitation sleaze, whatever. It just needed to have that piece.

159

So it was decided: Mr. Ric would direct our first-ever video.

Eventually we got a budget. I don't know how much it was, but let's just say the finished video looks . . . cheap. I honestly couldn't tell you what the high-flung concept was. I think we were trying to make fun of a David Lee Roth–type video? Like "California Girls" or "Hot for Teacher," except on a crappy beach near JFK Airport with three fully dressed MCs? Basically it was just us screwing around on a beach in decidedly non-beach attire, with a woman in a bikini nearby.

The most mind-opening part of the trip was our sleepover at Rick Rubin's parents' house in Lido Beach, Long Island, the night before the shoot. Unlike us, Rick had grown up in a bona fide suburban home. Staircase in the middle like *The Brady Bunch*. His dad had a real 1950s workaday look; his mom, Linda, looked kind of like a Divine Miss M—era Bette Midler. We showed up, and Linda was super excited to have Little Ricky back for a night. She never stopped offering us all manner of snacks, soup, matzo balls, you name it. Anything that a good Jewish mom could do, she did, embarrassing Rick the whole while.

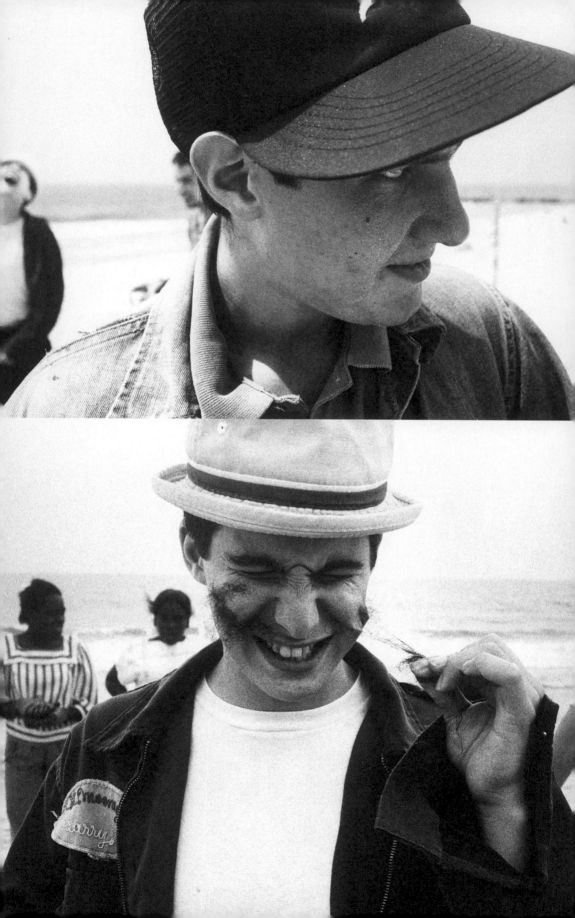

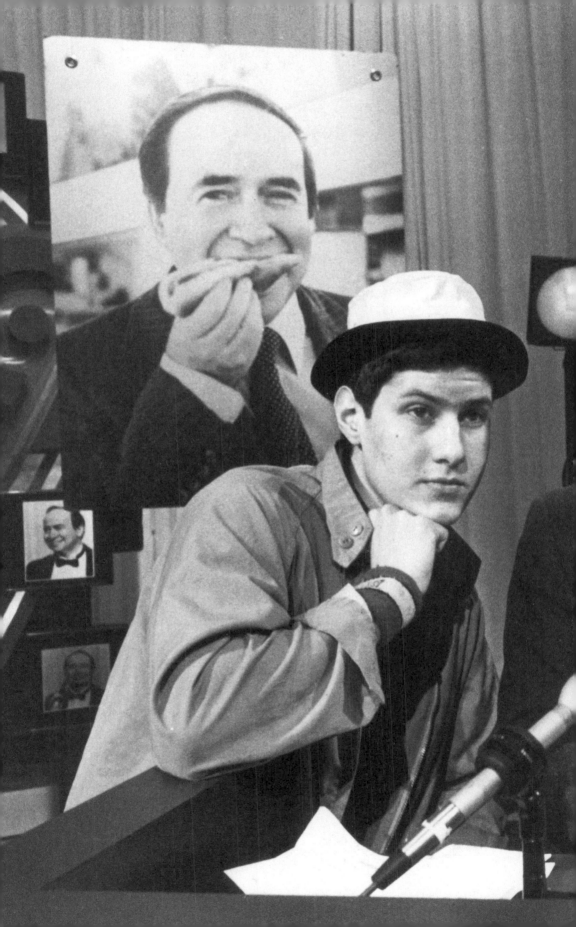

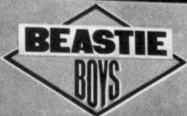

Sweet 16
(AH)

Beastie Boys was exploding on television. Channel U68 was playing our video "She's On It" every hour on the hour. Unfortunately, no one ever tuned in to those weird UHF channels and so no one knew about this Tri-State Area music video channel.

One person, however, *was* watching U68 regularly, and that was the daughter of record executive Charles Koppelman. When you have some free time, google Charles Koppelman. He's a fascinating example of someone who went from here to there, to there, to whoa . . . there? Made a ton of fucking money, and did it with some random-ass people. I say this because I just googled him and discovered that, at one point he teamed up with the dude who built LeFrak City, a neighborhood just off the BQE that I'm mildly obsessed with when I see it on the way to the airport. (Not just because Russell Simmons lived there, or because the basketball great Kenny Anderson grew up there; I'm just intrigued by it, okay?) At the time, I had no idea who Charles Koppelman was. I just knew that some rich dude was paying us to play a song at his daughter's Sweet 16 party. When you're me at eighteen years old, you think every grown-up is a clown. I rarely factored in that I really knew nothing, and maybe that square grown-up had seen and done some wildly crazy-ass shit. Now I try my best to take the advice a five-year-old kid gave me in a park last year, as he was about to run up a slide . . . "Watch and learn."

Anyways, Charles Koppelman had a daughter and apparently she and her friends loved these Beastie Boys and their video. She was about to turn sixteen and was going to have a big blowout party at the Koppelman residence in Roslyn, Long Island, and wanted us to perform our smash-hit song from that video on U68. A Sweet 16 party, in Long Island . . . !?! OH SHIT! YES! The other "Oh shit" detail to this is, the headlining act for the musical performance part of the evening was none other than Run-DMC. They were the biggest band in NYC at that moment, and what young Koppelman wants for her Sweet 16 party . . . young Koppelman gets.

We were so excited to go and check out an actual Sweet 16 party. To the best of my knowledge, this sort of thing didn't happen back in NYC. And if it did, none of us had ever been to one. I mean . . . what goes on at a Sweet 16 party? Safe to assume there's gonna be a bunch of teenage girls there, right? We were teenage boys, and we wanted to mingle. A limo was sent to get us from Manhattan, and drive us all the way out to where this party was at. For us, just leaving Manhattan in a car was a big-deal road trip. We brought a bunch of friends and we were fucking psyched! We get to the Koppelmans' and it's

massive. At least, it was to us. We get out of our comfortable limousine, and one of the Sweet 16 birthday party staff shows us where we can put our stuff and hang out before we go on. But we weren't brought into the actual house. We were kind of steered into this other house. Like a small guesthouse detached from the huge house. As we looked around the guesthouse, we realized that the friendly staff member had *locked us in.* Mr. Koppelman must've heard about us, or seen our video, and was like "Fuck these jerk-offs. They will not be mingling with *my* Sweet 16." (He did leave us refreshments, though, which was nice.)

In this weird, suburban, leather-chaired, dark-wood, *Sky Mall* lockup mini version of an '80s Long Island mansion, there was one little window, and it looked out toward a swimming pool. After a few refreshments, our friend Doze (of Rock Steady Crew fame) decides that he wants to go swimming. So of course, it being a Sweet 16 party and all, he takes off his clothes, climbs up, and kind of shimmies out of the window. Streakin' and skinny dippin'. It was wonderful. The record executive's staff was not impressed or amused; Doze was locked back in the room within seconds. But . . . he was brave and bold; he made an escape and saw the other side.

Moments later, we were told that it was time for us to go on. To play our one song to the teenagers before Run-DMC performed. We were a little drunk and a lotta ugly. We get out there on the backyard party platform/stage under a tent, and start to play our smash hit single. The crowd of soon-to-be almost young adults goes wild. Miraculously, by the second verse of the song, all of the power onstage goes dead. Lights still on, but the speakers are cut off. No sound. What's going on? We just assumed that it was technical difficulties, so we just stood around on the platform/stage, mics in hand, tipsy+awkward. Enter a big tuxedoed securityish guy from platform/stage left. He took the mics from our hands and was like, "Thanks a lot, fellas, that'll be all. It's time to go now." The Koppelman staff quickly let us know that yes, in fact, it was time to get the fuck off the platform/stage and go away. The record executive would rather cut his losses and give us a couple hundred bucks than have to endure another moment of us. Being us. In front of his daughter and her friends. Run-DMC was a *way* better idea. And of course, they were. *Way better.*

So we all got in the limo and fell asleep on the ride back to Manhattan. Our friend Dave Scilken had a video camera and was gonna tape the whole night. He got so drunk that he did the thing where you turn it off when you think you're turning it on and then turn it on when you think you're turning it off. So the only footage from that entire night is an hour-long close-up still shot of his dirty sneakers on a limousine floor, in the dark, with the sounds of an engine humming and dudes snoring.

It was pretty sweet.

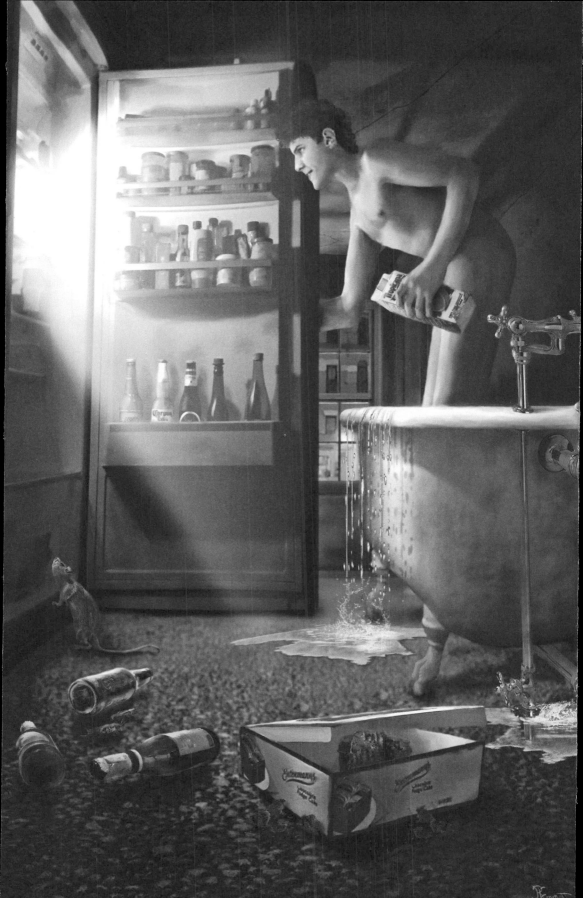

A Room Paved with Asphalt

(AH/MD)

Go to 59 Chrystie Street. Chinatown, NYC. Enter that building, walk past some trash cans in the hallway, and climb over some rats and up the stairs. On each floor you climb, there's a hallway running on either side of the stairs. Each room you see on those floors is a kind of sweatshop. Bunches of older ladies in tiny, grimy rooms, sewing fabrics of some kind. Keep walking up. Get to the fourth floor, walk through a door, and enter a room. There's no walls in that room. It's just an empty, dilapidated space. Except for a small kitchenette and a bathtub. Right in the middle of the room. It's like the scene in a movie when the landlord opens the door to show the goofy couple a dump of an apartment in a totally run-down tenement-style building on a grimy NYC street. This was Mike+Yauch's first apartment. As awful as this place was . . . hey, they had an apartment. They were kind of almost like grown-ups now.

Remember when I said that there was a bathtub in the middle of the apartment? Not a bathroom, a bathtub. Well, there was. And this one thing happened at least a couple times . . . I'd be on the phone at my mom's talking to Yauch and in the middle of the conversation he'd be like . . . "Aw, man . . . come on. . . ." I'd say, "What?" and he'd tell me that Mike was taking a bath, and while bathing, he would stand up to get a snack out of the fridge. And kind of linger there. Like . . . fridge door open, nude snacking. YES . . . go ahead and picture this . . . a nineteen-year-old Mike D. Fully nude. Standing upright in a bathtub that's in the middle of a room. He's leaning over as far as he can to reach and open the refrigerator door. He gets it open, stands there for a minute. Naked, and thinking to himself. For whatever reason, I've always pictured Mike having a handful of Entenmann's mini chocolate chip cookies. With one foot up on the side of the tub. Then lying down and continuing his bathing process in a soapy and crumb-filled bath. Oh, another thing you should know is that Mike used to be one of those people who would kind of talk at the same time he was eating. So add that to the picture. For some of you reading this, this might be fantasy becomes reality, but my guess is that this visual has a niche audience.

Look, Adam. Like you, I grew up with the relative NYC luxury of having the use of a separate bathroom complete with a shower and a tub. But hey, Yauch and I moved on *down*—def *not* like the Jeffersons. It was like we took a turn living in the NYC Tenement Museum. But to be honest, I got used to it. It was kinda great to be able to reach into the fridge from the tub and grab a juice. (Remember, we had no shower; this was our only bathing mechanism aside from going back home to our parents' or using a friend's shower, and we did plenty of both of those.) (MD)

I was at 59 Chrystie Street almost every day, and sometimes I wished that I lived there with them 'cause it seemed so fun and grown-up to have an apartment but . . . well . . . I was happy still living with my mom and . . . you

know . . . the thing with Mike and the bathtub, and the rats and all . . . I preferred to just hang out there. Yauch+Mike got a couple of friends who knew basic construction stuff to build out two "bedrooms": a couple of walls with curtains for doors. The rest of the place was a practice space.

Yauch+Mike might always remember that place as a dump. A shitty apartment during that transitional phase from young adult to almost actual adult. The apartment that gets totally trashed and so you just kind of move on. But for me . . . when I think of that place, my mind goes right to the night of the Fourth of July. Yauch+Mike's rooftop party. NYC can be fucking magical in the summertime, especially when you're nineteen and you're drunk and you're in a band. That night was a kind of transitional night for all of us. At least, it felt that way to me. Us and our group of friends were all up there on that roof in Chinatown. Drinking, laughing, and living life. In the moment. We were mini grown-ups, and that night, we knew it. (AH)

Sometime in 1984 or 1985, Yauch was working at a studio called Shakedown, owned by producer Arthur Baker. Yauch was an "assistant engineer" or something, but mostly he ran around and grabbed coffee or picked up recording gear. One of the main engineers at Shakedown, Jay Burnett, lived at 59 Chrystie Street first. He had a great loft-type place; you could hear the rumble of trucks on the ancient Manhattan Bridge and see it looming high above.

One day Jay told Yauch that there was another empty loft-type space at the building. We went to see it, thinking it'd be as nice as his, and . . . well . . . it wasn't. It was an absolute dump. The floor was literally blacktop, as in asphalt. Not the shiny, clean, gleaming concrete of art galleries—it was exactly like the surface of a street. It wasn't possible to really clean it. If you walked around barefoot for five minutes, the soles of your feet would turn black.

Yauch and I were like, "We can play music whenever we want?"

Jay said, "Sure."

Pause.

"We'll take it."

Jay introduced us to our new landlords, Quong and Eddie. They were basically like, *This is the rent, if Jay says you guys are okay, then you're okay. Give us*

Arthur Baker had an in-house editing duo called the Latin Rascals to work on his remixes. The editing technique they used was fucking nuts. They would chop up reel-to-reel tape with razor blades for hours and days and weeks to create a new and unheard-of sound. It's hard to grasp what they were doing back then. Everyone knows, and it's obvious to say, that editing anything . . . text, music, film, etc., is *so* much easier on a computer. But the Latin Rascals were working with ancient-times tape. They had their own brand-new style of manipulating songs for their remixes. They'd chop up parts of the music to rearrange the song, but their signature thing was taking different vocal lines and having them repeat in this manic way. Like a hundred times in a row, rapid-fire. But in order to get that sound, they would have to record that one vocal a hundred different times in a row, then take that tape from the reel-to-reel and find the exact place where the one single word would start and stop. Take a razor blade to the tape, cut it off, and Scotch tape it to the other reel-to-reel tape that was on a tape deck next to the one they were working from. The sounds they got were amazing, but what a fucking pain in the ass to get there. Relentless craftsmanship. They were the human analog version of the digital future of music. Imagining that you could do what they did is like watching Pistol Pete, Jason Williams, and Hot Sauce videos on YouTube and thinking . . . *Shit, I bet I could do that.* (AH)

a check and here's the lease. Back then, if you were willing to live in a room paved with asphalt and some guy could vouch for you, you were in.

I have two distinct memories from right after we moved in. One time, Yauch's parents came by to check the place out—Yauch's dad was an architect, after all. Yauch's mom looked at what little there was in the way of a kitchen, then saw the bathtub in the middle of the room and said, "Oh, you could put wood over the bathtub for another work surface." For years afterward, Yauch and I repeated that line like it was from *Fletch* or something. Later, my mom also came to check out the place. While I was showing her around, we discovered this huge dead rat on the windowsill by the toilet, which was in its own tiny closet. Fully rigor-mortised, stiff as a board. My mom somehow remained totally calm and detached and was just like, "Oh, good luck with that, Michael." (She had once been a social worker in the South Bronx.)

Turned out the place was rat-infested. Not as in, once in a while you would hear scratching inside the walls—most people who live in New York City have experienced that uneasy sound. But at 59 Chrystie Street, we had full-on packs of rats, roaming the hallways like Stegman from *Class of 1984*. Every night, the sweatshops would put jumbo black trash bags—seemingly stuffed with food—out in the halls, and a late-night feeding frenzy would ensue. Our main concern with the rat issue was, yeah, the rats freaked us out, but they were a deal-breaker if we were going to try to bring girls back from the clubs. I mean, going into a sketchy Chinatown building at three A.M. was bad enough, but then walking up the stairs with rats flying out of black garbage bags? No way.

When we mentioned the rat problem to the super, he suggested that if we killed a rat and left it for dead, and then did that a few times, the rest of the rats would vacate the premises. *Huh?!* When he told us that, though, Yauch and I looked at each other and had this simultaneous lightbulb go off:

Rat hunting.

We went out to Long Island somewhere and bought these pellet guns, some CO_2 cartridges, and a gang of pellets. Then we hatched a plan: We would stash the guns in our mailbox on the ground floor. (Possibly a federal crime?) That night, when we came home from being out (at three A.M. or so), we would grab our pellet guns, proceed up the stairs, and blast away at vermin, *Starsky & Hutch*–style. It was wintertime, so we'd have on down coats, plus hats and gloves; we'd be good and protected from any stray ricocheting pellets.

So . . . late that night, we rolled in a bit buzzed. We grabbed our loaded pistols, headed up the stairs, and started kicking the huge garbage bags. Sure enough, rats came streaming out of them. Somehow, we actually nailed a couple, then left them, dead, in the hallway for a few days.

I would like to interject at this point to say two things. 1) You guys are awful, murderous, animal-hating people. And 2) I didn't know the "rat hunting" thing was your own idea . . . nice one. (AH)

Turns out that particular urban legend is fucking *true*. Problem solved.

Now we were free to go about inviting girls back to our place or to play

instruments at high volume or to bathe while snacking. There were a few other impediments to relaxed living at 59 Chrystie, though. For one, a giant steam press from the sweatshop above us would sometimes start going like *kuh-joo, kuh-joo* and literally bend the ceiling above my bed. Like, you'd see it go up and down a few inches. At other times, there was something up there that would overflow or leak or whatnot and all this burning hot gross rusty water would come through our ceiling onto my bed. There was no warning or schedule or method to it; every now and then it would just randomly rain down on me, and I'd be like, *Ah, what the fuck?!*

When we got our first electric bill, it was something like $500. We turned white and weren't sure what we were going to do. Just then the landlord sent the super down saying he needed to speak to us. Now we were *really* freaking. We went up to his top-floor office, which was actually warm and clean, unlike the rest of the building. (Lots of marble tile.) He asked us, "Have you gotten your electric bill yet?" We looked at each other. "Um, yes." "Good, you must have seen it was for a lot of money?" "Um, yes." "That's because the business on the first floor uses your same power. Don't worry, I'll introduce you to Peter, he'll take care of it."

A few minutes passed, and in walked Peter: a skinny man sporting short-shorts and a Fu Manchu mustache. Peter looked at the bill and said, "No problem, come with me." We followed him down to his ground-floor "business," which turned out to be a worn-down Chinatown brothel. Now we got the picture. We waited uncomfortably while women in lingerie walked by. He asked us if we wanted "anything." Now we *really* got the picture. We were so freaked out and just wanted the money so we could pay our bill. He pulled out a big knot of hundred-dollar bills, the likes of which we had never seen before, and peeled off the bills. He paid our part of it too, and told us to just come see him every month when we got our bill. Phew. In less than an hour, we went from maybe moving out without paying the bill to staying and getting all bills paid for us.

Then there was the time we were doing a band interview in the apartment and our toaster oven got shot. I don't mean shot as in ruined. I mean shot with a gun. A gun using real bullets and everything. We were talking to some music journalists. Suddenly, we heard this really loud sound, and the little glass window on the toaster shattered, and the toaster fucking exploded. We looked closer and saw that the hole was a bullet hole. *What the fuck?!* We ran upstairs, to where we thought the bullet had come from. In full MacGyver mode, we barged into the sweatshop above us, which should have been packed—it was the middle of the day. Instead, it was completely empty. One of life's unanswered mysteries.

Things were just like that during the year or so we lived at 59 Chrystie. We had tons of band practices and, yes, Adam, that super-epic July Fourth party on the roof, when a pre-Giuliani NYC got lit up. Literally. Chinatown

and Little Italy were the epicenter for selling illegal fireworks, especially the eastern stretch of Canal Street, near our apartment. M-80s, blockbusters, Roman candles, mortars, bricks of firecrackers, you name it. The Canal Street operations were as fine-tuned and ritualized as any drug corner: you'd pull up in a car; a kid would approach and, in semi-discreet fashion, grab the appropriate knot of cash; he'd run back to a stash spot and return, arms filled with your order, and dutifully load it into the open trunk of your Buick Century or Ford LTD. This would go on every day and night for weeks leading up to the Fourth. Once in a while, cops would cruise by, and the runners would have to "cool it" and run inside a deli or act like nothing was happening.

The best part of that system was, by the time the day itself rolled around, all those illegal vendors would have tons of unsold fireworks left over. What were they gonna do, pay to put them in storage for another year? Oh hell no. And we had the perfect rooftop view: they'd take the grated-metal city trash cans you find on every corner and put them in the middle of the street, load a bunch of cardboard and trash in each one, and light the shit on fire. This effectively stopped all car traffic. Then they proceeded with the largest, most amazing, 100% unlicensed and illegal free-fireworks show ever. They'd toss every unsold firework, en masse, into the burning trash cans. They'd line up mortars down the middle of the street and ignite them, sending them high into the sky. It was a beautiful and chaotic drunken war zone, and we had the perfect perch.

At some point we left to go on tour.

We gave the keys to friends so they could use the place to practice while we were gone. We came back and the place was disgusting, totally trashed. Looking back, I'm not sure if our friends actually trashed it or if we had forgotten how bad it was from being on tour, where we stayed in decent hotels. Regardless: it was time to move out, and move on up. . . . (MD)

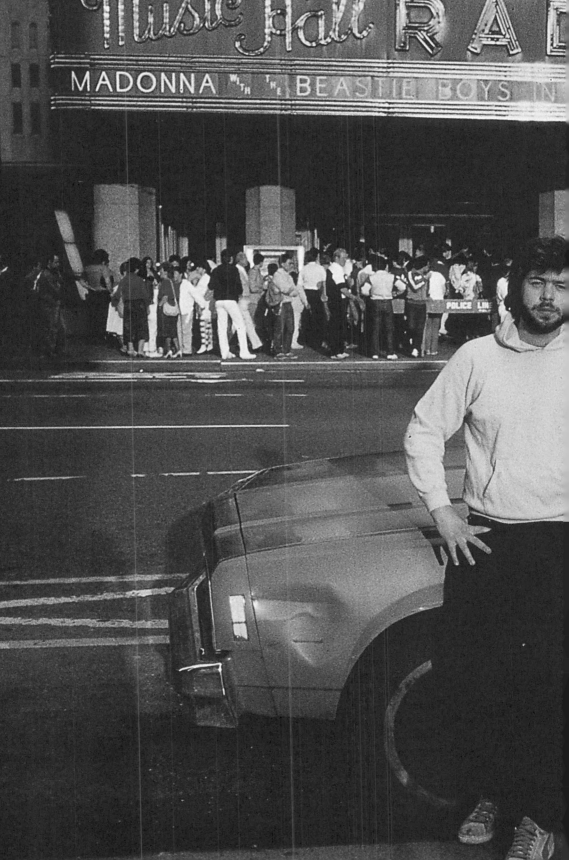

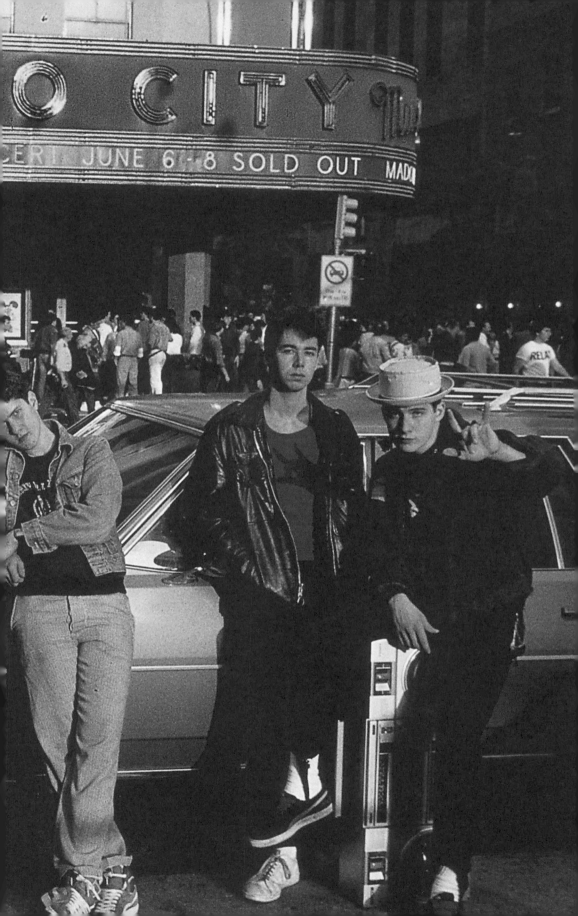

Something Kind of Like a Virgin
(AH)

The story of how we ended up opening for Madonna is as follows: Since Russell Simmons was Run-DMC's manager, he got a call one day from Freddy DeMann, Madonna's manager, asking if Run-DMC would like to open for her on her first-ever tour. Russell said, Yes but they get twenty grand a show. Madonna's manager said thanks anyway. He called back later to ask if the Fat Boys were available for the tour. Russell said that they were busy at the time and couldn't do it. (Russell did not manage the Fat Boys.) *But* . . . he said he had another rap group, Beastie Boys, that'd do it for five hundred bucks a show. I have no idea why Freddy DeMann said yes, but he did; and the next thing you know, we're flying out to Seattle with Rick Rubin and Scott Jarvis to start the tour.

Here's two things about Madonna in 1985 . . .
1. At that very moment when Freddy DeMann called, she wasn't the global superstar that everyone now knows. She was just a great singer/performer, with an awesome debut album that people were talking about. But then her record *Like a Virgin* was released, and started getting a lot of attention. Within the first week of that tour, she blew the fuck up. People went berserk for Madonna. Every other song from both her records became a hit. She was Beatlemania *and* Elvis combined. Every twelve-year-old girl wanted to dress, look, and be like her.
2. We kind of came from a similar sort of scene that she came from. She performed at Danceteria a bunch of times. Knew Haoui Montaug, Anita Sarko, Johnny Dynell, and all the early '80s downtown celebrities. So, to us, it wasn't *that* weird of a combo. We didn't know each other, but we ran in similar circles.

Here's four things about us in 1985 . . .
1. As a band, we'd never stayed in a hotel before. The first hotel we stayed at on this tour was the Four Seasons in downtown Seattle, and that shit was FAN-CEE. And really expensive. But fuck it. We're supposed to be staying here, right? This is what big bands do on big tours, right? We'd been playing gigs for a few years, but we'd never been on tour before. We didn't know what to do, or what it was gonna be like. We were something kind of like a virgin.
2. We basically did the entire tour in a rented Lincoln Continental.
3. We didn't really bring luggage on this tour. Meaning, I think we just wore the same clothes all summer.

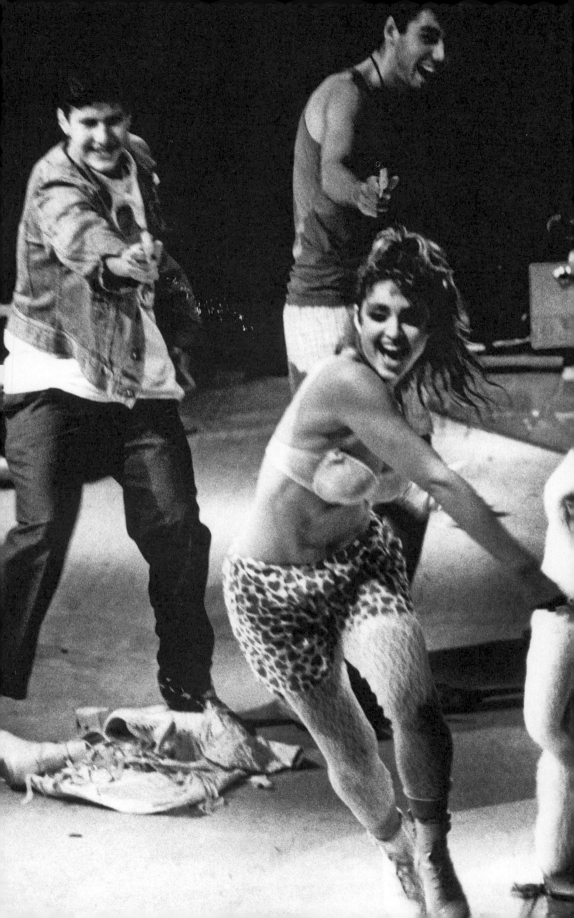

4. Rick Rubin was our DJ. But after the first week, he had to fly back to New York for some reason, and he never came back. He told us that a doctor said he shouldn't fly because of an inner-ear situation, but my belief is that he made up the story because he just didn't wanna be on tour.

Here's two things about Scott Jarvis...

1. He was our friend from a couple years back and recorded the *Polly Wog Stew* 7-inch. He came on tour with us as the "roadie," mainly because he had a driver's license and could therefore drive the rented Lincoln Continental.

2. We needed someone to take over for the missing Rick Rubin. So Scott was now the DJ. He was also *not* a DJ. At all. Zero DJing experience. It worked out fine 'cause all he had to do was start and stop two, or three, records onstage. We only had a couple rap songs. It's not like we played "Egg Raid on Mojo" for the Madonna audience. And so that's all we did. Our two or three rap songs.

Madonna's band were all hired-gun session dudes. It was a weird and professional scene that we'd never seen before. The drummer, Jonathan Moffett, had toured with fuckin' Michael Jackson. This was some big-time shit. He had a huge gong as part of his drum kit. He did this thing, like, forty times a show, where he'd hit these two big cymbals that were hanging behind him and catch them like frisbees with each hand as he hit them. Sticks in his hands, never missing a beat. It was truly fascinating. We'd never known anyone in a band that didn't start in high school. This was super-duper professional stuff. SHOW BIZ. This was the kind of shit that we made fun of, and now here we were. On the same massive stage with professional musicians, backup dancers, and MADONNA.

Before the tour, we talked about a game plan with Rick+Russell. *What could we do that would make these people remember us?* It certainly wasn't gonna be our microphone mastery. Our big idea was that we should be as rude and awful as possible onstage. If we just went up there and played a couple songs and said our thank-yous and good nights, like, who would care? Instead, we would be memorable. Memorable fuckin' jerks. The Madonna audience at that point consisted of mostly eight-to-twelve-year-old girls, and their moms, all dressed in Madonna clothes—bangle bracelets, fishnet shirts, etc. (By the way, I believe this look was created by our friend from the neighborhood Simone Reyes.) We literally made children cry. We were that obnoxious.

I guess that crying children and angry parents weren't what management had in mind, so Freddy DeMann wanted us kicked off the tour. But Madonna wanted us to stay. I'm not sure why, but she did. And we stayed. Maybe she felt bad for us. Maybe she thought it was a good thing to have other NYCers out there on the road. Or really, and probably . . . she knew that the audience hated us so much that by the time she hit the stage it would be fucking glorious. Like an ice-cream sundae after the dentist.

I totally do not know Madonna. Not then, and not now. I wish I were friends with her. How fucking cool would that be? And . . . it's not really a stretch. I mean, we had a bunch of people in common, right? We hung out at the same places. But maybe it's that thing where girls are just more advanced than boys, and even though I was, like, nineteen, I seemed more like a thirteen-year-old scrub. A pimply freshman. And I kind of was. And she for sure was way beyond whatever I was into. She seemed like a grown-up who'd traveled and knew what wine to get and had friends with nice teeth whose picture you'd see in the party pages of some magazine like *Elle* or something.

She for sure did *not* have to keep us on that tour, but she did. And it was huge for us. We learned so much from being out there. What a tour was like. What a real *show* show was like. It was eye-opening and inspiring to us to be around a performer who was so awesome and totally professional and who was out to handle her business and just have fun. Madonna, thank you.

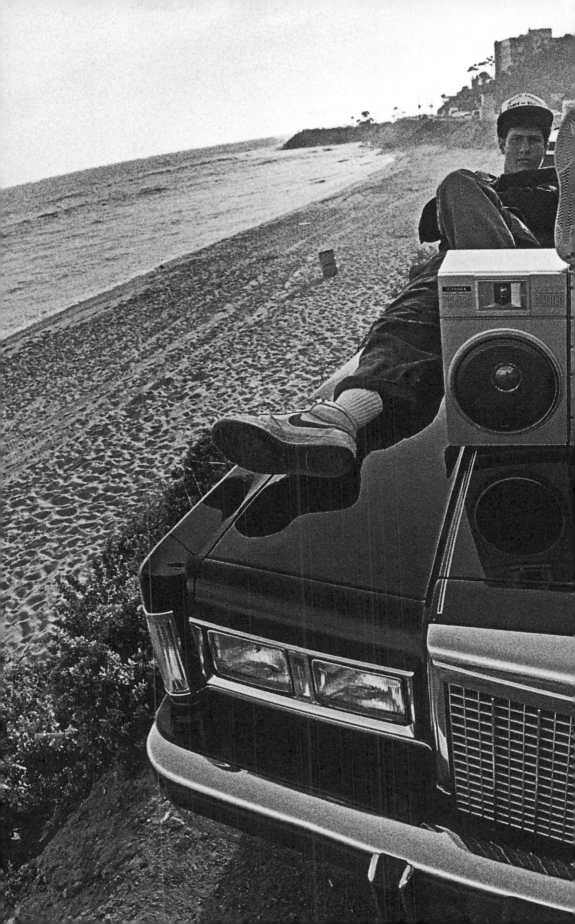

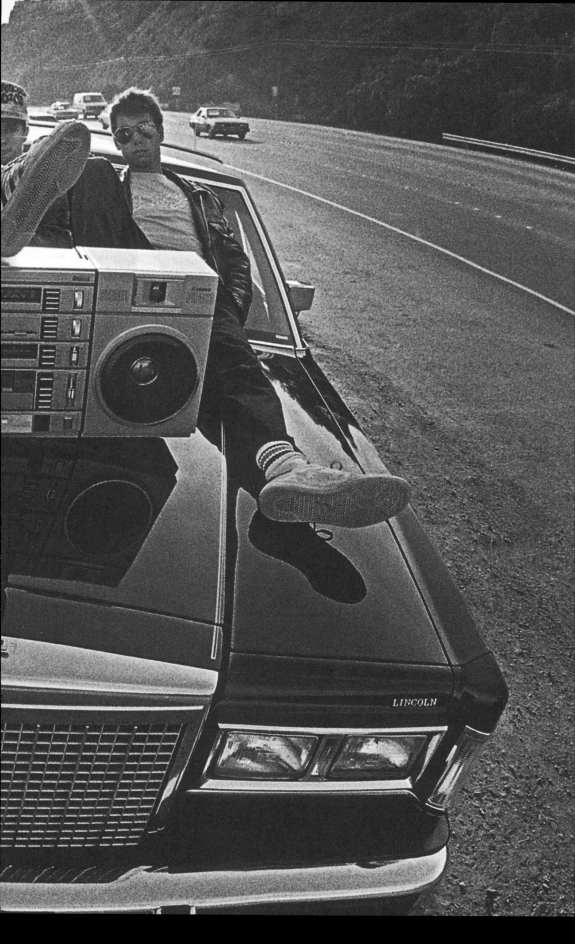

Madonna Tour FYIs and BTWs

(AH)

IHOP

The first night of the tour was in Seattle; then down to Portland. Oh . . . speaking of Portland . . . we got there late at night, after the drive from Seattle, and we were hungry. So we wandered around downtown trying to find a place to eat. Mike was running ahead to look around each corner to see if anything was still open. He ran up to a corner, looked around, turned to us, and from far away we hear Mike scream . . . *IHOP!!!* He jumped in the air, hands waving above his head, landed, and crumpled to the ground. He twisted his ankle so bad, we had to take him to the ER. I blame the '80s for this. If it was now, we would've Yelped the shit out of "late night spots Portland." We'd have

DISCLAIMER: I may or may not have been very excited and/or very stoned—and I definitely was hungry! (MD)

slowly and calmly Wazed to a restaurant and had delicious pierogies (instead of almost eating at the International House of Pancakes). We also had no idea what it was like to be on tour. Night after night. Next new place, away from home. No idea where to get food, do laundry, get a shitload of quarters to call home with. It was the final days of having to just find shit out as it happened.

SHOWBIZ

For us, just being in hotels was awesome. Room service was a very new and exciting thing. So much so that I ordered escargot to the room in our fancy hotel because . . . why not? The short story here is that we were all hanging out in a room, I got my escargot, and for whatever reason, I was eating them in bed while wearing only underwear. Why, I don't know. But again . . . why not? I was so overexcited that I spilled a plate of steaming-hot snails, garlic, salt, butter, and oil onto my bare legs. So there . . . it's been properly documented. (You guys can stop laughing at me now.)

TASTY LICKS

Rodger Clayton (from L.A.'s legendary and influential DJ/production crew Uncle Jamm's Army) filled in for the first two shows after Rick left the tour. In the middle of one of the L.A. shows, Uncle Jamm came out from behind the turntables and was doing a kind of air-guitar thing to the audience. He was also making that *I'm a nasty shredder on this axe* face, and it was all over. It was just a thing that people do, but not us. Not at A7. I know it's a totally childish way to make a business/professional decision. We could've talked about it with him and moved forward, but it was an unfortunate pantomime that could not be unseen, so we parted ways.

EVERYTHING YOU'D HOPED IT WOULD BE

Just being out of NYC, really for the first time, was thrilling. Being on tour. Seeing cities I'd heard of but never been to, like Seattle. Portland. Miami. Cleveland. Chicago. Places with unpronounceable-to-me names like La Jolla. Oh, speaking of Miami . . . did Madonna have a wild party at some crazy mini-mansion when we were in Miami? Yes. Of course she did. Was it all you could imagine and want it to be? Yes, it was. Was John Salley getting freaky in a hot tub? Yes, of course he was.

PICKLE MAN

One morning in Cincinnati I woke up and had a couple weird itchy splotches on my arm. I didn't pay them any mind until the end of the night, after the show, I noticed that they had spread over my entire body. I had some kind of insane allergic-reaction hive breakout. Having a face that looks like an itchy pickle is not a good look when trying to talk to girls after the show. The next day we were given the address of a doctor and got lost. We asked somebody waiting at a bus stop for directions, and he said, "Oh, I don't know . . . I'm a little . . ." He pointed at his head and made the *I'm crazy* signal with his finger. We kept going. When we finally got to the doctor, he gave me a shot of what he called "adrenaline." I was tweaking for about two hours straight, and then the hives went away. Not the kind of sexy or raucous details you were looking for in a book about a band?

HOLLYWOOD SWINGIN'

We'd never been to L.A. before, and somehow we hooked up with a friend of a

friend, Glen E. Friedman. Glen kind of grew up in L.A. and decided to be our tour guide. Glen is vegan, but for whatever reason, he took us to Fat Burger our first night in town. I got a fried egg on my burger. Glen kept referring to eggs as liquid flesh. We made fun of him, he made fun of us, he cried from laughter, and we became friends for years. I think punk rock tipped the scale over veganism for Glen because the next night he took us to a grimy outdoor hot-dog place called Oki Dog. It was some kind of L.A. punk rock landmark because X did something there, or Circle Jerks, or the Germs, or the Go-Go's . . . I can't remember. But the important thing is this . . . an Oki dog is a burrito stuffed with beans, cheese, two hot dogs, and pastrami, and it's fucking delicious.

When we were in L.A., Madonna had a big party to celebrate the success of *Like a Virgin*. So we were there, drinking free drinks and loving it. Now . . . growing up in New York, you would occasionally see a famous person on the street, but this was for-real Hollywood. We went with our new friend Glen, who's a great photographer, and he's taking pictures of us with, like . . . Sean Penn, E. G. Daily, Weird Al. The most random list of, like, oh shit . . . *that person?!* We gotta get our picture taken with them. Pre-selfie, pre-self-conscious. It was fucking fantastic, and, like, so totally L.A. Fer sher.

TAPES

I brought more cassette tapes with me on tour than clothing. The other thing I brought was a massive box (or boombox, as the kids never used to say). Because I brought the box, I was usually in charge of the music. That, and also because I can get a little control-freaky sometimes when it comes to song selection. We listened to a ton of music on that tour, either on the box or on the Lincoln Continental's stereo. Two selections come to mind as standouts.

1. *Forward*—A Greensleeves Records reggae compilation
We listened to the shit out of that shit. In particular, the musical compositions . . . "Fattie Boom Boom" by Ranking Dread, and everyone's favorite, "Bathroom Sex," by the one and only General Echo. The music is phenomenal and the lyrics are about as abstract as you can deal with.

2. *"Good Times Bad Times"*—Led Zeppelin
We were just letting our guard down about listening to classic rock, and well . . . Led Zeppelin was fucking greater than great. That song being blasted out of speakers is similar to dipping lobster into melted butter.

Songs are like markers in time. You hear them, and your brain catalogs where you're at while they're playing. "Fattie Boom Boom" was playing while we drove through the intersection of Franklin Avenue and Cahuenga Boulevard that Los Angeles summer night in 1985. An intersection I would drive through nearly 486 times just a few years later.

THE HOTTEST PARTY IN L.A.

On the first night we ever spent in Los Angeles, we saw Freddie "Boom Boom" Washington . . . twice. He was in an open Jeep-type car. I'm gonna say it was a Suzuki Samurai because I want him to be in one. We were only a few nights into the Madonna tour, and we ended up in Los Angeles with a couple nights off. Not always, but sometimes when you're in a band on tour, you find out about stuff that's happening in the town you're currently in. People want you to be at their thing. Their bar, club, house party. Weird people and their parties gravitate toward you, and you to them.

So one of these nights in L.A. . . . somehow . . . we meet this guy named Riki Rachtman. I really don't remember how or why we hooked up with him, but we did. He was like an L.A. version of a dude from Queens. He wasn't a burnout. He was more like a metalhead with a hustle. (A couple years later, he became an MTV VJ for a show called *Headbangers Ball*.) He kept saying that he was gonna hook up "the hottest party in L.A." And it was gonna be in our shitty hotel room at our shitty hotel, the Franklin Plaza Suites. He just kept saying he was gonna get all these girls to come down and that it was gonna be *hot*. A word that was only spoken in NYC when referencing the temperature, unless you were making fun of an "L.A." person.

No one showed up. It was the three of us, this dude Riki Rachtman, and his friend. It was one of those parties where it's a bust so you split and try to find something else to do. I think we left them there in our room 'cause we really wanted to not be there anymore.

IT WAS NOT *HOT*.

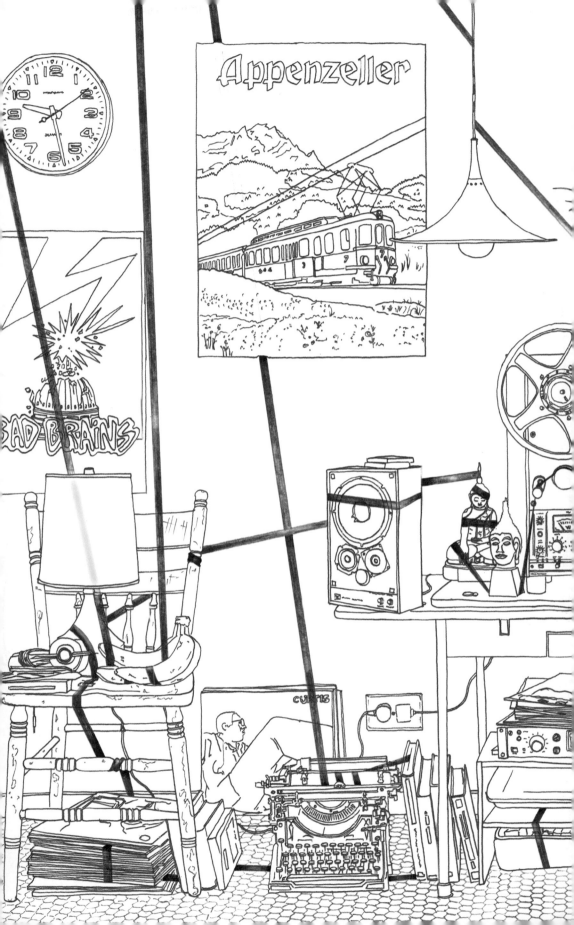

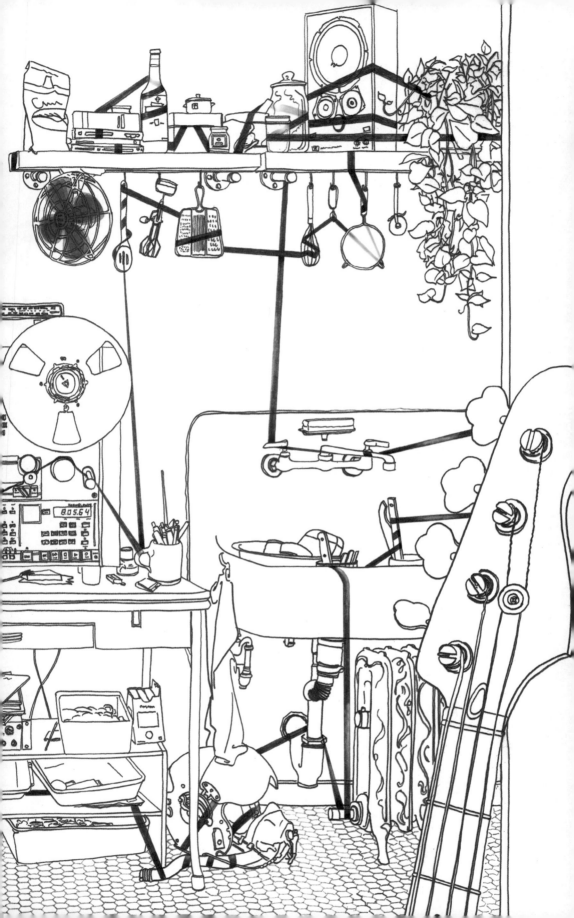

You Should Loop That

(AH)

After we got home from the Madonna tour, we had nothing to do but do nothing. On a typical night I could walk over to Mike's new place on Barrow Street, or I could go out to Yauch's cool new ground-floor apartment in Brooklyn Heights. I guess I was in the mood for a road trip because I chose the latter. I took the train to Clark Street. Walked past the bagel place where all the cool girls from St. Ann's high school worked. Hit the deli on the corner of State+Henry for a couple 40s of Ballantine on my way (you know . . . Ballantine Ale, with the puzzle on the cap) and got to Yauch's. Weirdly, Yauch was the super for the building. He would occasionally get calls from tenants asking him to come look at the radiator, or check to see if their fridge or window or what-have-you was broken. He had zero qualifications for that job, other than that he could kind of do just about anything.

It was dramatically different from 59 Chrystie Street. It was a tiny place, but it was clean and very grown-up. It had a nice little backyard. (If you've never been to NYC, a backyard here means a four-square-foot area that is outside your apartment that is not the sidewalk or a fire escape.) It was the kind of apartment where you'd drink wine from a wineglass.

Anyways . . . I get there and Yauch has a tape deck up on the counter in the kitchen. Not a cassette deck, but a quarter-inch reel-to-reel tape deck. I didn't even know he had one. He'd pulled the tape out of the machine and wound it around a mic stand and a wooden chair close to the reel-to-reel. When he pressed PLAY, the tape came out one side of the tape deck, went tightly around the mic stand, then the chair, then back into the other end of the machine.

He had the intro drumbeat to Led Zeppelin's "When the Levee Breaks" going around and around his kitchen. The sound and the visual were so magical to me. It was like he was on some Doug Henning shit. He said that he recorded the intro part of the record onto the tape, and then edited just that intro part, and wanted it to keep going around and around like what a DJ would do with break-beats. So, what I'm saying is . . . Yauch was on to tape loops before "You should loop that" was a ubiquitous phrase. He told me that he'd heard about Hendrix and Sly Stone doing tape loops and he wanted to try it. *Where* did he hear about it? There was no Google or YouTube. No library had a section on beats. He must've seen the Latin Rascals editing at Shakedown Studios, and thought . . . *Can I do that? I'll just try to make that little drumbeat edit keep going around and around and see what happens.*

What Yauch was working on that day became "Rhymin' and Stealin," the first song on our first album.

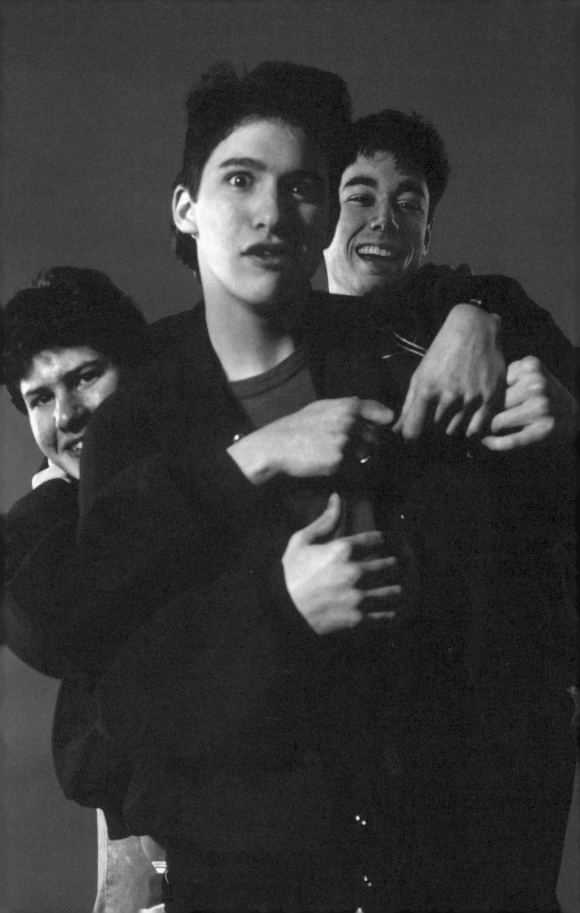

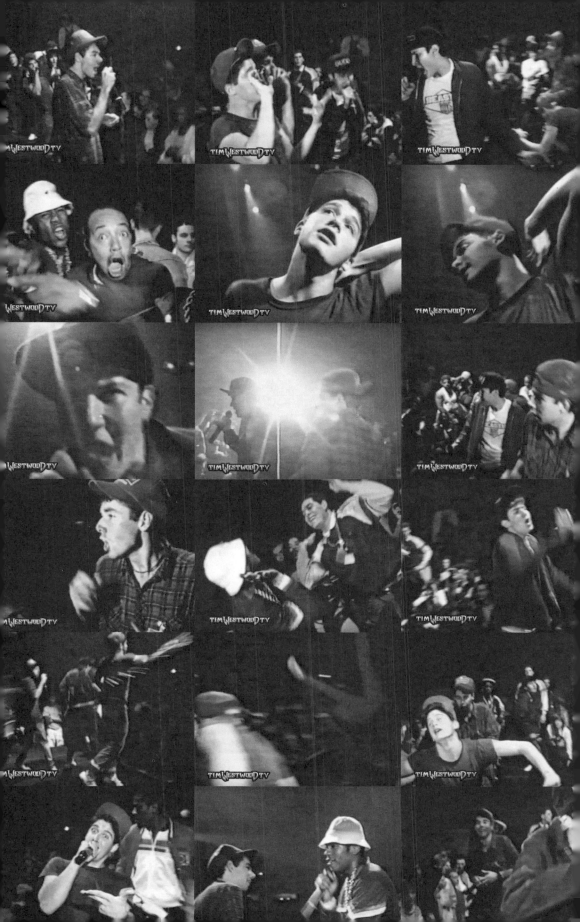

London '86
(AH)

So . . . early 1986. We all go to London.

Def Jam signed a distribution deal with CBS UK, and there's gonna be a big party to launch this "hot" new rap record label into the United Kingdom. So me, Adam, Mike, Rick, Russell, and another Def Jam recording artist, LL Cool J, fly to the UK to make it happen.

Driving from the airport into London takes, like, a long-ass time. (Like in that Jam song "London Traffic.") But seeing the city for the first time is so fucking cool. Actual fish-and-chips places. Just like you thought there'd be. Tons of curry houses. Big British taxis. Tiny winding streets. (You guys, there really is an actual Electric Avenue in Brixton.) We finally get to the hotel and have nothing to do for a while, so we go out. Walk around. Do what people do. Get snacks. But since we're away from home, we get a ton of "local" snacks. You know how you do that when you're somewhere else? Like, *I should probably get all four different bags of potato chips 'cause they don't have those styles back home.* It actually worked out this time because I got fuckin' chicken tikka masala–flavored chips. (Sorry . . . I mean . . . flavoured crisps. We're in England.) Back home, we'd call the place we got the snacks from either the deli or the bodega. Here, it's called . . . "the shops." *Gonna go 'round to the shops. Pop down to the shops.* Cornershop. Everyone's got a cool British accent. Like on *Monty Python* or *The Young Ones.* We're spending pounds and pence. The shop people are a little rude to you 'cause they can tell you're American. But that's kinda how you want them to be.

One of the snacks we got was something called a Scotch egg. I don't know if you know what a Scotch egg is, but as we learned, it's a hard-boiled egg, wrapped in sausage meat, breaded, then fried. Looking out the hotel-room window we see a British gentleman right out of central casting walking down the street. Maybe, like, sixty years old. Wearing a nice black suit and a bowlerish-style black hat. A proper gentleman. So, of course, the first thing that comes to your mind is . . . *I wonder if . . . from up here . . . can I hit that guy with this Scotch egg?* I mean, throwing a bag of chips (sorry, crisps) out a fifth-floor window at someone doesn't make sense. It'd take a while to get down there . . . it's an odd object to throw, and obviously, the wind would be a factor. But a Scotch egg is perfect. Kids, I'm neither encouraging nor condoning this behavior, I'm just letting you know what happened on our trip to England.

We're in London for a few days to "work." Do some interviews, meet the people at the UK record label, etc. But that was daytime. At night we were on our own. Our friend from New York, photographer Josh Cheuse, was

friends with Mick Jones from The Clash. He worked with them a little bit and hooked it up for us to go hang out with him one night. AT HIS FUCKIN' HOUSE! I'd like to preface this by letting you know that this was one of my favorite nights. Ever. It was one of those times where you can't believe this is actually happening to you. (But in a really good way) So, we go to Mick Jones's house. He lived in a normal house, not the kind you'd think one of The Clash would live in. It wasn't a dark and depressing tiny British house like in *Quadrophenia*. His house was grown-up and fancy. Three or four floors. Nice furniture. Paintings and shit. And by the way, he is one of the nicest people in the world. We meet, hang out, have a little tea, a couple beers, and then he shows us his studio in the basement. Not a practice space, but a nice little studio,

with all kinds of equipment. While Mick Jones is showing us a guitar of his, Yauch asks him to play "Clash City Rockers." I don't know what possessed him to do that but, I mean, *fuck yeah*, I wanted that to happen. He kind of laughed and said that he forgot how to play it, and so Yauch took the guitar and taught Mick Jones how to play the song. Yes! Mick Jones from The fucking Clash. To quote my friend Bridget . . . "Story doesn't end there." Oh wait . . . Someone's at the door. Yup. It's Joe fucking Strummer! Our new close friend Mick Jones had said some people were coming over; and maybe we could have some beers, hang out, and go see a movie. We could've either gone back to the hotel to eat, then sleep, or done this. Tough call. Now Joe Strummer's here and we're all drinking Red Stripe Crucial Brews, which are delicious, and the doorbell rings again. . . . It's fucking Johnny fucking Rotten! He's with this cool-ass German lady (who was the mom of Ari Up from the Slits) and we are now officially drunk, and freaking out. In Mick Jones's living room. We're getting ready to go see a movie, and one more person shows up on our way out. Take a guess . . . could be any-fuckin'-body, right? It is one of the coolest people in the world. Ever.

Paul Simonon.

Oh . . . the movie we're about to go see is called *Re-Animator*. (A great movie. Not quite on par with *TerrorVision*, but still a fine, fine film.) Now . . . Picture yourself with your two best friends . . . real tipsy. Driving around the streets of London at night in two cabs with, basically, The fucking Clash and Johnny Rotten. Stopping at red lights, laughing, screaming, and throwing things at each other out the windows. I mean . . . just a few years ago, these people made music that changed our lives. We absolutely and totally fucking

love them. And now we're getting drunk with them and we're on our way to go see a slasher movie together. IN LONDON!!!

We were getting our incidentals paid for by the record label, which means free room service. (Obviously nothing is free. We'd soon learn that. "Wait . . . they said that the flights and hotels were paid for. . . . You mean they're gonna just charge it back to us later . . . ?") So one night we have some people over to our hotel, and order a ton of food and drinks. By now it's really late so we figured the right thing to do before going to bed was to order a fish entree and some salad, break into Rick Rubin's room, and slip it all under his sheets while he's sleeping. I can't remember for sure, but I think we put a big plant or small tree on Russell Simmons while he was sleeping too. I don't know if it still works but . . . if you know what hotel room someone's staying in, you can go down to the front desk, looking really sleepy and out of it, and tell them that you're that person in room whatever and you somehow locked yourself out of the room and can you please have an extra key to let yourself back in. This was something we made a steady practice of. (Chuck Eddy . . . where you at!?!)

So now we've thrown all kinds of snacks at British pedestrians, had a big party, broken into other guests' rooms, and well . . . the long and short of it is . . . we found out the next morning that we were banned for life from the wonderful chain of Hilton hotels. We had to move on. No big deal.

Actually, Adam, it was Holiday Inns. (MD)

There's plenty of other places to stay in London.

I feel like I'm telling you all about a vacation I went on, but it felt just like that. Every day of this London trip something amazing and memorable happened. We met a ton of new people and hung out with some of the great ones. Like Don Letts. For some reason he likes us and gives us some dancehall reggae mixtapes that changed the way we thought about making music. Through another New York friend, Peter Dougherty, we go to a recording studio to hang out with this little-known band maybe you've heard of called Madness. We were so overwhelmed and excited and jet-lagged and drunk from drinking snake-

A snakebite, of course, is lager and hard cider mixed. And a black-and-tan is pale lager and dark lager mixed. (AH)

bites and black-and-tans in the studio that me, Adam, and Mike passed out asleep on a couch in the corner of the recording studio. I think all the stimulation of the past few days got to us and we just shut down.

Everything on the trip led up to the big launch party for Def Jam. The party ended up being like the finale of a movie when everything gets wrapped up all neatly. Everyone we met that week was there. Even Paul Simonon. Our performance that night was awful, but for us it was as fun as cannonballing into a swimming pool. London is awesome.

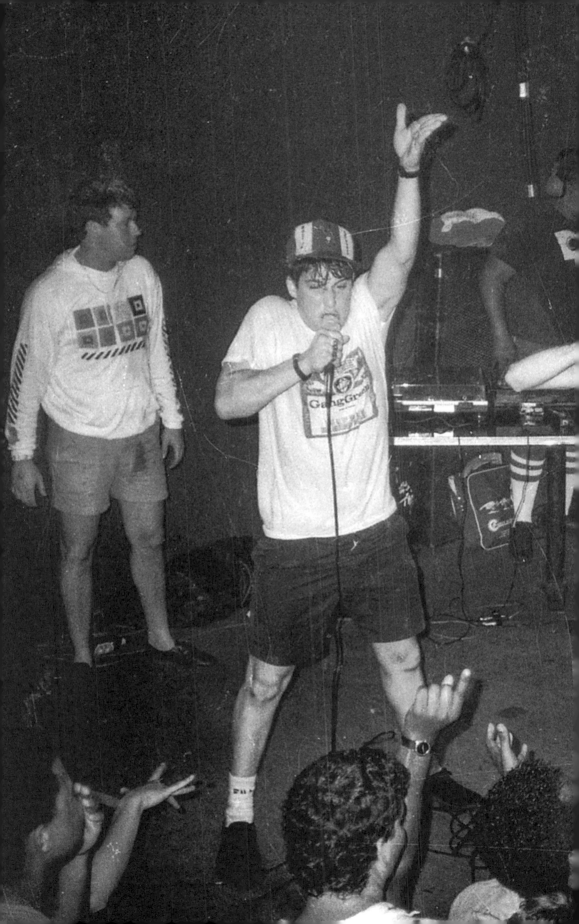

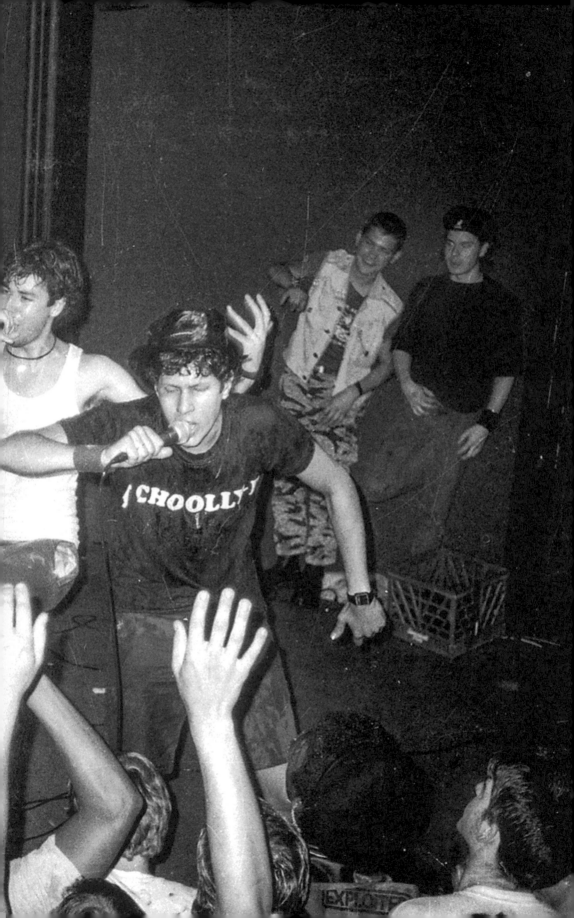

The Song That Changed Everything
(MD)

Sometime in early 1986, we started to focus on making another 12-inch for Def Jam.

Even though our first two had sort of been duds, the label was doing really well, and we'd been on tour with Madonna, so there was momentum, even if it hadn't exactly been created by us.

Our creative process wasn't complicated: mostly we spent a lot of time just hanging out. By now, we were all out of school. Aside from crappy part-time jobs, we really had no responsibilities; when we weren't working, we'd just wander around. No mission and no permission. We'd drink Ballantine Ale sheathed in brown paper bags. Critique graffiti pieces and tags. Listen to music blasting from boxes or cars or large wooden speakers set up in storefronts. All of a sudden, there were rap shows on the radio where there hadn't been before. Great shows, like Mr. Magic on WBLS, the *Zulu Beats* show on WHBI, and DJ Red Alert on KISS-FM.

On one of these afternoons, Horovitz and Rick started going back and forth with little bits from records we loved or just thought were funny. That part at the beginning of Kurtis Blow's "Christmas Rappin'," when he interrupts the Christmas carol by saying "Hold it now!" The way Slick Rick says "Hit it" at the end of the intro to the Doug E. Fresh hit "La Di Da Di." That "Yo, Leroy!" shout from "The Return of Leroy Pt. 1" by the Jimmy Castor Bunch. Phrases, horn stabs, drumrolls: the more records we bought and listened to, the larger our "internal libraries" became. We would voraciously consume sounds and lyrics, fractions of a bar, and just get them stuck in our heads. Then, against the backdrop of New York City, they'd come shooting back out of our mouths. So picture some eighteen-year-old kid walking down the street saying "Hold it now" in a fake low voice to his friends, and his friends answering back with a high-pitched "Hit it!"

At the time, we were working on and off at a studio called Secret Society. It was up in this maze of a loft building on Lafayette Street in Chinatown. Secret Society essentially had an open-door policy with Rick; the owner didn't need the studio to bring in money, because at the time the studio was mostly being used for "other purposes." The only people working there legitimately were the people working with Rick, so it wasn't like you had to call up the studio and say, "Well, in regards to our session on Monday . . ." We could just leave our shit there—drum machines, records, turntables, whatever—and kind of wander in and out. So that was where we went—without Rick—and got down to the brass tacks of trying the idea we'd stumbled upon while walking

When *Licensed to Ill* was finished, we liked the studio so much that we didn't want other people to start booking it—we wanted the studio to remain like it was, someplace we could just sort of use whenever. So on the album's credits, instead of putting that the music was recorded at "Secret Society Studios," we said it was recorded at the "Chung King House of Metal." But John King, who owned the studio—hence the name Chung King—outwitted us and just changed the name. Then it immediately became a real professional studio that was booked all the time. And still is. (MD)

around: a song built around the "Hold it now" and "Hit it" samples.

The first thing Horovitz did was make a drumbeat. A few months before, he'd bought a used 12-inch at St. Mark's Sounds: "Let's Get Small" by Trouble Funk. That shit was banging. Trouble Funk was a go-go band; go-go was *the* regional music of Washington, DC. It was a localized variation of funk that could be identified mostly by its rhythms: kick drums on the upbeats or the "and"s, with bongos or percussion kind of dancing over the beat. It was instantly recognizable. We loved it.

Inspired by Doug E. Fresh's "The Show" and Trouble Funk and Chuck Brown & the Soul Searchers, Horovitz programmed a beat on the DX drum machine that had real go-go swing. We combined that with a simpler 808 beat that had a big sustained kick drum. Then Horovitz scratched in the "Hold it now," "Hit it," and "Yo, Leroy" parts, as well as the whistle and horn parts. We were left to our own devices (literally) and loving it. When Rick was producing, he brought a more set agenda and sound into the studio—there was less experimentation. Left alone, we felt comfortable and excited with this new kind of collage format we had stumbled upon.

Once it got down to writing the lyrics, we were loose. On our first couple of Def Jam 12-inches, the lyrics were self-conscious—we were trying to sound and write like other rap groups that had come before us. Here, we just started writing about the ridiculous stuff we did and saw. A combination of personal experience and fantasy, but fully our own vision. Our main goal was really just

to crack each other up. A bunch of the lines probably make no sense to anyone but us. Like the last one: "Surgeon general cut professor DJ Thiggs." DJ Thiggs wasn't an actual DJ; he was just some guy that DJ Run knew. Run would always tell us that Thiggs would be a great DJ if he were a DJ, so we name-checked him, sight-unseen. Turns out he couldn't spin, really, at all—which made the whole thing funnier to us. The whole song was like that, just whatever crazy shit we came up with.

After a few days, we'd finished putting the song together. Rick came by and we played it for him. He kind of flipped out. *Don't change anything. It's great. I want to play it for Russell.* Russell came over, straight out the club and fueled by who knows how many screwdrivers. He flipped out too. *We need to just put this out.* We were surprised, but excited. Rick mixed it, making it sound bigger and more professional—just generally more legit. Most important, he made that 808 sound crazy.

A few weeks later, the song—now titled "Hold It Now, Hit It"—came out as our third 12-inch. Mix shows up and down the East Coast started playing it. It was in record pools. Legit rap DJs really wanted it. We're not talking about the quirky Danceteria success of "Cooky Puss." Our shit was getting played on hip hop radio and in real hip hop clubs, at block parties, in schoolyard jams. In this world, no one knew who we were or what we looked like or even where we came from. It didn't matter. What mattered was when the intro to that record dropped and crowds heard that "Hold it now" phrase followed by the roll and the 808 kick on the verse, they went crazy. You could hear that 808 rattling the rear glass on cars up and down the East Coast. It also detonated many a PA, overloading the low end and making shit just shut right down.

In retrospect, "Hold It Now, Hit It" changed everything for us. Instead of trying to act and sound like someone else, we were just being ourselves, writing from our own lives and experiences for the first time since *Polly Wog Stew*. We figured out how to piece together different elements that we loved (beats, samples from our favorite records, turntable scratches) and turn them into a song. We had, in short, found our voice.

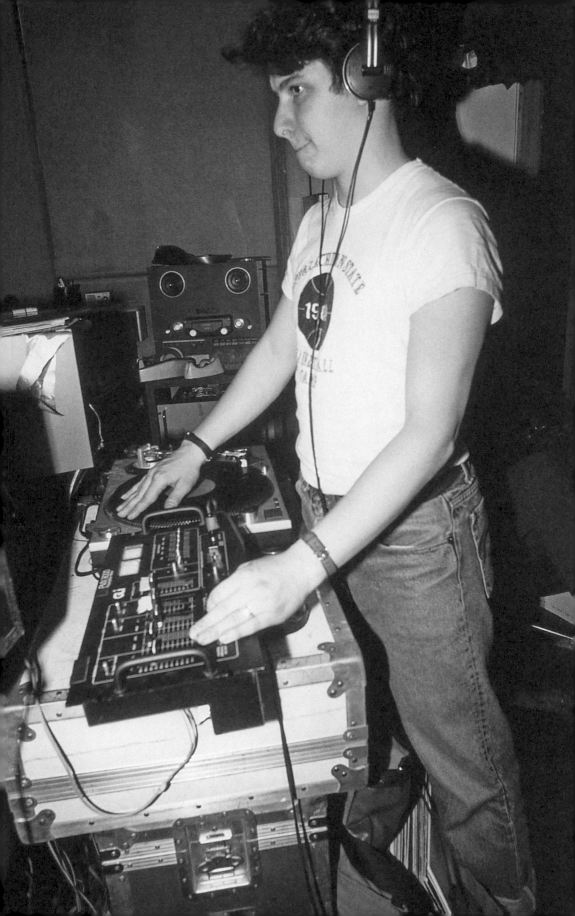

MC SHY D

AND
A DOZEN EGGS

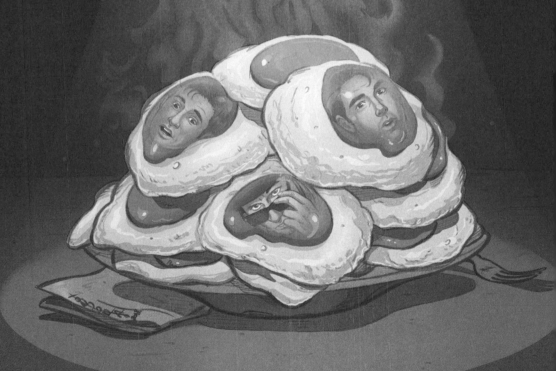

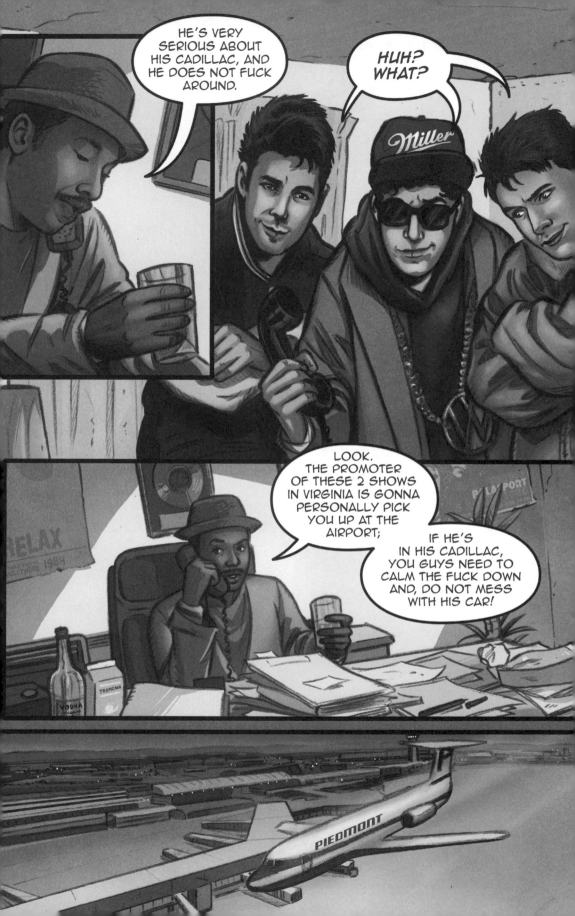

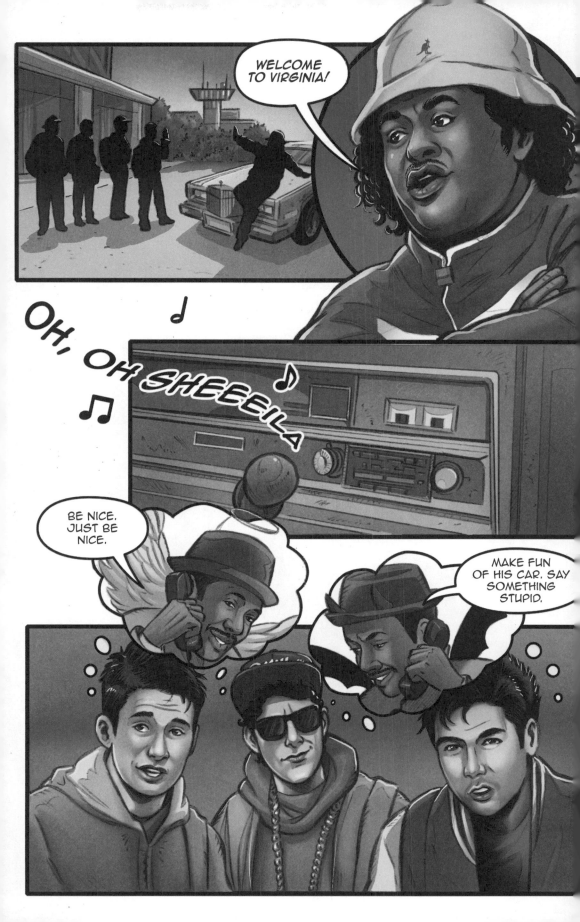

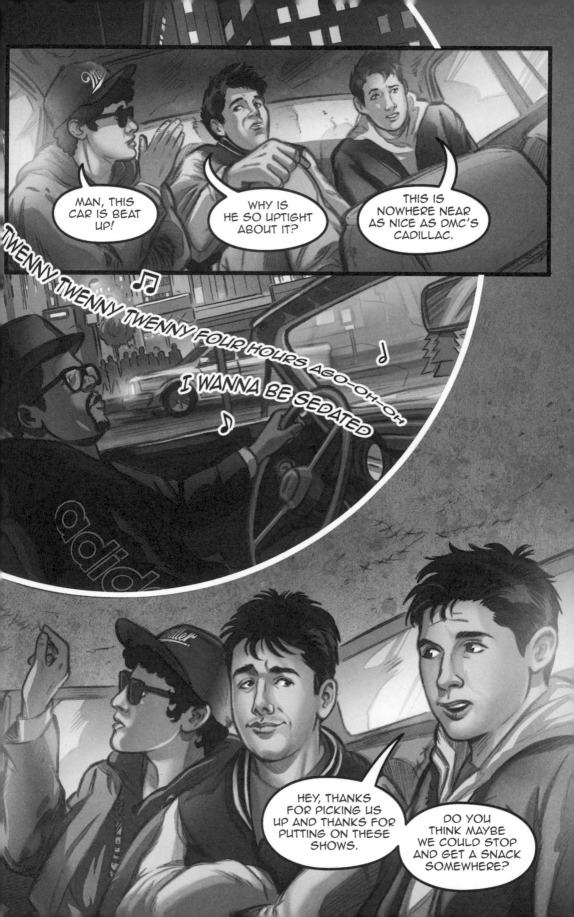

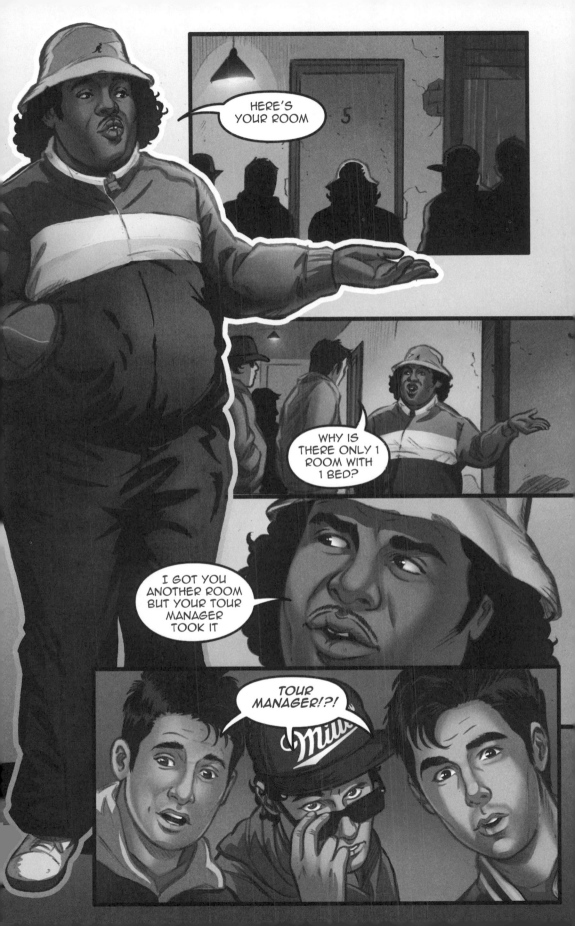

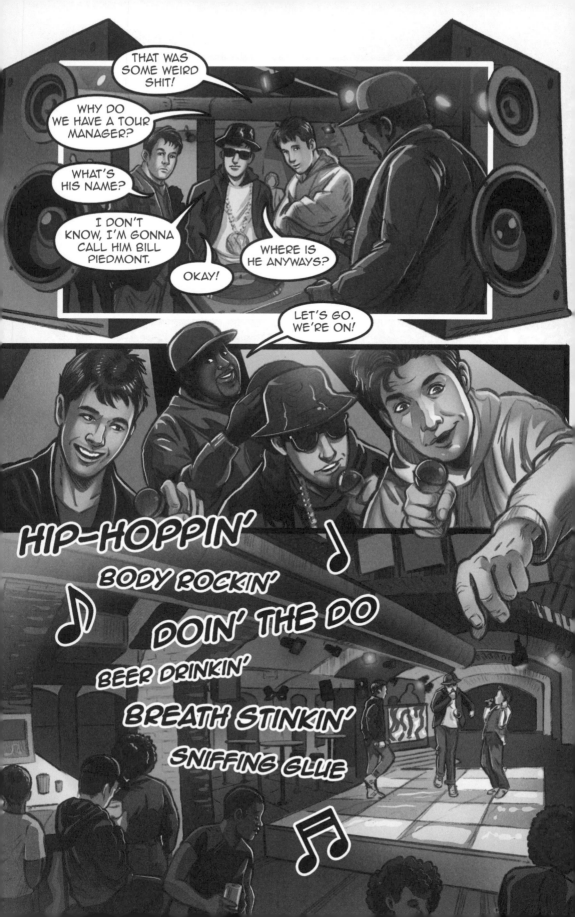

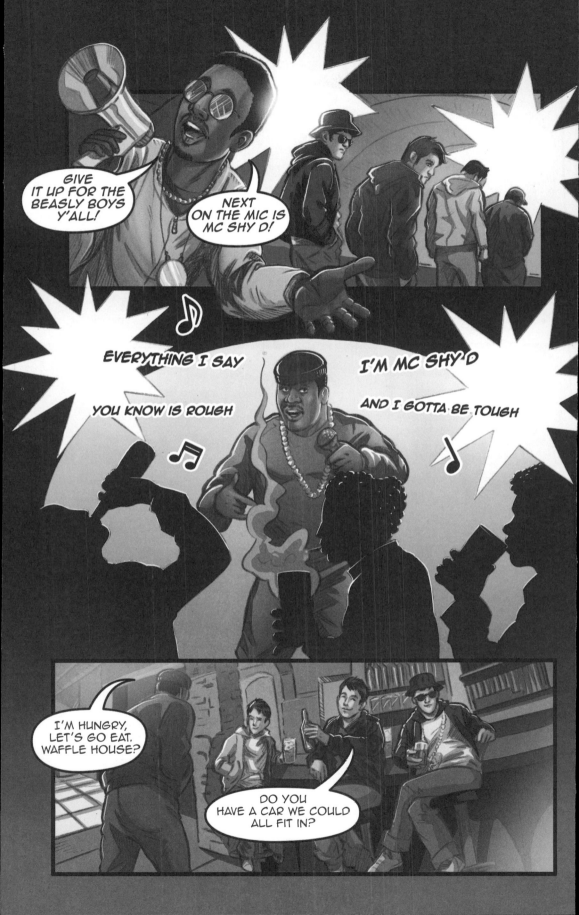

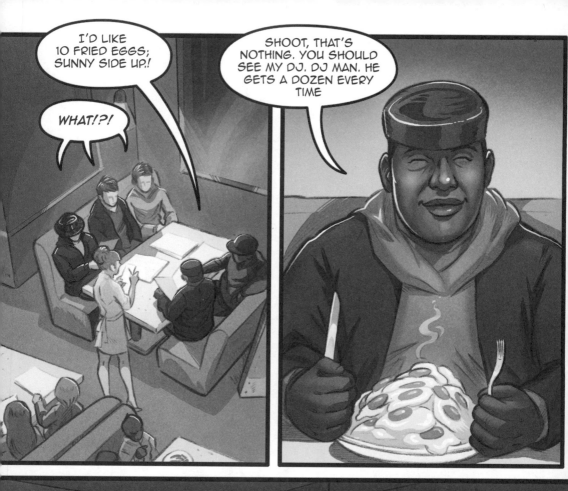

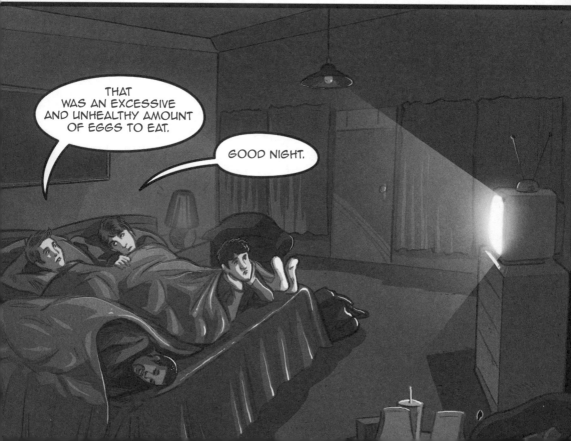

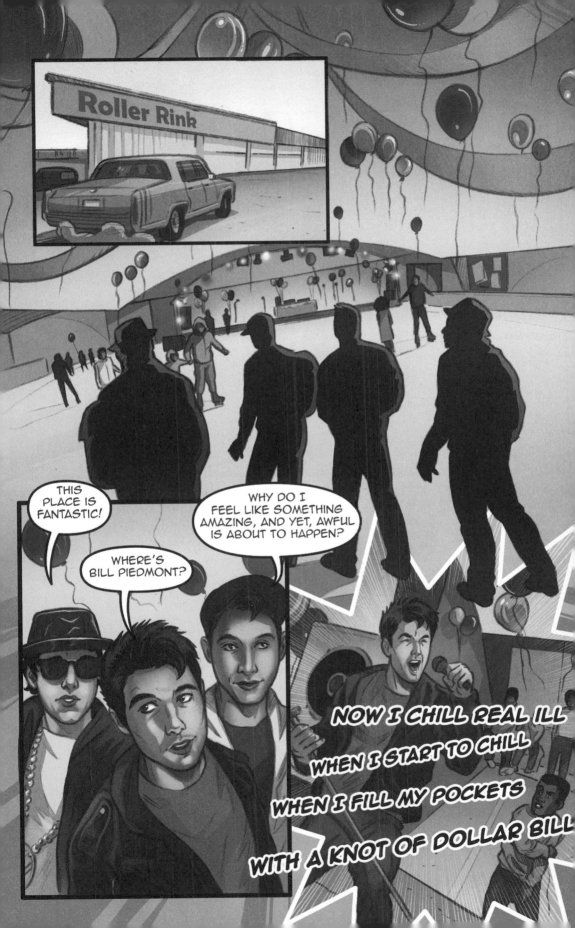

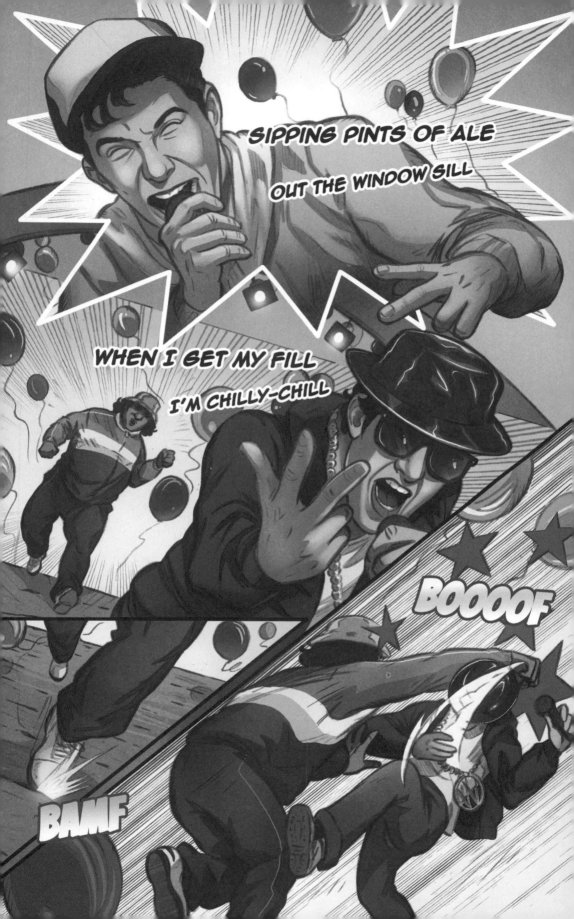

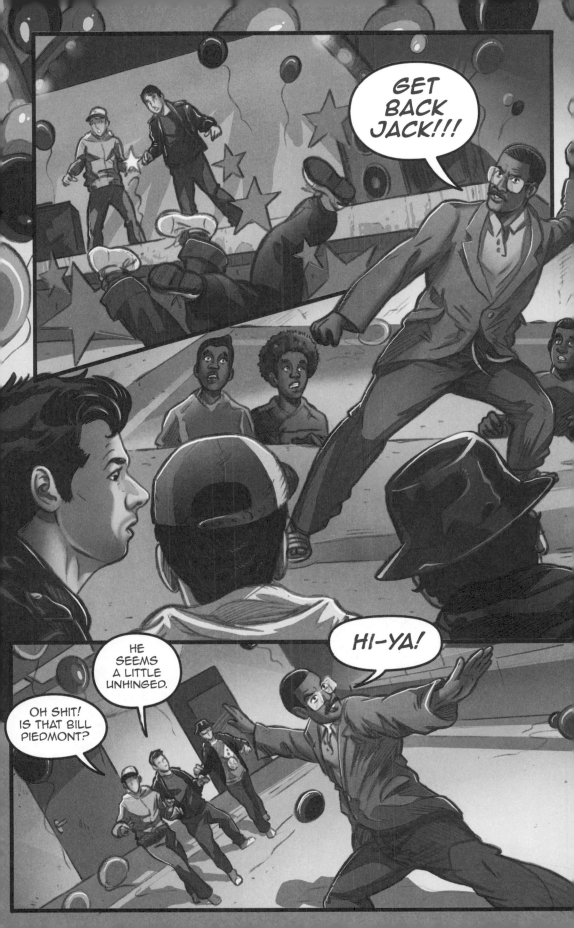

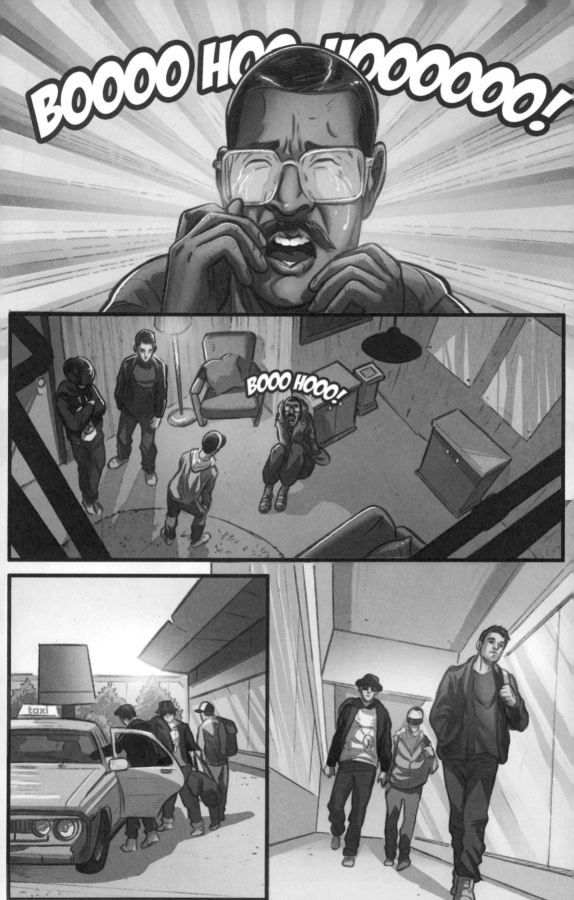

HAAHHA - HAHAHA

IT WAS TOTALLY CRAZY. THE DUDE JUST RUSHED THE STAGE AND...

WAIT, DID HE HAVE JUICE WITH THE 10 FRIED EGGS?

CAUSE IT'S THE JUICE THAT FILLS YOU UP

Walk

Rick Rubin was getting ready to start producing Run-DMC's next record, *Raising Hell*, and he had this idea that they should do a new version of the Aerosmith song "Walk This Way." The original version starts with a nice breakbeat, and so it'd be an interesting idea to use that and see what a rap version would sound like. He took it a step further and contacted Joe Perry and Steve Tyler (from Aerosmith) to see if they'd want to play guitar and sing the chorus on this new Run-DMC version. They said yes. There was no way we were gonna miss that shit, so we made sure to be in the studio when they recorded it. Joe Perry seemed just like what you'd think he'd be like. (Do you think about Joe Perry a lot?) He seemed quiet, cool, and laid-back in the cut. Steve Tyler was also just what you'd think he'd be like. He did not stop talking the entire time. He wasn't really making sense, and would randomly just start scatting. Like boogety-woogety-boo-type stuff. Run, D, and Jay were kind of loving it. Like, *Who the fuck is this ancient court jester wearing silk clothing and thirty scarves?* He's definitely making us laugh (uncomfortably). "But wait . . . Rick, you're sure this is a good idea, right?"

This

I don't know if you've ever been in a room, or on a random small-town street, somewhere, and it's just you, a *really* famous person, and one other person that's uncontrollably screaming or crying with excitement and disbelief at seeing that famous person. It's really awkward. Going to do anything with Run-DMC in 1986 in America was bizarre. They were fucking HUGE. We'd go with them to a restaurant, mall, gas station, whatever, and people would come running from their houses and apartments and leave work to see them, because word of mouth started spreading around the neighborhood that they were there. People would freak the fuck out. They were so large that by the time their *Raising Hell* tour got to Miami, the promoters upgraded their venue from basketball arena to baseball stadium. THOUSANDS+THOUSANDS of people. Joe Perry and Steve Tyler were flying down to Miami just to do the song with them. It was bound to be a fucking spectacle. We were one of the opening bands on that tour, and Yauch, for whatever reason, happened to have a bass with him, and someone, probably Jam Master Jay, said it would be okay for him to play bass with them and Aerosmith for the big song onstage in a baseball stadium in Miami. YES!

Steve Tyler and Joe Perry didn't do a sound check, and so they had no idea who Yauch was.

CUT TO: The big moment when Aerosmith is about to hit the stage to join Run-DMC to play the #1 song on the entire planet. They walk out, and the crowd goes wild. But . . . now there's also some other guy onstage. Yauch. And he was *LIT UP*. We all were. Super drunk all day, waiting for this moment. And Yauch fucking delivered: majestically. The look on the Aerosmith guys' faces was fantastic bemusement. Who is this dirty drunk guy onstage? And why is he playing bass? With us? Throughout the whole song, Yauch kept trying to go back-to-back rock-guitar-player-style with Joe Perry, who was having none of it. It basically turned into Yauch chasing him around the stage, running backward after him. And all of us were on the side of the stage watching, screaming, laughing, and *lov—ing—it*.

Way

Not for nothing, but . . . I feel like there was always a spin on "Walk This Way" that Aerosmith was this HUGE band that blew Run-DMC up. This little-known group with this new sound called "rap music." As if Run+them would be nowhere without Aerosmith. Yes . . . the original "Walk This Way" was an insanely big record, but Aerosmith's days of being an arena rock band were behind them. No offense, but no one really gave a shit about them in 1986. Real Talk™. If it wasn't for Run-DMC doing that song with *them*, who knows what would've become of Aerosmith. I mean, shit . . . we might not have ever had to endure "Love in an Elevator" or "Dude Looks Like a Lady." Thanks a lot, Rick Rubin, for your brilliant fucking ideas.   (AH)

Perhaps the Shortest Headlining Gig in History
(MD)

August 1986. We were playing the Oakland–Alameda County Coliseum Arena on the *Raising Hell* tour, and playing our first-ever L.A. headlining gig later that same night. The plan was that we'd get offstage in Oakland at around 7:45, fly to L.A., and play a late show at the club Power Tools, which was located in an amazing old ballroom at the former Park Plaza Hotel on MacArthur Park. At the time, Power Tools was to L.A. what Danceteria was to NYC: an underground nightclub that catered to art students, aspiring musicians, club kids, and everything in between. We were psyched; playing two shows on the same night in different cities was like some Phil Collins Live Aid–type shit to us, especially if one of the gigs was headlining an underground club.

The people from Power Tools told us that a driver'd be waiting for us at LAX, so when we landed, we were on the lookout for, like, a driver in a suit holding a placard. Instead, we were greeted by a short kid who legit looked twelve years old. His hair was brushed back, rocker-style, and he was wearing a leather jacket; instead of making him look older, though, all of that made him look even younger, like a kid sporting a *Grease* costume for Halloween. His name was Max Perlich, and he was driving this ginormous white Chrysler Imperial. I'm sure he didn't actually sit on phone books to see over the steering wheel, but that was the vibe.

On the way to the club, he told us we needed to buy booze for the DJ booth. To us, this was already an odd task—like what club wouldn't have that squared away before now? But then, instead of just walking into the liquor store, Max had to ask people walking in and out of the store to buy the booze for him; he was only eighteen, and he definitely didn't look like he could pass for twenty-one. It took a while for someone to say yes. While we waited and then drove to the club, Max regaled us with various tall(ish) tales, the kind that I later discovered were his forte. He was a successful character actor—as in, that was literally his job—but Max was fundamentally an L.A. club kid, a real music fan. Like, if it were this day and age, he'd be a DJ. In that era, even though he knew a lot and had tons of vinyl, Max was just an actor who was really into music.

Soon we were up in the DJ booth having some drinks. Power Tools was packed. The DJ—and co-owner/mastermind of the club—was a guy named Matt Dike. That night, he played everything from the Junkyard Band to Doug E. Fresh to Led Zeppelin. People were *into* it. We were getting all psyched, thinking, *Wow, we are finally getting to kill it headlining our own show in L.A.* (It didn't

Horovitz and I were only nineteen and twenty then; Yauch would have just turned twenty-two, but obviously he didn't feel like volunteering for this mission. (MD)

213

hurt that the place was packed with beautiful L.A. women, whom we imagined meeting immediately following our soon-to-be-triumphant gig.) In the audience, we'd find out later, were musicians from Fishbone and Jane's Addiction—kindred spirits who made up an L.A. scene similar to ours in New York; Bob Forrest, the singer of Thelonious Monster, was running sound for our show.

Right before we went onstage, a dude with long, straight hair bum-rushed us and said, "Hi, I'm Anthony and I'm going to say something and introduce you guys." Before we could even react, he went onstage and read some spoken-word thing that we couldn't hear anyway. (The guy, we soon realized, was Anthony Kiedis from the Red Hot Chili Peppers, with whom we'd played a show earlier that year.) Then DJ Hurricane played some kind of intro, and we went onstage as he dropped "Slow and Low."

Then we started rapping.

The sound was utter garbage. You could barely hear the music, our vocals were way too loud, and anytime we all rapped at the same time, the whole thing got distorted and the sound started to cut out entirely. Bob Forrest, by his own admission, was not a soundman. He definitely didn't know hip hop or understand low end or 808 kick drums.

We somehow made it through that first song, but on the very first beat of the next one, "Hold It Now, Hit It"—when that 808 kick drum dropped—the entire PA blew out. Completely gone.

Now, by this point in our careers, we'd played a good batch of shows and had some idea of what they took, both musically and professionally. So when the entire sound system got blown while we played a headlining gig to 1,500(ish) paid audience members, did we tap into that reservoir of professionalism and experience to get the problem worked out?

No, we most certainly did not.

Transcript of our stage banter during the first song: "Yo, man, what the fuck is wrong with you, turn the music up!" "I don't know about you, but in New York we're not a bunch of suckers. Did I say that?"

Transcript of our stage banter after the PA blew: "We gotta get outta here." "Yo, the sound system sucks my dick, no offense to anybody." "Y'all come down to the Palladium on Monday, we're gonna kick some fucking ass."

And then we left.

A few things happened in the club after we took off—which we wouldn't find out about until years later—that had a far greater impact on our trajectory as a band than the disastrous show itself. One of the angry attendees we left behind was a young engineer and musician named Mario Caldato, who tracked down Matt Dike and his co-owner Jon Sidel and said, *This place is a joke. I have a PA system. I should set up my PA at your club and you need to let me run the PA and the sound.* Matt hired Mario on the spot.

Power Tools closed the following year, but by then Matt wanted to start recording as a producer. So Mario started bringing some of his recording

equipment over to Matt's apartment in (a shady part of) Hollywood and became his engineer. That crap apartment was where Matt co-wrote and produced massive hits for Tone Lōc ("Wild Thing," "Funky Cold Medina") and Young MC ("Bust a Move"). It was there that we later made (most of) our second album.

Before all that, though, we needed to make our first.

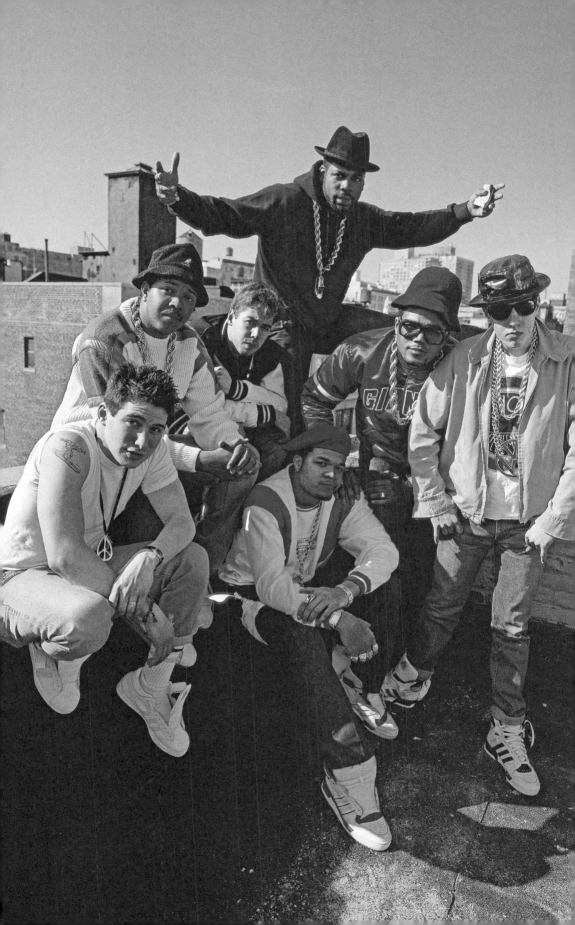

Here's a Little Story (I Got to Tell...)
(AH)

Me, Adam, and Mike were sitting on a stoop, outside a random recording studio Russell had booked for us, on Twenty-First Street between Broadway and Park. We were waiting for Run and DMC. The plan was for us to write and record a song together. It was probably nine P.M. Probably summertime. We probably had bags of beers. What I know for sure is that I was thinking as we sat there waiting on that stoop . . . *Just a couple years ago, me and Dave Scilken got busted for writing graffiti, so we ran and hid from the police in a stairwell leading to a basement, two doors down from where we are sitting now. And here we are, waiting to record a song with the greatest of all time, Run-DMC.* We were sitting there on that stoop, with our probable bags of beers, waiting in fucking psyched anticipation.

Then we heard a sound. A voice. It was getting louder. We looked down the block, and it was Run. He'd turned the corner and was now barreling toward us . . . screaming . . . "Here's a little story I got to tell!!!" over and over. (Run was total walking comic mania. Him *and* his brother Russell. Frantic energy. They must've been insane toddlers.) Run caught up to us. Way out of breath. We saw D, far behind him, turn the corner and slowly stride toward our stoop. "Here's a little story I got to tell!!! The song'll be like a story. Your story. Here's a little story I got to tell, about three bad brothers you know so well. It started way back, in history . . . with ADROCK, MCA, and me, Mike D." DMC walked up. "Yup. That's it. That's the intro."

So remember . . . the three of us were just sitting there on a stoop, and there's Run fuckin' DMC. Wearing their Run-DMC outfits. Hats and all. They were standing right there. Seemingly almost as excited as we were. And they were giving us an intro to a song. Me, Adam, and Mike are trying to contain our exhilaration. When LeBron passes you the ball, you don't just hold it and yell, "Oh my God oh my God, LeBron James just passed me the ball!" No. You crossover the sucker who's trying to guard you, and you drive the lane furiously.

We all went up to the recording studio, and began the process of writing and recording a rap song: make a beat, record that beat to tape, and then record yourself rapping over that beat. It was lucky for us (and Suzuki Samurais throughout the country) that we thought to bring my Roland TR-808 drum machine with us. We were talking about what the beat should be like, and Yauch, seemingly out of nowhere (like a thousand other ideas of his) said . . . "Let's just make a simple drum pattern, but flip the tape over and record the drum machine backwards." We all looked at him like Shaggy+Scooby. *HUH!?!*

"Yeah . . . you flip the reel-to-reel tapes upside down, press Play on the drum machine, and play and record on the tape deck. Then after three to five minutes, stop recording, flip the tape right side up, and listen back. The drum machine will have recorded backwards." It was fucking magical. (And very typical of Adam Yauch. "Oh yeah . . . I heard how you could pull a rabbit out of a hat and so . . . here's an elephant.") Up until that moment, in 1986, there had never been a beat that sounded as funky fresh, dope, hype, or def. We *never* said this word back then but really . . . the "Paul Revere" beat that Yauch made was fucking AWESOME. The beat was so nice that we must've just gotten lost in it 'cause we didn't actually record any vocals that night. We probably just drank 40s with Run and D and then walked down to the Palladium, knowing that we'd be back at Chung King to finish this song very soon. We hadn't forgotten our priorities; music can wait . . . drink tickets and digits were more important.

A few nights later, Rick and I were walking around, hanging out, and I was telling him how great being in the studio with Run and D was, and how Yauch made this crazy fucking beat and Run was screaming "here's a little story" to Manhattan passersby . . . all of it. We were sitting on the stoop of St. Mark's Sounds record store and I had my little rhyme book and pen on me. So me and Rick started to write the little story we had to tell. The horse's name, Paul Revere, comes from *Guys and Dolls* but . . . you knew that already. I know how deep into show tunes you are. We had just seen the movie *Once Upon a Time in the West* and really liked it. We were in a western kind of mode. So of course . . . Now we're high plains drifters.

During the *Raising Hell* tour, Adidas did a special presentation for Run-DMC at their L.A. offices, and, of course, we tagged along. Adidas presented them with these huge golden Adidas shell-toe sneaker sculptures on rope chains. It was the coolest thing you ever saw, and we were super jealous. After everyone applauded and showered Run, DMC, and Jam Master Jay with the love and golden sneakers they so richly deserved, the room died down a little, and then . . . *our* magical moment. Adidas presented each of us with our very own miniature version of the golden shell-toe. I covet the shit out of that shit. (AH)

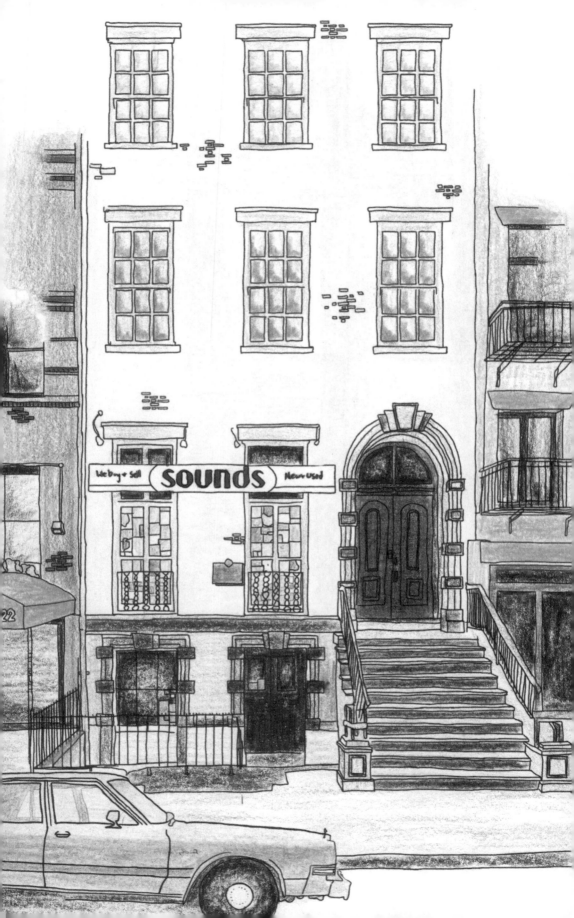

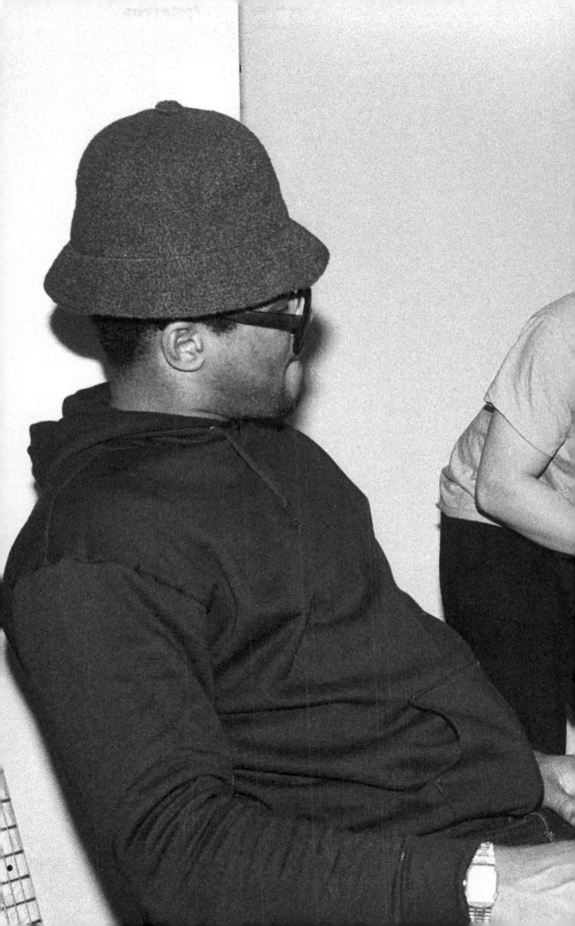

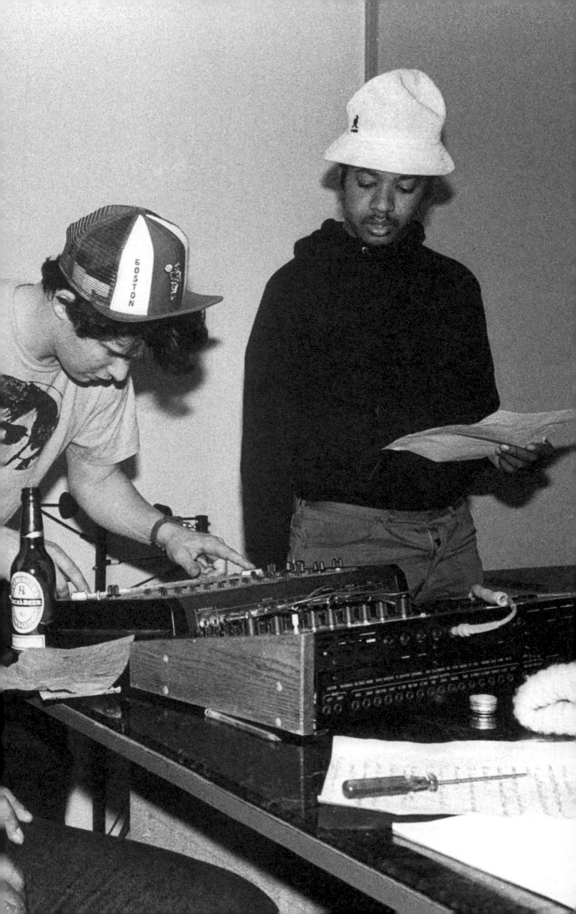

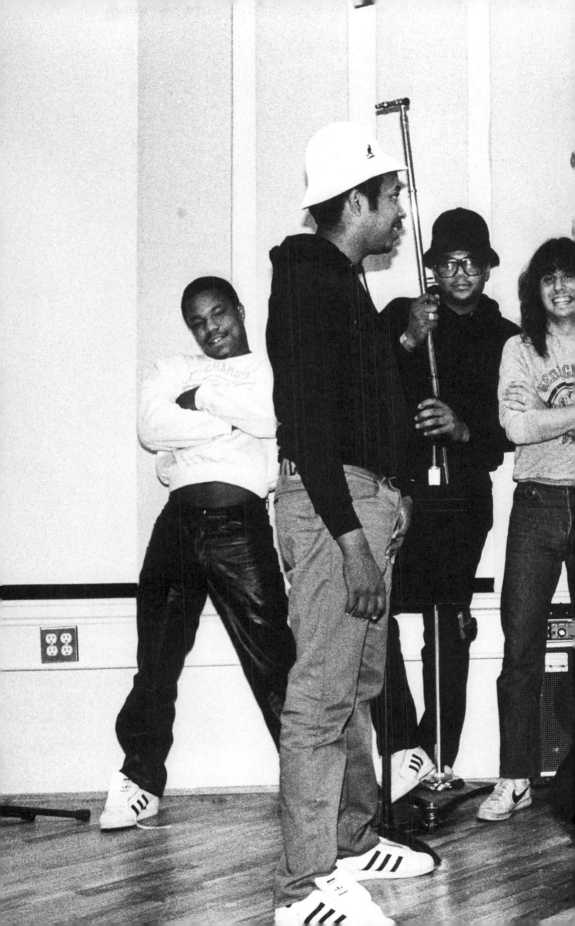

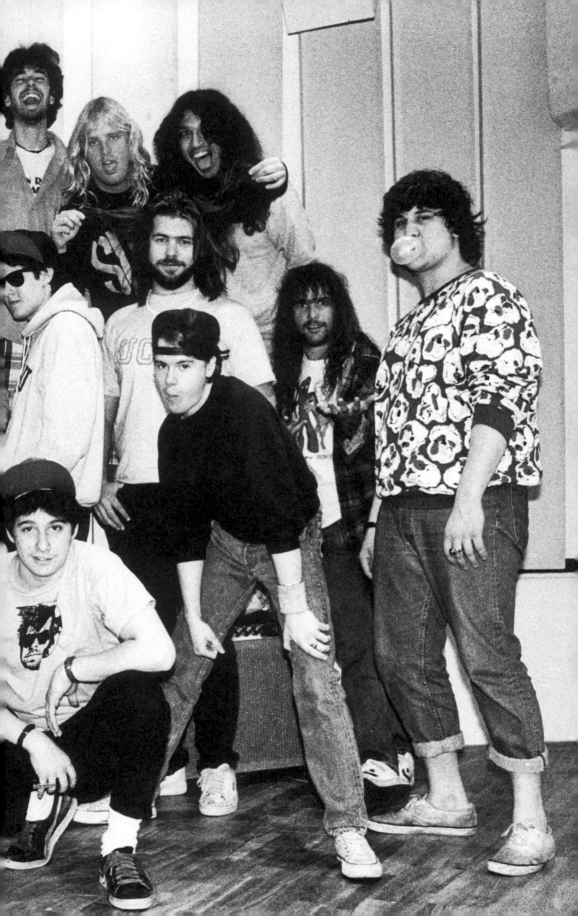

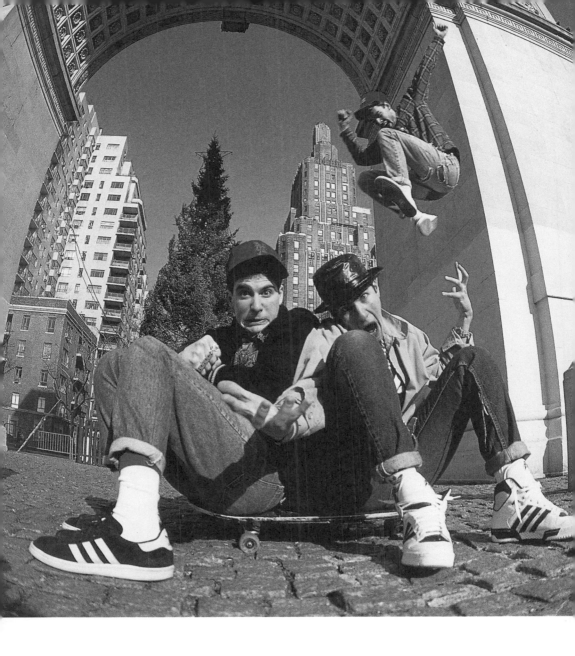

We Liked It. We Hated It.

(MD)

After we moved out of 59 Chrystie, I found a place on Barrow Street in the West Village. The apartment itself was a second-floor walk-up above a bar. Not a glamorous bar at all, kind of like a cop/FedEx-guy hangout. The jukebox speakers were right below my bedroom; that shit would get fucking *loud* on Friday and Saturday nights, blasting Bob Seger and Loverboy until four in the morning. But it wasn't a bad apartment, and we started meeting there to write. I had a stereo, and I hooked up an 808 drum machine and a Tascam 4-track cassette recorder to it, and the three of us started to make demos.

We'd sit around drinking tall boys and coming up with ideas. One came from listening to a Motörhead live album called *No Sleep 'til Hammersmith*. We started batting that name around and came up with the idea of writing this fantasy song about being a huge touring rock band and our hard life on the road. The joke was that we were, like, the opposite of big. I mean we'd played three headlining shows outside of NYC. So all the stuff we put in there was a fantasy version of us as clichéd rock stars. Even the title—"No Sleep Till Brooklyn"— was a joke: Brooklyn is now the hipster capital of the world, but at the time, much of BK was infamous in the hip hop world because it was so rough and dangerous that literally no rap shows could get booked there. Similarly, "The New Style" was a fantasy version of our actual lives. I mean, "Coolin' on the corner on a hot summer's day"? Yes. "A lot of beer, a lot of girls, and a lot of cursing"? Maybe sometimes. "A .22 automatic on my person"? Yeah, maybe not.

One of the things that would serve us well throughout our careers was that we'd usually all sit around and write lyrics together. We'd write for a bit and then—almost like we were playing a game of Boggle—decide that some arbitrary self-imposed timer had gone off and it was time to read aloud what we

had. This could be both intimidating and frustrating—one of us might have a rhyme that we really liked, but that didn't mean the other two guys would vote it in. As ruthless as this process could be, we became each other's best editors.

After inferior lines were vetoed, we'd then organize the mutually approved bits and divide up who was saying what. So as opposed to me writing my own parts, Adam writing his, and so on, all of us co-authored, then divided up the lines after we'd voted on what should stay. In the process, we stumbled

upon what defined *Licensed to Ill*: fantasies of a life that we pretended to have, delivered in interweaving, accented, occasionally doubled and tripled vocals. We loved the Treacherous Three, Funky Four Plus One More, Grandmaster Flash and the Furious Five, and of course Run-DMC, so much that we couldn't wait to switch off rhymes and double lyrics like our heroes had before us. Old-school-crew-style.

The recording process—writing lyrics on Barrow Street, going into Chung King to try music ideas, honing everything into songs that we were happy with—took place over a few months in the spring of 1986. We were becoming more confident songwriters. The only time there was doubt was at the end of making the record, and that was the regular creative doubt you get when you're finishing something and you're like *God, is this really good enough? Does it suck? 'Cause I don't know, I can't even tell anymore. I've listened to this thing ten thousand times now.* We've made eleven albums, and every time I still had that same level of doubt when we got to the end. If I *didn't* have it, I'd feel like something was wrong.

CUT TO: Fall 1986: I was sitting with Run in his car—it was like hanging with your favorite rich uncle, who also happens to be your favorite rapper. Run had a 3-series BMW. Black. Two doors. At the time, it was a huge deal to have one. Only drug dealers had that car. Somehow, the all-powerful Run had scored a cassette of our now almost-complete album. He suggested we listen to it on the only stereo that mattered: the tape player in his BMW.

He popped it in the tape deck. I was fucking nervous. It didn't matter that we had toured together all year and become friends (despite us once having put a selection of cold cuts on the seat of his dressing-room commode). I respected Run so much as an artist that I'd have been devastated if he didn't like the new songs.

From the first song that played, Run seemed into it. I mean, he was playing it LOUD and wasn't fast-forwarding through shit. In the cassette era, that meant you were on to something.

When the tape finished playing, Run said, "You know you're gonna have at least a gold record, right?"

Huh?! That blew my mind. It hadn't crossed any of our minds to have actual commercial aspirations for the record, beyond hoping that the radio stations and DJs we respected would play some of the songs. It seemed enough of an accomplishment that we'd made a record at all.

The New Style—This song has a real chorus, just not a repeated vocal line like a normal pop song. ("Wait a minute, Mr. Postman"; "I can't get no satisfaction"; etc.) "The New Style" has a combination of scratches and beats that make the hook. We started making these songs that had no specific connection between the content of the verses and choruses, and I guess we accidentally did end up with a new style.

(You Gotta) Fight for Your Right (To Party)—Yauch and our friend Tom Cushman wrote the basic idea for this song at 59 Chrystie Street. It was meant to be for a side band that they had called Brooklyn, but they never recorded it. When we were trying to come up with ideas for songs, Yauch offered this one up.

Brass Monkey—One night in 1984, Dave Scilken and I were at a recording studio in Queens with Rick Rubin, a few grown men and women that we did not know, DJ Jazzy Jay, and a rapper named T La Rock. We had all met up there because Rick was recording what would be the first official rap release on Def Jam records, *It's Yours*. We were psyched to be in the presence of a legitimate DJ and rapper. It was an incredible night—we got to go on a road trip all the way out to Queens, eat at a White Castle, hang out with grown-ups and the legendary DJ Jazzy Jay, and we were introduced to Brass Monkey.

It happened so casually. People were passing around a bottle of booze, and when it got to me, I took a sip. Whatever it was that I drank set off an alarm, and as I passed the bottle to Dave Scilken, the thought hit me: *Oh shit. This shit is delicious!* Except I said it out loud. Like, the thought escaped because it had to. Just then I saw the same recognition dawn on Dave's face. I asked DJ Jazzy Jay, who had passed the bottle to me, "Yo, what is this?" and he replied, "That's Brass Monkey, man. You don't know about that?" I didn't. I mean, on second thought, I kind of recognized the bottle from the lower shelves at the deli, where it gathered dust next to bottles of Night Train and Mad Dog 20/20. I'd had those before but just assumed that everything down there was gross. But as Felix Unger observed, "When you assume . . ." (AH)

We wanted "Brass Monkey" to be a song about a dance. Like, say, the Twist, or the Pee-wee Herman. It's not for me to say, but I kinda feel like the up-tempo 808 beat on this was a precursor to Miami bass music. I have had a number of people tell me that they use this song to test the low end in a new car sound system.

Slow and Low—This was actually a cover of a Run-DMC song that they recorded but didn't release for their *King of Rock* LP. We thought it was great and were completely baffled that they'd left it off their album, so we covered it.

Their lost track was our gold mine. We changed the lyrics to include our own names and remade the track completely with Rick.

Licensed to Ill came out on November 15, 1986. "Paul Revere" and "The New Style" had been released as singles. Both did well; they built

on the success of "Hold It Now, Hit It," got played by the same mix shows and club DJs. By early February 1987, the LP had gone platinum. DJ Run had been proven correct. This seemed incredibly fast; we were barely out of high school. Being small-time celebrities in our little NYC nightclub world had been fun; getting a chance to make records was incredible; opening for Madonna and Run-DMC was surreal. But this was something else entirely. And nobody—us, Rick, Run, nobody—could have imagined what happened next.

In February, "(You Gotta) Fight for Your Right (To Party)" came out as a single and video. It wasn't even something we picked as a single; the label chose it. To us, it was practically a throwaway. But in a matter of days, the song blew up on the radio. Not hip hop radio—rock and pop stations were spinning it in heavy rotation. Then MTV started playing the video. The only rap group getting played on MTV was Run-DMC. The "Fight for Your Right" video was a simple, ridiculous thing directed by Mr. Ric (Menello) and Rick Rubin's friend Adam Dubin; we were making fun of the current trend of cheesy pop-metal videos (Mötley Crüe etc.), with a healthy dose of *Blackboard Jungle*, courtesy of film geek Mr. Ric. But MTV played the shit out of it. Obviously, us being white had a ton to do with that.

Weirdly, the moment that this new level of success dawned on us wasn't when MTV started playing the video—it was when the label called us to say we had the front window display at the Tower Records on Fourth and Broadway, a three-story fortress of a store. There was nothing underground about Tower; it was a one-stop shopping mall of music. Yauch's uncle Freddie would stand outside Tower and stop people walking down the street and be like, "My nephew's in this band. They're great. You gotta go in there and buy one of his records."

Overnight, we went from being New York famous—maybe the best kind of famous you can be, actually—to being national MTV star–type famous. We went from Rat Cage to

Tower, from rap mix shows to Casey Kasem's top 10, from U68 to *American Bandstand*. A lot was happening. To capitalize, we toured for twelve months straight—first as headliners, then on the co-headlining "Together Forever" tour with Run-DMC. We decided to see how far over the top we could make everything we did, in any way we could imagine (and even some we couldn't)—from hiring a stupid-long limousine (with exterior jump seats in the far back) for our NYC homecoming gig at the Ritz to having a giant hydraulic penis onstage just because we could. We were suddenly rock stars, and we definitely embraced it.

Over the course of those months on the road, we went from being like, *This is the most exciting thing ever, I can't believe we're actually rock stars* to thinking, *God, people really expect us to be these idiot caricatures of ourselves night after night. This kind of sucks.* I know that might sound ungrateful or ungracious. It's just that we only saw ourselves as a band that played music we loved. We didn't see ourselves having to act out a role, having to go onstage and be the three guys who throw beer and have a giant dick for a prop. And it had never occurred to us that it would start to be demanded of us. We honestly just didn't know.

We never performed "(You Gotta) Fight for Your Right (To Party)" after 1987. Partly because it was a marker in time for when things went sour, but mainly because the song turned corny, quick.

It took a few years for us to be able to look back at the good stuff on this record. (AH)

We came from this punk-rock background. There was a conscious identity choice in that. Then, being in a rap band, we felt pretty sure that we were still speaking to our people. But when it became this huge thing, and all these, like, frat dudes were buying our records and coming to shows, we realized we couldn't control any of it. You appreciate anyone who appreciates you, as long as they're genuine to a degree, but we weren't ready for something so big. *What the hell just happened . . . and what do we do now?*

Designer labels always get ripped off.

People have been sporting our Volkswagen badge for years.

Proudly displaying it on the front of their cars.

Recently, though, many have been heard to out-swear a Beastie Boy (the result of finding their badges have gone missing).

Their protests haven't fallen on deaf ears.

Because, as of now, our badge is a positive steal.

In fact, it's free.

You can lay your hands on one of your own (as opposed to somebody else's) simply by writing to us at the address below.

Let it never be said that we're averse to youth cults.

After all, who brought you the Beetles.

42

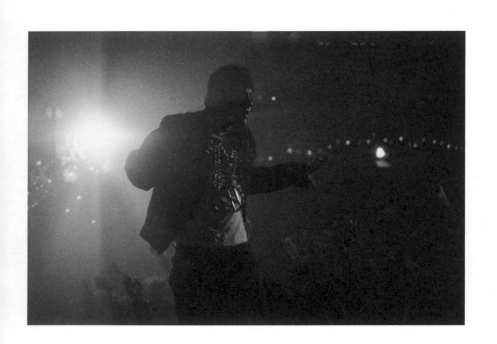

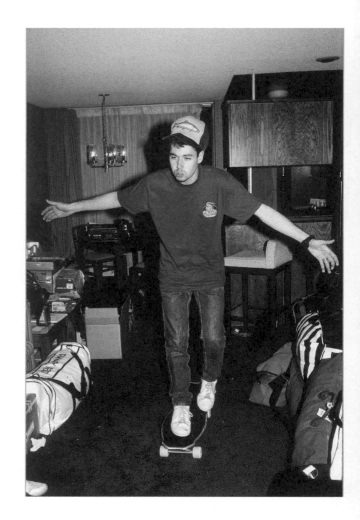

231

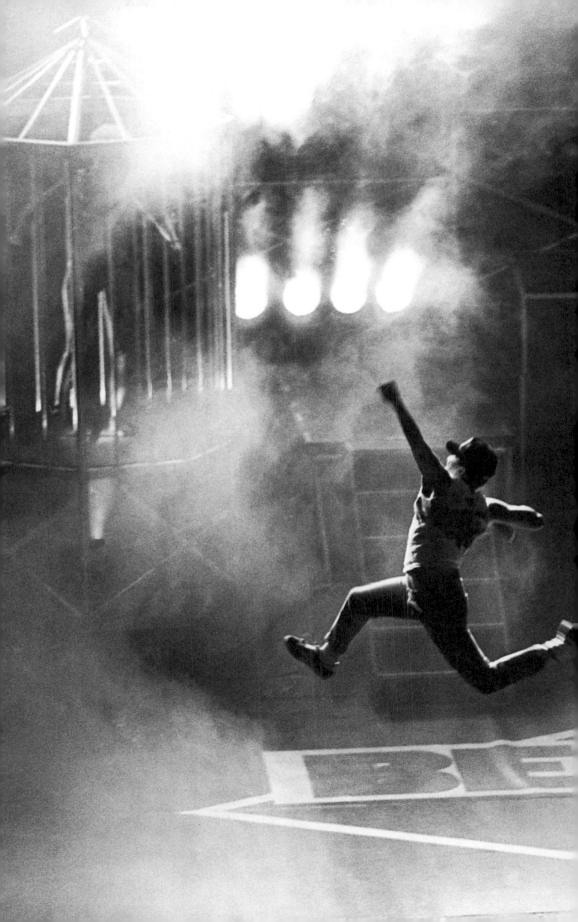

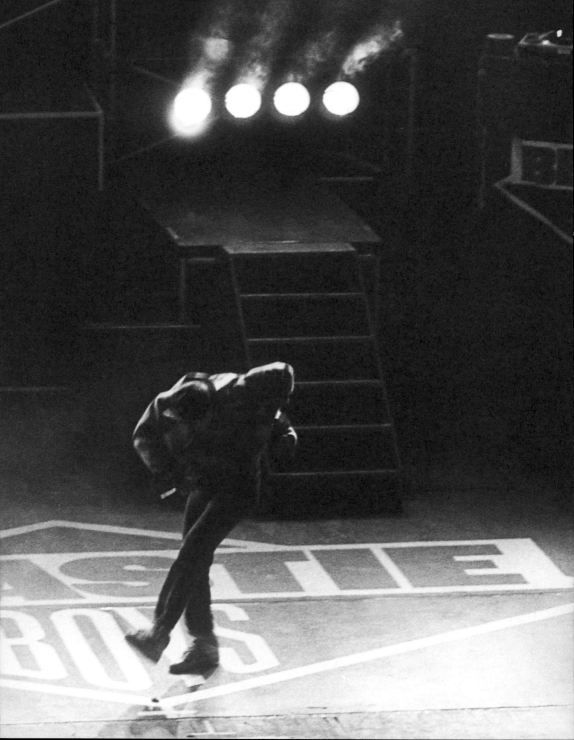

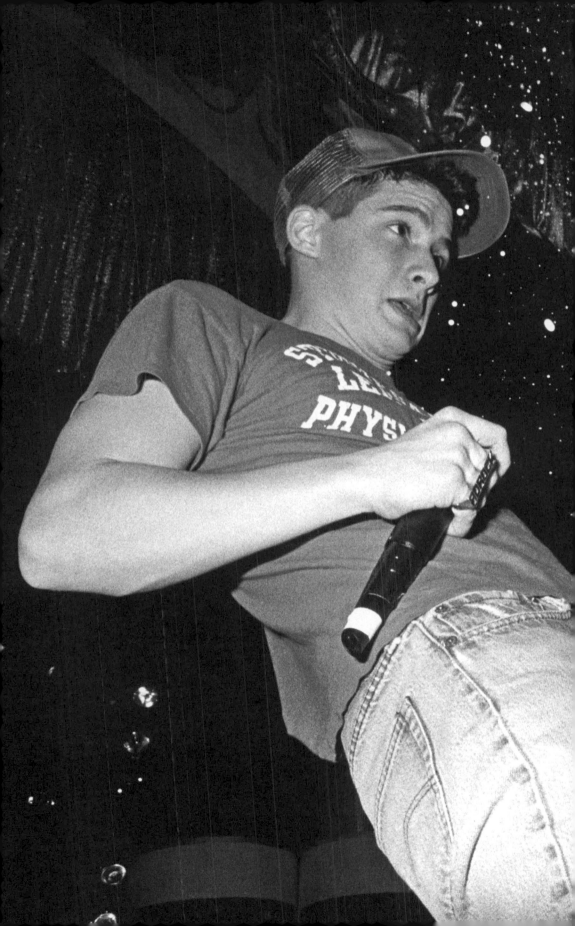

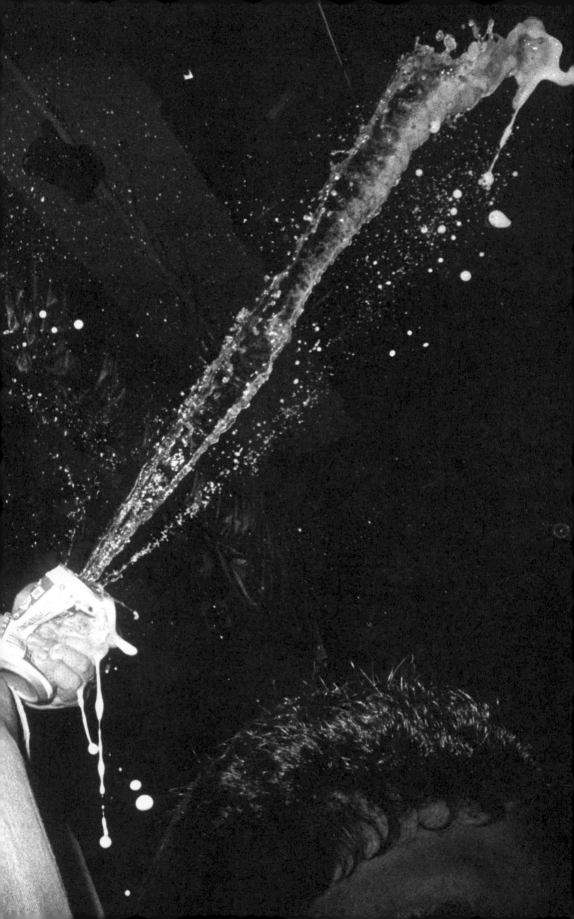

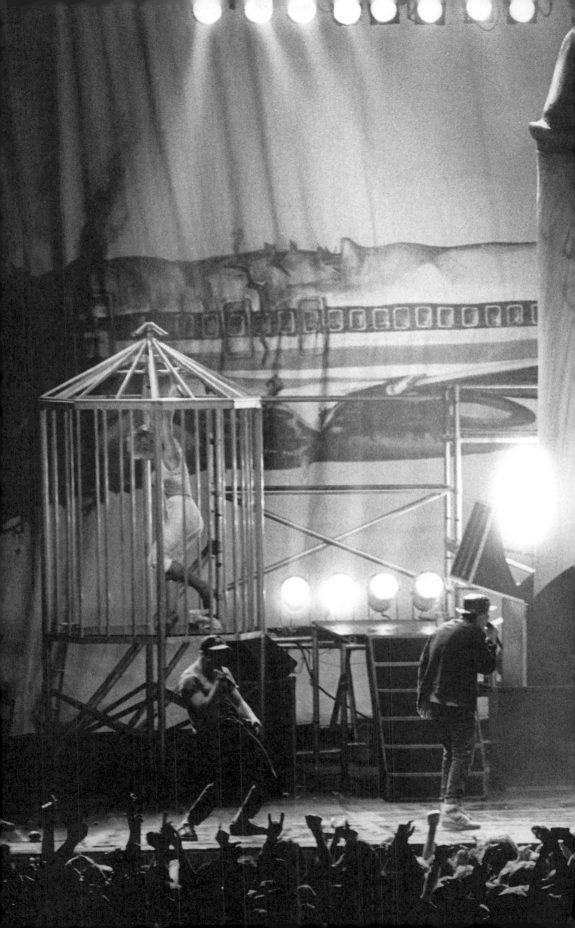

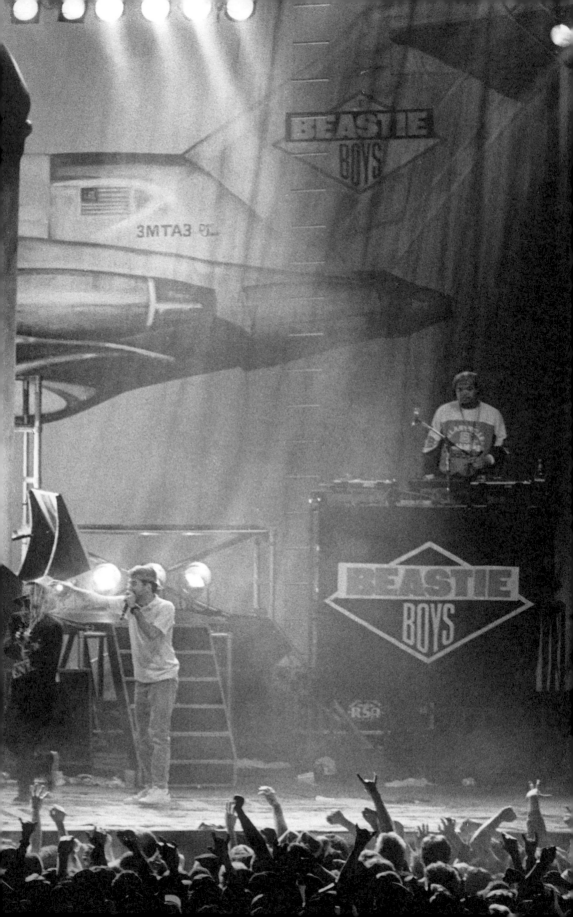

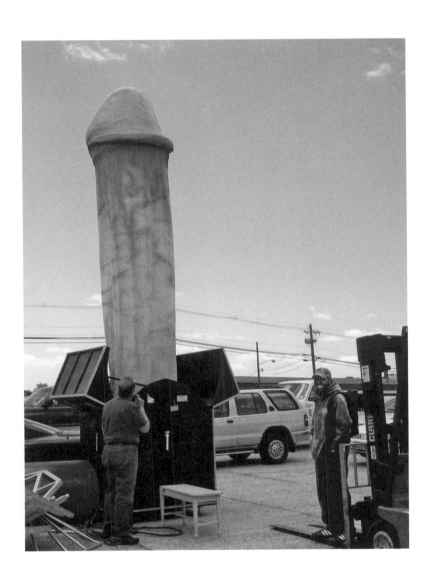

The Original Dick in a Box
(AH)

It's been referred to, many times, as an inflatable penis.

It is *not* an inflatable penis.

It's a *hydraulic* penis.

And it lives in a 5-foot-by-5-foot wooden box. In New Jersey.

Every show we played in 1987 would end with "Fight for Your Right (To Party"). When that song would start, someone would flip the switch and out, and up, went the dick. In retrospect, of course, this was a really unfortunate move. But it seemed funny at the time. . . .

The *Licensed to Ill* record had just come out, and Russell started arranging a tour for us. Our first actual headlining tour. He had us meet with this guy Eric Moskowitz, who ran a company that made stage stuff for big tours. This guy Eric asked us . . . "Well, what do you want onstage? Do you want some platforms? Some stairs? Or, like, a walkway? You can have whatever you want." We were explaining that we'd never had anything like that. They didn't have room onstage at CBGB for a couple of swings or a double staircase. Wherever we played, we always just used what was up there. Which was always . . . nothing. But he kept saying to us that we could have some stuff up there. Onstage. It's gonna be a big-time tour, and big-time headliners had a bunch of stuff onstage. This whole idea, and conversation, felt so ridiculous. Really . . . ? Who wants to walk up and down a small flight of stairs during a show? And who in the audience wants to watch that? So we started saying anything stupid we could come up with, like . . . we should probably have a huge dick come out of a box for the big finale. Right?! Eric Moskowitz was like, "GREAT. That's easy to do. We'll use a hydraulic system."

Now we have stuff onstage. We're a real big-time band, ready to go on a real big-time rock tour, with *that* onstage with us. We also had a '60s-style go-go dancer cage, and an 8-foot-high DJ riser that was in the shape of, and painted to be, a massive six-pack of Budweiser beer. Again: *Seemed funny at the time.* But here's the thing I need to express . . . You gotta really think before you say or do some dumb shit. Not always, but usually . . . take a moment. Think of yourself in the future looking back. Think about the people you care about most. Will they be embarrassed for you, and *of* you? Yes . . . they will think you're an asshole. And . . .

You'll end up paying thirty years' worth of storage locker fees in New Jersey for a 5-foot-by-5-foot dick in a box.

LAB REPORT

ADA CALHOUN

PROBLEM:

We hate sexism.
We love Beastie Boys.
Is this a contradiction?

It's the early 1990s. Throughout our New York City childhoods, we've been catcalled on corners and flashed on the subway. When we close our eyes we see the smiling penises of Keith Haring's safe-sex paintings.

We've just emerged from the bullying gauntlet of middle school bra snapping and teasing. In high school, the lascivious old history teacher has the hottest girl in class help him playact Mussolini's rape of a reporter, with him in the role of Mussolini. In the margins of a test, the science teacher writes a dirty joke: "Q: What makes a hormone? A: Don't pay her."

Figuratively and literally, there are Just. So. Many. Dicks. Fifteen-year-old radical feminists of Stuyvesant High School carry around *Backlash*, bell hooks, and Bikini Kill fanzines. We long for deliverance from the sexual violence of Guns N' Roses and the numbing sexism of '80s sitcoms and beer commercials.

And yet, Beastie Boys, with their song "Girls" and their tour's cage dancers, do not disturb us. We sing along, we include their songs on mixtapes alongside Ani DiFranco and the Indigo Girls.

Why?

I. Materials

a) Sexist Song Lyrics, e.g.:

- "We rag-tag girlies back at the hotel. Then we all switch places when I ring the bell."
  ("The New Style," 1986)
- "Girls! To do the dishes. Girls! To clean up my room. Girls!
  To do the laundry! Girls! And in the bathroom. Girls!
  That's all I really want is girls. Two at a time—I want girls!" ("Girls," 1986)
- "And I'm always out lookin' for a female companion. I threw the lasso around the
  tallest one and dragged her to the crib. I took off her moccasins and put on the bib."
  ("Hey Ladies," 1989)

b) Feminists who grew up with the band's music. I am one, and I called a few more.

II. Hypotheses

Hypothesis A:

Our critical faculties are disabled by lust.

> "If I pondered the lyrics at all, it was to lament the fact that I would never have a chance to fondle ADROCK's silverware or glimpse his dirty socks," says feminist historian Karen Abbott. "After I heard their tour planned to skip Philadelphia, I sent them a Polaroid of myself, wearing a fringe bikini and standing in the shallow end of a wave pool. When they came to Philly after all (persuaded, no doubt, by my Dorothy Hamill haircut and aggressive overbite), it was, at that point, the best moment of my life. Their trademark twenty-foot inflatable phallus held, for me, all the exquisite wonder of the Eiffel Tower. I wanted to be a dancing girl in a cage."

In the rest of our lives, the penis could be menacing: pushing up against us on public transportation, symbolizing the threat of infection in sex-ed videos. But onstage at those shows, the penis is a giant, joyful, celebratory toy.[†] In its dopey joyfulness, it's almost cathartic. And also sort of hot.

Hypothesis B:
We assume they're joking. And many of us feel let in on the joke.
As with so many teenagers navigating New York in this era, the band is arrogant and sarcastic. To some, this was adorable; to others, deeply irritating.

"I think we thought of them as kind of doofuses, like *of course these dorky white boys are trying to sound cool and tough and misogynistic*," says Asia Wong. "*So cute!*"

Priscilla Forsyth says, "My thinking is that they got a pass (for their sexism, but also for their general annoyingness) because they were 'good, smart, cute' middle-class white boys."

Growing up in Brooklyn (and attending the same artsy high school as Yauch, though some years later), Daisy Rosario, now a radio personality, says that to her they just offered a universally accessible good time. They spoke her language. It didn't make a difference to her that they were boys and she was a girl, or that they were white and she was a woman of color: "I was just attracted to the freedom they had," she says. "They were a group of friends being silly and bizarre and fun. I didn't want to date them. I wanted to *be* them."

(When Daisy became a stand-up comic in her twenties, the vast majority of comics were still men, and MCs often played the song "Girls" as she got onstage, as if to say, *Look! A girl!* Daisy says, "*They* didn't get the joke.")

III. Conclusion:

Jeez, We Just Liked Them, I Don't Know. And Their Feminist Reformation Validated Our Initial Tolerance.

My Stuyvesant friends and I didn't get much satisfaction back in high school. Those teachers never got in trouble. We never did get apologies from the flashers or harassers. But New York is different now, and so are Beastie Boys. Those of us who trusted our positive instincts about the band have had our enthusiasm repaid a million-fold.[*]

---

[*]Data
- Before the 1990s end, Beastie Boys express regret for their early sexist and homophobic lyrics. "Time has healed our stupidity," Adam Horovitz writes in a letter to *Time Out New York* in 1999.
- They go on to write explicitly feminist lyrics, such as: "What makes you feel/And why you gotta be/Like you got the right/To look her up and down/What makes this world/So sick and evil." ("Song for the Man," 1998) And: "I want to say a little something that's long overdue/The disrespect to women has got to be through/To all the mothers and sisters and the wives and friends/I want to offer my love and respect till the end." ("Sure Shot," 1994)
- They boldly address the issue of rape when giving an acceptance speech at the 1999 MTV Video Music Awards.
- They marry feminist women and advance women's causes and women's work.

[†]As of press time, the penis remains in a storage unit in New Jersey. Every year, the employees inflate it for their holiday party.

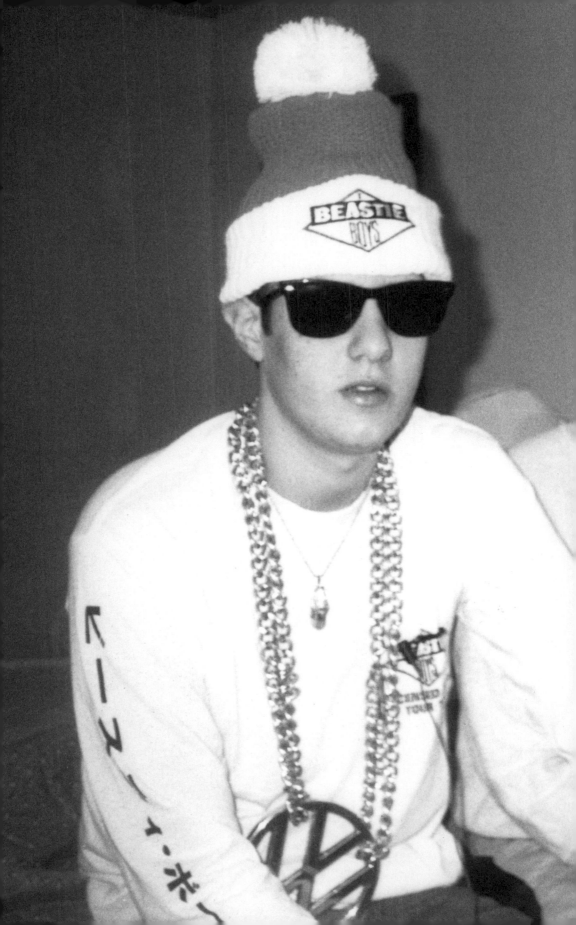

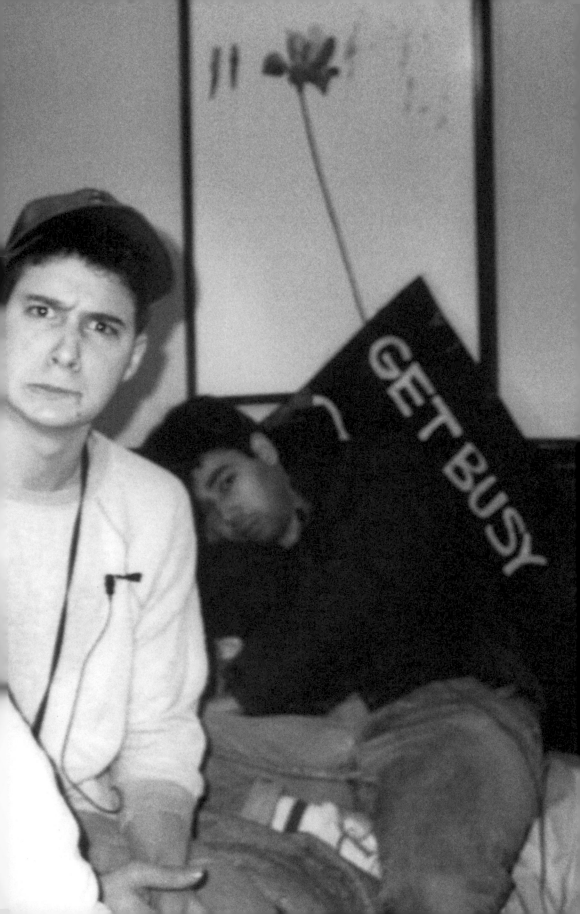

Tadlock

(AH)

Our first real tour bus experience was in 1987. The bus was driven and owned by Tadlock. (He was one of those people whose own mother would call them by their last name.) In its glory days, Tadlock's bus was part of a small fleet that had gone on tour with Elvis Presley. Our bus had carried the road crew for Elvis's backing band, the Stamps. This bus was state of the art (in, like, 1962). It had a ton of something that was new to the marketplace back then . . . Velcro. Everything had a huge Velcro strap on it to keep it from moving around. Curtains, cabinets, even the interior doors. It was tough to get any sleep because of the constant *rrriiippp* sound. But the coolest thing by far about the bus was Elvis's big TCB logo on the outside. And Tadlock, he was great. A really nice dude. Fun and funny. But we were from a different generation and planet. I don't know that he'd seen it all, but it's safe to assume that touring for years with Elvis Presley, he'd seen a hell of a lot. So he just kind of rolled with all the weird and fucked-up shit that was happening on the *Licensed to Ill* tour. Our getting chased out of cities by the police for foul language, and fouler behavior, seemed funny to him. Like, "Crazy kids these days with their rappin' music."

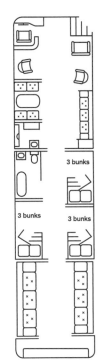

3 bunks

3 bunks

3 bunks

Tadlock used to wrestle (wrassle) alligators. (Maybe that's what every older Floridian guy tells New Yorkers.) He always wore these huge gold sunglasses. Always. One day, he told us the story of how he came upon these spectacles. We all crammed into the front of the bus while he was driving and listened with fucking fervor.

At the end of one particular Elvis tour, the King gathered everybody in a circle. He thanked his band and crew and gave everyone a pair of these golden shades. Except Tadlock. They all hugged and said their goodbyes, then Elvis left the building. Tadlock was fucking bummed out. He told us that he kind of went off to the corner of the room and started tearing up: *Why has Elvis forsaken me?* Of course, as he's telling us the story, especially this detail, we're trying as hard as we can to not burst out laughing. (I don't need to remind you that at this time we were a bunch of snobby twenty-ish-year-old jerks from New York City.)

So Tadlock's in the corner, almost full-on crying, when out of nowhere comes the King himself, Elvis Presley, and his entire entourage. They're all pointing and laughing at Tadlock. Elvis says, "C'mon, Tadlock, you know we'd never forget about you." And he presents him with a pair of the coveted golden sunglasses. Elvis gives Tadlock a big old bear hug, and Tadlock begins to sob in the King's embrace. "Elvis was just like that . . . fun. Fun, and generous." As Tadlock told the story, he had tears in his eyes. Like he's describing to us the single greatest moment that's ever happened to him.

We responded with . . . silence.

Tadlock regained his composure, and we all kind of headed toward the back of the bus to nap or eat potato chips or whatever, mumbling "Wow . . . yeah . . . that's great . . . awesome glasses, man. Elvis must've been a really cool dude." Actually, he sounded kinda like a dick, but no way were we gonna say something negative about the King in Tadlock's presence. Because, remember . . . he used to wrassle alligators.

Paul Williams (The Singer/Songwriter)
(AH)

In a way . . . the night we played at the Hollywood Palladium, in 1987, was the tipping point for all the really crazy and stupid shit that we'd done during the *Licensed to Ill* era. We were in Hollywood. We had a number-one record on "the charts." And we were *really* feeling ourselves. When you're a "famous" person, you mostly receive positive feedback. At least from the people that are in the room with you. And when you're, like, the brand-new super-hot famous star . . . you're the shit. Everyone tells you, *Yeah, man . . . that is a fucking GREAT idea.* That's why so many people fuck up. You'd think it'd be easy when you become a "famous" person. All you have to do is keep your good friends and trusted family members around so you don't fuck up. *But* . . . they're the ones who tell you *not* to do those drugs or not to set that thing on fire. But you really want to do those drugs and act like an asshole so . . . you turn your back on them and you go with these new people 'cause . . . *yeah . . . that is a really good idea. You should get super high, Krazy Glue the hotel room's shower door closed, and fill it up with water so it'll be like a seven-foot soaking tub.*

Yauch rented some kind of ridiculous sports car for the few days we were in L.A. Like, a red Lamborghini convertible or something. It was a red Ferrari—just sayin'. (MD) He thought it would be a funny "Hollywood" thing to do. It kind of was. He also liked to drive really fast back then. After the show was done at the Palladium, we were in the park- I dunno, Mike, I really think it was a Lamborghini. (AH) ing lot getting ready to all go somewhere, or split up and do whatever was next. Yauch pulled up in this crazy, low-to-the-ground, huge red sports car.

Top down. Blasting a cassette of Paul Simon's *There Goes Rhymin' Simon.* The song playing was "Kodachrome." I remember thinking, *That is NOT what you're supposed to be blasting out of a huge red convertible sports car.* And that is why I love Adam Yauch. 'Cause he is so fucking weird.

Yauch tells us that he's gonna go drive up and around Mulholland, a winding and sometimes treacherous one-wrong-move-and-you're-flying-over-a-cliff street at the top of the mountain that separates Hollywood from the Valley. There've been car-chase scenes on Mulholland in about seven thousand movies. He'd heard it was a cool way to see the city, and off he went. The next day we get the story . . . and this is one of the things I loved about being on tour. Almost every "next day," someone had a story to tell.

So . . . Yauch was driving this red sports car, winding through the Hollywood Hills, taking the sharp twists and turns of Mulholland Drive. As he got to a particularly hairy curve, he slowed down and saw some crazy shit out

of the corner of his eye. He pulled over to the side of the road, and there he saw the exact same red sports car dangling over the side of the mountain. Like in a movie, it was teetering and could fall right off at any moment. And sitting on a tree stump a few feet from the car was the singer-songwriter Paul Williams. Hands over his face, hands through hair, shaking his head, like, *Whoa . . . what the fuck just happened?* Yauch slowly walked over to him and quietly asked . . . "Hey man, are you okay? Do you need some help?" He said that singer-songwriter Paul Williams just kind of looked up at him and shook his head . . . no. Yauch was thinking . . . *You sure? Because you look REALLY fuckin' wasted and your red sports car is about to fall off the mountain and roll into a bunch of houses in the Valley.* Yauch kind of stood around for a couple minutes just to make sure that the singer-songwriter Paul Williams didn't do some crazy shit like try to get back in the car. At this point a bunch of different people had pulled over, and Yauch decided that they were probably more capably helpful than he was, so it was fine for him to cut out. So he did.

I'm pretty sure that was the night Yauch decided that driving really fast is pretty fuckin' stupid, and soon after, he bought a Subaru and was very cautious. He switched his interest in going fast to things that he could only really hurt himself doing if something went wrong. You know . . . like jumping out of a helicopter to snowboard down a mountain.

Sean and Brad; Robin and Batman at Rad

doesn't in any way tie the acts
contracts, and, should a
h to take on one of his bands

Immaculate as ev
suit, the singer sits t
lunch hour and ian

The Captain
(AH/MD)

The first time I really remember meeting the Captain was at Danceteria. At this point, the Captain wasn't the Captain yet. He was this British guy named Sean Carasov. It was around Thanksgiving 1985, and he kept talking about a twenty-two-pound turkey that he had to pick up and deliver somewhere, or someone won it in a raffle, or some odd thing. (Think of it being said by a funny little guy with an exaggerated British accent, really drawing out the *Turrrr* and *keeeey*.) It turned out that Sean was renting a room at our friend Gerb's apartment, and soon he became part of our circle. He was kind of fucking wild. He was a loyal friend, really smart and really funny, but not someone you'd lean on for a heart-to-heart conversation when you needed one. There was definitely something very heavy that he'd left behind in London. Sean loved his life as a New Yorker. And as a Yankee fan. When you think of different people that you know, you picture them in a certain place or setting. My picture of Sean would be at Yankee Stadium. Day game. No shirt, soaking up the sun, drinking a beer. Happy.

Oh, by the way . . . Sean was a drinker. Well, at times, a drunk. Or as they say now, he had a substance-abuse problem. He had very detailed ways of navigating his booze consumption. He'd have a day off for every day on. On his off days, he would run. He was actually really physically fit. But on his on days, he would really just get lit up. And that led to his nickname: in the '80s we used to call getting drunk "getting pissy drunk" or just "getting pissy." Sean was given the name Captain Pissy. Soon enough it morphed into just the Captain (a more palatable nickname). So the Captain became his new identity—and it fit.

When you're twenty-two, you have nowhere you need to be. At least, after work hours. And for us, that was most days and nights. We'd always be meeting up somewhere. As friends do. Where do you wanna get dinner? What time should we meet there? The Captain always arrived a few minutes early, and had a penalty system for tardiness. You would owe him one drink per every five to ten minutes you were late. Show up a half hour late, and you'd have to pay for whatever he wanted that night at the restaurant. He was a totally organized wreck. (AH)

We asked the Captain to be our tour manager for the *Raising Hell* and *Licensed to Ill* tours. He was the only one in our social circle with genuine applicable tour experience. Before he moved to New York, he had started out selling T-shirts for The Clash and worked his way up to being the right-hand man

< I collected the first twenty copies of *The Face* magazine when they came out. In an article about the Specials, a band I loved, there was a picture of a rockabilly-ish kid. He looked really cool and British and stuff. Lo and behold . . . it's the Captain. (AH)

of tour manager Kosmo Vinyl. So he knew the ropes. And at that point with Rush Artist Management, the people in their pool of tour managers were far less qualified than the Captain. He could be incredibly responsible and detail-oriented, and to his credit, he took his job with us very seriously. Perhaps way more seriously than we did. I mean, *someone* had to get us to *The Joan Rivers Show* and back, or to some random radio station and then to the show on time. Pay hotel bills, book flights, etc. And he did it all well; for the most part he

was a really good tour manager. But the minute he was "off the clock," he was on the sauce.

Quick story: One time we were on tour in Amsterdam, and we all ate pot in multiple edible forms and went out. And of course we weren't patient enough in terms of waiting for it to kick in. And so we got way, *way* more stoned than any of us had thought possible or planned on. At, like, five in the morning, we all called each other, like, "Dude, I don't know, I think I'm gonna have a heart attack. I'm freaking the fuck out." The Captain's reaction to his own potential death was to pack all his bags and have them perfectly placed by the door. That's where his paranoia went—in his bad trip or whatever, he was like, *Well, if they come to take me away, I've got all my affairs in order.*

At some point during or after the *Licensed to Ill* tour, the Captain moved into my apartment on Barrow Street. He was Felix Unger fastidious. He wouldn't go out without being showered and shaven and having literally not a hair out of place. Everything would stay perfect until he'd had enough drinks. When he was sober, he was a bit of a homebody: he'd be a real listen-to-music, watch-a-movie, read-a-book type of person. He was also a true cat enthusiast. It wasn't just that he preferred them to dogs; he was obsessed with them, became a little kid when one was around. We had a cat on Barrow Street, and I'm 99% sure he liked it more than he liked me.

After we moved out of Barrow Street, we all kind of ended up in L.A. around the same time, but as me, Adam, and Adam were becoming way more focused on making music, our relationship with the Captain started to fade. He stopped being a tour manager and got a job doing A&R for Jive Records. (He actually was the person to sign A Tribe Called Quest to a record deal.) But the record biz wasn't for him, and he didn't stay in the industry very long. Eventually we kind of lost touch. We seemed to be headed in different directions.

He had originally fled England because he knew what the future might have held if he'd stayed: a life spent on the dole, day drinking, going nowhere. The fact that he lived his dream of moving to beautiful Southern California must have meant a lot to him. But ending up out of work and going nowhere must have been a tough pill to swallow.

We heard about him one last time in 2010, when he killed himself. We never heard the details, and didn't need to. He'd been fighting something ever since we met.

One thing I'm reasonably sure of, though: when the end came, his bags were packed, and his affairs were in order. (MD)

DAILY Mirror

Thursday, May 14, 1987   FORWARD WITH BRITAIN   20p

Shame of rampaging stars

POP IDOLS SNEER AT DYING KIDS

SHAMEFUL: The Beasties who drove tragic children to tears.

'Go away you *!*! cripples'

DYING child cancer victims were in tears last night after being cruelly jeered by the Beastie Boys pop band.

First the youngsters, mainly terminally ill leukaemia sufferers, were told "Go away you f****** cripples" when they shyly asked the group for autographs.

Then they were sworn at and roughly pushed aside as the three-man cult band rampaged through a plush hotel after a five-hour drinking spree which left a trail of destruction.

Tory MP Peter Bruinvels immediately demanded the banning of the cult band from playing in Britain.

But when the group's Adam Horowitz was asked about the incident he sneered:

"Who cares about a bunch of cripples anyway?"

From GILL PRINGLE in Montreux

Pop idol Paul Young paid for their flights and Duran Duran, Simply Red and Kim Wilde were among those who chatted happily with them.

But when they approached The Beasties, whose stage act has got them banned all over the US, all they were met with was abuse.

The band laughed at the children—aged from ten to 17 and some of them on crutches—and shouted: "Look they're baldies."

Then they were brushed aside. One child — unsteady on his feet — staggered and nearly fell.

Last night Dreams Come True founder Margaret Hayless was too distressed to comment on the incident.

But a spokesman said: "We are absolutely

○ Turn to Page 2

The Mrs Tha

● The reveals popu NOT the Pri

WHAT

● Yet, JOE HA the of h

MAGGIE DEATH PLOT FOILED

World's nastiest pop group arrive today but British hotels give them the elbow

GET LOST

THE BEASTIE BOYS: Over the top, over-wealthy and coming over here—but nobody in Britain wants them

BEASTIES

Doors slam on vile US band

The world's vilest pop group will fly into Britain today to be told — GET LOST!

Hotel after hotel here refused yesterday to take the revolting Beastie Boys, the U.S. trio who taunted leukaemia victims, calling them cripples.

Their sickening jibes at

By GORDON HAY and GILL PRINGLE

young cancer sufferers have made them outcasts on the eve of their first British tour.

Last night the swaggering Beastie Boys defiantly told the Mirror — and Britain: "We are going to be the nastiest bunch of

teenagers you have ever seen!"

But first they will have to find somewhere to stay.

The top hotels in the Brighton area have all turned them away after their rampage at the

● Turn to Page 2

Guess who's arrived in Britain?

WE HATE ◎△✳!◎△! ENGLAND

'HORRIBLE': Horowitz   Picture: NIGEL WRIGHT

THE Beastie Boys, the crudest pop band in the world, hit Britain yesterday . . . screaming a torrent of obscenities.

Almost the first words from the millionaire American pop group after landing at Heathrow were: "We hate England."

Well, England's not too keen on them, either. There were many demands to ban them after they taunted leukaemia victims in Switzerland, calling them cripples.

Fifteen bodyguards were waiting at the airport, and they lined up in front of the group at a bizarre Press conference in a terminal building.

First the group wanted to bar some papers who had reported the mayhem on their European tour.

They failed.

Then one of the band, Adam "Horrible" Horovitz flew into a foul-mouthed tirade.

"There will be no ***** questions," he shouted at reporters. "Because whatever we say you don't ***** listen. It's a bunch of bullshit lies.

"We've come to London to play for the kids we want to play to.

"We are not making music for the Press. We are making it for the kids."

BACK-SEAT BEASTIES: Leaving Heathrow.

Yes, it's those Beastie Boys

By GORDON HAY

After that, the strong-arm men forced their way through a throng of reporters and cameramen and escorted the three slightly-built Beasties to waiting cars.

Their plan to speed off hit trouble immediately. Their cars were caught in a traffic jam, and photographers quickly surrounded them.

The minders threw themselves across the car windows to try to block photographers.

Three minutes later the Beastie Boys were on their way to a West London hotel which agreed to take them when many others refused.

Their first concerts are in Brixton this weekend, when riot police will be on stand-by.

On their flight from Amsterdam the Beasties caused no trouble at all.

They sat quietly, refusing all drinks and listening to their stereo head sets.

But all that stopped when they landed

FELL IN, YOU 'ORRIBLE LITTLE PUNK

By STEVE CROWTHER

PUNK rocker Jason Crompton was a shocker when he volunteered to join the army.

His spikey hairdo, fishnet body stocking and skeleton ear rings would have made even the toughest drill sergeant cringe.

But now young Jason has finished his basic training and yesterday he was voted the smartest Coldstream Guardsman at his passing out

You're a soldier now, son

Hong Kong to be reunited with another reformed punk—his best pal Phil Sharples who joined the Guards last

quit his job as an upholsterer in Bolton, Lancs, to get fell in with the lads at Pirbright Barracks, Surrey.

His proud mother Dawn said last night: "I could hardly believe my eyes when I saw him with short back and sides.

"Before he joined up his appearance was atrocious, an absolute mess.

"He wore those awful weirdo clothes. But

The Liverpool Riot

(AH)

So, yeah, basically . . . we blew up in England in 1987. I don't know what the deal was, really. Like, why it happened. *Licensed to Ill* was big and getting played on the radio a lot and we were playing big shows and stuff, but this was really weird next-level stuff. All of a sudden, we were on the cover of the newspaper. Every day.

Well . . . what had happened was (that's my favorite thing that people always say on judge shows) the week before our first British tour, we went to the Montreux Jazz Festival in Switzerland with Run-DMC, and there were some industry-ish parties, and we got a little buck-wild and stood out as these kooky rap mayhem-makers. And since there was a ton of press there, they wrote about us as such. The first headline of our first newspaper cover story (in the *Daily Mirror*) in bold letters was

POP IDOLS SNEER AT DYING KIDS.

Wait . . . say what?!

It quoted us as saying, "GO AWAY YOU *!*! CRIPPLES." One of the press people at Montreux was a writer for the British tabloids and had decided to write a story that we were at the airport in Switzerland and a "crippled" kid asked for our autographs and we told the kid to go to hell and made fun of him. I mean . . . I've done some pretty awful and shitty things in my life, but I really have never told a kid with a disability to go to hell.

ANYWAYS . . .

After Montreux, we played a few shows in Europe, and then went on to the UK. When we got to the airport in London, a bunch of reporters asked us all these questions about why we're so awful and mean toward "crippled children" and suggested that we should go back to the US of A, where that sort of thing is okay. The whole thing snowballed into this sort of Sex Pistols scenario where we were these outrageous punk rap guys from America who don't give a shit about nothin'. The next day's headline was . . . WE HATE F@#KING ENGLAND! With a picture of us from that airport press conference on the cover.

Things kept getting crazier. There were tabloid interviews with the "crippled" kid saying how hurt he was; then it turned out that the "crippled kid" was a fake and wasn't actually in fact disabled at all, and of course we'd never actually in fact met the kid. It was nuts. And every day, we'd be on the front page. Again. It was like a tornado building up power, and it just kept growing in size.

Some context: While we were on tour in the Deep South of the U.S., local municipalities caught wind of our act and the "foul language" and "lewd acts" involved. They decided they should impose an age limit on our shows or ban them altogether. We had a UK music journalist covering the tour who wrote about it, amping the whole thing up to eleven. (MD)

It certainly was a weird-ass way to start a tour that we were so psyched to go on. We'd been really looking forward to seeing these places we'd only heard about in, like, *The Face* magazine—Birmingham, Manchester, Brighton. But because of all these newspaper stories, there was this weird expectation for us to be fucking maniacs. With each city we went to, the crowds developed a *You motherfuckers ain't shit compared to us here* vibe, and so by the time we got to the last show of that tour, in Liverpool, the punters went berserk. They were chanting football chants and throwing shit, and then it turned into a hailstorm of beer cans and bottles; so mid-show, we broke the fuck out and drove back to London. We got back to our hotel really late at night. We were exhausted and so happy to be going home for a few days before heading off to wherever we were gonna head off to next.

I got to my hotel room, put my bags down, sprawled out on the bed, and heard a knock on the door. "It's the police. We've come to arrest you for what's happened up in Liverpool." *Wait . . . say what?! Arrest me for what's happened in Liverpool?!* I cracked open the door and saw two cops in the hallway. As it's all happening, I am totally freaking out, but also there was a split second where I was like, to myself, those cops are bobbies just like on *Monty Python*. One of the cops told me not to try to jump out the window because there were two more of them out around the back of the hotel. *Jump out the window?! Why would I jump out the fuckin' window? And also . . . What the fuck did I do?*

It turned out that someone in the audience said that in the middle of the melee, I threw a full can of beer from the stage and hit her square in the grill, and she got a big black eye and was all fucked up and was pressing charges against me. Have you ever thrown a full can of beer at a crowd of a few hundred angry people? Well, I haven't either.

I got put in a police car, and was driven back to Liverpool. In the car with me were one good cop and one bad cop. I remember during the drive, the bad cop was asking me all these weird questions like, "Are you high on drugs right now?" The good cop would be like, "It's okay. We won't tell anyone. We just want to know so we can help you." It was real cornball stuff, and would've been funny except that it was actually happening to me. I wasn't watching fuckin' *Barnaby Jones*. After I got to a Liverpool police station, I was fingerprinted and processed and was in holding for four days because of a long weekend/bank holiday. Was I gonna actually get sentenced to jail time? I didn't know what was going to happen next. I just sat in a cell (by myself, which was nice) and tried my best to lounge a little. I actually hadn't been by myself and quiet in a while, so, in a way, it was quality me time. I was going through a pretty heavy Velvet Underground phase at the time, so I just sang to myself and took it easy. The highlight was when I got moved to another facility late one night. They got, like, ten dudes out of holding and cuffed us all together and put us in a throw-back Keystone Cops–style paddy wagon. I got cuffed to this super-old and drunk Andy Capp–looking Irish guy. All the cops knew him, and were giving him a hard time about being drunk and disorderly . . . again. He was like . . . "Aye, I'm doin' bedder den da likes of you coppers." If you were directing a movie, you would've asked him to dial down the Irish stereotype a little.

Anyways . . . after the four days, they brought me into a courtroom, and first thing I see is a judge wearing one of those olden-times white curly powdery judge wigs. You know, like in a comedy. The court appearance was to set a trial date, and then I was free to go until that date. But I didn't know that when I first walked in. I was in handcuffs and thought sentencing was about to go down. I was all alone. Everyone cut out. In that moment, I was really feeling that *Oh shit, this could be bad* feeling. I looked around the crowded room for anyone I knew. No one. Wait, someone *was* there for me. He was in the very back row. Wearing a white-on-white Adidas tracksuit, white-on-white Adidas shell-toes with no laces, a furry white Kangol hat, and with a pen clipped to his ear. Not resting behind his ear; it was like someone played a practical joke on him and clipped it to the outside of his ear. And . . . he was dead asleep with his feet up on the row of chairs in front of him. Like a bum that just needed a warm room to crash in for a few hours.

That's my man . . . the Captain.

The judge set a trial date for me, and I was free to leave. While all of this was happening, my dad had totally stepped up and found me a lawyer in London. Sir David Napley. After I got home, I had to fly back and forth

to London a couple times to meet with this guy. He was great; he hated me. He was of a different and older generation, and did *not* care for rock 'n' roll types. Hooliganism was not his bag. The thing about Sir David Napley is . . . he was a big-deal lawyer. Of course, I had never heard of the guy, but everyone in England had. He was kind of a celebrity lawyer. And when the trial started, the judge (wearing an olden-times white curly powdery wig) watched my guy deliver his opening speech like he was watching a fuckin' TED Talk. He literally had his elbows on his desk and his hands cradling his face. Like how a four-year-old does. It was a spectacle. I knew I was already walking out of there because of how into my lawyer the judge was. And when the witness took the stand, she said that she *did* get hit with something at our show, but she didn't know what it was or where it came from. So the accusation of me throwing something and hitting her with it was false. (And to clarify . . . I really did not do it.) And I was free to leave.

The next day, me, my dad, and Sir David Napley got some breakfast and took the train back to London from Liverpool. We were all happy about the outcome. We were getting along. Then we pass a newsstand on the train platform, and see the cover of that morning's newspaper. It was a big picture of me screaming and giving the double-bird fuck-you to the camera. I think BEASTIE BOY WINS might've been the headline.

The train back to London was more quiet than pleasant.

Clear the Air
(MD)

From the beginning, hip hop was a battle format; dueling MCs would take the stage at a club to see who could win a crowd, bragging about themselves and dissing the other guy. Once people started making hip hop records, disses could turn into beefs when committed to vinyl, where they became permanent and far-reaching, and the "diss" record became a hip hop staple.

Any and all readers who haven't already done so should immediately seek out the MC battle of Kool Moe Dee vs. Busy Bee. (MD)

We didn't really diss a lot on our records. Kool Moe Dee dissed us on a "rapper report card" he put on one of his record sleeves (he gave us a lot of C's), but didn't call us out on a song. Our big beef was with MC Serch, one third of the hip hop group 3rd Bass.

I first met Serch at Payday, a really good once-a-week club night started by these guys Patrick Moxey and Beaver, the latter of whom I know now from the rare-wine world. (Did I just write that sentence? You're goddamn right I did.) Serch was a white MC from Queens, and everyone was like, *You should meet this guy*. Probably because we were the only other white MCs that anybody knew. It was like that scene in *Animal House* where the nerds keep getting reintroduced to and seated next to each other at the jocks' fraternity rush party. *Kent, Lonny, I'd like you to meet Mohammet, Jugdish, Sidney, and Clayton.*

Here's how Serch described us ten years later in *Spin*: "They were the Antichrist—they didn't go to Harlem World, didn't go to Union Square. I was [a white MC] busting my ass in the streets going through what I considered the proper hip hop urban channels and these guys go on tour with Run-DMC. To me, they were the worst possible thing to happen to hip hop culture." (MD)

One day Serch was around the corner visiting Russell, who had just moved into a yuppie West Village condo half a block away. I don't know if 3rd Bass had officially signed with Def Jam yet; they definitely hadn't put out a record. I guess Russell thought we could give Serch advice, or perhaps he simply had a female visitor coming over and needed to get rid of Serch. At any rate, he told him, "Mike D and the Captain are just up the block. You should stop by and play them your shit."

Unfortunately for Serch, he happened to buzz our door after we'd been out all night on a bit of a psychedelic bender. The Captain and I were in no condition to hang out and listen to his music, let alone give anyone helpful advice. No disrespect to Serch or his music. As I remember it, we dragged our asses out of bed and opened the window to see who it was. Instead of telling him to come back or even saying hello, we just started throwing shit at him and laughing. I can't remember exactly what we threw; it wasn't like water balloons or an Acme anvil, but it wasn't cool. Maybe trash? Or my plastic Mr. T piggy bank?

REPORT CARD

	VOCABULARY	ARTICULATION	CREATIVITY	ORIGINALITY	VERSATILITY	VOICE	RECORDS	STAGE PRESENCE	STICKING TO THEMES	INNOVATING RHYTHMS	
Kool Moe Dee	10	10	10	10	9	10	8	8	10	10	95 A+
Melle Mel	10	9	10	10	9	10	8	10	10	9	95 A+
Grand Master Caz	9	10	10	10	10	9	7	10	10	9	94 A+
L.L. Cool J	10	10	9	6	10	9	9	10	9	8	90 A
T. La Rock	10	10	10	9	8	9	8	7	10	9	90 A
Rakhim	8	10	10	9	8	10	10	7	9	10	91 A
KRS One	7	9	9	9	10	9	9	9	10	9	90 A
Spoonie G	7	8	9	9	8	9	9	7	9	7	82 B
M.C. Shan	7	9	9	9	9	7	9	8	9	7	83 B
Doug E. Fresh	7	9	10	10	9	8	9	10	9	9	86 B+
Bizmark	7	7	9	8	8	8	9	9	9	9	83 B
Kurtis Blow	7	7	7	8	9	9	9	9	9	7	81 B
Just Ice	9	8	8	9	8	8	8	7	8	9	82 B
Run DMC	6	9	8	8	7	8	10	10	9	7	82 B
Fat Boys	6	8	8	9	8	8	8	9	10	7	81 B
Whodini	7	8	9	9	9	8	9	9	10	8	86 B+
Beastie Boys	6	7	7	6	6	6	8	8	10	6	70 C
UTFO	7	9	9	9	9	9	8	10	9	10	89 B+
Heavy D & the Boyz	7	9	8	8	8	8	8	10	9	8	83 B
Boogie Boys	7	8	8	8	8	7	8	7	8	8	77 C+
Ultra Magnetic	10	7	8	8	8	7	8	7	8	9	80 B
Public Enemy	7	9	8	9	8	9	8	7	8	7	80 B
Stetsasonic	9	7	9	9	8	7	8	9	8	8	82 B
Grandmaster Flash and the Furious Five	9	8	7	10	7	8	7	9	9	7	81 B
Jazzy Jeff and the Fresh Prince	8	9	10	10	9	8	8	10	9	7	88 B+

Here's how Serch described the incident, also ten years later in *Spin*: "The Beastie Boys were huge at the time. One day I saw Mike D on the street and I ended up talking to him in his apartment, because I needed some advice. He gave me really good insight about Russell. I was leaving his apartment and all of a sudden he started throwing shit at me, like foam balls and stuff lying around his apartment. There was no reason for him to do that. Two months later there was a piece in *Spin* and the writer asked them what they thought of 3rd Bass, and Mike D said how he threw shit at me and shooed me out. I didn't know any of them before I met Mike that day. He was a real asshole." (MD)

We weren't looking at it like we were throwing shit out the window at MC Serch. It was more, *Why does this guy keep bothering us and ringing our bell?* (The lingering psychedelics in our system couldn't have helped.) Regardless, Serch took off, pissed, and who could blame him? We were hungover douches.

I didn't think much about it after that—until the first 3rd Bass album. They came out the gate swinging. The song "Sons of 3rd Bass" is one long diss on us, and it ends with an unbroken chain of insults:

> You know about that silver spoon havin'
> Buckshot acne showin', L.A. weak-ass sellout
> Non-legitimate, tip-doggin', Jethro pseudo intellectual
> Dust-smokin', pretty boy playwrite posin'
> Folks wiggin', whinin' annoyin' Def Jam reject devil
> White bread no money havin' slum village people clonin'
> Step children.

Once *that* happened, then it was like, *Okay, this is on.* On *Check Your Head*, Yauch did a great verse on the song "Professor Booty" in response.

> So many wack MCs you get the TV bozack
> Ain't even gonna call out your names 'cause you're so wack
> But one big oaf who's faker than plastic
> A dictionary definition of the word spastic
> You should have never started something that you couldn't finish
> 'Cause writin' rhymes to me is like Popeye to spinach
> I'm badass move your fat ass 'cause you're wack, son
> Dancin' around like you think you're Janet Jackson
> Thought you could walk on me to get some ground to walk on
> I'll put the rug out under your ass as I talk on
> I'll take you out like a sniper on a roof
> Like an MC at the Fever in the DJ booth

It goes on a little bit . . . he *is* going in pretty hard on Serch. I'm feeling kind of bad now. But that was the end of it. We ran into him a few times after all that. It was awkward at first, obviously, but eventually we hugged and made up, followed by a spirited discussion about family, loyalty, and mezuzahs.

Here's how Serch described his perspective ten years after the fact, also in *Spin*: "Now, in retrospect, I think they're brilliant orators and storytellers. If we ever do a new 3rd Bass record, I might have to put an apology song on there." (MD)

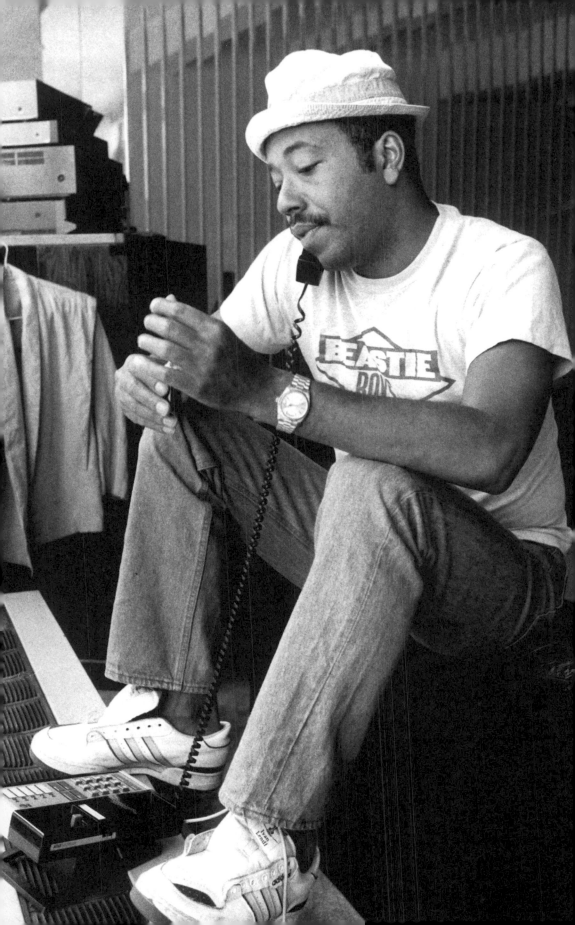

The Fallout
(AH)

It was kind of like that thing that sometimes happens when you're in a relationship and you choose to ignore how fucked up things have gotten. The fun and exciting phase has worn off. You now really know each other, and you now know that you really don't like each other. But you've kind of slipped into your roles and so you stay in it. Until something snaps you out of it and you realize that you don't have to be with that person. Neither of you is getting anything out of it. That's sort of how the big fallout between us and Rick+Russell came to be.

When we started, we were just a band. Friends in a band. We'd never thought of having a producer or manager or record label. Never really thought about the future of things in general. Then Rick+Russell came along, and they had big ideas. Things seemed to be going great, so we just rolled with it all. Going on tour opening for Madonna, and then Run-DMC . . . it was like a dream that we didn't even know existed for us had come true. We'd become a big group of friends having ridiculous fun, making music, playing shows, traveling, and getting paid money to not actually have a job. But at a certain point, Rick+Russell started coming up with ideas and making decisions for us. When you're young and someone tells you "Trust me. Do *this* thing. It'll be fun, and you'll make a bunch of money doing it" . . . you do it. And so we did. But it felt a little weird, like we weren't in control anymore.

For example: In late 1985, early 1986, we made the rough demo version for the song "Fight for Your Right (To Party)." Shit sounded funny to us. But a couple weeks later, Rick played us a new version that, unbeknownst to us, he'd been working on. All of a sudden it sounded clean and full, like a song that a professional would've made. Rick had not only totally remixed the song, but he replayed the guitar line that Yauch had recorded. *Wait, what? M'okay.* I guess it doesn't really matter, right? It's still the same song. It's just more . . . "polished." And that sort of thing happened a lot on that record. Even down to the artwork for the cover. Rick just kind of showed it to us one day. Like, *Oh, I had some guy make this, and this is your album cover.* All we really knew up to that point was that punk rockers went to the Xerox store to make their flyers and 7-inch covers and stuff. But we were like, *I guess this is how it's done when you have a producer and a manager and you're on an actual big-time record label like Columbia.* We were too busy living the high life to pay attention. Big mistake. Kids . . . when someone's making decisions for you, you can bet that they've also decided to take what's yours.

Rick told us that we were gonna make a video for "Fight for Your Right (To Party)," and so we showed up where we were told to go. We didn't question

it, 'cause that's how things are done, right? The video came out on the newish MTV network, and for whatever reason, people went berserk. The song and video were everywhere. Beastie Boys was large. So large that we decided to make a movie. (Every other band decides to do this when they blow up big.) Yauch and our friend Tom Cushman wrote a script. Rick was gonna direct, and Russell would produce. The movie was called *Scared Stupid*. It was like a drunken haunted-house party kind of situation. Like Abbott+Costello–ish . . . sort of. In retrospect, I'm *so* happy we didn't end up making it, but that's beside the point. What I'm saying is . . . We were gonna make this movie. We had meetings with Hollywood people and everything. One night, a few weeks later, Rick and I were outside Blanche's, a bar on Avenue A that all us kids used to hang out at, and we were talking about the movie, and Rick made a quick comment about splits. He was saying that Beastie Boys would get 10%, and him and Russell would get 90. This for real happened. He said something to me like, "Well . . . you know . . . We're doing all the work and you've never made a movie before." Red fucking flag. For me, that was the point at which things really started to unravel.

Yauch was already always kind of pissed and disillusioned with Rick because of the studio stuff. Yauch was into engineering and learning about how to get certain sounds through amps and speakers and microphones and stuff, so Rick taking over as "producer" and not including him was not cool with him. Neither was the notion that Rick was the video/movie director and ideas guy, because Yauch was also into film and making videos.

At some point Yauch quit the band. Sort of. He told me about this conversation he had with Russell in '87. It was after, like, twelve straight months of touring. He was sick of it. Done. Shit got old fast. He felt disconnected from his family, his friends, and himself. He was sick of being the drunk guy at the party. (In a flash, Beastie Boys went from being the funny tipsy guy with the lampshade on his head to the ugly drunk dude that people were trying to figure out how to get out of their apartment.) Yauch said that Russell wasn't trying to hear him and kept trying to convince him that it was all fine, that he should just *pretend* to be the drunk guy at the party and get back on tour and, you know . . . put water in a beer can and splash it around, and a whole bunch of other clown stuff. That was enough for Yauch. So he told Russell that he quit. He never actually told me or Mike, so neither of us had any idea that we weren't a band anymore. We had spent so much time together in the studio, on tour, and just being friends, that by the end of touring in '87 . . . we went our separate ways for a minute. I had a girlfriend who lived in L.A., so that's where I went. Yauch went back to his band Brooklyn, and Mike had started a new band called Flophouse Society Orchestra.

As for me, my mom had just passed away and I was running from all kinds of things. The chance to escape into becoming a different person couldn't have come at a more perfect time. That's the thing with dealing with tragedy when you're young and/or a drunk and/or stoned: you can't really comprehend the severity of what's actually happening. It's easier to go into denial mode and shut off what's real. But that's a story for my personal memoirs. Which I just set on fire in my bathtub.

During all of this madness we'd stopped being paid royalties on our record. We made money for playing shows. Big shows. Madison Square Garden shows. But zero dollars for the multiplatinum smash hit *Licensed to Ill*. The fucking record that a group of friends made together. Had intense and real fun making together. And now, for whatever reason, one of those friends, the one that is half owner of the record label, decides that the other three should not receive the earnings for the sales of that record. THEY DID NOT FUCKING PAY US! Rick+Russell . . . our friends. Def Jam. We'd been there with them from the beginning. I was there in the studio with Rick when T La Rock recorded "It's Yours." I was there in the studio with Rick when the Junkyard Band recorded "Sardines." I made the beat for LL Cool J's first single for Def Jam, "I Need a Beat." We felt that Def Jam's success was success for us. And vice versa. 'Cause we were all friends.

So what happened? Allegedly Rick and/or Russell said that we were in breach of our contract because we hadn't started to record our second album for Def Jam yet. I mean . . . Russell was our manager, as well as the owner of the record label. If he wanted us to record a new record by a certain date . . . he shouldn't have had us on tour during said date. Right? Why not just have a conversation about it all? Or an argument. Or whatever friends are supposed to do with each other to figure things out. But basically . . . $ was what it was all about. How $ad is that? We were all making a $hitload of money but, for whatever reason, it wasn't good enough.

We never got the chance to actually even have creative differences. Things just spun out of control. Allegedly Russell threatened to put out a record of unreleased songs of ours, call it *White House*, and have someone remix them to the theme of this hot new sound, house music. Ferreealz!?! The whole thing was just a real bummer 'cause we really *were* friends and things could've gone a different way. Not that I regret what-all happened next. I don't. 'Cause walking away from those dudes was actually the best thing to happen to us as a band, and as friends. It's just . . . I don't know . . . sad.

We didn't really run into them that much during the next few years, and when we did it was in a crowd of people at a party or something. Not the time or place to have a serious conversation. So time passed, and in the way that it does, it eased tensions. And after a while the fallout didn't really matter. We'd all moved on.

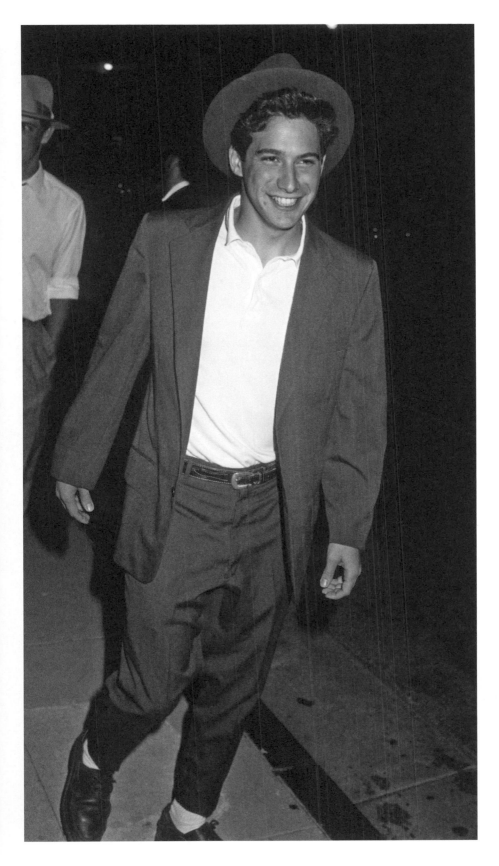

'88

(AH)

WARNING: THE METAPHOR I'M ABOUT TO USE IS KIND OF GROSS.

The three years leading up to the end of the *Licensed to Ill* tours in 1987 were like watching a pimple on your face grow into a huge and amazing spectacle. As though you really wanted it there. You want people to see it. Want people to admire how big and ghastly it is. But when you're alone, looking in the mirror, you know it's gross. You have to pop it, but you can't. It's your calling card. It's what gets you attention and fulfillment. *There goes Pimple Face. That's one crazy motherfucker right there.* But you remember when you were younger and were humiliated by pimples on your face. You used to furiously Buf-Puf those shits. (Or did anything your best friend Nadia would tell you to do to get rid of them. Like putting toothpaste on them. Which, by the way, Nadia, doesn't work.) And then you wake up one day to realize that you *are* that fucking pimple, and oh jeez . . . get this pus outta my face. So you set aside some time, go to the bathroom, take a deep breath, and squeeze. And what flies out from beneath your skin is three full years of growth, bad decisions, outrageous fun, love, hate, friendships, and the idea of a new beginning.

As I was putting new 1988 calendar pages into my Filofax, I was reflecting on what had just happened. We'd been spit outside the craziest fucking whirlwind. And for the first time in a long time, I was on my own. Sometime in '87 I auditioned and got the part in a movie called *Lost Angels*. Please, if you care about me, do not look it up on YouTube or Netflix (or whatever the thing to do is by the time you're reading this). I had a lot of fun making it, but I'm kind of pretty awful in it, and I'm mildly mortified as I type. But anyways . . . the movie was filming for a couple months in San Antonio, Texas; and then Los Angeles for a couple weeks. Since me, Adam, and Mike were so burnt on being Beastie Boys, we went our separate ways for a little while. Doing something totally different, like acting in a movie far from home, was just what I needed at the time. So I excitedly went to Texas.

One day, I got back to the hotel after filming, and someone at the front desk told me that a package had been delivered for me, and that it was in my room. I get up to my room, and there's a *huge* box waiting for me, and it's from Yauch. It was the closest thing to a care package at sleepaway camp I'd ever received. I hurriedly opened it, and there was another huge box inside it. Then another box inside of that one. Then another. It kept going until there was a big Ziploc bag filled with coffee grounds. Inside all that mess was another Ziploc bag with a cassette tape. It was the demos from his band, Brooklyn. (Man,

267

I miss him and the dumb, and detailed, stuff he'd do like that.) I didn't think for a moment about being hurt that he was in another band and was having fun with other bandmates. It just made me so happy to have the friend that I loved so much go to crazy lengths to keep our friendship intact.

After a few weeks in San Antonio, the production moved to L.A. I'd only really traveled places with Adam and Mike, and so this was new for me. Being somewhere else on my own. I wasn't lonely, though, because luckily my sister Rachael happened to be in Los Angeles for a bit when I first got there. Before she left, she introduced me to someone who would be my first friend in L.A., Dono. Donovan Leitch. We hit it off right away. It's that thing when you meet someone who grew up thousands of miles away from you but you feel like you could've and should've been friends forever. You're into the same stuff. Understand all the reference points, etc. Dono introduced me to his friends, and I quickly became part of their circle. One night Dono took me to this crazy Hollywood party at the house of this big-time Hollywood manager, Sandy Gallin. It was me and Dono and a bunch of his friends, and it felt like I was with my friends back home. Crashing a party at some weird rich person's house. But in the context and trajectory of our band, this party would turn out to be much more significant than that.

Because it was L.A., we were hanging out by the swimming pool. (Nighttime pool parties in Hollywood are *exactly* what they look like on TV.) I bumped into this guy Matt Dike, who had put on a show for us a couple years earlier at his club in L.A., Power Tools. He was about to start a record label called Delicious Vinyl. Matt was with these two guys he was making music with who called themselves the Dust Brothers. They were playing a cassette of some instrumentals they were working on: smooth and psychedelic and with layers of sounds stacked on top of other layers of sounds. It was so nice and precise and funky to death. The music, the friends, the weird parties . . . I was really enjoying this new lifestyle I was living in Los Angeles. Sunny days are every day. There's always some kind of fragrant flower smell in the air at night. And it was just nice being away from garbage-truck-filled New York for a minute. I also really liked these new people I was becoming friends with. I did feel like Rhoda Morgenstern most of the time I lived in Los Angeles, though. I knew I was out of place. I always felt kind of . . . schleppy. I guess being super stoned all the time added to the many conversations going on in my head. Thinking that the

268

people around me were like, *The Jewy New York guy is interesting, right? Why are his shirts always so dirty?* But a big draw to sticking around out there was those amazing instrumentals the Dust Brothers played. I called Adam+Mike soon after I heard their music and suggested that they come out to L.A. and meet these guys. Maybe potentially work on some music together. And so they did.

And so we did. Made music with Matt and the Dust Brothers. At Matt Dike's apartment. It was a big and long sprawling apartment in a kind of nowheresville neighborhood on the fringe of Hollywood. Rent was cheap back then, and you could find a place that had space for a couple bedrooms and a makeshift recording studio in the living room. On each side of the long hallway of the apartment were all these doors painted by Jean-Michel Basquiat. Matt said that Jean-Michel used to come to L.A. and stay at his place, and some nights they'd drive around in Matt's big old pickup truck and look for stuff for Jean-Michel to paint on. Stuff that people had thrown away, like discarded doors from construction dumpsters or something. Matt, to us, was a totally weirdly fascinating and interesting guy. It was similar to when I started to get to know Dono; we shared the same reference points. Got the same dumb *Barney Miller* jokes, understood the different connotations between Adidas Countrys and shell-toes. We also believed that Chef Boyardee was of culinary icon status.

For a couple months, me, Adam, and Mike each rented a room at an expensive hotel, Le Mondrian, on Sunset Boulevard. Are you wasting money when you're having an intense amount of fun spending that money? Tough call. But there we were, living that L.A. life. We had a bunch of new friends out there, and they'd all come by the hotel and we'd get food and swim in the pool and stuff. It was young and wonderful. None of us had actual jobs, so we could really focus on what was important: pot, snacks, mixtapes, going out to clubs, and, oh yeah . . . making new songs with Matt and the Dust Brothers.

And that was 1988.

MONDRIAN

HOTEL DE GRANDE CLASSE

MEMORANDUM

TO: Mr. Yauch, Suite #801

FROM: Klaus Ortlieb, General Manager

RE: Falling Items From Window

DATE: August 8, 1988

Dear Mr. Yauch,

I have received several complaints that there are items falling out of your window and hitting people on the sidewalk.

Please let me know, if there is anything defective on your windows so we can eliminate this problem.

I am looking forward to your cooperation in this matter.

Respectfully,

KO/tg

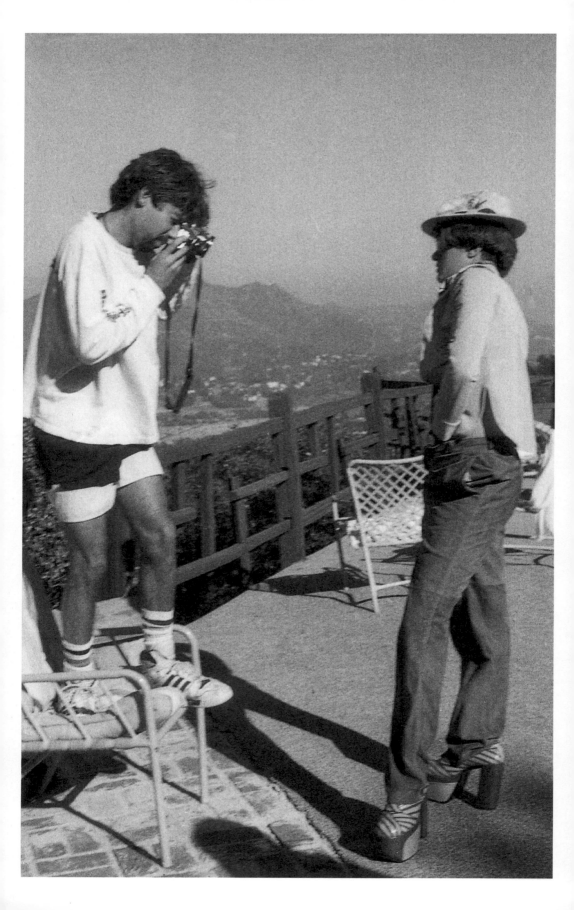

Expensive Shit
(MD)

In Los Angeles, dense layers of infrastructure exist to rapidly separate you from your money: You can find (and pay) any number of people to locate a great vintage guitar you don't need, to sell or lease you cars and homes you can't afford, and extravagantly groom the dog you don't have.

After the success of *Licensed to Ill*, a bunch of people thought they knew exactly what our future should look like. After we parted ways with Def Jam, we started meeting with other labels and eventually signed with Capitol. In the music business of the late 1980s, fortunes could still be made, and Capitol was betting millions of dollars on us. They wanted a new record immediately. We were . . . in less of a hurry.

Matt Dike introduced us to Mario Caldato, the engineer with whom he'd built a makeshift studio at Matt's down-and-out apartment on Santa Monica Boulevard in Hollywood. They were recording instrumental tracks there with these two hip hop fanatics named John King and Mike Simpson, who recorded under the name the Dust Brothers. We loved the Dust Brothers' shit the second we heard it and immediately wanted to work with them on our next record; their stuff had an entirely different vibe than the tracks on *Licensed to Ill*: funkier, jazzier, less classic rock, more R&B. It also pushed the boundaries of what we thought was possible with sample-based music.

We started working together and ended up recording most of the music and a fair number of vocals for *Paul's Boutique* at Matt's apartment. We really could have just recorded our entire album there, and in hindsight, I'm not exactly sure why we didn't. Capitol may have started to get nervous that we were holed up in a shitty apartment in the middle of a drug-and-prostitution zone. Or maybe we were just insecure and thought that to make a "big-time" record, we had to do it at some "big-time" studio with dudes with mullets crouched and poised to set up a mic or coil a cable. Or maybe we thought it was funny to record where Debbie Gibson and Lionel Richie might have recorded.

Anyway: we ended up at the Record Plant.

This place was the exact opposite of the Chung King House of Metal, not to mention Matt's apartment: An iconic L.A. studio. Platinum Eagles records lining the halls. Now, don't get me wrong. The Eagles are a big name in the game. Been in the game a long time. But what the fuck does that have to do with what we were making?

So we booked time at the Record Plant, and spent days just redoing the shit we'd already done at Matt's. We re-tracked every loop and scratch. Redid our vocals. Tweaked everything on the giant Solid State Logic mixing

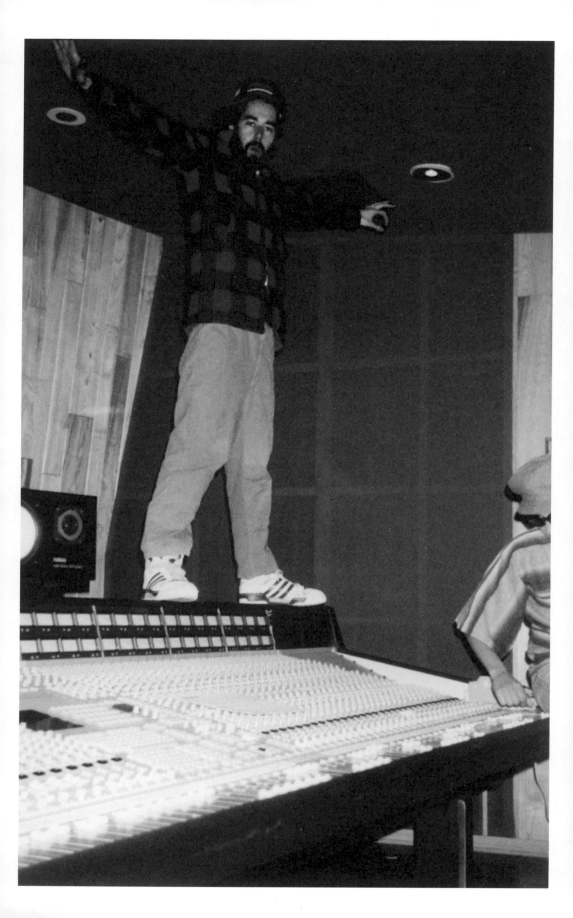

consoles you see in every super-fancy studio. Ran tracks through expensive outboard gear with every variety of knobs, faders, lights, and meters in abundance. It was the same crew— the three of us, Mario C on the faders, Mike and John behind desktop PCs (that's right, people, laptops were not the go-to yet), Matt Dike (RIP) kinda bobbing his head with a smile of approval every so often. And it took what seemed like forever.

One day while we were doing all this, a huge video crew rolled into the studio across the hall from us. Craft services times ten. An army of dudes with rolls of tape hanging from their belts and walkie-talkies on their shoulders. Persian rugs were suddenly everywhere. Lots of booze bottles placed around the studio, just-so.

Turned out Guns N' Roses was there to film the video for "Patience."

First we ran into Slash, briefly. Nice guy. Big hat. Then, by the reception desk, we stumbled into the bass player, Duff McKagan. We started talking about hardcore, and it turned out he was in this band we'd heard a lot on *Noise the Show* in our hardcore days: the Fartz. A Seattle hardcore band. So here we're meeting someone from a ginormous band traveling around the world on floating magic carpets, their feet never touching the ground, and we realized we had more in common than we'd ever have thought.

We never ran into Axl.

Anyway, back to the (re)recording of our album. After we got through a couple of songs—"Shake Your Rump" and "Car Thief"—we listened to what we'd done and realized, *Fuck—what we had from Matt's house was better*. Yeah, some of the new vocals were stronger on the new versions, but overall we were disappointed. We went more "pro" and lost some of the grit. This happens often when bands rerecord their demos—they get a more polished recording but lose some of the magical essence of the demo. Yeah, that's right: magical essence.

So did we cut our losses and go back to Matt's apartment? No, we did not. Instead, we doubled down on our bad idea by deciding to go record at some other big L.A. studios, on the off chance that they had some . . . *magical essence* that the Record Plant was missing.

We did some work at a studio where Quincy Jones had supposedly worked on those amazing albums he made with Michael Jackson. This spot had a crazy Harrison mixing console that looked like it belonged at NASA mission control. It was the first generation of digital console, a fucking humongous thing with all kinds of micro green and red lights. The wave of the future. Unfortunately, at that time, the future still sucked: nothing—and I mean *nothing*—worked on this

thing. We'd sit around for hours while guys in button-down shirts ran in and out of the room in panic mode, unable to figure out why the entire studio was inoperable. After several days of doing nothing, bored out of our minds, we finally just canceled the session.

So after all that, did we go back to Matt's apartment at last? No, we fucking did not: *We decided to just return to the Record Plant even though we didn't like what we'd already gotten there.* We booked it for weeks on end to finish the record, tracking final vocals, scratches, overdubs, and mixing. It might have been a productive plan if we hadn't also decided to rent basically an entire arcade's worth of games and put them in the main room of the studio. We're talking full-on air hockey, pinball, etc. It's not like we needed room for an orchestra— it was just the three of us doing vocals in this huge room, with a large staff to order us food and bring us coffee. We recorded ourselves playing Ping-Pong in stereo, so it could be panned left and right in the headphones. I guess it just made us feel big-time.

The upside was that we finally did finish *Paul's Boutique* in that second push at the Record Plant. The downside is that we wasted So. Much. Fucking. Money. I don't know the exact amount, but it was hundreds and hundreds of thousands of dollars fronted us by Capitol, which would come out of our royalties. It was even more of a fucking waste because we still liked many of the instrumental tracks from Matt's apartment best anyway. Soon enough, though, the amount of money we'd just wasted would be the least of our problems.

Not long after *Paul's Boutique* came out, I ran into our old friend Dante Ross. He told me that he had just heard our new record. He said (in a positive way), "Yo, I just heard your new record, it's all right. It's got like two songs on there." There's actually fifteen songs on the track list, so I assumed that he meant that only two of those fifteen were anything that anyone would want to listen to. We've used this quote about a thousand times since. "Yo, you heard that new Radiohead joint? It's got like one and a half songs on there."

Shake Your Rump—All kinds of sampled funk bass lines and beats coming at ya in stereo at a super-fast pace and even a bong rip that we recorded at a fancy Hollywood studio. Yes, we paid handsome amounts of $ to record a bong hit in a fancy studio where certainly many bong hits had come before but maybe none of them were recorded? Also, the dude that says "Is your name Michael Diamond?" was just a very tall messenger who happened to be delivering a cash

advance to us at the studio. We would get so excited every time this would happen, even though it was our money. We would nickname the messengers Louie.

Johnny Ryall—Johnny Ryall was a bum on our stoop. As in: Johnny Ryall was a homeless guy we frequently found sitting or sleeping in front of our place on Barrow Street. This was at a time when grimy shit like that could happen in NYC—when cops and politicians *let* grimy shit like that happen. Many blocks had their regular homeless characters, who might disappear from time to time (to go to various shelters or mental-health spots or maybe jail) but would invariably return and be welcomed back by everyone on the block.

Johnny was super weathered and leathery, but also looked like a 1950s rockabilly star. Widow's peak and all that. We never got him to talk much about himself, but we'd heard that he was a forgotten early rock star whose extensive booze-filled adventures—in addition to getting screwed on royalties—had led him to our stoop. We eventually expanded this story into the lyrics for "Johnny Ryall."

One day, when it was cold outside, I gave the real-life Johnny Ryall my Def Jam satin jacket to stay warm. At some point, Russell saw him in it and was super pissed. "Mike! Mike D! Why you give a Def Jam jacket to a bum? I don't want motherfuckers seein' that!" He didn't think Johnny was the best brand ambassador. But we did.

5-Piece Chicken Dinner—You know what? I am proud of this cut. Not because we spent so long making it, weaving in intricate ideas, or because we spent days on lyrics (there are none). It's just that this idea is so damn stupid and juvenile and we did it and it's super short and kinda great and starts off side 2 of the vinyl version. So there!

Shadrach—Allegedly, a very long time ago, there were these three Jewish dudes who would not bow down to a golden idol in the image of Nebuchadnezzar, the new king of Babylon. He was super pissed, and a lot of people got jealous of the three dudes, so the king threw them into a fiery furnace. They were like, *Fuck it, go ahead and throw us into a fiery furnace, God will make this right. We don't care about your bullshitty golden statue, and besides, we prefer the warm weather anyways.* When the king looked upon them in the fire, he saw that they were not only still alive, but they were singing songs and a fourth band member had joined them amongst the flames. None other than Jesus Christ himself. The king, being a total starfucker, was like, *Get those dudes out of the fiery furnace.*

#nebuchadnezzar #sad #failingempire (AH)

B-Boy Bouillabaisse—We wanted to make our own psychedelic rap manifesto inspired by listening to the Beatles' *Sgt. Pepper*, the Beach Boys' *Pet Sounds*, and Hendrix super loud in various automobiles and Yauch's bedroom. We had nine

song ideas left over. We could have spent time working on them and developing them more fully, but instead we decided to shove them all together into one medley and call it a bouillabaisse. One of these ideas featured Yauch's vocals recorded at his apartment using a military helmet with a microphone built in that he bought at a thrift store ("A Year and a Day"). Also, coming from hard-core, we always loved the economy of super-short songs. (Please listen to "I Like Food" by the Descendents.) So what if we tried some rap songs like that? Then throw in for good measure a completely crazy (said with a thick French accent) 808 beat that Yauch recorded onto an 8-track in his kitchen ("AWOL"), backward loops, fuzz bass, b-boy routines, and a hundred NYC shout-outs, then chop up and mix and cut it all together with a Ginsu II.

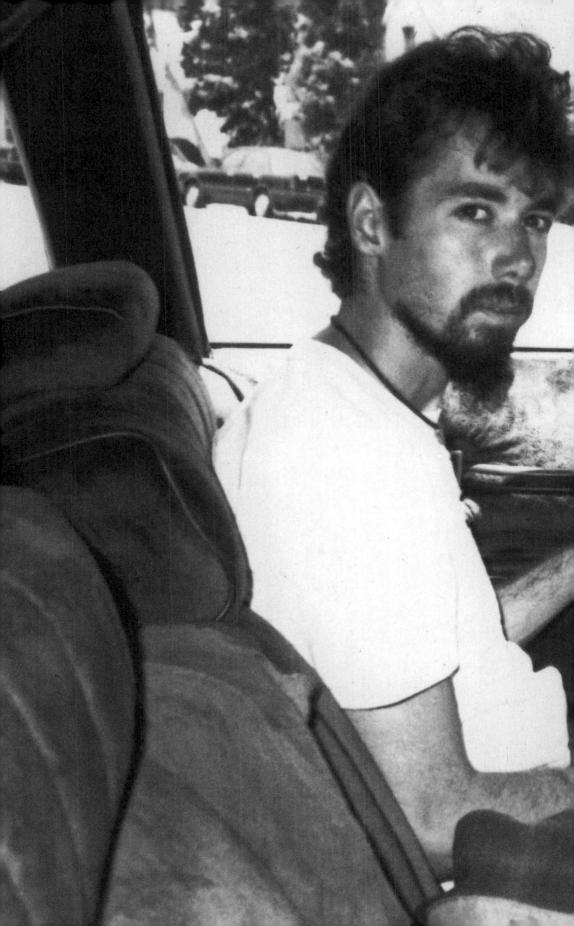

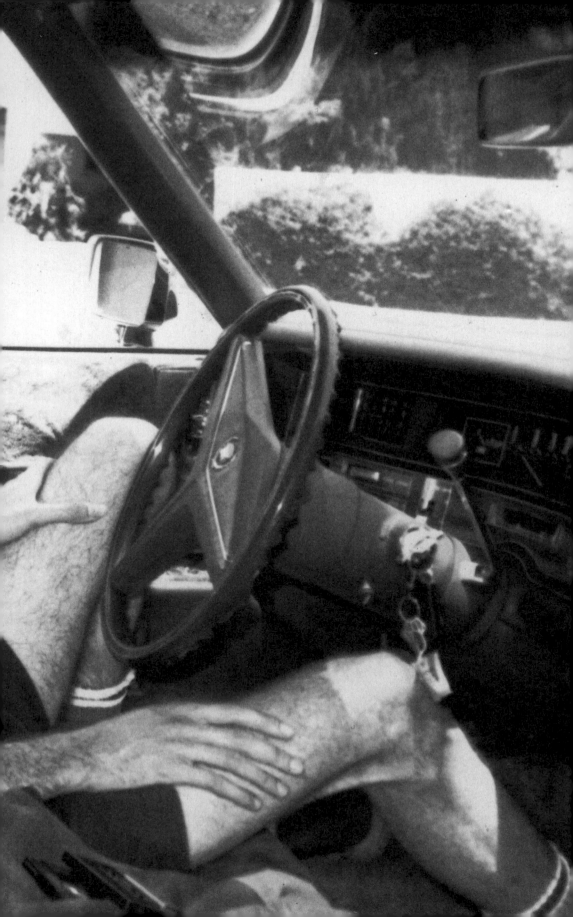

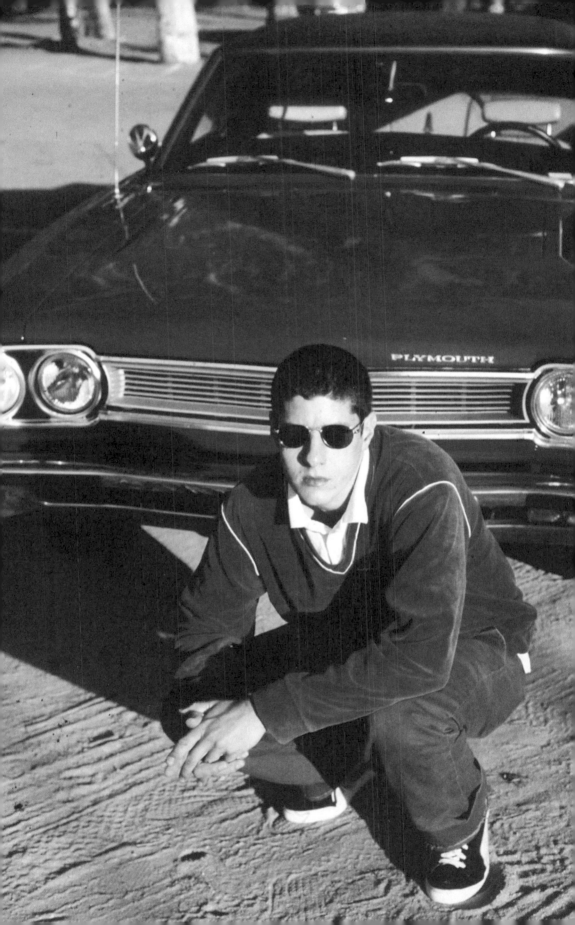

Barrel-Chested Randy

(MD)

Growing up in New York City, none of us had a car. None of us needed a car. We took the subway. We walked. Sometimes, if we had some extra cash, we piled into taxis.

When we started hanging out with Run and them, they lived in Queens. It was b-boy to drive a car, a whip, whatever. In certain areas—like the Hollis that Run-DMC came from, the Brooklyn where Eric B and Rakim came from, or the Roosevelt, Long Island, where Public Enemy came from—only drug dealers, pimps, celebrity reverends, and crooked politicians drove nice cars. On "Sucker MC's," when Run rhymed "now Larry put me inside his Cadillac," that was some vivid and real shit; as soon as Run-DMC made some money, DMC got a Cadillac, Jam Master Jay got a Jeep Wrangler, and Run had his BMW 3-series. After Russell signed Eric B and Rakim, Eric B wowed us all by spending a sizeable amount of his advance money on a used burgundy four-door Rolls-Royce. I mean, this was some Thurston Howell III–type shit. It seemed way out of our reach.

> You seem to have detailed knowledge about things that "only drug dealers" have, Michael. . . . (AH)

> Larry refers to Larry Smith, hip hop producer extraordinaire, who produced the first few Run-DMC albums, Kurtis Blow, etc. When his records started becoming hits, Larry bought a Cadillac real quick. (MD)

As soon as we started spending time in L.A., though, we followed suit. We had a manager at the time named Andy Slater, and he introduced us to this guy Randy.

Randy wore glasses, was always well groomed. He had a big barrel chest and wore tight polo shirts tucked into even tighter pants. He was one of those guys who repeated his spiel over and over every single time he talked to you, as if he'd never said it before: "I'm going to get you into the right car at the right price." Randy would always be talking about what cars he was handling for whom. Inevitably, any conversations about your car would segue into a discussion about what Randy was doing for Kenny Rogers or Lionel Richie, how fabulous they were, and how even more fabulous their cars were. This was Hollywood 101. You're only as successful as your clientele.

Say what you will about Randy's spiel, though; he *meant* that shit. He could get you anything. Some old muscle car: check. A brand-new Range Rover: done. Vintage Cadillac: you got it. And he'd get you any kind of accessories you wanted—the booming system, the interiors, the ginormous car phone. And yeah, we could have just gone to a Range Rover dealership, but remember (a) this whole buying-a-car thing was completely new and foreign to us; (b) we looked like, acted like, and were still teenagers basically, so some slick dude at

a luxury car dealership in Beverly Hills with a mustache and aviator glasses was not looking to spend time showing us around anything; and (c) we *had* to customize that shit: boomin' system, phone, car fax machine, etc. Yeah, that's right, a fax machine so I could write a rhyme about getting a fax in a car and then fax it to you. We definitely didn't know where to start with that, but Randy had an endless list of suppliers who would gladly help lighten our pockets.

We were kids in a candy store. We'd sit in the studio with Randy, stoned, looking at pictures of cars and talking about them. Of course, this service came at a very steep price—one that was frankly out of our league, though we didn't realize it at the time. Adam Horovitz went with a beautiful, dark green Range Rover. Very b-boy, but elegant at the same time. He also added some crazy subwoofers in the back; I don't think there was much trunk left, but he had a shit-ton of bass. Only problem was, this thing was a lemon and had to go into the shop all the time.

I opted for a crazy vintage muscle car: A 1968 Plymouth GTX with a 440 engine. Red, with white decal stripes. I kind of pimped out the interior, adding b-boy burgundy piping to the white seats and putting in a crazy sound system that—when it worked and if you were properly stoned—was pretty transcendent. We also built a custom box between the two front seats for the massive car phone. The car would have been great, had I possessed any mechanical know-how whatsoever. I did not.

The backseat area of Yauch's car was wild. All burgundy pleather, with the secret flip-up bucket seats that faced backward. When the seats were folded down, it was like a plush, carpeted, sleazy moshpit. (AH)

It constantly required tinkering with the carburetor, fuel lines, hoses, and spark plugs so it would run right—or actually run at all. I had to call AAA so many times I started to wish they had frequent flier miles. Though I probably didn't help my own cause by putting a sound system appropriate for a nightclub in a car from the 1960s with an AM radio.

Yauch won the prize for most esoteric and least practical choice: an early '70s black Cadillac Fleetwood Brougham d'Elegance. (Best name ever.) This thing was basically a limo. A ride for a '70s diplomat or maybe a studio chief. An early '70s Maybach, if you will.

It was huge and thoroughly impractical to park. But it was incredible to cruise in. It also rode really low to the ground, so any bumps or dips would make it bottom out and

DAT stood for digital audio tape. It was the next step in the evolution of the cassette: a smaller tape, and a huge step up sonically. You could record your own music and not have the hiss and loss that you got on cassette. (MD)

scrape the ground. Yauch put in an incredible sound system that featured a DAT player, which was completely unheard-of at the time. We would drive around, blasting DATs of stuff we were working on or mixes of music, and just drive and pretty much have the best time ever, bought for us at a markup by our new friend Randy.

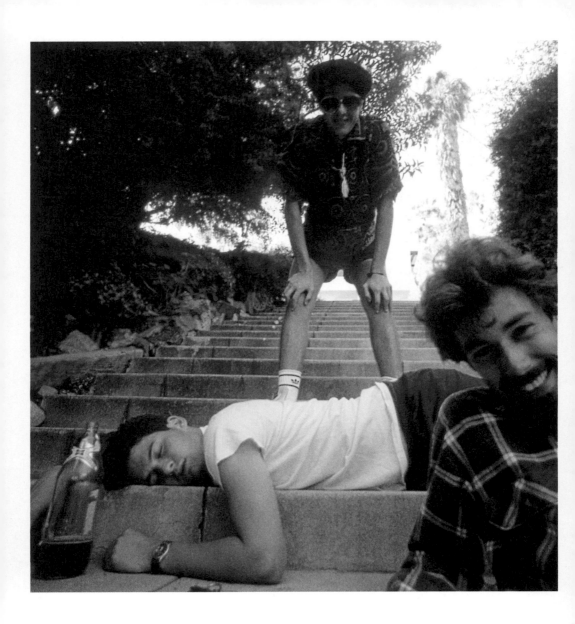

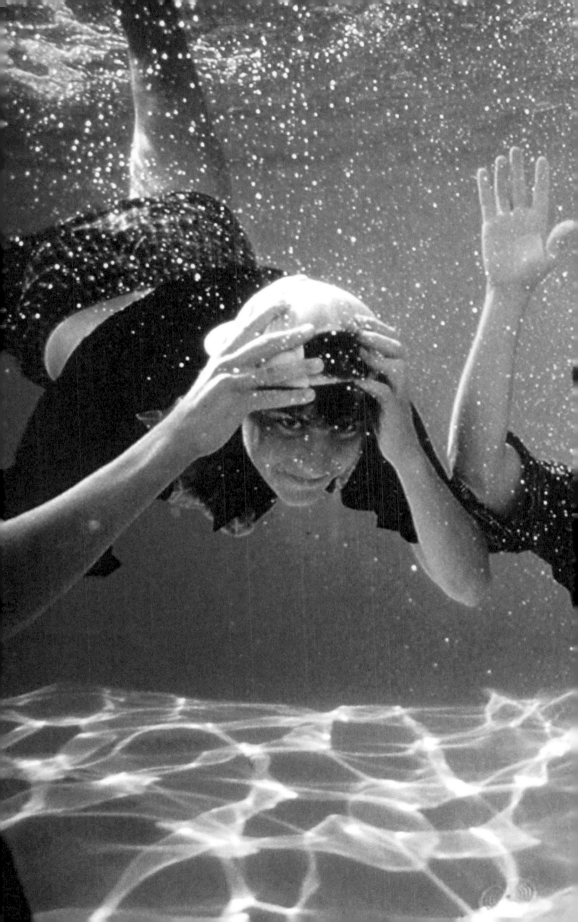

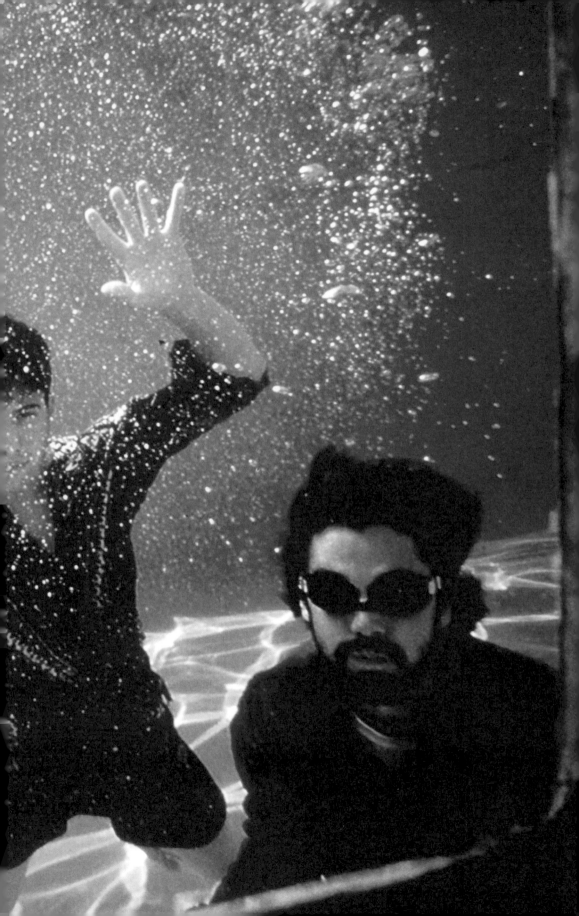

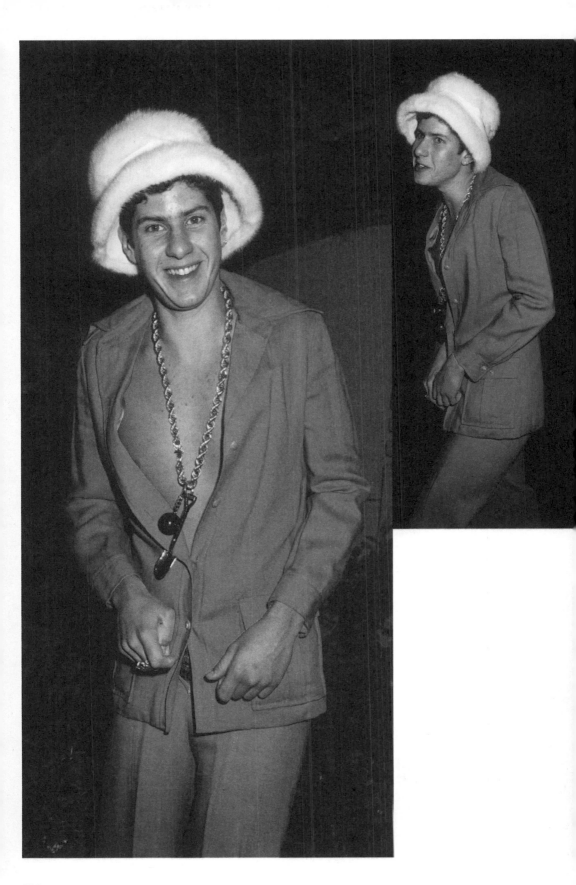

It All Started at Dolly Parton's Birthday Party
(AH)

At some point in 1988, me, Adam, and Mike had decided that since we were together pretty much all day and night already . . . we might as well rent a big house and just do it up family-style. Enter the G Spot. It was a crazy house off of Mulholland Drive. (Just down the street from the spaceship-looking house from the movie *Body Double*.) There was a gate at the entrance to the house with a big *G* on it. Hence the name. You'd go through the gate and you'd drive down this little driveway, and straight ahead where you parked you could see right into the house, right into this crazy entryway with a rock wall, a bunch of fake plants, and a pool table. Outside the house was a swimming pool with a little bridge that went over it. It was butter on a roll at a shitty spaghetti place. THE BEST.

The interior-decoration scheme was like the restaurant that the cast of *Quincy* hung out at, or the Regal Beagle from *Three's Company*. The house had a burgundy vinyl restaurant-style booth for dining at, and an olde-tyme lamppost in the living room. You know . . . just 'cause. We fucking loved it. And made ourselves right at home. We each picked our own room. Mike's was the master bedroom suite upstairs. The one with the view and the huge bathtub. Yauch's was the media center/library room. It had a massive '80s television and oversized reclining

It was adorned with nude statuary that involved the feeding of grapes. (MD)

leather bad-boy chairs and couches. My room was the pool house, separate from the main house. It was right on the side of the mountain. It had a bar in it, and there was a window that looked right into the bottom of the pool. So fucking great. (The inside sleeve picture from *Paul's Boutique* was taken from inside that bedroom.) Some nights I'd fall asleep to the sounds of wild animals. Ones we didn't have in Manhattan. Deer, raccoon, coyote, fuckin' bobcats. And some mornings I'd wake up hearing loud banging. I'd look up and see Yauch, fully clothed in the swimming pool, harassing me through the little pool window. Trying to get me to wake up so we could do . . . nothing.

The owners of the G Spot were an older couple named Alex and Madilyn Grasshoff. In one of the bathrooms there was an illustration of a few people surrounding a movie camera that said **GRASSHOPPER UNIT** on it. We were curious about this, and so we did some research on the Grasshoffs (by going through most of their personal stuff inside the house). We discovered that Alex was a TV director, and had made this massively popular after-school special in the early '80s called *The Wave*. Damn, the G Spot jumped up to another

level. The house with a fucking lamppost in the kitchen and all the crazy '70s trimmings is owned by the dude who made *The Wave* . . . and homie's got a unit!?! The Grasshopper Unit.

If you can picture the movie character Dolemite, in 1975, having a meeting with contractors and architects, sitting down to discuss building his dream home . . . the G Spot would be it. The main thing about our rental home, though, was this . . . in the room Mike was staying in, there was a locked closet. And when you're mostly stoned and really have nothing to do all day . . . you get curious. So, we broke into the closet. Inside was what we assumed to be Madilyn's wardrobe. A fucking barrage of crazy shit from the '70s. Like, if you would have said that Sly & the Family Stone wore this stuff on the *There's a Riot Goin' On* tour in 1972, we would've been like, "Ooohh shhiitt!!!" So, of course, we started wearing Madilyn's clothes around the house . . . often. She had, like, long ankle-length brown leather coats. Fur items. Straw shower-cap things. So many signature pieces. Then we started to wear them out. On the town, that is. And that brings us to . . . Dolly Parton's birthday party.

What had happened was, we got invited to the big-time music manager Sandy Gallin's house to celebrate Dolly Parton's birthday, and what do you do when you get invited to Dolly Parton's birthday party? You fucking go to that shit psyched as hell.

So . . . day of . . . we're at the G Spot and we're getting pumped and prepped for Dolly's party. While trying on various ensembles, we were like, "Yo . . . We are for sure wearing the most fucked-up outfits to the party tonight, right?" "Yes." We split up for whatever reason, and me+Yauch said to Mike and his girlfriend (and future wife) Tamra, see you at the party tonight. Then, before me+Yauch left, we decided that there was no way we were wearing this stuff tonight. This party's gonna be awkward enough already. But we did not convey that decision to Mike+Tamra. Hey, it was pre-cellphone. *I'm sure we tried.*

Prior to Dolly Parton's gala birthday event and after our fallout with Russell Simmons, we met with Sandy Gallin to see if, potentially, he would be our manager. He was the manager for people like Dolly Parton, Michael Jackson, Cher, and Barbra Streisand. So why not us, right? The meeting took place one afternoon at Mr. Gallin's big crazy awesome house in Beverly Hills. The sun was out. Birds were chirping. Dude had a big crazy landscaped lawn, a koi pond with a walking path that led you to the big front door. Me, Adam, and Mike were feeling a little out of our league/element. Three schleps from New York in this lush environment. We rang the bell and waited. The door opened and it's Sandy Gallin in just his tighty-whitey Fruit of the Loom underpants. M'okay. We said our hellos and introductions, and he led us through the big foyer and into a huge living room. He said, "I'll be right back," and soon returned in a white terry-cloth robe. He sat on the couch, and we had our meeting. As they say in Hollywood, we weren't the right match but . . . that shit was super big-time Hollywood, and kind of fuckin' gangster. (AH)

Me+Yauch get to the party, and there's Mike. Now, I don't remember the exact outfit he had on, but it was something like this: Satin or velvet pants. Ankle-length patchwork leather coat. No shirt. And a huge white fur hat. Tamra was in basically the same outfit. Now, remember, this was before any kind of '70s throwback/*Austin Powers*/Deee-Lite–esque scenario, so Mike+Tamra just looked like crazy, perhaps homeless, people at the super-fancy

Actually, it was a green leisure suit–type deal. Not just green, but super-bright lime green. Something you could spot from hundreds of yards away. A matching jacket and super-wide flared bell-bottom pants. And to top this look off, literally, I had on a white fur hat kinda like Sly Stone meets your grandma–style. (MD)

Interestingly, it was still somehow close enough to the '70s that people really got uncomfortable for a minute seeing this kind of throwback commitment. The party's attendees were older than us and had actually worn these clothes in the '70s. At this particular point in time, people were not checking that era for fashion cues. (MD)

Hollywood party. For Dolly fuckin' Parton. In retrospect it's funny, but to Mike+Tammy, in that moment, maybe not so much. But there we were, hanging out at the party. You know, us, Kenny Rogers, Barbra Streisand, and people of that stature, ilk, and genre.

We saw Bob Dylan there. Mike's a huge Dylan fan, and I don't know what he was thinking but he went right over to talk to him. He's like, "Hi, I'm Mike, I'm in a band called Beastie Boys, and . . ." Dylan doesn't flinch at his crazy outfit, but he asks the age-old question . . . "How many you good for?"

MIKE
(TAKEN ABACK A LITTLE)

What?

Bob Dylan is seated on the arm of a sofa with his back turned to a small group of people that are still in conversation with him.

BOB DYLAN
(SPOKEN WITH A BOB DYLAN ACCENT)
Tickets, man. How many you good for?

MIKE
You mean, like, how many people come to see my band play?

BOB DYLAN
Mmm-hmm.

MIKE
(AWKWARDLY)
I don't know. Like, a few hundred maybe. Sometimes a few thousand, maybe. I don't know.

BOB DYLAN
(MATTER-OF-FACTLY)
Good. I'm putting together a pro-smoking concert, and I'm trying to get people involved.

MIKE
(NOW NOTICEABLY UNCOMFORTABLE)
Oh . . . wow . . . huh?

(PAUSE)

MIKE (CONT'D)
Pro-smoking . . . like, cigarettes?

(ANOTHER PAUSE)

MIKE (CONT'D)
Benefit . . . concert?

Now very aware of his outfit and out-of-placeness in this adult Hollywood party, Mike sort of mumbles some other words as he slowly backs away from Bob Dylan, retreating to the comfort of his friends.

END OF SCENE

Mike came back to me, Yauch, and Tammy, and reported what just happened. Like . . . where do you go from there? When you get out-weirded by Bob Dylan, what do you do next? Walk away, I guess. We snooped around the house for a bit, looking for Dolly Parton. But we never saw her, so we split. On our way out, though, we walked by someone playing this amazing grand piano, and Mike said, "Oh shit . . . that's Burt fucking Bacharach!" Oh shit . . . that *is* Burt fucking Bacharach. Hollywood is awesome!

This night marked a new future for us. We were now part of the fucking Grasshopper Unit.
WHAT.

S SHACK
22/7887

LET TELL YA LITTLE STORY BOUT MY MIKE D [DD]

ROLLIN FROM N.Y. TO CALIFORNIE

THOUGHTS OF FARMERS DAUGHTERS ~~& A~~ AND A ROLL IN THE HAY

BUT YA KNOW WHAT THEY SAY EVERY DOG HAS HIS DAY

NAUGAHIDE INTERIOR, CHROME EXTERIOR

TIMOTHY'S LEARY BUT I WAS LEARYER

LOOK IN THE LIST TO CHECK THE GOLD ROOF DISPLAY
FEAR + LOATHIN CROSS THE COUNTY LISTNIN TO MY 8 TRACK

REACH¹ᶜᵒ BEHIND THE SEAT AND GRABBED A COOL 1 FROM THE

CHECK THE ODOMETER I WAS WELL ON MY WAY
LONG DISTANCE FROM ~~A~~ MY GIRL TALKIN ON THE CELLULAR ~~PACK~~ BACK
~~TOOK CHECK THE REAR~~

SAY SHE WAS SORRY ~~SO~~ BUT I SAID THE HELL YOU WERE

DO 120 PLOWIN OVER MAIL BOXES

RADAR DETECTOR TO TELL ME WERE THE COPS IS

PABST BLUE RIBBON
SPEND ANOTHER NITE AT A MOTEL SIX

IN MY BRANDY SNIFTER I'M A MANIAC KLEPTO
FIVE DOLLAR EXTRA ~~TO WATCH~~ GOT THE PORNO FLICKS

K-MART SHOP LIFTER
CASH FLOW GETTIN LOW AND I HAD TA PULL A JOB

FOUND A NICE PLACE TO VISIT BUT A BETTER PLACE TO ROB

PARKED ~~THE~~ WIT
~~LEFT THE CAR~~ ~~THE LIGHTS WERE ON~~ THE ENGIN STILL REVIN

OH THANK HEAVEN FOR 7-11

WENT INSIDE TO MAKE MY WITHDRAWL

SAW WHAT HE HAD AND I HAD TO TAKE ~~IT~~ ALL

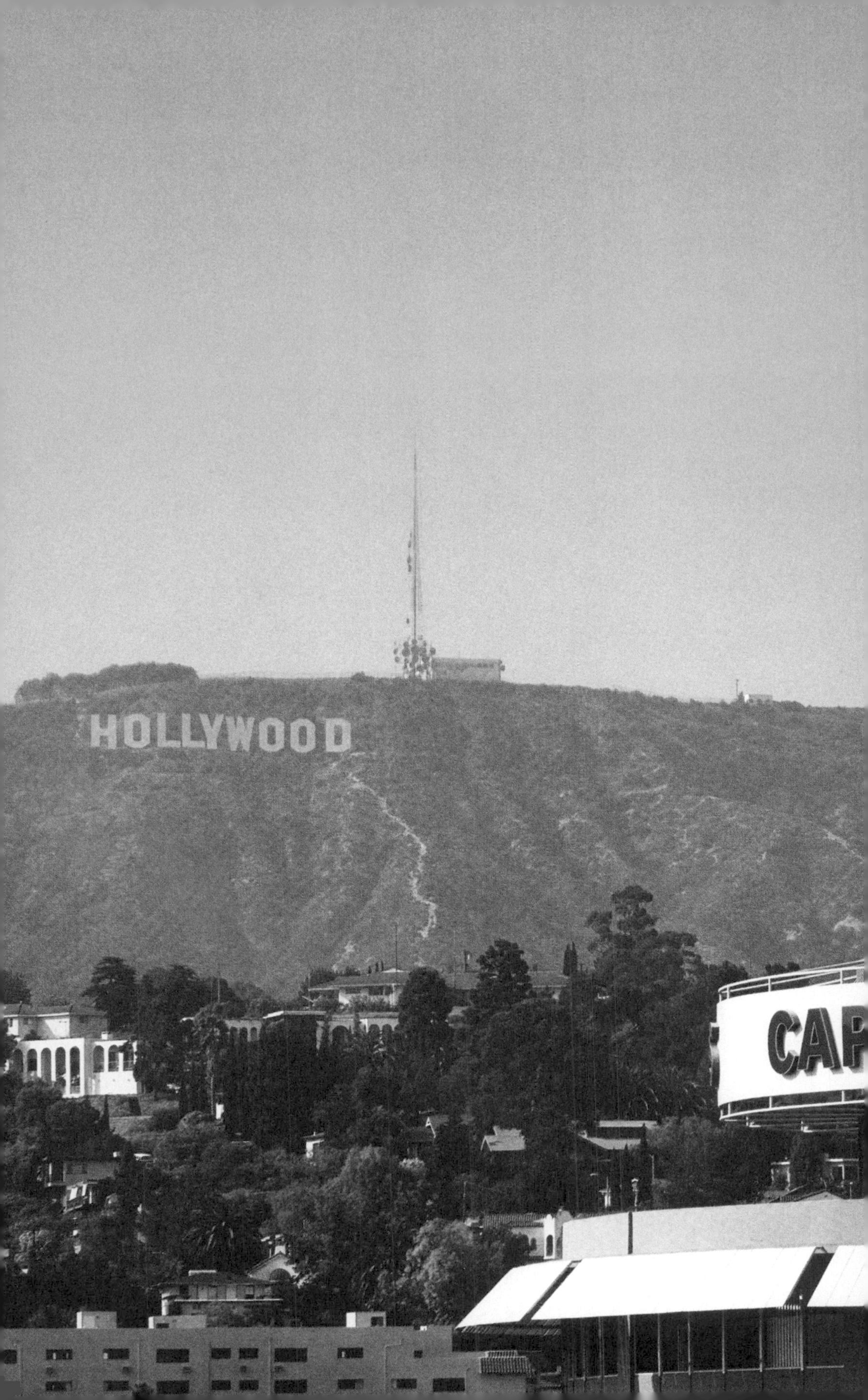
HOLLYWOOD
CAP

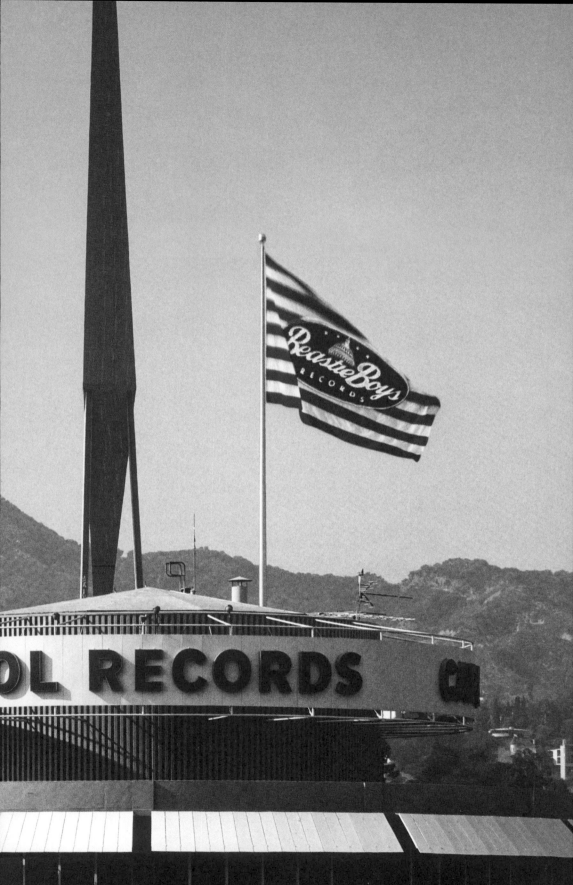

The Business of *Paul's Boutique*

(AH)

It's not like we wanted to burn the fuckin' flag or anything. We just wanted a huge American flag that said Beastie Boys on it, flown on the roof of the Capitol Records Building. And when *Paul's Boutique* was done, finished, and handed in to Capitol, that flag was raised for all of Los Angeles to see. We had a big record-release party up on the roof of the building. Hollywood's own Empire State Building. The party coincided with George Bush's campaign to protect the American flag from desecration. We weren't trying to burn it or anything. We were the multiplatinum fight-for-your-right-to-party guys . . . we were just *really* feeling ourselves. And we wanted the world to know. Like, this *was* Frank Sinatra's building, but now it's ours. We truly believed that we were shot callers. (It's like when Tamra Davis was gonna direct a video for Cher. The first day of the shoot Cher walks right up to Tammy D, introduces herself, and says . . . "I'm gonna be wearing leather. A lot of leather. Get used to it.") And that's when things started to get a little . . . odd.

Right after we handed in the final version of *Paul's Boutique*, the president of Capitol Records quit. Around the same time, the A&R guy who brought us in and signed us quit. New faces at the label. New band on the label. Then this happened: Capitol brought us in for a marketing meeting to launch the record. They had us sit down with their "street team" to figure out how to get the word out to "the streets." (Yikes.)

The street team had a plan. They had been given the title Street Awareness Program. And so on their presentation paperwork it spelled out SAP in big letters across the top of each page. Already funny. SAP, SAP, SAP. Their marketing plan was for us to make a diss record against MC Hammer. They said that diss records always get some kind of attention, and 'cause Hammer was so huge, that'd be great. Oh, and that because Hammer was also on Capitol Records, it'd be easy to contact him to let him know that it wasn't for real. We told the SAPs that we'd never met Hammer and had nothing against him, and that he seemed like a nice enough guy. Maybe we should just try to get the songs on the radio and in clubs and stuff instead. To be fair . . . me, Adam, and Mike were sitting in that meeting obviously high as kites and dressed in our best Madilyn Grasshoff outfits looking like we were on our way to a Cymande concert. I'm sure the lack of confidence was mutual.

But the most weirdest and most bummerish thing happened *after* the record came out. We just assumed that because *Licensed to Ill* sold a billion copies, *Paul's Boutique* would do the same. But, like, it didn't. I went to the Tower Records on Sunset Boulevard a couple days after it came out, and they didn't

have any copies. So I thought, *Great, this shit is flying off the shelves and we are still large.* It turned out that they did sell out quick, but Capitol had only sent, like, I don't know, a hundred or so copies. No back order, nothing. Seriously . . . Capitol is literally down the street from Tower Records. Can't someone drive a couple boxes over? I mean, shit . . . *I'll buy the goddamn stamps.* We don't know who we were supposed to call to be like . . . "You know, there's no copies at Tower Records" or . . . "Is there a better game plan than us humiliating ourselves by making a record trying to pick a fight with MC Hammer?"

"That's insane, you're stupid. You should sleep late, man; it's just much easier on your constitution." (Bill Murray)

So we were kind of in a holding pattern. We kept trying to arrange a meeting with the new president of Capitol Records. But he wasn't really getting back to us. A solid couple weeks go by and then we finally meet with him. We go to the top floor of the Capitol Records Building and wait on some nice new couches. The president is ready for us, so we go in. The first thing I notice is *Man, this is a nice office.* It's kind of huge and has a *crazy* view. You can see all of what L.A. is made of. But the most striking visual inside the room is the new president himself. My man is, like, mid-fifties, balding on top with a teeny ponytail in the back, and he's rocking a brand-new crispy fake tie-dyed Grateful Dead tour T-shirt. (*Eesh.*)

So, we sit down, and before we can ask our whats and whys, he's like . . . "Look, guys. I'm a Deadhead so I know where you're at. The company's just really busy right now. We're all just focusing, and working really hard on the new Donny Osmond album so, next time. Okay?" *Wait . . . What?!* What he had just said to us, the multiplatinum fight-for-your-right-to-party guys, is . . . *Forget about the record you just spent the past couple years making. Forget that you made a huge and bold move severing ties with Rick, Russell, Rush, and Def Jam. Forget all this life-changing shit that's happening to you as a band, people, and friends. Because . . . Donny Osmond's new record is just a little more important than yours. Just go back, make another record, and we'll see what happens when that happens. Everything's gonna be fine.*

INDUSTRY RULE NUMBER 4080: RECORD COMPANY PEOPLE ARE SHAAADY.

The teeny ponytailed/phony-baloney hippie costume/looking like an undercover cop guy was replaced soon after by . . . some other middle-aged white guy record executive. To quote the great Donny Osmond . . . "One bad apple don't spoil the whole bunch, girl."

Important note: besides this glitch, Capitol Records has always been really supportive of us and what we make. I'm not talking shit on the label, because really, for a major label with a big business to run, they left us alone to make what we wanted to make, and we probably couldn't have done that somewhere else. That being said . . . for a good time, look up "Donny Osmond Sacred Emotion" on YouTube. That's what this Deadhead had the company locked down with.

STOP THAT TRAIN

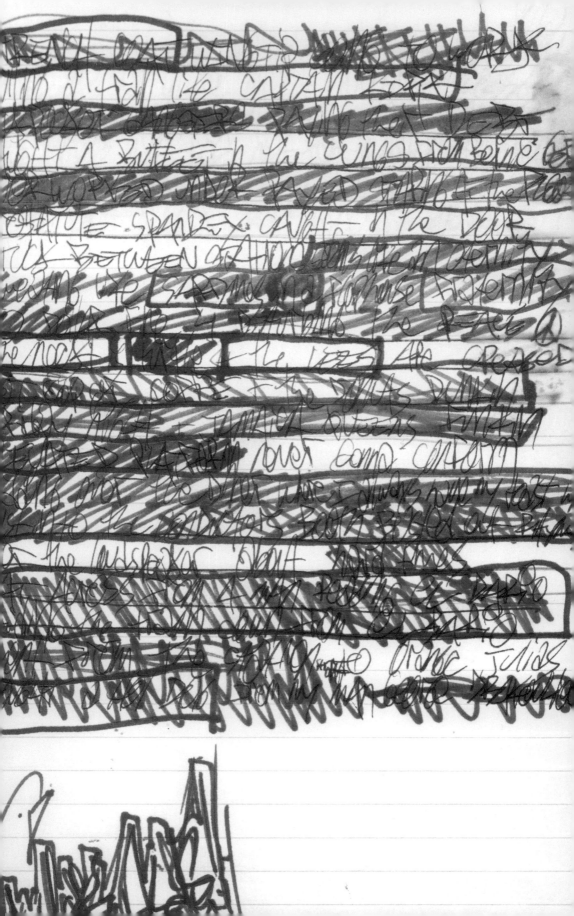

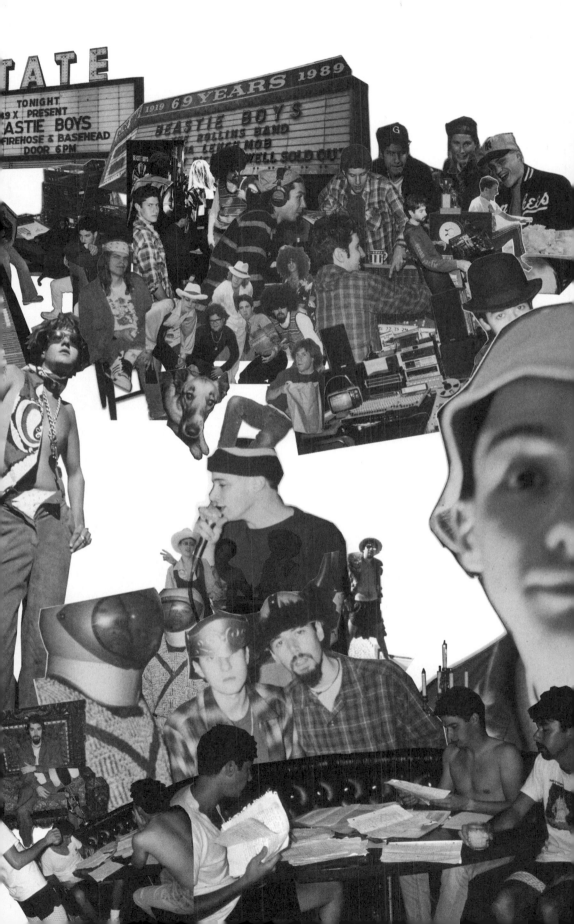

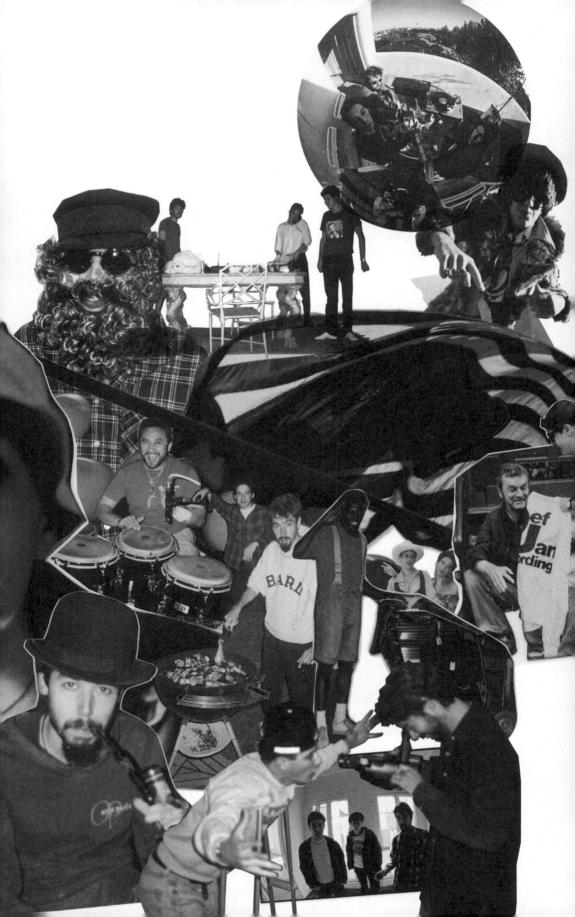

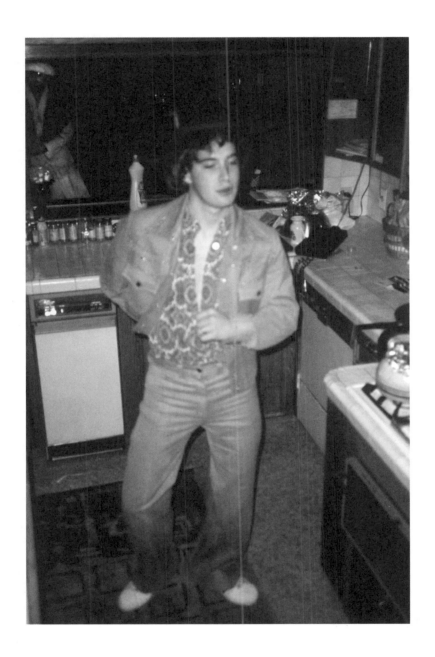

Zero Recollection
(AH)

It happens to all of us. I think. (I hope.) You see an old picture of yourself, and you're like . . . *I have zero recollection of what that is.* The memory of that moment is just . . . gone. You scan the room for clues. Nothing. It's fascinating. Like that picture over there . . .

Where the fuck am I? I *do not* recognize the location. It wasn't taken at the Grasshoffs' house. Where is it?! I'm kind of intrigued by all the lost memories in this picture. When, where, and why did I get rid of that paisley shirt? I'm sure that I wanted it when I got it, right? I mean, it was the '80s and I must've been like, *That's a cool paisley shirt, I'd like to own that.* And then time moves on and you're over it. At one point we were so happy together. Even no matter what other people said. Especially when I wore you with overalls. And now something's happened. Maybe you lost interest. We never see each other anymore.

It's not a paisley shirt. I see no tears.
(Conny, the book designer)

But man . . . that awesome denim outfit, though. Where did I get it, and where did it go? Did I give it to someone? Did I just leave it somewhere? That's not my actual hair. What am I holding behind my back? The wondering goes on and on. I know I must've been *super* high when this picture was taken, and so that's a partial puzzle piece right there, but I digress. . . .

My favorite thing about this picture is *not* that I have zero recollection of anything going on or where it went down. It's not my little denim outfit or the pose I'm striking. And it's not the aluminum foil over the teakettle in this shitty kitchen. My favorite thing about this picture is that Yauch is creeping over my shoulder there in the background, wearing an even crazier outfit.

Soul Train
(AH)

No one you know has been on *Soul Train*, right? Well, I just wanna say how fuckin' cool it was that we got to be on *Soul Train*. And not once but twice. The first time was in '87 to promote *Licensed to Ill*. And like most things at that time, it went by in a blur. Everything felt unreal. All of a sudden being a big band. Not being the opener but the headliner. And now we're on TV. Fuckin' ... *American Bandstand*, *Soul Train*, *The Joan Rivers Show*. Yes. *The Joan Rivers Show*. Out of all the talk shows we've ever done, Joan Rivers was the best. She came to our little dressing room before the show to meet us. We could hear her coming down the hall screaming, "Who's from Brooklyn?" She was awesome and hilarious and really nice to us. So there.

But *Soul Train*? Being on *Soul Train* was like being on *Bugs Bunny*. That show was so embedded into our fabric, our DNA. It was unreal to go from being seven years old, lying on the couch eating fuckin' Entenmann's pound cake watching *Soul Train* to us being on that stage. With those dancers. With none other than Don, the Don, Cornelius. *Mind-blowing*. If I could've told my fifth-grade class that I was gonna be on *Soul Train* twice, I would have had baller status at PS 41 for sure ... even Mr. Goldstein would've been like ... "OH SHIT!!!"

The second time we were booked on the show, in '89, we made sure that shit was tight. I'm sorry to spoil this for you, but no one actually performed their music on *Soul Train*. Or *American Bandstand*. Or almost any of those old shows. Have you ever been onstage and had to lip sync? But do it like you want people to believe that you're actually singing and playing? Well, it for sure makes you feel like a doofus and it's kind of mortifying. That's why we fucked around so much.

So, before we went to do *Soul Train* the second time, we recorded a new "live" version of the song we were gonna perform. We figured at least it'd be different. And if we added some call-and-response it'd be funny and maybe some-
one in the know watching would think, *Wait... are they actually doing this song live right now?* So we're up there, doing the song. Cameras are rolling. Dancers are dancing. And we came to the part where we had recorded "somebody say Don ... DON! Cornelius ... CORNELIUS!" My friend Dono was there watching Don Cornelius watching the little TV monitor off to the side of the stage, and when Cornelius

heard his own name, he got super confused. Looking at the monitor, then the stage, then the monitor, then the stage. For a moment he thought, *Are they actually doing this song live right now?*

When the song ended, he comes out onstage to plug our new record that's available in the marketplace, and to say thanks for being here and all that other TV-show-host stuff. The same thing he'd done with James Brown, the Commodores, Roberta Flack, etc. But now it's us. You tell me how you would feel if that was you being greeted by Don Cornelius. On the actual *Soul Train* stage. Unreal, right? Anyways . . . Don Cornelius hesitantly walks out onstage toward us. Cameras still rolling. But . . . he seems weirded-out by us. Me+Mike had brought copies of Ronco *Soul Train's Greatest Hits* records with us. We asked him to autograph them for us right there on the air. He probably thought that we were fucking with him. He was used to having legends on his stage. Not three scrubs potentially trying to clown him. But really . . . we weren't.

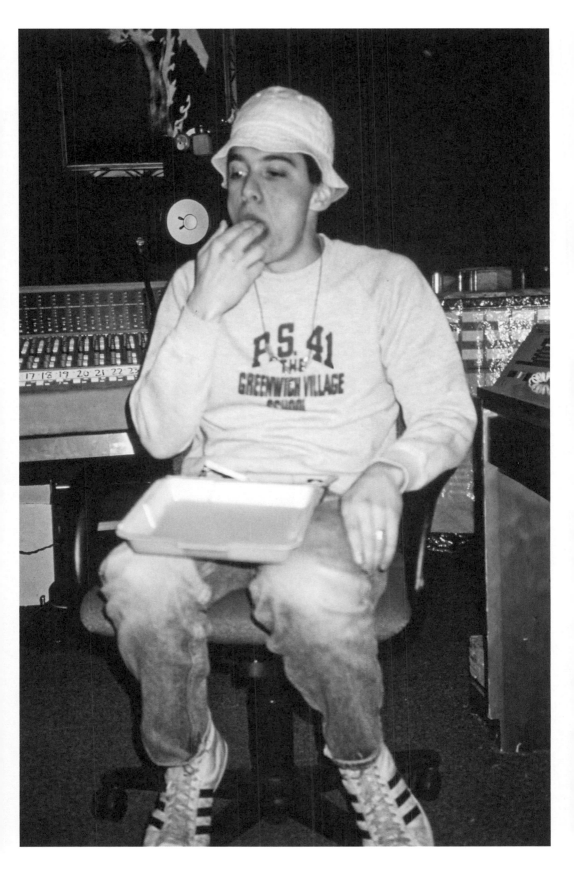

G-Son
(MD)

When I accidentally slammed a rental car into the gate outside the Grasshoffs' house, I wanted to avoid calling the landlord—better to just quietly have it repaired ourselves. Mario Caldato, the engineer on *Paul's Boutique* who was now part of our regular crew, recommended his old friend Mark. *He's great with this stuff, he'll fix it no problem.*

Mark's full name was Mark Ramos Nishita, and he *was* great. Fixed the gate perfectly and talked to us a lot about music. Next time we saw Mario, we were all kind of like, "This guy's awesome. What's the deal with him?" Come to find out, Mario and Mark had grown up together and played in a bunch of the same bands. Mark apparently could play anything, was an especially good keyboard player, and had all kinds of great music gear. But more important for our immediate needs, he was an excellent carpenter.

It had been pretty heartbreaking when *Paul's Boutique* didn't work. So we did what we do best: just hung out. Got breakfast, got stoned, bought some records, listened to records, talked about what parts of what records are amazing. Drove around. Made mixtapes. Listened to mixtapes. Sampled some music, programmed some beats. What I'm trying to say is, we would absolutely and completely obsess over records. Then, eventually, we got around to talking about making a new record.

We'd been super-inspired by a bunch of the soul, funk, and jazz records we were buying and sampling. We also felt that we'd pushed sample-based songs as far as they could go on *Paul's Boutique*. Plus, that shit was getting mad expensive. So the idea for our next record became, *Let's go in the opposite direction*: Instead of sampling records, we'll *play* the music. Like, on instruments. *Ourselves.* Music that was influenced by those records we'd been buying and that sounded like them, using that exact sort of instrumentation. *Yeah, we never trained as musicians, but we're going to play like the music we sample, even though that music was played by guys who spent decades learning jazz.* You might say it was stoned, arrogant, or straight-up crazy, but you can't say it wasn't ambitious.

This was all possible because nobody at Capitol wanted anything to do with us. The new people were like, "I just got this new job. I don't wanna get fired. I ain't messing with that, you do it." Like a bunch of kids in a schoolyard looking at a dead bird. Their lack of interest gave us free rein to do whatever we wanted. We were on paid vacation.

By then, we'd moved out of the G Spot (the Grasshoff house) and each gotten our own place, so we set up our instruments in Horovitz's West Hollywood apartment. Me on drums, Yauch on bass, Horovitz on guitar. Mario

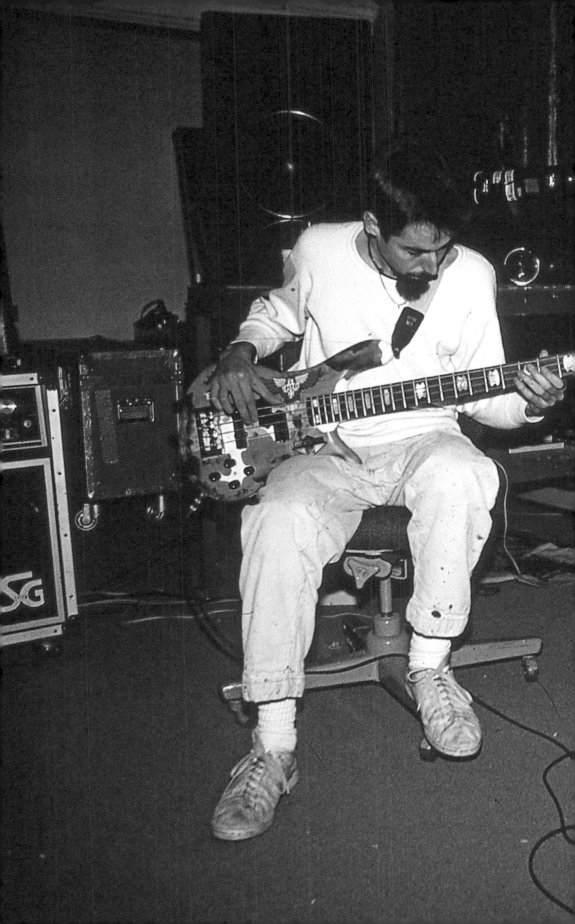

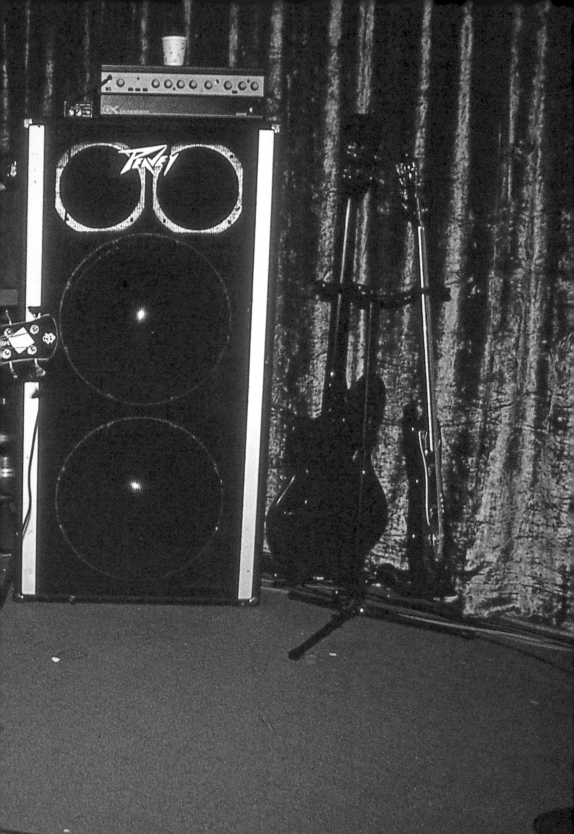

helped us set everything up and was there all the time, recording everything using these weird, flat, low-tech but cool-sounding PZM microphones bought at Radio Shack. Mario was very much on the same page as us, and understood what we wanted to achieve—even if on some days that just meant smoking pot and listening to Lee "Scratch" Perry.

Pretty quickly, we realized we needed a keyboard player to pull off the sound we were after. Someone who could play the Wurlitzer, the organ, the Moog, and the clavinet. Like on the funky records we'd been devouring by Jimmy Smith, Stevie Wonder, Groove Holmes, etc. That's when it occurred to us: Mark Nishita, aka Keyboard Money Mark. The guy who repaired the gate. We brought him in, and he was even better than Mario had led us to believe. The five of us began to play regularly until one day when Adam was leaving his apartment and ran into his downstairs neighbor, who told him that (a) he'd been cleaning all his guns and couldn't wait to use them, and (b) some loud music from upstairs had been seriously disturbing him.

We needed to find a studio. Next stop was Cole, a clean but thoroughly unglamorous Hollywood rehearsal space that we would book by the hour. Again, Mario would set up the Radio Shack mics, and we would set up our instruments, smoke some weed, play, record to DAT, and hope for the best. Thing was, we would do this for a few hours and would then have to break it all down so the next group could come in. Most definitely a drag.

We'd learned our lesson after *Paul's Boutique*; we now wanted a super-cheap space that we could take over indefinitely. Leave our shit there. Try any crazy idea we had, with the room to fail, and without the running meter, pressure, and cost of a big L.A. studio. We looked at some places in downtown L.A., but at the time, DTLA still had too much of a *Night of the Living Dead* vibe. This was at the height of the crack epidemic. Then a musician friend told me about this no-name studio in Atwater Village where he'd just worked. The owner was a musician who worked out of the studio, but things seemed really slow, so maybe we could figure something out with him. In 1990, Atwater was a sleepy little neighborhood just over the L.A. River from Silver Lake. It had a main shopping strip with a small-town-USA vibe and not much else. The studio was in a building on that main strip, above a drugstore. The place didn't look like much from the outside, but inside, it was perfect.

The main room was a big, open ballroom—I think it used to be some kind of Rotary Club or Lions Club or something—with a parquet floor and a high round ceiling. Tony Riparetti ran it. Very nice guy. Had a minor hit in the early '80s as a member of the L.A. band Sue Saad and the Next. Was now doing film scores out of the studio. (Mostly cyborg and slasher-type stuff.) Another guy had a room there, Country Mike. He too had a couple of minor hits in his past. Seemed like he'd been through a lot. His room smelled of cheap weed and bad wine. Empty wine bottles on the floor. He had this routine of coming in

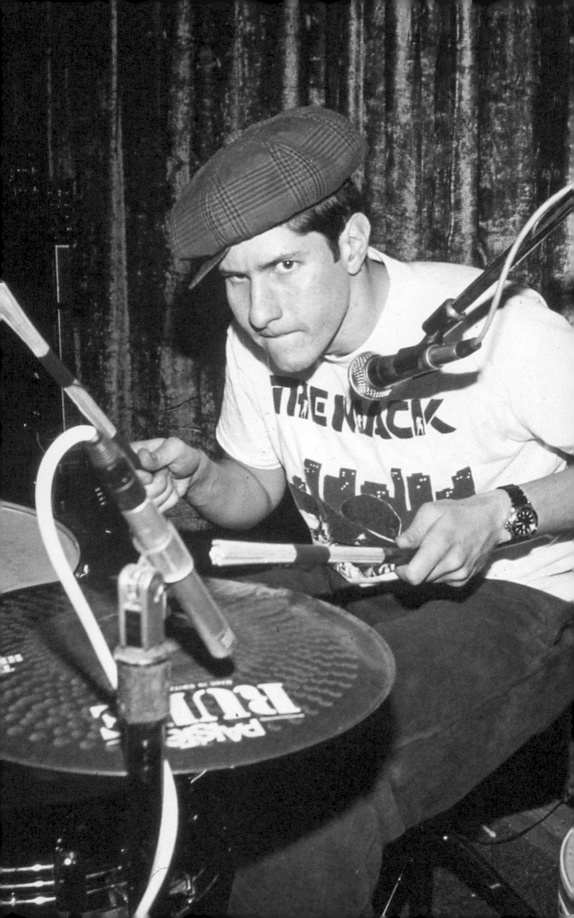

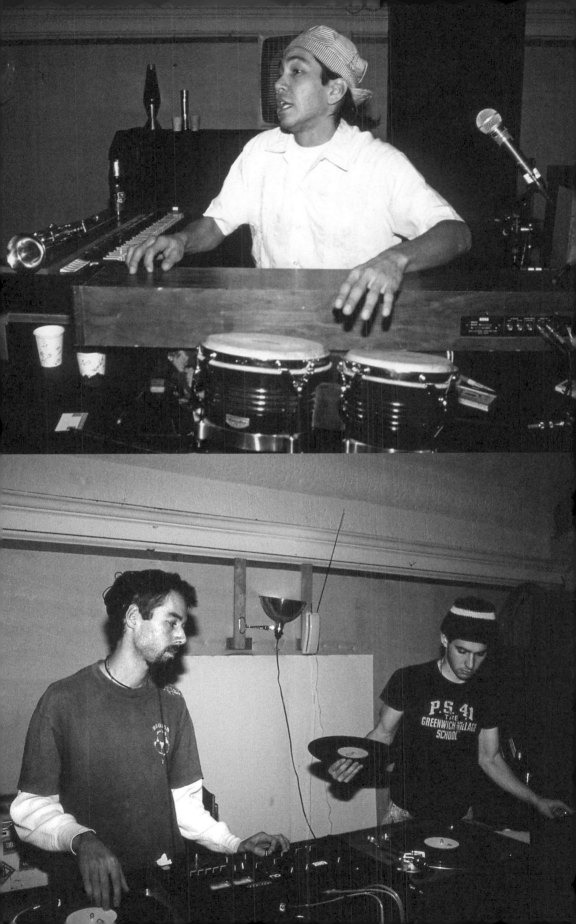

and writing one song a night. He'd ride the bus over from Angelino Heights as a way to find inspiration in the faces and conversations of the other commuters. He'd come in, brew a big pot of coffee, and get to work. He may or may not have been slightly intoxicated by the end of the day, but he'd have a new song.

We took the place immediately.

Tony had his two rooms, Country Mike kept his, and we took the big ballroom. To make a separate control room, we decided to tear up and combine two adjoining closets. Then we'd need to build out that control room and get the main room right. And by "get the main room right," I mean we had to build a skate ramp and install a basketball hoop in there. And also extend the stage a bit so we could leave all our instruments set up. It was crucial to have everything ready to go at all times, so whatever dumb idea one of us came up with, we could play and record it immediately. We lacked the discipline to sit on an idea while equipment got set up—we'd never remember it—so it was paramount that we could record pretty much anything right away.

Pre-Internet, finding used instruments and vintage studio gear was a real pain in the ass. You could go to music shops, but that entailed a day of listening to some guitar-noodling, mullet-sporting owner hold forth on whatever topics struck his fancy until he decided whether or not to sell you the thing that he knew you really wanted.

In L.A. circa 1990, the gold mine for used gear was this weekly, small-sized newspaper called *The Recycler*. Basically all it contained was pages and pages of classified ads. The key to getting anything good or underpriced was being the first person to call about something, so you had to buy *The Recycler* right when it came out every week.

We outfitted our entire studio with gear we found via *The Recycler*. The timing was perfect for buying the type of vintage instruments we wanted—they were considered obsolete by "pros" and hadn't yet been adopted by collectors. Pros at that time wanted brand-new keyboards that had Clavinet and Wurlitzer and organ sounds all built in with digital technology, so they all wanted to get rid of their Hohner D6 Clavinets or their Minimoogs or their Rhodes 88s. You'd get that stuff ridiculously cheap.

The weirdest part was when you'd go deep into the Valley to pick up a piece of gear at a stranger's house. It would give you uncomfortable insight into their whole life story. Pretty much every purchase for us was the result of some other guy having to give up his dream. It definitely added a tinge of the bittersweet to our otherwise good fortune.

After a few months of work, we finally got our new studio up and running. There was an old sign on the roof that originally said "Gelson Plumbing," but all that was left was an aging G, then a few spaces, and then "son." So we named the studio G-Son. G-Son with the parquet floor.

Now all we needed to do was make another record.

1. Staircase to the back entrance. It may be familiar to you from our "Pass the Mic" video.
2. Grand Royal's first office / G-Son broom closet
3. Entryway
4. Studio G. Home to AH and his SP-1200. It later became Bob Mack's *Grand Royal* magazine office, where spilled bong water was a staple.
5. The lounge. We had bummy thrift-shop furniture, not leather bad boys.

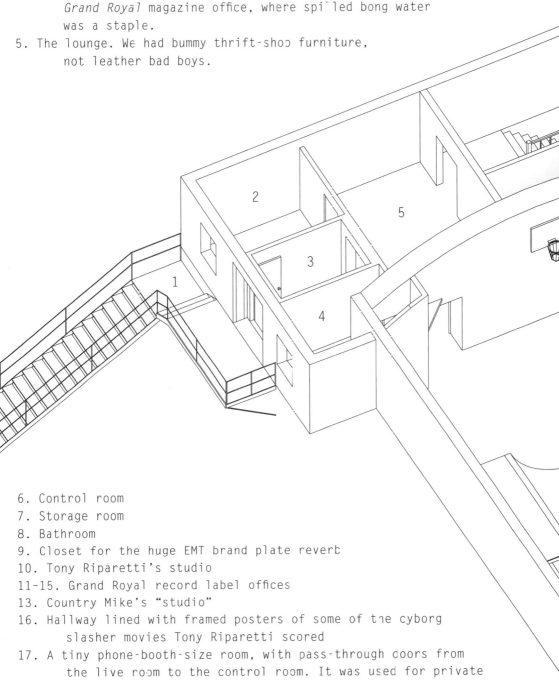

6. Control room
7. Storage room
8. Bathroom
9. Closet for the huge EMT brand plate reverb
10. Tony Riparetti's studio
11-15. Grand Royal record label offices
13. Country Mike's "studio"
16. Hallway lined with framed posters of some of the cyborg slasher movies Tony Riparetti scored
17. A tiny phone-booth-size room, with pass-through doors from the live room to the control room. It was used for private phone calls and isolated vocal recordings.
18. Live room with a stage for recording and playing music, skateboard ramps, and a basketball hoop

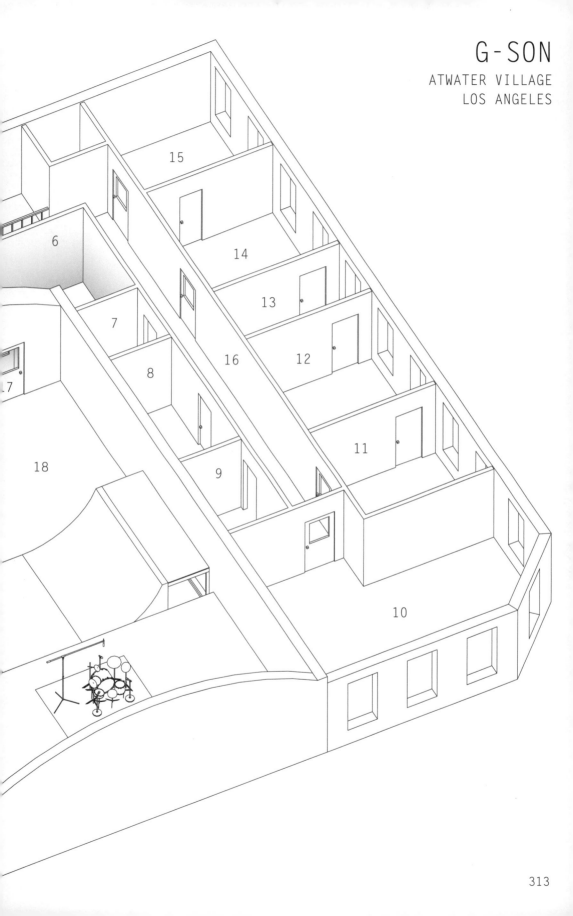

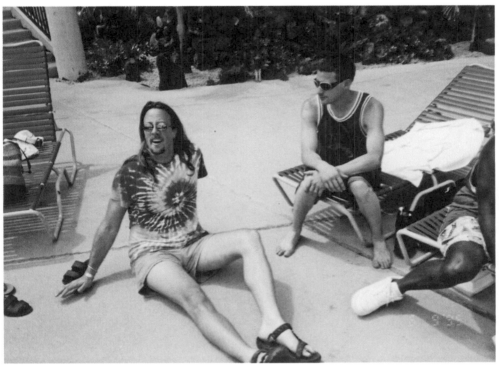

Oooo girl.

Hippie Steve
(AH)

Of all the people who've come and gone in our friendship circle, Hippie Steve is one of my favorites. He was our L.A. pot dealer in the late '80s/early '90s. He's a really nice dude, it's just . . . he was comically hippie. He *really* looked like an undercover cop. He drove a nice car and always wore new tie-dyed shirts and billowy, hippie Hammer pants. It's tough to trust a well-groomed and clean hippie wearing expensive hippie clothes. My brother Matthew lived in L.A. in the early '90s, and one day he drove out to Hippie Steve's place in Brentwood to buy some weed. He said that Steve lived in an apartment above the garage of his parents' expensive house. The whole time he was there, Steve kept complaining about how his square parents just didn't get it; how they were part of the Man's corrupt corporate capitalist society. Meanwhile, my brother's just trying to get weed, get out of this weird super-rich-people neighborhood, and get back to his crappy apartment so he and his roommate could get high and listen to Smiths records.

I'm certainly not into hippies. At all. But I do prefer my hippies dirty, shoeless, and stealing shit from my apartment. Hippie Steve was like a white-collar hippie. A hippie with a hustle. We bought a fucking ton of pot from him throughout the years. It was such a regular occurrence that we wouldn't give him cash. He would just make weekly trips to our business office and pick up a check. Don't all big-time L.A. rock stars have their drug dealers go to their business office? I very much doubt that Slash made his pot dealer wait in the car while he ran into the bank to get cash. Or gave him a personal check signed: Slash. Pay to the order of: Hippie Steve. For: Money for pot.

We spent a lot of time with Steve. As one does with one's pot dealer. He'd come to the studio and hang out. He'd come by the house. He and Yauch went on a few snowboard excursions together. He knew a lot about music and music gear, and so we did have plenty to talk about. It's just . . . as a punk rocker, I was trained for disdain when it came to hippies. But something about Steve was different. It almost felt as if he was a method actor studying the role of hippie.

I always had this idea of Steve only being a hippie when he sold pot. Like, he'd strap on the Tevas, Dead shirt, and hemp cargo shorts when he was leaving the house with different strains of weed and hash oils. And when he sold cocaine he probably wore a nice Armani-ish suit, had a gun, and went to discos. And he'd wear super-tight ripped black jeans and a Pantera T-shirt, tease his hair up, and head to the Ralphs supermarket on Sunset to sell heroin. *But* . . . I'm pretty sure he's always been a nice, harmless, upper-middle-class dude trying to make a buck selling pot, who just wants to jam out and play didgeridoo all day with his friend that makes didgeridoos.

L.A. Gear
(MD)

After we'd lived in L.A. for a while, we got obsessed with a certain type of work gear that we'd seen people sporting around town. The gear was mostly Carhartt and Ben Davis. I knew of Carhartt as the construction standard from back east, but Ben Davis was a below-the-radar, regional brand—family-made, simple, stayed creased with ease, and only available on the West Coast. Best of all their emblem had a monkey on it. Trouble was, the only places you could find this stuff were Army/Navy stores in wayward industrial areas of greater L.A. The trips were generally worthwhile, but it'd end up taking an hour each way for us, if you didn't hit traffic.

Around that time, I was always at the Silver Lake dog park with my girlfriend (and future wife), Tamra. We became friends with a crew of regulars there, among them these two RISD grads, Adam Silverman and Eli Bonerz. One day, I was telling Adam and Eli about the lengths I'd have to go to get the work gear I was sporting, Yeah, that's right, I just admitted I was "always at the dog park,' fool. I guess if you break it down, we were young urban creatives with dogs. Yups with pups, what? (MD) and a lightbulb just kind of went off. "What if there was a spot in our neighborhood that carried all this stuff?" I asked them, then promptly went back to scooping my dog's shit.

At this point in my life, I must have had, I don't know, five thousand "great ideas" like this, and invariably the idea I was excited about would be either forgotten or—if it was a genuinely good idea—ignored until someone else did it. But Eli and Adam got off their asses and made this shit happen. They found a small storefront on an up-and-coming stretch of Vermont Avenue in the Los Feliz neighborhood of northeast L.A.—adjacent to Hollywood and Silver Lake. At the time, it wasn't high-rent at all. Once they got the space, me and a few other folks put in a modest amount of money, and within weeks, we opened up shop. That was the first X-Large store.

At first, the stock was limited to Ben Davis, Carhartt, some X-Large T-shirts, and dead-stock sneakers. We'd search sporting-goods and shoe stores everywhere, looking on high shelves for dusty, abandoned boxes of Puma Clydes, Adidas shell-toes, and so on. We were so into it that we had a guy named Concave Dave who scoured the Tacoma and Seattle area. Pretty quickly, we got bored with the small amount of other designers' clothes we actually liked, and just started making more and more clothes ourselves: sweatshirts, button-down flannels, jackets, jeans. Eli and his brother churned out designs on their computer. Before we knew it, X-Large was shipping to Japan and worldwide, and this was an actual business.

Not that you'd have known it from walking into the shop. A daily crew of skater kids "worked" there, which mostly entailed them doing bong rips in a loft at the back of the store. It was a funny crew. Jason Lee was around a lot; he was mostly still just a skater then. Spike Jonze would stop by almost daily. Once in a while a random Japanese film crew would show up, talking about what these crazy kids are doing in L.A. Eventually, a design studio and warehouse were set up around the corner from G-Son in Atwater, and X-Large became a fairly legit international "streetwear" brand. Stores opened in Tokyo, Osaka, New York, Taipei.

There was a groundswell of new DIY clothing brands in L.A. that were started out of parents' garages, studio apartments, and crap dorm rooms. You had brands like Fuct and Jive, and skateboard companies like Supreme and Girl. And all of it crossed over with the L.A. hip hop scene. Cypress Hill was definitely associated with Carhartt jackets and beanies; N.W.A. with oversized white T-shirts, Dickies, and L.A. Raiders caps.

It seems like so long ago now, because present-day hip hop has become all about big-name fashion: Tom Ford and Gucci and Rolexes and rappers sitting front and center along the runways at Fashion Week, pulling up in their new Bugattis and touting their new capsule collections and $1,000 signature sneakers. The original impulses behind b-boy and skater fashion—imagination, daring, and swagger—were all done with little or no money. Which is exactly the way it should be.

Yo, Paul, This Is Allen

(AH)

The best in men's clothing. Call Paul's Boutique and ask for Janice and the number is (718) 498-1043. That's Paul's Boutique, and they're in Brooklyn.

At the height of our collective mixtape-making and -sharing era, I used to put a commercial I recorded off the radio on tapes I made for Adam+Mike. It was an ad for a clothing store in Brooklyn called . . . Paul's Boutique. For whatever reason, we loved the commercial and thought it'd be funny to put it on our record, which ultimately we titled . . . *Paul's Boutique*. Unfortunately, the actual store closed down not long after our record came out. I don't think the two incidents were related in any way. I hope not. There's no way, right? That'd be crazy.

Anyways, unbeknownst to me+Mike, Yauch contacted the phone company, paid some kind of fee, and took ownership of Paul's Boutique's phone number. He had it routed to an answering machine in the basement of his parents' house in Brooklyn. He left some kind of outgoing message that was basically, "Hey, it's Paul. Things are pretty busy around here lately, so I'm not sure when I can get back to you, but leave a message anyway. Thanks." He would check the machine every now and then when he'd visit his parents. *Is that the fuckin' best, or what!?!* He told me+Mike about it a couple months after he did it and obviously we were like . . . *This is your greatest achievement, ever.* And so one day while skimming through the message tape, Yauch was intrigued by a message left by a gentleman named Allen. The phone message was so bizarre that we loved it and put it on our third record, *Check Your Head*, before the song "The Maestro," and it is as follows . . .

"Yo, Paul, this is Allen, and you can kiss my ass.
I ain't interested in you anyhow.
I'm just interested in the B-Boys.
So fuck you, my man."

Now, I'm not sure I understand. How and why would Allen have thought that that message would get to us? Did he think that we put the commercial on our record because we were part owners of the boutique? Did he think that maybe one of us might've answered the phone when he called? I believe that deep down in his mind, body, and spirit, Allen knew that the message he was leaving was for someone named Paul. A gentleman who owned a store in Brooklyn that boasted it had "the best in men's clothing." But really, though . . . how would it have made Paul feel to hear that message? It'd be 10:15 in the morning. He'd

have just met Janice out front. (Or maybe they'd arrive together. Not to start any gossip or anything.) Together they'd roll up the huge metal security gate. Unlock the door to the store. Turn the lights on. Do some general getting-ready-for-another-day-of-business stuff. You know, listen to the answering machine to see if there were any deliveries for today, maybe a special order. But what they'd get that morning instead would be a slurry, Robitussin-induced message from a stranger that says "Fuck you, my man!"

What the fuck, Allen? I mean . . . c'mon!

It turns out, when you put a phone number on a record that half a million people own . . . there's gonna be more than a few who decide to call it. After a while, shit got pretty odd. The answering machine's cassette tape would fill up, causing the phone line to have a busy signal for weeks at a time. But people kept calling. The messages started to get pretty heavy, and then started to not make any sense. Yauch realized that someone had cracked the four-digit code to the answering system and was now not only able to listen to the messages other people would leave but could change the outgoing message too. Some anonymous person created some crazy-ass outgoing messages. They got pretty fuckin' hostile. Yauch would change the outgoing message, only to have it changed again the next time he'd listen to it. He'd unplug the machine for a while. Plug it back in six months later. Only for more weirdness. So he left the machine off for years. Every once in a while it would come out of retirement for a couple weeks. And maybe, just maybe, it still does.

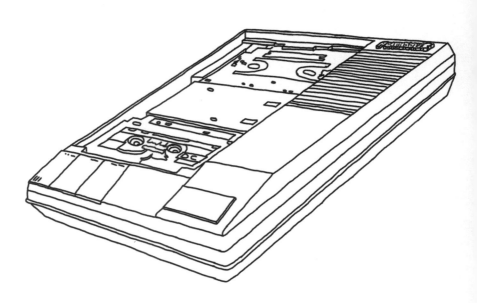

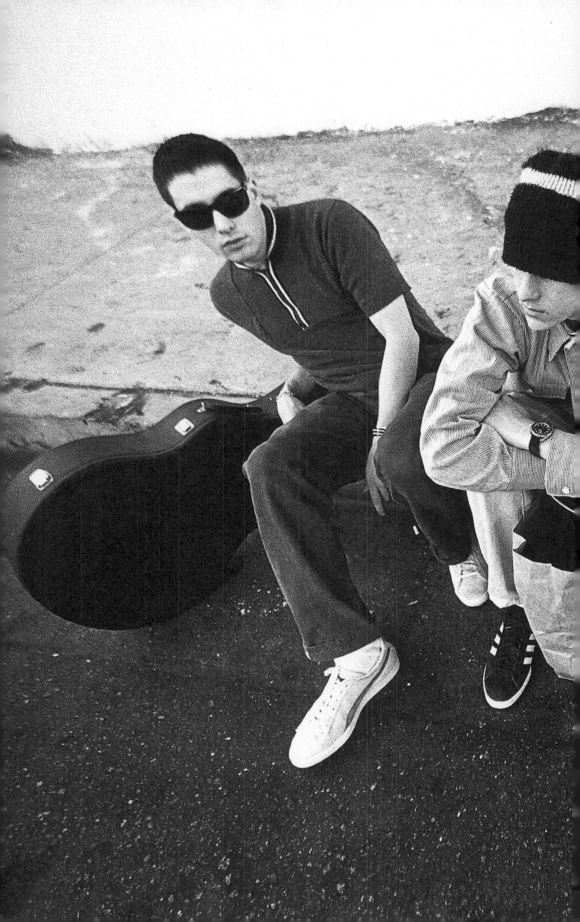

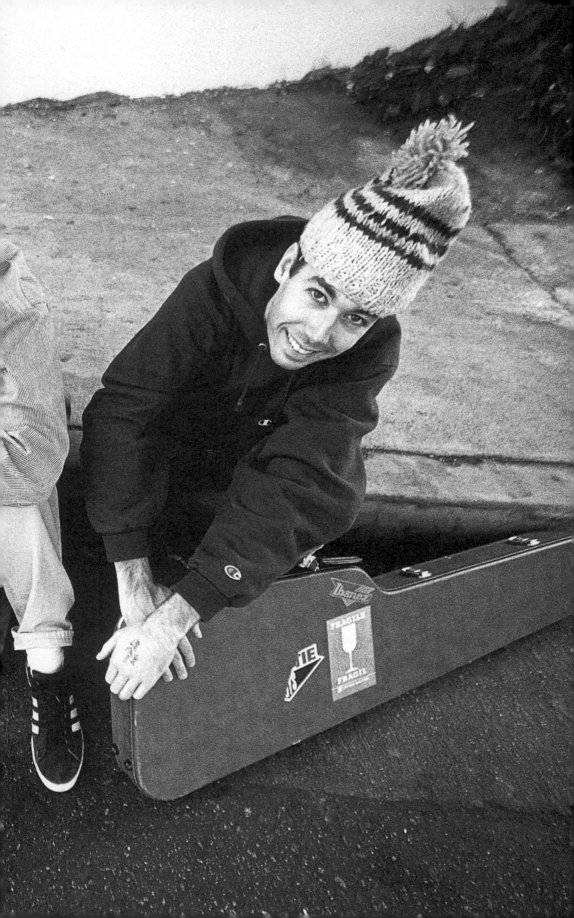

Toyota Corolla Mixtape
(AH)

Back in '91, my girlfriend, Ione, had a *really* beat-up burgundy Toyota Corolla. We went a lot of places, and had some weird and fun times together in that car. All four doors were different colors because they'd been replaced over time due to several big dents either she or I had made. It had graffiti, stickers, and trash all in it. The whole car started to shake if you drove over 50 mph. I loved it. I drove it to the studio every night. It was basically my home office. Ashtray piled over. Two hundred Del Taco wrappers in the backseat where your feet go. The car's stereo was busted, so I just had a box in there. (I also kept a guitar and a Casio keyboard in there, just in case. It was a young, fun, and creative time.) I had a rotating stack of tapes that I'd listen to when I drove from my house up to Mulholland Drive and over and through the Hollywood Hills to G-Son. Here are a few songs I was listening to then . . .

Come Along—Lee "Scratch" Perry
The greatest. People love Kanye 'cause he produces and raps. And they should 'cause he's fantastic, but . . . give this song a listen when you get a sec. (It'd help if you were super-stoned and driving in the mountains in eighty-degree weather with the windows rolled down.) This whole *Upsetters Chapter 1* album is great too. The song "Bushweed Corntrash" is another gem. The song was mixed to have the vocals on one side and all the music on the other, so I could be a DJ rocking an imaginary crowd while driving on Hyperion Boulevard. Turn the Left/Right knob all the way left to drop out the music; and you've just got Lee Perry on the mic. Turn it all the way to the right and the crowd keeps dancing.

People Funny Boy—Lee "Scratch" Perry
Yes. Another Lee Perry song. But I was *really* into Lee Perry then, and now.

Croaking Lizard—Prince Jazzbo
Just a great space-out jam. One of those ones that's magical. I love reggae so much but have always been nervous to try to perform it myself. Like Bob said: "If you explain to musicians . . . they know it, but they can't do it." There's not that many people who make you wonder when you hear their voice not just what they're like but what it would be like to be them. Sly Stone, Ari Up, a handful of others. Prince Jazzbo was one of those people. I had no idea what he was like. And . . . especially as a musician; I hear 98% of recorded music and I understand how it was made. I can picture the person/people making it but . . . Prince Jazzbo?

322

I Gotta Stand for Something—Professor and the Efficiency Experts
I got this 45 from Skate Master Tate (RIP) via my friend Max Perlich. Look this shit up and you'll see why this song was such a big deal to me. If I was a different person, one that could sing and play an instrument really well and make great-sounding records, this is what I would've wanted all of my records to be like. Similar song, similar idea: "Misdemeanor"—Foster Sylvers

Plantagenet—Back Door
This shit is just real, real funky. And . . . it's nice and short like a punk song. The way great songs ought to be.

Sweetie Pie—Stone Alliance
This is actually not that great of a song. It's funky for sure, but way too long. It's just, I got it at the height of our record-collecting days. And so it went into heavy mixtape insertion. And when it came on, I most likely just spaced out and looked out over the Hollywood Hills.

Mr. Brown—Bob Marley & the Wailers
This is just a great song. And oddly/not oddly, very punk.

Fried Neck Bones and Some Home Fries—Willie Bobo
In the midst of digging deep into dirty record crates, we discovered these new and awesome sounds that were there all along. I'm sure we heard it a thousand times when we were kids in New York but . . . who knew about boogaloo? It's the fucking best. Honorable mixtape mention . . . "Soul Sauce" by Cal Tjader

and "Mira Ven Aca" by Johnny Colon. And over the next few years, all three of us got deep into boogaloo and samba, and other types of Latin sounds.

Answer the Phone—Cheech and Chong
All great mixtapes, and/or pause tapes, have skits on them. Cheech and Chong delivered some of the G.O.A.T.

New Bell—Manu Dibango
This is how I wanted to play guitar, and this is what I wanted our instrumental music to sound like. Honorable mention for guitar playing: "House of Rising Funk" by Afrique and "Tippi Toes" by the Meters.
P.S. I love Eddie Hazel.

Give It Up or Turn It Loose—Dick Hyman
If you just found this record for a dollar and brought it home and listened to it, it would blow your mind too. Old '60s electronic-music guy doing a James Brown classic?! Yes, please.

I Walk on Guilded Splinters—Dr. John
"Right Place, Wrong Time" was the jam when we were kids, of course. But as I got older and deeper into music and records . . . the Meters/Dr. John connection put me on to Dr. John. This is a burnout classic.

You Are the One for Me—Charles Wright
Just a fresh cookie from the jar. Baked and crate-dug.

The Humpty Dance—Digital Underground
Needs no explanation, right? It's one of the greatest songs ever recorded since the invention of music.

Lovely Is Today—Eddie Harris
For whatever reason, I decided that Eddie Harris was my hero. This song is what led me to that decision. I didn't own all his records; I didn't actually know anything about him. I wouldn't hear his record *The Reason Why I'm Talkin' Shit* for another year or two. It was just this song and his song "Drunk Man" that did it. Well . . . actually, a big factor in that decision is the cover of the record that "Lovely Is Today" is on, *Plug Me In*. In the picture on the cover of the record, he's holding his saxophone in one hand, and in the other, he's pushing a Maestro FX pedal toward the camera. I HAVE ONE OF THOSE. I bought it at this used music store on Larchmont in L.A. that me+Mike used to go to. The store is long gone, as is anything old on Larchmont. This pedal looked cool to me but I never really gave it its due until my hero, Eddie Harris, told me to plug it in.

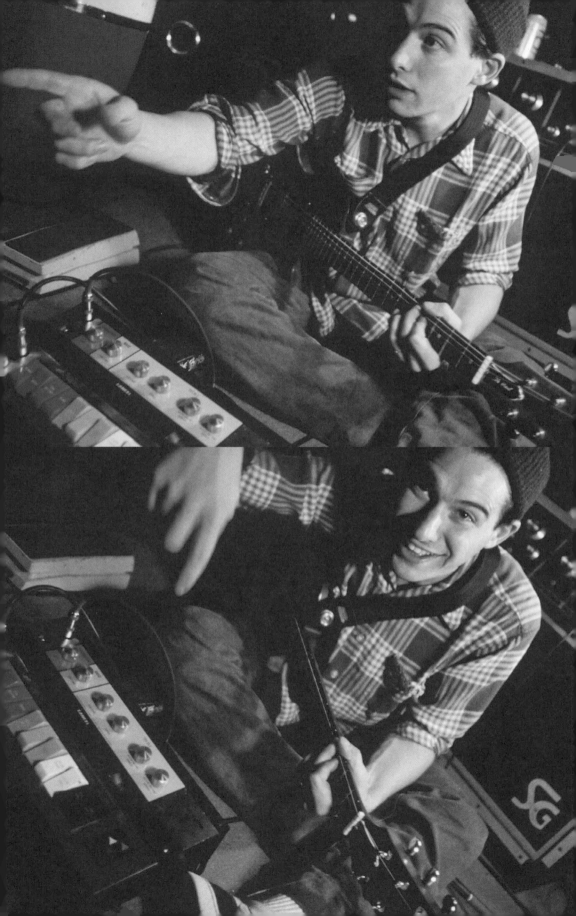

The Diabolical Biz Markie

(AH)

"Yo, you know where there's a candy store?" That was the first thing Biz Markie said to us when he first came to G-Son to "work" together. We didn't really know him, or what he was about, so we didn't know what that meant. Was it code for drugs, or for actual candy? Turns out he meant actual candy. Like . . . before we got started, he *needed* to have Tootsie Rolls, a Butterfinger, and maybe some jelly beans. Asking for a candy store seemed really specific and odd. For one, it was nighttime when he arrived. So you'd assume that a candy store would be closed by then. And at that time, Atwater, where our studio was, was a dead neighborhood. We told him that the only thing open around us was a liquor store across the street called Kopper Keg, and they might have, like, a Snickers or something. So off he went. A fantastic introduction, if you ask me. Sober, grown-up rappers that need to have candy right away.

In rap, you're weird if you don't have a bunch of guest rappers on your record. We never really did that. I guess up until the early '90s no one really did that. It's not like Stiv Bators would guest on a Blondie track. Or Josey Wales would do a verse on a Bob Marley song. We loved the Biz, and thought it would be so cool to hang out with him, and make something weird together. I did not expect Biz to be as Biz-like as he was. Let's just say . . . as an artist . . . the Diabolical Biz Markie is not about process. He is about as on-the-fly as you can be. You better have the tape rolling when the Biz is around. He's an all-freestyle, off-the-dome type of artist. The thing that we recorded and used of him on *Check Your Head* happened like this: He grabbed a record off the shelf in the studio and was like, "Yo, this record has a crazy beat on it. Gimme a mic." Mario hits Record. And as the record is playing . . . the Biz just freestyles . . . "The Beatsie Booooys . . . they are they're coming home. They're coming hooome . . . whoa they're coming home." For us this was a truly magical moment.

He came by the studio a couple more times, and we would hang out, eat together, play basketball (Biz playing sports is a spectacle), and make music. We'd be playing our instruments, and he'd just shout out random songs for us to play so he could sing them. "Yo . . . play the Beatles, 'Yesterday.'" *We don't know how to play that.* "Yo . . . Seals and Croft." Seriously, what? It was great that he assumed that since we were "musicians" . . . obviously we'd know how to play Captain and Tennille's "Love Will Keep Us Together." It was like this weird dream of being able to perform his seven-year-old AM radio greatest hits.

Footnote about the Biz: If you mentioned any item . . . he'd say he had it. Still sealed in the original packaging. Rock 'Em Sock 'Em Robots . . . "Yo, I got those." Grover Washington Jr.'s *Mister Magic* . . . "Two copies, sealed."

In '93 when I asked Biz if he had a cassette tape of mine that we had been listening to together in my blacked-out Volvo station wagon, Biz replied with one of our top twenty most favorite quotes, "If you don't have it, I probably got it." (MD)

Well, apparently he didn't have Parliament's *Rhenium* record, 'cause he "borrowed" mine and I never got it back.

But probably my favorite of all of our Biz stories was when we were recording *Hello Nasty*. He was supposed to come down to the studio to do some stuff. He was running a little late and we got a call. "Yo, it's me . . . Biz. I'm downstairs in the car, I'll be right up." We didn't see or hear from him for another two years.

THE DIABOLICAL BIZ MARKIE.

Our New A&R Guy

(AH)

I know it's not nice to clown people but . . . sometimes it just has to happen. Right or wrong. I also know that most often, clowning someone is a fuckin' boomerang. Case in point: 1991—our new A&R guy. By the time we were recording *Check Your Head*, everyone new at the record label had already been replaced by someone newer. There was now a *new* new A&R guy, and he wanted to come to the studio to hear what we were making.

Back to the clowning part; I know I'm an awful person and that it's wrong to judge somebody just because of their personal style but . . . to me, unless you're riding a horse . . . I just don't think that you need cowboy boots in Hollywood. So . . . the breakdown of our new A&R guy's style goes like this: cowboy boots, tight black jeans, leather jacket (dad-style), long and straightened dyed black hair, driving a Porsche convertible. Top down, everything. The guy that immediately gets picked in a police lineup for '80s Hollywood A&R guy douchebag. I'm sure he was really nice, it's just . . . we didn't give him a chance. He was just not on to what we were into. He seemed to be stuck in a Loverboy "Lovin' Every Minute of It" moment, and just really wanted to keep his paychecks coming. (New boots are pricey.) So when our new A&R guy was on his way to our studio to hear what we'd been working on, we decided to go through all our tapes and select the most awfullest garbage we'd made so far to play for him. Like eleven-minute super-stoned slow jams where you could hear us still playing music while someone just walks away and starts playing basketball. Or, mid-eleven-minute space jam where a couple of us are having a conversation about ordering food while the rest are still playing. It was a really weird way to clown someone. We played these tracks and just waited for any kind of reaction. Nothing. After an hour or so, he was like . . . "Wow, you guys . . . that's some great stuff here. I'm really excited about this." And then he left. Who was more confused? Him or us? Did he get to his car and think . . . *Shit! These guys suck. It's way worse than I thought. Someone's gonna get fired 'cause of this dumb pothead jam band, and it might be me.* What *was* he thinking? The music we played for him was way worse even than you're imagining it to be. Why did we do that? This person was supposed to be looking out for us, and we just so obviously clowned him. Why? It *must've* been the boots. Footwear is so very specific. And fucking important. (As is having a tight sock game.)

When everything was done with *Check Your Head*—written, recorded, mixed, and mastered—we handed it off to the record label. To our new A&R guy. We didn't know if Capitol would tell us to wait again because fuckin' Whitesnake was back and their heat was hot. We had to go into the Capitol

Building a few days later to meet the A&R guy and to discuss the choice of the first single. What song (and video) would make the most impact and let the people know that Beastie Boys is about to make heads explode?

We got to his office and he seemed way too relaxed. We were fuckin' amped up. We had a whole finished-and-ready-to-go record. We started talking about songs off the record, and he was acting weird. He casually picked up the prerelease cassette tape and said, "I think 'Jimmy James' should definitely be the first single." Nothing against that song. I really like it. It's just . . . it doesn't have a hook. A chorus. Most songs you hear on the radio, most of the songs you love, have a chorus. A hook. The thing that reels you in and makes it so you can't help but sing, scream, or rap that damn chorus. Over and over. "Jimmy James" doesn't have that.

We asked him about other songs and suggested "So What'cha Want" as the first song to go with. If we're gonna come out, let's come out big. Right? Our new A&R guy kind of scanned the tape, looking at the track titles, and was like, "I don't know . . . I think 'Jimmy James' is the one." We asked him if we could just play "So What'cha Want" for him and see what he thought, and he begrudgingly said okay.

.

.

.

(Long awkward moment when you have to fast-forward and rewind a tape to find the beginning of the song you're looking for.)

.

.

.

A half a minute into "So What'cha Want" . . . he's like . . . "Wow . . . what's this? I like it."

He hadn't even ever listened to our record! He only just glanced at the tape and said "Jimmy James" because it was the title of the first song on the track list. Because it was the nearest to him. He couldn't have given two shits about us. And you know what, why should he?

The fuckin' clowns just got clowned.

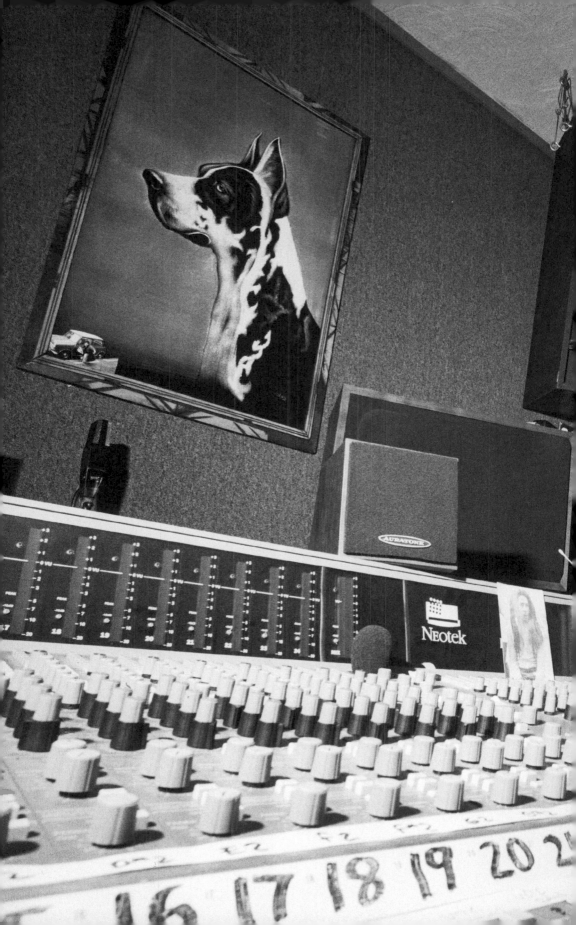

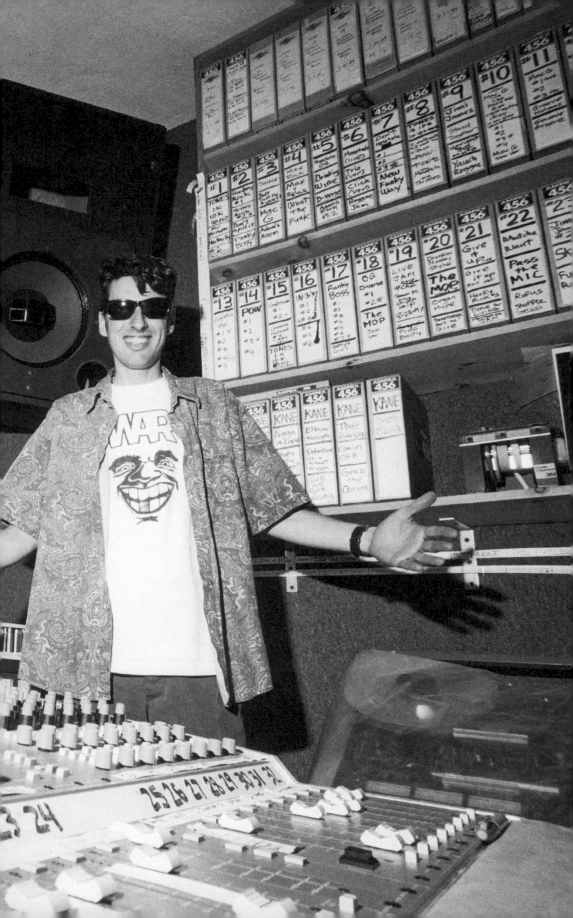

Check Your Head
(AH)

So after we found G-Son and officially set up shop there, we started sifting through the tapes we'd recorded at the Cole practice space. (You know . . . the stuff Mario recorded using those cool Radio Shack PZM mics.) Most of the stuff on those tapes was garbage playing and us talking about where to order food from, but there were a couple gems hidden inside. On one particular tape was a long space-out jam that had a few sensational-sounding bars of playing on it. We sampled those bars on Mike's MPC60 sampling drum machine, put them in a kind of arrangement, Yauch wrote a few lyrics, and we each took a turn singing the words. In a sample-y kind of way, we muted and unmuted the vocal takes that sounded good. The end result is the song "Something's Got to Give." It certainly is odd that a three-and-a-half-minute song would take two years to finish, but that's how this record was made. Like you'd make a dough, then put it on top of the fridge for a while to rise. You make a sauce, add ingredients, let them sit together, and coalesce into deliciousness. Then . . . you get where I'm going with this, right? I'm making a two-year-old pizza.

Pass the Mic—Yauch was on a mission. He was standing in the middle of the live room at G-Son, directing traffic. We were several months into the recording of *Check Your Head*. The process had been loose but productive. We had never made a record like this. We knew how to play and we knew how to sample and program and scratch and MC, but doing all of the above was uncharted territory. We didn't know what we were doing, in the best way possible. There was a lot of experimentation. Which was what Yauch was consumed with that day.

We'd been fans of John Bonham's booming drum sound long before we became associated with that sound on *Licensed to Ill*. Now that we'd resolved to play our own instruments, we wanted to create that sound ourselves. The G-Son live room was a ginormous ballroom (by NYC standards)—certainly big enough to give us the reverb and echo we needed—so why couldn't we? But just

recording the drums in the room didn't make them sound big enough. "Let's put the drums in the middle of the room," Yauch said, "so the sound bounces everywhere." We pulled the drums down off the stage and set them up in the middle of the floor. Better. More room sound and reverb for sure. But still not big enough. It needed to knock people over and break speakers.

Yauch grabbed a bunch of empty cardboard boxes still lying around from when we moved in. We broke them down and then refashioned them into a long cardboard tube, about ten feet long and the same diameter as the kick drum. We put one opening of the tube flush against the kick drum and duct-taped it there. Then Yauch had Mario place a couple mics inside the tube itself and one at the open end of it. It was like that scene from *Apollo 13* where they had to make a carbon dioxide filter out of plastic bags, cardboard, and duct tape.

Once this was all set up, I played the drums for a while and headed into the control room to listen back. The sound was epic, truly huge. We had it. Who thinks of things like this? Adam Yauch, that's who. Was there some kind of using-cardboard-to-get-better-drum-sounds manual I hadn't read? And the whole time he was acting like, *Yeah, this will work*. And it did. His self-confidence was both necessary and contagious. That big drum sound, made from the magic of cardboard, is what you hear on "Pass the Mic." (MD)

Gratitude—Yauch's Univox Super Fuzz distortion pedal was more than an object, a keepsake, or a cool piece of music gear he liked to have around. For him, this fuzz box had a life of its own. A personality. When he played his bass through this box, it was as though he'd transform into this other being. A much grimier and more badass person. He's a great musician, and can play the acoustic and electric bass fantastically without it, but when Mr. Super Fuzz showed up . . . shit got different. This song features that distortion pedal and, really, it's about being thankful for the simple things: love and friendships and life. And dumb little objects that make us human.

So What'cha Want—Every rapper on the planet has publicly denounced biting, yet we all do it. You can't rap and not have Spoonie Gee, Biggie Smalls, or Melle Mel in the back of your head. Trust me, if you're rapping, you're biting Sha-Rock whether you know it or not. So kids . . . If you're gonna bite, do it right. But biting is not a crime. (No, that's not a lead-in to a Marv Albert joke.)

All musicians, artists, writers, etc., get "inspiration" from some other musician, artist, writer, etc. There can be a fine line between biting and stealing. But really, there's a thousand songs where the music goes . . .

Dunk, da-Dunk.

Dunk, da-Dunk.

So to me, biting the Southside Movement's song "I've Been Watching You" is not a crime. I had a little setup in a big empty closet at G-Son that we called Studio G. It consisted of a turntable, a DJ mixer, speakers, and my SP-1200 sampler. I was chopping up (sampling) that Southside Movement song for a potential song of ours, and that shit sounded fucking great. I added some kicks and snares . . .

Dunk, kack, da-Dunk, kack.

Dunk, kack, da-Dunk, kack.

I looped it up, and we put that shit on blast. Listened to it over and over again. And while we were writing lyrics, someone (I'm sure it was Yauch) said . . . *Why don't we just bite this, and play it ourselves?* I mean, we were playing our instruments all night every night already, why not give it a try?

When you think about it, you've heard that *Dunk, da-dunk* in a ton of other songs, but once Money Mark started to play his organ with our guitar, bass, and drums . . . it sounded different. It sounded a little sample-y, a little sloppy, and kinda funky. And it was now *ours*. We added our distorted microphone style, and we changed the course of history forever. Or at the very least, we made a banger for you to blast.

We were feeling pretty hesitant about doing vocals, and up to a certain point *Check Your Head* was entirely instrumental. These karaoke mics were ceremoniously given to us one day by Mario C, who randomly found them in a music store. When he presented them to us, it was like some kind of CGI effect of glistening diamonds and rainbows happened as a heavenly "ahhhh" soundtrack came on. These mics distorted our voices in just the right way, making us instantly comfortable just freestyling, talking mad shit, and whatever. You could just go off, and we sure did. (MD)

Time for Livin'—This was the hardest song to write lyrics for. We liked the music and wanted to include it on the record, but lyrically, we were at a loss. We had been listening to a lot of Sly & the Family Stone. On the *Small Talk* album, there's a song called "Time for Livin'." We'd play that in the studio all the time, put the vinyl record on when we were playing basketball and whatnot. So one day, everyone kept pushing me to record something—anything—for vocals on the hardcore song. I got frustrated and just went in and sang the lyrics to the Sly Stone song verbatim, through a karaoke mic. Anyway, the "Time for Livin'" version wasn't intended to be the final vocal, just a placeholder. But then we listened back later and thought it was kind of good. So we kept the vocal as-is, and credited the song to Sly in tribute. (MD)

The Blue Nun—This one is self-explanatory because Blue Nun is a delicious beverage.

Stand Together—Oh my goodness . . . this song was gonna drive me nuts. I love it, don't get me wrong. It's just . . . we recorded Mario drilling a screw into a piece of wood because we wanted to have that be a funny and odd percussion sound. Which it is, but . . . when you make a record, you end up hearing the songs a thousand times because of writing and recording and mixing and mastering and performing and so on. (I've heard my least favorite Beastie Boys song, "What Comes Around," a hundred times more than I've heard one of my all-time favorite songs, "Kleenex," by Generation X, just because I had to.) Anyways . . . for this song, Mario recorded Yauch playing a ton of Univox Super Fuzzed guitar. Then he played that recorded guitar from the mixing console out and into a DJ mixer, and then back out of the DJ mixer and into a different track on the mixing console, so we could rerecord the guitar through that DJ mixer. Yauch wanted to do this because the mixer had a little switch that could cut the sound off+on when you wanted to. It's known to DJs as the terminator switch. When a record's playing through a mixer and a DJ is cutting the sound off+on really fast, it's called terminating. If none of this is making sense, either I'm an awful describer or you know zero about DJing. (I blame you.) Yauch recorded his guitar-playing knowing that he wanted to terminate it after it was recorded. He wanted to have the end result become this new and fragmented re-creation of what once was. A chopped-up cyborg of the original. Although it took hours and hours to record (it was like watching someone who loves to play video games, play video games), the end result sounds amazing to me. And it was all for the common cause of experimentation. Yauch's big idea for this one was . . . I wanna make a rap song with crazy terminated fuzz guitar that has super-positive lyrics. Something about like . . . "Stand Together." Okay, let's do it.

Mark on the Bus—We were still getting to know Mark Nishita, and I guess he was going through a transitional phase during this time. (He briefly went under the moniker Keyboard Liquor Mark. "Always drinkin' wine.") We met practically every night at the studio, and unbeknownst to us, he sometimes spent the night there, on the couch. His drive back to Gardena was a long one. Especially at 3:26 A.M. and two bottles of wine deep. He'd do the safe thing and just crash on the couch. Anyways . . . Mark was the best musician of the four of us. We'd never played with a piano player before, and something about that instrument made things sound a little more like real music. And when he broke out his clavinet, he was on some Stevie Wonder shit. Also, Mark is the only one of us who could actually sing a song without sounding like a toddler. We showed up at the studio one night, and Mark played us a song that he'd recorded the night before after we'd all gone home. He must've done it at, like, four in the morning. He had recorded all the instruments and vocals by himself. Drunk as a skunk. Even though he wrote and recorded everything, and we had pretty much nothing to do with it . . . it's one of my favorite songs we ever made.

Professor Booty—There's nothing outrageously remarkable about this song. We just looped a beat and wrote lyrics. We switched back and forth with our rhymes so often that we wanted to each take a verse for a change. It's dumb and funny and the music is funky. What else do you want? But on a side note . . . we played a festival in the late '90s (somewhere in the world), and this older gentleman approached me and asked if I was in Beastie Boys. I said yes. *Why?* He said that he wanted to thank me. *For what?* He said that we sampled his music and that he actually got paid for it. He said that his music had been sampled a bunch of times and he rarely received clearance or payment. Of course I asked, *Who are you?*, and he said, *I'm Willie Henderson.* I knew right away who he was. We sampled his song "Loose Booty" for this song, "Professor Booty." I was like, "OH SHIT, no way. Oh, man . . . C'mon . . . Thank *you.*"

In 3's—This was one of the last songs we recorded for this record. We were starting to lock into each other's playing style. We were starting to *have* a style. A new style. This song started because someone (not me) casually said, *Hey . . . let's play something in threes* (instead of 4/4 time). Mike started playing a beat, Yauch came up with a bass line, I got my wah-wah going, and Mark got busy with his clavinet. It was coming together and it felt fun, like playing funky hardcore. (Note to self: Please don't say "funky hardcore.") But . . . we didn't know where to take it after that. We decided to take this other, slower thing that we'd recorded sometime earlier, and Scotch tape it to the end. Mario muted all the instruments and echoed out the guitar part to have it blend into this new/old ending part. Done and funky.

Namasté—I'm assuming it's the same for everyone who makes records: each record you make is like a time capsule, looking back as a marker for what was going on in your life then. *That* phase. And this song was a perfect way to end this record. It ends with more of a comma than an exclamation point. We were all going through life changes, but Yauch was in a full-on transformation. He had started learning about, and practicing, Buddhism. He was traveling the globe any chance he got. India, Nepal, Tibet, Egypt. He needed to soak up every experience he could. He left Los Angeles and didn't really have a home. He was spending a lot of time in Utah snowboarding. He was all over the place, but in a really thoughtful, balanced, and introspective way. He was making new friendships in the form of Tibetan monks and knuckle-head snowboarders. He would hang with anyone, so long as they were fun. His demeanor had an odd, thrilling calmness. One night at the studio he said that he had some thoughts that he'd written down (not lyrics) and he'd like to try saying them over an instrumental track that we had waiting for just this occasion. And like most of the songs on this record, we were like . . . *m'okay. If you wanna take the lead, go ahead.* And so this song kind of tells us where he was at, and where he was headed.

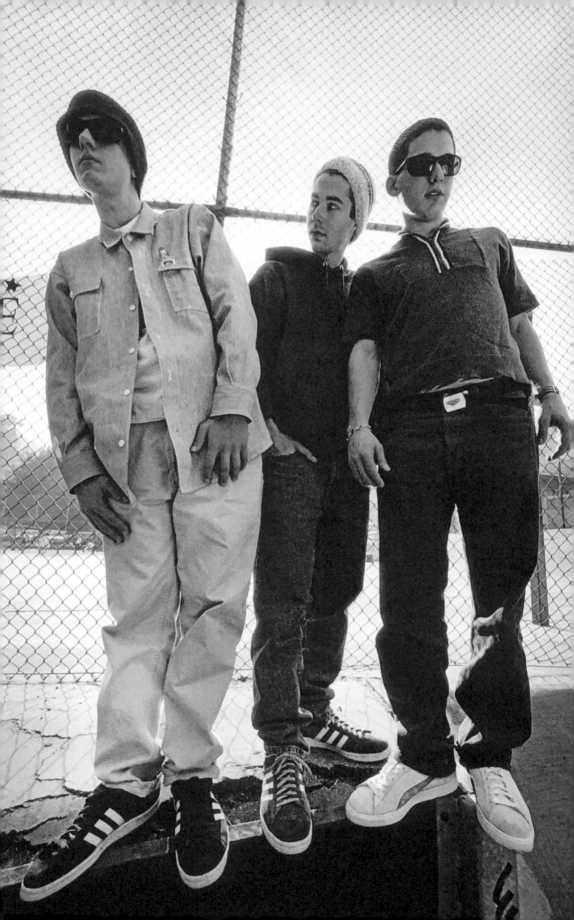

Kiss the Monkey on the Nose
(AH)

Just before *Check Your Head* was released, me, Yauch, and Mike did a photo shoot for some magazine. We were in promo mode. Doing tons of interviews, photos, and generally whatever it is you do to let people know that you have a new, purchasable product in the marketplace. So, for this particular photo shoot, we went to some random photo studio somewhere in L.A. and it was like something off a TV show or movie. Straight *Zoolander. Can I get you some water? Flat or sparkling? Cold or room temperature? Espresso?* There's a DJ playing crappy music. There were a lot of people hanging around for just one person to take pictures of three dudes.

So . . . Someone brings us into a room and says that the photographer has picked out a few different looks for us to wear. No offense, but we already picked out our looks when we got dressed this morning. As schlubby as we've always been . . . that is all our own doing. No stylist has ever picked out our shitty T-shirts and pants. But this guy has rented animal costumes, Roman centurion outfits, weird "fashionable" clothing, etc. We try to explain that we really just want to take the pictures of us how we *are*. That's kind of our thing.

The photographer hears about it and comes in looking a little heated. He is a kind of bigger, older Swiss gentleman. We start explaining that all we need is someone to take some pictures so we can be in a magazine and sell records, and you know what I mean . . . we're only here for schpieling purposes. Generally.

Mike Watt of Minutemen and Firehose fame referred to all band promotional activity as "schpieling." (MD)

He is Swiss and pissed. "Why won't you wear the animal costumes?!" I say, "Look . . . if you take a bunch of pictures of us with the clothes that we came in here wearing . . . I'll put on the gorilla mask and we can take a few pictures like that." Compromise. Everyone's happy. He calms down a little.

We start chitchatting while people are setting up whatever they needed to set up. Because this guy is Swiss . . . Yauch starts talking about his uncle Nathanial Hörnblowér, the great and innovative Swiss film director. He's telling him about his early experimental work in the '50s, and how he's been living in seclusion in the mountains of the Appenzell region on the Swiss/Austrian/German border. *Now* the photographer is interested, and we're okay with him.

We start taking the pictures and it's fine. He starts getting a little animated. Like a fashion photographer in a movie. We take a break for a minute so I can put the gorilla mask on. We resume poses and pictures. The photographer is *loving* it. He's shouting at us over the house music. "Action! More action!

Move around! Jump up and down! Do something with your hands! More action again! Get closer! Kiss the monkey on the nose!"

Wait . . . what?!

"KISS THE MONKEY ON THE NOSE!"

We stop dead. What do you want us to do? What? He screams at us, over the blasting dance music, that he wants Adam+Mike to be on either side of me and that they should kiss my gorilla mask on the nose.

Game over.

I take the mask off. We start thanking him for all his hard work and for the room-temperature water and we leave.

That experience left a big impression on us, though. It gave us a new phrase and framework for selling out . . .

KISSING THE MONKEY ON THE NOSE.

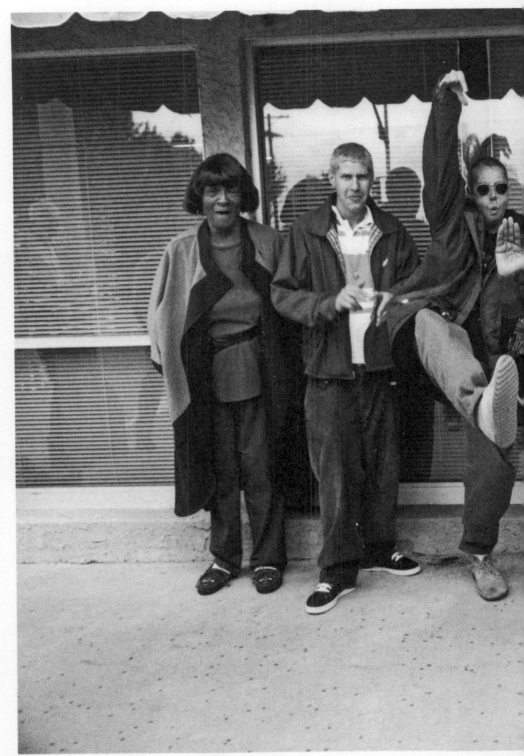

Queen Bee, DOLOMITE. AND CR

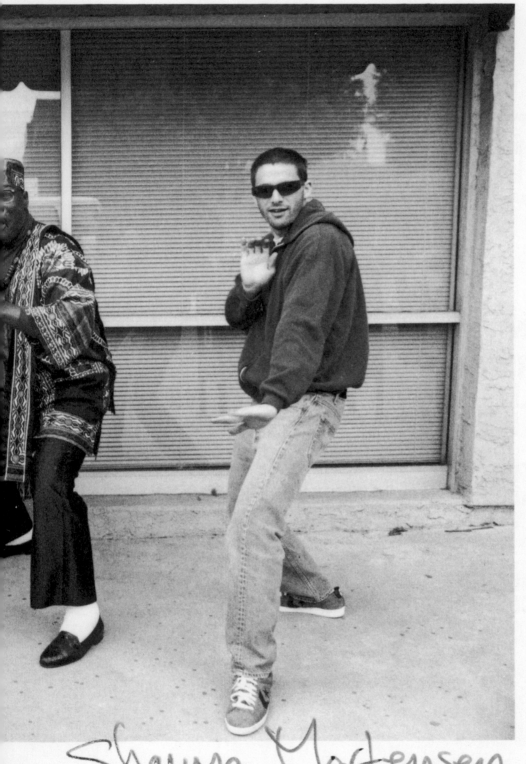

Shawn Mortensen

Hey, We Should Put That Out

(MD)

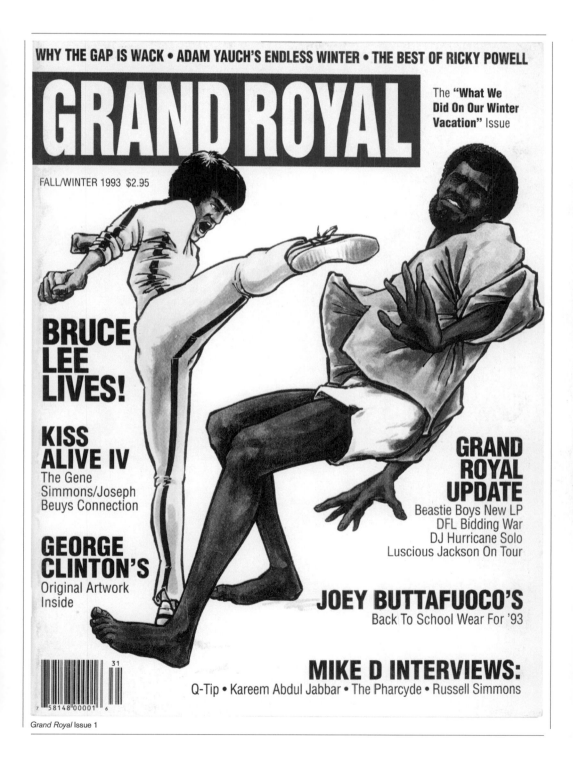

Grand Royal Issue 1

At first, Grand Royal was just a logo. A logo and a vague notion. When we signed with Capitol, the only other labels we'd been on were Rat Cage and Def Jam. Both of them had an us-against-the-world, antiestablishment outlook—even after Def Jam partnered with CBS—and we fed off of that. Capitol Records, on the other hand, *was* the establishment. We were never 100% comfortable with that, so as part of our deal, we negotiated the right to put our records out on our own label within Capitol. No, we didn't have a label or intend to start one. Instead, we spent a bunch of time coming up with a name and logo for our nonexistent label and slapped both on *Check Your Head*. *Look, we've got a label! The logo proves it!*

The name Grand Royal and accompanying catchphrase "Guaranteed, Every Time" were copped from Biz Markie, who said both into the mic, probably after consuming half a bag of candy.

Sometime right after *Check Your Head* came out, we got a cassette of demos from a couple of old friends: Jill Cunniff and Gabby Glaser, two of the original Bag Ladies. Their band was called Luscious Jackson. Jill asked if we could help with getting the demo to people, to see if a label might be interested in putting it out. At that point, the three of us were becoming slightly less self-involved, meaning that instead of ignoring such requests, we actually wanted to help our friends if we could. So we listened.

The demo was really good. It had elements of hip hop—sampling beats, looping stuff—but was definitely not a rap demo. It was fresh, unlike anything else out at the time, with musical references that we all appreciated. I was trying to think of what record labels to send it to, when Yauch just said, "Hey, we should put that out ourselves." Of *course* this was Yauch's idea; he was (definitely) the most generous of the three of us, and he was always undeterred by thinking big. At the same time, he (and we) didn't think of it as just helping friends; he genuinely loved the music and thought it deserved to be heard.

I told Jill our idea, and she accepted. Just like that, Grand Royal was an actual record label. Immediately we were confronted with the next inescapable fact: we had zero infrastructure, and even less of an idea of what we were doing.

Actually, wait: we had this kid named Max. Long story short: When we couldn't get the lyrics for *Check Your Head* to fit on the cassette insert, we promised anyone who sent us an SASE that we'd send them back a printed lyric sheet. This seemed cool in theory, but *way* more people wrote in than we expected. We actually had to hire someone to deal with it, and that someone was Max.

Besides Max, though, we had zero else. So while Luscious Jackson tweaked the recordings that would become their debut EP, we had to figure out how to manufacture, distribute, and promote a record. We'd seen hardcore bands do it—how hard could it be?

Answer: really fucking hard.

Pretty quickly, we managed to figure out the easy part—getting the LP/CD/cassette manufactured. It was an 8-song EP: *In Search of Manny*. The finished version was even better than the demo, and as a cosmic bonus for us, our old drummer Kate Schellenbach—whom we'd rather shittily kicked out of the band eight years before—had joined Luscious Jackson. It wouldn't make up for how we'd treated her, but maybe we could start repairing a friendship at least.

The EP came out and people liked it, which alone was gratifying—we hadn't totally failed our old friends. But the actual release of a record is only the beginning of a label's work. What good is it if people hear *about* a record but can't find it in a store? (Online sales—and online piracy—were still a few years away.) We had no fucking idea that all these little record stores all over the world had to be called and told that a new record was out and which distributor they could get it from. Even worse, we had no idea how to get paid by independent record distributors—nor did we understand that for most of them, their "business model" was to only pay the people they absolutely *had* to pay. But even before any of *that*, we had to solve the biggest, most basic problem—finding ways for people to hear or hear about the record so they'd want to buy it in the first place. Pre-Internet, there were only a handful of ways that people could experience new music—hearing it on the radio, in a record store, or at a club, or reading about it in the press. Each of these avenues of exposure had its own subculture and its own gatekeepers.

We also stumbled upon another way to communicate with people about the music we were putting out. In his broom-closet-turned-office, Max had this super primitive, early Mac computer. Whenever he'd get one of those SASEs for *Check Your Head* lyrics, we somehow had the foresight to enter that person's name and address into a master spreadsheet. This gave us something that, once we started a record label, suddenly became invaluable. Data. Data that we could theoretically use to tell all these people that we had an awesome new record by Luscious Jackson coming out. Today, this kind of mailing-list-driven direct marketing is so common that it's taken for granted,

We actually had to hire someone to deal with it.

"Guaranteed Every Time"

but it wasn't common at all in those days. Certainly a bunch of dipshits in a band and a kid in a broom closet wouldn't have thought to create such a database. Instead—through the random, possibly bad decision of promising lyrics in the mail—a database just fell into our lap.

Since we were already mailing lyric sheets to these folks, somebody came up with the idea of also sending a newsletter that would inform the recipient what we were up to, both in the band and with Grand Royal. The idea felt incredibly practical—and incredibly boring. But instead of just bagging the idea and moving on, we talked ourselves into something way bigger and more ambitious: *Let's make a magazine that covers all the kinds of stuff we're into.* The truth was, we just weren't interested in producing some xeroxed fanzine. We wanted our shit to look legit, like a real magazine. Like a cross between *Spy* and *The Face* and *Thrasher*, with the humor of Monty Python and *Mad* magazine.

So we decided to do it.

Once again, we had absolutely no idea what the hell we were getting ourselves into. I mean, the premise of covering topics we were interested in seemed straightforward enough, but the logistics of producing an actual magazine were way beyond any of us. The first order of business was finding an editor. I can't remember exactly how we ended up hiring Bob Mack. What I *do* remember is that he had written a *Spin* magazine article about us that in his mind was flattering; in our minds, it was . . . not. But that's kind of how Bob's mind works.

He's also inspired and idealistic, so we hired him and gave him an "office" (read: desk in another broom closet) at G-Son. Soon we discovered a problem: for Bob, deadlines were like a totally alien concept. "Moving target" would be generous. Pretty quickly, we found ourselves in the unlikely position of having to tell someone else they had to quit messing around and actually finish something. I wish I could say it worked.

Often, our days went something like this: We'd walk into the studio at our regular(ish) afternoon(ish) time and decide to check in with Bob to see what had been happening all day on the magazine front. We'd enter Bob's "office" to find him in a hacking-cough fit from doing one or several overly large bong hits. Every inch of his desk was completely littered with random papers, so there was no visible writing surface. We'd ask him for updates, he'd give us vague, evasive answers, and eventually we'd have to take him to task.

Somehow, we put out a first issue. The cover story was about Bruce Lee, and our man Bob really went deep. Beyond the piece about Bruce himself, we thought it would be cool to interview Kareem Abdul-Jabbar about the four years he spent learning martial arts from Lee, and somehow, miraculously, Bob made it happen. All of a sudden, there I was, interviewing one of my all-time heroes. Dreams becoming a reality. Crazy.

Now we were all hooked; we wanted the next issues to tell even more elaborate stories. Bob was determined to track down the reclusive Lee "Scratch" Perry, and he eventually did, finding him in a rural alpine region of Switzerland. He became our cover story for issue number 2 (which came out a year late). In future issues, we researched Moog synthesizers, made free flexi discs and posters as inserts, staged a verbal confrontation between Bob Mack and Ted Nugent, and even, at one point, built a demolition-derby car that we entered and drove in an actual demolition derby.

Another great thing about all this was that we were able to involve a ton of talented and creative co-conspirators. Spike Jonze shot photos. Andy Jenkins (art director for *Dirt* magazine) designed *GR* before handing over the reins to artist Geoff McFetridge. On the label side, a kid named Kenny "The Tick" Salcido, who started as an intern, would show up before anyone in the morning with a Big Gulp–sized 7-Eleven coffee to keep amped while he called radio stations all over the country to beg for airtime. Miwa Okumura, now a successful music executive, dealt with the record stores.

And then there were the bands we released. Luscious Jackson. Solo albums by Sean Lennon and Ben Lee. To this day, Buffalo Daughter's "303 Live" can hang with songs by Can or Silver Apples. Atari Teenage Riot was on some crazy ahead-of-its-time shit that combined the energy, noise, and raw power of hardcore punk with glitched-out digital music. We also released a few of our own side projects: a hardcore EP (*Aglio e Olio*) and Adam Horovitz's BS 2000 and DFL (Dead Fucking Last).

Looking back, most people who start labels (or magazines) usually have a manifesto, a specialized focus, or, you know, just a basic business plan. We had none of those things; all we had was the energy to dive in and keep things going until exhaustion or combustion overtook us. It was a blast, at first. Making cool shit with a bunch of creative people, running around in our studio and out at shows. Going from a single employee who answered fan mail to a full-blown operation that released records and a magazine was all-consuming for everyone who worked with us. We definitely never made money and probably lost a good amount. But that was never the point.

Eventually, though, we realized it was spreading us too thin. Fundamentally, all we cared about was being in a band; to become publishers and label executives was never part of the plan. The magazine eventually petered out after six issues. With the label, there got to be too many chefs in the kitchen, with too much $ being spent to have any real fun. We had drifted far off course from the fun and creative reasons we started it. Grand Royal had become like any other business—we *had* to sell records and magazines to survive. We became disenchanted and finally closed it all down in 2000 so we could refocus on the only thing that really mattered: making music.

THE GIRL IN THE BAND
OR
GOODBYE TO YOU AND YOUR INFLATABLE PENIS

Kate Schellenbach

In August 1984, I was eighteen years old and still a Beastie Boy. I had just gotten back to New York from a monthlong trip exploring the nightclub scene in Europe with my best friend, during which I proudly rocked my hand-screened Beastie Boys graffiti-logo hoodie. Every day I wore my custom-made belt buckle with my "rap" name: MATE. I drunkenly tagged bathrooms all over Amsterdam, Berlin, Paris, and London with "Beastie Boys—NYC." Back in the city, I went out with my friends to the happening club at the time, Area, and ran into Mike, Adam, and Adam, with Rick Rubin. I immediately noticed they were wearing matching black-and-red Puma tracksuits, matching Puma sneakers with fat laces, and—most ridiculously—do-rags. Someone told me Rick had bought everyone the outfits. I immediately recognized this as a tactical move to solidify the band and distance me from them. Rick had flat-out told me he didn't like the sound of women rapping, so I knew I'd never stood a chance with him.

Yauch must have noticed my confusion; he pulled me into a dark hallway to "have a talk" and fill me in on what had been going on while I was away. They had been spending a lot of time with Rick, working on their raps and music, and he had convinced them that he could break them as the first-ever white rap group. I rolled my eyes, knowing what was coming next: Rick had given them an ultimatum—their future as Beastie Boys was going to be either with him or with me. They'd chosen him. I was blindsided. I could feel the heat rising up my body into my face. I was not one for public displays of emotion, certainly not at a trendy nightclub, so I turned away and tried to hide what I was feeling. We had always been in this together—it didn't matter if one of us went off to college, if someone had a day job, we were Beastie Boys. These were my compadres. It had never mattered that I was a girl. Never mattered until Rick Rubin came into the picture. . . .

Yauch assured me this wasn't the end of our musical collaboration. We could continue to play our punk songs as the Young Aborigines while Beastie Boys continued to pursue rap fame. But looking at them in their ludicrously matching do-rags, trying to come off like some kind of break-dancing crew from the Bronx, I felt alienated and embarrassed. Deep down, I knew I didn't have the chops or the confidence to be part of a rap group—but I also didn't want to lose my band and, more important, my friends. I felt dizzy and, no longer able to hide the tears welling up in my eyes, I ran into the bathroom to pull myself together. I had to find the friends I'd come with that night. I wanted to drink and get high and dance and try to forget what just happened.

The next few months, the boys spent the majority of their time working with Rick, writing their raps and creating backing tracks. Yauch would proudly play me their demos, tripping out on the sub-bass sounds of a Roland 808 drum loop played backward. As much as he and I continued to bond over music and sound, I knew I was losing my pals, who were more and more taking on Rick's meathead persona. When they were around him, they'd put on this hip hop swagger, make sexist jokes, and act like knuckleheads. Their raps focused on the size of their dicks and how many girls wanted to fuck them. It was hard for me to accept this assholian behavior from these nerdy boys who had never overtly sexualized me or any of the other girls in our scene. We continued to play our punk music and even did some recording together, but when Beastie Boys started making their first album, I stopped spending time with them and decided to focus on my college studies and my first girlfriend.

Licensed to Ill came out in the fall of '86, while my girlfriend and I were visiting her family in Miami. We bought a cassette of the album so we could listen to it in her mom's Bronco driving up to Disney World for my twentieth birthday. When I first pushed PLAY, I didn't know what to expect, and I was prepared to hate it. We listened to it over and over and thought it was hysterical. However offensive it was lyrically, sonically it was brilliant, and we blasted it while driving around Florida. I was proud of my boys, but deep down, I was sad to not be with them. Part of me was jealous of their success without me, but I had to accept the fact that I would never have fit into this version of the band. I mean, what would I be doing when they were rapping about fucking a girl with a Wiffle ball bat? I think it still holds up as one of the funniest comedy records of all time. But I was in on

the joke—sadly most of the world wasn't, and eventually even the Beasties forgot it was a joke.

I groaned while watching them make fools of themselves on MTV's Spring Break special in Daytona. I heard secondhand tales of tour-bus conquests, drunken hotel escapades, and prolific Budweiser-can smashing. They'd invite me to their gigs when they played in New York, but their live show featured a girl dancing in a cage and a giant inflatable penis, which my feminist brain really couldn't handle. This meathead mind-set was the exact thing we'd made fun of and been disgusted by as young punks navigating NYC, so seeing them flourishing in this environment was hard to swallow.

About a year later, after they finished touring, Yauch called me out of the blue. I hadn't talked to him on the phone in years, and I was excited and surprised to hear from my old friend. He wasn't trying to talk like a rapper. He was just his old self, and he confessed how miserable he was: He hated Rick. He wasn't getting along with Mike and Adam, who were "siding with Rick," whatever that meant. They were being screwed by their label and their management. He missed playing his bass in a band. He missed playing with me and asked if I'd consider making music with him again. My mind was spinning with the possibilities, but we never ended up getting together. He started singing in a short-lived rock band called Brooklyn, with the bassist from Bad Brains. I saw them play a show at the World and was amused by his choice of a cover song: Bachman-Turner Overdrive's "Taking Care of Business." We didn't connect again before the Boys relocated to Los Angeles and left Rick Rubin and Def Jam behind.

I was pretty out of touch with them by the time they released their sampling masterpiece *Paul's Boutique*. I was really impressed with their musical output, and it became very clear to me that they had rejected their meathead ways and their "fight for the right to party" personas and were focusing on creativity. In 1991, I was devastated to learn about the death of Dave "Shadi" Scilken, lead singer of the Young and the Useless, talented graffiti artist, and beloved mainstay in our downtown club scene. I saw the Boys and many of our friends from our teen years at his funeral. Dave's death seemed to have knocked them all back into reality, and they seemed anxious to reconnect with their New York City friends from pre–rock star days. Yauch and I went to lunch after the memorial, and he told me tales of living in L.A. He revealed that he, Adam, and Mike were back playing their instruments, and he was

excited about the music they were going to do next. It felt great to be with him again and geek out about music, just like we did when we were teens.

Around this time, a couple of girls I knew from the teen punk scene in New York, Jill Cunniff and Gabby Glaser, recorded a brilliant low-fi, sample-happy demo tape as Luscious Jackson. Pulling from many of the same influences as Beastie Boys, the songs were a mish-mosh of obscure samples, funky drum loops, humorous raps, and catchy choruses. They gave their cassette to the Beasties to get feedback and advice about what labels to send it to. The demo was such a big hit on the Beasties' tour bus that Mike D wanted to make it the debut release of their new record label, Grand Royal. Mike wanted the girls to record a couple more songs. This is when Jill asked me to join the band, and I played with them on some "live" tracks for what became our debut EP, 1993's *In Search of Manny*. I was finally back where I was supposed to be—playing drums in a band made up of friends from this magical time in New York when punk rock crossed paths with hip hop. I was reconnected with the Beasties in the most beneficial and holistic way, and each of them helped my band navigate the next decade of our music career.

The Beasties had used their advance for *Check Your Head* to build their own recording studio in L.A. They were filming and directing all their own videos, in charge of their marketing and output. They were growing their record label, launching a magazine, investing in a cool clothing line. We followed their model and tried to do the same—always fully in charge of our music, videos, marketing, publicity, logos, artwork, etc.

Yauch's spiritual awakening was parlayed into a foundation supporting Tibetan rights. They were actively outspoken about women's rights. They publicly apologized for homophobic comments they'd made in the past. They gave me a shout-out at their Hall of Fame induction. It was an honor to be associated with Beastie Boys and part of the Grand Royal family. People sometimes ask if the guys made any kind of formal amends, but I never felt like they owed me an apology. We were kids; we were all assholes. But we've always loved each other. And this went a long way for me personally: "I want to say a little something that's long overdue / The disrespect to women has got to be through / To all the mothers and the sisters and the wives and friends / I wanna offer my love and respect till the end" (Adam Yauch, "Sure Shot," 1994).

And, no, I haven't ever run into that meathead Rick Rubin.

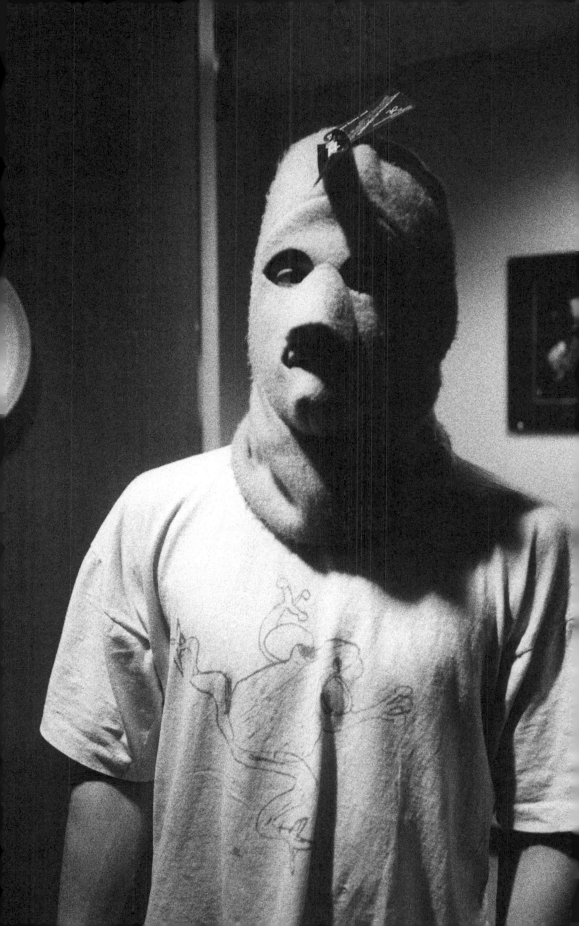

I'll Just Call Him Mitchell
(AH)

I don't wanna name names here, so I'll just call him Mitchell. Mitchell was a percussionist. He toured with us for a little while in the early '90s and recorded with us on a few songs too. We met him at a percussion store not far from our studio and invited him to come down and play some music with us. We got a little insight into his psyche when he arrived at G-Son and took out his three conga drums. He went into lengthy detail about how one was the mother drum, the other the father, and then with a special caress and fragile care he whispered that this third one was indeed . . . the baby drum. Mitchell seemed like a pretty intense, wound-up type of cat. *Super* positive, though. So much so that it seemed a bit much. Oh, also . . . he cried a lot. Whenever he had to have a difficult conversation, he'd get choked up and a little weepy. Mitchell missed the flight for his first gig on his first tour with us. He arrived the next day with an explanation. *What had happened was* . . . He was walking to the airport and was running late, and then these guys were eyeballing him and wanted to steal his gold chain and, you know . . . and so one thing led to another and he missed his flight. "But bro . . . now I'm here and ready to play."

There were a couple red flags in this story.

1. No one, not anyone, *ever*, has walked to the airport in Los Angeles.
2. He wore the skinniest gold chain. It really wasn't the kind that you see someone wearing and think . . . *That's a big chain to be wearing just walking around.*

BUT . . . now he was here and ready to play. And we needed a percussionist, and he was actually really fucking good.

It's weird to have someone you don't know that well playing onstage with you every night, but there was Mitchell. Getting weirder. After a show one night in Cleveland, we're all in the parking lot of a hotel, getting ready to go to the next city on our tour. Mitchell approached me and said . . . "Bro. I saw the light around you tonight, bro. It was the circle of Jesus, bro. Here, I have a Polaroid." He handed me a picture of myself with stage lights on behind me. I didn't know what I was supposed to say in response. I'm sure I was like, *Oh wow. Cool. Thanks for this Polaroid of me and Jesus, Mitchell.* And then a few nights later, Mitchell went missing. We had just played a club in Boston called Spit, and Mitchell was nowhere to be found. We waited outside the club for hours, and then said fuck it. He's a grown-up. He can figure out how to make his way from Boston to our next show, which was in Philadelphia. Greyhound and Amtrak are pretty easy.

We didn't hear from him until he showed up, just before sound check, at the club in Philly. He gathered us all together to explain what happened to him. "Bro, when we were all walking out of the club together in Boston . . . all of a sudden, bro, I got kidnapped by these two gay white Aryan fags, bro. They took me to their basement apartment and forced me to do coke with them all night. They said they were gonna cut my thumbs off, bro. When they went out to get more blow, that's when I made my escape." *This is actually what Mitchell told us.* For real. So which part do you like the best? The gay fag part, the white Aryan part, or the two cokeheads that kidnap people and force them to sniff their expensive drugs? I like the escaping-from-the-basement part best myself.

We did our sound check, and then a bunch of us ended up in the dressing room talking about Mitchell. This dressing room is the size of your bedroom. Not huge. It's empty except for some folding chairs. It's a perfect sunny summer day, and the windows are wide open. There's a fire escape right there. We started *going off* on Mitchell. Tearing him up. Making fun of his gold chain that no one would wanna steal, the circle of Jesus, being forced to do coke. All of it. We were loud and laughing and talking mad shit. Then, all of a sudden, we hear the sound of a toilet flushing, and out comes Mitchell from a tiny bathroom connected to the small dressing room. He'd been in there the whole time and had to have heard *everything*. It was so fucked up. And what did we do . . . ? Did we say, "Aw, man . . . Mitchell. So sorry you had to hear that. We were kidding. We're overexaggerating. We're assholes"? No. We all *ran* out of that room any way we could. Out the door or out the window and up the fire escape. We scattered like rats in a basement when you turn on the lights. We never, ever talked about this incident with Mitchell. We all just pretended like the whole thing had never happened. It was ice cold.

A couple weeks later we got to Dallas, Texas. It was the last show of this particular tour, and then within a week or so, we'd start a long tour in Europe. In *that* dressing room, in Dallas, Mitchell broke down crying. . . . "Bro. I can't go. I can't go to Europe with you brothers. I just can't. Look, I got your back on the stage, and in the streets, but I just can't go with you brothers." He was sobbing. We were like . . . "Okay, okay, enough. Don't worry about it. Just stop crying. Please." It was actually kind of fucked-up and unprofessional, 'cause now we had to find a new percussionist and teach them all our songs, and practice with them on the few days off we'd have for months. When you're on tour for a long time you cherish that few-day break, and Mitchell was impeding family and friend and dog time. But . . . it's just . . . he was such a fantastical yarn spinner that none of it really mattered after all. Mitchell made things totally weird and funny and memorable. And there's nothing worse than not being memorable.

And then all of a sudden Mitchell was gone.

THIS IS THE KEY
THAT THE LORD HAS
GIVEN TO ME,
THAT HAS HELPED
TO SET ME FREE,
I AM AT LIBERTY
WHEN I HAVE THE SPIRIT
OF JESUS IN ME.

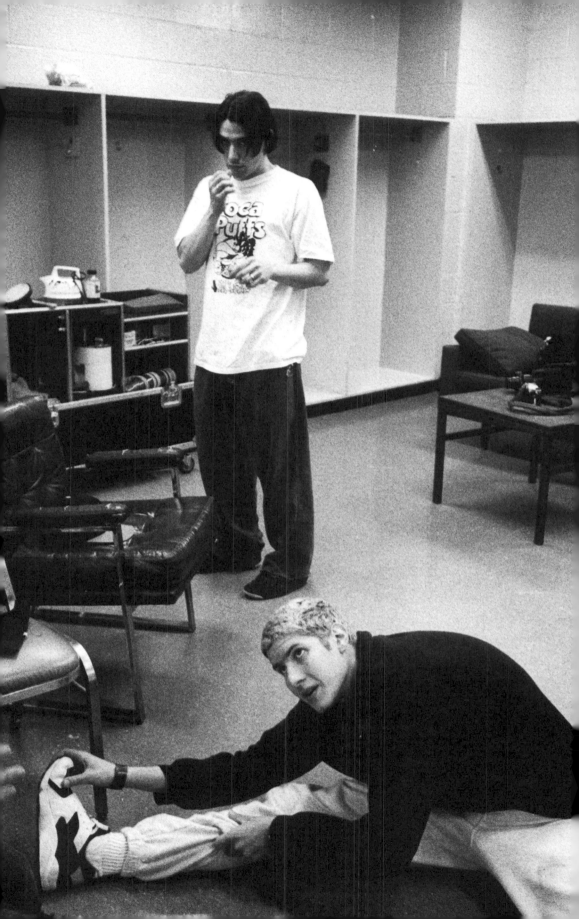

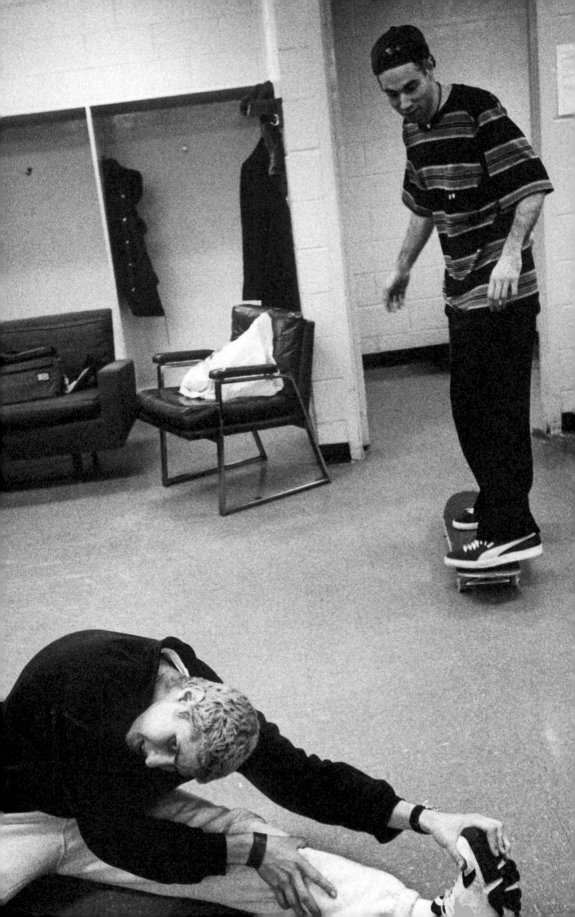

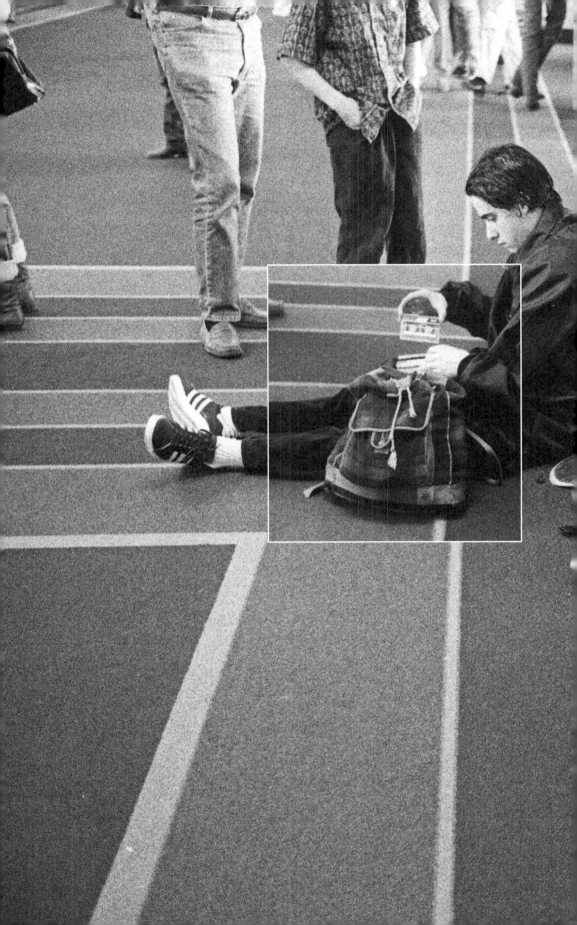

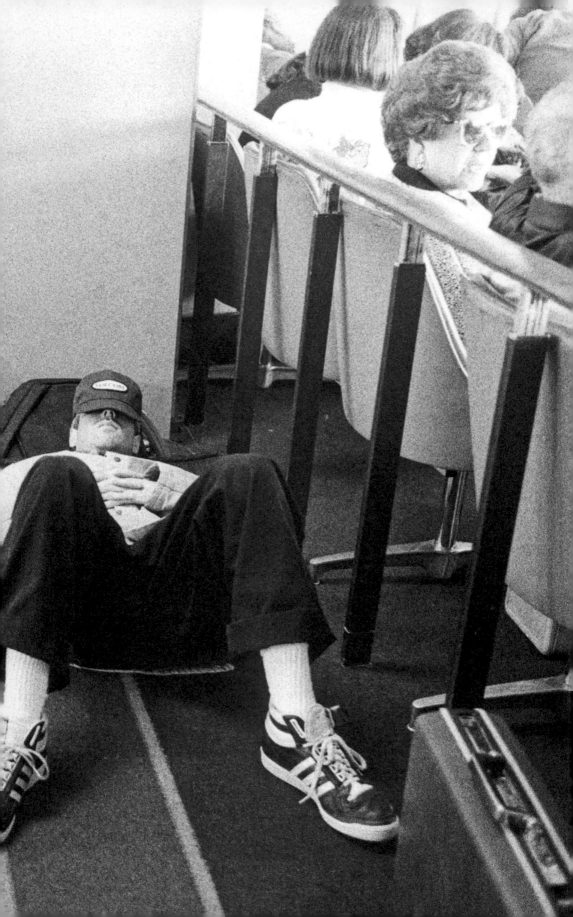

(Maybe) Don't Play Basketball While High on Mushrooms
(MD)

A Tribe Called Quest was based in NYC but came to L.A. often, and Q-Tip would invariably end up at G-Son. Probably because we had that basketball hoop, and it was just fun to hang and smoke pot and listen to records and play basketball. Sometimes he'd bring Afrika Baby Bam from the Jungle Brothers. We loved Tribe, but damn, the JBs were on some shit at the time. We couldn't get enough of *Straight Out the Jungle*, their first album, with its anthems "Jimbrowski" and "Because I Got It Like That"; their second album, *Done by the Forces of Nature*, was even better, a psychedelic, adventurous record that was more experimental stoned soul-jazz poetry than rap. We played that record over and over.

We met A Tribe Called Quest through the Captain. Q-Tip listened to a lot of the same records as us, searched for the same beats and grooves to sample at the same record stores and swap meets. The search was an infinite, crate-digging, until-the-edge-of-the earth quest for anything and everything that could be sampled or even just inspire an idea. Everything from Idris Muhammad to Alice Coltrane to Witch. We really loved Tribe. They were kindred spirits on a mission to make rap music that was as creative and free as the music we had discovered, listened to, and sampled. (MD)

Tip and Afrika were close friends but also competitors—in music and in basketball. *Especially* in basketball. They'd show up, sporting Africa medallions or Zulu beads and dashikis, with Timberland boots on their feet and tie-dyed bandannas around their heads—or maybe the Eddie Murphy *Golden Child* hat—and then go hard in a sweaty and heated game of one-on-one. Without changing their outfits. The shit invariably got to the point where they'd be dripping in sweat, shoving and yelling at each other. Things would escalate and cool down, escalate and cool down. Neither of them ever bothered to take off those clunky boots; it's a miracle that no one broke a toe. And then there were times they'd play when magic mushrooms were involved—those games would take forever because nobody could hit a shot.

We always wanted Q-Tip to get on a track. Earlier, when we were making *Check Your Head*, he was a little apprehensive. Or maybe just conflicted: *Licensed to Ill* wasn't exactly cool anymore, and *Paul's Boutique* kind of bricked on the commercial front. But during the *Ill Communication* sessions, he was in the studio one day and heard a song we were working on that made him instantly light up.

The track, which still didn't have vocals, was something I put together on my Akai MPC60 sampler. The MPC60 and the similar E-mu SP-1200 were revolutionary. Before those two machines came out around 1987 or '88, digital samplers only let you sample about one second of material. (Not a metaphor. Real talk, people: it was actually *one fucking second*.) If we wanted to loop

something when we were making *Licensed to Ill*, we had to make a literal tape loop. Like we'd wind a quarter-inch audio tape between machines and around shit in the control room so the loops would be just long enough that they'd play consistently and not warble as we recorded them.

On *Paul's Boutique*, we could still only sample two or three seconds, and that was only because the Dust Brothers were geniuses. But with the release of the MPC60, even an idiot like me could record and sample stuff relatively easily.

The track that Q-Tip liked was very simple: a beat I had looped, with a weird synth thing laid on top of it. Its simplicity may have been why he liked it; a lot of the great rap productions we all loved had been minimal and raw, mostly due to that era's low bit-rate and limited sample time. Reduced as much as produced. After Tip perked up, we looked around for a sample to add to the basic track. Both Beastie Boys and Tribe were listening to a lot of jazz then; in our band, we were all pretty obsessed with Miles Davis's amazing freeform psychedelic funk-jazz record *On the Corner*. Another discovery was this obscure album by Eugene McDaniels called *Headless Heroes of the Apocalypse*—an out-there jazz-funk LP from the early '70s. Tip knew and loved it too, so we kept trying to find a sample from it that would work on our track. Eventually, we took a line from the song "Headless Heroes" ("Get it together/see what's happening") and dropped it in. It was super weird—and worked perfectly.

By now, Tip was feeling it. We handed him a mic, and he just went to work. Tip's voice is totally original—stylistically and in its tone and cadence. He only did a few passes and then had to bounce. We ended up editing his freestyle, which gave it structure and allowed us to rhyme on there too. The finished track, "Get It Together," managed to mirror, in subtle ways, some of Tribe's stripped-down hip hop, with plenty of low-end and touches of funk, boom-bap, and out-there something. And to this day when I see Q-Tip, we laugh about that session.

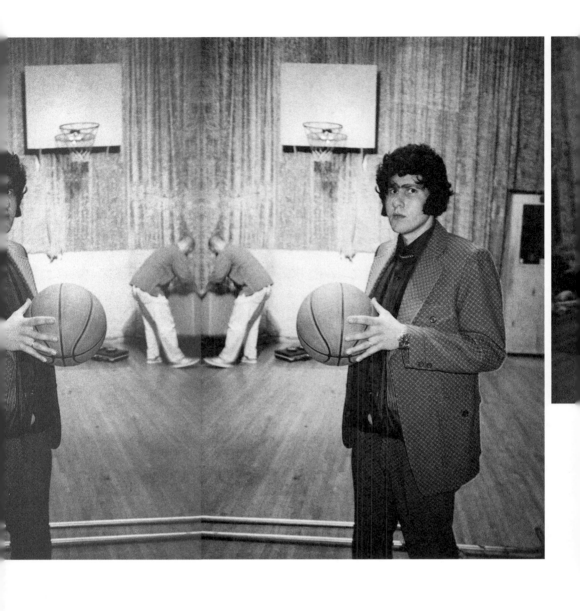

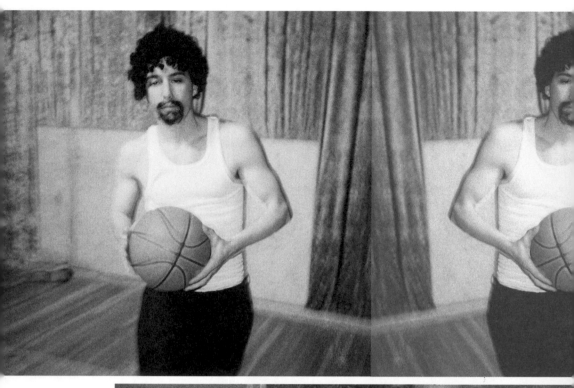
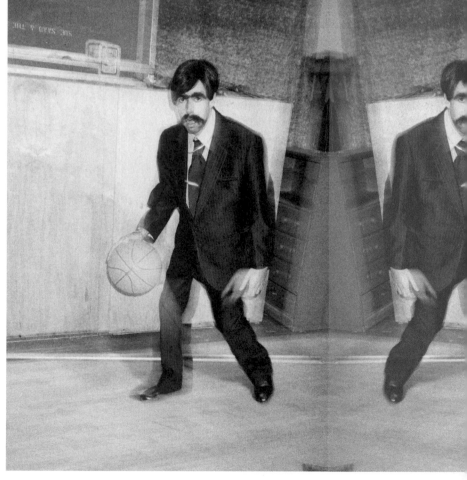

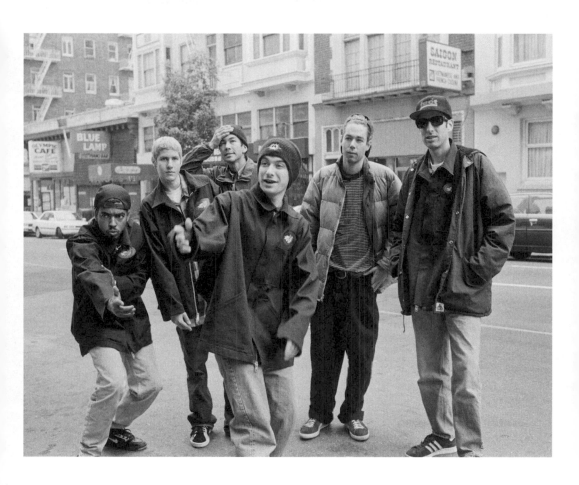

Sabotage

(MD/AH)

After *Check Your Head* came out, we toured a lot. Mark Nishita played the whole tour with us, and Mario was the front-of-house engineer. We'd also settled in with a regular percussionist, Eric Bobo. By the end of that cycle of touring, we'd grown comfortable with the musical language we'd developed together, and we wanted to keep that going. So instead of taking a bunch of time off after the tour, we decided to start recording again. Yauch lobbied for us to do the first stretch in New York. He missed his friends and family. So we booked a couple of months at this kind of old and neglected studio called Tin Pan Alley.

This time around, the process went a bit like this: We knew that we'd start by playing our instruments live, improvising ideas, playing around with stuff. Mario would record us as we went along, mixing a bit on the fly, adding effects or live-dubbing elements, and noting what might be a "keeper" of an idea. We'd sample some of the things we played and put songs together based on that, sometimes just keeping the original recordings and sometimes replaying sections or a song in its entirety. Then we'd add lyrics and otherwise turn the pieces into songs. In short, we weren't feeling the need to totally break all the rules of what we had done; we were happy to expand on them a bit.

One day early in the process, we were about to start working, and Yauch starts playing this incredible bass line on his vintage Fender Jazz bass. I remember it vividly because I immediately asked him, "What song is that from?" It sounded so good that I felt like it must already be somebody else's. Turned out it wasn't; he'd just come up with it. So I started playing drums, and this double-beat break was the first thing I came up with. Those two elements are what you hear at the beginning of "Sabotage"; we wrote the rest of the music in a matter of hours. Horovitz added those great, simple guitar parts. We recorded it at the end of the day, or first thing the next morning. (MD)

You know I'm gonna read this. It's a little passive-aggressive, don't you think? And such a drummer thing to say. *Oh, that guitar playing is just so simple.* Shame on you, Michael. (AH)

There was an engineer at the studio named Chris something-or-other, and he was a super-nice guy, but not particularly a b-boy head. Meaning, he was indifferent about the music we were making. He was just at his job. *But . . .* when Yauch+Mike started really playing this track, Chris went nuts for it and was like, "YO! *That* is the song!" I guess the track touched him and he couldn't keep his feelings for it inside. The track sat around for months without vocals, known only by the working title "Chris Rock."

I vaguely remember Yauch wanting to just keep it as an instrumental. We tried to make it a rap song, and the hook was a scratched-in sample of Queen

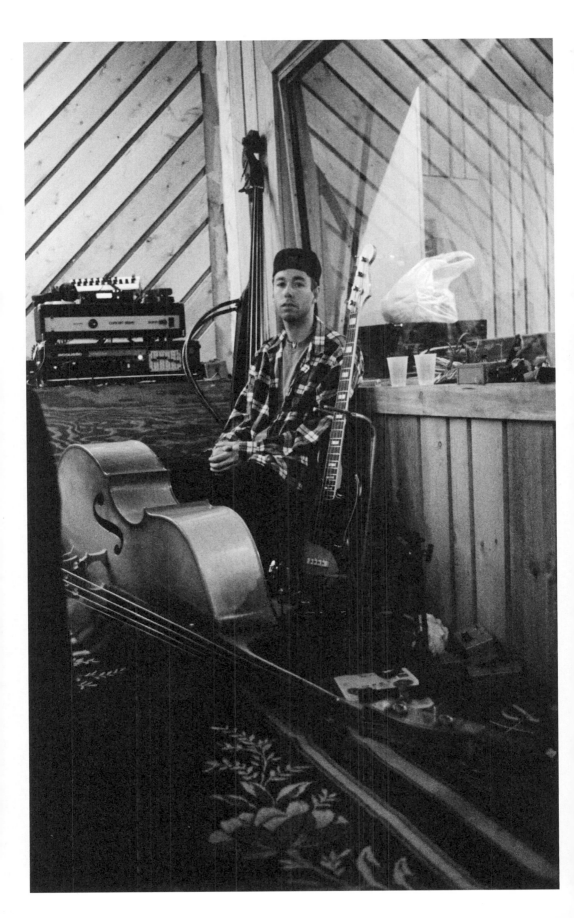

Latifah saying, "Get live, all right." Would've been nice for a different track. This one called for some good old-fashioned screaming, for sure.

We'd been in the studio every night for so long making *Ill Communication* (and *Check Your Head*), and we were totally indecisive about what, when, how, and why to complete songs. Mario was getting frustrated. That's a really calm way of saying that he would blow a fuse and get pissed off at us and scream that we needed to just finish something. Anything. A song. He would push awful instrumental tracks we'd made just to have something moving toward completion.

My favorite memory of him blowing a fuse: I was standing next to him and some piece of electronics wasn't working right and he was getting more and more frustrated. Trying this or that or testing something, just trying to figure out what it was that was making that electronic thing *not work*. He lost it and decided (to himself, not aloud) that it was the power strip that a bunch of things were plugged into. So he manically unplugged the electronic things that were plugged into the power strip, opened a nearby window, and threw the power strip out the window. All the while saying "GOD BLESS AMERICA!!!" in that voice you use when you're on the verge of an angry fucking breakdown but you're not whispering or shouting; the words are pushed through your teeth. (Mario had gone to Catholic school and didn't like to curse.)

Eventually we brought the music back to G-Son, and that's where we finished the songs that were gonna be on our next record, *Ill Communication*. But there was that one track left. "Chris Rock." It had to be dealt with. I decided that it would be funny to write a song about how Mario was holding us all down. How he was trying to mess it all up. Sabotaging our great works of art. So one night I went to Mario's house, and he recorded me screaming words into a microphone, over that track, all about some mysterious thorn in my side— the ubiquitous biters and the haters. (AH)

STICKING TO THEMES

TO

THEMES

———

15 PHOTOS

SPIKE JONZE

I met Adam, Adam, and Mike in 1991 and shot photos of them for *Dirt*, a magazine I did with a couple friends of mine. The guys were working on *Check Your Head* at the time.

They had always been one of my favorite bands, so I was of course really nervous and excited to meet them. But over the next couple years I got to know them better and hung out a lot at their studio, making stuff with them or helping them make stuff, or just getting ridiculous. There was always something bubbling up creatively around them, and if you were lucky enough to be close, you would get sucked up into it, which was a dream come true for me in my early twenties.

They were always playing. It didn't matter what they were doing—making music, playing shows, making videos, or getting dressed up in disguises for no reason—it was just all play. I got to see how they set their lives up, building their studio G-Son and their deal with the label to ensure that nobody could fuck with them. This small selection of photos gives a sense of what it was like to be one of the lucky ones that got sucked into their orbit in the early '90s.

Los Angeles, 1994

Hamburger Hamlet, 1994

At this lunch, we came up with shooting press photos with them as '70s cops. We loved the idea so much it became the "Sabotage" video.

This place was the hub of it all. They had their recording equipment, skate ramps, basketball hoop. And it usually was just a free-for-all: people stopping by, hanging out to skate or eat or fuck around. It was unusual for a band that well known to have that kind of setup. I thought it was so cool that with the record-label money, they made a place where creativity was built into the walls. They weren't just making records, they were making worlds.

They always did it their way. There was never anyone from a record label around telling them what to do. They made their thing, and then once it was all done—the photos, the videos, the record—they gave it to the label.

G-Son Studios, Atwater Village, Los Angeles, 1993
Jason Lee, kickflip pivot up the extension.

"Sabotage" shoot, Los Angeles, 1994

Once we discovered wigs and mustaches, it was over. This was from the "Sabotage" video.

Everything they did was always no-frills too. That was the coolest thing about Yauch. He knew how everything was made—he'd make videos, he took photos, he made music—so he knew you didn't need big, fancy Hollywood crews and budgets. Everything was so homemade and handmade—I think you could feel that, that it was made by these people. It was all very pure.

In those first few years, I had just started making music videos. So when they asked me to make the video for "Sabotage," I was very excited. I wrote up the treatment from the idea we had at Hamburger Hamlet, which wasn't much more than: "We are making the opening credits for that '70s cop show *Sabotage*. We need lots of wigs, moustaches, and a cop car." We submitted it to a production company I'd started to work for, and the budget they came up with was $85K. Yauch was like, "No, it shouldn't cost $85K." So we went in together and had a meeting, me and Yauch and the people who ran the company. We were like, "We don't need police officers, we don't need closed-down streets, we don't need makeup trailers . . . " and cut it down to its bare bones. And they said, "Well, this is the way a video's made, and this is the way we do it to ensure that we can deliver you what it is you want." And Yauch was like, "Okay, we'll do it with a different production company." Then they were like, "Wait, wait, wait, hold on a second." And instantly, $35k got cut. Yauch wasn't going to be told how or what to do by anybody. He was a true original and punk always, and really inspired me to keep that attitude in everything I did no matter what world I was in.

Adam Yauch's apartment, Los Feliz Manor, California, 1994

My friend Casey Storm brought in racks of clothes he got at thrift stores. He had never actually done styling before—he was just a friend of mine, and we didn't have much money—but he had good style, so I was like, "You wanna be a stylist?" And he was like, "Okay. What do I do?" And I said, "You go to thrift stores and buy a bunch of clothes that would be in a '70s cop show." He totally got the aesthetic and crushed it. So we started trying on different things and creating the characters from those outfits.

We ended up creating like ten characters. Adam, Adam, and Mike each played three or four characters in the video. I don't know which one Adam Horovitz is exactly in this one, but I think he's kind of a rock-'n'-roll '70s Sunset Boulevard Jim Morrison dude. And I think Mike D's putting a fat suit on.

So, this is the place that we bought the wigs from. Me and Mike and Yauch found this place in the phone book that was a wholesale wig warehouse. We went over there, and there was no real store there, it was just the warehouse and the front office where they took the orders over the phone. We were in this woman's office and basically told her what we wanted, and she pulled the wigs out of the warehouse. I don't think there was one wig or mustache she showed us that we didn't buy.

Wig warehouse, Los Angeles, 1994

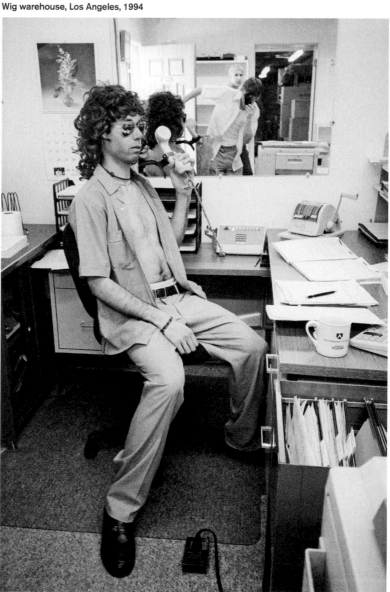

Basically, we made that video—really all the videos we made—in the way Yauch (and the almighty Hörnblowér) worked and in the way I had made skate videos. Just driving around town, stealing locations, getting dressed in parking lots, eating in the van. We had no permits, we would just see a spot and say, "Let's grab a shot there!"

"Sabotage" shoot, Los Angeles, 1994

Las Vegas, 1994

Right after *III Communication* came out, the guys were about to go out on the Lollapalooza tour. We wanted to do a more collage-y video. I always loved the "Pass the Mic" video, so, in a way, this was riffing off that style—a collage of shots and just running around. I would just write down shots: *performing in front of an airplane, swinging from a camera hanging from a crane, etc.* . . . and we would meet up and drive around and shoot stuff.

When they went to Vegas to rehearse for Lollapalooza, we all went with them and shot a bunch of the "Sure Shot" video that week.

This photo is in a casino, where we stole the last shot of the video. We wanted to shoot inside a casino, but you're not allowed to, so we rented tuxedos and covered the red lights on the 16mm camera with tape, and I held it down by my leg and pointed it backwards and up, and they just walked through the casino behind me . . . and we got our casino shot! It seemed very important at the time.

Mike D and Money Mark, Atwater Village. *Grand Royal* magazine, 1994

Milwaukee Mike, the Mullet. *Grand Royal* magazine, 1994

So, basically, once we discovered wigs and mustaches, we just couldn't stop, and we would go out in disguises every night.

Yauch had curated this incredible wig and disguise closet at his apartment. We'd go as Heshers or weird professors or whatever it is that Yauch is in this photo . . . I'm not even sure. We'd end up meeting people and going wherever the night took us.

We decided to go as professors, or as the principals of the school. Actually, I'm not sure what Mike decided to go as. Maybe the older dude who graduated a long time ago and still hangs around the high school.

Sofia Coppola's prom-themed birthday party, Los Angeles, 1994

Grand Royal magazine, 1993 or 1994

This is Adam Horovitz in a Joey Buttafuoco fashion shoot for *Grand Royal*. Not sure where or why Adam had the idea to do a fashion shoot inspired by him, but that never seemed to matter. If it made us laugh, we would just follow it.

Mike D, the sweetheart of the group, Las Vegas, 1994
[Mike's aunt's online dating profile picture —AH]

In another article for *Grand Royal*, Mike D explored the mullet hairstyle craze that had died in Los Angeles ten years earlier.

The best part of this day was Mike with a guitar in a bag, hanging out at Guitar Institute. It was this school for tech-y guitar players, who were mostly in metal bands. At lunchtime all the kids hung out in front of the school. Mike basically blended right in . . . he looked just like all them, hanging out with his guitar in front of the school.

Metal Mike, *Grand Royal* magazine, 1993–94

Yauch's Prince Street apartment, 1995 or 1996

I loved this apartment. It was on the corner of Prince and Mulberry. It was just one room, tiny. Barely big enough for a bed and a sofa. Yauch had very few things—the only expensive things in the whole apartment were his bass and a video projector and screen, which had theater-quality projection. He had this amazing DVD collection. He was living super-simply: making music, watching movies, and going wherever his creativity took him, like having an idea for a music festival to support Tibet.

There was something really simple about the way Yauch always lived . . . almost like a creative monk. Creativity was his guide, leading him wherever it would, with no rules. His friends were his travel mates, riding with him to places they would never have gone to on their own. I know that was true for me. Thank you, Yauch. And thank you, Beastie Boys, for bringing me along on your ride.

Those three friends are magic to me.

REVIEWS, LISTINGS, AND MORE

April 1994 / #288

Syncopation

Tempo is "Outta Time"

Boobie Knight's
Re-imagination

Shawna Frizzel
in Oslo

Rasheed Smith

The 411 on 4/4

IN REVIEW
ILL COMMUNICATION

Dianne Wentworth

Clayton Battershall

DON
AMBROSE
EARNS HIS STRIPES IN '64

GAIL GRANT
IMPORT(ANT)

III Communication

The first thing you notice, in appearance, about these three Beastie Boys is how strikingly unstriking they are. They're neither tall nor short. Handsome nor ugly. In a crowd of people they would easily blend, unnoticed. And within their musicianship, they're not particularly skilled, nor are they particularly awful. Rather, they embody all that is mediocre. Yet to my surprise, as well as that of the entire music journalist community, they've managed to create a new recording that some refer to as "pretty good." At first listen, I was underwhelmed. I was easily distracted; time passed neither quickly nor slowly. I was at home making a soup and so I assumed that I would have enough time to listen and make notes and then get back to what I was doing. But this record is a full-length LP. Full-length meaning, to me, a little too lengthy. There are twenty tracks here when they should have weeded out the weak and let the strong rise to the top. In this case, there might've only been four tracks left on here and I'm sure contractually that would not be enough material to constitute a full-length LP and so here we are: Beastie Boys' *Ill Communication* and its twenty tracks.

The lead-off, "Sure Shot." Certainly you've heard similar songs on numerous occasions. A very talented jazz musician's work being synopsized to a one-bar pattern and repeated to such a degree that it undermines all that musician has accomplished. Then layer three vocalists shouting words that rhyme alongside a drum pattern and you have popular music's current trend: rap music. I was surprised, however, when the next track, "Tough Guy," began. This was a totally different musical direction, and ultimately unrefreshing to my ears. This song is that of the hard-rock or heavy-listening genre. Your basic format of drum, bass, guitar, and a lead vocalist shouting. A format made so popular by the Beatles it has persevered throughout the generations. I recognized the capacities of this song immediately and felt staying around for it was superfluous. So I walked from my desk and went to the kitchen to check on the soup. This unfortunate song concluded well before I expected it to, and so that at least was somewhat of a positive.

The next song, "B-Boys Makin' with the Freak Freak," was so noisy and disjointed, I stayed in the kitchen to find my good ladle for the soup. I had purchased it on a recent trip to Luxembourg for the Geheien Ugrëff Vun Jazz. (Music and cooking have a symbiotic existence in my home.) To my mild delight, the next song, "Bobo on the Corner," commenced soon upon my return to my desk. An admirable attempt at creating that space where

"I was exhilarated..."

music and improvisation can lead you toward one's inner/outer mind/body concord. Whereas the attempt is mundanely middling, it is, nonetheless, adequate.

We now move on to the next track, "Root Down." I quite like the original version of this song. Jimmy Smith during his Verve Records era walked among the greats that caressed eighty-eight keys. Brahms, Rick Wakeman, and a handful of others. Beastie Boys, here coattailing on Smith's brilliance, receive a nod of acceptance from me because of their recognition of true virtuosity. The next song has the same title as an album I reviewed a few years back by a rock and roll group named Black Sabbath, "Sabotage." The song is really just a—wait, hold on. I'm sorry. I smell smoke coming from the kitchen. Okay, whew. It's fine. I was melting butter for a mirepoix to fill out my soup and it just overheated. I cleaned out the pan and started over. It's fine. Where was I? Right, track 7. "Get It Together."

This so far is a stand-out track. The groove is very interesting but most notably, a fourth voice is now heard. The voice is listed as someone named Q-Tip. He has a smooth yet bookwormish cadence to his voice that lends to the essence of jazz itself. I look forward to hearing more of this fellow in the future. Track 8, entitled "Sabrosa," is yet another attempt at instrumentation by way of heavy groove. While, yet again, it is commendable that the band harkens back to the days of formidable

BEASTIE BOYS, 1992

King Ad-Rock   MCA   Mike D

pioneers of the genre such as Stuff, Ekseption, and Simtec & Wylie, they fall just short of exceptional. I only barely heard the next few songs, "The Update," "Futterman's Rule," and "Alright Hear This," as I was in the kitchen working on my Ajiaco Cubano, a delicious soup I discovered when I was visiting the home of a balloonist friend of mine in Cuba during my autumn break in '67. My trip was overshadowed by the death of Che Guevara, and, as an American, I felt it was awkward for me to stick around and so I finished out my travels in Jamaica, where I heard wondrous new rhythms and horn sections, drank Red Stripes until dawn, and learned to make an enchanting oxtail stew. Upon my return to the States, via Toronto, I heard a remarkable violinist making his way onto the jazz circuit, Michal Urbaniak. Which leads me to the next track from *Ill Communication*, "Eugene's Lament."

This song is by far the stand-alone track from this album, and is reminiscent of the glorious Urbaniak himself, whom I had the pleasure of meeting and spending time with during the recording of *Body English* with Urszula Dudziak. By no means his best album, but there's a true musical ingenuity that lies within his body of work. "Flute Loop" is the next track on Beastie Boys' LP. I rather enjoyed this track, most notably because of its playing time. It falls just under two minutes long. Which I feel is the appropriate length for a person of the young generation to speak their mind. There were some other songs that played next, but I was distracted by straightening up my apartment, as I have a few guests coming over for my bimonthly "soup and readings of my poetry" gatherings. The titles, so you have them, are: "Do It," "Ricky's Theme," and "Heart Attack Man" (which was so noisy I had to turn my stereo down). The songs that followed were "The Scoop" and "Shambala." "Shambala" piqued my interest, as I am an enthusiast of the Far East and its mystical ways. Although I've never traveled to India, I feel as though John Coltrane took me there in my formative years as a student of jazz. The final two tracks, "Bodhisattva Vow" and "Transitions," were a pleasant surprise to me. It's as though Beastie Boys is headed in a new direction. One of interflection and calm. I was exhilarated when this album came to a close, as my doorbell rang and the first of my guests arrived. It was Judith and her new husband, Don. Judith was my longtime colleague at *Syncopation*. She was with me during those now-distant days and nights with Michal Urbaniak, and I guess after all these twenty songs I'm interested in discussing our time together with him, with her. And maybe, in some way, this Beastie Boys album will make its way into tonight's conversation as well. —*Tim Willoughby*

Beastie Boys' *Ill Communication* is set to be released through Capitol Records on May 31. Available on record, cassette, and compact disc.

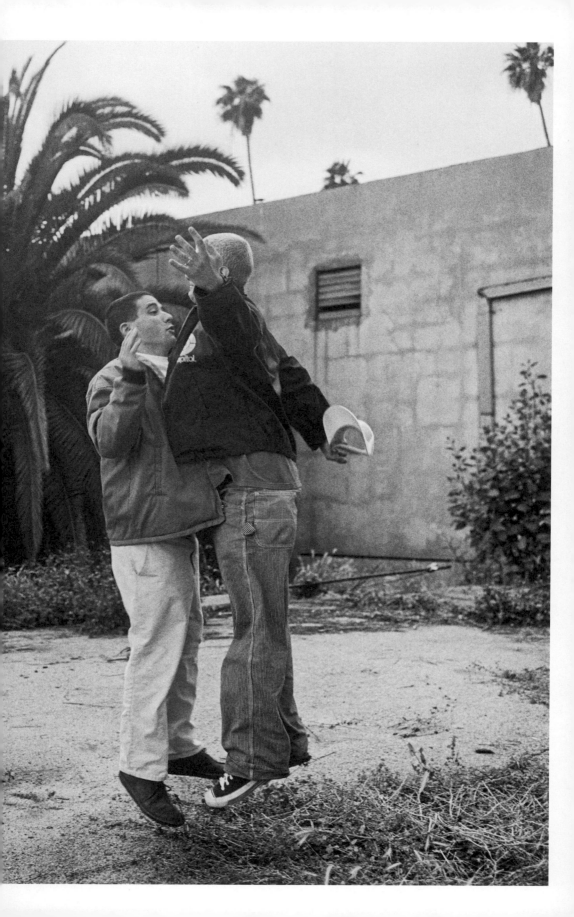

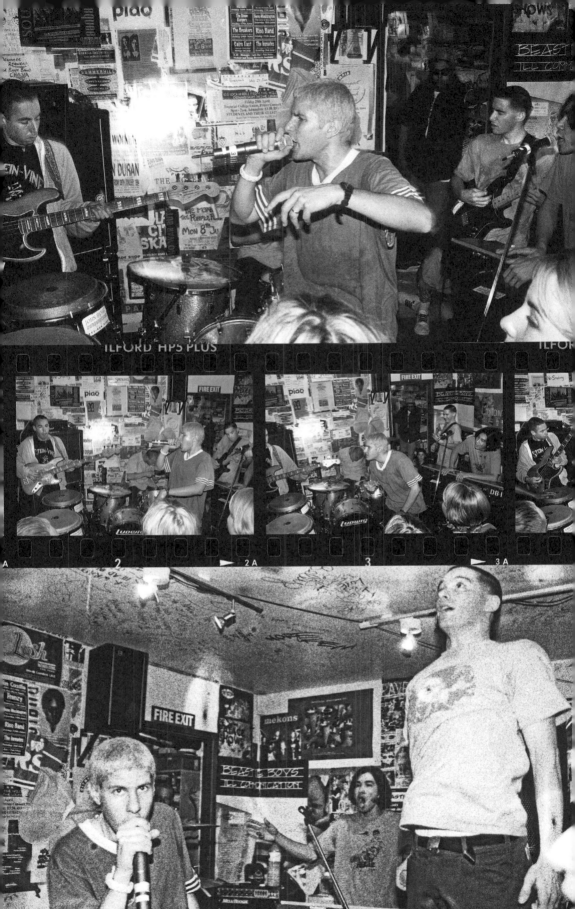

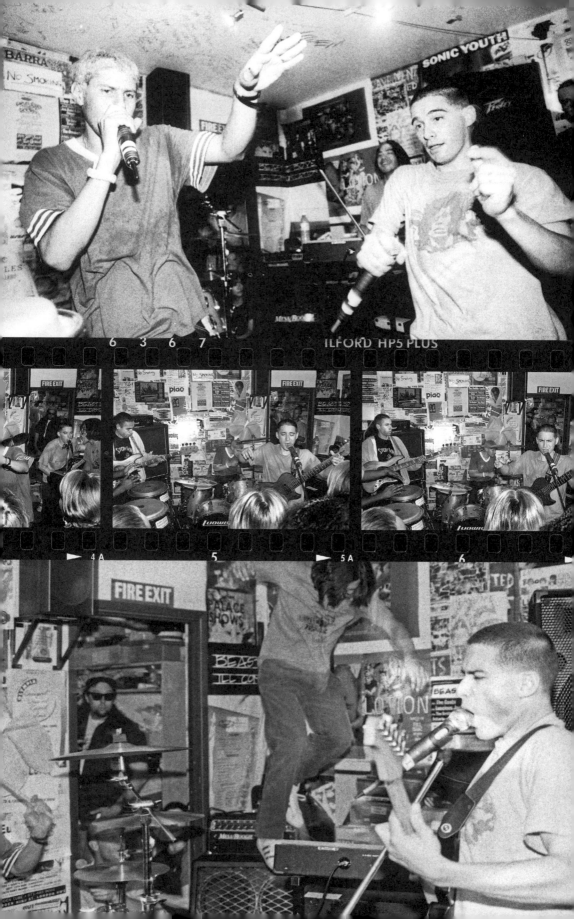

Who at this Table Sucks Dick?

(MD/AH)

When most New Yorkers talk about "The Dunk," they're talking about the famed John Starks posterization of Horace Grant and Michael Jordan in game two of the 1993 Eastern Conference Finals at MSG. But for us, the Dunk will always be the 6'3" Billy Corgan brutally flushing over the 5'9" photographer Ricky Powell, who was also high on mushrooms. It was nasty.

Well, *what happened was* . . .

In early 1994, while we were finishing *Ill Communication*, Lollapalooza asked us to play that summer's tour with Nirvana headlining. (We loved Nirvana—thought they were amazing and important—and we were immediately in. Then Kurt Cobain died. The sadness, and the loss of Nirvana at the top of the bill, gave us pause about the whole deal. Without Nirvana, we thought Lollapalooza was just corny. Straight-up. A name-brand MTV alterna-mosh party. But then the festival organizers came up with the idea of us co-headlining with Smashing Pumpkins.) (MD)

We were still interested in seeing what the lineup would be and how much $ we'd make and how it'd all play out, so we had a meeting. It was us; our booking agent, Don Muller; our manager, John Silva; his partner, J.C.; a couple Lollapalooza representatives; and this guy Billy Corgan, who was the singer of this band we'd never really heard of that was taking Nirvana's place as headliner. And also there was the founder of Lollapalooza, Perry Farrell.

I love Perry Farrell. He is fucking bonkers. A genuine weirdo. We're all sitting at this table in Hollywood at night outdoors, a pleasantish and grown-up evening, and Perry's getting *drunk*. It was kind of inspiring how little he appeared to be worrying about the right way to act or the right thing to say. The rest of us were talking about bands we wanted in the lineup. We were throwing out bands that we liked that we were also kind of friends with: A Tribe Called Quest, L7, Boredoms, and a couple others. Billy's telling us what he likes. After a while of going back and forth, Perry sits up and says loudly, "Who sucks dick?!"

Wait . . . what?

"Who at this table sucks dick?"

None of us really knew how to properly respond. Then we realized that the point he was making was that all the bands we were suggesting were super straight bands for straight people (a broad generalization, but . . .). He was looking out for gay kids who didn't want the usual rock music. Ultimately the lineup did not reflect what he had in mind. (I'm not sure what exactly he had in mind.

I feel like he might've said Morrissey, and we all said that that'd be awesome to tour with Morrissey. Or did he want Bette Midler? Again . . . would've been fucking amazing.) (AH)

Anyway, the lineup ended up being us, Smashing Pumpkins, Funkadelic, the Breeders, A Tribe Called Quest, Nick Cave, L7, Green Day, and Boredoms on the main stage, with numerous other bands, like the Pharcyde, the Verve, the Flaming Lips, and Luscious Jackson, on the other stages. It was a full-on traveling circus. Because we'd gotten a say, Billy Pumpkin had gotten a say, and Perry had gotten a say, there was all manner of different shit going on simultaneously at any given time. Starting with: on the main stage, the day's festivities got underway with Tibetan monks chanting. (Yauch's idea. If that wasn't strange enough, the monks were followed by Boredoms—a brutal and assaultive noise band from Japan.)

Backstage could be a lot of fun too—especially the pickup basketball games. Billy Corgan did not exactly have handle or a crossover move, but he was tall and surprisingly competitive, demonstrated by his thunderous dunk on Ricky Powell. There was Phife (RIP) from Tribe driving through the backcourt and Guided by Voices chucking up threes. On one pleasant summer afternoon backstage at the Bay Area's Shoreline Amphitheatre, I guarded Phife. A crowd had gathered to watch. He was sweating, running the court up and down in Timberland boots. Eventually, he got frustrated with a few things. Also, he was 5'3", so he had to really muscle or elbow his way anywhere near the rim. Eventually he went up for a shot, and I *had* to reject that shit. After I did, Phife gave me an icy glare that made me wish I had never guarded him in the first place. (MD)

Also backstage somewhere on the tour, a UPS delivery person walked in with a package. It was kind of quiet in the room/tent. Then she took off her UPS hat and said to us . . . "*Dude!* I can't believe that worked. I borrowed this UPS uniform from my friend, came here with a clipboard and an empty box, and security just let me walk right through. And now I'm in the fucking Beastie Boys' dressing room!" So yeah, of *course* we gave her all the tickets and all-access passes she wanted.

Oh, and one time we gave the Verve a ride on our tour bus and the singer told my brother that his father was a time traveler. And that was Lollapalooza. (AH)

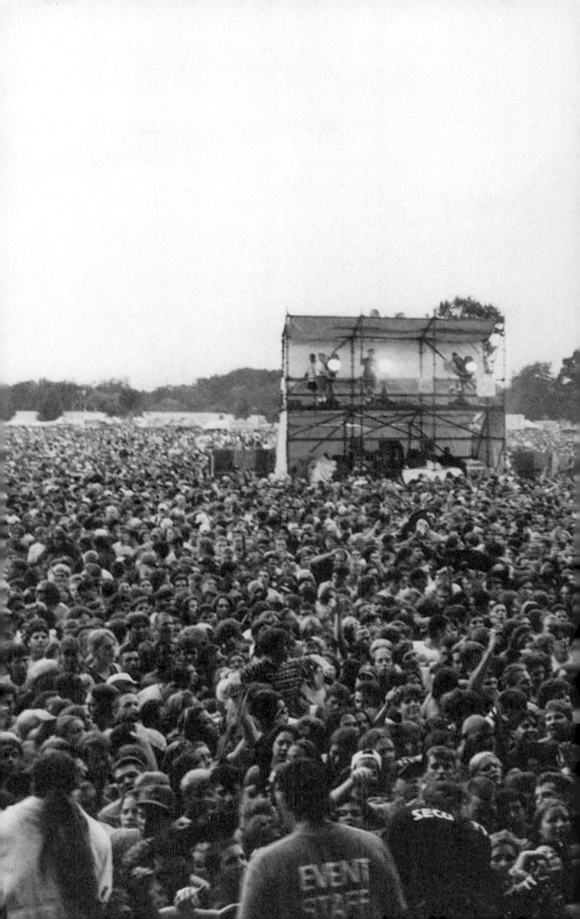

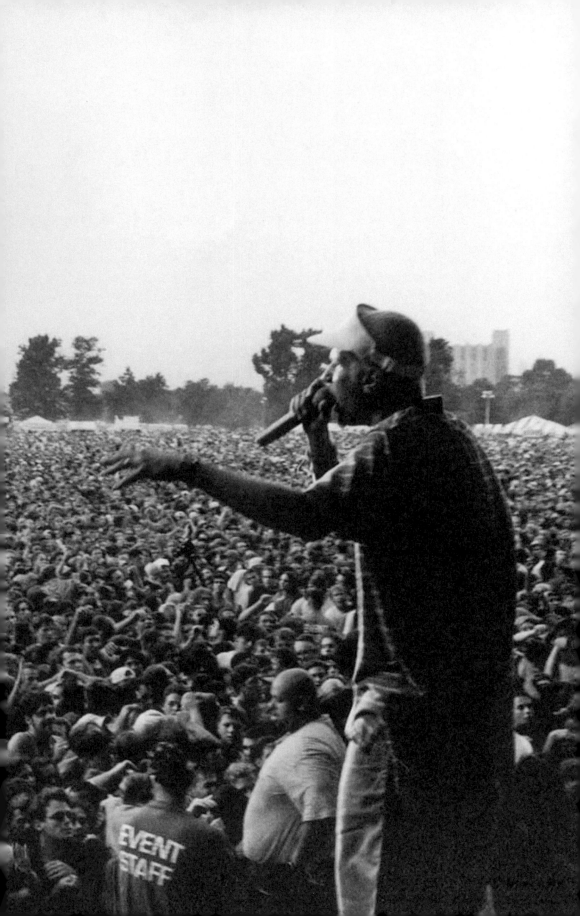

Like a Fanzine, but on a Computer

Hi, my name is Ian Rogers, and this is how I showed Beastie Boys the Internet. ¶ I grew up in a town of twenty thousand people in northern Indiana. My stepfather studied computer science, and we had an Apple II in the house when I was eight years old; by age ten I was an assistant instructor at an after-school computer programming center. I'd been obsessed with music since age five, and through skateboard mags and mail order, I found Minor Threat, Black Flag, the Misfits, and Bad Brains. I knew Beastie Boys as a band on the *New York Thrash* ROIR cassette and never listened to *Licensed to Ill* in the '80s, but *Paul's Boutique* hit the bull's-eye for me. I became obsessed with that record in a way we don't get obsessed with albums in the streaming Internet music age: memorizing every moment, identifying and making mixtapes from the samples, noting and looking for hidden meaning behind each lyrical reference. ¶ When I went to college in Bloomington in 1991, I bought a used IBM 8088 XT clone with an amber monochrome monitor and quickly discovered Usenet–international Internet message boards where nerds from around the world wrote endlessly about whatever they were into. I'm sure Usenet had professional uses, but I used it for the same reasons I use Instagram today–music and skateboarding. ¶ I contributed to Usenet in the two ways I was most qualified: transcribing and posting David Bowie lyrics, and maintaining the Beastie Boys "Frequently Asked Questions," or FAQ. For the Beastie Boys FAQ, I dutifully determined what the important questions were, made sure they were answered, and posted the organized document to a Usenet

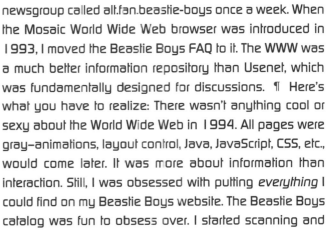

newsgroup called alt.fan.beastie-boys once a week. When the Mosaic World Wide Web browser was introduced in 1993, I moved the Beastie Boys FAQ to it. The WWW was a much better information repository than Usenet, which was fundamentally designed for discussions. ¶ Here's what you have to realize: There wasn't anything cool or sexy about the World Wide Web in 1994. All pages were gray–animations, layout control, Java, JavaScript, CSS, etc., would come later. It was more about information than interaction. Still, I was obsessed with putting *everything* I could find on my Beastie Boys website. The Beastie Boys catalog was fun to obsess over. I started scanning and

posting every magazine article I could find, because linking to the article in your favorite magazine was still several years away. So the website not only answered your newbie questions ("Is Screech from *Saved by the Bell* Mike D's brother?"), it also tipped you off to all this stuff you didn't even know existed. While I'm sure the audience was infinitely small by today's standards, the Beastie Boys website was one of the few "must see" sites for people just coming online, and that distinction made me all the more determined to make it definitive. ¶ Still, the notion that Beastie Boys or anyone they knew would ever see the site seemed absurd. I was no lawyer, but I was pretty sure the scanning of magazine articles and appropriating of logos and images wasn't legal without permission. So when I got a call from a woman named Bethann who worked with Beastie Boys, I was stunned and pretty sure the next step was a cease-and-desist. But when I talked to Beastie Boys' manager John Silva, he said, "Sue you?! No! I want you to do this for *all* my bands!" Not only did he not shut me down, he offered to pay me for the time I spent on the Beastie Boys site. I was making $6.50/hour working at the IU music-school library at the time, so I went in for the kill–I asked for $8.50/hour to build websites. ¶ By the summer of 1994, I'd still never had any contact with the band members themselves. One day I got a call from Bethann offering me tickets for Lollapalooza. I had seen Beastie Boys a few times between '92 and '94 in small venues, like a cow barn in Indianapolis. I really didn't have any interest in the big festival, and I would have been embarrassed to meet the band in a corny "Hi, I'm the nerd who made a shrine to you on this thing you've never heard of called the World Wide Web" way. So I thanked Bethann for the offer but declined. She called back a week later saying the band wanted me to give them a tour of the site: "They've never actually seen the Internet, and they want you to show it to them." ¶ "Okay! In that case I'd love to come." ¶ This was my first time ever having special access to anything. Yauch volunteered to show me around. We played basketball and rode skateboards. I played one-on-one basketball with Billy Corgan. I have a vague memory of George Clinton feeding me spaghetti off his plate. The entire day was thrilling. But we were more focused on hanging out than talking about this Internet business, and we ran out of time. I failed at my mission to bestow the wonders of the Internet on Beastie Boys. Yauch had the solution: "Come to Detroit!" ¶ I jumped in the Beastie Boys bus headed to Pine Knob Music Theatre. This time we had an appointment to get down to business, and after I hooked up to a modem in the production office and installed some software, we all huddled

around Mike D's PowerBook Duo (trackball and all) to catch a glimpse of this new thing called "The World Wide Web" on "The Internet." Mike, Tamra, and Yauch were in the room, along with a couple members of L7, Matt Sweeney from Chavez, and Lollapalooza co-founder Marc Geiger. No one in the room had ever laid eyes on the Internet except for Geiger (who was pacing around the back of the room insisting, "Guys! In a year you're going to sell *all* your records this way!") and Sweeney (who knew the URLs for black metal sites in the Netherlands by heart). ¶ Despite my lackluster presentation, Mike and Yauch got the potential of the technology immediately. They saw the value of a direct path to Beastie Boys fans (without MTV or radio in the middle). On the spot, we decided to put their magazine, *Grand Royal*, online, and take the out-of-print first issue and make it available in its entirety for free on the Web. It was like a fanzine, but on a computer. ¶ Later on the bus, the band's then–tour manager, Wilf, sat down and asked me how I was doing. "I'm having the time of my life," I said, "but I can't figure out why these guys want me hanging around." ¶ "Oh, that's easy," replied Wilf. "They think this Internet thing is important, and they're trying to figure out if you're going to be helpful or if you're going to be annoying." ¶ "How am I doing?" ¶ "You're doing great." And he walked away.

A few weeks later, someone named JC from the management company called. "We're gonna need you in L.A. for pre-production in March, and we need a budget." I told him I thought there was some mistake: Mike just asked me for an idea, and I gave him one. "Y'all should totally do it," I said. "I mean, I don't even know *how* to do it, I'm still in college. . . ." ¶ JC calmly said, "You wanna do this, kid. We will figure it out." ¶ We built video-game machines out of classic junked Space Invaders and Lunar Lander machines I found in Indianapolis and had trucked to Los Angeles. We begged Apple to give us hardware. We put joysticks on the front and used QuickTime VR studio as an interface to launch loud videos from Beastie Boys, DJ Hurricane, and other Grand Royal artists. We put loudspeakers and big monitors on top of the video games to make them a spectacle on the concourse level of the venue. They were cool in 1995, and even if they existed today you'd have to nod your head and give it up. Shit was dope. Nerdy but dope. ¶ In those days, you couldn't say "Check out my website," because maybe one out of every hundred people had ever heard of one. So on the 1995 tour, we launched our own grassroots campaign to get people to try the Internet. We handed out floppy disks at the shows. If you put them in your

Kids, do not hand out floppy disks at your shows. Morons will throw them at you. (AH)

computer, they signed you up to an Internet account (white label ISP through Spry) and dropped you right on the Beastie Boys webpage. ¶ Finally, on that 1995 tour we pioneered the idea of posting live from the show. No mobile Internet, so I was taking photos with an early Apple QuickTake camera, running backstage, and uploading grainy photos over a phone line while my best friend from college, Mark Thompson, wrote sarcastic stories about every show and every city we traveled through. ¶ That's the story of how Beastie Boys became Internet pioneers and I started a career in digital music. We did the tour diary again for the *Hello Nasty* tour, built the first online radio station for a label at Grand Royal, achieved the first day/date digital/physical album release with At the Drive-In's *Relationship of Command*, reissued every album in deluxe box sets online with director's commentary in 2009, and more. From my perspective, this story shows you a lot about how Beastie Boys worked. They were visionary and quick to explore something new, always making it theirs instead of using what other people were doing as a template. They could have worked with professionals, but instead they preferred to support a kid from Indiana they thought had some potential. They worked at it but had fun with it, and I'm proud to have been a part of early Internet history in exactly this way.

Antiques Nerdshow

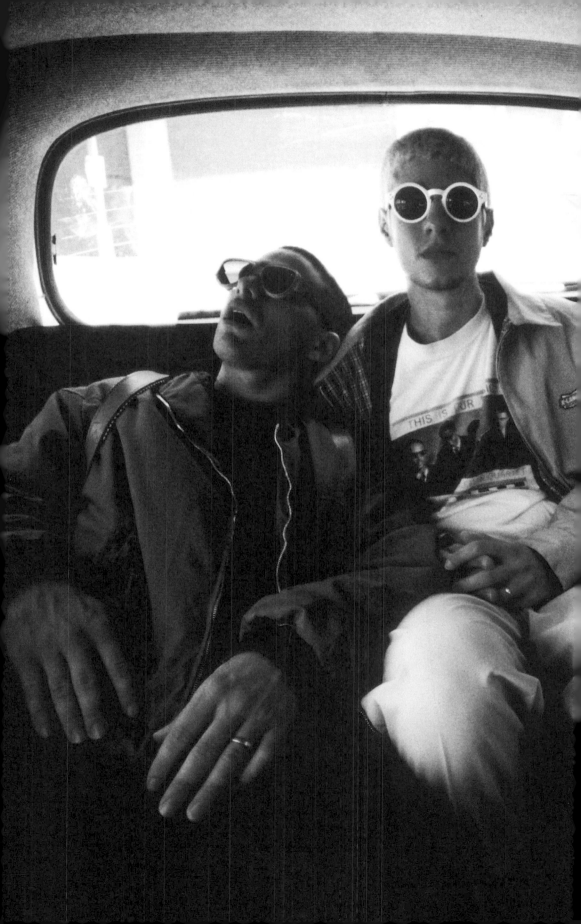

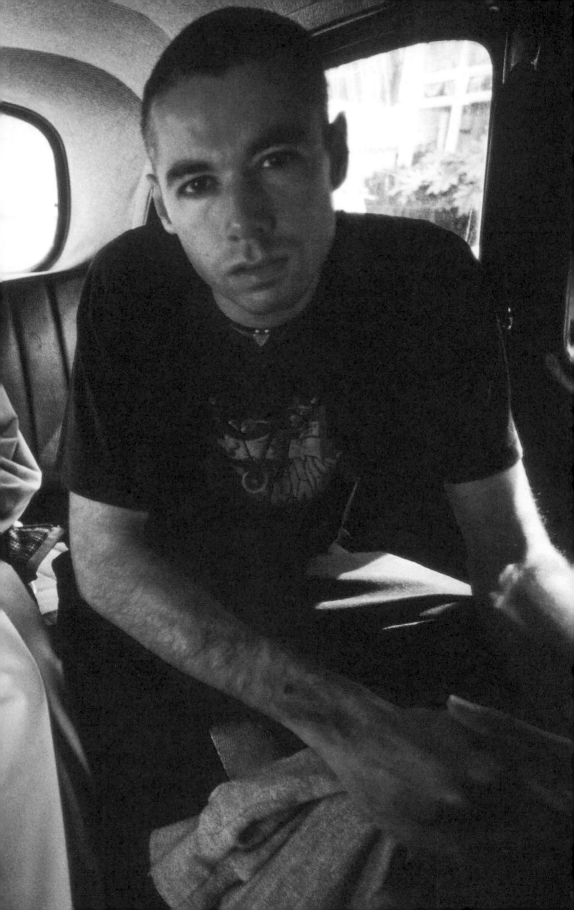

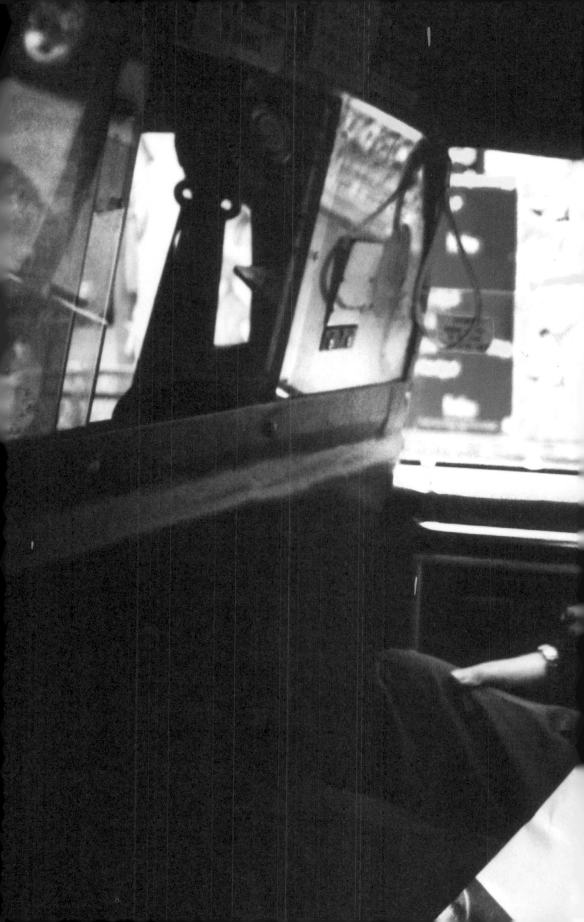

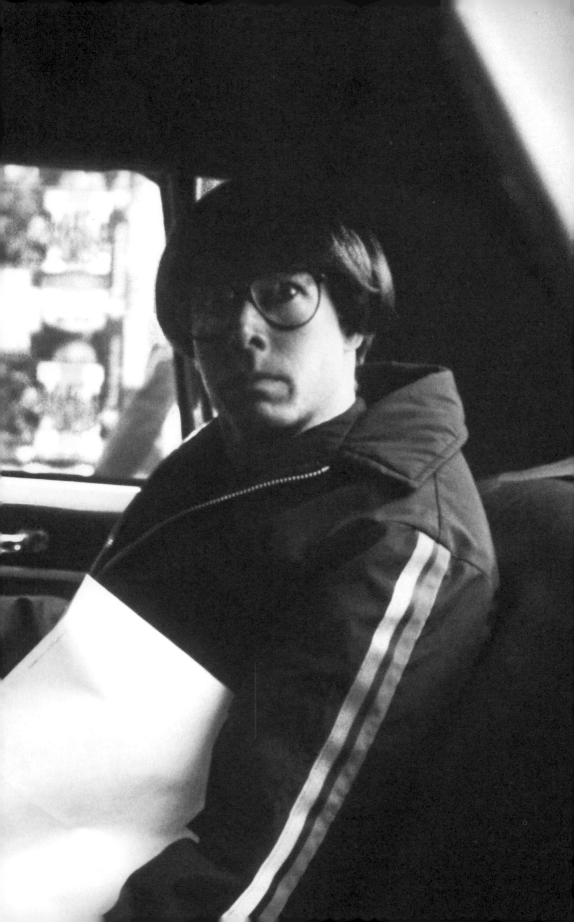

The Summer of Os Mutantes
(AH)

1996. I was madly in love with my new girlfriend (and future wife), Kathleen. The California life had run its course for me, and I had to get out. It was time to come home. Yauch had already left L.A. and was fully back in New York. Living in a (fucking tiny) apartment on Mulberry Street. Right in the thick of Little Italy's yearly San Gennaro festival. More specifically, his window looked down onto the "Drown the Clown" booth. So every day during the festival, from morning till the end of the night, there was some fucking guy barking at people to spend their money throwing balls at him to humiliate him, and make him fall into a dirty little bucket of water. Just to shut him up. (The annoying shit that you hear and see out of your NYC apartment window is its own book of stories and lists.) The past few years we'd been living in Los Angeles, and when we'd come back to New York, it was as though we were just visiting. We recorded some music there in '94 and '95, but felt disjointed from our city. I love Los Angeles, but how many sunny days in a row can a True Yorker take? So we moved home. And when you move, you start hanging out with new people. And when you make new friends, you end up hearing new music. Or new to you, at least.

Enter Os Mutantes.

I don't know who told me about them, but when I heard their song "Panis et Circenses," it instantly got bumped up to top fifty of all time. It was a psych-rock sound I'd *kind of* heard before (sort of), but it was coming from a different geographical place. Further expanding the notion of . . . *If they're making this music over there . . . what else are they doing and who else is doing it?* We got pretty deep into bossa nova and other Brazilian music. I'd already had the bigger, more classic records. The ones that made it in America. Sérgio Mendes, Herb Alpert, even Jobim and Gilberto, but no one had ever hipped me to Jorge Ben. Or this fucking Os Mutantes record. Soon enough I was on a new musical hunt. Not just for breaks and beats but . . . sounds. Lucky for me I didn't have a job to be at, so I had a lot of time to go hunting. I started getting back into old electronic records. Moog records. Digging a little deeper than the few *Switched On* records I had. Taking the real sonic plunge into Morton Subotnick and Jean-Jacques Perrey. (Who knew that Gershon Kingsley made the song "Popcorn"? And how was Hot Butter's version of it the biggest record when I was six? Everyone loved that song. Put it out now with the "Shack Up" beat, 808 kicks, and some crazy Trap hi-hats, and you have a hit record.)

When we moved back to New York, it seemed different. A little. It was changing. While we were gone, a lot of strangers moved in who seemed to

have extra cash to buy funny hats and shoes at these new fancy boutiques in what used to be forgotten neighborhoods. All of downtown was mid-facelift and was being given new names like Norbeca, or EaSo (east of SoHo?), or the Future District. But who cares? It was summertime, and NYC summers are the best. We were back and were living a grown-up version of our high school days. Nothing to do but wander around trying to link up. Hearing new music. Making new music. Hanging out with some new friends. And so on and on.

Here's my summer of '96 playlist . . .

Panis et Circenses—Os Mutantes
Psychedelic greatness.

Silver Apples of the Moon—Morton Subotnick
This record should've been titled "Music to Play Scrabble By."

Do the Math—The PeeChees
Punk brilliance.

E.V.A.—Jean-Jacques Perrey
Jean-Jacques Perrey, gettin' funky on *Moog Indigo*. What's not to love?

Mira Ven Aca—Johnny Colon
If someone you know doesn't know what boogaloo sounds like, play them this song and they'll be like, *Oh shit, I love this.* And they'll go on a hunt for records by the Lat-Teens, Ray Barretto, Joe Cuba, and so many more.

Lovefingers—Silver Apples
I'd never heard of this band, like Os Mutantes, until I got back to New York. This song has an amazing intro. One that we tried to bite for the next decade.

Elevators (Me & You)—OutKast
Whoa. Atlanta is on to some new shit.

Halleluwah—Can
Smoke a pin joint and walk around New York listening to this song on headphones.

Smilin' Billy Suite—Heath Brothers
This is what we wanted our laid-back instrumental music to sound like.

El Ratón—Cheo Feliciano
Simply one of the best songs ever recorded.

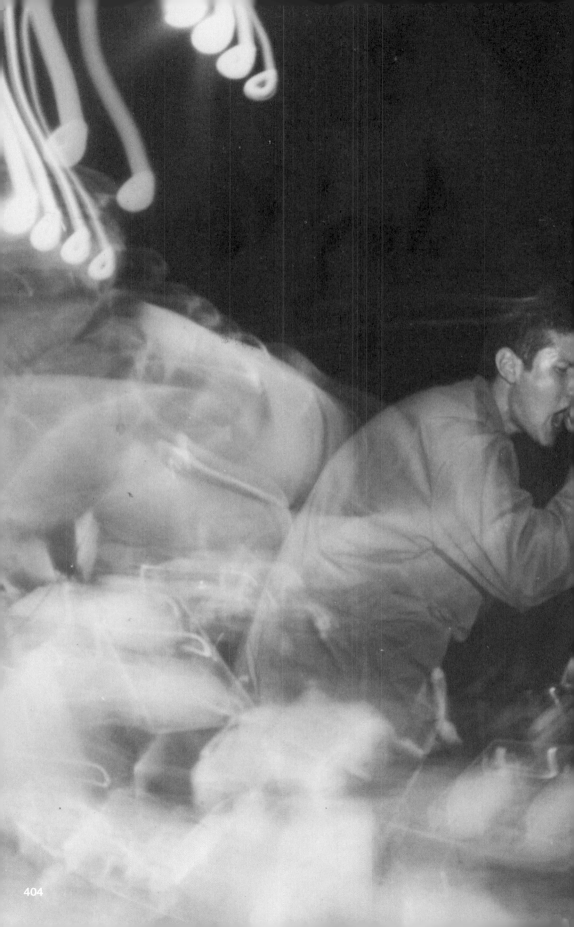

In 1995, we recorded and released a hardcore 7" called *Aglio e Olio*. We thought it would be fun to start an alter-ego band (called Quasar), go on a couple tours, and only play our old and new hardcore songs. (And a few covers too: "Wonderwall" by Oasis, "53rd & 3rd" by the Ramones, "I Am a Poseur" by X-Ray Spex, "Big Shot" by Billy Joel, "Red Tape" by Circle Jerks, and a couple Bad Brains songs for sure.) We played maybe fifteen shows in total, but each one was completely memorable and exciting. We toured the West Coast of the US, and did a few shows in Japan and Australia. We played punk clubs, an indoor skate park, outdoors at the bottom of a ski slope, some dude's house party in Lake Tahoe, and the best of them all . . . a cruise boat in the harbor of Sydney, Australia, dressed in a nautical theme. (Of course.) I would here like to acknowledge the glory that is our longtime friend and drummer, Amery "AWOL" Smith. He is simply the greatest hardcore punk rock drummer ever. Never to be rivaled when playing the typewriter beat. (AH)

405

Halloween with Lee "Scratch" Perry
(MD)

In terms of the way we made records, Lee "Scratch" Perry was one of our biggest influences for sure. I'd explain it like this: Since the first recorded music, most pop and jazz recordings have been made in as simple and straightforward a manner as possible. You have a bass guitar going through a mixing console going to a tape machine. You have drums mic'd and submixed with few effects, if any. Guitar, vocals, whatever—same. The idea being that you wanted the recorded version to sound as close as possible to the way the music sounded if you were simply sitting in the room while the musicians played it. Fair enough.

Lee Perry's approach is the exact opposite: Taking the instrumentation and whatever was being played in the room as the starting point, as his raw materials, he'll then endlessly manipulate and tweak and transform them until they sound *nothing* like they had in the room, and *everything* like whatever he has in his head. Usually he does this using some technology or other. Tape delay/echo. A reverb that makes something recorded in a closet sound like it's being played inside a giant hall or stairway. An EQ where you're only hearing a portion of the frequency of whatever is being played. Loops, layering, feedback, speed changes, playing stuff backward, slapping and pounding on spring-reverb units until they literally create explosions of sound, and hundreds of other ideas and effects. Instead of aiming for perfect reproduction, Perry sees the raw tracks as merely his paint; and *he* is the painter, not the musicians.

Like a lot of kids my age, I first saw his name on a Clash record. On the band's first LP, they covered "Police and Thieves," a song Perry co-wrote, and he later produced their amazing single "Complete Control."

But it wasn't until later, while we were making *Paul's Boutique*, that we started to buy a lot of dub records. During *Check Your Head*, we became obsessed with his song "Bushweed Corntrash" by Bunny & Ricky, produced by Scratch. The vocals sound literally otherworldly, swirling around like an alien spacecraft, and so much is happening in Perry's chamber of effects that the listener can't tell which way is up. Perry pushed the production and effects further than we'd imagined possible, and we really wanted to do the same, so his records became a blueprint of how we could get there. When stuck on an idea for a song, we'd ask, "What Would Lee Perry Do?"

Even though *Grand Royal* published a huge cover story about Perry, we didn't actually meet him until 1996. Oddly enough, we bumped into him in Hong Kong and had dinner with him. Perry had a video camera and was filming everything—the people, the buildings, the night sky. After a while he said there was no tape in his camera. I wouldn't say it was your average, normal

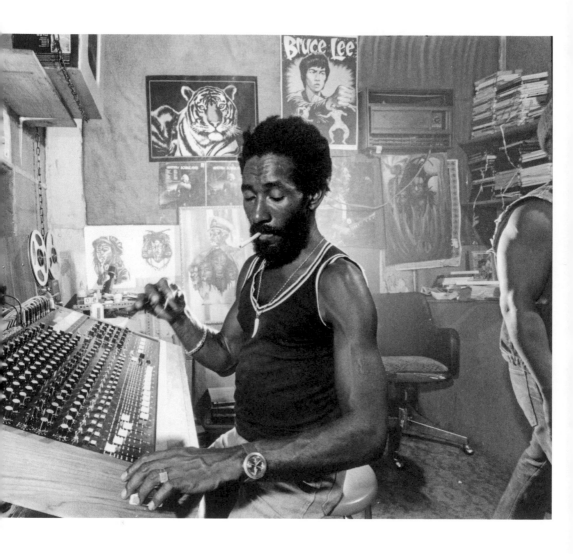

dinner conversation, like, "Oh, you live in Switzerland. What's your favorite thing about the Alps?" But there was nothing disappointing about meeting this particular idol; his personality was every bit as strange and captivating as his records.

Soon after, we were working on the *Hello Nasty* album at a studio on Downing Street in the West Village. A lot of our material at the time came out of just basically jamming an idea. We had this one unfinished song that revolved around an organ line by Keyboard Money Mark, a bass line that Yauch played, and a beat I had made with a big kick drum in G-Son's live room with the parquet floor. Perry's productions were always the primary reference for us with that song, but we didn't have what it took to finish it—a vocal idea, a hook, the thing that could take it from a sort-of-idea to an actual song. We tried a couple of directions and nothing really got it there. We *liked* it, but we couldn't quite figure out how to finish it. We had our dry-erase board up with a list of all these songs in various stages of construction, and that one just sat there. Then we heard Perry was doing a show on Halloween at a club in Tribeca called Wetlands. Mario Caldato, our co-producer on *Hello Nasty*, really started pushing—"Lee 'Scratch' Perry's coming to New York; we gotta get him in and see if he has some ideas." Long story short, Perry agreed to give us a few hours between sound check and show time on the night of that Halloween show.

The day of the show arrived, and it turned out we'd overlooked one minor detail: Halloween in the West Village is a huge fucking deal. There's always a massive parade. You've got tens of thousands of people, maybe more, dressed to the nines. People of all colors, all persuasions, all preferences, letting their freak flags fly. Sixth Avenue gets closed, and it's very difficult to get around—forget driving.

So now we had this very small window of time with Lee Perry, but he basically can't get a cab. So it was decided that Yauch and Mario would go down to the World Trade Center, where his hotel was, and bring him back through the thick of the Halloween Parade. Yauch and Mario dutifully showed up at the hotel and told Lee and his manager that the only way to get back was to take the train. The manager was immediately like, "What? You're gonna take Lee 'Scratch' Perry on the *train*? No." But Perry, with his worldly calm, simply said, "It's fine, it's fine." So the three of them took the train. Then they had to walk through masses of people from the station to the studio.

The amazing part is, the way most people dress for Halloween is the way Lee Perry dresses every day. He had rainbow-dyed hair and beard, and was wearing a super-tall baseball hat that was covered in mirrors and broken glass and buttons, and boots to match. Every bit of his outfit was covered in something. He'd stand out 364 days of the year, but he was perfectly camouflaged to walk through the middle of the Halloween Parade in the West Village.

After many hours, miraculously they walk into the studio. We played Perry a little bit of what we were working on. We were very nervous about it

because the song was kind of, uh . . . *inspired* by him. He could easily have just turned around and said, "Fire burn," and wandered off into the parade. Thankfully, he seemed good with it.

We didn't know where to begin, so Mario just started handing him random percussion instruments, and he did several takes playing them. We all had this *holy shit* fan moment when we realized that it was actually *him* playing percussion on a lot of his productions—you could just tell from the way he played. Then Mario sheepishly handed him a vocal mic and said, "Here, why don't you try this?" His singing was also revelatory, because we realized that on his productions, it's often *his* voice. On so many of the records he produced, it's impossible to tell who's singing what, but just hearing his phrasing, we realized how much of it was actually *him*.

All told, we got two to three hours of him in the studio. As sort of out-there as he is, he got it done, right? He was a consummate professional. He did what a session player would do if you said, "Here, be Lee 'Scratch' Perry." The track finally had what it needed to become a song, and it ended up on *Hello Nasty*: "Dr. Lee, PhD."

After we finished the session, we still had to get him back to Wetlands in Tribeca. It wasn't actually that far. Maybe a twenty- or thirty-minute walk. In the middle of all this Halloween madness, the seas just parted, and Lee Perry walked right through.

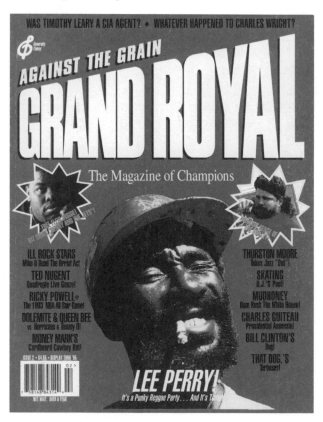

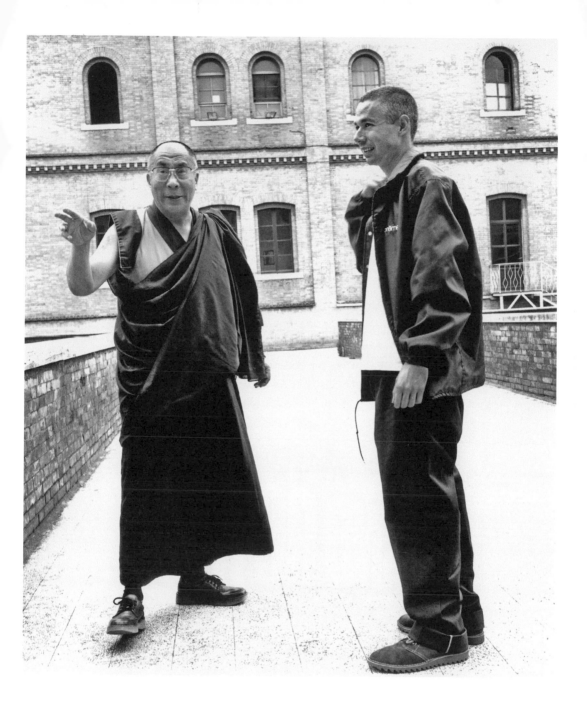

Milarepa

(MD)

> "The Bodhisattva Vow means striving for enlightenment to better help all other sentient beings attain enlightenment. That's an important issue—the objective of that Vow. Being enlightened is the best way to benefit all other beings—from that place you're able to help more. . . . And it clicked in my head. I thought, I need to write a song about this."
>
> —Adam Yauch, *Tricycle: The Buddhist Review*, Winter 1994

This is about Yauch and how he found something that made so much sense to him, he could actually believe in it.

When he was a kid, his parents would take him on trips to Mexico, Italy, and other places that weren't Brooklyn or Manhattan. He became interested in seeing the world and how other people live in it. By the time we started making music for what would become *Check Your Head*, we'd gotten used to him showing up at the studio, only to get a phone call from a friend about snowfall in Utah that would throw him into a panic, and he'd be on a flight the next morning. Around 1990, he'd gone to India and Nepal. To us, while this fit his nomadic ways, it was next-level far and hard to comprehend at first. While trekking in the Nepalese Himalayas, he met Tibetans in exile who told him what life was like for them under Chinese rule. He was moved by their vow of nonviolence in response to cruelty and oppression, their generous outlook, their belief in interconnectedness through past, present, and future lives.

Upon his return, we could see that Adam wanted to understand this vow of nonviolence. Why did they choose not to fight back against a government that would beat and imprison a person just for waving a Tibetan flag? He wanted to know more, so he traveled to India a few more times. In Dharamsala, he began his studies of Tibetan Buddhist philosophy and practices. He drank yak-butter tea with the monks and loved watching them debate one another in their customary style. He saw how laughter was a staple of their lives. Then he wanted to share this information. He went to Arizona in 1993, where His Holiness The Dalai Lama was giving teachings.

> "The people that I've met are really centered in the heart; they're coming from a real clear, compassionate place. And most of the teachings that I've read about almost seem set up to distract the other side of your brain in order to give your heart center a chance to open up. In terms of what I understand, Buddhism is like a manual

Here's a list of all the bands that played at the Tibetan Freedom Concerts. . . .

Alanis Morissette
Audio Active
The Avalanches
Beastie Boys
Beck
Ben Harper & The Innocent
    Criminals
Biz Markie
Björk
Blackalicious
Blondie
Blues Traveler
Blur
Bobby Chen
Boom Boom Satellites
Buddy Guy
Buffalo Daughter
Celibate Rifles
Chaksam-pa
Cibo Matto
The Cult
Dadon
Dave Matthews Band
De La Soul
Eddie Vedder & Mike
    McCready
Eskimo Joe

Foo Fighters
Fugees
Gang Chenpa
Garbage
Garpa
Gerling
Handsome Boy Modeling
    School
Herbie Hancock and the
    Headhunters
Jebediah
Joe Strummer and The
    Mescaleros
John Lee Hooker
The Jon Spencer Blues
    Explosion
Kan Takagi
Kiyoshirou Imawano
Kraftwerk
KRS-One
Lee Perry featuring
    Mad Professor & the
    Robotiks Band
Live
The Living End
LMF
Luscious Jackson

The Mavis's
Michael Stipe & Mike Mills
The Mighty Mighty
    Bosstones
Money Mark
Mutabaruka
Nawang Khechog
Neil Finn
No Doubt
Noel Gallagher
Not From There
NRA
Otis Rush
Patti Smith
Pavement
Pearl Jam
Porno for Pyros
Pulp
Radiohead
Rage Against the Machine
R.E.M.
Rancid
Red Hot Chili Peppers
Regurgitator
Richie Havens
The Roots
Run DMC

Scha Dara Parr
Sean Lennon
The Skatalites
The Smashing Pumpkins
Spiderbait
Sonic Youth
Taj Mahal and Phantom
    Blues Band
Thom Yorke & Jonny
    Greenwood
Thee Michelle Gun
    Elephant
Tizzy Bac
Tracy Chapman
Trans Am
A Tribe Called Quest
UA
U2
Urban Dance Squad
The Wallflowers
Wyclef Jean
Yoko Ono
You Am I
Yungchen Lhamo

to achieve enlightenment—there are these five things and these six things within the first thing, and all these little subdivisions. And despite all of that right-brain information, it's very heart-centered. At least that's the feeling I get from the Tibetans. Also the teachings of Tibetan Buddhism have been passed down for a long time now. They have that system pretty well figured out."

—*Tricycle*

He started writing lyrics and making songs that incorporated his new life findings, his new understanding of the connectedness of all things. He sampled Tibetan monks chanting for our song "Shambala" on *Ill Communication*, and wanted to donate some of the proceeds to an organization that could raise awareness for the Tibetans' situation. Unable to find a nonprofit that met his criteria, what did Yauch do? He started one, a nonprofit organization called the Milarepa Fund, which would oversee how the money got distributed.

And what he did next was global.

He wanted to spread the word far and wide about the plight of the people of Tibet and their message of nonviolence. With the help of our long-time managers, John Silva and John Cutcliffe, Yauch organized the Tibetan Freedom Concert, a massive two-day benefit in Golden Gate Park in San Francisco in 1996, a huge outdoor festival with mega bands like Red Hot Chili Peppers and Rage Against the Machine. It was the biggest charity concert since Live Aid. What he did was historic.

No one remembers that Yauch had Tibetan monks do a morning prayer onstage to open the Lollapalooza tour. It was out there and amazing. Watching the confusion on the faces of thousands of American kids who wanted to get a good spot for the Smashing Pumpkins and instead saw a dozen Tibetan monks chanting in prayer was fantastic. Playing basketball and video games with monks is pretty fun, but crying with laughter while sliding down a waterslide together is an experience that I can't believe we were lucky enough to have. (AH)

The next year, he organized an even bigger Tibetan Freedom concert on Randall's Island in New York. Then in 1998, a two-day festival in the 50,000-seat RFK Stadium in Washington, DC. Free Tibet '99 was actually four concerts on the same day internationally.

Hundreds of thousands of people had "Free Tibet" on their tongues and heard the call for nonviolence, because of that guy in Beastie Boys.

The choice today is no longer between violence and nonviolence. It is either nonviolence or nonexistence.

—MLK

The Draco Report

PLANETARY SURVEILLANCE—EARTH/HUMAN
DJMMM Chronicle Entry—Earth date June 20, 1995:

> I first encountered humanoid subject #A718 Adam Yauch at a youth gathering in Earth's subsector NY212-B.
>
> My mission was to observe and engage in human relational protocol at a location known as Rock Steady Park.
>
> The proceedings were referred to as a "hip hop jam."
>
> My initial transmissions with Earth's inhabitants were via the scratch communication device.
>
> In this gathering of "people," in the metaphysical form, I warned subject #A718 of his planet's impending danger from the Draco constellation.
>
> For generations, the beings of Draco have threatened the demise of this Earthling communication known as "hip hop."
>
> I offered our initial schematics of the Zektar turntable, and impressed upon him that its ultrasonic frequency rays were certain to have the capability to quell Draco's hostility.
>
> Before beaming back to substation 916-C (Sacramento, California), #A718 and I exchanged micron slips containing our digitational data.

PLANETARY SURVEILLANCE—EARTH/HUMAN
DJMMM Chronicle Entry—Earth date August 3, 1995:

> Several Earth days ago I sent an audio transmission (or answering-machine message) to subject #A718.
>
> It contained a brief example of my tactical tweak scratch skills using the Technic and Numark devices.
>
> I am still awaiting a response transmission.

PLANETARY SURVEILLANCE—EARTH/HUMAN
DJMMM Chronicle Entry—Earth date April 11, 1996:

> I received correspondence from #A718.
>
> He and his squadron had formed a secret alliance known as "Quasar," and they were to give a lecture on the human topic "punk music" in close proximity to substation 916-C.

Contact was initiated—Earth time 9:14:07 P.M.

The location of our deliberation took place at an exercise facility referred to as a "skate park."

There, we strengthened communication and locked in plans to join forces.

PLANETARY SURVEILLANCE—EARTH/HUMAN
DJMMM Chronicle Entry—Earth date November 4, 1997:

During my research and strategizing plan for the Anti-Theft Device mechanism inside the DS-1 Orbital Battle Station, I received another transmission from subject #A718.

He agreed that the situation involving the Draco constellation was dire, and we began laying the groundwork for our first strategic sonic strike entitled Code Name: Hello Nasty.

Seven Earth days hence, Beastie drone forces landed on the rooftop of DS-1 Orbital and transported me to subsector NY212-M. Manhattan.

PLANETARY SURVEILLANCE—EARTH/HUMAN
DJMMM Chronicle Entry—Earth date January 2, 1998:

We docked in audio sound station Barracuda beneath a large mass of H_2O, named the Hudson River.

It was there that we devised our first offensive strike.

With a few simple modifications on the original PROTON-K scratch, we reformed the Zektar turntable's usage in the form of the tweak scratch.

Subject #A718, his squadron, and I were successful in our first audio attack, given the human name "Three MCs and One DJ."

It was a crushing blow to the Draco Alliance, and a peaceful resolution was reached.

PLANETARY SURVEILLANCE—EARTH/HUMAN
DJMMM Chronicle Entry—Earth date September 14, 2018:

Fueled by Krispy Kreme doughnuts, games of Boggle, and injections of iced coffee, I find it difficult to return to the Zektar coordinate at this current date.

I would like to request an extension to continue my research here on planet Earth.

Hello Nasty Is Our Best Record
(AH)

And I'm gonna prove it to you if you believe otherwise.

1. It has twenty-two songs on it, the most we've ever put on a record, so you really get your money's worth, making it our most financially advantageous product in the marketplace. You may love Erykah Badu, or the Eagles but . . . Beastie Boys gives you more music for the same price.

2. Upon its release, it received a staggering amount of praise and accolades in the media. I just looked on Wikipedia, and it says that *Hello Nasty* not only ranked as the #22 best record of the year in Germany's *MusikExpress* and #44 in France's *Les Inrockuptibles*, but it received a B+ from *Entertainment Weekly* magazine and a 7 out of 10 from something called *PopMatters*. So, deal with that, Sean Paul and Adele. And Mumford & Sons too.

3. It has the song "Intergalactic," and that song is the fuckin' jam, right?!

4. It *really* is a weird record. Not a "Why be normal?" fake weird, but it's actually weird for the top-40 pop music medium. Especially in the late '90s. Most bands don't let themselves get loose. They stay in their lane. Since The Clash, name another band that sounds like a few different bands all on the same record?

5. *Hello Nasty* is more mixtape than record. A gift from us to you. When you get a sec . . . listen to the songs "Song for Junior," "Song for the Man," "Sneakin' Out the Hospital," "I Don't Know," and "Body Movin'." Are those songs supposed to be by the same band on the same record? Well . . . the wonderful people of Switzerland say yes, because on Wikipedia it says that *Hello Nasty* was #1 on the fuckin' Swiss charts. So wrap that around your brain, Tool, Celine Dion, and Fetty Wap.

6. Maybe this isn't a reason for you to think *Hello Nasty* is our best record but . . . does it help to know that it's my favorite? I love all the records we made, but this one is just a little more special to me. It was recorded during some major transitional life moments for the three of us. It started at G-Son in L.A. and ended on Twelfth Street in Manhattan, NYC. In the same building as my first ever New York grown-up apartment. Things just felt very full circle–ish. We were back in New York. We were still family. And we were still an NYC band. We shared a practice space with my friend Michael Rohatyn in a sub-sub-basement room on Mott Street. It was the NYC version of G-Son. Except G-Son was big and open and had an indoor basketball court. Mott Street was tiny and cramped and had water bugs and a serious mold infestation. It almost felt like a gross practice space in a submarine. The kind of gross where when you blow your nose, dirt comes out. It was perfect for me, and I loved it. I

would ride my bike there across Bleecker Street every day and make music. A lot of times I'd be by myself just recording drums or piano or guitar into the tape machine. Press PLAY+RECORD on the Tascam DA-88 tape deck, run back behind the instrument, and scramble to get the headphones on in time to start playing. Adam+Mike would do the same. And it was really cool to show up by yourself, to work by yourself, and hear what the other two had done the day or night before. By *themselves*. You'd add some little thing to the thing they were working on, or start some new idea for them to listen to and add to. It was a new and exciting way for us to make music.

7. It's our best record cover/artwork. We were stuck on what the cover should be, and so we had a show+tell presentation of other record covers we liked and talked (and talked) about them.

Herbie Hancock—**Fat Albert Rotunda**

Azuquita—**Azuquita y Su Melao**

B. B. King—**Indianola Mississippi Seeds**

Blood, Sweat & Tears—**Child Is Father to the Man**

Mad Professor & Patu Banton—**Mad Professor Captures Pato Banton**

Melvin Jackson—**Funky Skull**

Cal Tjader—**Latin Concert** or **Soul Sauce**

The 9th Creation—**Bubble Gum**

Dr. Early B—**Wheely Wheely**

Charles Wright & the Watts 103rd Street Rhythm Band—**Hot Heat and Sweet Groove**

Like . . . it should be a picture like this. No, what if it was more like that? And then Mario Caldato blurted out, "Yo, the cover should be a picture of the three of you guys packed in a sardine can." Of course it should. It was staring us in the face the whole time. We asked Michael Levine, a photographer friend of a friend, to shoot the shot. And he did. (It was, and he is, great.) Our friend Bill McMullen (and Yauch) created the inside image. *Our other world.* This was a throwback to when people used to listen to records and stare at the artwork and think about the band being otherworldly. The *Check Your Head* collage artwork was an invitation, or an insight, into our little circle of friends and family, but *Hello Nasty* was where we were headed. Interplanetary and outer space. Uranus.

8. "Sneakin' Out the Hospital" is your favorite song title ever.

9. The song "Dedication" is SBIA—"So bad, it's awesome." That's why it's on the record.

10. *Hello Nasty* is our best record to me also because it was the end of an era. It was the beginning of a new chapter, sure, but after this, things were different. After this we were grown-ups. Not as dumb. After this we'd get called sir at a coffee shop by some fucking asshole barista shithead that I just wanted a coffee from and not a whole lengthy situation, but . . . you know what I mean. After this we kind of knew what we were doing. After this we started to have kids and actual responsibilities. After this was totally great and new and exciting, but after this was also kind of just . . . after this. Shit got really real. After this, September 11th happened. Sandy Hook happened. Ferguson happened. Orlando happened. And, oh God, Donald Trump happened. Innocence passed at such a mass and rapid rate that after this there was only looking back . . . at this.

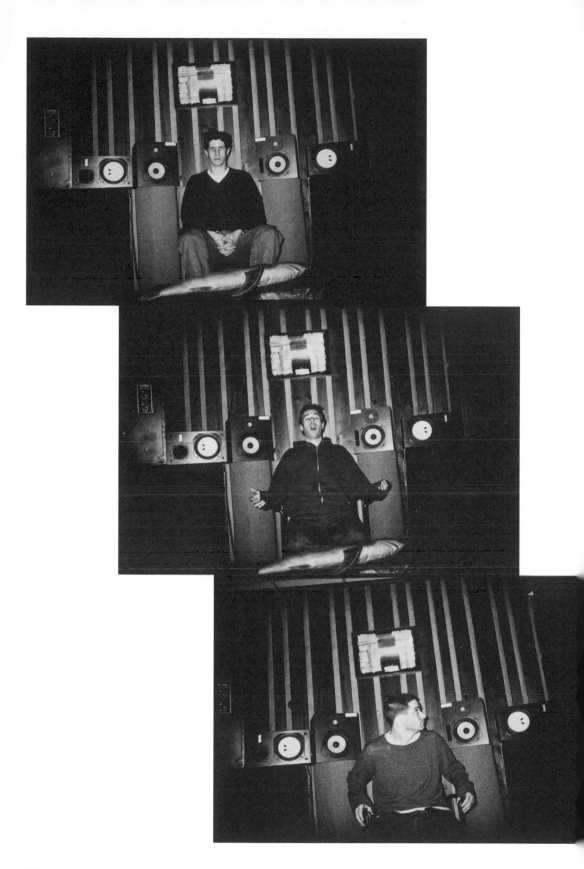

Hello Nasty was recorded all over NYC. We'd moved from L.A. and didn't have our own studio, so we asked around to see if anyone had space somewhere that we could borrow. And to our rescue came Sean Lennon, one of the most genuinely nice people I know. We were just becoming friends with him, Cibo Matto, Sonic Youth, the Jon Spencer Blues Explosion, etc. Sean has a practice space that belonged to his dad, and he said we could set up there for a few weeks. Not only was it incredibly nice of him, the space was fucking awesome. A big soundproof room in SoHo that we could all walk to and make a ton of noise in at night. Not to mention that there was gear in there, like a couple guitars and a Rhythm Ace drum machine, that each had a little '70s-style red label on it that read JOHN LENNON. It's pretty amazing to think that while I was using a big plastic label maker to make red labels on my bicycle and stuff so my brother and sister wouldn't mess with them, John Lennon was doing the same thing to his stuff.

We got to do the thing I'd always wanted to do as a band: have a bunch of places listed on the liner notes that we recorded at to make the record. We made demos at our apartments, as well as an office Sean's mom had but didn't use very much. We rented a studio on Spring Street and Sixth Avenue, but it was only available for two to three weeks. Mike's brother, David, was out of town for a couple weeks so we set up there too. (Mike, I'm assuming that he knew we were doing this, right?) We also recorded for months at our dungeon studio on Mott Street. We ended up booking a real studio to finish it, RPM Studios on East Twelfth Street. We spent a lot of time and money at RPM, but it was worth it, as this is our best record, right? And not for nothing, the guy that owned the studio was with Robert Moog when he/they invented the first polyphonic synthesizer. So there's that.

Remote Control—I made the basic demo of this on a cassette 4-track tape recorder at home. Adam+Mike liked it enough that we rerecorded it as a band. It needed lyrics, and it was decided that Mike would take the lead. The problem was that he had just gotten a cellphone that had this new text-messaging feature that he was obsessed with. He wouldn't put his new communication toy down. So me+Adam made Mike sit in a vocal booth with a tape of the song so he could listen to it over and over and write lyrics. We took away his phone and said he couldn't have it back until he was done. When he emerged from the closet-sized room, he'd written one of my favorite songs of ours. Focus is not Mike's strong point, but when forced, he can be magnificent.

Sneakin' Out the Hospital—This is one of the few songs of ours where I play the bass and drums. I'm telling you this not because I'm a mediocre bass player or 'cause I can't keep time as a drummer, but because this song is special to me. It's one of the ones that I basically made by myself.

I knew that Paul McCartney and Stevie Wonder would often record

· ELECTRIFY ·

words comin forth like water from the tap
claptraoks line the spaces places papers people stack
backtrack throught the minits when the thoughts wentinsane
i puleed the picture off the cover blew out the mind games
people say this is the playlist of the void non-bound
but i can pray this is the plainess of the peace ive found
its not the sorrow or the pity that we hope to dismantle
its the cast of past dyes lighting both ends of the candles
scandelescent in the means i have dreamed on the schemes
reunited in the times of such picturesque scenes
can i get a witness to testify
open your eyes realise and electrify

so i plan and i scam and write it off on my taxes
times like these ill just go with the decisions of the masses
and to the crowds whove come before with there profit massing ways
to'the greed that fucked it up and brought it down to today
no pain i stand sain and remain holding strong
as all around me those who clown me are now drowning by the throngg
can i get a witness to testify
open your eyes realise and electrify

No
space

its illogical the actions that are typically displayed
a set back aint all that much problem to invade
so i will glow like a lantern on a new moon night
ill fight violence with these hands that werent built to fight
but like a furnace burning coal my goals are bound to burn in flames
wether achieved or dismantled by the agendas displayed
can i get a witness to testify
open your eyes realise and electrify

420

a bunch of instruments on their records, so why not me too? Because of my sloppy drumming, this song has a different kind of funky to it than our other instrumentals.

I Don't Know (with Miho Hatori)— I love this song not so much for the song itself, but more for what it represents: Yauch pushing our band forward into new directions.

Electrify—The main loop from this song is from the soundtrack to the Broadway smash hit *Company*. Collecting cheap used records for the purpose of finding samples is like being a five-year-old kid who can buy fifty boxes of Cracker Jacks. You keep opening those shits and get a prize every time. I can't tell you how often I'd get home and listen to records I had just purchased at a Salvation Army and cry tears of joy after finding just one glorious bar of music to loop over and over. If you have a friend named Bobbi, or Rob, the first song on the *Company* soundtrack is the funniest song you've ever heard. When you get a sec, you should really go and listen to it.

Picture This (with Brooke Williams)—This is another song that I played all the instruments on, down in the dungeon. I'm not telling you that because I'm full of myself. I am, but that's beside the point. What I'm saying is . . . and I know it may sound weird, but it took me a really long time to admit to myself that I was a musician. Making music by myself in the dungeon is what, in my mind, transformed me from just being a guy in a band to being someone who's confident when writing the word "musician" next to the word "occupation" on a piece of paper. I was hanging out with my friend Brooke, and she showed me this cool portable Fender reverb box she would always sing her vocals through, no matter where she was. Gigs, studios, home demo tapes, etc. I asked her to write lyrics and sing on this track, and for lack of a better term . . . she killed it (through her portable reverb box). "Picture This" really reminds me of a beautiful summer's day looking out of a half-open window at the grimy glory that is NYC.

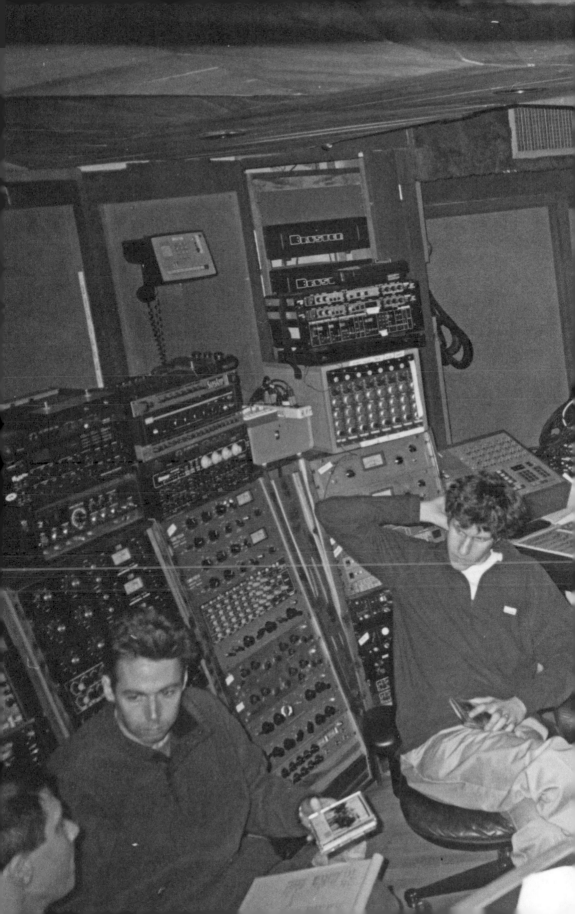

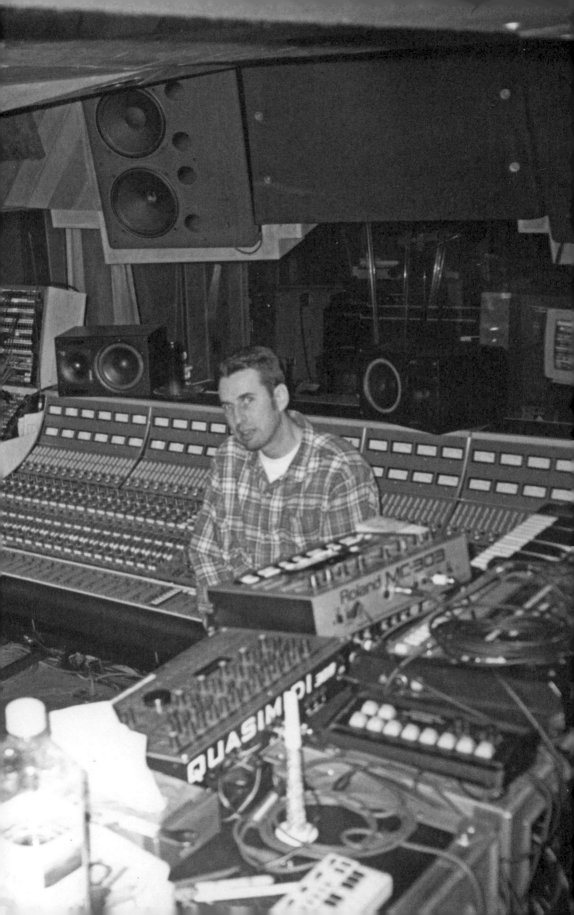

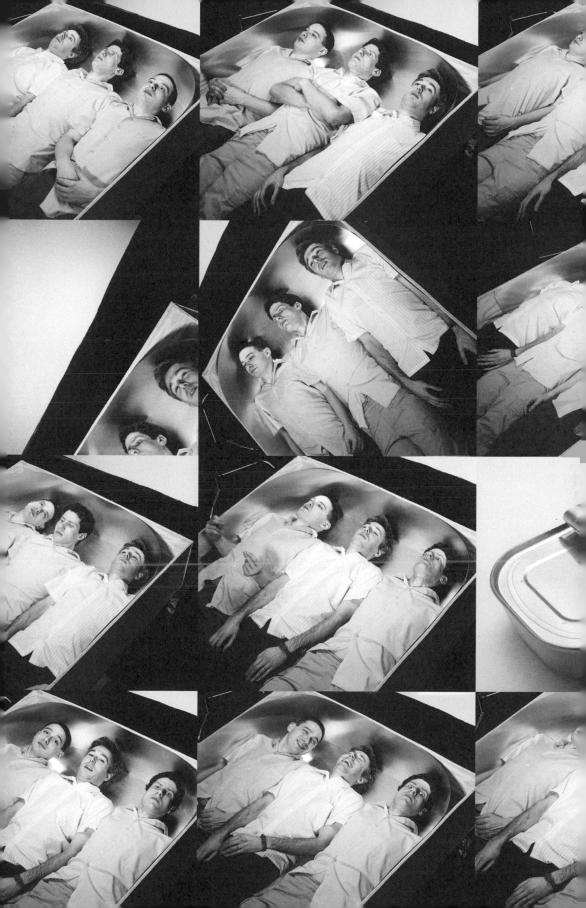

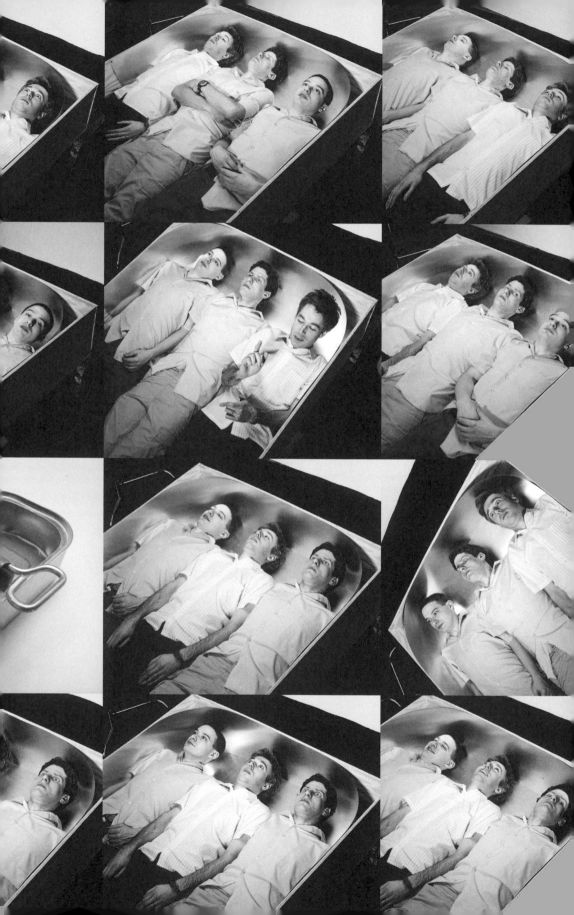

YoshimiO

Stop Soba Violence

I still don't know why I got punched . . .

Whenever the Beasties came to Japan, we would always go shopping for electronics and clothing and then eat at a soba stand. I have fond memories of doing this with them often.

So as usual, we went to a soba stand in Shinjuku, Tokyo, with some friends. We bought our meal tickets, and as soon as I walked into the restaurant, an old man I'd never seen before appeared out of nowhere and suddenly punched me!

I didn't know what had happened, but I grabbed the shirt of the drunken old man. Then Kodama, the owner of Time Bomb Records, stepped in and punched the dude.

Thurston Moore quickly grabbed Coco, who was a toddler, and stepped outside. Mike D, ADROCK, and Yauch were in total shock, but they also came in and helped me.

What just happened? Everyone was thinking the same thing, and our heads were filled with question marks.

The one who remained calm through the whole incident was Kim Gordon. She came up to me and said, "Hey, Yoshimi, those white boots that the people working in the kitchen wear look so *cool*."

So the next day, we went searching around Tokyo to find the "industrial white rubber boots" that the kitchen workers were wearing.

I still don't know why I got punched that day. . . .

STOP SOBA VIOLENCE . . .

What a classic song.

This Highly Coveted
GOLDEN MIC AWARD
Presented By
The Beatsie Boys
Is Awarded To

The Boredoms

*For Excellence Beyond
The Call Of Necessity*
1994

We presented Boredoms with this plaque somewhere on the Lollapalooza tour. We usually just sent a grasshopper cocktail over to your table to show our appreciation (we sent Grasshoppers to Steve Rubell, Ron Artest, E. G. Daily, and several other people of note), but Boredoms are on another level, and this plaque obviously conveys that. (AH)

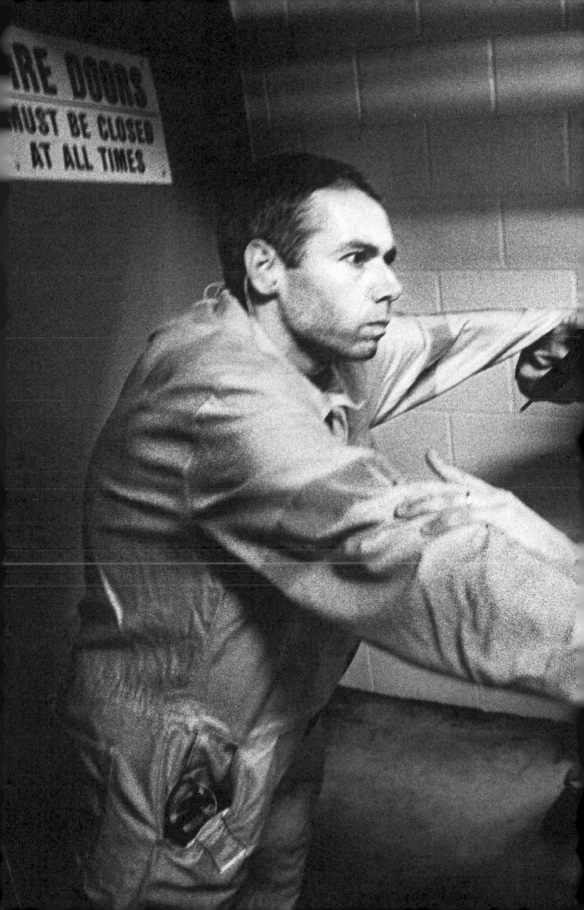

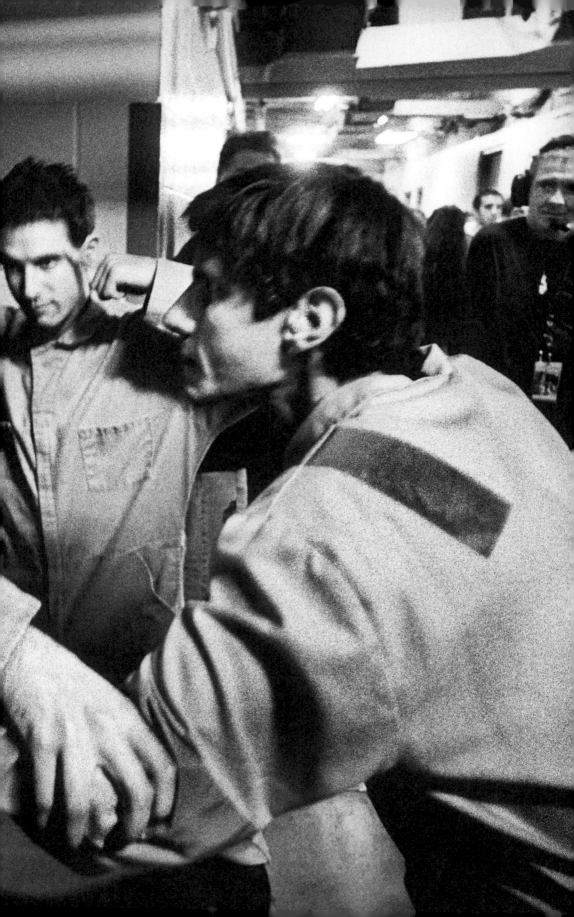

UNITE!

1. let me get some action from the back section
   we need bodyrokin not perfection
   . see i dont want to fuss and fight im
   im all about rappers delight
   < . but its a hectic life cause we all got plans
   ~ and when they conflict we all get mad
   . so the new square danders and the robotics
   lets get down to the new melodics
   ' let me get some action from the back section
   have you gotton down to your recollection
   ' do what you like its a free for all
   i could do a dance called the hectic stall
   ' i could do a dance called the mr spazz
   and i will and you know i have
   . do the porcupine and the cassanova
   make up your own dance and you might get over

Verse — . i catch wreck at thg discotech
   my . steps alone deflate your whole dome
   . walkin down the street its 96 beats per minit
   im ' in to win it
   . like a bottle chateau neuf du pap
   im fine like wine when i start to rap
   . we need bodyrockin not perfection
   let me get some action from the back section
   . mike dee with the rump shakin action
   gxkki do it like this for your satisfaction
   . im gonna sing this song
   gonna rock this party all night long
   , going off the hook like latrell spreewell
   with my fat brief balss you say "you know me fe well"
   kkkxxxkxkxdxfkxxkxnxdxwnxxxxxxxnxwxxxkkxkkxxxx
   . like birds will fly when theyre on the wing
   an mc will rhyme like a bee will sting
   . strip yourself naked of your pride and shame
   and let your body move to the groove were playin
   . i feel im comin down with the bugaloo flu
   explain to me really what doctors must do
   . we be kickin bass all in your face
   and when it comes to beats im the rhythm ace
   . so what if im a ham and cheese on rye   } — 7
   i got to do my thing and that is no lie   }   6
   . were the scientists of sound xxxx
   wre mathmatically puttin it down
   . when lightning strikes best grab a ground
   gotta get up to get down

WE NEED BODYROCKIN NOT PERFECTION
LET ME GET SOME ACTION FROM THE BACK SECTION
every day bringing life to dreams
fresh like a box of Krispy Kremes
like water from the tap tap tap on and flowing
heading down the tracks and we're not slowing

ATE O ATE

A Roy Choi Cookbook

Yo, I was fifteen maybe sixteen. Afternoon, after school, late afternoon. Burgundy Nissan with a SnugTop, fifteen-inch deep dish, carpeted truck bed with four fifteen-inch woofers in the back. So the 808 kick drum was boomin'. It was in his garage, my boy Carlos, my DJ, but I was no rapper. Carlos and I were inseparable at this time, always kicking it. He hardly ever drove his whip, so it was always in his garage and we just sat in it not getting it dirty listening to music, smoking weed, talking shit. The truck was so low to the ground that when you sat in it you could lounge your leg out the door and it would just be flush with the ground, like sitting on the floor watching TV with them funny-shaped back-pillow things from the '70s with the armrests that were shaped like a rhino. There was a lot of West Coast stuff being played at this time as we sat for hours in a car that never moved, listening to Egyptian Lover or Rodney O, waiting for his mom's chili verde to be done, never thinking about our homework. Then he put the tape in. This was the moment I think a part of my life changed.

> Here's a little story I've got to tell
> About three bad brothers you know so well
> It started way back in history
> With ADROCK, MCA, and me, Mike D.

Then everything shook, we bugged out, the bass changed everything within me, and we turned it up and up and up and popped a woofer and still turned it up. That was the first time I had heard Beastie Boys. I think—no, I know—I had seen them on *Krush Groove* by that time, but I wasn't really paying attention, not only to them but to anything really. I wasn't interested in anything but spacing out at that time and losing myself in a sea of bass. And "Paul Revere" that day warped me, and the chili verde never tasted so good.

As I grew, so did my taste buds, I found new buds, drank more than just Bud, smoked better bud, but the White Castle and the sound of "Paul Revere" were the beginning of that. I followed the music and the culture from there on, of course. *Paul's Boutique* to *Grand Royal* to X-Large to Mix Master Mike to "Sabotage" to all the weirdness. I got lost in videos, then I just got lost as a twentysomething, then found cooking. In kitchens we always play music, most of the time on shitty systems with shitty speakers, and now, as times have grown, a lot on phones propped up on the pass by a kitchen towel. Why we don't invest in better speakers and systems as chefs and cooks in kitchens I'll never know. Maybe it's because we're just gypsies like that, always on the run, moving from kitchen to kitchen, working our ass off and just being in the moment. What's great about cooking in restaurants is you spend hours standing around together

working and focusing. Time unfolds and you have nowhere to be except there with each other in the kitchen. I mention this because it is a perfect place to play albums out in their entirety. There was a lot of Beasties in my kitchen.

So I'm older now, been through some amazing twists and turns. I'm still humbled, but shit don't surprise me no more. I expect the unexpected to happen, but I never expected to meet Mike D. But I did. In my restaurant A-Frame, and my stupid ass played "So Wha'cha Want" loud as fuck to see if it was really him. I told my staff, *That's Mike D*, and they kept doubting me, so I played it. No reaction. But I knew it was him, so we kept turning it up like in the Burgundy Nissan and I kept pummeling the table with food until I got the courage to say what up, and it was him. And we clicked right in the moment. And now I'm here writing a cookbook for you to cook from in this Beastie Boys book. **Trip the fuck out!**

Ooowee. *Paul's Boutique* has so much food. I love this album because it thinks like a cook. Not in just the food references but in what the album did after the success of *Licensed to Ill*. As cooks and chefs, we love to take the most popular things off the menu because in many cases they weren't meant to incite that certain reaction or to become popular in the first place. We are a very neurotic tribe, and seeing our food become stale and looking at it every day can be tough, because we as cooks have moved on so much, as our struggles with flavor and development are constantly shifting. We love those dishes that become standards that everyone wants to come back for—but sometimes we just want to remove them all and make a *Paul's Boutique*.

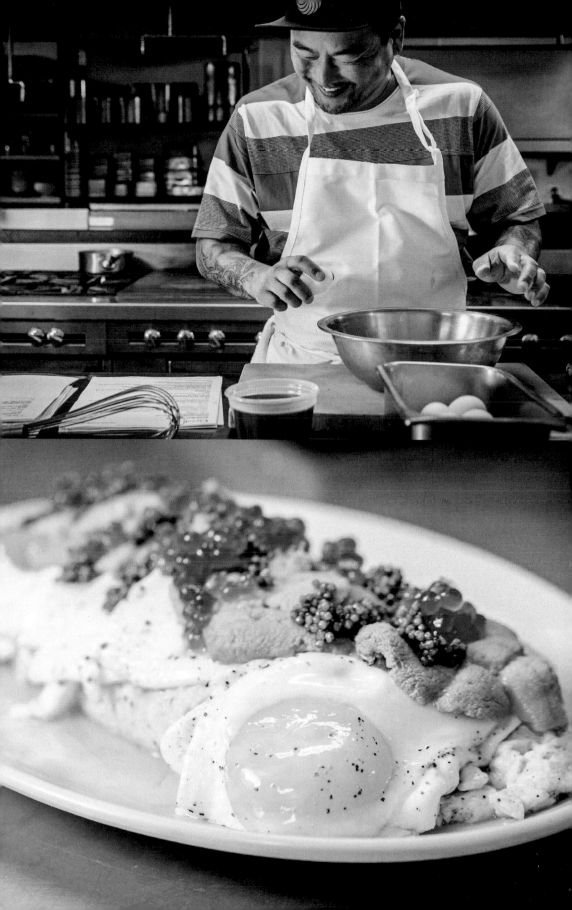

Egg Man

> *The egg a symbol of life*
> *Go inside your house and bust out your wife*
> *Pulled out the jammy he thought it was a joke*
> *The trigger I pulled his face the yolk.*

This is gonna be a trippy one. Egg on egg on egg on egg with egg garnish.
But you can do it because you're the Egg Man.

> Make this shit with a dozen eggs (6 for the omelets and 6 for the fried),
>   plus 2 more for the hard-boiled yolk
> ¼ cup milk
> salt and pepper
> olive oil
> butter
> box of sea urchin uni
> tin of caviar or a jar of salmon eggs (ikura)

First, hard-boil 2 eggs in boiling water for 10 minutes, then cool completely,
    peel and remove the hard yolk, and run the yolk through a strainer or
    a sieve to get powdered yolk. (A microplane works best.)
Now whisk 6 eggs with ¼ cup milk and season heavily with salt and pepper.
Heat a nonstick large pan to low-medium and dab in some olive oil and
    a couple knobs of butter.
Pour in the eggs and shake and swirl.
Then use a rubber spatula to keep shaking till it's a soft scramble.
Then let it set for a second, fold it over into an omelet, and put on a
    large plate.
Now wipe that pan and add a touch of olive oil and butter again and crack
    the other 6 eggs in and cook them sunny-side up.
Shingle each egg on top of the omelet in a row.
Now layer the uni and dollops of fish eggs on top of the eggs.
Then garnish the whole thing with the powdered egg yolk.
Boom.

Crack on your forehead here's a towel now wipe.

The Sounds of Science

Naugles, Isaac Newton, and Scientific EZ.
Ben Franklin with the kite, gettin' over with the key
Cheech wizard in a snow blizzard
Eating chicken gizzards with a girl named Lizzy
Droppin' science like Galileo dropped the orange.

All I can think is tacos when I see these rhymes. I think beer, *naranjas*, tacos, late nights, dusty roads, bean burritos, and Newports. That's what I think of. My friends used to work at a Naugles in Anaheim, and we used to go through the drive-thru, yelling into the speaker, buying one burrito at a time, then going back around into the drive-thru again and again till we filled our order. Stupid hungry stoner shit.

Chicken Gizzard Tacos
(Otherwise Known as Butthole Bites)

1 pound chicken gizzards
1 cup peeled garlic, pureed
1 tablespoon Korean chili powder, coarse-ground
1 tablespoon roasted sesame seeds
4 tablespoons sesame oil
4 tablespoons vegetable oil
salt and pepper to taste

Soak the gizzards for a couple hours in cold water and let sit, then drain, rinse, and dry.
Mix the gizzards with all the other ingredients, then fry in a pan till cooked, should take a few minutes on each side.

Onion mix: mince an onion with a cup of chopped cilantro and squeeze the juice of a lime in, with salt and pepper.

Heat up some corn tortillas and fill the tacos with the gizzards. Garnish with shredded cheddar cheese, Tapatío hot sauce, and the minced-onion mix.

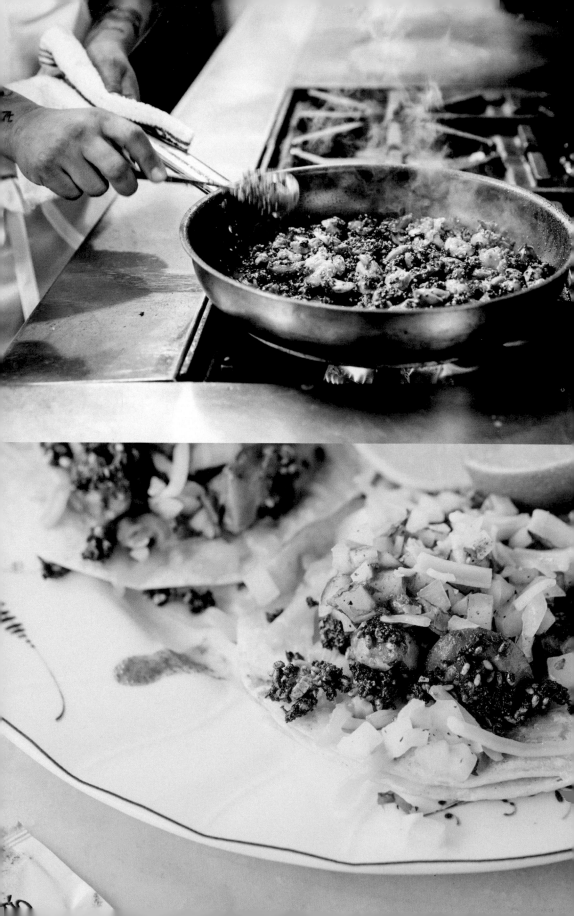

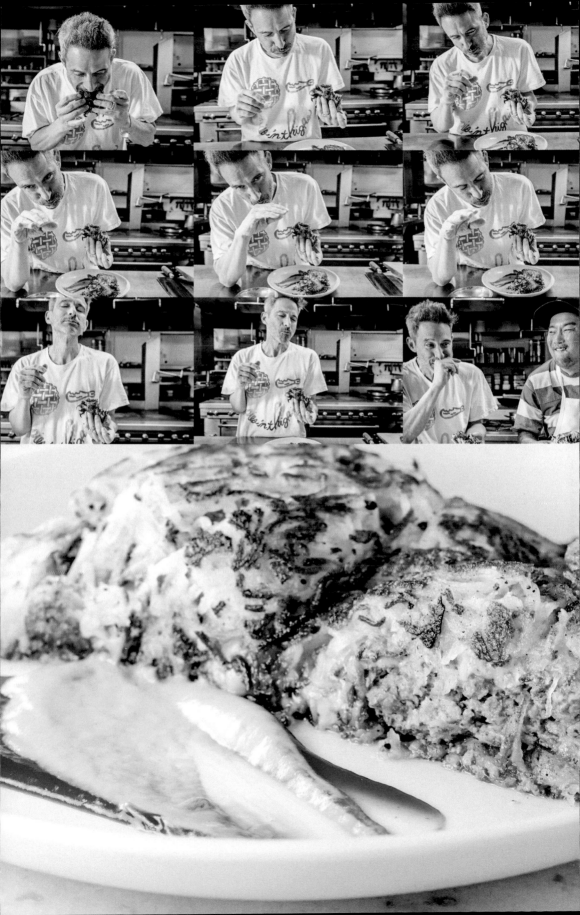

Car Thief

See, I'm a city slicker, I ain't no townie.
Right now I wish I had another hash brownie.

I grew up in the era of hash and 'shrooms. Now it's edibles and dab. We didn't have much money back then, so the resin was gold too. Scraping pipes, saving resin, unrolling roaches, and rolling resin-lined secondhand joints. I don't know, it was like my *mise-en-place*. It's like cooking, like storage, like fermentation, like pickling. I basically do the same shit now in my kitchens, not with weed but with food. Layering, scraping, saving, rotating, using everything.

Let's make brown burgers.

4 Idaho potatoes, washed and peeled and soaked in water
1 onion pureed in a blender with a touch of water
touch of olive oil
lots of butter
salt and pepper to taste
12 ounces hamburger meat
8 slices American cheese
ketchup and mustard

Grate the potatoes into clear water with a hand grater.
Drain them and mix with onion puree.
Heat a large pan or griddle to medium heat. Add oil and some butter.
Layer the potato mixture in the pan or griddle gently in one even layer.
Turn the flame down to low-medium and chill.
Season the potatoes heavily with salt and pepper and knobs of butter.
When the bottom is deep golden brown, flip and season and add more butter.
In a bowl, mix the burger meat, then season with salt and pepper and a
    touch of mustard.
In a separate pan or griddle, or the same griddle, heat to medium,
    form 4-ounce patties, and start to cook with some oil and butter.
Flip the burger and add two slices of cheese.
Just as burger is ready, layer on top of hash browns and squirt in some
    ketchup and mustard.
Now you can serve it open-faced like this or cut the damn thing down the
    middle and fold it over so the crispy potatoes are the buns.
Either way, it's pretty stoney.

Get It Together

I'm thinking the streets, smelling from skating all day, pants sagging, sun shining, wearing tropical colors, in puppy love like a dog.

BBQ Grilled Cheese

loaf of white bread or sourdough
1 cup butter, softened

Macaroni:
½ pound macaroni, boiled and cooled (You know how. Just the noodles.)
½ pound shredded cheddar, melted over a low flame with ½ cup milk

Mix those two together and reserve.

BBQ sauce:
Use a store-bought BBQ sauce
1 pineapple, peeled and cored
4 tablespoons olive oil

Drizzle pineapple with olive oil, sprinkle with a touch of sugar and salt, then roast at 350°F till brown and soft. Maybe 30 minutes or so.
Take it out and puree in blender with a splash of water.
Add this pineapple mixture to the BBQ sauce and incorporate.
Spread the soft butter on the outside of the bread slices, layer with the macaroni mixture inside, then drizzle the BBQ sauce all over the mac and close the sandwich.
Cook the sandwich on a griddle on low till crispy on each side.
Bomb.

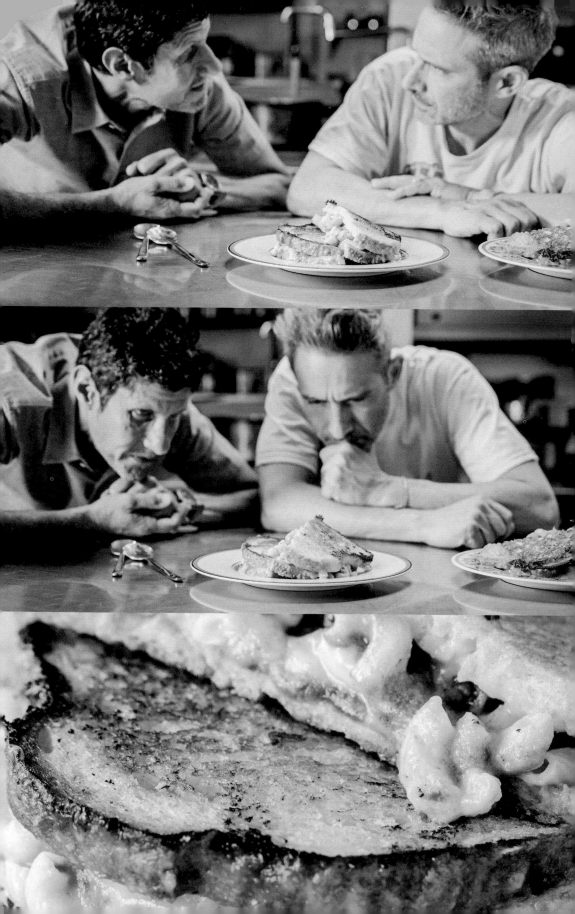

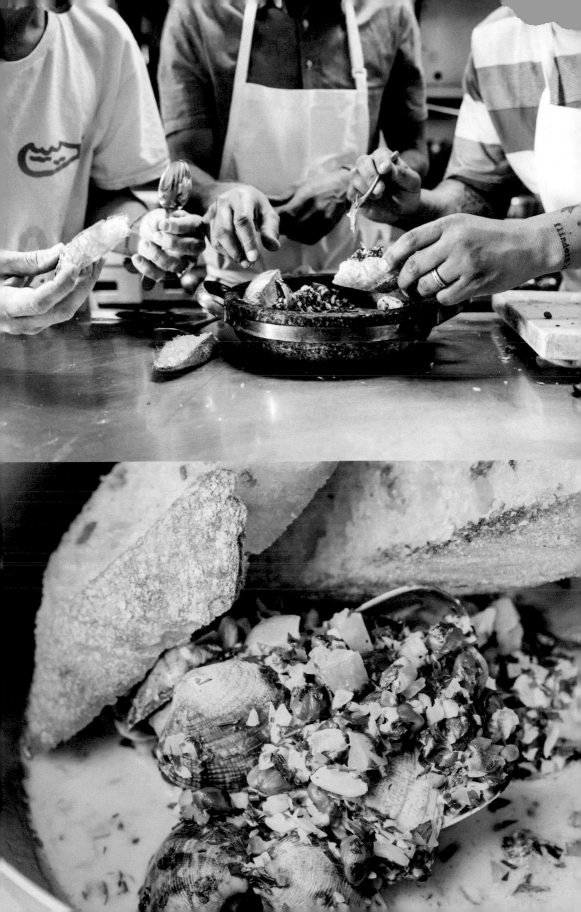

Don't Play No Game That I Can't Win

> *You try to play to win but now you lost*
> *Like clams with no tartar sauce.*

I'm a tartar sauce fiend. One of those little sauce cups will never do when I'm eating fried stuff. I truly don't understand how restaurants think it could. Let's do a big bowl of clams as if it were a pool of tartar sauce.

For the tartar sauce:
2 cups heavy cream
1 cup capers with juice
juice of 2 lemons
1 cup minced chives
2 tablespoons minced garlic
½ cup minced pickles
splash of hot sauce
1 teaspoon ground black pepper

Whisk all ingredients together.

For the bowl of clams:
olive oil
½ pound clams, washed
½ cup minced shallots
bottle of really good white wine
salt and pepper
knob of butter
1 cup chopped flat-leaf parsley

Heat a big pot with some olive oil, add the clams and shallots, then cook about a minute till it's really hot. Douse in about half your bottle of wine (and drink the other half). Cover the pot and reduce flame to medium. In a few minutes take off the top. The clams should be open. Season with salt and pepper, add the tartar sauce mixture, and reduce. Continue to shake the pot and move the clams around with a spoon. Add a knob of butter, turn off the flame, add the parsley—and don't put in a sauce cup.
You can eat this right out of the pot, or put it all in a large bowl and be primal. A good baguette would be nice.

One Potato Chip

I want to end this with the first conversation I had with ADROCK and Mike D about the book. The devil's in the details. How simplicity and attention to fundamentals can turn a single potato chip into a life-changing moment.

> *"That's cooking!"* —Roy Choi

1 Idaho potato, washed and peeled
a big pot of hot oil
salt and pepper

Slice that potato very thin, like paper thin, like rice-paper thin, like seeing through the veil of all your insecurities thin. Real thin.
The oil should be at 300°F.
Lay the potato slices in one at a time very gently, only as many as you think you can handle at a time.
Keep moving and flipping those chips and watch very carefully.
As soon as they turn golden, take those fuckers out, put on a paper-towel-lined tray, and season immediately.
Game over.

Peace up, out, and all around to Mike D, ADROCK, MCA, and you know, "We can't, we won't, and we don't stop."
Papi.

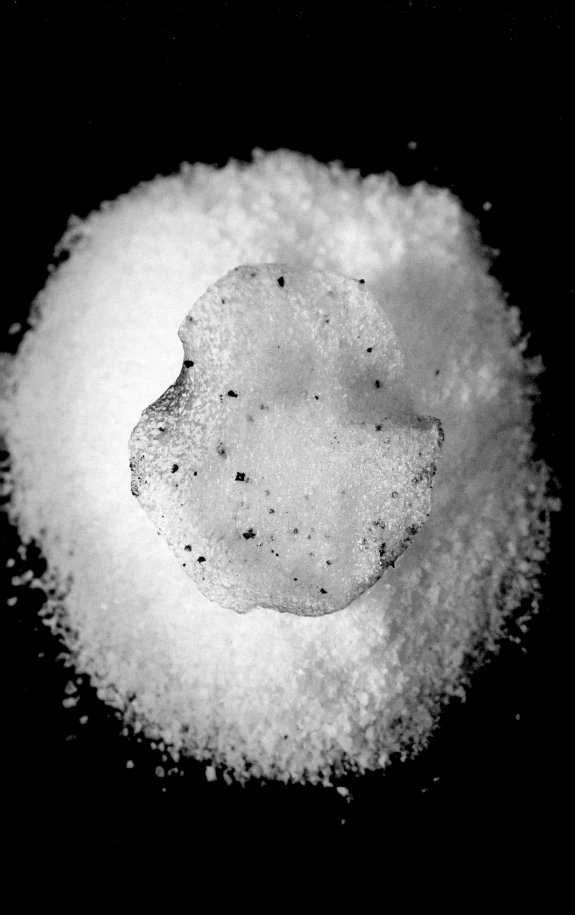

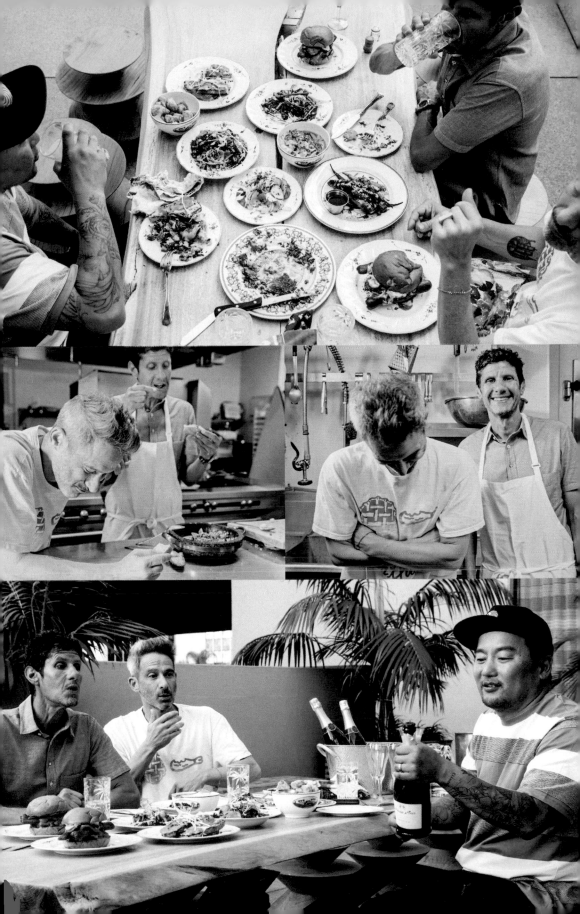

unite

```
 cause were the cats that got the raps
 and whe if you check my pulse it beats skull snaps
·from the land of lost kie an old sleestack
 i keep all my rhymes in my le sportsac
·its like that yall and you dont quit
 you know i come off with the off the hook shit
·now rhymes is montaquilla on a track by us
 safe    sorted    sussed
 whozmadexyouxthex
·aint you never heard of privacy
 who made you the judge of me
·so what if im a ham and cheese on rye
 i got to do my thing and that is no lie
·i feel im comin down with the bugaloo flu
 "explain to me really what doctors must do"
·cause we be kickin bass all in your face
 and when it comes to beats im the rythm ace
·to temporarilly remove the stress
 i got the beats with the most finesse
·i got a little water for your live wire
 shit is getting shocking break out the quagmire
·i went inside the deli and my mans like what
 i write the songs that make the wholeworld suck
·all this hi tech shit aint nothin new
 in the new milleneum ill still be old school
·in money moakin its how we do shoutsztoxrachelzandzmyxbro
 shouts to rachael and my brother matthew
·fresh outthe box like a pair of playboys
 listen everybody lets make some noise
·so come and cut the rug with me on the floor
 we dont gotta be robots no more
·we keep it movin to the broad daylight
 b girls of the world unite alright
```

jesse

maybe

1st verse

- OH MY MY IM REALLY NOT FEELING IT
OH MY MY SOMTHINGS REALLY WRONG
- GOIN OFF THE HOOK like LATRELL SPREEWELL
~~GOT THE FOR DROP BALLS~~ + YOU KNOW THE REST
- GOTTA ~~KEEP~~ FOCUSED GOT TO ~~KEEP~~ MOVIN
GOTTA STEER THIS SHIP like CAPT. STUBING
- PRACTICE ASANA DAILY SO YOU KNOW IM VERY FLEXIBLE
IM A SCORPIO SO YOU KNOW IM VERY SEXUAL
- DONT like TO FIGHT DONT HAVE NO PIECE
WEAR PERMANENT PREDS SO IM ALWAYS CREASED
- FROM THE EARS THAT ARE RINGING FROM THE SOUNDS IVE MADE
TO RECORDS THAT WERE CUT WHEN THEYRE ON THE LAYTHE
· I NEED TO BREAK IT DOWN EVERY CHANCE I GET
SO SSSSHHHH - WE KEEP it RAW ON THE SET
· HIGH ROLLER BIG BALLER
I CALL EM KILLERS BUT YOU KNOW THEY'RE CALLED OR

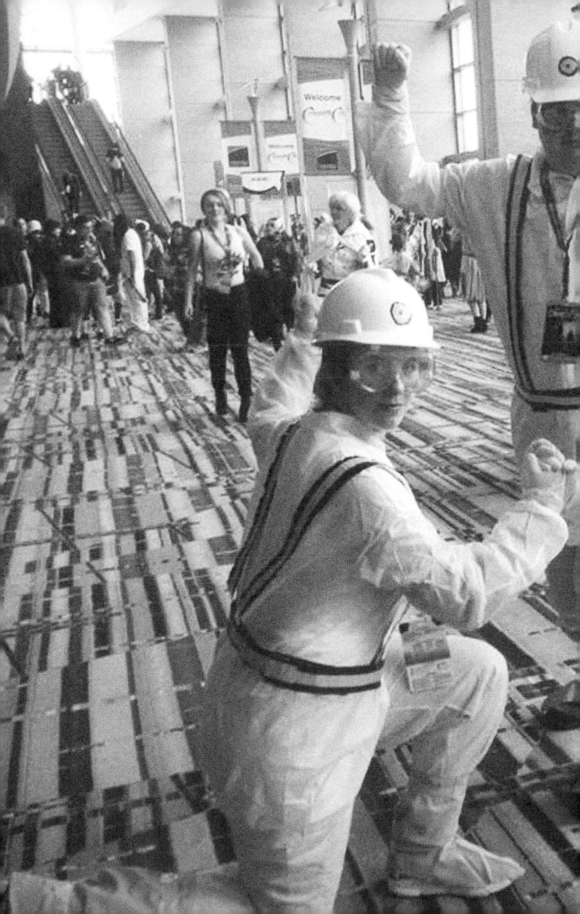

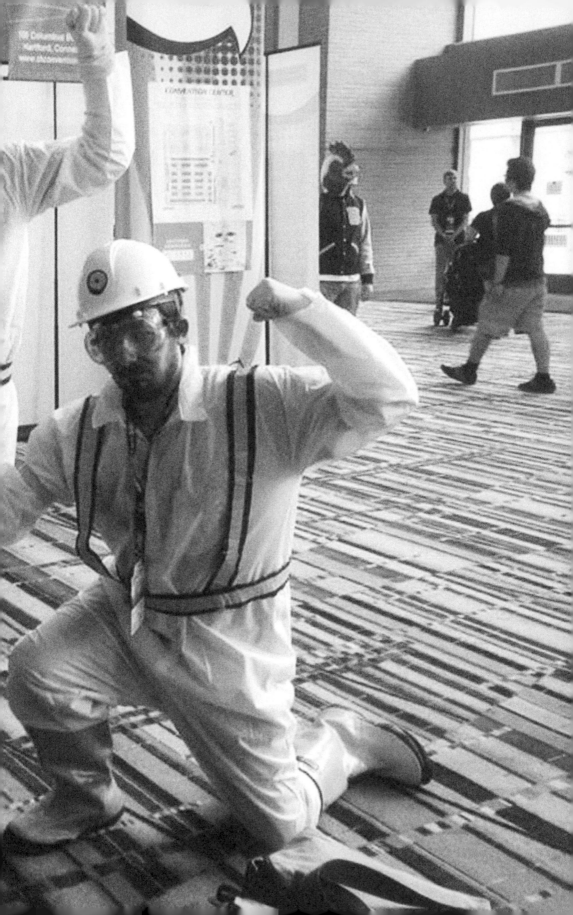

Approximately Grown-Ups

(MD)

After *Hello Nasty* came out and "Intergalactic" started doing well, it became clear we'd be doing another tour of arenas. We started to think about possible ways to make the shows a little more immediate and in-your-face, even, instead of being little ants on a stage at one end of the building with the sound echoing around everywhere. An idea was floated: What about putting the stage in the middle of the floor, as opposed to at one end? Like the sporting events these arenas were built for in the first place? We quickly concluded that it made sense, just based on simple math: you're cutting by half the maximum distance away from us that any one person could be, and doubling the number of good seats. So we decided, okay, we're playing in the middle. The obvious next problem was that you couldn't just play facing one side the whole time—the show had to be equally good whichever side of the building you were on. That's how the idea of playing "in the round" came about.

All the instruments would be placed near the center of the stage, and the center would rotate 90 degrees every ten minutes or so, so every audience member got four different perspectives in equal measure. Around the moving center was a stationary ring, separated by an inch or two from the moving part that we could step onto and MC from when we weren't playing our instruments, while running around to all sides of the audience. We called it the In the Round Tour. We meant that to be a little ironic; we felt a little self-conscious, like we were becoming Yes or something.

Once the tour started and we played a few shows, it became clear that the setup solved the previously mentioned problems very well—it was nothing like going to see AC/DC or Eric Clapton. But practically speaking, there was definitely a learning curve for us. It was weird. After fifteen years on conventional stages, you're not used to worrying about somebody looking at your ass, or how gross and sweaty the back of your shirt is, or how stupid some dance will look to anyone not directly in front of you. We just felt more exposed, and we hadn't considered that since we'd changed, the way we were perceived would change too. There was no place for us to hide while talking with each other onstage. No midshow me time. I'd like to say that we also did a lot of glute work to make it a better experience for the audience and for us, but that didn't happen. The audience probably suffered.

For whatever reason—maybe because "Intergalactic" was a pop hit—we had more women at our shows this time around, and fewer of the overexcited aggro dudes that had been a staple of the *Check Your Head* and *Ill Communication* tours.

The scene backstage was different as well. Yauch brought his wife, Dechen, and their newborn on tour. My wife, Tamra, and Adam's then-girlfriend (now wife), Kathleen, were around. For the first time, we had a "family bus." On this bus it was me, Yauch, his wife and daughter, and our tour manager, Robert. Horovitz was definitely *not* on the family bus. (He was on the pothead bus.) Money Mark would go back and forth between the two. Tamra and I would go on to have two boys who grew up their first few years touring around with us. For the rest of our time together as a band, we'd bring our families and kids on the road. It was almost like we'd gone and become grown-ups.

Almost.

I have a specific memory of a show in SF where I noticed that there were maybe four toddlers in our dressing room. They were on the floor playing with cars or trains or something. There were more little kids playing than there were grown-ups getting drunk. Times changed and it was nice. (AH)

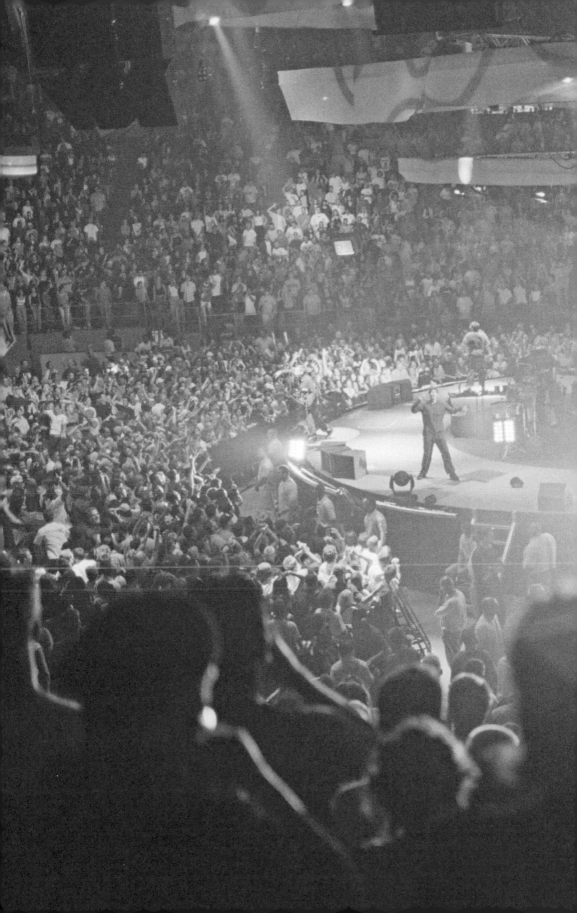

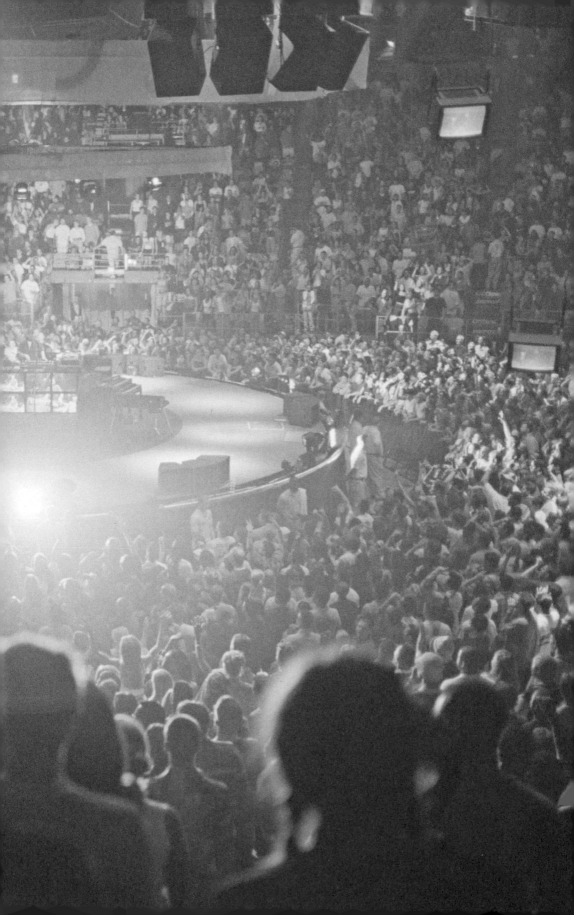

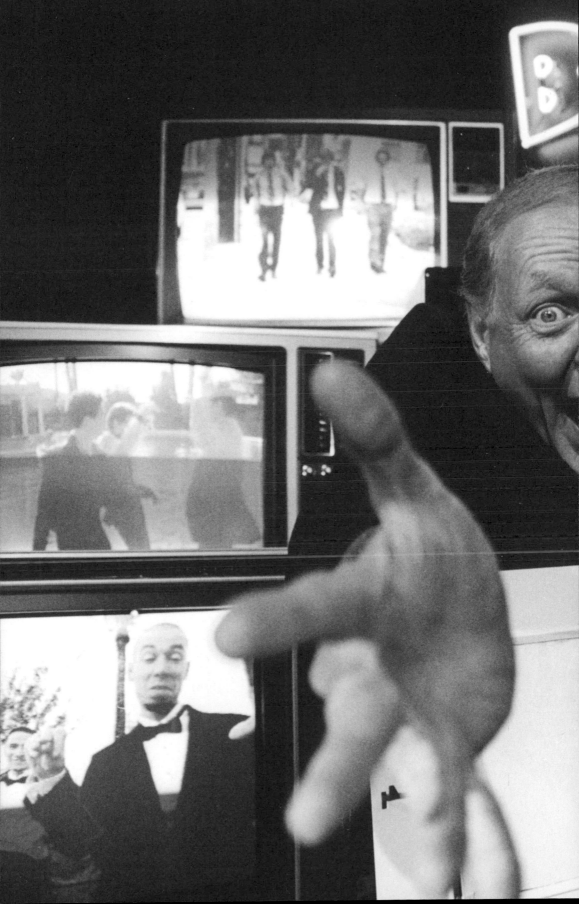

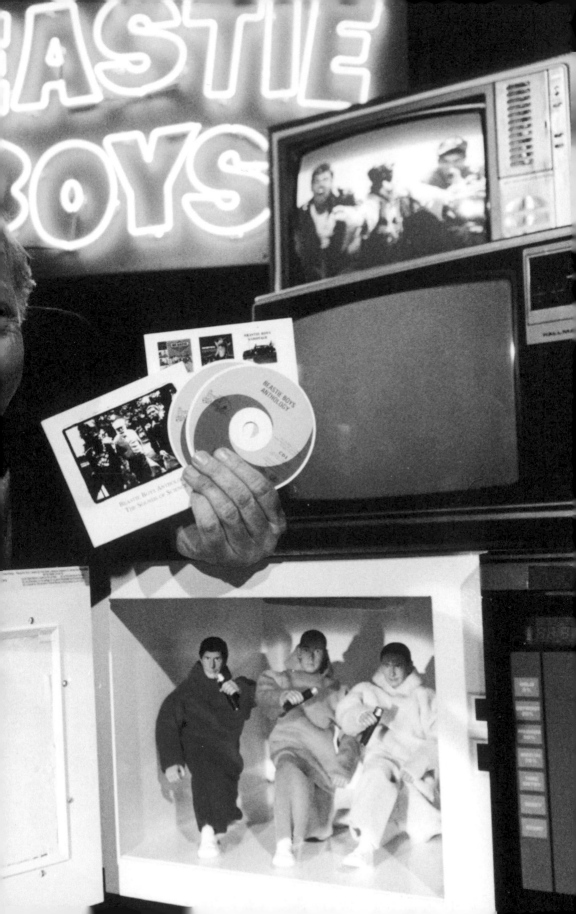

That's the Life I Wanted

(AH)

So one summer morning in 1998, I woke up in a hotel room in Kansas City. I had nothing to do all day until the show that night. I did what Michael "Sweet Lou" Diamond and I usually do on days off. Look through the phone book to find record stores and thrift stores. I went down to the front desk with my phone-book list of potential crate-digger gold mines and asked if any of the places on my list were nearby the hotel. You can really get a nice tourist view of a town/city by doing this. Almost never is there a Goodwill "with great records" listed in the Fodors travel guide to Davenport, Iowa. Outside bigger cities, good used record stores are usually near a college, or on the street that has the town's only "cool" coffee shop. (You know, the ones where Dave Matthews Band is playing on the radio, and the walls are decorated with paintings with shards of broken plates glued to them.)

It was a sunny summer weekday morning in Kansas City. Nice and quiet. I took a taxi from the hotel to the most promising-sounding store on my list. Places called something like Bill's Records or Sound Exchange are usually a good bet. The place that always tops the list for me is a used bookstore/ used record store combo. They always have jazz records. They almost always have at least one early '70s record on the CTI or Groove Merchant labels that I don't have. Some Monk Higgins–ish record with a song on it called, like, "Bumpin'." This Kansas City morning's cab ride dropped me off outside the Music Exchange. It was massive (by NYC standards). A big, wide-open space with just bins and bins of records. And they had everything. Not just jazz and soul but great rock records too. Like, if you were looking for the record by one of Billy Joel's first bands, Attila, I bet they had it. And for cheap too. My favorite part about this place was that no one else was in there. Just me and the records. Private sifting. I was quietly happy going through the aisles, feeling up the record covers, when I heard an intensely funky breakbeat playing faintly through the store's speakers high up there on the walls. I looked around the place and wondered where, why, and how this was happening. Was it just in my head? No. At the back of the store, behind the counter, was the one other person in this huge room of rows of bins. He was sitting down looking, and pointing, directly at me, and he was laughing. I stopped, turned, and fuckin' speed-walked right up to him and asked about the beat. He said, "Oh, you don't have this?" The perfect response from any collector of anything. I said no. He casually said, "It's the Niagara beat." Like I'm supposed to know what that is. *Shit, I AM supposed to know what that is. What is it? I want it!!!*

He told me that he couldn't sell it to me 'cause it was his. He explained

that his job at the store was to buy the used records from the people who brought them in to sell. (Because these CD things had taken over so they didn't want their big bulky records anymore. Or they needed money. Or drugs. Or money for drugs. Or they had outstanding hospital bills or . . . damn, you can't think about that now. Stop thinking of all the potential depressing scenarios that drive people to sell the stuff they used to love. Some people just don't care about records anymore, and for sure could use the couple extra bucks that selling them will bring. Right?) When the really good shit got brought into the store, he kept it for himself. I couldn't argue with that. Especially since this place had a fucking endless amount of great records. The store had *hundreds* of De Wolfe Music library records.

Library records are a collection of little one-minute pieces for soundtracks recorded by session musicians for movies, TV, student films, whatever. I don't actually know the story behind when, why, or where they were made but . . . there were a bunch of different labels that made them [and still probably do], and I was on the hunt for any recorded between 1969 and 1976. They all have random song titles like "Bouncy Strut," with descriptions like "hard-driving beat with percussion." So imagine how much funky shit is on them. For me, De Wolfe Music was the best. Maybe it was because they had the best artwork. (AH)

Since no one else was in the store, this guy had plenty of free time to bullshit about records and bands and stuff, as did I. My friends/bandmates were probably still sleeping back at the hotel while all this was happening. I was really happy that I went on a solo mission. A Tribe Called Quest was on tour with us too, and I'd played enough basketball with Q-Tip to know that he can box out. Today I wanted my own personal sifting space. I could've called Michael "Sweet Lou" Diamond, or Fredo, or Mix Master Mike, or Ali from Tribe to tell them about what I'd discovered, but you know what? . . . Forget those guys. These records were *mine*. The record-store guy, who had now introduced himself to me as Dante Carfagna, was fucking schooling me on all this stuff that I should've known. Records I never knew existed. Kind of blowing my mind with music knowledge. We hung out at the store for a while, and then he said he was going on break soon—did I wanna grab a coffee and some snacks and go to his house around the corner and listen to records?

HELL YES!

We walked a couple blocks to his house, a nice little two-story house with front and back yards and he said that his rent was 250 bucks a month. So, I'm thinking if *I* were *him* . . . I could wake up in the morning, go get some good coffee. Go to a great record store, sift through unknown potential gems all day. Go home. Smoke pot. Listen to more records. And then do it all over again the next morning . . . ?

That's the life I wanted.

I wonder how he felt about mine.

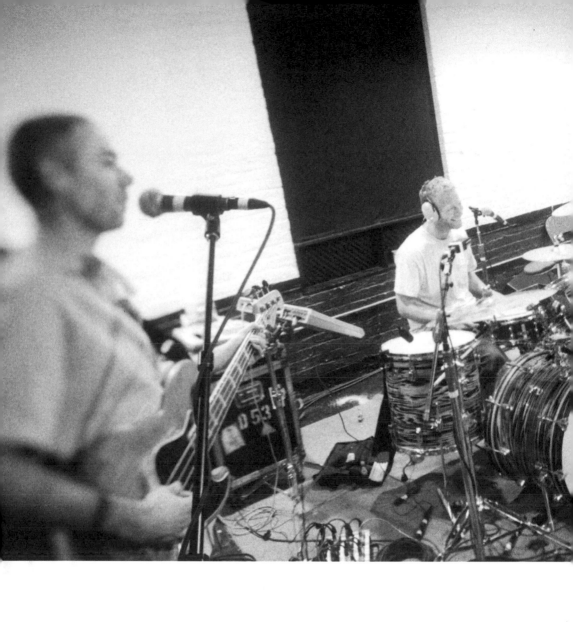

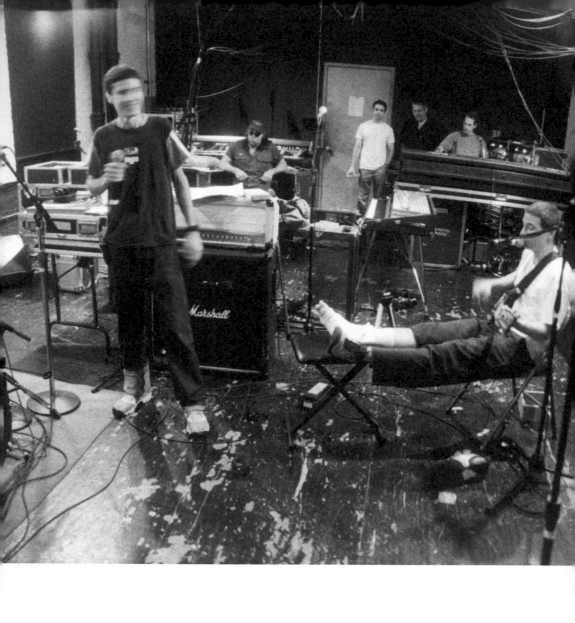

5 *Borough* Breakdown
(AH)

Similar, but so dissimilar, to the *Licensed to Ill* tour, *Hello Nasty* had spun into another type of whirlwind for us. It took us around the world again, but in a larger way than ever. By 1998, we had a string of records out, and a few "hit" songs that people were psyched to see and hear us perform. We sold out the Garden in a day. We weren't just the "Fight for Your Right" one-hit wonders anymore. Out were the wild tour days of beer-soaked shirts and freak shows; in were private chefs on tour, sightseeing, and family fun backstage. The only real similarities about those two tours were that me, Adam, and Mike were together having fun, and it was all-consuming. We lived and breathed music while making *Hello Nasty*, and were away from home, playing music, almost nonstop for the two years after it was released.

We had booked a co-headlining tour with Rage Against the Machine for the summer of 2000, but we had to cancel it because Mike broke his collarbone. Mike+Tamra were riding bikes up University Place, and Mike hit a pothole in the street. His front tire went in, and he was upended off the bike and came slamming down onto the concrete. Tamra said that when he stood up, his collarbone was sticking up out of his shirt. Mike said, "I'm fine, I'm just gonna lay down here on the sidewalk and take a little rest." He was way too fucked-up to go on a tour and play drums and jump around every night, so please don't be mad that we canceled those shows. They would've been fun, but c'mon; can you please just think about Mike's well-being for a moment?

First, I would like to second Adam's depiction here; he gets it right for a change. He is really showing us a compassionate side of himself, and I appreciate that. *He really gets me.* (MD)

The reason I'm telling you all this is because we took a break from touring for a while, and spent most of '00–'01 in New York doing nothing but being people who watched TV, went on errands, and walked their dogs. It was fantastic to be able to stay put for a real amount of time and not have a suitcase staring at you, waiting to leave home again. But after a while, the fulfillment of going to the hardware store or waiting around for the goddamn fucking Time Warner Cable guy to show up wore off, and we wanted to start making music again. Yauch was grossed out by our grimy, water-bug-infested basement-below-the-basement practice space, and wanted to get a real studio that we could call our own. *A place with a window* was all he said he needed. But instead, he found an entire floor in an office building on Canal Street and built a full-blown recording studio. Soundproof room, huge mixing desk, etc. It was perfect for us. Our own place that we could walk to and make music whenever we wanted. And it had a big, beautiful window to let light in. On one end the window looked onto a classic

NYC alleyway, and out the other end's window you could see the tops of the World Trade Center.

One day we met up to start thinking about what to make, and Yauch declared that whatever our next record was gonna be, it had to be an all-rap record. No instrumentals. I don't know what led him to that decision, but that was it. Me+Mike tried to argue with him about it—why did we have to decide now, why not just see what happened—but Yauch was not the wavering type. He was the most determined person I knew. Maybe it's something to do with him being an only child, and since Mike and I are both the youngest of three-kid families, we're used to not getting our way. Or at least giving in to battles that weren't that important to us. I mean . . . it's always been so much fun making music together, what's the big deal? An all-rap record it is. And we got to work.

In the midst of us doing our usual thing—hanging out at the studio, bullshitting, ordering lunch, and making music . . . September 11 happened. For obvious reasons, it cast a huge shadow over what we were doing. Also, our studio was just a few blocks away from the World Trade Center. Suddenly there were cops and military police on every corner. Checkpoints and everything. Walking past guys with assault rifles every day kind of set the tone for an un-slap-happy mood. Well . . . Osama bin Laden, Al Qaeda, fucked-up government policies, racism, hatred, etc., is what set the tone. The dudes with guns on the corner were just a part of it. Rapping about farts and Chef Boyardee in the wake of thousands of people being murdered down the street didn't feel right. Shit got serious. Quick.

I feel like the record we ended up making (*To the 5 Boroughs*) would've been way better if it wasn't limited to rap songs. Few rappers are successful when trying to get "serious" (i.e., political). Chuck D comes to mind as one who is; anyone else? Songs about racism, sexism, homophobia, etc., might've been better screamed in a punk-rock style. A good path to creating something mediocre is having rigid rules for what you're making and how you're making it; unfortunately this record took a stumble down the path of mediocrity. If you listen to our voices, something's a little off. We sound a little hesitant, right? Rarely do you wanna listen to a wishy-washy rapper. The rapper's confidence is usually the thing that draws you in. We got caught in this kind of middle ground/gray area of *This is a "serious" song* and *This is a "funny" one*. The serious ones feel a little forced, and the funny ones are a little flat. I'm not trying to shit on this record, though. (Out of all the slang phrases that've been introduced in my time here on Earth—dope, fresh, bangin', on fleek, hatin' on, etc.—shitting on something is by far the most vivid. It's really on the nose.) There are some really funny moments on *To the 5 Boroughs*. And I'm proud that in a serious time, we got serious.

Unfortunately, another downfall to this record is that we didn't work with Mario on it. We wanted to do it by ourselves, but in retrospect, he really helped

us capture a sound and a style that we loved. A blend of all the great sounds we tried to emulate, from Black Flag to Lee Perry to Os Mutantes. We brought in Duro to do the final mixes of the songs with us, and nothing against him, he is great at making records sound great (for little-known artists like Jay-Z, Mariah Carey, Alicia Keys, and so on). It's just, making shit sound fucked-up, dubbed out, and punk isn't really his thing. Making songs sound crispy, clean, and ready for the radio is more his specialty. So there's a computerized cleanness to this record that makes it stick out from our others. And not in a good way. If we'd pushed the sound of this record in a more psychedelic and grimy direction, it might've been more special.

The addition of computer recording, as opposed to direct-to-tape, was new to us. We'd made *Hello Nasty* (and a bunch of *Paul's Boutique*) on a computer, but me, Adam, and Mike didn't know how to use computer programs then, so someone else was touching the keyboard and mouse. Now, for this record, the three of us all had the same basic technical skill level, and we were in control. All the songs on this record were made using the programs Reason and Pro Tools. It can be so infuriating trying to work on something and have someone over your shoulder, breathing down your neck, telling you what to do. And it is equally aggravating to be the one standing over someone's shoulder. For the three of us, this process sort of magnified some personality things that frustrated us about each other. Yauch would be so meticulous with little nitpicky edits—and then have these ideas to run sounds through different FX machines and things—that it would totally sidetrack the thing we were trying to do in the first place. It was always fun once we got sidetracked, but in that moment, c'mon, this is taking forever. Mike is like Mr. Magoo. He totally knows his way around recording programs, instruments, drum machines, outboard gear, etc., but when he sits at the computer to record and edit, it's like he's never seen one before. He always gives the screen this big old once-over like, *Wow . . . okay . . . I see . . . this is what we're workin' with.* And then we'd continue working, real slow. As for me, I'm the only one in the room who knows what they're doing. If

You know what, I take back what I said earlier. FUCK YOU, ADAM. (MD)

you would just move and let me sit at the computer and stop looking over my shoulder, everything would work out much better. I'm not saying that I have control issues, it's just . . . it'd be better if you guys let me do it so it can be done correctly. That's not weird or annoying, is it?

Another thing . . . the record cover is a little too melancholy. It's a beautiful illustration, but it's kind of sad to look at. I'd rather pick up *Ill Communication,* 'cause I'm not sure if I'm in the mood to do all that heavy lifting. I really do like this record, though, just not as much as our others.

Right Right Now Now—I sampled a Partridge Family record 'cause the loop was great, but also because I knew it would make my sister Rachael happy to know that someone was rapping over the Partridge Family.

Oh Word?—Me+Mike wanted to make an '80s song. Pre-electroclash '80s Gumby hairdo polka-dot-shirt flashback freaky Friday. No one cared about this one except me+Mike. Not even Yauch. This song kind of sucks, but if this was the B-side to some 45 you found at a thrift store, you'd be like, *Oh word? Beastie Boys made this? This is my shit right here.*

All Lifestyles—Maybe this wasn't a big record for us because we did rap about very specific things like racism, an international ban on nuclear weapons, homophobia, and so on. People weren't trying to hear that. Any semblance of '80s pop-music gender ambiguity was done. Metal rap was still the spoiled milk in the fridge. Fred Flintstone had re-emerged in the form of George W. Bush and Fred Durst, and America was not in a good, open mood.

Shazam!—Mike has internal factual issues with TV shows, and pop culture in general. It's most noticeable in our song "Netty's Girl," wherein he sings the Seekers song "Georgy Girl" to the tune of Eddie Holman's "Hey There Lonely Girl." Maybe his mistakes are a well-crafted mixtape of dialect, but I think it's just that he has a bad memory. In this song he says, "I'm coming, Weezy." Now, everyone knows that Fred G. Sanford's deceased wife was named Elizabeth, and that Weezy was in fact a living character on the show *The Jeffersons*. Not a Sanford, a Jefferson. But he managed to bring an unnecessary sexual connotation to the lyrical mistake that's kind of creepily fantastic. So, Mike, don't worry about the actual facts of these things. It doesn't matter. Being funny is way more important.

Crawlspace—This may be one of my favorite songs we ever made. We wanted to make a super-creepy song about spying on MCs in their own homes. Not a lot of weirdo stuff in rap, and I hope in our own way we've injected some in our time on the mic. NO ONE else thinks this is funny. Yauch tells an imaginary MC that he looks a little chilly, and asks, "Can I get you a shawl?" It makes me laugh out loud every time.

The Brouhaha—S.D.I.G. (so dumb it's good) was always a theme for us. Like, we wanted to make these individual 8x10 pictures of each of us and sell them on tour. We'd each pick the ugliest picture of ourselves, and whoever sold the least amount of cheaply framed 8x10s was the winner. We didn't ever actually do it but that was the idea. The dumb idea is the good one. And so what's the dumbest old-person thing you can write a rap song about . . . ? A brouhaha. This song is so mediocre that I can't remember how it goes, which doesn't bode well for its freshness, but I can tell you now that it probably has at least seven rhymes that'll make me laugh out loud if I heard it. And I'm fine with that. A dumb idea that makes us laugh is a good one. This song is terrible and I'm laughing as I type this. *Let's put this on a record 'cause it sucks.*

MADISON SQUARE

Awesome, I . . .

What do you do when your band plays Madison Square Garden? You get a camera and you document that shit. But, typically, Yauch didn't want to do it in a normal way. He didn't ask a friend to film it. Or hire a camera crew. The day of the show, he went to an electronics store and bought fifty video cameras and that night he gave them out to fifty different concertgoers to have *them* document the show. It's a brilliant idea: All concert movies kind of look the same. They're usually filmed in a stale, slick way. But our concert movie is really like being at a show. People are screaming, dancing, sleeping, going to the bathroom, smoking weed in the cheap seats, etc. It's all in there. The computer kept crashing during editing because there was just so much information being processed. The best part of the whole movie isn't the dynamic Beastie Boys rappin' and rockin' the house. It isn't that Yauch got all fifty cameras back from the nice people. It's that he returned all fifty cameras to the store the next morning and got his money back. (AH)

464

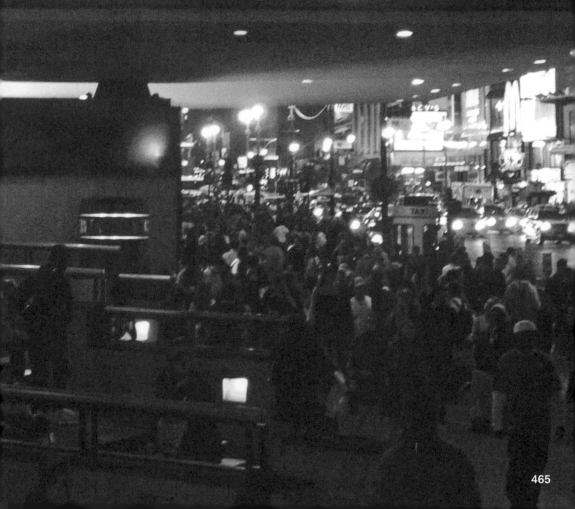

S.A.S.Q.U.A.T.C.H., Inc.
CANADA

Dear The Beastie Boys,

It was great working with you this past month. I don't
get down to the city that much and so it was really fun
to go sightseeing and dine in restaurants. And I LOVE
that High Line park. It was also special for me to dip
my toe back into the acting ocean. (I was in a very
low-budget amateur short film in the 1960s.) In any
event, I regret having to write this letter to you but I
feel I must. I still have not received full payment for
my work in your short music video film, "Triple Trouble."
I also submitted two invoices to your accounting firm
and have not heard back. I need to get this resolved
so I can keep my books in order. Winter is coming up
soon and it's more difficult for me to find a place
to stay during those months that meets my needs. Also,
I have an outstanding balance with a local trapper up
here, and fulfilling this payment will be a huge weight
off of my shoulders financially. I hope my reaching
out like this directly isn't overstepping or unprofessional, but I try to maintain a low profile and I would
feel repentant taking this through the court system. My
wish is to resolve this amicably.

Whew! Official business letter written.

I REALLY enjoyed working with you and that odd
Swiss director. It gave me a much needed respite from
mountain life.

All the best,

Sasquatch

S.A.S.Q.U.A.C.H., Inc.	CANADA	NUMBER 00004

Phone 5-3353   DATE May, 30th 2004

TO The Boothe Boys   NO.

FROM Sasquach   MD BILLED Lunch

VIA _____ FRT. BILLED _____

SHIPPER'S NO. Port Authority LOCATION Snacks-N-Wheels

4	Grilled cheese Sandwiches	14	00
1	Greek salad	7	50
6	Sun chips	6	00
2	vitamin water	5	00
1	Large French Fries	4	50
3	Iced Honey Buns	3	00
2	Newport cigarettes	20	00
1	coffee	1	00
(NO TAX INCLUDED)		$ 61	00

RECEIVED THE ABOVE IN GOOD CONDITION EXCEPT AS NOTED

SIGNED BY S. Daniels   P.K.A. Sasquach   T. MDSE.

S.A.S.Q.U.A.C.H., Inc.	CANADA	NUMBER 00005

Phone 5-3353   DATE May, 30th 2004

TO The Boothe Boys   NO.

FROM Sasquach   MD BILLED Travel

VIA _____ FRT. BILLED _____

SHIPPER'S NO. _____ LOCATION _____

| 1 | 1 way Greyhound Bus Ticket (ECONOMY EXTRA) New York, NY - Regina, SK (Canada) | | |
| | | $ 192 | 73 |

RECEIVED THE ABOVE IN GOOD CONDITION EXCEPT AS NOTED

SIGNED BY S. Daniels   P.K.A. Sasquach   T. MDSE.

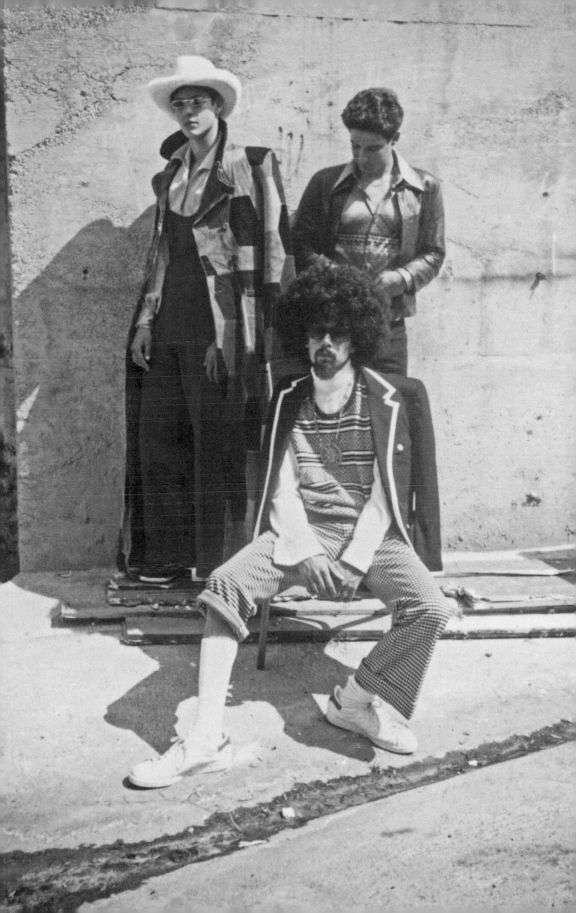

AMY POEHLER

BEASTIE BOYS VIDEO REVIEW

Beastie Boys mean a great deal to me. Their music was the soundtrack I heard while I sat in my room, drank in the woods, and rode my bike to my dead-end job. Their music played while I learned how to perform comedy and find a seat on the subway. Their music made me finally feel like a New Yorker, and like them, I grew and changed and went deeper and hopefully got better. These days, their music makes me feel old and young at the same time, which I am finding is a delicious space to surf. So when I was asked to write about their videos for this book, I felt a huge sense of responsibility. How do I watch, and rewatch, seventeen music videos that span an entire career and attempt to encapsulate what is so special about them? How do I comment on someone else's art in any kind of new or profound way? How do I try to insert my narrative into the impressive Nathanial Hörnblowér canon?

And then I remembered . . . a good number of these videos are pretty dumb, so it should be easy.

Holy Snappers

This video rules. I think we may have saved the best for first. When I was sitting on a rock in suburban Massachusetts, this is what I imagined it was like to be a New York teenager. A chaotic gaggle of feral youngsters jumping over mailboxes and hitting each other with sticks. I assume every single one of the young people in this video went on to start a band or record label. I wish I had a time machine and could be in this video as a cool girl sticking her tongue out on a fire escape.

She's On It

This video is so dumb.

The only thing that saves it is the band is just as embarrassed by the exploitation as we are. It was always funny to me when Beastie Boys would have sexy girls walking around while they acted like the Three Stooges and did their best De Niro impressions. Pick a tone, guys! I do really like the number of 1980s hair bows in this video.

I also think the woman is beautiful and I am impressed with her ability to beach-walk in stiletto heels. There is nothing complicated about this video, but it still confuses me. I'm not sure what Rick Rubin is disgusted by. Does he think they are being gross or not gross enough? What is she supposed to be on? Spanish fly? This video is the first of many times Beastie Boys will use humorous and oversized props, or what I like to refer to as their Carrot Top period.

(You Gotta) Fight for Your Right (to Party)

Nerds! Tabitha Soren! Mouth close-ups! Bad acting! More Spanish fly! Pies!

Hey Ladies

Everybody is growing up. Yes, we are still going to have a disco pool party, but we are going to move the camera around and shoot this sucker in Los Angeles. I forgot how many close-ups of shoes are in this video. There are a lot of nice dance moves in this, although I feel like halfway through, MCA went to lunch and never came back. This was directed by Adam Bernstein, who also directed an episode of UCB's Comedy Central show, *Upright Citizens Brigade*. But I checked Wikipedia and it is not on there, so I may be remembering this wrong—or Adam is ashamed of his work with us? I suspect both?

Shadrach

Shadrach is one of the three men from the Book of Daniel who is thrown into a fiery furnace by Nebuchadnezzar, the king of Babylon, when he refuses to bow down to the king's image. Pretty badass. This video is badass too. I had never seen it, but it's beautiful. Apparently every frame was painted by hand. It kind of reminds me of the great children's book *The Snowy Day* by Ezra Jack Keats. I would elaborate, but I just realized I have twelve more of these to go.

Pass the Mic

Check Your Head reminds me so much of riding my BMX bike in the freezing streets of Chicago and telling myself, "Be true to yourself and you will never fall." I loved that bike so much. It had cool stickers and big fat tires, and I took it with me when I finally moved to New York City a few years later. I wish I could tell you I still have it, but I put it in the designated bike room in my apartment building and completely forgot to respond to repeated emails by our building super to remove it or claim it. Just recently I asked our doorman if it was there, and he was like, "The bikes from 2002? Nah." I really blew it. Anyway, this cool video seems to be the first of many times the three Beasties sing in triangle formation to camera. It was also the first time I learned how to pronounce "Yauch."

So What'cha Want

Smoke weed smoke weed smoke weed smoke weed smoke weed smoke weed smoke weed smoke weed smoke weed all day.

Netty's Girl

I love you, Mike D, but I do not have time for this right now.

Gratitude

The Beasties are going to play their instruments in the hot sand and you're gonna like it! I like how everyone feels a little grouchy in this, like they are experiencing the right kind of growing pains. This makes me wish for the millionth time in my life that I was in a band and got to look cool and play guitar and stare off to the side while the camera was on me like I didn't give a fuck. Musicians are magicians and will forever be. I like to think that while ADROCK was shouting about gratitude in the desert, his future wife, Kathleen Hanna, was singing "Suck My Left One" in a small club many miles away. And then their vocal particles traveled across land and sea until it became a giant love cloud ready to rain awesomeness on them for years to come.

Sabotage

I truly believe there would be no *Anchorman*, no Wes Anderson, no Lonely Island videos, and no channel called Adult Swim if this video did not exist. It hit a lot of sweet spots for me. Bad wigs. Obvious dummies thrown off buildings. Shots of Yauch with tape on his mouth and then rack focus to a ticking bundle of dynamite. This song was kind of like Madonna's "Vogue," in that it had built-in moments for people to freeze frame and strike a pose. To capitalize on this in a video was genius, and I enjoyed it as much as my two young sons did when I just played it for them for the first time.

Sure Shot

Looks like Beastie Boys have been doing some yoga! Let's get those tuxedos on, boys! This video looks like one long selfie. I remember truly loving and believing MCA when he apologized for disrespecting women in the past and sending love and respect to the mothers and sisters. And I always loved the "b-boys" moment followed by the "b-girls" moment. I always knew I was in the club, but now I knew they knew. Cool.

Intergalactic

We have more bad wigs and oversized props, but now we've added a bald cap to the mix! I enjoy the robot dance moves but I was never a big *Godzilla* fan, so I have to admit that halfway through the rewatch of this video I started checking my phone.

Technology is crazy, right? Did you know that the camera on the *Voyager* spacecraft was less powerful than the one currently on our cellphone? Did you know that when *Voyager 1* was launched in 1977 it contained a golden record that not only had recordings of Bach and Chuck Berry, but contained greetings in fifty-nine languages and human and nature sounds such as footsteps and thunder and laughter? Jimmy Carter shot that shit into the Milky Way and it's still out there right now doing its thing. So cool. Anyway, great video.

Body Movin'
So many sets and locations.

Three MCs and One DJ
Mix Master. Cut faster. And he does. He does cut faster.

Triple Trouble
Sasquatch, y'all.

Don't Play No Game I Can't Win
Dolls, y'all.

Fight for Your Right Revisited
I love the idea that they can go back to their video so many years later and tease it out until it becomes a meta short film. This vid is jam-packed with cameos, including my own. I play a disgusted patron in a café, and I remember asking for a red beret and meeting Ted Danson for the first time. And most of the day was spent trying to be cool and stay quiet as I hung around the Beasties, who now felt like friends. It was honestly one of the biggest thrills of my life. And as I watched MCA direct and snuggle with his beautiful family, I could only think about one thing . . . why the fuck wasn't I cast as ADROCK? Or at least the older version of ADROCK? Goddamn it to hell. Well, at least the video ends with all the men peeing on each other, which just goes to prove you can take Beastie Boys off the roof in New York but you can't take the roof off of the . . . you get it.

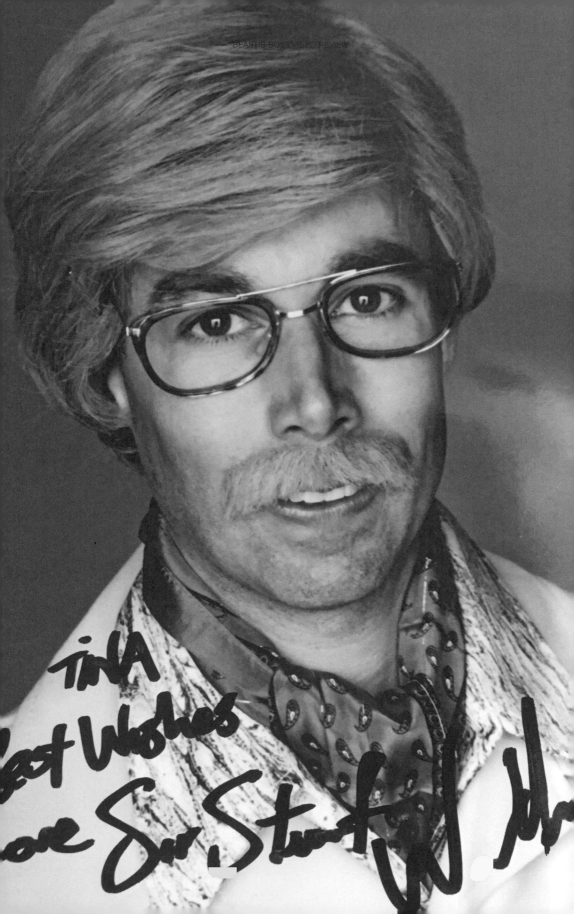

TINA
Best Wishes
love Sir Stewart Wallace

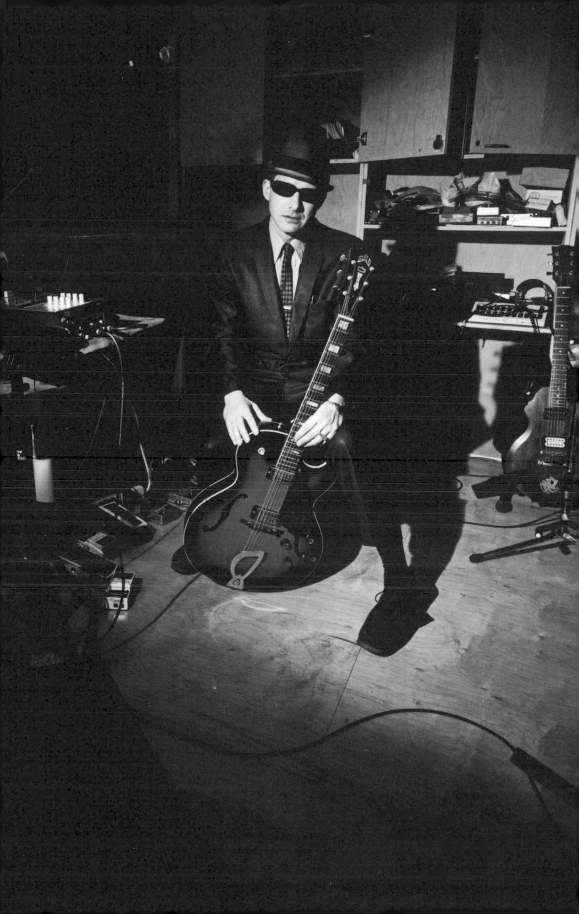

In a Mix-Up Fa-Shun

(AH)

If your band is gonna record an all-instrumental record, you should dress accordingly, like jazz cats. And so when we started to work on *The Mix-Up*, we implemented a very strict fashion rule. Every day we were in the studio, which was five days a week, we had to be dressed in clothes only from the years 1956–1964. This was pre–*Mad Men*, but it was *that* look. If that TV show had already been a thing, I'm sure we would've opted for a different look; probably 1969–1973 Mandrill/Kay-Gees style. (Which was our unofficial *Paul's Boutique*–era look, but anyways . . .) We went on crazy eBay shopping sprees, buying all the sharkskin suits, small-collared button-down shirts, ties, and tie clips we could find. Every day was going-to-work-suit day—except casual Fridays. And casual Fridays still had to be in the jazz-cat era, so we also bought a shitload of knitted shirts, bulky wool jackets, and Sta-Prest pants. Remember . . . *everything is a competition*, so we really stepped up our eBay game. It may not be the greatest record you've ever heard, but we looked fuckin' nice while making it.

You guys . . . outfits are fucking important.

Here's the thing about 94% of instrumental music: the title comes after the song has been recorded. Or at least the basic idea of the song. I'm 98% sure that no one has ever said, "I've written an instrumental song that starts in G minor, then transitions down to E, then has half-bar horn stabs of A to B, then holds on F-sharp for three bars while the hi-hat plays with conga fills and double-time güira runs. It's called 'Bump Town,' and it's about climate change and politicians deciding what constitutes a living wage." NO. When making instrumental music, musicians just improvise and play whatever comes to them. Usually someone starts playing something and everyone joins in. The social and political is on their minds, and so that somehow gets embedded in the music. But you'd never know. The title of the song is an afterthought. Like looking at a cat and thinking, *He looks like his name should be Waffles.*

After *To the 5 Boroughs*, we wanted to get back to playing instruments. It had literally been years since me, Adam, Mike, and Mark had made music together, and we missed that spontaneous feeling of improvising with physical objects, away from a computer. We had no big concept or specific goal in mind for what we wanted to make; we just knew we wanted it to be live and direct. And fun. The end result was an all-instrumental record called *The Mix-Up*.

We'd never made an instrumental-only record before, and thought it might be interesting one day to look back at all our records and be like,

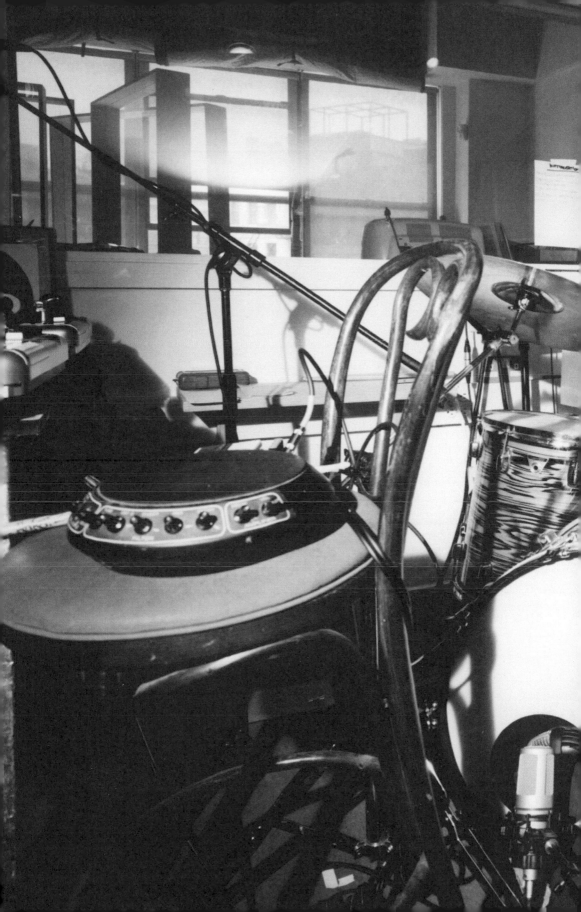

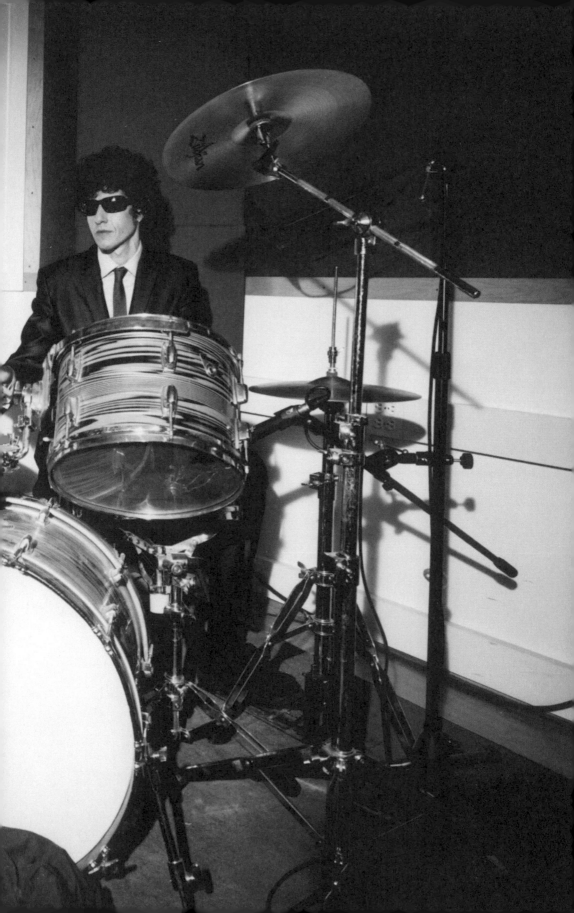

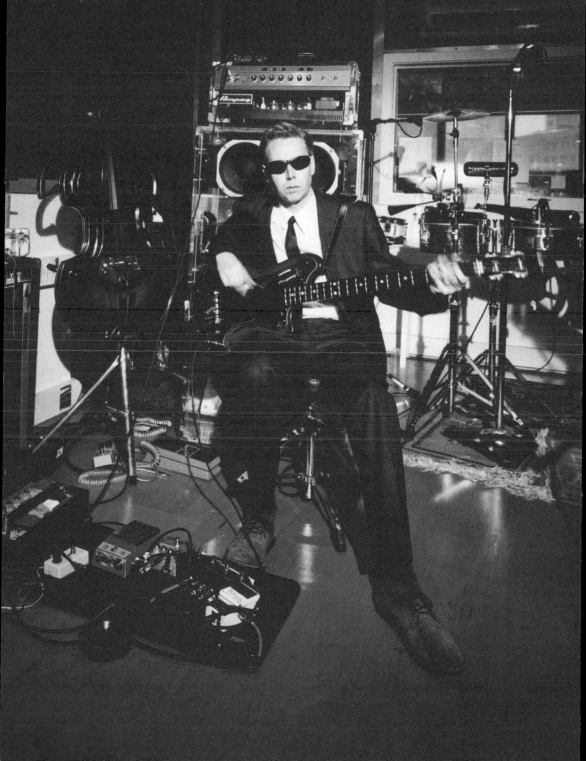

Oh, right, that instrumental one was kinda cool. So after a couple weeks of playing every day, we decided to go all in and put ourselves in the lineage of the great instrumentalists. John Coltrane, Miles Davis, Wendy Carlos, Sandy Nelson, Lalo Schifrin, the MGs, James Last, and so many more. We tried our best to fully embrace musicianship. The time had come for us to simply make music and not think too hard on it. No layering of samples and drum machines and computer programs or rhymes to switch off and back up. We just wanted to play forty-eight minutes of ball and have fun. Maybe we were just tired of talking. George W. Bush had us deflated, dumbfounded, and confused. Yes, shit was fucked up. Even way back in 2006, before Donald Trump was . . . I can't say it. Anyways, it felt right to us to be in the studio together playing our instruments. We were happy, and happy with what we were making.

I'm sure in our minds we wanted to make a full-on funky Head Hunters/ Meters/Politicians record, but there's just too many influences to ignore. Eddie Hazel, Greg Ginn, Ricky Wilson (B-52s), Wes Montgomery, Earl "Chinna" Smith, Jimi Hendrix, and Viv Albertine are all fighting for space in my brain when I play guitar. Mike's got Greg Errico, Pete Thomas, Ziggy Modeliste, Carlton Barrett, Clyde Stubblefield, Ringo Starr, and Pete Rock twisting up his inner syncopation. Ron Carter, Darryl Jenifer, Jah Wobble, Carol Kaye, and Aston Barrett are sending Yauch's bass-playing fingers in all directions. And Mark has an inner roll call of Elton John, Stevie Wonder, Jerry Dammers, Larry Harlow, Jimmy Smith, Jean-Jacques Perrey, and Steve Nieve doing the same. Because of this, *The Mix-Up* doesn't sound like any other record made by one band. It's as if ESG, Silver Apples, the Meters, PiL, The Clash, the Ventures, and the MGs recorded together and then released it through Salsoul Records.

> Memphis Mike,
Starz Restaurant
and Lounge,
Virginia Beach, 1978

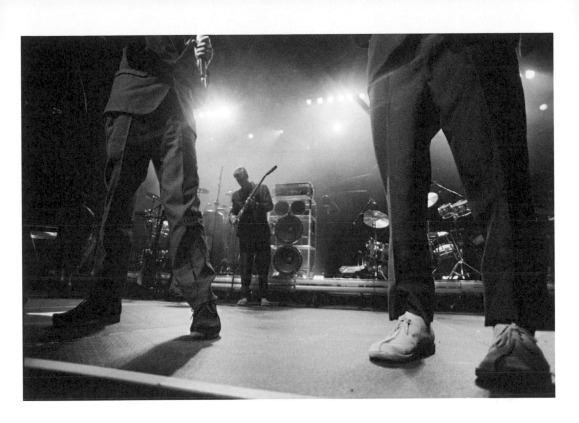

B for My Name—The title is a reference to Busy Bee in a scene from the movie *Wild Style*. He's laying out cash on a motel mattress in the shape of the letter *B*. You know, for his name.

Suco de Tangerina—Whenever we're in Rio de Janeiro, we head straight to BB Lanches. (Of course.) It's a sandwich/juice spot that in the '60s was allegedly renamed BB for Brigitte Bardot because she used to hang out there with Jorge Ben. Or was it Gilberto Gil? I don't know. But wherever Brigitte Bardot hung out in the early '60s in Rio de Janeiro sounds like a cool-ass place to be. BB Lanches looks exactly like where you'd find Brigitte Bardot drinking a coffee and having a sandwich in a black-and-white picture. Super mod. But mostly we went there for the intensely delicious fresh juice. Specifically, the Suco de Tangerina.

Alfredo Ortiz

Off the Grid—When you record using the computer program Pro Tools, you usually have your music set to a specific tempo. And therefore it's locked to that tempo. *On the grid*, it's called. This song is not set to a specific tempo. Thus its name. It's not my favorite title, as the immediate image it conjures is someone who's quit the rat race and moved to the mountains. Not that there's anything wrong with that, but really . . . what I want to tell you is this . . . the break in the middle of this song is a catapulter, one of my favorite musical left turns we ever made.

Dramastically Different—Yauch interviewed a gentleman by the name of Coach Bub for his movie *Gunnin' for That #1 Spot*. During the interview, Coach Bub said, of a young basketball player, that his style had vastly improved and was "dramastically different." And now "dramastically" is your new favorite word, right?

I'd like to end this little section with a quote from the great Nasty Nas:

> *It drops deep as it does in my breath*
> *I never sleep, 'cause sleep is the cousin of death.*

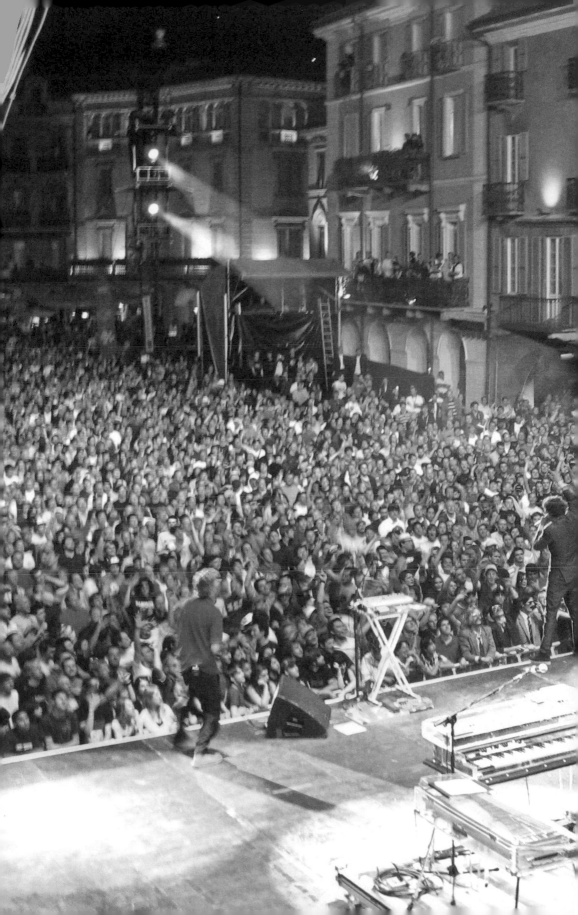

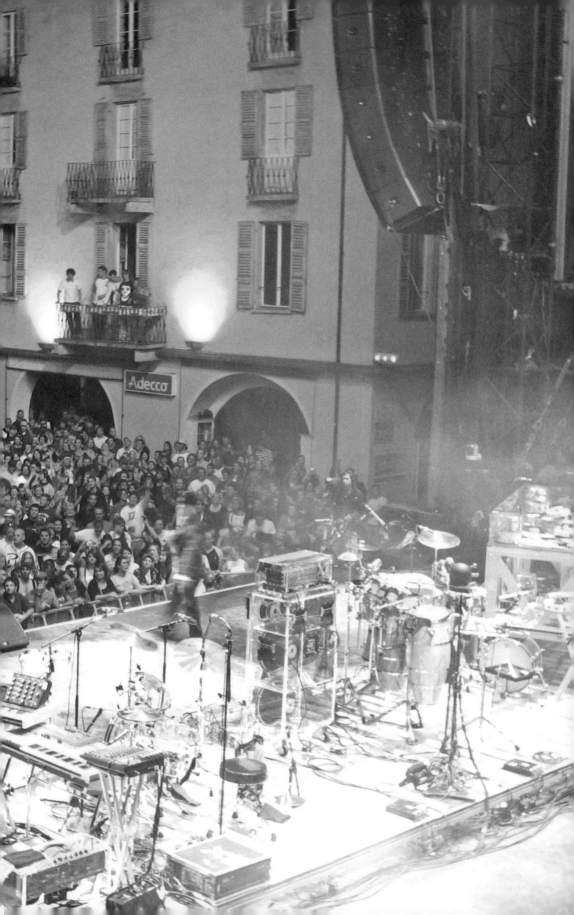

TOUR RULES (while playing)

MUST (DO'S) (MUSTS)

#1 MUST WEAR BLAZER

#2 MUST USE BRIEFCASE or purse or hat box

#3 MUST WEAR SLACKS or skirt

#4 MUST WEAR a TYPE of SHOE

~~#5 MUST WEAR SKIRT or PANT SUIT~~

#5 MUST WEAR OUTFIT With Coat/blazer

#6 MUST WEAR CLIP ON TIE Private
    or Some TYPE of SASH or NECK SCARF

#7 MUST WEAR DRESS SHIRT A/K/A button
                                         down
~~#8 MUST WEAR "SHITTY" belt~~   short or long
                                    sleeve except
#8 MUST WEAR "SHITTY" belt   able
        "DRESS UP"

#9 MUST TUCK SHIRT INTO PANTS

#10 FACIAL HAIR MUST be WELL Groomed

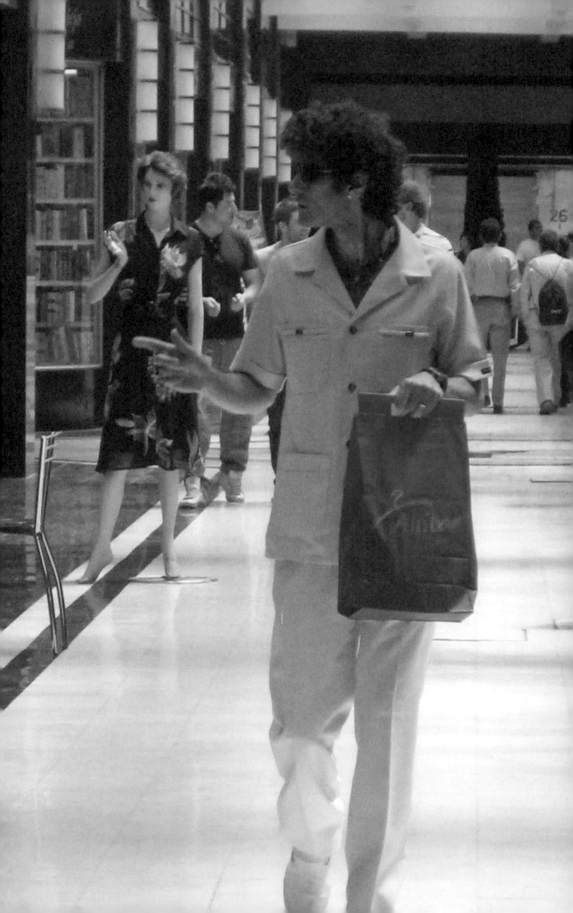

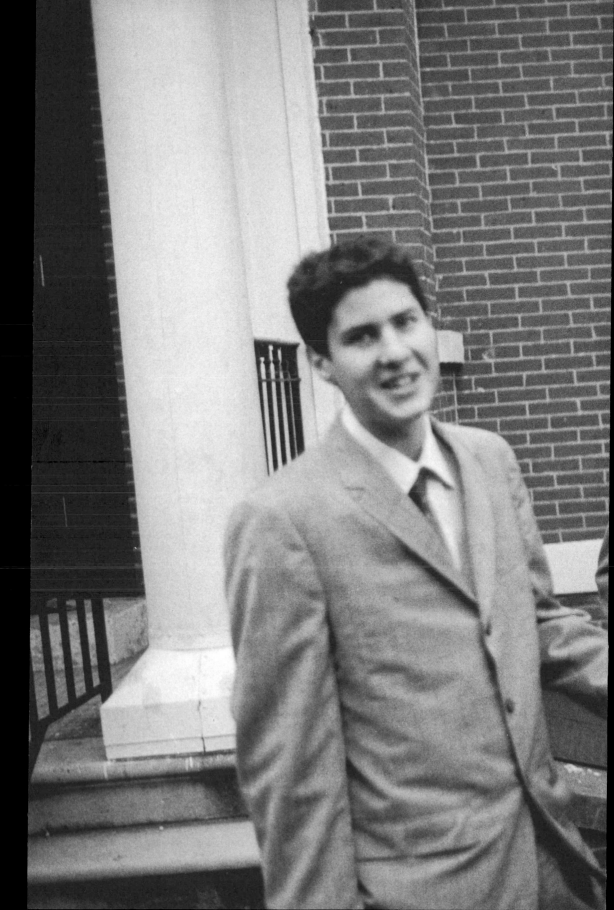

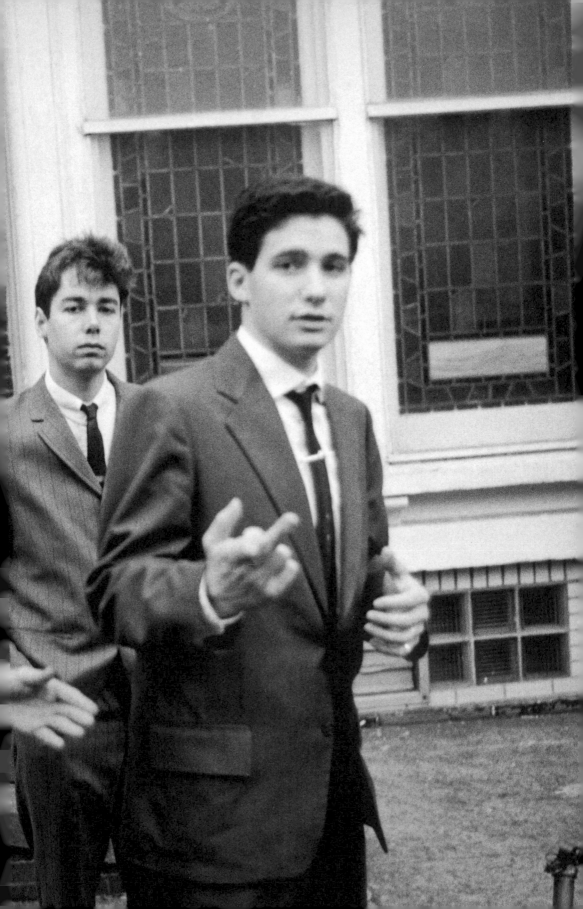

hello . . .

so . . . as you know . . . i don't usually do this . . . send reports on what's happening in the world of me . . . but this time i kinda had to . . . wow . . . i don't know where to start . . . we played last night in athens greece . . . the city that's still rebuilding . . . literally . . . from what i can tell athens takes its design from a really crappy and barren strip mall under the 5 freeway way out in covina or oxnard california . . . sorry if this story gets a little negative at times . . . i got fkn sick in barcelona and basically stayed in my hotel room the whole time . . . i saw a doctor who stuck a camera up my nose and down my throat and then told me that my throat looked scratchy . . . which is what i told him before he put that crazy-ass thing up in my face . . . okay enough kvetching . . . so . . . the trip starts out normal . . . we wake up . . . get our bags together . . . get in a van . . . get to the airport . . . fly to greece . . . the view from the plane is sick!!! . . . the greek islands look to be all that . . . as we were landing we all had visions of meeting up with jay-z and beyonce and having tzatziki and dolmades on karl lagerfeld's yacht . . . it didn't work out that way . . . as i said . . . we didn't get the glitz . . . we got the grime . . . kathleen said that when she went it was great . . . she hung out in old town, had a great show, and met a bunch of cool people . . . oh well . . . we did have a really good lunch including greek salad though . . . anyways . . .

THE GIG—

the van-driver guys kept getting lost and were both generally very new to the van-driver-guy job . . . they were getting us a little nervous . . . we get to the gig (which is outdoors, and is the size of a minor league baseball stadium) . . . everything's going okay . . . sort of . . . just before we go on . . . bailey . . . who does security for us on tour . . . comes into the room and said . . . "i just wanna warn you guys that upwards of 1,000 people just rushed the gates and it's a little weird out there . . . no one's fighting or anything . . . i just don't really like it . . . so keep an eye out." okay . . . we get onstage and play our show . . . with about 4 songs left in the set . . . i see bailey walk out onstage and call together a little huddle . . . he says . . . "okay guys . . . the show's gotta be over now . . . they're pepper spraying people and they've set fire to the dressing rooms . . . we gotta go NOW!" . . . we say our good nights . . . people are bummed . . . as we rush offstage we can hear the at least 5 or 6 thousand kids screaming . . . and it's not getting quieter . . . we get in a van that's waiting for us behind the stage . . . and the van-driver guy is frozen in panic . . . there's at least 12 people in the van screaming at this guy to drive . . . he's in shock. . . . he then starts to drive . . . real slow . . . we're yelling . . . he stops to talk to somebody . . . there's a truck blocking the exit and that's the only way out . . . bailey jumps out of the van and tells us not to move . . . he runs off toward the smoky dressing rooms . . . someone in the back has a walkie-talkie and a minute later bailey is screaming for us

to drive . . . there is total chaos in the background of his screams . . . the driver is
again frozen . . . we all start hitting him and scream at him to drive . . . it's totally
fucking nuts . . . and this is just the beginning . . . anyways . . . we drive up a dirt path
towards the exit and see bailey and total mayhem all around him . . . there's smoke
everywhere . . . he gets in and whispers as loud+quiet as he can . . ."everybody fuckin'
duck down now!!!" (he is a tommy lee jones movie character come to life) as he's
saying this we see about . . . shit . . . 40 kids wearing black motorcycle helmets all
holding baseball bats or pipes or big-ass knives . . . like for real . . . machetes . . . and
now we gotta drive through them to get out . . . i can't believe i'm even describing
this . . . we get towards the gate and see jerome (our tour manager) just standing
there . . . we stop real quick and throw him in and drive . . . SAFE . . . all our shit has
been left behind . . . wallets . . . cameras . . . phones . . . money . . . everything . . .
it is nuts . . . and then jerome tells us what he saw and then we meet up with the rest
of our crew the next day and the rest of the night's story is told . . . it goes like this . . .
while we were onstage . . . only a few people were in the dressing-room area . . .
they heard some noises . . . then glass starts shattering . . . then jerome starts seeing
these guys with the motorcycle helmets creeping all over the place . . . he's seeing
them breaking windows with bats . . . throwing chairs through windows . . . chasing
after a security guard . . . (oh . . . when jerome got in the van with us at the gate . . .
he said he saw tons of police cars driving AWAY from the venue . . .) people in our
crew saw kids setting fire to all the banners . . . the advertising crap . . . setting fire to
cars . . . one kid ran onstage and sprayed our equipment with a fire extinguisher,
which, because of the wind, ended up blowing back into the audience, which set off
tons of fights . . . one of our crew guys . . . brian . . . just before it all started to jump
off . . . left the stage to go get some coffee 'cause he was jet-lagged and tired . . .
by the time he got to the dressing room . . . he saw the flames and the helmet dudes
and the whole shit . . . he grabbed everything that he could see in our dressing rooms
and threw it into a huge road case and closed it . . . grabbed a couple backpacks
that were left, and ran . . . right when he hit the door he was face-to-face with a
motorcycle-helmet guy . . . he froze in his tracks . . . the guy lifted his face thing off
his helmet so he could talk to brian . . . he said the guy was totally casual and said,
"we're not after you . . . we want the security." he said that while he was saying this the
kid was grabbing a coke from this huge refrigerator . . . got the soda and then pushed
the fridge over onto the floor . . . brian ran . . . there's so much more to this trip to
greece . . . it was fkn NUTS! but i guess my favorite part was that after all that . . .
the same van-driver guy from the gig (we decided his name was sad sack sam)
came the next day to bring us to the airport and didn't get gas, so the van broke down
on the way . . . that was truly one for the books . . . thanks for letting me share . . .
adam

The Music Made It Stop
(AH)

This is a story about what happened at a gig we played in Ireland in 2000-and-something. Saying it was a gig sounds so blasé compared to what it actually was: a huge festival in a big, open field with a sea of, like, fifty thousand people. And way, way, in the distance was a castle. Someone's castle. The rumor was that there was an Irish prince living inside and he watched the festival every year from his throne. A prince doesn't get a throne, right? And do they live in castles in 2000-and-something? I don't know. When I tell you what happened next, you'll understand why my facts are all over the place. We had a chef on tour with us. He had a mobile kitchen, all packed in various road cases, and he made us delicious meals every day and night. It seems like a total extravagance, but it wasn't that much more expensive than buying everyone's food for each day. We had probably twenty-five people in total on our tour. Just for our band. It was factually probably way more fucking expensive, but this chef was named Wayno (RIP) and he was magnificent in the kitchen. Well . . . this one night in Ireland I had a little bit of a sore throat, but I had a hankering for some marijuana pot joints. Meaning, I wanted to get high, but I didn't wanna smoke because of the sore throat. And I did not wanna play a mediocre, scratchy-voiced show with the eyes and ears of the mysterious prince of all of Ireland judging my every move from his golden throne. So I asked Wayno two questions:

1. Do you have any pot?
2. Any chance you wanna make some pot cookies?

He did, and he did.

About an hour later, we were all hanging around in some commissary-type backstage communal eating zone, and Wayno presented me with a batch of freshly baked cookies for me to eat and get baked. He told me to go easy 'cause they were kinda strong. I gave him the *Oh-kay . . . don't you worry about me, Grandma. I been doin' this semi-pro for a while now. I can handle my weed intake.* I ate a little cookie, and so did Alfredo (Ortiz). Nothing. We hung out some more just bullshitting, killing time. And we did the classic amateur move . . . *These cookies aren't doing anything. I'm gonna have another.* So we did. The next thing I knew was that I was alone on a couch, in that same room, but now my friends seemed to be sitting in chairs that were moving rapidly away from me and they were laughing at me while floating backward. *OOH NOO.* My head felt like a punching bag and my limbs were like snakes trying to get away from

my body. *I am fucked up.* Just as it all hit me, a child in a motorized wheelchair zipped right up to me. Completely invading my personal interspatial perimeter zone. "Hi, I'm Sally. Money Mark told me to come over and say hi to you." *WHAT?!* I think the sound I made was *gwaagh* as I shoved my body upright and pushed past this kid. Young Sally must have thought I was an asshole, but sometimes, Sally, that's how it is. That person in that band you wanna say hi to might just be way too fucked-up to return a pleasant "Hello, nice to meet you."

I stumbled out of that room like I was in a spy movie and I just got dosed by the enemy secret double agent. *WAYNO! Why!?! Who are you, Wayno? What are you after?* In the moment, the thought came to me that if I could make it to a bathroom, I could splash a bunch of cold water on my face and that would make it stop. I was still in the espionage-movie scene, and suddenly I was stumbling down a fluorescently lit hallway, lined with small dressing rooms on either side, and I was bouncing off the walls. Bouncing off people trying to get to their gig or tour bus or whatever people are trying to do backstage at a huge festival. While plowing through strangers I passed Paul Simonon. *Oh man, I wish so bad I wasn't like this right now. I love you, Paul Simonon. Right, Gorillaz is playing this festival too. I wanna see them. Oh man. How did those two little cookies make me feel this way? This short hallway is getting longer and longer.* I was freaking out. *Must find cold water.* I got outside and remembered that it was a festival and the bathroom was a row of port-a-potties. Not a nice, clean bathroom at a nice hotel, but literally a shithole. The water that comes out of the sink of a port-a-potty is not refreshing, FYI. So I decided that I was gonna have a band meeting.

I gotta find Yauch. He's an in-charge type of person, and well versed in the ways of the world. Seedy and serene. He'll help me. He'll know what to do. As I lumbered back down that dreaded hallway, I looked in each little dressing room that was on either side. Yauch? No. Yauch? No. I turned and looked into the next one and there was Fredo, crouching on top of a four-foot-high road case. He had an audience of a few people in a semicircle watching him. He was wringing his hands together in a menacing way like that creepy creep from that creepy movie. And he was saying, "I want the precious." And his audience was laughing and I was on the verge of terror tears and suddenly there was Mike. "Dude . . . you okay? You look manic." *I do? I am. I'm freaking out. I had these pot cookies and they got me like whoa and I don't know how to, like, you know, like . . . make it stop. Can we have a band meeting please? Now. I need us to all be together.* "Okay. Okay. I'm here. We're here." "It's gonna be okay. Let's get you some water." He led me into our little dressing room. Why hadn't I thought to just go there in the first place? Yauch was there. Mix Master. Mark Nishita. (*Fuck you, Mark. Did you really tell that little kid to hassle me while my trip kicked in? I'm gonna remember that shit.*) Then Fredo was in the room and it was a band meeting. "Listen . . . here's the deal. I ate a couple pot cookies that Wayno made. I asked him to. My throat hurts a little but never mind. What I'm saying

is, those shits kicked in fuckin' hard and heavy and it's not stopping and I need this to just stop. I know I'm not gonna die. I mean, I know I'm not dying. Right now. Not tonight because of this. It's just, I'm really, really fucked up and I need it to stop. Yauch, do you know how to do that?" I know I must've looked nuts, and so I was okay that my friends were laughing at me right then. I knew that each one of them had been where I was at some other point in time because of some fuckin' laced cookie or brownie or Dutch bonbon. Yauch said that he was sorry, but he didn't know how to make it stop. "Maybe splash some cold water on your face." *Dammit.* He said, "Let's go see Wayno, he'll probably know what to do." Adam+Mike literally held my hands as they led me through the haunting backstage labyrinth. Which, had I not eaten that second cookie, would've been a beautiful outdoor place to hang out on a summer evening, under Irish trees and stars with my new best friend Paul Simonon. But no.

We got to where Wayno's road-case kitchen was and found him.

ME: Oh fuck. Wayno. Man, those cookies were *R.E.A.L.L.Y.* strong.
WAYNO: Yeah, they were.
ME: Yes. That's what I just said. I'm fucked up, though.
WAYNO: I put some hash in there too. I told you to go slow.
ME: I know, Wayno. I'm sorry. I didn't. I went fast and now it won't stop. We
      have to be onstage in fifteen minutes and I am the Blob. What do I do?
WAYNO: Uh . . . I don't know. Splash some cold water on your face?
ME: I tried that. The water was warmish, though. Does that matter?
WAYNO: Do you want some tea?
ME: Tea? I don't know. Do I? Will it make it stop?
WAYNO: It can't hurt.
ME: Okay.

So I drank some tea. Chamomile? Earl Grey? Throat Coat? I don't know what it was, but it did not make it stop. And there I was. A human baked pot cookie walking to the stage with fifty thousand people, and at least one prince, about to witness some real TMZ shit. "Jewish Rapper Hits the Deck" will be the headline. And the picture will be of me on the floor crying and pounding my fists. *I just want it to stop!*

We got out there onstage and it was beautiful. There really was a castle way back there. It was all lit up and it was magnificent. The audience seemed so nice and happy and excited to be in the great outdoors. Timmy Chunks (wonderful person and guitar technician extraordinaire) handed me my guitar and I put it on and instinctively went and stood by my mic in front of my amp. Mike stick-counted in the first song. It was one of our laid-back-playing cuts. Yauch, Mike, and Mark were playing some groove that was nice and funky. And I was frozen. I wasn't moving my hands or my body. I was just spacing out on all the space. The castle, the people, the

stage lights, the summertime. Something caught my eye, and it was Timmy Chunks. He was over on the side of the stage and he was yelling at me . . . "Are you okay!?!" It took me a second to realize what he was saying. I couldn't hear him so good and so I was kind of lip-reading. It snapped me into real time. Right. Pot cookies. Band meeting. The precious. Regurgitated pee water from the port-a-potty sink. Guitar. Stage. Lights. Music. Band. Showtime. I scanned the stage to see my friends and noticed that Fredo was frozen too. He was staring out into outer space, and his hands were just hovering above his conga drums. He was fucked-up. But like it is with an oxygen mask on an airplane, you gotta help yourself first before you can help others. Get your shit together. I figured out what song they were playing, and started playing along. It's lucky that we've played together for so long or else I wouldn't have instinctively known what to do. The next song started—*Hey, I know this one.* I was back in it.

The music made it stop.

The Ring
(AH)

"Naw, man, it's cool," I said to him as I nervously backed away. "I don't really wear jewelry. Thank you, though." Then he backed me into a wall in a dressing room at the Warfield Theatre in San Francisco. "But I just really want you to have my ring," he said, real creepy-like.

Maybe I was tired, or hungry, or just wanted to hang out with my friends after the show, but this fuckin' dude freaked me the fuck out. He was shortish, like me, but with arms that were noticeably too long, so his hands were well below his knees. His teeth were too big for his mouth, and they had spaces between them. They looked like Chiclets that had been neatly laid out on a table. And he had *fully* zoned in on me. Why me? Why not Yauch or Mike or Mark Nishita? I can't remember what he was talking to me about, but midsentence, he took a ring off his finger and told me that he really wanted *me* to have it. It was 1992, and he was wearing *several* pieces of early '90s tribal-y jewelry. Necklaces, piercings, bracelets, and rings. The thing he kept pushing on me was a silver-colored ring that had what looked to be iron crosses on it. The only way to stop what was happening was to just accept the ring and say thank you. When he left the dressing room, I put it in my backpack and out of my head.

A couple weeks later, when I got back to my apartment in New York, I emptied my bag and there it was . . . THE RING. What to do with it? Throwing it away felt weird for some reason. I was sure that I put it on a little shelf in my bedroom, but the next day when we were all on a train to Washington, DC, for a show, I reached in my bag to get something and there it was. I was kind of terrified. How'd it get from the shelf back into my bag? It made no sense. I must've *not* put it on the shelf but back in my bag. But why would I do that? The conversation in my head spilled out loud, and I stood up from my train seat and told everyone about the dude and the teeth and the ring and they started making fun of me. "Stop laughing at me." I threw the ring down to the other end of the train car, took a deep breath, and moved on with my life. I did. I really did. Every once in a while the dude's teeth and arms and hands would pop in my head, but it became more of an "Oh yeah. Remember that funny thing?" than a *Walking Dead* kind of thing.

CUT TO: Santiago 2007
I was in my hotel room packing my bags to meet everyone downstairs in the lobby. I reached into my backpack and there it was again . . . THE RING. I fucking froze. Suddenly I was in that *oh no* moment of every scary movie I'd ever seen. The one when the person figures out who the murderer is and then

494

the murderer is standing right behind them. What the fuck!?! I rushed down to the lobby in full panic mode to tell everyone that I found the ring. "I have the ring." "The ring?" "Remember? That dude in San Francisco who made me take his creepy jewelry from his intensely oversized limb? How he smiled at me with his fuckin' picket-fence grill?" No one seemed to care. They were all like, *Wow. Hmm. That's peculiar.* I was left still standing there with this fucking horror show in my backpack. I'm not a whatevs type of cat, and this was some fucked-up shit, and I couldn't shake it. There was a little fountain outside the hotel, and I went to it and had a private moment of observance with the ring. "Stop doing this to me," I said. And I tossed it into the fountain. And we left Santiago.

CUT TO: Singapore 2007 (a week or so later)
It's a regular day on tour. Everyone meets up and spends thirty-nine minutes trying to decide on where to eat. But this day Yauch pulled me aside. "Look, I gotta tell you something. *I* put the ring in your bag." Obviously my response was, "WHAT!?!" "Yeah, remember when we were on that train to DC and you threw the ring across the train? Well, when you went to the food car, I looked around, found the ring, and put it my bag." "Wait . . . WHAT!?! That was fifteen years ago!" "Yeah, I just kept it, and when we go out on a tour, I usually throw it in my bag and wait for the right time to sneak it back into yours." "No fucking way!" "I wasn't gonna tell you I did it, but you seem so genuinely freaked out that I feel bad seeing you this way. I had to tell you. To put your mind at ease."

CUT TO: Me, now.
Seriously though . . . who fuckin' does that? Who has the prank stamina to hold it back for fifteen years? I'm not only impressed by this, but I am proud to have a friend with such stealth practical, and tactical, joke skills. Thank you, Adam, for elevating the team that Coach built around you.

Key to that which follows

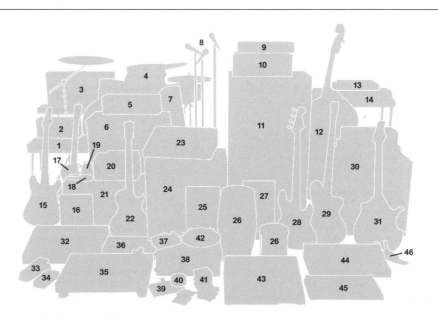

Equipment

(AH)

1. Hohner D6 Clavinet
This is like Mark Nishita's Superman cape. When he turns it on and starts playing the clav, he becomes a superhero.

2. Maestro Rhythm King
We don't have this drum machine recorded on any song, but we always had it around because it's just a cool drum machine to have around. Not just because it sounds great, but it also has the classic Maestro brand Technicolor Dreamcoat buttons on it.

3. ARP 2600
This thing is a beast to work with. Sometimes it would take hours just to figure out how to get cool sounds out of it. But with a combination of patience and some know-how . . . you could make some sonic magic. (Honestly, probably better suited to a virtuoso like Wendy Carlos or Dick Hyman than us.) Featured on the song "Dedications." (MD)

4. Ludwig drum kit
Tough to pick just one of Mike's drum kits. He has a few, and they're like markers in time. The green one is *Check Your Head*. The champagne one is *Hello Nasty*. But the Ludwig Tiger Stripe "student kit" model is Mike's favorite. No real reason, it just is.
Fun fact about Mike: He only owns used drums. He prefers the way they look, feel, and sound.

5. Acoustic 150 bass amp head
Yauch's first really loud bass purchase. He got this thing in 1982 and played through it for years.

6. Leslie speaker
The organ grinder. It has a rotary speaker that makes the sound feel like it's constantly in motion. It's like a psychedelic audio fidget spinner.

7. Korg CX-3
I know you're supposed to play a Hammond B3 organ if you want that awesome Jimmy McGriff/Booker T and the MGs style, but this Korg sounds fantastic (especially when played through a Leslie speaker), and it's so much easier to bring on tour.

8. Shure SM58 mic
The classic. The god.

9. Gallien-Krueger bass amp head
This thing is just so stupidly loud.

10. DA-88
A lot of the basic tracks for *Hello Nasty* were recorded on this (using a Mackie mixer). It's an 8-track recorder that uses Hi-8 video tapes only. It's so '90s. It's like the '90s version of an '80s cassingle.

11. Huge Peavey bass cabinet
Not sure if we've fully described this properly yet, but Yauch really wanted the bass loud when we played shows. And this bad boy had an 18" woofer, so no shortage of bass for your face. Just sayin'. (MD)

12. Upright acoustic bass
Yauch bought this beautiful old upright bass around 1990 at a store in L.A. called Stein on Vine. The two were almost inseparable there for a minute, Yauch+that bass.

13. Rhythm Ace
This drum machine isn't actually recorded on any of our songs, but Mike always kept it set up right next to his drum kit. Anytime he wanted to practice or record drums to a locked-in tempo, he'd plug in headphones and play along with his trusty Rhythm Ace.

14. Wurlitzer 200A
An instrument that, when played, will bring you right into the feeling of the era it was made. Play this Wurlitzer and you could easily imagine yourself being onstage with Steely Dan in 1973. But in a good way. (Featured on "Ricky's Theme.")

15. Hondo II professional guitar
My mom and her friends chipped in and got me an electric guitar for my twelfth birthday. I don't remember ever being like, *Mom . . . c'mon . . . please . . . I really want an electric guitar.* She and her friends just decided that I was meant to be a guitar player. (Shout-out to the Carlotti family.)

16. Tascam Porta One Ministudio 4-track cassette recorder
The game changer.

17. Gibson Melody Maker
My most favorite guitar I've ever owned. I got it in 1994 at a used-gear store in Chicago. It's light and beautiful, and I wear that shit way up high, mod style.

18. Sony Variety mic
A gift from Mario Caldato Jr. (Featured on "So What'cha Want.")

19. "Hey Ladies" promotional cowbell
Bill McMullen wanted this here.

20. Maestro Echoplex
"The sound sounds sweeter through an Echoplex." If you want something to be dubbed out and sound crazy, would you prefer to use this tape-delay machine or the Roland Space Echo? Tough answer, right? I prefer this one. Maybe it's because it's Maestro brand, or maybe I just love how shitty it sounds.

21. Fender Deluxe Reverb guitar amp
The dependable friend.

22. Gibson Firebrand
My first ever nice guitar. I got it at a used-gear store in the Valley in L.A. in 1991. I never wanted to play Fender guitars back then because they made me think of Bruce Springsteen and I wanted one that looked more like something Bob Marley would've had. I played this guitar on *Check Your Head* and *Ill Communication* (records and tours).

23. MPC-60 sampling drum machine
The go-to sampler of the '90s. When people first started saying . . . *oh, that's a cool sample.* This is the machine that sample was sampled on.

24. SG guitar amp
There's nothing that special about this amp other than I love it. I brought it on tour with me for all of 1992. It has a nice built-in phase effect and a nice little reverb plate. I eventually bought a used Fender Deluxe Reverb, which was more dependable than this beat-up old amp, but this beat-up old SG amp was the one that I became a guitar player through.

25. GLI PMX 9000 DJ mixer
Middle school rap DJ's required device.

26. Conga and guica
Add a little percussion, and your sound is gonna sound funkier.

27. Rave-O-Lution drum machine
This thing is pretty fuckin' cool. I did a live remix of every rap song on *Hello Nasty* while we were mixing the record. I have a cassette tape of it. Wanna hear it sometime?

28. Fender Jazz bass
Mike Watt once asked to hold this bass of Yauch's. He wanted to know how much it weighed. He said most people don't know what they want, and that's why you see guys playing a 6-string bass that looks like and weighs as much as a coffee table. Which is why for years we would look at someone's bass, and be like . . . *oh, that shit's a coffee table.* This Fender Jazz bass passed the test. Fun fact about Yauch: He installed a terminator switch on it.

29. Ampeg Scroll bass
My favorite of all of Yauch's basses. He played it with these awesome black La Bella flat-wound strings. It plays smooth to the touch, and sounds loud and low.
Also shout-out to the one Jah Wobble of PiL, whose low-end sounds were driven by this gnarly little tool. (MD)

30. Ampeg Portaflex flip-top bass amp
It's just a nice amp to play the bass through.
And pairs so well with the abovementioned Scroll bass. Just like the wine with the chicken. (MD)

31. Rogue sitar/guitar
I bought this on eBay for $200. It's a guitar with extra strings that vibrate to make a kind of sitar sound.

32. Oberheim DX drum machine
This was the first drum machine I ever used. Rick Rubin had one, and I used to cut school and hang out in his dorm room and mess with this thing all day and night. I eventually got my own, but his was the one. The one I learned to program on.

33. Dunlop Cry Baby wah-wah pedal
The first Cry Baby I owned I stole from some band off the stage at the Mudd Club in 1982. I never *really* messed with it until we started playing music at my apartment on Stanley Ave in L.A. in 1990. Just as we were setting up and about to start playing together for the very first time (as this new version of ourselves), Yauch said, "Oh, what about that old Cry Baby you have? You should go get that." So I did. And we got funky with it.

34. Univox Super-Fuzz
Anytime you hear a distorted bass sound on any of our records, that's Yauch playing through this FX box. (Featured on "Gratitude," "Sabotage," being terminated on the end of "Pass the Mic," and so many more.)

35. Technics SL-1200 turntable
The one and only.

36. Maestro Rhythm + Sound
This crazy box has a bunch of weird percussion FX that play at odd intervals when you touch your guitar strings. They're unwieldy and hard to control. BUT . . . it has a button on it that adds a deep, low sub-bass to whatever you're playing. And when you have the Fuzz button pushed down too, you've got "The Maestro." (And it comes in a special little suitcase, which is always the best.)

37. Boss DS-1 distortion pedal
My go-to fuzz box, especially for shows. It's not as cool as my Maestro Super Fuzz, but it actually sounds better, in that you have more control over it. You can be as clean or fuzzy as you want when playing through it, whereas the Maestro is just always dirty. The Super Fuzz is kind of like the Robert Horry of distortion pedals. You only want it around for one thing. And when it's crunch time and you need that three . . . it's a killer. (I can't believe that I just name-checked fuckin' Robert Horry.)

38. Roland Space Echo
I beg to differ from my dear esteemed colleague; this tape delay and the Maestro Echoplex are both glorious machines. (No need to slam each other on leather bad boys over this.) BUT, the Roland Space Echo has this magic combination of tape delay and reverb that you can manipulate with these dials, giving you a taking-off-for-space or a slamming-on-the-brakes-into-a-brick-wall effect, depending on which way you turn them. Plus it is no design slouch. The graphics and colors capture the late 1960s/early 1970s fascination with space exploration. (MD)

39. Realistic PZM mics
This microphone is unique because you can literally lay it on the floor, and with some of its Radio Shack magic, it captures the drums, the room, and everything, just right. (MD)

40. Roll of duct tape
You have to have duct tape lying around the studio (or apartment). You might need to fix that cabinet, or put some on the window to keep the cold air from coming in. BUT . . . be careful. The band Le Tigre might put a piece of orange or green duct tape on your guitar cable or Casio keyboard and say that it's theirs.

41. Floppy discs
These things are kind of like iCloud, but, like, way different.

42. Synare drum synthesizer pad
This is on the stoner's top 10 favorite musical instrument list. Careful, though—don't hit your hand with the drumstick. It'll kill your buzz.
Also, I would advise refraining from any engagement with this while hungover. It's pretty touch-sensitive, so if it's whacked too hard you just get a super-loud high-pitched disco *buooooww* sound that will ring your bell. (MD)

43. EMU SP-1200 sampling drum machine
I was never really the type of guitar player that would hide in my room and just play all the time, but I was like that with my SP-1200. If you've never seen the documentary about objectum sexuality, go see it, then think about me in the '90s with my SP-1200.

44. Moog Prodigy
I've had this thing forever, but for whatever reason, it was never on a song until "Make Some Noise."

45. Roland TR-808
Oh, you don't have one?

46. Donkey's jawbone
Percussionist extraordinaire Alfredo Ortiz showed up to record on *The Mix-Up* with this crazy thing. When you hit the side of the dried-up old jawbone, the teeth would rattle for days.

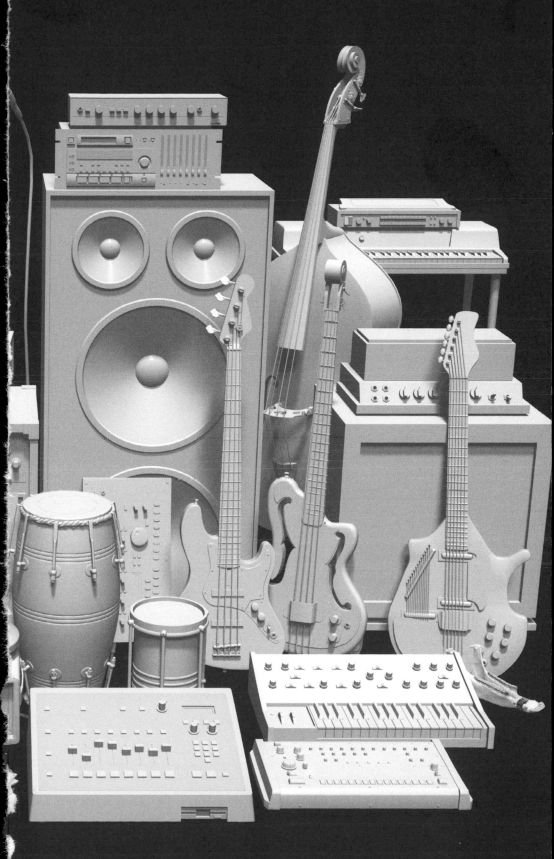

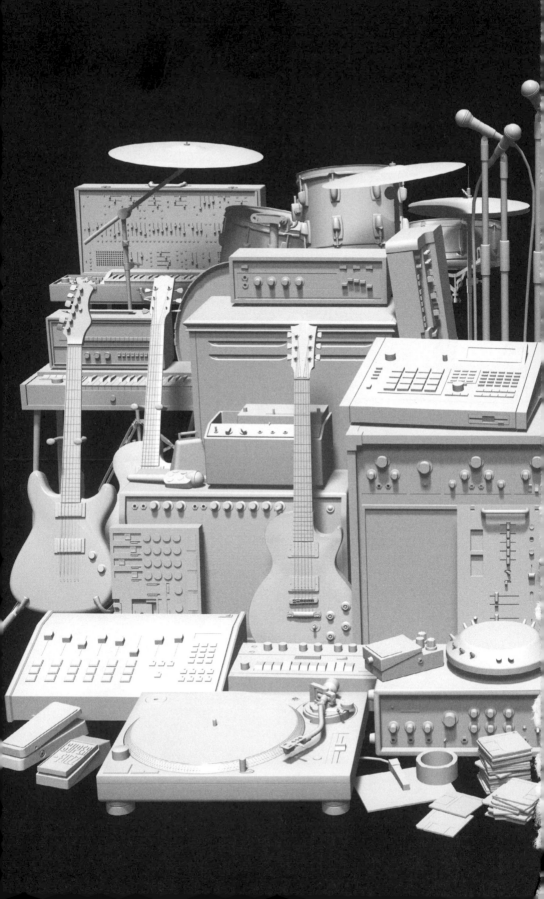

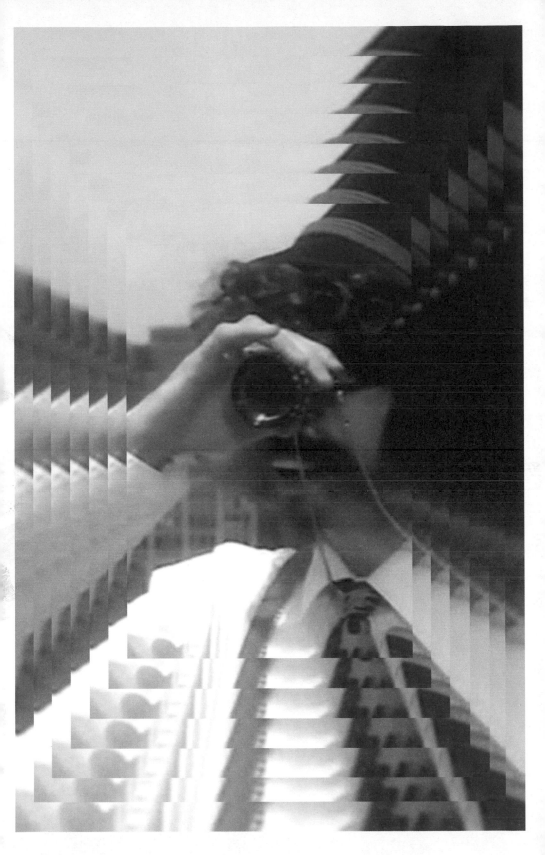

HÖRNBLOWÉR

Profile of a Shepherd

"The boy was born laughing—literally." So reads a notable entry in the diary of midwife Frau K, now long deceased, who bore witness to the first unaccompanied breaths of Nathanial Hörnblowér on an early winter morning in Wildhuser Schafberg, the Appenzell, Switzerland, December 1922. The boy's parents, Jan and Gaëlle, were modest third-generation goat herders. "They gave me what I needed: a brutally hard work ethic, a skin as thick as buck leather, and an immunity to pain, both physical and emotional." He was taught well in the family trade and learned the mysteries of milk, cheese, and mutton. But it was Hörnblowér's aunt—Lena Hörnblowér-Klapisch, an actress in the famous Lustig Bühne theatre company, based in Zürich—who awakened the boy to the possibilities of the dramatic arts and a life outside the village. Jan Hörnblowér: "Twice each year, my sister Lena came for *Knabenschiessen*. She would sit with little Nathanial around the *Tafelspitz*-pot and tell him about the latest roles she'd played. Meaning she would recite every line of dialogue from scene one to final curtain. It was agony." For the next six months, Nathanial would re-create the plays. He constructed a stage out of fallen timber and fence joisting. He painted spectacular backdrops on the walls of the milking barn. He stitched and sewed and rehearsed all night. Jan, again: "He was a peculiar, weird, *strange* little shepherd." On Hörnblowér's tenth birthday, Lena arrived at the cabin with a gift: an 11.5mm indirect-sound Leica *Kubbikam*. By the following September, Hörnblowér had written, directed, photographed, and starred in seventy-two short and feature-length *Film-produktions*. The only surviving print among this masterful juvenilia is an adaptation of one of Aunt Lena's greatest stage triumphs: Kiebler's *Those Roaring Americans*. It was invited to premiere at the prestigious Kinoteque Expo in Berlin that spring. Nathanial traded his winter earnings plus a slaughtered goat and three chickens and booked his train fare.

Then came Hitler. It would be a decade before Nathanial shot another foot of film.

The rest, we know. After the war, Hörnblowér would become one of the great voices of the Swiss New Wave. Inventive, prolific, enigmatic. "The most curious thing about Nathanial's pictures," wrote Frau K in a later entry, "whatever the story—comedy, tragedy, thriller—they invariably conclude with exactly the same gesture: the entire cast doubled over in absurd, hysterical, hopeless laughter. As if he knew, from the start, where he must end." Perhaps the midwife knew him best.

—*Jean-Michel Kubelą*

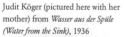

Judit Köger (pictured here with her mother) from *Wasser aus der Spüle (Water from the Sink)*, 1936

Fred Solberg in *Der Einsame Offizier (The Lonely Officer)*, 1950

Hörnblowér's diagram of two yodels crossing (seen in its original form on notebook page below), which William Royce credited for his profound discovery of "the two-hearted mind."

Hörnblowér at Studio 54,
New York City, 1977

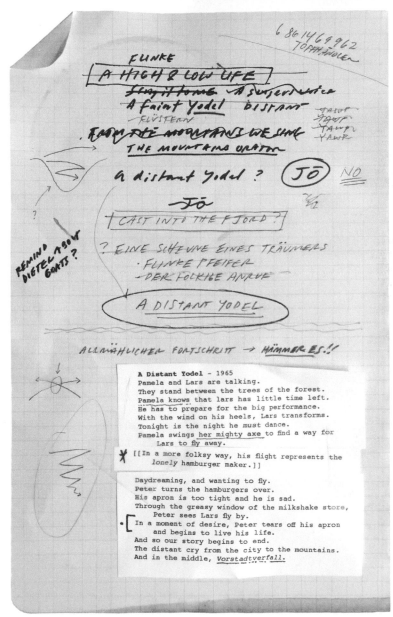

A Distant Yodel - 1965
Pamela and Lars are talking.
They stand between the trees of the forest.
Pamela knows that lars has little time left.
He has to prepare for the big performance.
With the wind on his heels, Lars transforms.
Tonight is the night he *must* dance.
Pamela swings her mighty axe to find a way for
      Lars to fly away.
[[In a more folksy way, his flight represents the
      lonely hamburger maker.]]

Daydreaming, and wanting to fly.
Peter turns the hamburgers over.
His apron is too tight and he is sad.
Through the greasy window of the milkshake store,
      Peter sees Lars fly by.
In a moment of desire, Peter tears off his apron
      and begins to live his life.
And so our story begins to end.
The distant cry from the city to the mountains.
And in the middle, *Vorstadtverfall*.

Nicky Carlotti, *Computer Brain*, 1983

Page from Hörnblowér's notebook, written c. 1964

502

A DISTANT YODEL

Franz Kniffle
The Nimble Whistler, 1962

Jürgen Ürnst
Fast Food, 1970

The following conversation takes place on the set of *A Distant Yodel*—the film that remains most revered among all in the N. H. oeuvre. The picture's young star, Blitzen Bergen, struggling through the eighty-ninth take of the famous extreme close-up of his tearful reunion with the mute lumberjack, cries to his master: "I've done it every which way I can think up! Can't you fix it in the cutting room later? Loop it or something. I'm losing my mind and my voice."

Hörnblowér clears the set, sending the crew off to smoke and mutter among the frozen cedars below. He motions to the boy, who follows him up the ram path to the crest of a frosty butte. He points across the vale to the stone emergency hutch at the peak of Mount Weisselwurst. He says quietly: "You see that emergency hutch up there? For three generations it has stood at the ready for climbers stranded by storm or avalanche. It has never failed them."

Young Bergen nods, interested but drawing a blank.

Hörnblowér continues: "It was built carefully, stone by stone, with unbroken devotion. If a stone fails, the hutch falls—and the climbers all freeze in their sleep and die."

Finally, the boy understands (and so, perhaps, truly begins his long career in Alpine cinema). He says to his master, "Every shot is a stone in the hutch."

The master shakes his head. "Every shot, Blitzen, is the hutch."

Apocryphal? Possibly. Nevertheless, this account perfectly encapsulates Hörnblowér's approach to his lifelong art. I went to visit the unremarkable but symbolic stone emergency hutch one winter afternoon five years ago, along with a group of friends, critics, and academics (all disciples of the maestro, who had died in his sleep one week earlier).

The climb itself was uneventful. The projection equipment had been carried up and installed in advance by a team of Tyrolean sherpas and stage technicians. A light lunch of smoked cheese and pretzels awaited us at the mountain's midpoint. A thunderhead rolled in like a Panzer division at sundown, and we were snowed into the cozy but poorly ventilated structure for the next nine days straight.

We had planned an overnight marathon of the cream of the crop: the best of Hörnblowér's cinema, his six great masterpieces, to be accompanied by a feast of sandwiches, wine, jerky, local beer, dry sausages, schnapps, and good Swiss tobacco.

By the time we emerged after the thaw, we had seen each of the films, projected on a flax-linen sheet stretched end-to-end across the interior of the sturdy building, a minimum of eleven times. One of them, sixteen. Indeed, the last jerky rations ran out three days before we could safely open the hutch hatch. The films themselves became our only sustenance. (It was our good fortune that electrical power to the projector was generated by a stout goat's-lard stove. Goat's lard was the one thing never in short supply that week.) Curiously, the projection was only enhanced by the slow evolution in the color of the flax linen from white to a yellowy beige due to pipe smoke, goat grease, and the stench of human sweat. It was like an igloo in there—an igloo of cinematic art of the highest caliber. In a sense, we felt we had never seen the films before. I can assure you, we will never see them again. But I think it was the most correct and fitting N. H. memorial one could ever have imagined: to see the films continuously, as if they were one.

One hutch.

(And, also, to see them *in* the actual emergency hutch.)

—J-M.K. *in Memoriam*

Blitz Bergen, production still from
A Distant Yodel, 1965

HÖRNBLOWŃ
(ANIMATED AUTOBIOPIC)

Zeitung der Nordostschweiz's infamous illustrator Köelmen Fitz captures Hörnblowér on the set of *Zug Geheimnis (Train Secret)*, 1954 (below, top), and Hörnblowér shooting *Fick diese Brücke (Fuck This Bridge)*, 1978 (below, bottom), for the animated autobiopic *Hörnblown*.

ANSCHNALLEN
(BUCKLE-UP)

Production still:
Anschnallen (Buckle Up), 1988

Swiss legend Nathanial Hörnblowér is back with explosive heat in his new action thriller, *Buckle Up*. His utterly modern take on the romantic spy farce is invigorating. He unnervingly tells us when, where, and how, and we love it. It is simply 90 minutes of pure curiosity.

The first-ever feature film written, shot, edited, mixed, and released all in the same day. And done while aboard an airplane traveling from Switzerland to the United States.

Gertrude Traub in her final Hörnblowér production. She appeared in as many as fifteen of his films in as many as two years. She recieved the prestigious Luxembourg Medaile vu Lëschtegen for her work in *Anschnallen (Buckle Up)*.

2

LUFTHANSA 2804 Zurich to JFK
1440 - 930
— NOEL & FRANCES Brooklyn Heights
MEET w/ Son ADAM ABOUT BAND's
YETI FILM

12:30 - 16:00 SHIATSU

LUFTHANSA 1067 JFK to Zurich
12:25 - 805

+ EYE PILLOW   *CALL*
DIETER
ABOUT
GOATS

3

EEDING

IZMEHUNG
FACHWEFLUTHEE
FADLEBOIZTAVEIE
IMBEILATWERI
9AD U6 ZUCKEBOLLE
SCHLUPFCHAAS

EIN LUTTER ASTRO - SHOOTING SCHEDULE
14, January, 1947

SCENE 2:
Albert wakes up to wreckage - space capsule -
interior/exterior - Day

SCENE 7:
Gruber and DroidBot Ally discuss flight charts -
SPACECRAFT - interior - Day

[LUNCH]

SCENE 5:
Princess Helga records transmission - SPACECRAFT -
interior - Day

SCENE 11:
Albert discovers father's true identity -
space capsule- exterior - night

- - -
NOTES FOR 15, January

SCENE 12:
(Battle scene) Gruber's flight deck - Interior - Day.
Helga, Gruber, Albert, Humanoid-J, Ally, and Dave.

THERE WILL BE NO LUNCH.

HÖRNBLOWÉR FACTS

The video game Pac Man was based on his experimental documentary *Witzige Knochen*.

His 1947 short film *Ein Lutter Astro* was the inspiration for the American film series Star Wars. (Years of litigation led only to an undisclosed but reportedly modest settlement.)

Hörnblowér's nephew performed in the American rap group entitled Beastie Boys. In his retirement, Hörnblowér himself directed several of the band's most memorable music-video pieces.

Hörnblowér has often been cited as the founding father of the "mAke" or "Hacking" movement.

Production still: *Ein Lutter Astro*, 1947

Bestival

(AH)

After *The Mix-Up* record came out we went on tour. It's the usual thing that happens. You make a record, then you go on tour to promote that record. Then after that, you do it all over again. But we'd been doing that usual thing for such a long time that we wanted to make this next traveling adventure different for us. A band on tour spends so much time together at airports, in vans, at restaurants, etc., that you start to feel like a sports team headed to a city to play some other sports team. We always wanted to travel in matching outfits to really give us that team look, but we never took the time to make it happen. So we decided that, finally, something had to be done about this serious issue, and we executed a mandatory *Mix-Up* dress code while we were traveling. No shitty backpacks, down coats, and beanies allowed. Briefcases, old suits, trench coats, and pens in button-down shirt pockets were required. We looked like a group of traveling insurance salesmen from 1966. We wanted the audience at our shows to dress up too. We called the tour the Gala Event, and said that if

you showed up wearing Tevas and cargo shorts, you'd get turned away at the door. Most people just arrived in their normal T-shirts and whatevers and were allowed entry, but it was wonderful to look out into the audience and see a few dichard B-Boys fans dressed for a gala event. We know who you are, and we love you. Thank you for taking this shit as seriously as we do.

But all of this is a nonstory, really. It's more of an explanation.

A backstory to a photograph.

This one here of Mike.

I took this picture of Michael Louis Diamond just after the very last show we ever played in the UK, at the Bestival Festival on the Isle of Wight. The rule of Bestival is that you have to go in costume, so everyone in the audience was dressed up. Bestival was in a big, open field somewhere in the middle of the Isle of Wight. A place you had to take a cool old ferry to get to. The view was spectacular. Like all the great seaside scenes from *Quadrophenia*. The ferry brought us closer and closer to a beautiful open British landscape. It

was a gorgeous sunny day, and it was so refreshing to not have to drive through a sea of miserable punters drenched in rain and mud, like every other UK festival we'd ever played. Instead, we were greeted by the Bestival attendees, who were as sunny as the day was and had put a lot of energy into the costumes they were wearing. They were prepped as fuck. There were, like, twenty Smurfs, a bunch of gnomes and wizards, and pirates. Five dudes dressed like a row of Foosball. Tethered together all day and night, and they were loving it. The unwritten rule was that bands didn't have to wear costumes. But since we were still in *The Mix-Up* dress-code mode . . . we arrived already ready.

Because we were that night's headliner, we could play an encore if the crowd wanted it. We finished our show, went to our designated backstage area, and waited a couple minutes to see if these nice people wanted just a couple more original classic smash hits from the legendary Beastie Boys. And you know what . . . they did. We went back out there onstage but soon noticed that Mike had gone missing. We waited an awkward couple of minutes and then Mike came barreling out onstage in a brand-new special outfit that he had stashed away, just waiting for the proper occasion to break it out. (The one he's wearing in the picture on the opposite page.)

Mike coming back out onstage in this special outfit was like if you went to the movies and your friend went to the bathroom and came back in a Cap'n Crunch suit. It was hilarious and necessary. And in retrospect, the perfect way to exit the country we love, and that loves us back. We've had a rocky relationship, us and England, but true love prevails. *Oi!*

P.S. We were later in a lengthy lawsuit with a beverage company, and this picture of Mike was introduced as evidence. The image was blown up to stand about three feet tall and then it was mounted on cardboard. It was suitable for framing. I'm not sure what their purpose was to have this wonderful photograph brought in as evidence, but to me it was proof that outfits are important, and that on this night . . . Mike fucking nailed it.

OFF THE GRID
GRATITUDE
TIME FOR LIVING
ROOT DOWN
SUPER DISCO BREAKIN'
SURE SHOT
OPEN LETTER TO NYC
TRIPLE TROUBLE
REMOTE CONTROL
ELECTRIC WORM
SHAMBALA
EGG RAID
BRASS MONKEY
PASS THE MIC
SKILLS TO PAY
TIME TO GET ILL
3MC'S
THE MAESTRO
THE GALA EVENT
TOUGH GUY
SABROSA
ALRIGHT HEAR THIS
CHECK IT OUT
NO SLEEP
SHAKE YOUR RUMP
BODY MOVIN
SO WHAT 'CHA WANT
INTERGALACTIC
HEART ATTACK
SABOTAGE

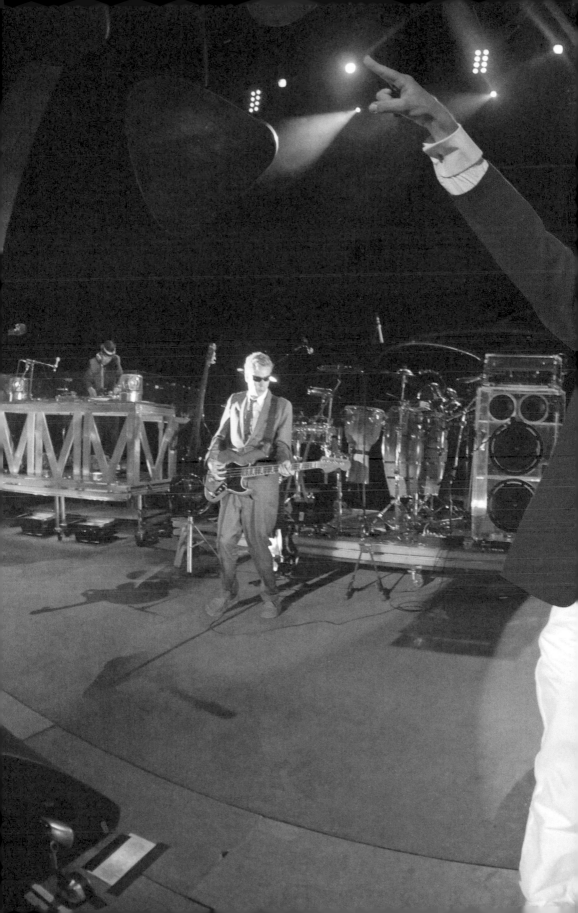

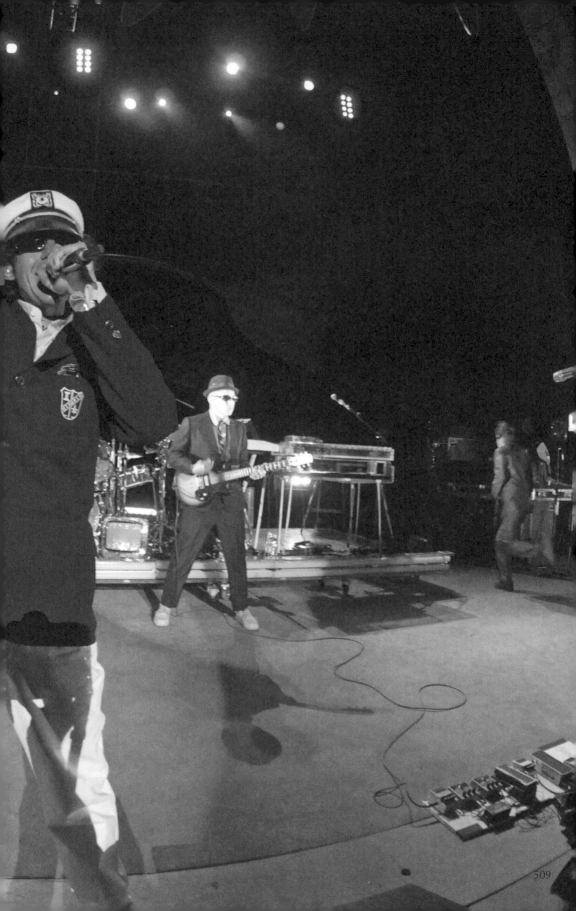

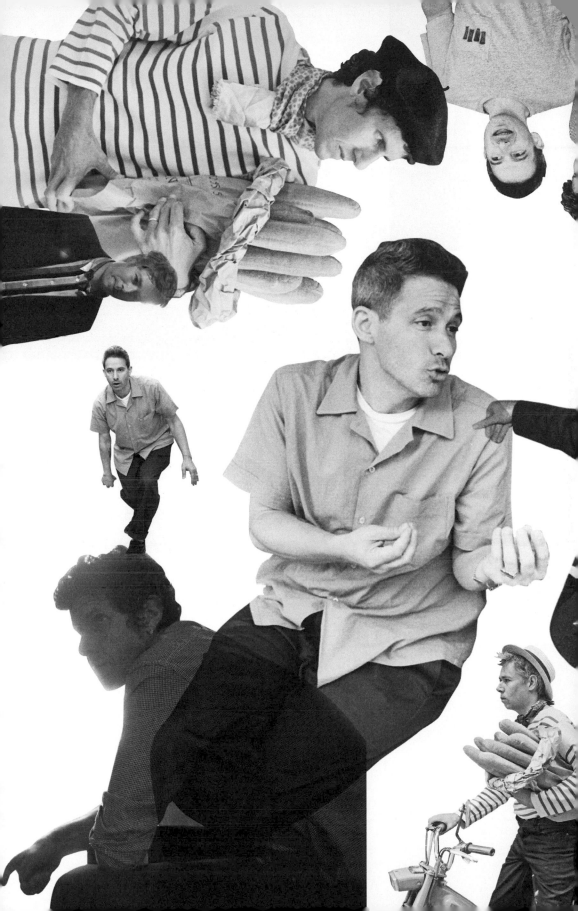

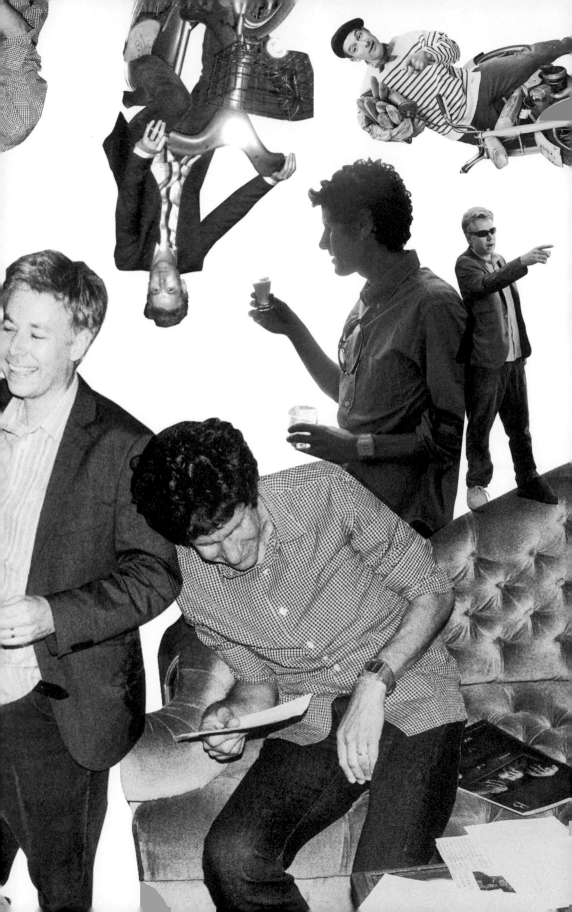

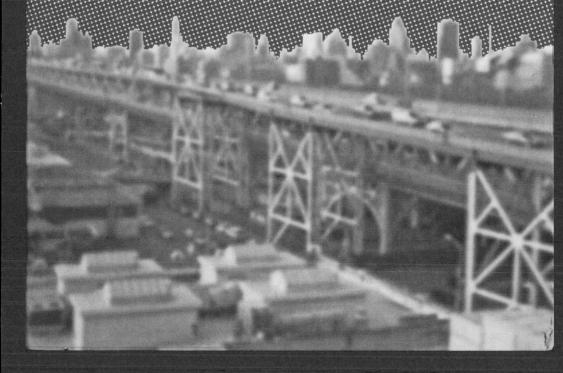

No One Seemed to Notice
(AH)

We had a big idea for the music going into recording our last record, *Hot Sauce Committee Part Two*. Every song would be made of fake samples. It was meant to be a sort of record collector's unattainable nightmare. *Wait, what's that record they sampled? I've never heard of it. How come I don't own that record?* We listed each fake sample in the liner notes on the artwork. Complete with fake song titles, band names, and fictitious record labels. Unfortunately, not only do people not study album art the way they used to, but big ideas are irrelevant in the pop music medium. The song itself will always trump whether it's an interesting idea or not. If there's no big beat to dance to or big chorus to sing along with, who cares? If you're not a hardcore baseball nerd, it doesn't really matter if that last pitch was a curveball or a slider. All you care about is that it struck out the side to eventually win the game. And now you're happy. Or your team lost and so you're sad. Either way, the curveball was insignificant. As a band, we've had both: the songs to get behind and scream with in your car, and the duds that have some cockamamie idea that only we are aware of and think is funny.

Making those fake samples was laborious, though. When you sample a piece of music, you don't just sample the beat or guitar part or vocal thing you want. There are always random, unintentional, and mostly unheard sounds that come with it. Maybe it's the sound of the bass player touching her strings, getting ready to start playing just *after* your sampled bar of music. Or the singer taking a deep breath before he's about to sing. Or the echo, or reverb, from the string section that just finished playing their part, and it's carried over into the little piece you want to sample. You don't notice it until you've looped it and heard it a hundred times. There's almost always some tiny obscure, off-chance sound that's buried in that drumbeat or guitar line you've sampled.

We wanted to experiment with unpremeditated audio. *Create* those slightly unheard sounds. To take imaginary recordings—that we imagined finding on imaginary 45s at imaginary yard sales, bookstores, and record shops— and then put ourselves in the studio with them. We spent days recording Mike's drumming. We'd mix the sound so it'd sound like a sampled beat. And then we'd sample Mike's drumming into one-bar, or half-bar, loops, to really have that chopped-up sample feel. Sometimes we'd quietly add the sounds off of actual old records popping from the needle to really make it feel like it was from an old, beat-up record. Then we'd record some weird vocal or horns or piano just before it, but not during, so you could kind of vaguely hear something else going on. The trail of the sounds that came before. Same went for any bass, guitar, or keyboard parts we recorded. We spent a ton of time making these fake samples and the fictitious musicians that created them to put in the credits, but no one

seemed to notice. Not one person has mentioned it to me. I guess no one ever says to you, "Yo, I heard your new record. Those liner notes are the shit."

We had recorded so much material for this album that we decided to break it up into two different volumes. Parts one and two. They had an elaborate idea behind them about the human ascension from cave dwellings to the Wright brothers' attempt at reaching the stars in Kitty Hawk, North Carolina, and onward past the Mars Rover. Unfortunately there's no interesting story behind why we only released part two. The long and short of it is this: While doing research on travel during the Great Depression for part two, we left the hard drive for part one on a boxcar somewhere outside Missoula, Montana. It's gone; only part two remains.

Getting into the details of what was going on personally with us after the record came out is a heavy thing to write about. It was unintentionally our last record. The band didn't break up. We didn't go our own creative ways. No solo project fucked things up to cause animosity. This was our last record because Adam got cancer and died. If that hadn't happened, we would probably be making a new record as you read this. Sadly, it didn't turn out that way. Sadly. Sadly. Too fucking sad to write about.

When we listened to what we'd recorded, we thought the songs sounded muffled and muddy and needed to be brightened up a bit. Yauch said, "How about if we work with Philippe Zdar?" Horovitz and I were like, *Philippe Z'who? Huh? What does that guy know about what we do?* Yauch (and his daughter, Losel) were obsessed with Phoenix's record *Lisztomania*, which Zdar had mixed. Yauch somehow sold us on seeing what Zdar could do on a few tracks. It turned out Zdar had a hip hop background pre–dance and pop music. But most important, he was really what we needed at the time. Zdar would obsess over every detail of sound. He is a master at gear manipulation. Yauch would join in, literally right beside him, hands on deck and fingers on faders at the legendary Electric Lady Studios on West Eighth Street, where Hendrix used to record. (MD)

This record is one of my favorites because of the writing/recording process. We were all in, together. It felt like 1992, creatively. We were getting deep with audio experimentation. We were on some new shit. Again. Ideas were overflowing. We spent a lot of time making this gift and I hope you enjoy it. But please don't bring up the fake sample credits in the liner notes the next time we see each other, because I'll know that you read this, and that you're just trying to be nice by mentioning it, and let's just not do that, okay? Thanks.

Make Some Noise—This might be my favorite of our songs. I used to think it was "Intergalactic." Or "So What'cha Want." Or maybe even "Gratitude." Hmm . . . I do really like "Right Right Now Now" too. Anyways . . . the thing about "Make Some Noise" is the track. It's kind of like what I wanted our instrumentals to sound like, but maybe never really achieved. Hard-driving funk. Funky like, Whoa. I love that it's us playing and rapping. We didn't really do that too much. Our rap songs had samples, and our playing songs were either instrumentals or had more traditional screaming style vocals ("Sabotage," "Gratitude," etc.). It makes me pretty sad that we never got to play this song live in concert. For a lot of different reasons, but for the most part . . . it would've been really fun to play, and you would've loved it. It would've been a show closer. One that would've sent you out onto the streets like, *What next?*

"Make Some Noise" contains material from "I'm Suped (Got It Like That)" performed by Pump, used under license from Ohio Sounds Records.

"Here's a Little Something for Ya" contains material from "Kein Fleisch" performed by Franz Konkle, used courtesy of Synthetisches Material/EMI Intl.

"Funky Donkey" contains material from "Twin City Hustler" by The Diamels, used under license from Freaky Thangz Records, and "(It's Called) Love Boat" by Pretty Ron and the Love Boat Crew, used under license from Rock Creek Records.

OK—We wanted to make a new wave rap song. That may not be so evident in the end result, but that was the goal going in. We've talked about punk rock and hardcore so much in this book, but I wanna give special acknowledgment to some of my favorite bands ever. Punks that made music that didn't have a traditional punk sound, so they got lumped into this other category called new wave. Devo, Blondie, Elvis Costello, B-52s, Adam and the Ants, and so many more.

Too Many Rappers (New Reactionaries Version) (featuring Nas)—Yauch was a terrible drummer. Worse than me. He oddly would only play this one specific John Bonham–ish beat every time he sat behind the drum kit. In typical Yauch form, he wouldn't do the simple thing. Just play an easy 4/4 pattern: kick, snare, kick, snare. Same with him being an untrained acoustic bass jazz musician or filmmaker. He'd always just swing for the fences. But again, the wonderful thing about sampling music is, you can kind of suck as a drummer but be able to find that one perfect bar to loop. And that's what this song has. He must've felt so satisfied after years of playing that same sloppy off-time beat, to now have it so locked in, sounding just the way he'd wanted it to. And that same thing that drove me+Mike crazy now sounded booming.

We made a basic idea for a track and sent it to Nas to see if he liked it and would possibly record a verse or two over it. Within a week or two, he recorded some vocals and sent it back to us. This never happens with big-timers in the popular music realm. Things take forever, with thirty emails back and forth between managers and publicists, and maybe after three months you'll get a yes, but the thing won't ever actually happen. Nas is a wonderful person, and a true professional. Thank you.

CUT TO: Six months later. We start doing final mixes on all the songs, and Yauch felt like this song wasn't all it could be, and needed something. Unbeknownst to me+Mike, he went into the studio at night, took away all the music that we made, and played his Super Fuzz terminator bass from the beginning to the end of the song. We show up to put the final touches on the song, only to find that the track is completely different. It never occurred to Yauch that it might be a weird thing to do. That maybe his bandmates might get upset that he totally changed the thing that we'd made together. Without consulting us. And that's the gift and curse of being in a band with Adam Yauch. He did a ton of stuff over the years without first checking with me or Mike. It drove us nuts. And it was just as infuriating that he was always right. In the end, the song sounded really good, and it was so satisfying to all three of us that Adam got to go wild on his favorite thing, the Super Fuzz terminator bass, and that his John Bonham dream got fulfilled.

The Bill Harper Collection—This is one of a hundred answering-machine messages from our longtime accountant, Bill Harper. We felt that after so many

"OK" contains material from "Where Art for Thou" performed by Plastic Revolution, used courtesy of Plastic Revolution/Parlophone Records.

"The Bill Harper Collection" contains material from "The Coming of the Triumvirate" from the motion picture soundtrack of *Brutus*, used under license from Dynamic Specialty Products.

"Too Many Rappers" contains material from "Journeys, Oscillations and Other Dreams" performed by Irv Greenwood, used courtesy of Blue Note Records, and material from "Stone Love Lady" performed by Rail, used under special license from Octavious Records.

years of him trying to track us down for mundane answers to mundane questions, we should at least honor him by giving him the weirdest of shout-outs.

Don't Play No Game That I Can't Win (featuring Santigold)—We wanted to make a real-sounding dub/reggae song, and rap over it (a track like "King Tubby Meets Rockers Uptown"). We also loved Santigold's record and were becoming friends with her because we had just played some shows together. *Wouldn't it be amazing to have her sing on this song?* So we asked her, and she said yes. That's basically the whole story to this song, except that Santi wanted Switch to co-produce. We were uncomfortable at first because we like to be in control of these things, but we loved Santi's record, and in turn loved Switch because he produced a bunch of it. Since *Licensed to Ill*, letting go of complete control was difficult for us. But the lyrics that Santi wrote were great, as were Switch's ideas for editing and production, and so there you go. We managed to collaborate on someone else's terms, and made a song that we love.

Long Burn the Fire—When you buy a lot of records looking for samples, there's always a couple that have a great little vocal line with music under it that sound amazing. But often those vocal lines are too odd to base a song around. We wanted to embrace those weirdo samples and made a fake sample from a fake song called "Shallow Water." It was an imaginary tale of the supernatural in the bayous of Louisiana. A line from that fake sample from that fake song went, "Long burn the fire . . . The truth shall set you free." We liked it so much that after we recorded the fake sample, we made a whole song that was the actual fake song from that fake sample. A totally backward way of sampling and songwriting. It was an experiment in experimenting, and it was intensely fucking fun doing it.

The role of the '70s New Orleans crooner Dianne Wentworth was played by my best friend, Nadia Dajani.

Crazy Ass Shit—The thing of audible note on here is Mike's kids. We told the two of them to say "on and on to the break of dawn" and recorded it. They were such adorable children, and now they're knucklehead teenagers who surf and listen to Black Flag all day. (Just like their dad.) I know it's not as cool to them as guesting on a Slayer record when they were four, but I hope that at least one kid in their school thinks it is.

The Lisa Lisa/Full Force Routine—This song is actually from the tail end of *Hot Sauce Committee Pt. 1*. It was meant to be the bridge between the two records. The first half of this song is on a hard drive somewhere. It was in a small maroon-and-purple duffel bag with gray piping on the sides. If you find either of these things, the drive or the bag, please contact me. I really want them back.

"Lee Majors Come Again" contains material from "All Aboard the Rocket Ship" performed by Chip Welson, used under license from For Kids Only/Dynomatic Records.

"Long Burn the Fire" contains material from "Shallow Water" performed by the Supernatural Folk (featuring Dianne Wentworth) used courtesy of BayouTones/Capitol Records.

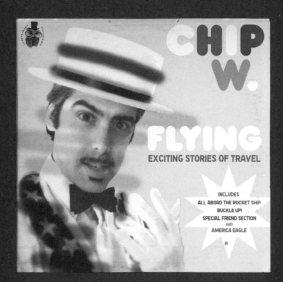

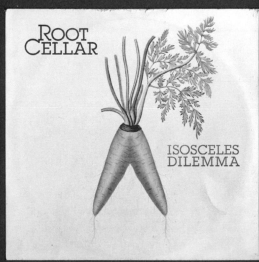

"Crazy Ass Shit" contains material from "Isosceles Dilemma" performed by Root Cellar, used under special license from Buabhaill Records.

"The Lisa Lisa/Full Force Routine" contains material from "Mighty Corporal Winston" performed by the Argonauts, used under license from Tempo Recordings.

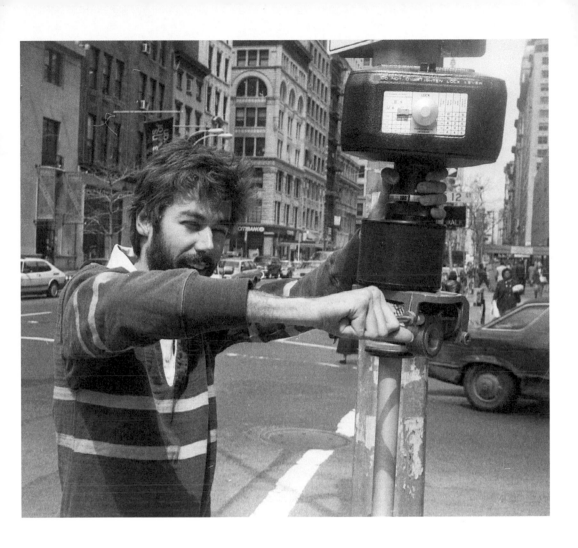

Yauch, Filmmaker
(AH)

What fucking if . . .

Recently I did an interview for a documentary about Spike Jonze. It was about his movies and how they affected people and what it was like to work with him. All that sort of stuff. In the middle of talking about how weird and funny and wonderful Spike is, I unconsciously said something about how easy it would be to be sitting here talking about what a great filmmaker Adam Yauch is. I paused on that and kind of drifted off for a moment. In my mind, I could see a movie montage of the documentary about the film director Adam Yauch. He was accepting awards. Giving charming and inspiring speeches. Film-school teachers were lecturing to students about the career of Adam Yauch. About how he and Spike Jonze and a handful of others changed the way we think about filmmaking. Reimagined the guerilla style. A style that's simultaneously disheveled and frantic, yet introspective and thoughtful. Smart and dumb. A quick cut to an interviewer commenting to Yauch about how amazing it is that he'd created such a diverse body of work, and how he'd finesse his actors into giving performances for the ages. Specifically that most recent film. The one that made you cry and barf and want to drive like a maniac. All made with a seemingly effortless, fun technique. "Hey, you guys, let's make a movie." And then . . . in a flash . . . I was snapped back into the room, talking to a camera about Spike.

I've certainly had these thoughts about Adam plenty of times before, but they all came into focus that day. He had greatness in him. He knew it and so did we.

What fucking if, right?
Damn.

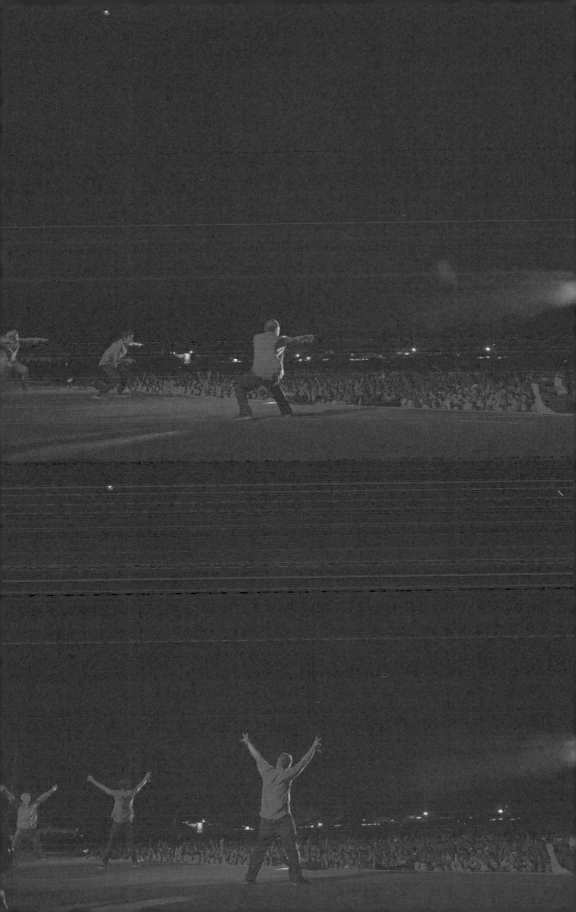

The Last Gig
(AH)

We didn't know it was gonna be the last gig we'd ever play. Everything that happened that day was totally normal. The gig was headlining a huge festival in Tennessee called Bonnaroo. Thousands and thousands of people were gonna be there, and we were the headliner. We went down to Tennessee early, because we were gonna shoot a video for a new song that hadn't come out yet. It was us, the rapper Nas, and Roman Coppola, the director. It was oddly normal for us to play these huge concerts and to have Roman with a Bolex camera filming us and Nas running around a supermarket and on some train tracks, in Tennessee. The weirder, the more normal for us by then.

We'd only met Nas a couple times, so we didn't know if he'd be cool with our style of making videos. Which is basically . . . walk, or drive, around until you see something interesting to stand in front of, or do something stupid in front of. Not all big-time professionals are into the sort of winging-it thing. Nas seemed right at home. Which was great, because we didn't have a plan B. He did seem a little thrown off at first, though, like, *Wait . . . we're literally gonna just walk around this random supermarket and lip-synch the song into the camera? That's it? We don't have to wait around for hours while someone has to move a light or wait for some person to get some other person a Frappuccino? Great! Let's roll.* So that's what we did all morning. We made a video. When we'd finished, we went to the massive field where the festival was happening to hang out and then play our show.

Things in life never come full circle. Maybe once or twice they're hexagonal, but to me they're almost always misshapen, as if drawn by a toddler in crayon. There's common threads, sure. Yauch+me+Mike were still together. Still laughing. Still family. Al Green was finishing his set on one of the many stages at the festival, and so hearing his voice in the distance was comforting. Just like how it was when I was in high school. In my bedroom waiting for my friends to come over. But now was such a great distance from then. The rearview was nearly impossible to reposition. Kate wasn't there with us in Tennessee. Jill Cunniff and Rhana Harris and Tania Aebi. John Berry wasn't there. Dave Scilken, Bosco, the Captain, Dave Parsons, Mike's dad, my mom, and so many more. Not there. Me, Adam+Mike were older and we knew it. Still very much in the game, though, getting ready to start all over again. Headlining a huge festival is very different from a nice turnout at CBGB. But shit, man, we didn't know it was gonna be the last show we'd ever play.

Yauch Mixtape
(MD)

One of the many things I loved about Yauch was that he could really fixate on a song. We all do this to a degree—playing a record over and over again, lifting the needle up, dropping it back down, pressing STOP and REWIND on a cassette. But Yauch would take it exponential: he would listen to a song again and again, memorizing every word, phrase, bass line, and production trick. He just absorbed music in a slightly different way. I think this is why he was technically a better rapper than either Adam or me, and a better musician too. He put the time in. He obsessed in a good way. Here are some songs that would be guaranteed to be on a Yauch mixtape.

Bad Brains Roir tape
Maybe the single record that changed the world for Yauch. (Actually, it was a cassette tape.) It stayed in constant rotation for as long as Yauch sported Bad Brains T-shirts—and that was until the very end, y'all. I think this inspired him to want to be in a band and play bass.

Alternative Ulster—Stiff Little Fingers
When I went to Yauch's house for the first time, this was the very first song he put on. I knew the song already but definitely had not played it as many times as he did. I preferred The Clash, but Stiff Little Fingers was *his* band for sure.

What Do I Get—Buzzcocks
This was on heavy rotation in Yauch's State Street bedroom. I also remember listening to this a lot at our friend Sarah Cox's Crosby Street loft, where we gathered on many a weekend, running around a desolate and deserted SoHo. We all *loved* this song. The hyper, overambitious drums and bass, the vocals, the lyrics, all of it.

Kiss Me Deadly—Generation X
I have a specific memory of sleeping over at Rhana Harris's house in the West Village and all of us young teen punk rock kids waking up in this very cool actual artist's loft, and Yauch playing this corny song over and over.

Public Image (and also **Careering**)—Public Image Ltd.
Yauch played the Public Image bass line hundreds of times. I am sure so many people learning to play bass did the same thing.

Pressure Drop—Toots and the Maytals

From the soundtrack to *The Harder They Come*. We loved this film—one of the all-time great soundtracks *ever*. I remember going to see this and *Rockers* with Yauch at the New Yorker theater on the Upper West Side. These movies lit a fire and made us want to discover reggae.

Fite Dem Back—Linton Kwesi Johnson

"Smash their brains in, 'cause they ain't got nothin' in 'em" became kind of an anti-skinhead anthem for a minute. LKJ inspired us.

Exodus—Bob Marley and the Wailers

Who hasn't listened to Bob Marley 1,000,000 times? If Yauch put this on and saw that you weren't feeling it, this mischievous smile would appear on his face and he would kind of dance over to you and get you excited to hear it again after all.

Spoonin' Rap—Spoonie Gee

The first rap song where Yauch had every word, every inflection, every cadence *down*. Just a few years later, he would perform a verse from this record when we were on the Madonna tour, as we had only three rap songs we could play as a group at that point.

Sucker M.C.'s—Run DMC

The rap song that changed the game for us and everybody. It was a true summertime anthem of a melting-hot, sticky NYC summer during which you would hear the signature drum machine handclaps and Run's "two years ago a friend of mine" bouncing off buildings and flooding avenues with this revolutionary sound. That same summer, Yauch had a Frozade™ cart, and we'd go hang out with him on the street and blast this song out of a transistor radio. Frozade was this supersweet frozen lemonade that kind of blew up for one summer and then just as quickly the carts disappeared. Yauch caught the Frozade wave.

Baby, Let Me Follow You Down—Bob Dylan

When we lived together on Chrystie Street, Yauch co-opted my copy of Bob Dylan's first album and played the shit out of it. Yauch loved this record and would recite the spoken-word intro to this song all the time, mimicking Dylan's voice, sounding like he had a cheek full of tobacco: "I first heard this from Rick Von Schmidt. . . ."

By the Time I Get to Arizona—Public Enemy

Yauch couldn't believe someone other than us had made a rap song over a crazy fuzz bass line. It merged one of his favorite rappers of all time with his favorite instrument of all time: epic fuzz bass. We were also alternately inspired by and jealous of P.E.'s "It Takes a Nation of Millions," which Yauch played on the

boomin' system in his Cadillac Fleetwood Brougham D'elegance, because it made us question whether what we were making was even worthwhile. "Damn, they did it! We will never make something this good."

Freedom—Jimi Hendrix
This could have come at any point in this playlist, because Jimi Hendrix was probably the most influential solo artist for Yauch. He has so many different amazing songs and albums, it's kind of a disservice to pick just one. . . .

Take It Easy—Jackson Browne
Another anomalous cut. I mean, who knew? Yauch? A Jackson Browne fan? Yauch volunteered at the NYC No Nukes concert and it really stuck with him. Just goes to show—speak your mind, organize, you can influence people in untold ways. Yauch listened to this on the LTI tour bus. He also played it on guitar, and it borderline influenced what he wanted to do with his side band, Brooklyn.

Promised Land—Big Fat Love
This was my side band, but Yauch loved BFL more than I ever did. Especially this song. He even recorded this on his own—all sneaky like, just an acoustic guitar, bass, and vocals—in different studios at different times without even telling us.

Slivadiv—Back Door
A G-Son *Check Your Head* era classic that we would listen to on repeat. Yauch would next-level study this jam, bunkered down in his Laurel Canyon log cabin.

The White Album—The Beatles
Of all the Beatles albums, Yauch was most inspired by the innovative and varied production of this one. (Fun fact: for one of Adam Horovitz's teenage birthdays, Yauch gave him every Beatles studio album because he only owned *Rubber Soul* at the time.)

Águas de Março—Antônio Carlos Jobim and Elis Regina
While we were making *Hello Nasty*, we went through a major Brazilian music phase. All types of stuff, traditional to psychedelic. Yauch favored the classics.

Two Words—Kanye West
Yauch would often fixate on non-album cuts. Example A: Yauch really wanted to work with Duro on *To the 5 Boroughs* based on some of the records he mixed for Kanye.

1901—Phoenix
This ultimately led to us working with mixer/producer/esteemed colleague Philippe Zdar.

Honorable mentions

Typical Girls—The Slits
Change—Killing Joke
Fade Away—New Age Steppers
Brand-New-Life—Young Marble Giants
Filler—Minor Threat
Subculture—Cockney Rejects
Genius Rap—Dr. Jeckyll & Mr. Hyde
Freedom—Grandmaster Flash and the Furious Five
I'm Somebody Else's Guy—Frederick "M.C. Count" Linton
Buffalo Gals—Malcolm McLaren
Yo! Bum Rush the Show—Public Enemy
The Well's Gone Dry—The Crusaders
Roc the Mic—Beanie Sigel and Freeway
12:51—The Strokes
When the Sun Goes Down—Arctic Monkeys

ADAM: Adventures of Super Rhyme—Jimmy Spicer • **Africa Must Be Free by 1983**—Hugh Mundell • **Ain't Got Me**—Anti-Pasti • **Ain't No H Steppin'**—Big Daddy Kane • **Al-Naafiysh (The Soul)**—Hashim • **Alien She**—Bikini Kill • **All Your Goodies Are Gone**—The Parliaments • **Alternat Ulster**—Stiff Little Fingers • **Amen, Brother**—The Winstons • **The American in Me**—The Avengers • **Another Nail in My Heart**—Squeeze • **Another C Bites the Dust**—Clint Eastwood & General Saint • **Apache**—Incredible Bongo Band • **Armagideon Time**—Willie Williams • **Around the World**—Daft P • **B-Side Wins Again**—Public Enemy • **Baby I Love You So**—Jacob Miller • **Baby, Let Me Follow You Down**—Bob Dylan • **Baby Let Me Take You My Arms)**—The Detroit Emeralds • **Bam Bam**—Sister Nancy • **Bang! Bang!**—The Joe Cuba Sextet • **Barb Wire**—Nina Soul • **Barbwire**—Nora Dea Barracuda**—Heart • **Basketball Jones**—Cheech and Chong • **Bathroom Sex**—General Echo • **Battery**—Metallica • **Be Black Baby**—Grady Tate • **Be-B A-Lula**—Gene Vincent and His Blue Caps • **Be Thankful for What You Got**—William DeVaughn • **Beat Bop**—Rammellzee and K-Rob • **Because I Go Like That**—Jungle Brothers • **Bela Lugosi's Dead**—Bauhaus • **Bellevue Patient**—Funkmaster Wizard Wiz • **Beware of the Boys (Jay-Z Remix)**—Pan MC • **Big A Little A**—Crass • **Big Yellow Taxi**—Joni Mitchell • **Billie Jean/Mama Used To Say**—Shinehead • **Billy Boyo in the Area**—Billy Boyo • **T Bird**—Jimmy McGriff • **Black Superman (Muhammad Ali)**—Johnny Wakelin and The Kinshasa Band • **Blackberry Jam**—Leroy Hutson • **Blow Y Head**—Fred Wesley & The J.B.'s • **Blue Train**—John Coltrane • **Body Rock**—Treacherous Three • **Bold Soul Sister**—Ike and Tina Turner • **Bon Bon (Gimme the Good Life)**—T. S. Monk • **Boogaloo Down Broadway**—Fantastic Johnny C • **Boogaloo Tramp**—A. C. Reed • **Boogie Nights**—Heatwa Boon Dox**—EPMD • **Boops**—Super Cat • **Bootleggin'**—Simtec & Wylie • **Bouncy**—Sandy Nelson • **Bout It Bout It**—Master P • **Brand New Key**—Mela • **Break Dance—Electric Boogie**—West Street Mob • **The Breakdown**—Rufus Thomas • **Bredda Gravalicious**—Wailing Souls • **Breeze Off**—Lady Bring the Pain**—Method Man • **Bubble Gum**—The 9th Creation • **Buddy Rich tape** • **Buffalo Gals**—Malcolm McLaren • **The Bump**—Alvin Cash and Crawlers • **Burn Rubber on Me (Why You Wanna Hurt Me)**—Gap Band • **Bustin' Loose**—Chuck Brown and the Soul Searchers • **Busy Bee vs. Kool Dee tape** • **By the Time I Get to Arizona**—Public Enemy • **C30 C60 C90 Go! (Spanish Version)**—Bow Wow Wow • **Ça Plane Pour Moi**—Plastic Bertr • **California Über Alles**—Dead Kennedys • **Call Me Animal**—MC5 • **Can You Get to That**—Funkadelic • **Candy Girl**—New Edition • **Caravan**—Theloni Monk • **Cars That Go Boom**—L'Trimm • **Cavern**—Liquid Liquid • **Celestial Blues**—Gary Bartz • **The Champ Is Here**—Jadakiss • **Change**—Killing J • **Check It Out**—Biz Markie • **Check the Rhime**—A Tribe Called Quest • **Checking Out the Checkout Girl**—Wazmo Nariz • **Cherry Bomb**—The Runa • **Chico and the Man**—Jose Feliciano • **The Choice Is Yours**—Black Sheep • **Close to Me**—The Cure • **C'mon N' Ride It (The Train)**—Quad City D Coffee Cold**—Galt MacDermot • **Cold Sweat**—Mongo Santamaria • **Cold World**—GZA • **Come Along**—Lee "Scratch" Perry • **Come and Get It**—Badfi • **Come Around**—Collie Buddz • **Common People**—Pulp • **Computer Love**—Kraftwerk • **Cramp Your Style**—All the People • **Crazy Love**—Van Morri • **C.R.E.A.M.**—Wu-Tang Clan • **Croaking Lizard**—The Upsetters and Prince Jazzbo • **Da' Dip**—Freak Nasty • **Daisy**—Buffalo Daughter • **Dance to Drummer's Beat**—Herman Kelly and Life • **Dancing Shoes**—Arctic Monkeys • **Darkest Light**—Lafayette Afro Rock Band • **Davy Crockett (Gal Hey)**—Thee Headcoatees • **The Day the World Turned Day-Glo**—X-Ray Spex • **Day Tripper**—Sergio Mendes and Brazil '66 • **Dazz**—Brick • **Dead Citie The Exploited • **Decepticon**—Le Tigre • **The Def Fresh Crew**—Roxanne Shanté and Biz Markie • **Definition**—Black Star • **Different Strokes**—G Washington and the Ram Jam Band • **Dirt off Your Shoulder**—Jay-Z • **Dirty Deeds Done Dirt Cheap**—AC/DC • **Dirty Old Town**—The Pogues • **D Baby**—Red Holt • **Do It, Fluid**—The Blackbyrds • **Do It ('Til You're Satisfied)**—B. T. Express • **Do Me**—Jean Knight • **Do the Math**—The PeeChees • **You Believe in the Westworld?**—Theatre of Hate • **Dog Eat Dog**—Adam and the Ants • **Doing It to Death**—The J.B.'s • **The Dominatrix Slee Tonight**—Dominatrix • **Don't Bring Me Down**—Electric Light Orchestra • **Don't Let Me Be Misunderstood**—The Animals • **Don't Stop 'Til You G Enough**—Michael Jackson • **Door Peep Shall Not Enter**—Burning Spear • **Double Dutch Bus**—Frankie Smith • **Down Home Girl**—The Coasters • **T Drag**—Ike and Dee Dee Johnson • **Dukey Stick**—George Duke • **Ears Hard**—Vybrant • **East of the River Nile**—Augustus Pablo • **Easy**—The Commod • **Ego Trippin' (Part Two)**—De La Soul • **El Ratón**—Cheo Feliciano • **El Rey Y Yo**—Los Angeles Negros • **Elevators (Me & You)**—OutKast • **Erase Yo ESG • **Eric B Is President**—Eric B. and Rakim • **E.V.A.**—Jean-Jacques Perrey • **Everybody Loves the Sunshine**—Roy Ayers • **E-Vette's Revenge**—E-V Money • **Expansions**—Lonnie Liston Smith • **Family Affair**—Mary J. Blige • **Far Out**—The Hip Sound • **Fattie Boom Boom**—Ranking Dread • **Fencewal Mandrill • **Fiche le camp, Jack**—Richard Anthony • **54-46 (That's My Number)**—Toots and the Maytals • **52 Girls**—The B-52s • **Fight the Power**— Isley Brothers • **Filler**—Minor Threat • **Fire Fire**—Peter Tosh • **Fite Dem Back**—Linton Kwesi Johnson • **Flash Light**—Parliament • **Flash to the Bea Grandmaster Flash • **Flat Beat**—Mr. Oizo • **Flava in Ya Ear**—Craig Mack • **Flirt**—Cameo • **Float On**—The Floaters • **Flute Thing**—The Blues Proje Flying**—The Beatles • **Folsom Prison Blues**—Johnny Cash • **For Mods Only**—Chico Hamilton • **Fox on the Run**—Sweet • **Freak Out Skank**—The Upset • **Freak-A-Zoid**—Midnight Star • **Freaks for the Festival**—Rahsaan Roland Kirk • **Free Soul Live**—John Klemmer • **Free Your Mind**—The Politicia Freedom**—Jimi Hendrix • **Fried Neck Bones and Some Home Fries**—Willie Bobo • **Friends**—Whodini • **Fug**—Cymande • **F.U.N.K.**—Betty Davis • **Fun for Jamaica**—Tom Browne • **Funky Broadway**—Dyke & the Blazers • **Funky Penguin**—Hap Palmer • **Funky Robot**—Dave "Baby" Cortez • **Future Shoc Curtis Mayfield • **Galang**—M.I.A. • **Gangbusters**—DJ Grand Wizard Theodore • **Gangster Boogie**—Chicago Gangsters • **Gangsters**—The Specials • **Ger of Love**—Tom Tom Club • **Get Me Back on Time, Engine Number 9**—Wilson Pickett • **Get Stupid Fresh**—Mantronix • **Get the Funk Out Ma Face**— Brothers Johnson • **The Ghetto**—Donny Hathaway • **Gimmie Gimmie Gimmie**—Black Flag • **Gin and Juice**—Snoop Doggy Dogg • **Give It Up or Tu Loose**—Dick Hyman • **Good Times**—Chic • **Got My Boogaloo**—Jackie Mittoo & the Soul Brothers • **Got to Get a Knutt**—The New Birth • **Got to Le How to Dance**—The Fatback Band • **Governor General**—Pampidoo • **Grazing in the Grass**—Hugh Masekela • **Greedy G**—Brentford Rocker • **Gre Onions**—Booker T and the MGs • **Groove to the Beat**—Keith + Ken • **Groovin'**—Willie Mitchell • **Gucci Time**—Schoolly D • **The Guns of Brixton**— Clash • **Guns of Navarone**—Roland Alphonso & the Skatalites • **Gwarn**—Mad Professor & Pato Banton • **Ha Ha Ha**—Flipper • **Halleluwah**—Can • **Hand the Pump**—Cypress Hill • **Happy Birthday**—Curtis Knight • **Hard Times**—Baby Huey & the Babysitters • **Hard to Explain**—The Strokes • **Harlem R Drive**—Bobbi Humphrey • **Heartbeat**—Taana Gardner • **Heaven**—The Psychedelic Furs • **Heaven at Once**—Kool & The Gang • **Hey DJ**—World's Fam Supreme Team • **Hey! Love**—The Delfonics • **Hey There Lonely Girl**—Eddie Holman • **Hihache**—Lafayette Afro Rock Band • **Hip Drop**—The Explosic Hippie Hippie Hourrah**—Jacques Dutronc • **Hippy, Skippy, Moon Strut**—The Moon People • **Hold You**—Gyptian • **Holy Ghost**—The Bar-Kays • **H and Sling**—Eddie Bo • **Hospital**—The Modern Lovers • **Hot (I Need To Be Loved, Loved, Loved)**—James Brown • **Hot Pastrami (with Mas Potatoes)**—Joey Dee and the Starliters • **House of Rising Funk**—Afrique • **Howlin' for Judy**—Jeremy Steig • **The Humpty Dance**—Digital Undergrou Hurry on Now**—Alice Russell • **Hush**—Deep Purple • **The Hustle**—Van McCoy • **Hyperballad**—Björk • **Hyperbolicsyllabicsesquedalymistic**— Hayes • **I Am a Poseur**—X-Ray Spex • **I Can't Explain**—The Who • **I Can't Get Next To You**—The Temptations • **I Can't Stand the Rain**—Ann Peeb I Drink Milk**—The Teen Idles • **I Feel Love**—Donna Summer • **I Feel the Earth Move**—Carole King • **I Know But I Don't Know**—Blondie • **I Still Live My Moms**—Thirstin Howl III • **I Walk on Guilded Splinters**—Dr. John • **I Wanna Be a Lifeguard**—Blotto • **I'll Be Your Mirror**—The Velvet Undergro and Nico • **I'll Take You There**—The Staple Singers • **I'm Chief Kamanawanalea (We're the Royal Macadamia Nuts)**—The Turtles • **I'm Gonna L You Just a Little More, Baby**—Barry White • **I'm Not in Love**—10cc • **Ice Cream**—Raekwon • **Impeach the President**—The Honey Drippers • **In Jungle**—The Messengers • **Inside Straight**—Cannonball Adderley • **It's a New Day**—Skull Snaps • **It's About Time**—Tanya Stephens • **It's Just Begu The Jimmy Castor Bunch • **It's My Thing**—Marva Whitney • **It's Your Rock**—Fantasy Three • **It's Your Thing**—Cold Grits • **It's Yours**—T La Rock • **Jac Blue**—The Ozark Mountain Daredevils • **Jah War**—The Bug (featuring Flowdan) • **Jane Says**—Jane's Addiction • **Jazzy Sensation**—Af Bambaataa and the Jazzy Five • **Je T'aime . . . Moi Non Plus**—Jane Birkin et Serge Gainsbourg • **Jealousy**—Tony Allen & Afrika 70 • **Jeeps, Lex Cou Bimaz & Benz**—Lost Boyz • **The Jerk**—The Larks • **Johnny Thunder**—The Kinks • **Jolene**—Dolly Parton • **The Jungle Is a Skyscraper**—Orn Coleman • **Just Dropped In (To See What Condition My Condition Was In)**—Kenny Rogers and the First Edition • **Just Kissed My Baby**—The Me • **Keep on Truckin'**—Eddie Kendricks • **Killer Queen**—Queen • **Kingston Hot**—Beenie Man • **Kiss Me Deadly**—Generation X • **Knockin Da Boots**— Town • **Kuff**—Shelly Thunder • **La Machine á Rêver**—X Ray Pop • **Laisse tomber les filles**—France Gall • **Lasso**—Phoenix • **Last Night Change

—Esther Williams • Le vaudou—Telephone • Lean Back—Terror Squad • Les Fleur—Minnie Riperton • Lesson 2 (James Brown Mix)—Double Dee
Steinski • Let Me Take Your Photo—The Speedies • Let the Music Play—Shannon • Let Your Lovelight Shine—Buddy Miles Express • Let's Get
all—Trouble Funk • Let's Go—The Cars • Let's Stay Together—Claude Denjean • Lexicon Devil—The Germs • Life from a Window—The Jam • Light
Fire—Astrud Gilberto • Light My Fire—Erma Franklin • Like Glue—Sean Paul • Linus and Lucy—Vince Guaraldi Trio • Lions Paw—Rogue State
uid Swords—GZA • Live at City Gardens—Venom • Live at the Funhouse—Run-DMC • Longshot Kick de Bucket—The Pioneers • The Look of
e—The Electronic Concept Orchestra • Look Sharp!—Joe Jackson • Loose Booty—Willie Henderson • Loran's Dance—Idris Muhammad • Lost Love
le Joey and the Flips • Lost Ones—Lauryn Hill • Loud Fast Rules!—The Stimulators • Love Comes In Spurts—Richard Hell and the Voidoids • Love Is
Drug—Roxy Music • (Love Like) Anthrax—Gang of Four • Love Ritual—Al Green • Love T.K.O.—Teddy Pendergrass • Love Will Tear Us Apart—Joy
ision • Lovefingers—Silver Apples • Lovely Is Today—Eddie Harris • Love's Theme—Love Unlimited Orchestra • Lowdown—Boz Scaggs • Magic—Pilot
ake It N.Y.—Max Tannone • Man in the Street—Don Drummond and the Skatalites • Man Pon Moon—Derrick Morgan • Manteca—Dizzy Gillespie
ry Wanna—The Lat-Teens • Mashed Potato Time—Dee Dee Sharp • Mass Appeal—Gang Starr • Maybe Your Baby—Stevie Wonder • Me and My
ow—Harry Nilsson • Memphis Soul Stew—King Curtis • Message from the Soul Sisters—Vicki Anderson • Metal—Gary Numan • Mighty Mighty—
e Anderson • Mind Playing Tricks on Me—Geto Boys • Mind Your Own Business—Delta 5 • Mira Ven Aca—Johnny Colon • Misdemeanor—Foster
ers • Mister Magic—Grover Washington Jr. • Momma's Boy—Chromeo • Money Changes Everything—Cyndi Lauper • Money, Money—Reverend
oo • Mongoloid—Devo • Mongoose—Elephant's Memory • Monte Carlo—The French Connection • More Bounce to the Ounce—Zapp • Moshitup—
-Ice • The Most Beautifullest Thing in This World—Keith Murray • Move Your Hand—Lonnie Smith • Mr. Blah Blah—Ray Barretto • Mr. Brown—Bob
rley & the Wailers • Mr. Jaws—Dickie Goodman • My Boy Lollipop—Millie Small • My Mic Sounds Nice—Salt-N-Pepa • My Neck, My Back—Khia •
Opinion—Pato Banton and Mad Professor • My Perfect Cousin—The Undertones • Negative Creep—Nirvana • Never Get Enough—Bobby Byrd •
w Aryans—Reagan Youth • New Bell—Manu Dibango • New Dance Craze—Five Stairsteps and Cubie • New Rose—The Damned • Nic Fit—The
ouchables • Nights X 9—Slant 6 • Nika—Vicious • The 900 Number—The 45 King • 96 Tears—? and the Mysterians • The Nitty Gritty—Gladys Knight
The Pips • No Diggity—Blackstreet • No Feelings—Sex Pistols • No Heathen (Ghetto Plazma Mix)—Com.a/Wicked Act • No Matter What Shape
ur Stomach's In)—The T-Bones • (Nothing Serious) Just Buggin'—Whistle • Now I Wanna Sniff Some Glue—The Ramones • Nuh Dis Me—Lady
• O Pato—João Gilberto • The Odd Couple—Al Hirt • Oh Honey—Delegation • Oh Shit!—Buzzcocks • On My Radio—The Selecter • On the Radio—
sh Crew • One Draw—Rita Marley • 101—The Mob • One Teenager to Another—Brenda Lee • Only Good for Conversation—Rodriguez • The Only
ng Boy in New York—Simon & Garfunkel • The Oogum Boogum Song—Brenton Wood • Ooh Ooh the Dragon—Marvin Holmes & the Uptights •
en Your Box—Yoko Ono • Opening Titles (Miller's Crossing)—Carter Burwell • Organ Donor—DJ Shadow • Organ Donor—Lefties Soul Connection
ut in the Streets—The Shangri-Las • Out of Focus—Blue Cheer • Out on the Tiles—Led Zeppelin • Over the Top—Motörhead • Panis et Circenses—
Mutantes • Paranoid—Black Sabbath • Paranoid—Hugo Strasser und Sein Tanzorchester • Pay Yo Dues—Jacki-O • Peg—Steely Dan • Person to
son—Average White Band • Planet Rock—Afrikaa Bambaataa and Soul Sonic Force • Plantagenet—Back Door • Players Ballin'—Ohio Players • Poison—
. Biv DeVoe • Pon De Floor—Major Lazer • Popcorn—Hot Butter • Poptones—Public Image Ltd. • Prison Oval Rock—Barrington Levy • Psycho
er—Talking Heads • Psychotic Reaction—Count Five • Public Jestering—Judge Winchester • Pull Up to the Bumper—Grace Jones • Punk Rock
•—The Cold Crush Brothers • The Rainmaker—The 5th Dimension • Rappin' Duke—Shawn Brown aka the Rappin' Duke • Reach Out of the Darkness—
nd & Lover • Red Clay—Freddie Hubbard • Red Onion—Richard "Groove" Holmes • Red Tape—Circle Jerks • The Regulator—Bad Brains • Represent—
• Return to the Underground—White Lightnin' • Reuters—Wire • The Revolution Will Not Be Televised—Gil Scott-Heron • Ring the Alarm—
or Saw • Riot Music—Donae'o • Rock Steady—Aretha Franklin • Rocket in the Pocket (Live)—Cerrone • Rocket Man—Elton John • Rockin' It—
rless Four • Roman Soldiers of Babylon—Freddie McGregor • Root Down (and Get It)—Jimmy Smith • Roxanne's Revenge—Roxanne Shanté •
xanne Roxanne—UTFO • Rudy, a Message to You—Dandy Livingstone • Ruff Ryders' Anthem—DMX • Rumours—Gregory Isaacs • Rump
aker—Wreckx-N-Effect • Run the World (Girls)—Beyoncé • Samba de Amor—Yusef Lateef • Sara Smile—Hall and Oates • Sardines—The Junkyard
d • Satellite of Love—Lou Reed • Satta Massagana—The Abyssinians • Scenario (Remix)—A Tribe Called Quest (featuring Leaders of the New School) •
orpio—Dennis Coffey and the Detroit Guitar Band • Searching for Soul—Jake Wade and the Soul Searchers • Seasons in the Sun—Terry Jacks • Set
ff—Strafe • Sexy Coffee Pot—Tony Alvon & the Belairs • Shack Up—A Certain Ratio • Sharevari—A Number of Names • Shattered—The Rolling
nes • She's a Bad Mama Jama—Carl Carlton • Shock Me—Kiss • Shoot You Down—APB • Show and Tell—Al Wilson • Sittin' on Chrome—Masta
Inc. • 6 AM Jullandar Shere—Cornershop • Skinny Papa—Willie Colón • Skull Session—Oliver Nelson • Skylarking—Horace Andy • Slip-in Mules—
ar Pie DeSanto • Slippin' Into Darkness—War • Smilin' Billy Suite—The Heath Brothers • Smokin' Cheeba Cheeba—Harlem Underground Band •
urf Across the Surf—The Micronawts • So Hungry, So Angry—Medium Medium + • So into You—Atlanta Rhythm Section • Sol's Glasses—The
y Boys • Soldier Soldier—Spizzenergi • Somethin' Else—Eddie Cochran • Sonic Reducer—The Dead Boys • Soul Clappin'—Pretty Purdie • Soul Heart
nsplant—Ebony Rhythm Band • Soul Love—David Bowie • Soul Popcorn—Doc Oliver • Soul Sauce (Guachi Guaro)—Cal Tjader • Soul Struttin'—1910
tgum Company • Sound of da Police—KRS-One • Spoonin' Rap—Spoonie Gee • Stand for Something—Professor and the Efficiency Experts • Stanga—
le Sister • Stick 'Em—Fat Boys • Stoop Rap—Double Trouble • Stories—The Chakachas • Straight Up and Down—Eric Dolphy • Strange Ones—
ergrass • Strawberry Letter 23—Shuggie Otis • Strychnine—The Sonics • Stutter—Elastica • Summer in the City—Quincy Jones • Supersonic—J. J.
• Sweet Pea—Tommy Roe • Sweet Shop—Doctor P • Sweetie Pie—Stone Alliance • Synthetic Substitution—Melvin Bliss • T Plays It Cool—Marvin
e • Tainted Love—Soft Cell • Take Five—The Dave Brubeck Quartet • Take Me to the Mardi Gras—Bob James • Take the Money and Run—The Steve
ler Band • Tea for the Tillerman—Cat Stevens • Tell Me Something Good—Rufus and Chaka Khan • Tempo—Anthony Red Rose • Temptation—New
er • 10 Crack Commandments—The Notorious B.I.G. • The Tender Trap—Leroy Randolph • Thankful n' Thoughtful—Sly & the Family Stone • That's
Joint—Funky Four Plus One More • That's the Way of the World—Earth, Wind & Fire • They Punctured My Yolk—The Flaming Lips • They
miniesce Over You (T.R.O.Y.)—Pete Rock and CL Smooth • Tighten Up—Archie Bell & the Drells • Time to Flow—D-Nice • Too Many Creeps—Bush
ras • Top Billin'—Audio Two • Totally Wired—The Fall • Tous les garçons et les filles—Françoise Hardy • The Traffic Jam—Stephen Marley • Tramp—
Redding and Carla Thomas • Trash—New York Dolls • (Turn on Your) Love Light—The High Spirits • T.V. Eye—The Stooges • 21 Questions (Featuring
e Dogg)—50 Cent • 2-4-6-8—The Jackson 5 • Two Pints of Lager and a Packet of Crisps Please—Splodgenessabounds • Two Sevens Clash—Culture
pical Girls—The Slits • U.N.I.T.Y.—Queen Latifah • Uh! Oh!—The Nutty Squirrels • Uhuru—Ramsey Lewis Trio • Under Me Sleng Teng—Wayne Smith
nhooked Generation—Freda Payne • Up in the Air—Kasenetz-Katz Super Circus • Up on Cripple Creek—The Band • Uptown Top Ranking—Althea
Donna • Use Me (Live)—Bill Withers • V.G.I.—Julie Ruin • Wa-Do-Dem—Eek-A-Mouse • Waiting Room—Fugazi • Watching the Detectives—Elvis
tello • Watermelon Man—Herbie Hancock and the Headhunters • Way Back Home—Jazz Crusaders • Weed and Grabba—King Baucho and Beenie Man
lcome to Jamrock—Damian Marley • Welfare City—Eugene McDaniels • Wet Look Crazy—Macka B • What About You (In the World Today)—
Real Artists • What Is Hip?—Tower of Power • Whatcha See Is Whatcha Get—The Dramatics • Wheely Wheely—Early B (The Doctor) •
ere Eagles Dare—The Misfits • The Whip—Billy "The Kid" Emerson • Who Got The Props—Black Moon • Who Has the Last Laugh Now—Bloodstone
ho's the Boss—Antoinette • Why Can't We Live Together—Timmy Thomas • Wide Open—LeShaun • Witch Hunt—Frog • Wolf in Sheep's
thing—Big Youth • Won't Tell—Babes in Toyland • Work It—Missy Elliott • Wu Banga 101—Ghostface Killah • Wut—Girl Unit • X'mas Weather—
dent Teachers • You Are the One for Me—Charles Wright & the Watts 103rd Street Rhythm Band • You Don't Mess Around With Jim—Jim Croce •
 Don't Love Me (No, No, No)—Dawn Penn • You Don't Own Me—Lesley Gore • You'll Find a Way (Switch + Sinden Remix)—Santigold • You're
 Great—Blur • You Sexy Thing—Hot Chocolate • The Young Mods' Forgotten Story—The Impressions • 007 (Shanty Town)—Desmond Dekker

MIKE: A Minha Menina—Os Mutantes • **Africa Must Be Free by 1983**—Hugh Mundell • **Aht Uh Hed**—Shuggie Otis • **Ain't No Half Steppin'**—Big Daddy Kane • **Ain't No Sunshine**—Harlem Undergrou Band • **Ain't You**—Kleenex • **Al-Naafiysh (The Soul)**—Hashim • **Allah Wakbarr**—Ofo The Black Compa • **All I Need**—Radiohead • **Always Let U Down**—Blood Orange • **Answers Me**—Arthur Russell • **At All** Kaytranada • **At Last I Am Free**—Robert Wyatt • **Baby**—Gal Costa + Caetano Veloso • **Back That A Up**—Juvenile with Mannie Fresh and Lil' Wayne • **Ballad of a Thin Man**—Bob Dylan • **The Ballad of Dorot Parker**—Prince • **Bam Bam**—Sister Nancy • **Battery**—Metallica • **Beautiful**—Snoop Dogg • **Beware Darkness**—George Harrison • **The Bewlay Brothers**—David Bowie • **Beyond This World**—Jungle Broth • **Big Pimpin'**—Jay-Z • **Big Take Over**—Bad Brains • **Billy Jack**—Curtis Mayfield • **Black Beatles**—R Sremmurd • **Black Satin**—Miles Davis • **Bling Bling**—B.G. • **Blue Train**—John Coltrane • **Blu Connotation**—Ornette Coleman • **Boneman Connection**—Nicodemus • **Bongo Rock '73**—Incredi Bongo Band • **Bonnie and Clyde**—Serge Gainsbourg & Brigitte Bardot • **Boops**—Super Cat • **Booty Clap** DJ Funk • **Bra**—Cymande • **Bring Em Out**—T.I. • **Bring the Pain**—Method Man • **Brooklyn Zoo**—Ol' Di Bastard • **Buddy Bye**—Johnny Osbourne • **Buffalo Gals**—Malcolm McLaren • **Bushweed Corntrash**—L Perry & the Upsetters • **Buzz Saw**—The Turtles • **C30 C60 C90 Go!**—Bow Wow Wow • **Ça Plane Po Moi**—Plastic Bertrand • **Cappuccino**—MC Lyte • **Change**—Killing Joke • **A Change Is Gonna Come** Sam Cooke • **Childhood's End**—Pink Floyd • **Children's Story**—Slick Rick • **Citgo**—Chief Keef • **Co World**—GZA • **Colomb**—Nicolas Jaar • **Computer Love**—Kraftwerk • **Contort Yourself (Augu Darnell Remlx)**—James White & the Blacks • **Corn Fish Dub**—Lee Perry & the Upsetters • **Crank Dat (I Godfather Detroit Ghetto Tek Mix)**—DJ Godfather • **C.R.E.A.M.**—Wu-Tang Clan • **Creator**—Santigol **Crosstown Traffic**—Jimi Hendrix • **Dancing Is the Best Revenge**—!!! (Chk Chk Chk) • **Dangerous** Conroy Smith • **Darkest Light**—Lafayette Afro Rock Band • **Davy Crockett (Gabba Hey)**—Thee Headcoat • **A Day in the Life**—Wes Montgomery • **Death Disco**—Public Image Ltd. • **Deceptacon**—Le Tigre • **Didn't Darondo • **Diseases**—Papa Michigan & General Smiley • **Disorder**—Joy Division • **DNA**—Kendrick Lama **Don't Let It Bring You Down**—Neil Young • **Doo Wop (That Thing)**—Lauryn Hill • **Dopeman**—N.W • **Dougou Badia**—Amadou & Mariam • **Dreamland**—Marcia Griffiths • **Dreamland Version**—U-Roy • **E Trippin'**—De La Soul • **Electric Frog**—Kool & the Gang • **E-Musik**—Neu! • **Everybody Loves t Sunshine**—Roy Ayers • **Fama Allah**—Idrissa Soumaoro Et L'eclipse de L'I.J.A. • **Feel So Good**—Mas **Fingerprint File**—The Rolling Stones • **First Time Around**—Skyy • **Fisherman**—The Congos • **Fite De Back**—Linton Kwesi Johnson • **Fly Like an Eagle**—The Steve Miller Band • **400 Years**—Bob Marley & Wailers • **Free (Diplo Remix)**—Cat Power • **Free Man in Paris**—Joni Mitchell • **Fusion Beats Vol Future**—Kevin Saunderson • **Galang**—M.I.A. • **Gangsters**—The Specials • **General Penitentiary**—Bl Uhuru • **Genius of Love**—Tom Tom Club • **Get Ur Freak On**—Missy Elliott • **The Ghost (Marc Garvey)**—Burning Spear • **Ghost Rider**—Suicide • **Girls and Boys**—Blur • **Give It Up**—Lee Dorsey • **Goi Back to My Roots**—Lamont Dozier • **Going Underground**—The Jam • **Good Name**—William Onyeal • **Govinda**—The Radha Krishna Temple • **Grindin'**—Clipse • **The Grunt**—The J.B.'s • **Greetings**—Half P • **Gucci Time**—Schoolly D • **Halleluwah**—Can • **Hanging on the Telephone**—Blondie • **Heart**—Darks • **Heartbeat**—Taana Gardner • **Heaven and Hell Is on Earth**—20th Century Steel Band • **Here**—Paveme • **Here I Come**—Barrington Levy • **Hero Worship**—The B-52s • **Hey Ma**—Cam'ron • **Hold the Line**—Ma Lazer • **Holidays in the Sun**—Sex Pistols • **Holy Thursday**—David Axelrod • **Horror Business**—The Mis • **Hot Pants**—James Brown • **How Deep Is Your Love?**—The Rapture • **How I Could Just Kill A Man** Cypress Hill • **How Soon Is Now?**—The Smiths • **Hyperbolicsyllabicsesquedalymistic**—Isaac Hayes **Can See Clearly Now**—Johnny Nash • **I Got The**—Labi Siffre • **I Heard It Through the Grapevine**—T Slits • **I <3 U So**—Cassius • **I Shall Be Released**—The Band • **I Walk on Guilded Splinters**—Dr. John **Wanna) Testify**—The Parliaments • **Ice Cream**—Raekwon • **Identity**—X-Ray Spex • **I'd Rather Go Blind** Etta James • **I'll Bet You**—The Jackson 5 • **I'm Coming Out**—Diana Ross • **(I'm) Stranded**—The Saints • **I Your Puppet**—James & Bobby Purify • **Impeach the President**—The Honey Drippers • **Impregnab Question**—Dirty Projectors • **Is It All Over My Face?**—Loose Joints • **Ital Corner**—Prince Jazzbo • **Itch a Scratch**—Rufus Thomas • **It's Just Begun**—The Jimmy Castor Bunch • **It's Your Rock**—Fantasy Thre **James Brown Ride On**—Orlando Julius & His Afro Sounders • **Johnny Thunder**—The Kink

ene—Dolly Parton • **Journey in Satchidananda**—Alice Coltrane • **Judy Is a Punk**—The Ramones •
cy Fruit—Mtume • **Just Kissed My Baby**—The Meters • **Justice Tonight/ Kick It Over**—The Clash •
g Tubby Meets Rockers Uptown—Augustus Pablo and King Tubby • **Kissing My Love**—Bill Withers •
now You—A.A.L. (Against All Logic) • **La Di Da Di**—Doug E. Fresh and MC Ricky D • **La Vie en rose**—
uis Armstrong • **Lavender**—BadBadNotGood • **Lazy Bones**—Witch • **Let's Do It Again**—The Staple
gers • **Life Is Strange**—T Rex • **Live at the Barbeque**—Main Source • **Live Forever**—Oasis • **Loose**
e Stooges • **Love Child**—Diana Ross & the Supremes • **Love Like a Sunset Part 1**—Phoenix • **Love Ritual**
wana Mix)—Al Green • **Love to Love You Baby**—Donna Summer • **Lovefingers**—Silver Apples • **Maiden**
yage—Herbie Hancock • **Malukayi**—Mbongwana Star (feat Komono No1) • **Marijuana**—Richie Spice •
rquee Moon—Television • **Maybe Your Baby**—Stevie Wonder • **Messiah Garvey (extended)**—Big
th • **Mind Your Own Business**—Delta 5 • **Minor Threat**—Minor Threat • **Misdemeanor**—Foster Sylvers
oney, Money—Horace Andy • **Mongoloid (45 version)**—Devo • **Moody**—ESG • **More Bounce to the**
nce—Zapp • **Mother**—John Lennon • **Mother and Child Reunion**—Paul Simon • **Murder She Wrote**—
aka Demus & Pliers • **My Jamaican Guy**—Grace Jones • **My Melody**—Eric B and Rakim • **Mystery of**
ve—Mr. Fingers • **Neat Neat Neat**—The Damned • **Needle in the Hay**—Elliott Smith • **The New Rap**
nguage—Spoonie Gee & the Treacherous Three • **The Next Episode**—Dr. Dre • **N**as in Paris**—Jay-Z
Kanye West • **Night and Day**—Toots & the Maytals • **93 'til Infinity**—Souls of Mischief • **No Diggity**—
ckstreet • **No Problem**—Chance the Rapper • **Norf Norf**—Vince Staples • **Not Great Men**—Gang of Four
othin'—N.O.R.E. • **Now's the Time**—Charlie Parker Quartet • **Numbers on the Boards**—Pusha T •
. State of Mind—Nas • **O-o-h Child**—The Five Stairsteps • **Optimo**—Liquid Liquid • **Pablo Picasso**—
e Modern Lovers • **Pale Blue Eyes**—The Velvet Underground • **Pink Moon**—Nick Drake • **Ponta**
Lança Africano (Umbabarauma)—Jorge Ben • **Pump It Up**—Elvis Costello & The Attractions • **Put**
ur Hands Where My Eyes Could See—Busta Rhymes • **Rebel Girl**—Bikini Kill • **Rebel Without a**
use—Public Enemy • **Reclamation**—Fugazi • **Red Tape**—Circle Jerks • **Ring the Alarm**—Tenor Saw •
c the Mic—Beanie Sigel and Freeway • **Ruff Ryders' Anthem**—DMX • **Rumours**—Gregory Isaacs •
naway—Kanye West • **Runnin' (Dying To Live)**—Tupac & The Notorious B.I.G. • **Satta Massagana**—
ce Buster • **Save Me**—Aretha Franklin • **Scenario**—A Tribe Called Quest • **Scorpio**—Dennis Coffey and
Detroit Guitar Band • **Shangaan Shake**—Tshetsha Boys • **She Don't Use Jelly**—The Flaming Lips •
uation—Yaz • **6 AM Jullandar Shere**—Cornershop • **6 Foot 7 Foot**—Lil Wayne • **Skin I'm In**—Sly &
Family Stone • **Sleeping Beauty**—Sun Ra and His Intergalactic Myth Science Solar Arkestra • **Slippery**
ple—Talking Heads • **Slow Down**—Brand Nubian • **Snowblind**—Black Sabbath • **Someone Great**—
D Soundsystem • **Something About Us**—Daft Punk • **Sonic Reducer**—The Dead Boys • **A Song For**
—Leon Russell • **South Bronx**—Boogie Down Productions • **South of Heaven**—Slayer • **Speak No**
—Wayne Shorter • **SpottieOttieDopaliscious**—OutKast • **Sprawl II**—Arcade Fire • **Stand on the**
rd (Larry Levan Mix)—The Joubert Singers • **Step Into a World (Rapture's Delight)**—KRS-One • **Still**
t a Player—Big Pun • **Strange Fruit**—Nina Simone • **Strictly Business**—EPMD • **Sucker MC's**—
-DMC • **Sunny**—Bobby Hebb • **Supernatural Thing Part 1**—Ben E King • **Sweet Green Fields**—
ls & Crofts • **Temptation (7" Mix)**—New Order • **10 Crack Commandments**—The Notorious B.I.G. •
at Lady—The Isley Brothers • **THat Part**—ScHoolboy Q • **That's the Joint**—Funky Four Plus One More
hese Days—Nico • **They Reminisce Over You (T.R.O.Y.)**—Pete Rock and CL Smooth • **Thinkin Bout**
—Frank Ocean • **Three Imaginary Boys**—The Cure • **Throw**—Paperclip People • **Tomorrow Never**
ows—The Beatles • **Tonight**—Iggy Pop • **Too Many Creeps**—Bush Tetras • **Too Much Pressure**—The
ecter • **Top Billin'**—Audio Two • **Trash**—New York Dolls • **T-Shirt**—Migos • **Tusk**—Fleetwood Mac
ptown Top Ranking—Althea and Donna • **Venom Live 7"** • **Walking on Sunshine**—Rockers Revenge
asted—Black Flag • **Water No Get Enemy**—Fela Kuti • **Way Back Home**—Jazz Crusaders • **What It's**
About—Slum Village • **Wheely Wheely**—Early B (The Doctor) • **White Mice**—Mo-dettes • **Wrath**
My Madness—Queen Latifah • **Yama Yama**—Yamasuki Singers • **Yègellé Tezeta**—Mulatu Astatke • **Yo**
Sé—Los Dug Dugs • **You and Me**—Penny & The Quarters • **You and Your Folks, Me and My**
ks—Funkadelic • **You Don't Love Me (No, No, No)**—Dawn Penn • **You'll Never Find Another Love**
e Mine—Lou Rawls • **You're the Man Parts 1 & 2 (Mono Single Version)**—Marvin Gaye

ANDRÉ LEON TALLEY

No. Nah. Oh no. Ucch!

I met with André Leon Talley (at Dapper Dan's Boutique in Harlem, of course) to discuss fashion. Specifically Beastie Boys fashion. We selected a few pictures that we felt best represented our band's schmatta narrative, and he, with his authoritative knowledge, offered his critique of our looks. (AH)

ANDRÉ LEON TALLEY: Oh, the boombox, oh God. *Oh!* This is an appropriation of the hood. This is appropriation of the hood and the street—you're giving us like baaad hip hop, thuggerish, but it's not thuggish enough. Ooh—that little stand, that little pose. Look at that little pose. Clean sneaks—and what's that over here? Is that like a hat or hood or snood or something?

ADAM HOROVITZ: It's a do-rag.

ALT: A *snood*. I would say it's a snood, not a do-rag. Oh, well, this is—is that a girl?

AH: That's me.

ALT: It cannot be you! Is that a girl? Look! It looks like a *girl*!

AH: Is that a problem?

ALT: Nooooo. But it's got the body of a girl! Oh, I've enjoyed this because I'm—I mean, do you want this? I mean, ucchh! The only great thing about this is the boombox. And the stripes. And you all are posing too much—you're posing like the supermodels. You're giving us a supermodel pose. Strike the pose—*Vogue*.

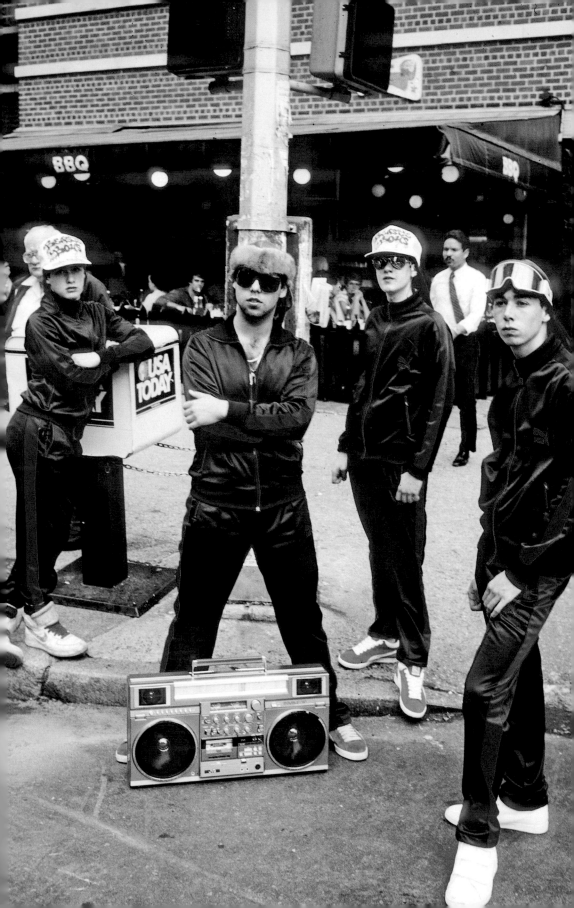

ALT: This one passes muster because it's kind of neutralized. It's neutralizing—it's not really a disruptive look, but it is a look that's safe. You're safe here, you're playing it safe. I wouldn't know they were pop stars unless you told me they were pop stars. Pop stars tend to take much more risk. Why did you wear these clothes then? You had no money to buy outfits? You were just experimenting—this was comfort—you didn't want to branch out into style. Okay. The VW accessory. That beeper—ucchh! How could you have a beeper as an accessory?

ALT: Moving on and you're a bit more upwardly mobile, you're taking a bit more of a risk. You've got a lot of beer. Mostly it's a T-shirt phenomenon here. [Points to MD and Yauch.] It's *pre*–Banana Republic over here. [Points to AH.] You're wearing *pre*-WASP, high WASP. It's high WASP. WASP-meets-biker boy. So you're, you're experimenting here, it's a bit more of a style moment, it's a bit edgier. I would say that you were aspiring for the moment of being a pop star.

ALT: Ooohh, you're trying to get hot here, sexy! What's that crotch pose? Vanilla smoke shot, vanilla, ooooohhh, I would say this is a look that you might find today on Grindr. This is your pre-Grindr look. And it is *not* working. Whoever that is in the middle should have known not to look like that. That is not sexy.

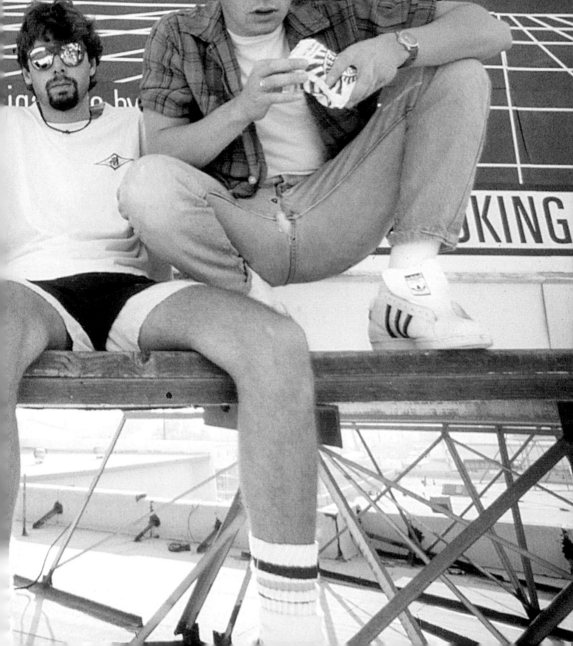

ALT: This was a moment in 1992. This is the way people *looked* in 1992. This was the precursor to the athletic wear of 2018, 2017, 2016, 2015. So therefore you were a pioneer here, you were pioneering with this athletic urban streetwear look. You hit the nail here. This is very good. The shoes, the pants—oh yeah, that's *very* good. I'd say you hit the mark there.

ALT: It's sooo scripted, it's so arch, it's sooo perfect, it's sooo unreal—these lumberjack grungy shirts—but this is grun-GE. That was the moment when grunge came about, you know, Seattle? So you're feeling the grunge, but you knew what grunge was—so you got sort of grungy without being grunge, 'cause grunge would be dirtier. So there's no dirt here. I don't feel any soil, I don't feel you rubbed around, you haven't gone into the earth, there's no dirt on it—it's like perfect grunge, okay?

ALT: Uh, I, I don't know what to say because it's like Kraftwerk. You remember Kraftwerk? They did it bett-ah. Is this not correct? Kraftwerk did it bett-ah.

ALT: This is just so bad. I mean why would you go from a Grindr look to this nerdy, Hush Puppy, Clarks desert boots, faux Ivy League blazers and turtlenecks in front of Lincoln Center—isn't that Lincoln Center? This is how the Beastie Boys go to Lincoln Center. You didn't have fun, you didn't have fun with this one. This is not fun.

UNKNOWN: It's sad.

ALT: Isn't it sad? It's what you put on. Didn't you have other choices at home? Other choices of shoes? You can't wear those Clarks shoes and Hush Puppies—*why* are you wearing Hush Puppies? Uh—you're a *Beastie* Boy, you're a pop star, why would you wear Hush Puppies and Clarks? This is so *nerdy*! You're so, like, postgraduate Princeton, Ivy League, but it doesn't work, you are not convincing. No one aspires to look like this. This is not an aspirational look. This is a look that you try to run *away* from. You want to *run* from that.

ALT: O-kay. This is like Adam Sandler meets Tom Hanks at a baaad former bank building in the Suburban Diaspora of New Jerrrsey. In New Jerrsey. What's that, what's that musical—*The Jersey Boys*? This is—so, *so*, so predictable. *Who* styled you there? You did. OH! Mmmm. What were you thinking? Didn't you know that you could go to Tom Ford and get something that was very snappy, svelte, soigné, impeccable, shapely, and directional? Have you not heard of Tom Ford? Have you not heard of Hedi Slimane? Have you not heard of, of *Gucci*? Have you not heard of Dapper Dan? Hmmm. And you dressed like *this*?!

ALT: I know this was meant to be hip with the sweatsuit moment, but you look like airport workers, like people who are part of a union, who load the planes up, you know, the cargo. This is *so nerdy* and *boring*. I mean, what were you trying to establish, what, what—? Good lord, I can't even comment on this, this is too union. This is union gear. You shouldn't be matching. Have you ever heard of Mick Jagger? Do you know what Mick Jagger wears? Do you know that Mick Jagger and his band—they do not *match*. You don't need to match.

*

Okay, let's flip through them again. No, no, no—nah—oh no! Oh no! Ucch! It's so fake! Nassau County. Paramus Mall, Kraftwerk. Nooo! Ooh! Airplane union, no, no. Is that the last picture? This!

ALT: Moving, moving—fabulous. I love that. It suggests that there is something edgy, there is something celebrity—could be a rock star, could just be the boy on the corner with a skateboard—but the mix of plaid and the mix of the print—the dashiki look—the beard, the Austrian felt hat—*and* the boots work here. I would say this is a step forward to the right moment. I like this look. This suggests originality. Who is that—which one is that? He's the one that's got the style here. He takes *big* chances.

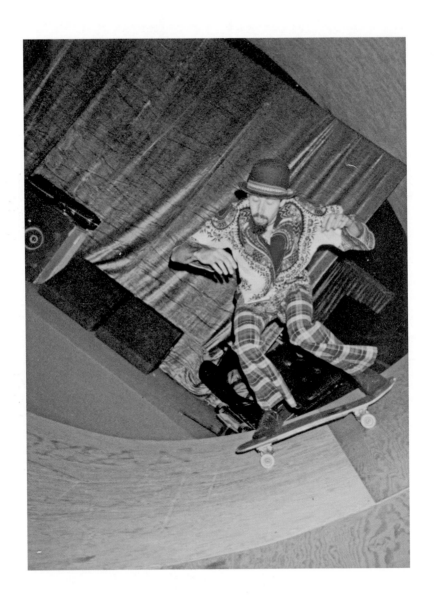

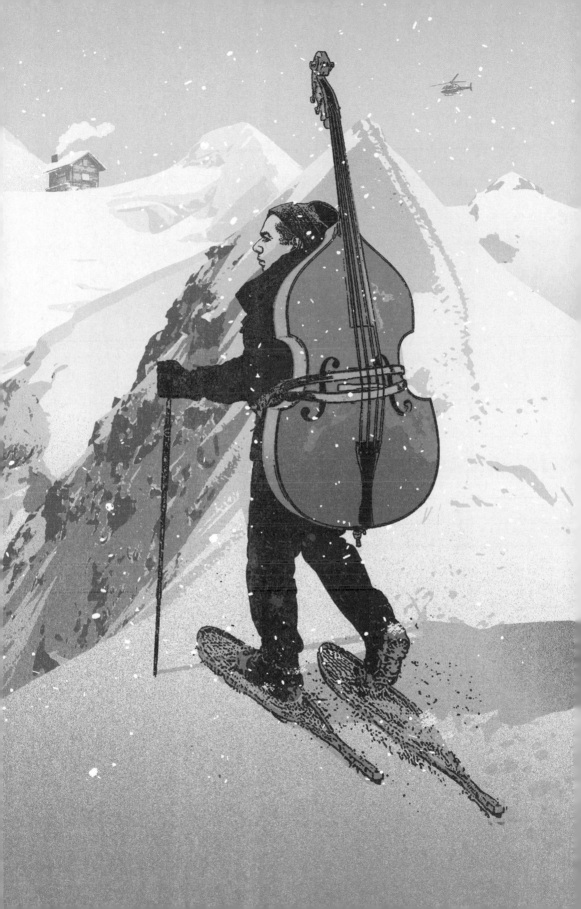

Outro

(MD)

Congratulations! You read the entire book. It probably wasn't easy, and it certainly wasn't quick. I wish I had a golden ticket or a prize that I could give you, but I don't. Yes, we were, and are, some lucky ducks. We were teenagers living in a chaotic city where anything was possible and everything was okay, even when it wasn't. We were young, making music, becoming famous, then infamous, and then not so famous; making money and losing money, making friends and losing friends, making mistakes and (sometimes) learning from mistakes. And through it all we were super fortunate to somehow remain close friends. To Adam and me, Yauch was like our older brother, and even more, a mentor.

Over the years the band transformed from a nonstop recording and touring machine into something sustainable, something that we could all come back to when we wanted and needed it. Grown-up things happened to us. We had our own families, kids, separate interests, the whole deal. But we would still come together to have fun and make stuff. And we would be coming back together today if Yauch were still alive.

So we leave you with this picture: Yauch flies to some mountains at the edge of the earth, hops out of a helicopter to perfect snowboarding conditions—"virgin pow," as they say. No one is around. Sure, he packs his gear—but what else? A pillow, a favorite stuffed animal to cuddle? Nope—he brings a ginormous upright bass and carries that shit up the mountain. Physically and metaphorically this is a big deal: crazy and funny and amazing and something that your mom, travel agent, accountant, and manager would all advise against. But it captures the spirit that marked a lot of the adventures Yauch led us on. And this is why, whenever I have the opportunity to do a random, kind of crazy thing, something I feel I have no business doing, I ask myself, "What would Yauch do?"

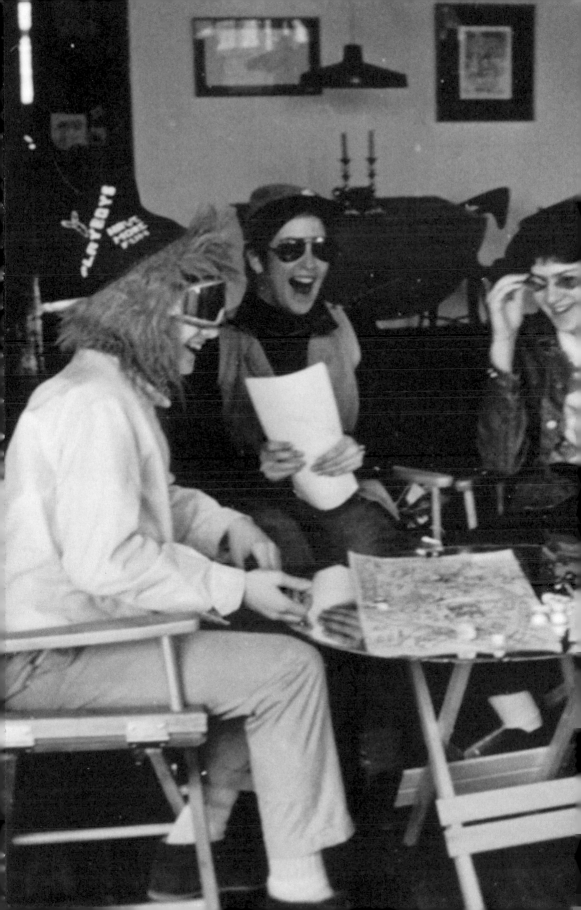

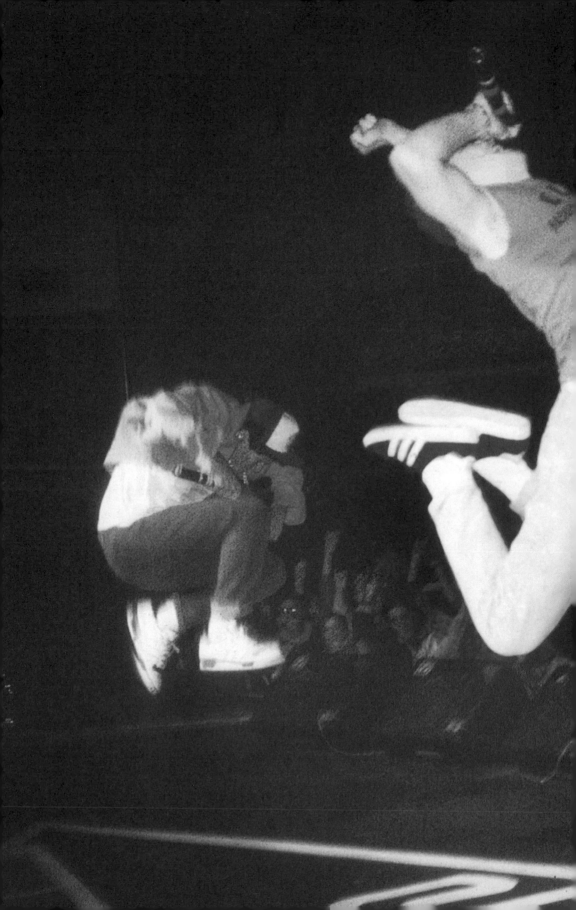

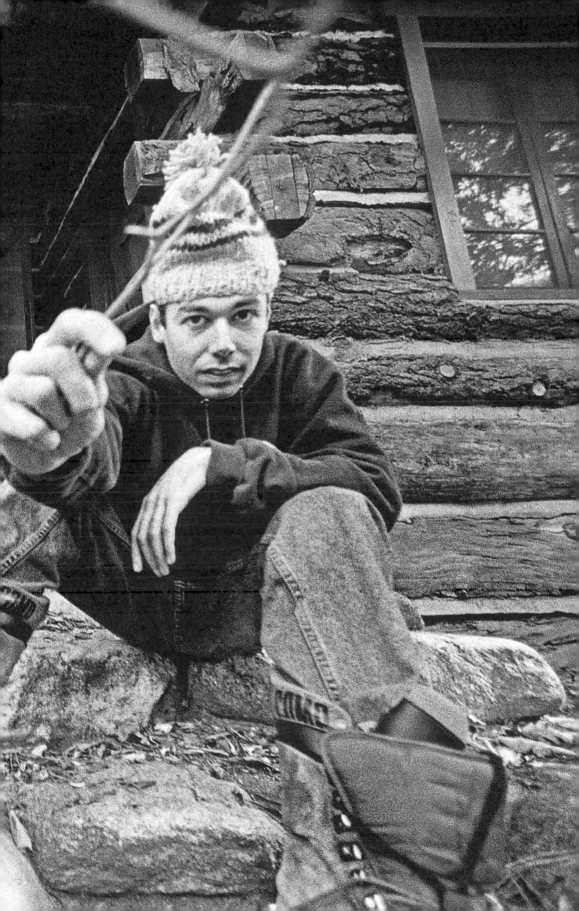

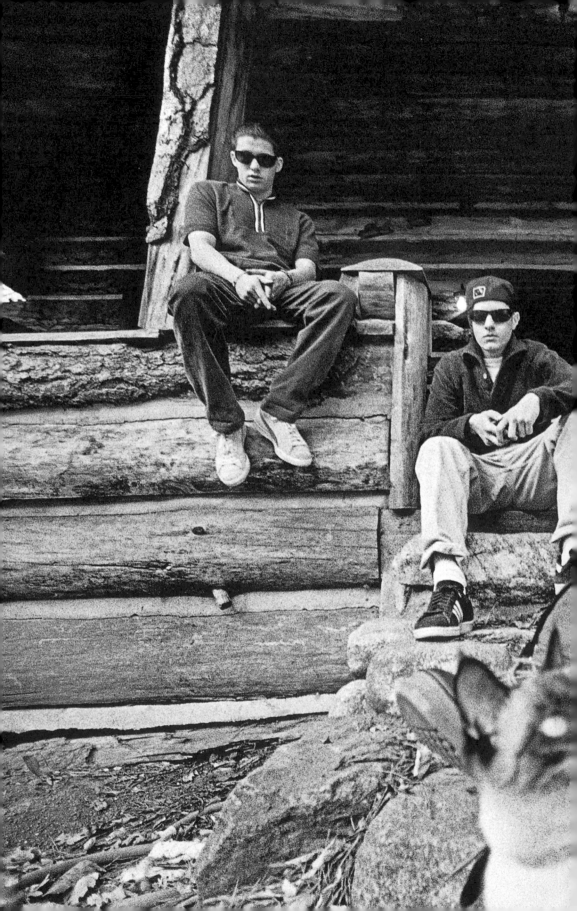

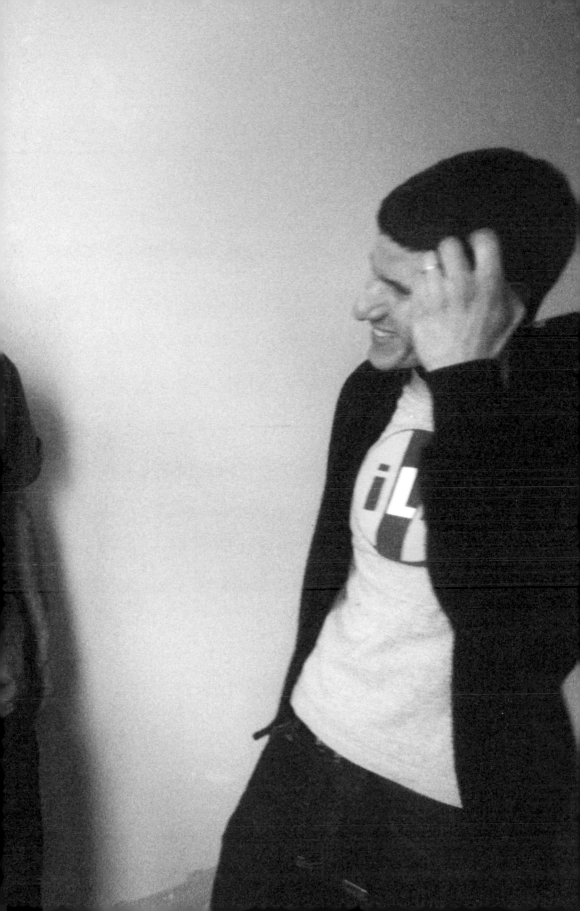

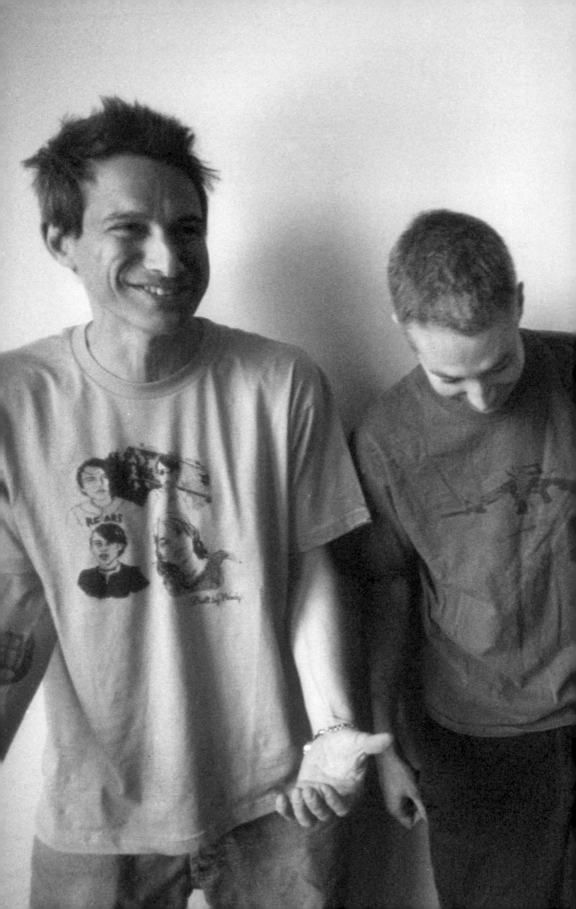

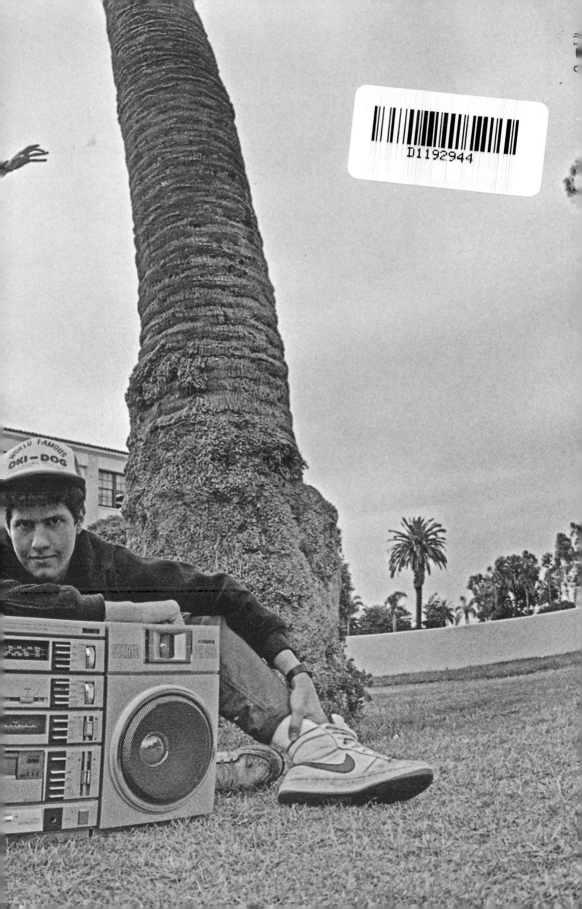